NEW MEXICO AND THE PIMERÍA ALTA

NEW MEXICO and the PIMERÍA ALTA

THE COLONIAL PERIOD IN THE AMERICAN SOUTHWEST

edited by **John G. Douglass** and **William M. Graves**

UNIVERSITY PRESS OF COLORADO

Boulder

© 2017 by University Press of Colorado

Published by University Press of Colorado
5589 Arapahoe Avenue, Suite 206C
Boulder, Colorado 80303

All rights reserved
First paperback edition 2018

 The University Press of Colorado is a proud member of Association of American University Presses.

The University Press of Colorado is a cooperative publishing enterprise supported, in part, by Adams State University, Colorado State University, Fort Lewis College, Metropolitan State University of Denver, Regis University, University of Colorado, University of Northern Colorado, Utah State University, and Western State Colorado University.

ISBN: 978-1-60732-573-4 (cloth)
ISBN: 978-1-60732-868-1 (paperback)
ISBN: 978-1-60732-574-1 (ebook)

Library of Congress Cataloging-in-Publication Data

Names: Douglass, John G., 1968– editor. | Graves, William M., editor.
Title: New Mexico and the Pimería Alta : the colonial period in the American Southwest / edited by John G. Douglass and William M. Graves.
Description: Boulder : University Press of Colorado, [2017] | Includes bibliographical references and index.
Identifiers: LCCN 2016044391| ISBN 9781607325734 (cloth) | ISBN 9781607328681 (pbk.) | ISBN 9781607325741 (ebook)
Subjects: LCSH: Spaniards—Pimería Alta (Mexico and Ariz.)—History. | Spaniards—Southwest, New—History. | Indians of North America—First contact with Europeans—Pimería Alta (Mexico and Ariz.)—History. | Indians of North America—First contact with Europeans—Southwest, New—History. | Ethnoarchaeology—Pimería Alta (Mexico and Ariz.) | Ethnoarchaeology—Southwest, New.
Classification: LCC F799 .N47 2017 | DDC 979/.01—dc23
LC record available at https://lccn.loc.gov/2016044391

An electronic version of this book is freely available, thanks to the support of libraries working with Knowledge Unlatched. KU is a collaborative initiative designed to make high-quality books open access for the public good. The open access ISBN for the PDF version of this book is 978-1-60732-701-1; for the ePUB version the open access ISBN is 978-1-60732-722-6. More information about the initiative and links to the open-access version can be found at www.knowledgeunlatched.org.

Cover photograph, Ruins of a room block and the San Gregorio de Abó church at Abó Pueblo in the Salinas Pueblo Missions National Monument, by William M. Graves

To Jane Dempsey Douglass, Gordon Douglass, and
the late Ralph Douglass for their inspirational examples

and to Jill Onken for her love

and

To Helena Rodrigues and Matilde Graves
for their love and encouragement.

Contents

List of Figures | **ix**

List of Tables | **xiii**

Foreword by David Hurst Thomas | **xv**

Preface | **xxi**

Acknowledgments | **xxiii**

1. New Mexico and the Pimería Alta: A Brief Introduction to the Colonial Period in the American Southwest
   John G. Douglass and William M. Graves | *3*

Part 1. The New Mexico Colony: Native and Colonist Worlds Colliding

2. "The Peace That Was Granted Had Not Been Kept": Coronado in the Tiguex Province, 1540–1542
   Matthew F. Schmader | *49*

3. Meeting in Places: Seventeenth-Century Puebloan and Spanish Landscapes
   Phillip O. Leckman | *75*

4. Hopi Weaving and the Colonial Encounter: A Study of Persistence through Change
   Laurie D. Webster | *115*

5. The Pueblo World Transformed: Alliances, Factionalism, and Animosities in the Northern Rio Grande, 1680–1700
   Matthew Liebmann, Robert Preucel, and Joseph Aguilar | 143

6. Comanche New Mexico: The Eighteenth Century
   Severin Fowles, Jimmy Arterberry, Lindsay Montgomery, and Heather Atherton | 157

7. *Aqui Me Quedo*: Vecino Origins and the Settlement Archaeology of the Rio del Oso Grant, New Mexico
   J. Andrew Darling and B. Sunday Eiselt | 187

8. Becoming Vecinos: Civic Identities in Late Colonial New Mexico
   Kelly L. Jenks | 213

9. *Moquis, Kastiilam,* and the Trauma of History: Hopi Oral Traditions of Seventeenth-Century Franciscan Missionary Abuses
   Thomas E. Sheridan and Stewart B. Koyiyumptewa | 239

Part 2. Divergent Histories and Experiences in the Pimería Alta, Southern Arizona

10. Population Dynamics in the Pimería Alta, AD 1650–1750
   Lauren E. Jelinek and Dale S. Brenneman | 263

11. Missions, Livestock, and Economic Transformations in the Pimería Alta
   Barnet Pavao-Zuckerman | 289

12. Life in Tucson, on the Northern Frontier of the Pimería Alta
   J. Homer Thiel | 311

13. O'odham Irrigated Agriculture Response to Colonization on the Middle Gila River, Southern Arizona
   Colleen Strawhacker | 331

Part 3. Discussion and Comparative Viewpoints

14. The Archaeology of Colonialism in the American Southwest and Alta California: Some Observations and Comments
   Kent G. Lightfoot | 355

15. Materiality Matters: Colonial Transformations Spanning the Southwestern and Southeastern Borderlands
   David Hurst Thomas | 379

List of Contributors | 415

Index | 417

Figures

1.1. Map of the American Southwest, including the approximate location of both the Pimería Alta and the New Mexico Colony | 6

1.2. Map of approximate early Spanish colonial routes through modern-day Arizona | 13

1.3. Map of approximate early Spanish colonial routes through modern-day New Mexico | 14

2.1. Approximate route of the Francisco Vázquez de Coronado expedition, February 1540 to June 1542 | 52

2.2. Map of Vázquez de Coronado's "Tiguex Province" (middle Rio Grande valley) | 54

2.3. Sample of sixteenth-century metal artifacts recovered from Piedras Marcadas Pueblo | 64

2.4. Military-related metal sixteenth-century metal artifacts recovered from Piedras Marcadas Pueblo | 65

2.5. Sample of slingstones recovered from surface context at Piedras Marcadas Pueblo | 68
3.1. LA 162's location in the Middle Rio Grande Valley | 79
3.2. Local watersheds and drainage systems in the vicinity of LA 162 | 80
3.3. North-south elevation profile of the Arroyo San Pedro watershed | 81
3.4. Major Early Classic–period sites in the East Mountains | 83
3.5. Site map of LA 162 illustrating major divisions and roomblocks identified by Nels Nelson (1914) | 84
3.6. Map of the seventeenth-century plaza group at LA 162 | 85
3.7. Rectilinear structure constructed in the southwest corner of Paako's seventeenth-century plaza | 89
3.8. Corrals erected within Paako's seventeenth-century plaza | 91
3.9. Precontact- and contact-period Arroyo San Pedro community settlement patterns | 94
3.10. Colonial-period water-management features at Paako | 95
3.11. Estimated precontact-period ceramic density along the Arroyo San Pedro floodplain | 96
3.12. Estimated contact-period ceramic density along the Arroyo San Pedro floodplain | 97
3.13. Density of major Middle Rio Grande pueblo sites during the Early Classic Period | 101
3.14. Density of major Middle Rio Grande pueblo sites during the contact and colonial periods | 102
3.15. Paako and neighboring communities at the beginning of the contact period | 103
3.16. Paako and neighboring communities in the mid-seventeenth century | 104
4.1. Map of Hopi Reservation | 117
4.2. Excerpt of map by Don Bernardo de Miera y Pacheco, ca. 1760, illustrating the "Dress and Dance of the Indians of New Mexico" | 126
4.3. Wàlpi kiva interior showing Hopi man weaving on a traditional upright Pueblo loom, 1899 | 131
6.1. The Vista Verde Site (LA 75747), located within Rio Grande Gorge at the confluence of the Rio Grande and the Rio Pueblo | 165

6.2. Probable Jicarilla Apache rock art from the Rio Grande Gorge | **167**
6.3. Lightly abraded and pecked rock art at the Manby Trailhead Site (LA 102341) | **167**
6.4. Map of the central tipi encampment (Area 6) at the Vista Verde Site | **169**
6.5. Scratched and abraded rock art from the Vista Verde Site (detail of Panel 2014-009A) | **171**
6.6. Scratched and abraded rock art from the Vista Verde Site (Panel 2008-353) | **171**
6.7. Scratched and abraded rock art from the Vista Verde Site (panel 2008-408A) | **172**
6.8. Scratched and abraded rock art from the Vista Verde Site (Panel 2008-374B, overlying graffiti removed) | **173**
6.9. Scratched and abraded rock art from the Vista Verde Site (panel 2008-298) | **174**
6.10 Scratched and abraded rock art from the Vista Verde Site (Panel 2008-059, overlying graffiti removed) | **174**
6.11. A. Panel 2009-234 at the Vista Verde Site (overlying graffiti removed). B. Rock art details from the Tolar Site, Wyoming (based upon Loendorf and Olsen 2003) | **175**
6.12. Scratched and abraded rock art from the Rio Grande Gorge, just north of the Vista Verde Site (Panel 2009-209) | **179**
7.1. Villages mentioned in the text | **190**
7.2. Changes in population growth rate from 1700 to 1900 using the formula for exponential population growth | **192**
7.3. The expansion of the Vecino Homeland after Nostrand (1970, 1975, 1980) | **194**
7.4. Rio del Oso grant genealogy | **198**
7.5. Early and late component structures in the Rio del Oso Valley | **201**
8.1. Sample of twenty-five excavated Hispanic Sites | **220**
8.2. Pueblo potting areas | **222**
9.1. Hopi History Project Workshop with the Cultural Resources Advisory Task Team (CRATT) of the Hopi Cultural Preservation Office, Kykotsmovi, Arizona, October 21, 2009 | **247**
9.2. Katsina Buttes (Kaktsintuyqa), where Hopis performed ceremonies in secret during the Franciscan mission period | **248**

Figures | **xi**

9.3. Ruins of mission church at Awat'ovi on Antelope Mesa | 252
10.1. The Pimería Alta | 265
10.2. O'odham distribution in the Pimería Alta as reported by Kino and Manje | 268
10.3. Pimería Alta sites and landmarks | 270
11.1. Map of the Pimería Alta in the eighteenth century | 291
11.2. Summary of zooarchaeological remains from Mission San Agustín | 299
11.3. Summary of zooarchaeological remains from Mission Cocóspera | 299
12.1. Map of the Pimería Alta | 313
12.2. A Piman bean pot found in a trash-filled pit inside the Tucson Presidio | 319
12.3. Northern Puebloan ceramic sherds found in the Tucson Presidio | 320
12.4. Brightly colored Mexican majolica vessels were used by women at the Tucson Presidio to serve meals | 321
12.5. Religious medal and forty-four European glass beads found in a soil-mining pit adjacent to the Tucson Presidio | 323
12.6. Brass gunstock appliqués on an escopeta found in New Mexico | 324
13.1. Map of major Spanish missions and presidios in Arizona and the study area of focus in this chapter | 333
13.2. Settlement extent of O'odham villages along the middle Gila River during the historic period | 339
13.3. Population numbers of the middle Gila River Valley from historic documents. | 340
13.4. Map of middle Gila River historic canals and villages | 343
13.5. Estimated irrigated acreage in the late historic period, select years, 1850–1921 | 346
13.6. Grain production on Gila River Indian Community | 347
15.1. Plan view of the Spanish mission at Abó (New Mexico) after its first reconstruction circa 1652 | 395
15.2. This mission bell was found at San Cristóbal Pueblo in New Mexico's Galisteo Basin | 400

Tables

5.1. XRF provenience of obsidian artifacts found at revolt-era sites of the Jemez Valley | 148

7.1. Comparison of late colonial and Vecino occupations in the Rio del Oso | 203

8.1. Sample of Hispanic New Mexican sites | 218

11.1. Inventories of livestock holdings at Pimería Alta missions and presidios | 298

FOREWORD

Columbian Consequences in Quarter-Century Perspective

DAVID HURST THOMAS

John G. Douglass and William M. Graves, the editors of this volume, have told me that the *Columbian Consequences* project served as a catalyst for the initial symposium entitled "Transformations during the Colonial Era: Divergent Histories in the American Southwest," subsequently published as this volume. They also asked me to write a few words about the *Columbian Consequences* effort, from a quarter-century perspective.

The roots of *Columbian Consequences* run back to the late 1980s, a time of considerable stress and not a little self-reflection in the Americanist archaeological community. A decade of repatriation and reburial debate would culminate in the 1990 The Native American Graves Protection and Repatriation Act (NAGPRA) legislation. Competing paradigms of processual and postprocessual archaeology generated lively conversations about future directions of archaeological theory. The rapid growth of applied archaeology (in the form of cultural resource management) tested the conventionally academic structure of the archaeological profession. Long-standing issues of gender bias clouded archaeological interpretations of the past and the practice of archaeology in the present.

DOI: 10.5876/9781607325741.c000

With the Columbian Quincentenary just a few years off, the Society of American Archaeology (SAA) puzzled its role in anticipating the inevitable events that would surround the 500th anniversary of European–Native American interactions. I was a member of the Executive Committee of the SAA at the time, and the president asked me spearhead the society's efforts for observing the Columbian Quincentenary.

Thanks to the support and encouragement of key SAA officers Don Fowler, Prudence Rice, Bruce Smith, and Jerry Sabloff, we were able to develop a plan. After exploring a number of options with the board, we settled upon a series of topical seminars that we dubbed *Columbian Consequences*.

These nine public seminars, to be held over a three-year span, were designed to generate an accurate and factual assessment of what did—and what did not—transpire as a result of the Columbian encounter. We specifically tasked ourselves to probe the social, demographic, ecological, ideological, and human repercussions of European–Native American encounters across the Spanish Borderlands, spreading the word among both the scholarly community and the greater public at large.

Although sponsored by the SAA, the *Columbian Consequences* enterprise rapidly transcended the traditional scope of archaeological inquiry, drawing together a diverse assortment of personalities and perspectives. We invited leading scholars of the day to synthesize current thinking about specific geographical settings across the Spanish Borderlands, which extend from St. Augustine (Florida) to San Francisco (California). Each overview was designed to provide a Native American context, a history of European involvement, and a summary of scholarly research.

The structure was fairly simple. Each of three consecutive SAA annual meetings (in 1988, 1989, and 1990) hosted three *Columbian Consequences* seminars. The resulting three volumes were published by the Smithsonian Institution Press, which remarkably published each volume less than a year after the seminar papers were presented.

The initial book, entitled *Archaeological and Historical Perspectives on the Spanish Borderlands West* (Thomas 1989), tackled the European–Native American interface from the Pacific Slope across the southwestern heartland to East Texas, from Russian Fort Ross to southern Baja California. The archaeologists involved addressed material culture evidence regarding contact period sociopolitics, economics, iconography, and physical environment. Other authors attempted to provide a critical balance from the perspectives of American history, Native American studies, art history, ethnohistory, and geography.

In the intermediate volume—*Archaeological and Historical Perspectives on the Spanish Borderlands East* (Thomas 1990)—nearly three dozen scholars pursued a similar agenda across La Florida, the greater Southeast, and the Caribbean.

Volume 3 of *Columbian Consequences* (Thomas 1991), entitled *The Spanish Borderlands in Pan-American Perspective,* explored Borderlands processes in action—past, present, and future. The volume began with a look at previous Columbus-related "celebrations," particularly the Columbian Quatercentenary, manifest as the Chicago World's Fair of 1893, which heavily impacted the next century of Borderlands scholarship. Several authors explored Spanish mission strategies across the Borderlands, particularly addressing various Native American survival strategies. Some participants also examined then-revolutionary approaches to the demographics of European contact.

The *Columbian Consequences* enterprise was grounded in what I termed a "cubist" perspective (Thomas 1989), an argument for approaching the contact-era past from multiple directions simultaneously. I believed that an analogy to the early twentieth-century cubist movement was appropriate because of the way the cubists deconstructed and invalidated the restrictive conventions that had come to dominate Western art. Conventional canons of Renaissance art held, in effect, that reality is best perceived from a single, time-honored perspective, tasking artists to perfect their craft for abbreviating three-dimensional visual realities into artificial, two-dimensional art forms.

Cubists such as Pablo Picasso and Georges Braque broke with this European illusionist tradition by arguing that one's perspective can (and should) be shifted at will. Questioning the pretense of absolute visual truth, cubists rejected classical norms for the human figure, refusing to paint their images as snapshots of objects as they appeared momentarily to the eye.

Columbian Consequences was structured along cubist lines by approaching the past from multiple directions simultaneously. Traditional Borderlands scholarship was viewed like the works of the Renaissance masters. Both involved a snapshot-of-the-past approach, bent on capturing perceived reality from a single perspective. Just as the Renaissance masters used light, color, and texture to generate their single-view imagery, Borderlands scholarship had long championed special-interest groups, promoting and perpetuating their single-point version of the "truth"—the way it *really* was. While not rejecting most conventional Borderlands scholarship outright, we (like the cubists) argued that the past was best addressed by fresh, sometimes conflicting, perspectives as well.

With this cubist imperative in mind, we scanned the Borderlands for participants who represented both traditional and novel perspectives, attempting to augment conventional Borderlands scholarship with fresher insights from historical archaeology, Native American studies, historical demography, and ethnohistory. At its base, the *Columbian Consequences* seminars tried to serve as an overarching mechanism for balance, criticism, and synthesis—reassessing throughout the importance of recognizing multiple pasts and the necessity of decoupling intellectual inquiry from its associated mythologies.

The ninety-three chapters of *Columbian Consequences* enlisted a broad sweep of scholarly opinions from a diverse range of disciplines. In all, there were 64 archaeologists, 11 historians, 9 physical anthropologists, 9 ethnohistorians, 6 cultural anthropologists, 5 art historians, and 3 geographers. Included in this group were four archaeologists hailing from Latin America, two Native American scholars, one Franciscan historian, and one Jesuit ethnohistorian.

Today, of course, looking back at the roster from a quarter-century perspective, our "diverse range" was disappointingly narrow, even parochial. Even at the time, this shortcoming was apparent; as I wrote in 1992, "the results remain somewhat frustrating and dissatisfying. Any objective assessment of the *Columbian Consequences* inquiry.... would point out that not only are the Native American, Latin American, and Hispanic perspectives seriously underrepresented, but less than one-third of the participants are women... despite our best efforts to elicit an extended suite of opinion and perspective, the final result remains biased toward white, Anglo, male scholarship" (Thomas 1992:615).

Further, like some of the cubist paintings themselves, the results of *Columbian Consequences* were not uniformly pleasing or universally accepted by the public. Conventional Renaissance scholars had, to be sure, produced exceptional artwork more pleasing to the eye than those of the cubists. Some readers of *Columbian Consequences* were disappointed that the series did not produce a "definitive history" of Hispanic–Native American interactions across the Borderlands. Grounded in the belief that multiple distinctive histories had played out during the Columbian encounters, we explored the range and evolution of Hispanic objectives, but also considered Native American counterstrategies for coping with European intrusions. Some critics, more personally comfortable with their own single-perspective histories, resented and protested the intrusion of such collateral, sometimes contrarian viewpoints. Choosing diversity at the expense of harmony, we broke ranks with traditional Borderlands historiography by exploring non-Hispanic, nonwritten records of the past (including archaeology, oral history, and tribal tradition). Some grumbled that arguments from oral history and tribal tradition were "out of place" in serious Borderlands scholarship.

The *Columbian Consequences* exercise highlighted some of the significant obstacles remaining for minorities and women seeking to pursue careers in scholarship—Borderlands or otherwise. The series sold pretty well, with *Choice* magazine selecting *Columbian Consequences* volumes 1 and 2 as Outstanding Academic Books of 1989 and 1990 (respectively). Recognizing the growing tensions over repatriation issues and acknowledging the acute challenges facing Indian people seeking higher education, all royalties from *Columbian Consequences* were earmarked to establish the Native American Scholarship Fund of the Society for American Archaeology. Since renamed the Arthur C. Parker Scholarship, these funds have been augmented by royalties from dozens of additional archaeological books and continue to support archaeological training for Native American students.

The contributions in the present volume continue in the *Columbian Consequences* tradition. The editors emphasize that their intent was not an all-encompassing overview of the American Southwest. They argue instead that this book is the first since *Colombian Consequences* to address the broader themes of colonialism in a number of case studies from the Greater Southwest. In his overview, Kent G. Lightfoot (chapter 14) agrees these chapters underscore the promise of the American Southwest for new directions in the archaeology of colonialism, particularly in exploring the distinctive historical trajectories that unfolded there. He adds that the major advances in the archaeology of colonialism, as clearly demonstrated in this volume, set the stage for another *Columbian Consequences*–style synthesis and critique of the Spanish Borderlands.

REFERENCES CITED

Thomas, David Hurst, ed. 1989. *Archaeological and Historical Perspectives on the Spanish Borderlands West*. Columbian Consequences, vol. 1. Washington, DC: Smithsonian Institution Press.

Thomas, David Hurst, ed. 1990. *Archaeological and Historical Perspectives on the Spanish Borderlands East*. Columbian Consequences, vol. 2. Washington, DC: Smithsonian Institution Press.

Thomas, David Hurst, ed. 1991. *The Spanish Borderlands in Pan-American Perspective*. Columbian Consequences, vol. 3. Washington, DC: Smithsonian Institution Press.

Thomas, David Hurst. 1992. "A Retrospective Look at Columbian Consequences." *American Antiquity* 57 (4): 613–16. http://dx.doi.org/10.2307/280825.

Preface

This volume began as an idea for a symposium at the annual meetings of the Society for American Archaeology (SAA) in 2012. Both of us had been interested in colonialism and colonial studies for quite some time, and we wanted to work together on a personal research project. Billy had done research on and off in New Mexico since his graduate school days, and John had been doing research on the Mission period in California for a decade or so. John was particularly interested in work that could widen his viewpoint on colonialism by studying another area for a comparative perspective. As a result, we organized a symposium at the 2012 SAA meetings in Memphis entitled "Transformations during the Colonial Era: Divergent Histories in the American Southwest." It turned out to be a very fun and stimulating symposium that brought together many of the scholars who are currently engaged in colonial studies in the Southwest. Immediately, we knew the symposium would be the foundation of a worthwhile edited volume. We are thankful that all of the original participants of the symposium—save Jun Sunseri, who sadly had to bow out—agreed to be a part of a book project. To round out the line-up of participants, we also asked David

Hurst Thomas to be a part of the project and to write a second comparative chapter for the end of the volume. Dave graciously accepted, and his chapter on the American Southeast (chapter 15) provides a wonderful complement to Lightfoot's comparative chapter on Alta California (chapter 14).

While Billy has worked in the American Southwest his entire career, John is more of an archaeological "mutt," having worked some in the American Southwest, but also in California, in the Midwest, and in Mesoamerica. Because of our different geographical foci and our different trainings and experiences, we feel that we have complemented each other well in this project and have found it very easy to exchange ideas and to write together. Our different backgrounds and our different theoretical viewpoints have come together in unexpected ways. We have learned much from each other, and even more from all of the contributors in this volume.

We ought to be clear that the content and topics that are contained in this volume are in no way meant to be viewed as comprehensive of the wide breadth of colonial studies in American Southwest archaeology. Rather, we included a number of friends and colleagues who we felt would bring strong topical or theoretical contributions to the project. There are a number of important scholars, research issues, and cultural groups that are not included in this volume for one reason or another. Realistically, we tried to be as inclusive as possible while keeping in mind our ultimate goal—to create something new and interesting that would have comparative importance to the study of colonialism in archaeology more generally, but not something that would be too huge an undertaking to pull off.

JOHN G. DOUGLASS
WILLIAM M. GRAVES
Tucson, Arizona

Acknowledgments

This volume had benefited from the hard work of many individuals. Foremost, we thank each of the volume contributors. Their enthusiasm for the project, perseverance, and excellent scholarship have allowed us to assemble an exciting and thought-provoking volume, and we have enjoyed working with you all as we moved from conference presentations to publication. We would like to thank Statistical Research, Inc., for institutional support the volume received throughout the process of writing and editing. Graphic designer Jackie Dominguez prepared Figures 1.1, 1.2, 1.3, and 5.1. Our families also need to be acknowledged, as they lived the volume with us while we spent weekends and evenings working on it, and we greatly appreciate their patience. And, finally, we thank the staff at the University Press of Colorado for their assistance and guidance throughout this project.

NEW MEXICO AND THE PIMERÍA ALTA

ONE

New Mexico and the Pimería Alta

A Brief Introduction to the Colonial Period in the American Southwest

JOHN G. DOUGLASS AND WILLIAM M. GRAVES

INTRODUCTION

The American Southwest is notable for its unique physical and cultural landscapes. From the low Sonoran and Chihuahuan deserts to the vast uplands of the Colorado Plateau to the Rio Grande valley and beyond, this region has witnessed a diverse and complex social history spanning more than 10,000 years. For the vast majority of this long span, this history was a Native American history that reflected the diversity and complexity of the indigenous groups who inhabited the region's various landscapes. By the AD 1500s, the region was home to hundreds of village settlement and scores of mobile hunter-gatherer groups who spoke dozens of different languages—the direct ancestors of many of the Native Americans who live in the Southwest today.

In 1539, the history of the Southwest was irrevocably altered with the arrival of the first Spanish expedition, led by Fray Marcos de Niza (Bolton 1990). The expedition was sent in advance of the Coronado expedition of 1540 by Antonio de Mendoza, the viceroy of Mexico. Members of Niza's group reached as far north as the Zuni area, where a member of his party, Esteban de Dorantes, a

DOI: 10.5876/9781607325741.c001

member of Pánfilo de Narváez's failed 1535–36 expedition to what is now the American Southeast, was killed by the Zuni (Bolton 1990:33–35; Riley 1999:29). Encouraged by exaggerated reports of gold and the potential for wealth from the Niza expedition, Mendoza organized a larger expedition and appointed the governor of Nueva Galicia, Francisco Vázquez de Coronado, to lead it (Bolton 1990; Riley 1999:30) (see chapter 2, by Matthew F. Schmader, this volume). In the spring of 1540, Coronado and a group of over 300 soldiers, as well as numerous *indios amigos*—generally Nahuatl speakers and other indigenous conquerors, primarily from central and western Mexico, who outnumbered the Spanish many times over (including the Mexica, Tlaxcalteca, Oaxacan, and Tarascan cultures)—headed north from Compostela, the capital of Nueva Galicia, continued along the western slopes of the Sierra Madre Occidental, continued through the upland valleys of Sonora, and reached as far north as the Hopi Mesas and the Grand Canyon (Bolton 1990). Over the next two years, Coronado's forces made contact with numerous Pueblos and Plains groups and reached as far east as Wichita, Kansas. His well-documented encounters (e.g., Bolton 1990; Flint and Flint 2005; Hammond and Rey 1940; Hartmann 2014) with Native American groups mark the beginning of the colonial period in the Southwest—an era characterized by what were often conflictive, violent, and tumultuous relations that distinguish much of the more-recent history of the region.

Within the Southwest, colonial encounters and the processes of colonialism played out in notably divergent manners through time and space. Colonialism and the process of state expansion into new territories far from capital and motherland have occurred for thousands of years across the globe (see chapters in Stein 2005). The Spanish intrusion into the Southwest was not the first, widespread extraregional interaction witnessed by the inhabitants of the region. However, similar to Mesoamerica (e.g., Matthew 2012), it was by far the most far-reaching and influential in terms of dramatically altering the historical trajectories of both native and foreign cultures. For millennia, various cultural groups in the Southwest had interacted with foreign societies and experienced influxes of new peoples into the region. A good example of such interactions is the widespread evidence for Mesoamerican influence in architecture, material culture, and ideology among the Mimbres, the Mogollon, and the Hohokam, and throughout the Ancestral Pueblo world seen in the centuries around AD 1000 (e.g., Creel and McKusick 1994; Di Peso 1974; Gilman et al. 2014; Harmon 2006; Schaafsma 1999; Somerville et al. 2010; Whittlesey 2004; Whittlesey and Reid 2013). In this case, archaeologists are still sorting out what form these interactions took and how they were structured—for example, direct or indirect interregional trade, population movement, diffusion of ideologies and cultural traits, or some combination of phenomena—but the presence of strong cultural ties between cultures of the American Southwest and of greater Mesoamerica seem undeniable. The later arrival in the 1400s of Athapaskan speakers, the ancestors of the modern Navajo and Apache, and the arrival of the Comanche in the 1700s are other examples of interregional interactions, this time marking the introduction of new cultural groups to the American Southwest (see, e.g., Wilshusen 2010:193).

Unlike these examples of extraregional cultural influences and movements of populations into the Southwest, however, the arrival of Spaniards in the 1500s was clearly the most "foreign" intrusion into the region and would irrevocably alter the histories of both native and colonizer groups. The American Southwest was the northern frontier of the Spanish Empire, and like Guatemala on its southern edge, was a place of conflict, persistence, and ethnnogenesis (see Comaroff and Comaroff 1991; Hu 2013; Matthew 2012; Palka 2005; Rice and Rice 2005). The Spanish colonization of the Southwest was part of a hemispheric approach to colonialism, one that bears striking resemblance to many other examples of colonialism in both modern and ancient state examples (Alcock 2005; Brown 2013; Deagan 1995, 1997; Gosden 2004; Gosden and Knowles 2001; Hart et al. 2012; Hartmann 2014; Hu 2013; Lapham 2005; Liebmann and Murphy 2010; Liebmann and Rizvi 2008; Lightfoot 2005; Lightfoot et al. 1998, Lightfoot et al. 2013; Lydon 2009; Lyons and Papadopoulos 2002; Mathers et al. 2013; Matthew 2012; Oudijk and Matthew 2007; Mitchell 2013; Oland et al. 2012; Oliver 2010; Panich 2013; Panich and Schneider 2014; Rice and Rice 2005; Riley 2001; Rojo 2001; Scheiber and Finley 2011; Scheiber and Mitchell 2010; S. Schroeder 2010; Stein 2002; Stojanowski 2010; Thomas 1989; Trigg 2005; Tiesler et al. 2010; Voss 2008a, 2008b; Wade 2008). These examples show us that, through such colonial encounters, cultures undergo dramatic transformations in identity and social, economic, and political relations, and that to understand such encounters, we must turn away from simplistic models of colonialism drawn from world systems theory or models of domination and resistance (see Gosden 2004).

The chapters in this volume focus on the two major areas of the American Southwest that witnessed the most intensive and sustained colonial encounters: (1) the New Mexico Colony which extended from present-day northeastern Arizona to north and central New Mexico; and (2) the Pimería Alta in the northern Sonoran Desert (Figure 1.1). The particular mix of players, sociohistorical trajectories, and local and regional social relations within each area both led to, and were transformed by, markedly divergent colonial processes. Understanding these different mixes of players, history, and social relations provides the foundation for understanding the enormous changes wrought by colonialism in both New Mexico and the Pimería Alta. Such an understanding also allows us to create models of the colonial process that highlights processes of ethnogenesis and cultural transformation among and within the colonizing state, colonists, and Native Americans, as well as a more realistic picture of power relations, autonomy, and

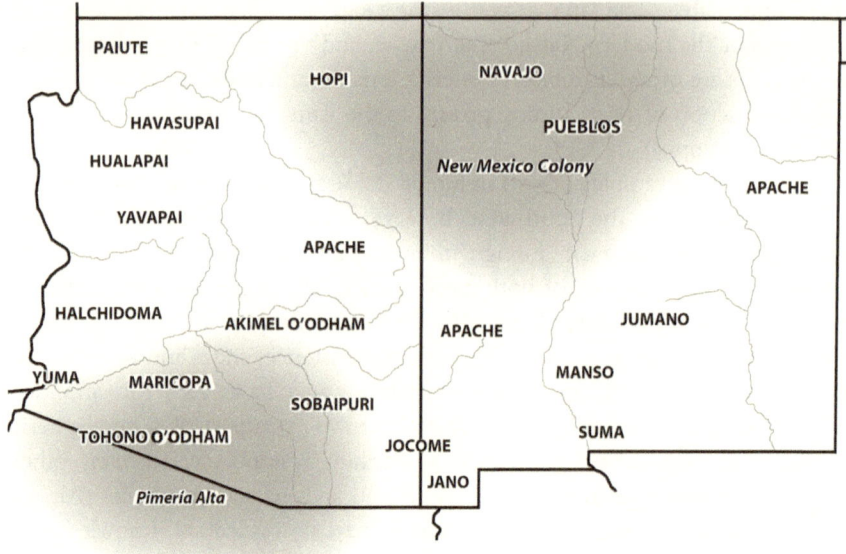

FIGURE 1.1. *Map of the American Southwest, including the approximate location of both the Pimería Alta (below) and the New Mexico Colony (above) (after Majewski and Ayres 1997:fig. 4).*

inequality among these groups. As a group, the chapters in this volume highlight such transformations and relations and focus on the experiences, perspectives, and actions of both Native Americans and European colonizers.

NATIVE AMERICANS, COLONISTS, AND TRANSFORMATIONS

Gil Stein (2005:25–26) has recently argued that colonial encounters should be viewed as having three participants: (1) the colonial homeland, (2) the colonies themselves, and (3) the indigenous societies living within the established colonies. This is a reaction to traditional views of the process of colonialism portrayed in a binary way with two primary players: the active, dominant colonizer and the passive colonized. One of the primary issues with this historical viewpoint on colonialism is that it is unidirectional (change occurs from colonialist to native peoples) and is, therefore, overly simplistic. Scholars today view colonialism as being highly complex in the nature of social relations that existed among various agents. In contrast, more traditional anthropological concepts such as "acculturation" and "assimilation" are unidirectional processes in which the passive indigenous groups alter their cultures to incorporate behaviors, practices, and material culture of the dominant colonizer (see Mitchell and Scheiber 2010:13–14). In pluralistic communities such as colonies, however, there are much more complex relations and interactions among different groups (e.g., Liebmann and

Murphy 2010). Without taking these complexities into account, there can be no recognition or conception of individual or social agency (Van Buren 2010:158; see also Hart et al. 2012; Lightfoot et al. 1998). Identifying social agency in colonial studies is important because (1) colonial processes are always grounded in history, (2) social actors are knowledgeable about the structure of society, and (3) the power and position of social actors vary (Mitchell and Scheiber 2010:16–17). Rather than being a unidirectional phenomenon, cultural interaction in colonial settings is better modeled as multidirectional, wherein cultural traditions evolve, change, as well as persist in a variety of ways (e.g., Deagan 2005; Haley and Wilcoxon 1997, 2005; Voss 2008a, 2008b). This is made abundantly clear by the chapters in this volume, which show great variation through time by both native and colonial groups in the American Southwest.

Colonialism is, at its essence, about unequal power structures (e.g., Gosden 2004; Hart et al. 2012). One important goal in the study of colonialism is to not view colonialism as an event or a defining moment in history, but as a context or a process in which one can view what Alexander (1998) originally referred to as "cultural entanglements." The resulting transformations, on the parts of both indigenous and colonial cultures, must be seen as part of the long-term histories of those groups (Hart et al. 2012; King 2012). These aspects of long-term histories affected and reflected the daily practice and general response of indigenous people to these newest foreign invaders to the Southwest (see Lightfoot et al. 1998). Changes or continuity of traditions in the face of colonialism should not be seen as an either/or situation, but rather as processes of responding and adapting to newly emerging and evolving cultural surroundings (Lightfoot 2012; Silliman 2009, 2012). Colonialism, in one form or another, was alive and well long before Spaniards arrived in the Americas. As we discussed elsewhere in this chapter, the American Southwest was no stranger to new groups and foreign ideas arriving from elsewhere and becoming incorporated into the cultural patterns and social histories of the region. Whether prehistoric interactions between the American Southwest and Mesoamerica were colonial in nature is debatable, and certainly the Spanish entry was several orders of magnitude different from anything seen previously, but it is important to acknowledge the nature of past cultural connections. Similar extraregional interactions and influences, certainly on a much larger scale, were present in central Mexico—from where Spaniards and their indios amigos originated (King 2012; Matthew 2012).

While some scholars conceive of Spanish colonies as being occupied by Spanish soldiers, settlers, and missionaries, it is clear from documentary and genetic records (see, e.g., Johnson and Lorenz 2010 and Snow 1998, 2010) that many colonies across North and Central America contained a mixture of peoples of different backgrounds that included many Mexican indigenous groups (such as the indios amigos discussed elsewhere in this chapter). The colonial era in the American Southwest, as well as neighboring Alta California, offered opportunities for colonists to reinvent themselves socially, away from the core of the Spanish colonial political economy in central Mexico. In Alta California, for example, colonists who in early censuses self-reported as being *mulato* or *mestizo* were later recorded as being of Spanish descent (e.g., Haley and Wilcoxon 1997, 2005; Voss 2005, 2008a). In one case, the 1781 census of the Pueblo of Los Angeles classified fewer than 5 percent of its residents as being of Spanish decent; just nine years later, nearly half of these same residents classified themselves as Spanish (Pubols 2010:132). By 1790, census records in Alta California began recording only two categories, *gente de razón* and *indio*, rather than the previously more complicated identity of race, thus creating a system that increasingly helped to contrast colonists (who most likely were of indigenous descent themselves, albeit from Sonora, Mexico) with resident indigenous groups. As we see in chapters by J. Homer Thiel (12), J. Andrew Darling and B. Sunday Eiselt (7), and Kelly L. Jenks (8) in this volume, similar processes were occurring in the American Southwest, as well.

As Spanish policies further and further restricted traditional subsistence practices, political economy, and self-reliance, Native Americans created novel solutions allowing the continuation of traditional practices and belief systems. The process of identity transformation was a reflexive one in which identities were transformed and communicated only with reference to previous identities (Casella and Fowler 2005:4). While many scholars have referred to these transformations as ethnogenesis (e.g., Haley and Wilcoxon 1997, 2005; Voss 2008a, 2008b), more recently Lee Panich (2013) has argued that these changes ought to be seen within the long-term histories of the perseverance among indigenous groups, rather than as "terminal narratives" (e.g. Wilcox 2009) of dramatic changes in identity and group constitution.

It is clear that Pueblo groups, in particular, transformed aspects of their lives and identities through the alteration of traditions. For example, the Hopi integrated many new concepts, material goods, and foods derived from colonists into their daily life, while simultaneously and actively maintaining core aspects of their culture (see, e.g., Laurie D. Webster, chapter 4 in this volume). In essence, the Hopi offered Spanish missionaries what they expected, and then went on to continue to perform traditional activities either in secret or after Spaniards left the Hopi Mesas (Dongoske and Dongoske 2002). Some scholars have referred to this as "passive" resistance (e.g., Adams 1989), while others have argued this was an active response to colonization—"Hopification" as Hartman Lomawaima (1989) has referred to it (see also discussion above of Brown's [2013] similar concept of "Pueblofication," as well as Clark [2005, 2012]). To be sure, native resistance to colonialism in the Southwest was multifaceted and reflected adaptations to the new and emerging colonial reality (see Mitchell and Scheiber 2010:17–18).

While many Native American groups incorporated aspects of colonial material goods and iconography into their everyday life, the message conveyed by those native people through the use of such items and images was not necessarily the same as when they were used by colonists. For the postrevolt period in New Mexico, for example, Matthew Liebmann (2012a:138–141; see also Liebmann 2002) describes the creation of variations on the image of the Virgin of Guadalupe in Puebloan portrayals of masked Pueblo dancers and the sun kachina (Frank 1998:46). In these cases, Pueblo artists appropriated and transformed Spanish iconography and imagery for their own purposes and needs. Such appropriation is an example of how Pueblo groups took, adapted, and used colonial symbols "to forge their way in [a] new colonial world" (Silliman 2005:68). By studying how agency and history combine to create new traditions that relate to particular long-term histories and circumstances, one can begin to understand transformations in colonial settings (Mills 2008:261). These trajectories continued well past initial colonial interaction in the American Southwest (see Liebmann [2012b]) and chapters by Thomas E. Sheridan and Stewart B. Koyiyumptewa [9], and Colleen Strawhacker [13], this volume, for discussions of colonialism extending into modern times).

It is through agency and shared histories that both colonists and indigenous groups transformed and created new identities during the colonial era. The histories of these groups defined the meanings of places on the landscape, how such places were used, and how people related to both these places and each other. Following Pauketat (2001, 2003), these histories can be seen as intertwining and creating webs of relations that connected people to each other and to their ancestors, and transformed the world around them during the colonial era. The concluding chapters to this volume, by Kent G. Lightfoot (chapter 14) and David Hurst Thomas (chapter 15), sum up these transformations in the American Southwest and compare and contrast them both to themselves, as well as to, respectively, Alta California and the American Southeast.

A PERSPECTIVE ON COLONIALISM IN THE AMERICAN SOUTHWEST

The colonial encounters in the American Southwest comprised a complex interaction involving multiple players and multiple agendas. Colonialism is generally defined as a dual process involving the "attempted domination by a colonial/settler population.... and the resistance, acquiescence, and the living through these by indigenous people" (Silliman 2005:59). With regard to the initial Spanish incursions into the Southwest during the 1500s, many might offer the view that resulting exchanges between indigenous groups and Spaniards were examples of culture contact, as these were relatively short-term encounters (e.g., Silliman 2005, 2009). However, with the official settlement of the New Mexico Colony in 1598, the policy of Spanish colonial domination became entrenched, and, to use Ferris's (2009:168–70) terminology, continued to "creep" forward (see Liebmann 2012a; Sheridan and Koyiyumptewa, chapter 9 in this volume). Stephen Silliman (2005:62) puts it well when he states, "Colonialism is not about an event but, rather, about processes of cultural entanglement, whether voluntary or not, in a broader world economy and system of labor, religious conversion, exploitation, material value, settlement, and sometimes imperialism." The establishment of missions, presidios, and other institutions of the Spanish Empire (see chapters by Strawhacker [13], Thiel [12], and Barnet Pavao-Zuckerman [11], this volume) formalized and structured relations with native groups who had lived in the Southwest for millennia, and inevitably drew cultures into a complex system of global colonial processes that transformed both groups in ways not captured by simple acculturation models or conquest narratives that have long dominated anthropological and historical thought on colonialism (see Wilcox 2009).

Chris Gosden describes colonialism—and, in particular, modern European colonialism—as a "total social fact" that has "infiltrated all areas of people's lives in all parts of the globe" (Gosden 2004:24; see also Gosden and Knowles 2001). These statements capture the transformative nature of the colonial process for all involved and highlight the roles of power relations, and social "creativity and experiment" (Gosden 2004:25). The unfolding outcomes of colonial processes were and are created by those who have *both* power and agency and are capable of enacting change. The Spanish conquest of the Southwest can be modeled as an example of Gosden's (2004:24–30) *terra nullius* form of colonization. Spanish colonizers would have viewed the cultural practices of indigenous groups as socially or politically illegitimate and would have asserted a natural right to control land, resources, people, and labor and forced new political and economic systems on native inhabitants. This colonization led to the transformation of native cultures and the recreation of existing social relations between native groups, as well as the death of many people through violence and the introduction of nonnative diseases (see Hull 2009:12–13; Ramenofsky and Kulisheck 2013). While Gosden's classification of colonialism is useful, scholars such as Spielmann and her colleagues have argued that he inadvertently deemphasizes "the actions of the living" (Spielmann et al. 2009:103). In their case study from the central New Mexico Salinas pueblos, Katherine Spielmann and her colleagues demonstrate with archaeological evidence that there were diverse and varied actions and reactions to colonization that were shaped by a combination of local environments, histories within specific pueblos, gender, past and present subsistence strategies, and the specifics of the establishment of missions. As they and others, such as Mark Mitchell and Laura Scheiber (Mitchell and Scheiber 2010), remind us, gender, ideology, and political economy all played important roles in guiding colonialism.

Despite such critique, Gosden's terra nullius concept provides a framework that allows us to recognize and begin to understand the roles that power and violence played in the Southwest colonial encounter (Gosden 2004:114–52). Traditionally, archaeologists and historians have tended to deemphasize violence and how it was used as a means of domination, culture change, and the establishment of control in social and economic relations with indigenous groups (see Wilcox 2009). By explicitly taking into account aspects of colonialism such as violence, the forcible usurpation of land and other critical material resources, and the religious and racist policies that drove much of European colonialism, we can critically examine indigenous resistance, culture change, and ethnogenesis within the colonial process. At the same time, though we do not wish to overemphasize violence by itself, it was at times an empowering factor for Pueblo groups (e.g., Wilcox 2009). While the violence of colonial encounters is undeniable (see chapters by Schmader [2], and Sheridan and Koyiyumptewa [9], this volume, for example), the focus on long-term histories, rather than on specific events, is also important to understanding its larger role and effect (Hart 2012:92; Silliman 2012:115). Colonialism in the American Southwest is much more complex than the Grand Narratives of domination and resistance (see Thomas [15] for a detailed discussion).

THE NEW MEXICO COLONY

In the following sections of this chapter, we briefly discuss the early colonial histories of the New Mexico Colony and the Pimería Alta to provide background for the rest of the volume. While each area was settled by Spanish missionaries, ranchers, and other colonists, their trajectories and individual histories are markedly different. We start with a discussion of the early history of the New Mexico Colony. This discussion below is meant as a brief overview; for some discussion of nuances, the reader is referred to the chapter by Thomas [15] in this volume.

The Pueblos and Their Neighbors

At the time of the first Spanish incursions into what would become known as the New Mexico Colony, the area was home to a diverse set of Native American groups, intertwined by complex sets of social relations and rich histories of living in the region that spanned thousands of years. Population estimates for the region preceding the colonial period have been placed in the high tens of thousands (e.g., Barrett 2002; Riley 1999). Multiple Pueblo Indian groups were living in large, multistoried, multifamily settlements, each consisting of numerous roomblocks in a vast area spread from the Hopi Mesas on the west to Pecos Pueblo on the east, and throughout a large portion of the Rio Grande valley and its tributaries—from Taos and Picuris Pueblos on the north to the Piro-speaking pueblos along the Rio Grande near modern-day Socorro (Barrett 2002; Cordell 1991; Spielmann 1998).

These Pueblo groups practiced irrigation and dryland farming and engaged in complex systems of trade and exchange that involved the community specialization of products; the extraregional distribution of bison products, shell, and other exotics; and the movement of raw materials (cotton, salt, obsidian, etc.) throughout the region (Shepard 1942; Snow 1981; Spielmann 1989, 1991; Warren 1969, 1979; see also chapters in Spielmann 1998). By the end of the sixteenth century, it is estimated that as many as 100 individual pueblos were occupied in the region, with many having populations of 500 to 1,000 people (chapters in Adams and Duff 2004; Barrett 2002; Graves 2002; Riley 1999). Pueblo groups spoke up to eleven distinct dialects or languages: (1) Zuni, (2) Hopi, (3) the Western Keresan dialect of Acoma and Laguna Pueblos, (4) Towa among the Jemez Pueblos and at Pecos, (5) Tewa among the villages along the Chama River and down the Rio Grande to its confluence with the Santa Fe River, (6) a possible distinct Tanoan or Southern Tewa dialect among the pueblos of the Galisteo Basin, (7) Northern Tiwa at Taos and Picuris, (8) Southern Tiwa among the pueblos of the Albuquerque Basin and along the eastern slopes of the Manzano Mountains, (9) Eastern Keresan among the villages of the lower Jemez River and along the Rio Grande to its confluence with Galisteo Creek, (10) Tompiro among the Jumanos pueblos, and (11) Piro among the southernmost pueblos along the Rio Abajo portion of the Rio Grande valley (chapters in Adams and Duff 2004; Cordell 1991; Eggan 1979; Hale and Harris 1979; Schroeder 1979). As well documented by over a century of anthropological and historical study, the entire Pueblo world was marked by both similarities and distinct differences in social organization, religion, economy, and political relations (e.g., Dozier 1983; Eggan 1950; Fox 1967; Levy 1992; Ortiz 1969; Sando 1992; Spicer 1962; Whiteley 1988), and these differences and similarities appear to have characterized the Pueblo world at the time of initial Spanish contact (e.g., Adams and Duff 2004; Barrett 2002; Graves 2002; Simmons 1979; A. Schroeder 1979).

In addition, there were a number of nonsedentary, primarily hunter-gatherer groups who occupied those regions to the south, east, and north of the Pueblo world. To the south lay the Mansos, who occupied areas in and around the Rio Grande valley near El Paso (Benavides 1996; Beckett and Corbett 1992; Riley 1999). To the south and east were the Teya/Jumanos, who are considered to have been Wichita- or Caddoan-speaking groups by many Plains anthropologists. Athabaskan-speaking Plains Apaches or Querechos also occupied areas to the north and east of the Rio Grande at the time of Spanish contact (Bolton 1990; Riley 1999).

The Early Colony

After Coronado and his forces returned to Mexico in 1542, it would be another four decades before the next Spanish incursion into what would become the New

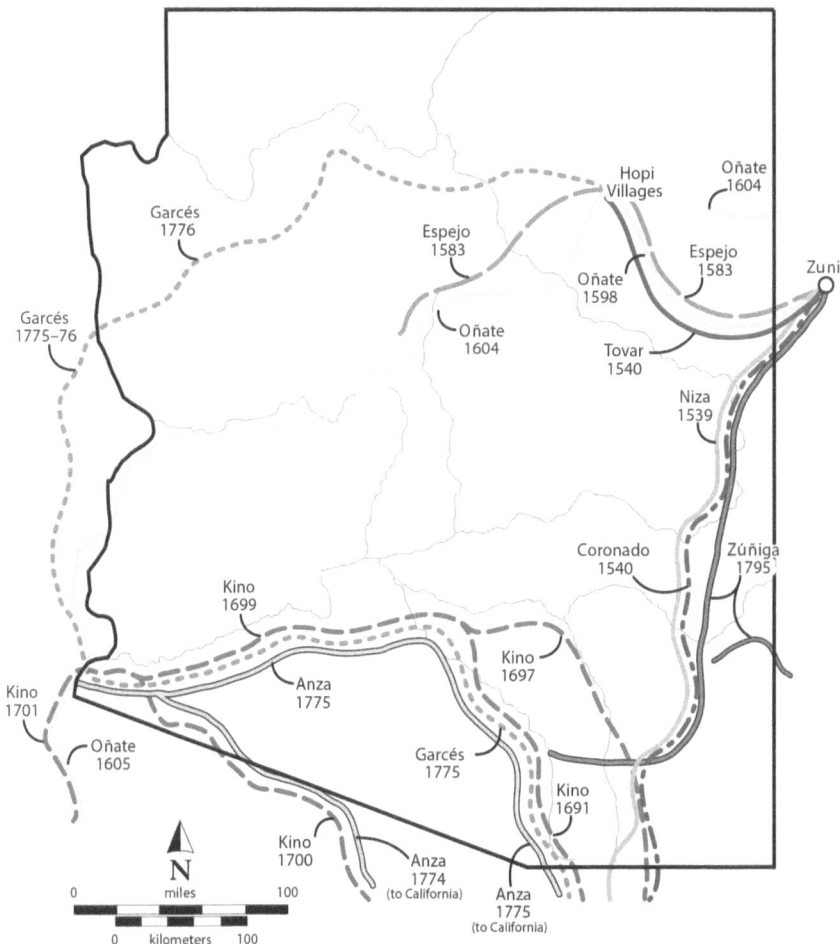

FIGURE 1.2. *Map of approximate early Spanish colonial routes through modern-day Arizona (after Majewski and Ayres 1997:fig. 2).*

Mexico Colony (Figures 1.2 and 1.3). As Linda Cordell (1991:27) discusses (see also Gutiérrez 1991:45–46; Hadley et al. 1997; Kessell 1979; Polzer and Sheridan 1997; Spielmann 1991), this hiatus can be attributed to the discovery of silver deposits in Zacatecas and the resultant shift in focus of colonial administrators from further exploration to the exploitation of this particular resource. In 1581, the expedition of Francisco Sánchez Chamuscado and Agustín Rodríguez entered the region with the joint mandate of missionization and exploration for mineral wealth (Barrett 2002:6; Bolton 1979 Cordell 1991:27; Hammond and Rey 1966). After only a few months and not finding any mineral wealth to exploit, the expedition returned to Mexico, but without Fray Rodríguez and another Franciscan

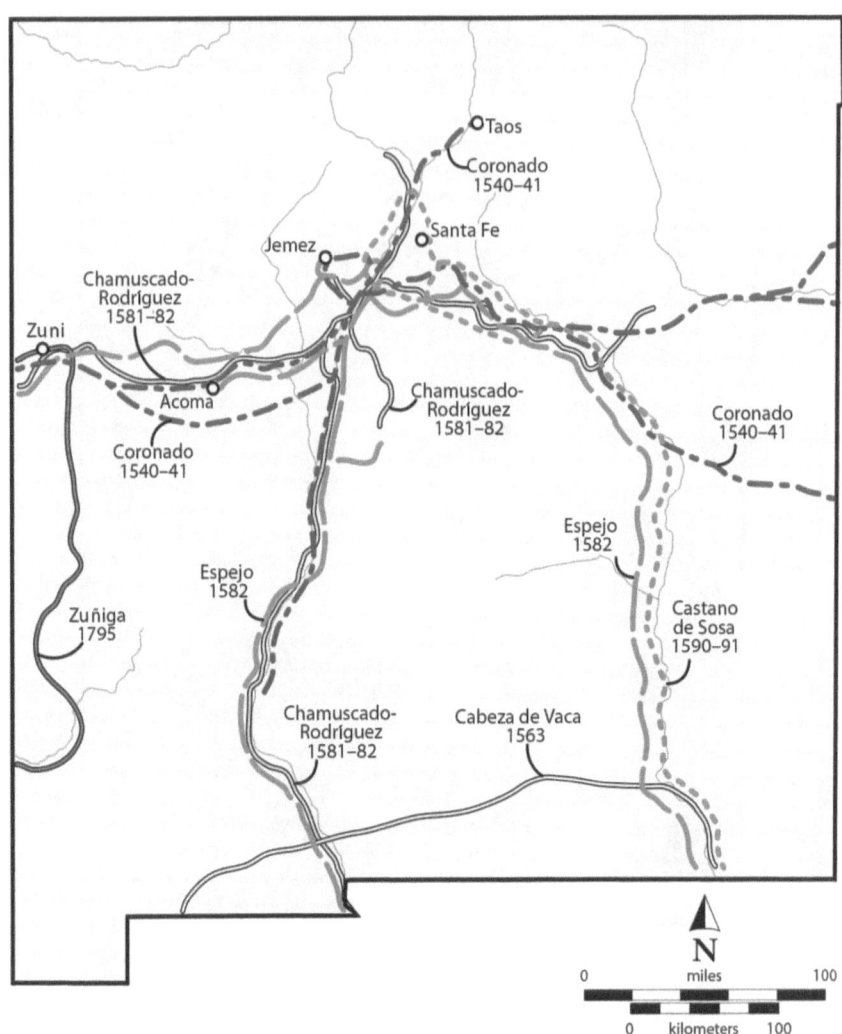

FIGURE 1.3. *Map of approximate early Spanish colonial routes through modern-day New Mexico (after Hartmann 2014:map 6; and Majewski and Ayres 1997:fig. 3).*

priest, who stayed behind to missionize the native people. A year later, another expedition was launched, led by Antonio de Espejo, to investigate reports that Rodríguez had been killed. After confirming Rodríguez's death, Espejo and his forces traveled west to Hopi and the Verde River valley, and then returned to Mexico, only spending five months in what is now New Mexico and Arizona (Barrett 2002:6; Cordell 1991:27; Hammond and Rey 1966).

Nearly a decade later, the early 1590s witnessed two attempts to colonize New Mexico that were not officially sanctioned by the colonial government of

New Spain and the Spanish Crown. In late 1590 / early 1591, Gaspar Castaño de Sosa led a small group north to the Pecos River and then west into Pueblo territory (Barrett 2002:6; Cordell 1991:27; Hammond and Rey 1966). After only seven months, this party was captured by forces led by Juan Morlete, who had been sent to return the illegal expedition to the colony. A second unsanctioned expedition into New Mexico with the intent of establishing a colony was launched in 1593 by two military captains, Leyva de Bonilla and Antonio Gutiérrez de Humaña (Barrett 2002:6; Hammond and Rey 1966). Little is known of this expedition as all members except one were killed while exploring the Plains east of the Pueblos along the Rio Grande (as reported to Juan de Oñate by the lone survivor five years later).

In addition to providing much ethnohistoric information regarding indigenous Southwestern groups, these expeditions in the late 1500s also reflected a renewed interest in colonizing the northern frontier of Mexico by both the Spanish Crown and the administrators and leaders of the colonial provinces of New Spain. In 1595, Juan de Oñate, the *alcalde mayor* of San Luis Potosí, was granted the contract to launch an expedition to establish the Colony of New Mexico (Hammond and Rey 1953; Riley 1999:42). Oñate, born around 1550 in Zacatecas, was the son of the lieutenant governor of the colonial province of Nueva Galicia (Riley 1999:40). After a significant delay due to changes in the viceroyalty of Mexico and considerations of competing applications by the Council of the Indies, Oñate and his forces began the journey northward in early 1598 (Hammond and Rey 1953:309–14; Riley 1999:42–43). On April 30, 1598, Juan de Oñate and his group stopped a few miles south of the Rio Grande and formally established the Colony of New Mexico by decree; and, on May 4 the expedition crossed the river near present-day El Paso (Hammond and Rey 1953:16, 315). These first colonists consisted of soldiers, Franciscan priests, servants, slaves, and their families. The group may have totaled between 400 and 560 people, including women and children (Cordell 1991:27; Riley 1999:46). On July 11 of that year, Oñate established the first Spanish settlement in New Mexico named San Gabriel across the river from the Tewa pueblo Ohkay Owingeh (the former San Juan Pueblo) (Hammond and Rey 1953:17; Simmons 1991). The official colonial capital would later be moved to the settlement of Santa Fe in 1610 by the second governor of New Mexico, Pedro de Peralta (Cordell 1991:27).

Almost immediately, Oñate and his forces traveled to scores of pueblos throughout the region to exact obedience to the Spanish Crown and colonial authority. Oñate's governorship lasted only until 1607, the year he resigned under pressure from the Spanish Crown and the viceroy of Mexico (Hammond and Rey 1953:32). His tenure was marked by what were often brutal and violent dealings with Pueblo groups throughout the colony and the forcible extraction of labor, food, and other commodities from these communities (see chapters by Sheridan and Koyiyumptewa [9], and Webster [4], this volume). Oñate never found the mineral wealth he sought in the new colony, and traveled as far east as Wichita, Kansas, and as far west as the Gulf of California looking for riches and a route to a Pacific seaport (Cordell 1991; Hammond and Rey 1953; Riley 1999:83–86). By the end of Oñate's governorship, the colony was considered a failure by the Spanish Crown and colonial authorities in Mexico, and there was talk of abandoning the effort (Riley 1999:86–87; see also Fontana 1994:79). In 1608 or 1609, Phillip III made the colony a royal province with missionization and the conversion of indigenous groups to Christianity as its principal objective (Hammond and Rey 1953:33–34; Riley 1999:87). Moving forward, missionization efforts and the continued extraction of Indian labor, land, and resources by both mission and secular officials and colonists became the main focus of the colonial effort.

Multiethnic Nature of the Colony

Although the first expeditions to New Mexico as well as the early colonists are often described as Spanish, it is important to note that these early explorers and colonists comprised diverse peoples from varied racial, ethnic, and social-status backgrounds, much like the native groups they encountered (see Severin Fowles and colleagues, chapter 6 in this volume). The work of Kathleen Deagan and Jane Landers (Deagan and Landers 1999) at Fort Mosé near St. Augustine, Florida, provides a good example of the potential cultural and linguistic diversity of Spanish colonial communities and how social identities may have been forged in settlements composed of individuals of many different traditions, origins, and social statuses. It is important to remember that while there were often clear or specific goals set by the Spanish Crown for the colonizing of the Americas, there were many times diverse and at times conflicting interests and goals of the members of these early expeditions and settlements themselves. Thus, these early colonial encounters and the colonists involved must be viewed as multiethnic interactions with the resulting colonial communities having been pluralistic in their compositions.

The presence of indios amigos among many early colonial and military expeditions also illustrates the multiethnic or multicultural nature of Spanish colonial encounters (see Schmader, chapter 2 in this volume). Alliances with native warriors such as these were used repeatedly by Spaniards to aid in conquering new areas and putting down indigenous rebellions across the Americas. Guatemala, for example, was conquered by a combination of hundreds of Spanish soldiers and thousands upon thousands of indigenous indios amigos consisting of groups from central Mexico and Oaxaca (Asselberg 2008; Matthew 2007, 2012; Oudijk and Mathew 2007). Indios amigos from central Mexico also accompanied the Spanish to other areas of conquest further removed, including Peru and the Philippines (Asselberg 2008; Richard Flint, personal communication, 2016).

The Coronado expedition may have included up to 2,000 indios amigos. Richard Flint (2008:10–12) argues that in helping to explore the northern frontier, those indios amigos on the Coronado expedition were at least partially motivated by the Spanish policy of allowing native warriors to keep captives captured in battle, or by the Spanish reduction of tribute obligations to native central Mexican communities who provided soldiers for the expedition (see Asselberg 2008 for discussion of similar Spanish colonial policies on the southern frontier with Guatemala). In addition to indios amigos, there were also *naborias* (also called *auxiliares*), who were generally laborers and former Indian slaves or individuals from defeated populations (see Yannakakis 2011:656).

While some scholars have suggested that the principal indigenous military ally with early Spanish expeditions to New Mexico were Tlaxcaltecas, because they were early allies of Hernán Cortés and were enemies of the Aztecs, Richard Flint and Shirley Cushing Flint (Flint and Flint 2005:165), David Snow (1998, 2010) and William Wroth (2010) argue that they see little documentary evidence specifically identifying Tlaxcaltecas. Snow (2010:50–52; see also Snow 1998) does not believe there were Tlaxcaltecas with the Coronado expedition, though he argues that perhaps there were several with either Juan de Oñate in 1598 or Diego de Vargas in 1693. Wroth (2010:176) argues that some scholars may have assumed indios amigos on early Spanish expeditions to New Mexico were Tlaxcaltecas since they helped the Spanish subdue northern Mexican indigenous groups, which were referred to in Nahua as *Chichimeca*. In addition, the Tlaxcaltecas were known to head to the edge of the Spanish frontier and establish barrios or communities; for example, Analco Araval in Oaxaca (see Yannakakis 2011 for details) and also Coahuila and Nuevo León (Wroth 2010:176), among other locations. During this same general time period, the mid-1500s to mid-1600s, other Spanish colonial settlements that contained barrios of indios amigos of various central Mexican origin included the Guatemalan communities of Totonicapán, Santiago, and Ciudad Viejo Sonsonate; San Salvador and San Miguel in modern El Salvador; Ciudad Real in Chiapas; San Esteban de Nueva Tlaxcala at Saltillo; Chalchihuites and Nombre de Dios in Durango; and Antequera in Oaxaca (see Asselberg 2008:113; Matthew 2000; Snow 2010:51).

In any case, while in early expeditions only a few indigenous conquerors may have stayed in what is now New Mexico (the few who stayed at Zuni, e.g., [see Flint and Flint 2005:166–67]), later indios amigos from central Mexico who arrived at the New Mexico Colony founded a barrio community in Santa Fe called Analco on the south side of the Santa Fe River. Wroth (2010:177) argues that while Tlaxcaltecas residing in ethnic barrios in other portions of the Spanish frontier edge gained special status and privileges (see also Snow 2010:49), those indios amigos residing in the Barrio Analco were not granted the same special status and were, instead, a "service class assisting the Spaniards in various realms such as labor, herding, hunting, and artisanal vocations, which placed them above the level of domestic servants and slaves, but below the level of full autonomy which, on paper at least, existed for the Tlaxcalans in their settlements." Indios amigos in Guatemala for generations after initial conquest also had difficulty in obtaining certain rights or levels of status they had been led to believe they would obtain for aiding the Spanish in conquering the area (see Matthew 2012 for a detailed examination).

The frontier of the Spanish Empire, even at this early stage, was a place for colonists to reinvent themselves, to create new identities (see chapters by Darling and Eiselt [7], Jenks [8], and Thiel [12], this volume). For example, Flint (2008:60; see also Flint and Flint 2005:166) states that when the Espejo expedition arrived in New Mexico, it found indios amigos still living in the Zuni area who had arrived with Coronado nearly forty years earlier. Stanley Hordes (2005:89) has argued that a motivation of the unsanctioned Castaño de Sosa expedition was leading persecuted crypto-Jews to "a secure haven in the far northern frontier." Crypto-Jews were also part of the later expedition to New Mexico led by Oñate, including some who had been a part of Castaño de Sosa's failed expedition (Hordes 2005:111). Barbara Voss (2008a, 2008b) and others (e.g., Haley and Wilcoxon 1997, 2005) have argued persuasively that in early overland expeditions to Alta California, from the moment many settlers left the confines of the strict caste system in the colonial core, their identities were being transformed. Settlers were able to refine and reinvent their identities in new surroundings far from the colonial heartland. Frontier settlements generally provide useful avenues for transformation of identity (see Comaroff and Comaroff 1991; Rice and Rice 2005; Matthew 2012). Similar motivations and similar transformations and fluidity of identity must have characterized the colonization of New Mexico over a century earlier.

Means of and Motivations for Colonization

The means of and the motivations for colonizing New Mexico fall into two categories: (1) the desire for economic wealth and power, and (2) the Franciscan missionary program. Initially, the primary motivation for attempts to colonize New Mexico was the desire for mineral wealth. Early explorers and the early colonists under Oñate's governorship held out hope that the silver and other mineral riches of the northern provinces of New Spain could be found along the far northern frontier. As discussed above, these dreams were not realized and the economic underpinning of this particular colonial intrusion would have to be found elsewhere.

From the beginning of the New Mexico colony through the 1700s, the real basis of the Spanish colonial economy lay in the colonists' ability to control and exploit land and the products and labor of Native Americans. The primary structural means by which this control was exerted were the *encomienda* and *repartimiento* systems. The encomienda system refers to the practice of conferring control of specific lands to preferred subjects of the colony (Anderson 1985). With this control came the right to exact tribute from indigenous groups living within and around the land grant (see Liebmann 2012b:32–33). Through the encomienda system, Spanish colonists were able to take as tribute Indian lands, labor, and food products and significantly "weakened the economic foundations of Pueblo society" (Liebmann 2012b:33). The abuse of this system, its inherent inequality, and the devastating effects it had on Pueblo economy and society were apparent to both the colonial administration in New Spain and Franciscan missionaries (Anderson 1985:360–61; Hammond and Rey 1953; Liebmann 2012b:32–33; Scholes 1944). Throughout the 1500s and 1600s, the Spanish Crown and viceregal administrators in Mexico enacted measures to control the granting of encomiendas and the ability of *encomenderos* to exact tribute and labor from Native Americans (e.g., Anderson 1985:355–57, 367). In the New Mexico colony, clergy members protested the exploitation of Native Americans by encomenderos and the exacting of labor and tribute by governors and their administrators (Anderson 1985:361, 364–66). However, such acknowledgment and denunciation of the exploitation and inequity of the encomienda system did nothing to eliminate such practice.

Along with the encomienda system, the repartimiento system provided the means for other early colonists to exploit Indian labor. Under repartimiento, Spanish landholders could force Native Americans to work on farms and ranches and to provide labor for other colonial pursuits (Anderson 1985:354; Liebmann 2012b:33–34). As Katherine Spielmann and her colleagues have shown, these increased labor demands made of the Pueblos by Spanish colonists had deleterious effects on the health of Pueblo communities (Spielmann et al. 2009). Such labor demands also took away from the labor necessary to produce food, and surpluses dwindled at pueblos throughout New Mexico in the century following the first colonial encounters. An important component of the exploitation of Indian resources and labor through the encomienda and repartimiento systems was the harsh and sometimes violent tactics that Spanish colonists employed to exact tribute. Over the course of the seventeenth century, colonists increasingly employed either threats of violence or direct violent actions in their efforts to take Pueblo labor and commodities (Liebmann 2012b:34; see also Hadley et al. 1997:232).

Missionization and the conversion of Native Americans to Christianity can be seen as both the primary means by which the colonial process was sustained in New Mexico following the first decades of the colony's establishment, and the primary motivation for sustaining such colonial efforts (see Gutiérrez 1991). Missionizing efforts in New Mexico began in earnest with the very first Spanish expedition into the region by Fray Marcos de Niza in 1539. Despite the clear economic motivations behind the early colonial expeditions, proselytizing and the conversion of native groups were always a major concern of the Spanish Crown in all of its colonizing efforts globally.

In New Mexico, economic and missionizing motivations to colonize can be seen as complementary. Both required the successful control over and exploitation of indigenous labor and production to succeed, and the control of indigenous populations was key to the overall colonial strategy (Galgano 2005:9). For the Spanish, the New Mexico Colony was fraught with difficult transportation routes, geographically isolated colonial settlements, droughts, and numerous autonomous native communities. As a result of these concerns and priorities, the establishment of missions in native settlements was seen as an important factor for success of the New Mexico Colony. In fact, given the lack of mineral resources in New Mexico, missionization became the primary function of the colony when it became a royal colony financed by the Spanish Crown (see Liebmann 2012b:34–35). By the mid-1600s, nearly fifty Franciscan priests were located in Pueblo communities throughout New Mexico, and the program of church and mission construction was well underway (see Sheridan and Koyiyumptewa, chapter 9 in this volume).

Spanish missions were constructed immediately adjacent to or within Pueblo communities, at times incorporating kivas to metaphorically draw on the power of traditional Pueblo religion the Spanish were attempting to simultaneously alter (Gutiérrez 1991; see also chapters by Phillip O. Leckman [3], Lightfoot [14], and Thomas [15], this volume). The overall agenda spearheaded by Franciscan missionaries in the New Mexico Colony was to create "a program of religious and social conversion calculated to undermine native institutions and sources of cultural strength in order to make the Pueblo people into Catholics and Spaniards" (Frank 1998:50). To do so, they had to confront and attempt to alter the native political, social, and religious structures that lay opposed to their conversion (see chapters by Leckman [3], and Sheridan and Koyiyumptewa [9], this volume). As a result, colonial Spanish religious structure was placed in such a way to mediate that opposition while also attempting to overpower it. In the Hopi village of Awatovi, for example, Franciscan priests filled in the village's kiva with clean sand and constructed the altar of the Mission church on top (Dongoske and Dongoske 2002). Leckman, chapter 3 in this volume, describes a possible similar situation at the Pueblo site of Paako. Other times, as in the case of Abó and Quarai, while the missionaries supervised the construction of church complexes, they allowed the construction of kivas adjacent to these buildings (see chapter by Thomas [15], this volume, for further discussion of this and alternative viewpoints).

This may have been, according to Robert Galgano (2005:73–74), ways for friars to "smooth" the introduction of Christianity to the native Pueblo populations.

Missionaries may have wanted to encourage "a Christianity that allowed for local flavor and permitted native expression" (Galgano 2005:75). However, it is clear that most missions and priests in New Mexico actively discouraged the continuation of, and tried to eradicate, traditional Pueblo religious rituals as part of their program of conversion (see Sheridan and Koyiyumptewa, chapter 9 in this volume). At the same time that Spanish religious institutions were created and imposed to negate native ones, Spanish missionaries also attempted to destabilize the native spheres of authority and leadership, as well as the sexual division of labor, both inside and outside Pueblo households and communities (see insight into this process at Hopi before and after conquest by Webster, chapter 4 in this volume). For example, while the Spaniards introduced domesticated animals as a food source (see Yetman 1994), it had the indirect effect of aiding to negate the traditional role of the male hunters (Frank 1998:51; Gutiérrez 1991:77; Pavao-Zuckerman 2011). In fact, many roles that females had traditionally performed were now, under Spanish leadership, afforded to males, and vice versa—activities such as weaving, hunting, community defense, and construction. Such dramatic shifts in the sexual division of labor likely altered and destabilized central aspects of Pueblo society (Gutiérrez 1991:76).

Despite the convergence of motivations among secular Spanish colonists and Franciscan missionaries, "the political climate of New Mexico was characterized by significant church-state tensions for much of the seventeenth century" (Liebmann 2012b:35). Franciscans and secular colonists were often at odds for control of indigenous labor and production, and such struggles and the deleterious effects of such tribute on Pueblo communities were main factors in the mission program and the political power wielded by the Franciscan order in the new colony (Gutiérrez 1991). In fact, high demands for tribute and labor from Pueblos have been argued to be reasons why mission recruitment was relatively strong in the early colonial period. For example, Andrew Knaut (1995:62–65) argues that so much food tribute was commanded by Spanish troops in 1600 and 1601, on top of a drought, that Pueblos could not sustain themselves. Many Pueblos had several years' storage of corn which was demanded by colonial administrators and encomenderos, leaving little remaining for those communities themselves. Much like later mission recruitment in Alta California in the early nineteenth century, the increase in neophytes in New Mexico appeared to partially be based on the needs of native populations for food, which missions could provide (see Hackel 2005, Larson et al. 1994, among others, for Alta California parallels). By 1607, another enticement for mission recruitment that resulted from the tribute demands made upon Pueblos was Spanish protection from Athapaskan raiding (Knaut 1995:66–67). Raiding was a response to the colonists' disruption of traditional trade networks, as well as the depletion, in part, of Pueblo stores of food and products devoted to such trade in the past. In the face of these difficulties, recruitment to missions can be seen as a reasonable response to ensure basic survival. As discussed below, however, such recruitment to missions many times did not equate to anything other than an outward facade of compliance by Pueblo groups.

Native Resistance and the Pueblo Revolt of 1680

In 1680, the Pueblo Revolt forced Spanish colonists and missionaries out of New Mexico (e.g., Hackett and Shelby 1942; Knaut 1995; Liebmann 2010, 2012a; Liebmann and colleagues, this volume; Preucel 2002a; Preucel et al. 2002; Silverberg 1970; Sheridan and Koyiyumptewa, chapter 9 in this volume; Spicer 1962; Wilcox 2009). This resistance to, and rejection of, Spanish colonial hegemony was one of the "pivotal events in Southwestern history" (Preucel 2002b:4) and provides a context within which to understand issues of native autonomy, power relations, domination and resistance, and processes of ethnogenesis and cultural transformation in the New Mexico Colony. During the revolt, twenty-one Franciscan missionaries—half of all Franciscans in New Mexico at that time—were killed and 400 or so colonists lost their lives (Preucel 2002b:3; Yetman 2012:73). Many of the physical signs of Spanish colonialism—churches, missions, homes, and government buildings—were burned, otherwise destroyed, or altered and subsequently occupied by Pueblo groups. Those colonists and priests who did not die in the revolt fled to safety in El Paso. It would be twelve years until Spanish colonists and missionaries returned and reestablished the New Mexico Colony, along with a renewed military effort (see examples of Spanish correspondence and analysis related to this in Hadley et al. 1997).

The Pueblo Revolt of 1680 and its aftermath were important in several ways (see chapters by Liebmann and colleagues [5], and Sheridan and Koyiyumptewa [9], this volume). First, until August of that year, many of the Pueblos were independent of one another, and while some were allied with one another, others were allied, at least tenuously, with Spanish colonists and thus against other Pueblos. Through time, such tenuous alliances with colonists became more difficult and strained. The revolt joined together much of the Pueblo world against a common enemy—the foreign invaders who had occupied their land for nearly a century, demanded tribute, and served extremely harsh treatment against the inhabitants of the entire region.

Second, the revolt appears to have wrought significant changes in Pueblo identity and the social relations that existed among disparate Pueblo communities. Liebmann (2012a:147–58; see also Whiteley [2003] for a more longitudinal view) argues that there was an emergence of a postrevolt pan-Pueblo identity, signified in part by changes in architecture and ceramic manufacture. For example, after 1680, plain redware became popular throughout the northern Rio Grande and was used in Jemez, Keres, and Tewa communities, as well as at

Pecos Pueblo (Kidder 1936; Liebmann 2012b:149–50). Plain redware in the northern Rio Grande may have symbolized a spreading pan-Pueblo consciousness and is similar to other undecorated redware from other portions of the Rio Grande region that was produced before the revolt; such as Salinas Red from the Salinas pueblos of Gran Quivira, Abó, and Quarai (Hayes et al. 1981:101). In addition, after 1680, there appears to have been an emergent unity of design among different decorated pottery types across parts of the northern Rio Grande (Liebmann 2012b:153–56). Four motifs—feathers, hooked triangles, key motifs, and cap steps or "sacred mountain" motifs—were adopted and commonly depicted on decorated ceramics at Jemez and Keres communities and at Pecos, Acoma, and Zuni, as well as among Tewa communities. The widespread use of these motifs among Pueblo potters may have been the result of artists "downplay[ing] their historical heterogeneity" (Liebmann 2012b:151), and could mark the unification of different Pueblo identities. At the same time, see Liebmann and colleagues' (chapter 5, this volume) study of Post-Revolt factionalism.

Across the Pueblo world, the manipulation and control over signs and symbols (*sensu* Liebmann 2012b) played an important role in colonial resistance and the preservation of native ideology and religious practice. Such manipulation and control are most obviously witnessed in changes in the use and the depiction of iconographic designs on pottery. Images such as feathers and stylized depictions of birds, serpents, and masked figures—seemingly benign images to the Spanish colonists and missionaries focused on eradicating Pueblo religious practices—were representative of core elements of Pueblo religion associated with prayer sticks, altar decorations, ritual costumes, or shields (Mills 2002:95). For example, while feathers are seen in ceramics across the Pueblo world in the 1600s and later in a wide variety of contexts, Barbara Mills (2002:95) argues that "similarities at the regional scale in the use of feathers is quite striking and suggests a unity that cross-cuts language groups and other important social differences among the Pueblos." In another example, Spielmann and her colleagues, argue that radical design changes in the iconography of domestic pottery at Gran Quivira, specifically among Tabira Black-on-white and Tabira Polychrome vessels, were attempts by female potters to express important Pueblo ritual knowledge in the face of active Franciscan suppression of such symbolism (Spielmann et al. 2006:640). Many new iconographic symbols introduced to the design of domestic black-on-white vessels—including masked katsina figures, feathers, possible deities, and birds—were previously found only in kiva murals and other ceremonial contexts (see also Mobley-Tanaka [2002] for similar arguments). Spielmann and her colleagues argue that different vessels, with distinct combinations of icons and signs, could represent specific religious societies or rituals performed at Gran Quivira (Spielmann et al. 2006:639). Through the production and decoration of these vessels, it was possible for religious knowledge to be conveyed and sustained clandestinely. Thus, it appears that ceramic decoration was an important medium that played a crucial role in resistance to Spanish hegemony and in the expression of complex messages and identities across the Pueblo world, whether in secret or hiding in the open, both before and after the revolt (see Mobley-Tanaka 2002).

The New Mexico Colony Postrevolt

After several unsuccessful Spanish attempts at recolonization, Vargas led groups of soldiers and colonists to reestablish the New Mexico Colony in 1692 and 1693 (Kessell and Hendricks 1992; Preucel 2002b). Through a series of brutal suppressions of Pueblo opposition over the next several years, he was able to exert control over the colony once more (Hadley et al. 1997; Kessell and Hendricks 1992; Kessell et al. 1995, 1998; Knaut 1995:179–84; Liebmann 2012b; Preucel 2002b). As the eighteenth and nineteenth centuries in New Mexico apparently witnessed a decrease in the level of violence in Spanish colonial policies and actions toward native groups in New Mexico (Knaut 1995:184–85), the organized resistance to Spanish colonial domination that characterized the latter part of the seventeenth century would not be seen again. Perhaps the centuries after the Pueblo Revolt may be seen as exemplifying the transformative nature of the colonial process (see Gosden 2004). As groups exerted agency, power, and their capacity for social "creativity and experiment" (Gosden 2004:25), identities and relations were transformed and, though they were clearly unequal in terms of power, both colonists and Native Americans found themselves intertwined in an uneasy relationship in a transformed world as the colonial encounter and their shared history continued to "creep forward" (*sensu* Ferris 2009).

For example, during the eighteenth century, Pueblo and other non-Pueblo native communities continued to culturally negotiate their relationship with colonial powers and colonists (see chapters by Fowles and colleagues [6], Liebmann and colleagues [5], and Webster [4], in this volume). Economically, politically, and spiritually, native peoples were incorporated into aspects of this new colonial society. Simultaneously, native peoples incorporated aspects of newly introduced colonial traditions into their everyday life, though the meaning and internal perception of these new traits were not necessarily what colonists understood them to be (see chapters by Thomas [15], and Webster [4], this volume). Because the government in New Mexico was generally weak (see chapter 5, by Liebmann and colleagues, this volume), the colonial state had little ability to "completely negate the power of Pueblo people to make choices about what elements of the Spanish lifestyle they were going to accept or reject" (Brown 2013:15). In her recent examination of eighteenth-century interaction between New Mexico colonists and native peoples, Brown (2013:17) has argued the power relationships between these groups, while unequal, allowed Pueblos to "dance" with colonists and colonial powers, at times Pueblo groups being led, while at other points native peoples leading this interaction. Much like Lomawaima (1989) conceptualizes Hopification, Tracy Brown (2013:17–20) argues for Pueblofication, in that Pueblo groups created new identities through allowing flexibility in the incorporation of new traditions into their cultural matrix. Some concepts, material goods, or traditions could be viewed as things easily discarded, while others became wholly integrated into Pueblo society. As Brown (2013:168) notes, "[Pueblos] expanded political, economic, and ritual traditions to meet demands and burdens placed upon them by contact, and they also sometimes conformed practices to Spanish expectations, especially when those expectations aligned with their own practices and beliefs."

Colonists, as well, adapted and transformed as time progressed in the New Mexico Colony (see chapters by Darling and Eiselt [7], and Jenks [8], this volume). During the initial stages of colonization, everyday life must be met with an open mind to survive, especially on the frontier. Rather than focusing economic output on one task, economic diversity was key for many (Trigg 2005). While initial colonists identified themselves as Spanish (even if they were of other descent), they slowly transformed themselves into New Mexican colonists. Through time, that identity became more solidified, a pattern seen in other colonies as well (see Deagan 1997; Voss 2008a, 2008b), though there was an increasing amount of interaction—social and otherwise—between these colonists and the native inhabitants. Furthering this, it has been suggested that in rural areas, the colonial economy was centered in Pueblo villages (see Trigg 2005:216). Soon after reconquest, many of these colonists transformed their identities from colonists to *vecinos* (Hispanic citizens), which further differentiated them from native peoples (Frank 2000; see chapters by Darling and Eiselt [7], and Jenks [8], in this volume, for detailed discussions of the process and context of becoming vecinos in late colonial New Mexico).

THE PIMERÍA ALTA

To the south and west of New Mexico, in the area of the northern Sonoran Desert known as the Pimería Alta, sustained colonial efforts began in the late 1680s with the establishment of a series of Jesuit missions by Father Eusebio Francisco Kino (e.g., Bolton 1919, 1936, 1979). The term "Pimería Alta" hails from early Spanish visitors' (including Kino's) distinctions between different dialects of the Piman speakers. While the native speakers of this language referred (and continue to refer today) to themselves as the O'odham, the Spanish used the term *Pima* and therefore defined the Pimería Alta and Pimería Baja to distinguish the physical boundaries of these languages and people (Fontana 1994:93). In this chapter, we use a combination of both modern and colonial terms for native groups of the

Pimería Alta; examples of colonial names for these groups, some of which are still used today, include Papago, Pima, Sobaipuri, Sand Papago, and Apache. In what is now central Sonora, missions were established among the Yaqui in 1617 and among the Pima Bajo (Pimería Baja)] Eudeves, and Ópatas in the 1620s and 1630s (see Spicer 1962). Settlements in Sonora were first established around 1640 and were located along river valleys in the northeastern part of the present-day state, to the south and east of the Pimería Alta. Missions expanded farther north into the Pimería Alta in the late 1600s based on Father Kino's plans to extend the mission system to the Colorado and Gila rivers (Mirafuentes Galvan 1994:103; see Spanish correspondence related to this dating from the 1700s for this region in Polzer and Sheridan 1997). These missions in the Pimería Alta were maintained by the Jesuit order until 1767 and were then taken over by the Franciscan Order when the Jesuits were expelled from the Spanish colonies across the New World. During the Jesuit period, numerous missions were established, while during the subsequent Franciscan period, the Franciscans only established a *visita* at Santa Ana de Cuiquiburitac to the northwest of Tucson, in 1811 or 1812. As in the New Mexico Colony, the mission system in the Pimería Alta had two fundamental duties: to represent the Spanish Crown and convert native groups to Christianity. Throughout their history, these missions relied on Native American labor for economic support. As the Pimería Alta became more economically and politically important to colonial efforts in the early 1700s, settlements and military posts called presidios were also established by colonial administrators, as were mining enterprises and small support settlements (Donohue 1969; Kessell 1970; Officer 1987; Polzer and Sheridan 1997; Spicer 1962) (see chapters by Thiel [12] and Pavao-Zuckerman [11], this volume). The first presidio in Sonora was established in 1691 and had no fixed home base or facility. By the early 1700s, it had become settled at the site of Fronteras in what is now Sonora. No other presidios were established in Sonora until 1742, when garrisons were established at Terrenate and Pitic (see Naylor and Polzer 1986 and Polzer and Sheridan 1997).

Native groups were quite diverse in the Pimería Alta and contrasted significantly in settlement patterns to indigenous groups in the New Mexico Colony (see Lauren E. Jelinek and Dale S. Brenneman, chapter 10 in this volume, for a detailed discussion of these groups; Seymour 2011, 2012). When Kino first passed through the Pimería Alta, the area was inhabited by speakers of the Piman language, which is a Uto-Aztecan language. Kino referred to many of the various groups as Pima, a term derived from the Piman word *pimahaitu*, meaning "nothing" (Doyel 1989; see also Fontana 1996). Groups inhabiting the Pimería Alta included Pápagos (now considered a derogatory term for the Tohono O'odham); Pimas, Sobaipuris, and Gileños (Akimel O'odham); Sobas and Areneños (possibly Hia Ced O'odham); and the Yuman-speaking Coco-maricopas and Opas (Maricopas, or Pee Posh). Neighboring groups along the region's periphery included Jocomes, Apaches, Yumas (Quechan); Quíquimas (Halyikwamai or possibly Cócopas), Seris, Nébomes (Eudeves), and Ópatas (Doyel 1989:140–42; Fontana 1996; Seymour 2011, 2012; Spicer 1962). Spaniards in general, however, tended to combine these numerous groups into larger subgroups, likely due to the mixing of populations brought about through Spanish and missionary influences (see Jelinek and Brenneman, chapter 10, this volume).

The timing of the colonial effort in the Pimería Alta is an important and obvious difference when compared to that in New Mexico. Whereas the New Mexico Colony was established in the northern frontier in 1598, nearly 100 years passed before similar efforts were initiated in the Pimería Alta, although numerous previous Spanish expeditions had passed through the area. In the Pimería Alta, the indigenous inhabitants of the region had long-standing knowledge of, and experience with, Spanish colonizers as missions and colonial settlements had been established to the south for generations (Spicer 1962).

Although one of the primary economic reasons for the initial interest in and establishment of the New Mexico Colony was mining, it was the northwestern portion of New Spain, a region including the Pimería Alta, that was rich in mineral resources (Spicer 1962; see Pavao-Zuckerman, chapter 11 in this volume). While the drive for mineral riches through mining and the conversion of native groups to Christianity through missionization were both important components of colonization in the Pimería Alta, these two objectives at times lay at odds with one another (Jackson 1999:62–65). Jesuits believed strongly that forced labor was counter to their conversion efforts. As missions were established in the Pimería Alta, Father Kino specifically requested and obtained from Spanish colonial officials a five-year exemption from recently converted Pima and other indigenous groups being drafted for labor at nearby mines (Jackson 1999:64). At the same time, a royal decree arrived in New Spain ordering that recent converts be exempt from forced labor for a period of twenty years.

The missionization of the Pimería Alta and the conversion of indigenous groups to Christianity differed in some significant ways from efforts in the New Mexico Colony. As described previously, missions, churches, and other religious institutions in New Mexico were built within or immediately adjacent to settled towns and communities. At times, churches were built on top of, or generally incorporated, sacred indigenous religious architecture, creating complex relations between Christian and native religious practices. There were also heavy tribute demands made by Spaniards on Pueblo communities. In Sonora and the Pimería Alta, in contrast, differences in settlement patterns and sociopolitical organization of groups strongly influenced the conversion efforts of the Jesuits and created different strategies of missionization. For example, while missions and Spanish towns were established near native villages in Sonora, if faced with tribute and labor demands, entire villages may have simply fled the area

(McGuire and Villalpando 1989:162). Unlike the New Mexico Colony, native villages and settlements in the Pimería Alta were less formal architecturally and the inhabitants of settlements were generally more mobile. Rather than the single- or multistory roomblocks, native residences were primarily individual thatch- or brush-covered structures (Doyel 1989:142). While there was aggregation of settlement, many native inhabitants of the Pimería Alta lived in dispersed settlements referred to by the Spanish as *rancherías*. Some native groups, such as the Tohono O'odham, were known for a shifting settlement pattern of well (winter) and field (summer) villages (Doyel 1989:141; Fontana 1996:20–23). As a result, by the mid-1700s, some Spanish decisions regarding where to establish new presidios had less to do with the location of native villages, and more to do with other physical requirements, such as access to water and pasturage. In addition, in the case of the establishment of the presidio at Tubac, it also was based in large part on symbolic meanings to the Spanish, as Tubac was the location where the Piman leader Luis Oacpicagigua had surrendered to the Spanish after the Upper Pima Revolt in 1751 (see Polzer and Sheridan 1997:407–42 for analysis and Spanish correspondence related to this topic).

This more dispersed, less nucleated, nature of settlement that characterized Sonora and the Pimería Alta would have allowed native groups greater freedom to leave an area where Spanish missions or settlements existed or were being established. For example, many Yaquis left southern Sonora in the 1740s and dispersed across the Pimería Alta following a Spanish repression of the Yaqui Revolt of 1740. As the colonial agricultural economy expanded in the Pimería Alta, the demands of missions and colonist for the limited arable agricultural land of the region increased. As a result, through time there were fewer areas where native agriculturalists were able to move. The rise of *ranchos* in the region (see Pavao-Zuckerman, chapter 11 in this volume) continued to increase the strain on land for traditional activities. Groups practicing agriculture such as the Pima also relied significantly on the collection of mesquite beans, cactus fruits, and other native foods to supplement their crops (Doyel 1989:141).

By the end of the eighteenth century, roughly 100 years after the first establishment of missions and other colonial settlements in the Pimería Alta, the cultural and physical landscapes had been significantly altered (see Strawhacker, chapter 13 in this volume). Periodic disease spread throughout the region, increasing mortality among native populations, whether gentile or neophyte. In the southern Pimería Alta, along major drainages such as the Santa Cruz, what had once been a landscape of dispersed, autonomous villages inhabited by diverse groups was transformed into nucleated settlements of indigenous groups living within or in close proximity to growing colonial settlements (see Doyel 1989:147–48). At the same time, large portions of the greater Pimería Alta were essentially unchanged by colonial intrusions. Tohono O'odham and Areneño groups were still inhabiting nonriverine desert regions outside of the major drainages. Along the northern edge of the Pimería Alta, Gileños and Cocomaricopas were living along the Gila River, essentially beyond the influence of Spanish missions and settlement. As we discuss below, colonial transformations of social landscapes in the Pimería Alta were not met passively by their native inhabitants, but rather occurred, in part, through a series of repeated acts of resistance and rebellion against colonial powers. At the same time, there were uneasy, yet seemingly positive, relationships between some native groups and colonists (see Thiel, chapter 12 in this volume). In comparison to Pueblos or Seris and Yumas, Pimas, for example, more readily converted to Christianity, allowing Spaniards more access to labor required for mission and nonmission pursuits than in other colonial situations. In return, Pimas had access to goods of Spanish origin, such as horses and wheat, which were important in the colonial economy and became especially important in native economies in the Pimería Alta at a time when traditional subsistence practices were rapidly transforming (Ezell 1961:45; 1983:152–56). While alliances between native groups and Spaniards ebbed and flowed continuously during this era, Pimas were generally viewed by Spaniards as allies against their mutual enemies, the Apaches and Seris (Doyel 1989:148; Sheridan 1999). As a result, Spaniards were able to turn one native group against another based upon traditional (or more recent) animosities.

Native Revolts and Resistance in Sonora and the Pimería Alta

Much like the New Mexico Colony, there was resistance to and revolts against the colonizing powers in this northwestern section of New Spain. Unlike the New Mexico Colony, however, revolts in Sonora were less unified and were generally of smaller scale. To the southeast of the Pimería Alta in Sonora, news of the Pueblo Revolt came relatively quickly, and settlers were concerned that a similar type of uprising could occur along the northern frontier of New Spain (Yetman 2012). Although the Jesuits had by this time established missions as far north as the upper Río Sonora valley, and were just beginning their missionizing efforts in the Pimería Alta, missionaries and colonists were under the constant threat of attack by various native groups, including Apaches. As David Yetman (2012:75) points out, the Apache had been helpful to Pueblo groups in accumulating information used in the revolt, and there was concern among Spanish colonists in Sonora that they could conduct similar activities in the south to aid in a rebellion. In addition, groups in Sonora and the Pimería Alta were generally perceived by colonists as more nomadic compared to the more permanently occupied Pueblo villages and therefore were viewed as members of potential insurrections (Yetman 2012:77). Yetman (2012:118–21) has suggested that many native groups in Sonora were inspired by the success of the Pueblo Revolt and strove to create their own unified attack against the colonists, but that there was no unified plan across the many different language and cultural groups in the region. Despite this lack of more widespread unification, alliances of Janos, Jocomes, Sumas, Apaches, and Chinarras attacked and raided native and European Christianized settlements during the 1680s and 1690s.

Significant uprisings and acts of resistance by native groups also occurred in the Pimería Alta after Kino's program of missionization was underway. Robert Jackson (1999:89–95) concludes that in the Pimería Alta there were two generalized patterns of resistance among indigenous inhabitants: resistance by northern Pimas associated with missions, and raids by Apaches and Seris on Spanish settlements (Jackson 1999:89; see also Jackson 1998). Two significant revolts by baptized northern Pimas occurred in 1695 and 1751 (Fontana 1994:97–98). To the south, the Seri had two significant revolts in 1748 and 1750 (Mirafuentes Galvan 1994). In the 1695 Pima uprising, a native Ópata overseer and his assistants were killed at the mission of Tubutama, as were the newly stationed Jesuit priest and his assistants at Caborca. The subsequent killing of Pimas by Spanish soldiers led to an even larger Pima uprising, resulting in the destruction of several missions in the area (Polzer and Burrus 1971; Spicer 1962:124–25). The second revolt, in 1751, resulted in the deaths of more than 100 people at the hands of the Pimas—including colonists, Spanish sympathizers, and two missionaries (Ewing 1934:72–88). There were also subsequent and repeated raids by Pima, Seri, and Apache groups against missions and other colonial settlements in the region. The Spanish response to these revolts (including the establishment of the presidio at Tubac [see Polzer and Sheridan 1997]) may have inadvertently led to increased raiding on colonial settlements, as these native groups remembered the brutal retaliation of the Spanish, such as the Spanish *matanzas* (mass killings) of native groups after the 1695 uprising (Fontana 1994:153). As Jackson (1999:91) points out, these raids, while not unified like the 1680 revolt in the New Mexico Colony, were "a serious challenge to the Spanish in Sonora [and the Pimería Alta] as well and threatened the stability of the colonial order being created on the frontier."

However, as Jackson (1999:92) also points out, while raiding and the two Pima rebellions in 1695 and 1751 were significant, Apache raiding across the northern frontier, including the Pimería Alta, proved to be a much more constant and serious threat to Spanish colonial establishment efforts. While there were relatively small numbers of colonists killed by Apache attacks compared to overall deaths due to disease and other ailments, Apache raiding took significant economic and emotional tolls on the native and nonnative residents of missions and other colonial settlements (Jackson 1999). Livestock raiding also led to significant economic losses for colonial settlements. In response, by the mid- to late 1700s, Spanish military units were more strongly positioned in the Pimería Alta to repel these native attacks, with an increased reliance on establishing more presidios (see Polzer and Sheridan, 1997; see also Thiel, chapter 12 in this volume).

CONTRIBUTIONS TO THE VOLUME

This volume presents varied views and voices on the colonization of the Southwest. Scholars demonstrate the intertwined relationships between cultural continuity and change during a time of immense upheaval in the region. Chapters address aspects of everyday life and practices, and the interactions and relations between colonists and Native Americans.

The volume is divided into three parts and is primarily organized around geographic regions with chapters ordered roughly chronologically. After this introductory chapter, Part I of the volume focuses on the New Mexico Colony. Chapters in Part I discuss issues of factionalism and alliances; perspectives on landscapes and mobility; social memory; the strategy of abandonment; production and consumption; indigenous and Spanish imperialism; warfare and military strategies; and ethnogenesis, identity, and demography. In chapter 2, Matthew Schmader focuses on the initial Spanish expedition by Coronado into New Mexico. Here, he details the expedition itself, including description of the hundreds of indios amigos from central Mexico who accompanied Spanish soldiers on this first large expedition to the American Southwest and Great Plains. In addition, Schmader provides details of an important siege and battle Coronado undertook at a Tiwa village site called Piedras Marcadas Pueblo to offer a sketch of the types of brutality early native groups faced when encountering Spanish expeditionary forces. Next, in chapter 3, Philip O. Leckman explores the interplay between Puebloan and Spanish conceptions of landscape and their potential impacts on the early New Mexico Colony through a consideration of seventeenth-century spatial organization and land use practices at Paako, a large village and *visita* site. Here, Leckman discusses and analyzes the transformation of the cultural and physical landscape in both Pueblo and Spanish settlements and concludes there was a lack of penetration of Spanish religious beliefs and customs among Pueblo groups. Hopi weaving traditions prior to, during, and after the Pueblo Revolt is the topic Laurie D. Webster details in chapter 4. While Hopi technology and materials involved in weaving changed during the colonial era, Webster documents how this evolution is connected to Hopi long-term histories and how, even as it was transformed by colonial encounters, a weaving tradition persisted.

In chapter 5, Matthew Liebmann and his colleagues discuss northern Rio Grande Pueblo communities during the period immediately after the Pueblo Revolt of 1680. Many Spanish records gloss over the complexities of the Pueblos' alliances and factionalism; however, archaeological evidence documents enduring alliances among communities. Their contribution offers important insight into internal and external Pueblo alliances, rifts, and negotiations based on fluid political and economic needs before and after the Pueblo Revolt. In chapter 6, Severin Fowles and colleagues delve into the Comanche presence in New Mexico during the era of Spanish colonialism. Beginning in the 1740s, and lasting over a decade, Comanche "imperialism" plays an important role in understanding the dynamic and complex multiethnic landscape the Spanish encountered in the New Mexico Colony as well as the quick adoption and incorporation of new technologies (such as equestrianism) into native cultural traditions. J. Andrew Darling and B. Sunday Eiselt (chapter 7) and Kelly L. Jenks (chapter 8) explore the concept of Spanish colonists in New Mexico becoming vecinos, building on the initial work done by Ross Frank (2000) on the concept (see also Trigg 2005). This transformation of colonist identity in eighteenth- and nineteenth-century New Mexico has its origins in the late seventeenth century, when the concept of vecino (a civic status) overshadowed caste and race. Both chapters discuss the integrative processes and social transformation of late colonial New Mexico related to becoming vecino. As Jenks (this volume) states, the ethnogenesis of becoming vecino indicates that "the most salient aspect of Spanish colonial identity in late colonial New Mexico was not Spanish identity but one's residence and accepted membership in a Spanish colonial community." Interestingly, similar types of transformation took place in Alta California in the late eighteenth century with the creation of a *Californio* identity (see, e.g., Lightfoot 2005; Voss 2008a), which provided important integrative privileges to colonists on the furthest edge of the Spanish frontier. Finally, Thomas E. Sheridan and Stewart B. Koyiyumptewa in chapter 9 provide a unique perspective on past and present understandings of the interactions between the Hopi and Franciscan missionaries during the seventeenth century. These scholars compare and contrast Spanish historical records of Franciscan abuses at Hopi with recorded Hopi oral traditions of the same events to explore and better understand what they call "intergenerational memory of colonial trauma." Their use and comparison of both Hopi oral traditions and Spanish ethnohistoric documents offer new insight into the connection between the colonial past and the present.

Part II of this volume details the colonial encounter in the Pimería Alta. Topics discussed in this section include Native American population dynamics of the region, military settlements and colonial strategies, ranching economies and influences, and indigenous agricultural responses to colonialism. In chapter 10, Lauren E. Jelinek and Dale S. Brenneman focus on the Native American demographic landscape during the early colonial era to provide insight into native population diversity and interaction. Analysis of ethnohistoric and archaeological data suggest that during the early period of Spanish contact, there was an extremely diverse and varied cultural landscape and that different groups in the Pimería Alta interacted with each other a great deal. Next,

Barnet Pavao-Zuckerman in chapter 11 focuses on the economic transformation of the Pimería Alta during the colonial era. Part of her discussion delves into the gradual, and patchy, transformation of native everyday life and activities through missionization and other colonial structures. Overall, based on both archaeological and ethnohistorical research, she argues that the introduction of livestock into the area led to deleterious effects on the sustainability of traditional native subsistence strategies, and the co-option of native labor led to profound effects on the daily life of the native populations. J. Homer Thiel in chapter 12 offers insight into the everyday life and experiences of soldiers and settlers at the Tucson presidio. Far removed from the comforts of home in what is now Mexico, by the late eighteenth century, these colonists and settlers slowly transformed their identities from those associated with race and caste, which created distinctions among them, to other identities, which integrated them as community members, much like similar processes in both California and New Mexico during the same time period. Finally, in chapter 13, Colleen Strawhacker explores the dynamic responses of the O'odham to colonialism through the nineteenth century. Specifically, Strawhacker argues that during the eighteenth and nineteenth centuries, the O'odham intensified their use of irrigation agriculture to meet demands of missions and, later, market demands, both resulting in relatively positive economic outcomes. Strawhacker also suggests that, like Fowles and colleagues do for the Comanche (chapter 6), the adoption of new innovations also led to changes in social structure. In the case of the O'odham, it appears that centralization of leadership may have aided in the adoption of intensive agricultural practices.

Finally, in Part III of the volume, Kent Lightfoot (chapter 14) and David Hurst Thomas (chapter 15) provide discussion and commentary on the other contributed chapters. Lightfoot and Thomas also compare the colonial encounters in the American Southwest to, respectively, Alta California and La Florida (the American Southeast). These two discussants offer valuable comparative perspectives with which to meaningfully contextualize the colonial process in the American Southwest and further our understanding of this transformative historical process that has created the Southwestern world as we know it today.

ACKNOWLEDGMENTS

First and foremost, we would like to thank all the contributors to this volume for offering detailed and informative insight into the nature of the colonial experience, from the perspective of both native and colonist. The topics they explore, and the commentary they offer, inspired the topics we discussed in this chapter. We thank the very helpful and thorough comments of Kathleen Hull (University of California, Merced), Tom Sheridan (University of Arizona), and Dale Brenneman (Arizona State Museum), as well as those of several anonymous peer reviewers; this chapter is much clearer because of their feedback. Any bizarre twists of logic or errors in facts, however, remain our responsibility. Both of us acknowledge and appreciate the support of Statistical Research, Inc., for administrative and financial support related to this chapter and the volume in general. In addition, John Douglass has been a Visiting Scholar in the School of Anthropology at the University of Arizona during the writing of this chapter and appreciates the support he has received by colleagues there, as well as University resources.

REFERENCES CITED

Adams, Charles. 1989. "Passive Resistance: Hopi Responses to Spanish Contact and Conquest." In *Archaeological and Historical Perspectives on the Spanish Borderlands West*, Columbian Consequences, vol. 1, edited by David Hurst Thomas, 55–91. Washington, DC: Smithsonian Institution Press.

Adams, E. Charles, and Andrew I. Duff, eds. 2004. *The Protohistoric Pueblo World*, AD 1275–1600. Tucson: University of Arizona Press.

Alcock, Susan. 2005. "Roman Colonies and the Eastern Empire: A Tale of Four Cities." In *The Archaeology of Colonial Encounters: Comparative Perspectives*, edited by Gil J. Stein, 297–330. Santa Fe: School of American Research.

Alexander, Rani. 1998. "Afterword: Toward an Archaeological Theory of Culture Contact." In *Studies in Culture Contact: Interaction, Culture Change, and Archaeology*, edited by James G. Cusick, 476–495. Center for Archaeological Investigations, Occasional Paper No. 25. Carbondale: Southern Illinois University.

Anderson, H. Allen. 1985. "The Encomienda in New Mexico, 1598–1680." *New Mexico Historical Review* 60 (4): 353–77.

Asselberg, Florine. 2008. *Conquered Conquistadors: The Lienzo de Quauhquechollan: A Nahua Vision of the Conquest of Guatemala*. Boulder: University Press of Colorado.

Barrett, Elinore M. 2002. *Conquest and Catastrophe: Changing Rio Grande Pueblo Settlement Patterns in the Sixteenth and Seventeenth Centuries*. Albuquerque: University of New Mexico Press.

Beckett, Patrick H., and Terry L. Corbett. 1992. *The Manso Indians*. COAS Monograph No. 9. Las Cruces, NM: COAS Publishing and Research Center.

Benavides, Alonso de. 1996. *A Harvest of Reluctant Souls: The Memorial of Fray Alonso de Benavides, 1630*. Translated by Baker H. Morrow. Boulder: University Press of Colorado.

Bolton, Herbert E. 1919. *Kino's Historical Memoir of Pimería Alta, 1683–1711*. Cleveland: Arthur H. Clark Company.

Bolton, Herbert E. 1936. *Rim of Christendom: A Biography of Eusebio Francisco Kino, Pacific Coast Pioneer*. New York: MacMillan Company.

Bolton, Herbert E. 1979. "The Missions as a Frontier Institution in the Spanish American Colonies." In *New Spain's Far Northern Frontier: Essays on Spain in the American West, 1540–1821*, edited by David J. Weber, 49–66. Dallas: Southern Methodist University Press.

Bolton, Herbert E. 1990. *Coronado, Knight of Pueblos and Plains*. Albuquerque: University of New Mexico Press.

Brown, Tracy L. 2013. *Pueblo Indians and Spanish Colonial Authority in Eighteenth Century New Mexico*. Tucson: University of Arizona Press.

Casella, Eleanor Conlin, and Chris Fowler. 2005. "Beyond Identification: An Introduction." In *The Archaeology of Plural and Changing Identities: Beyond Identification*, edited by Eleanor Conlin Casella and Chris Fowler, 1–8. New York: Kluwer Academic/Plenum. http://dx.doi.org/10.1007/0-306-48695-4_1.

Clark, Bonnie J. 2005. "Lived Ethnicity: Archaeology and Identity in Mexicano America." *World Archaeology* 37 (3): 440–52. http://dx.doi.org/10.1080/00438240500168525.

Clark, Bonnie J. 2012. *On the Edge of Purgatory: An Archaeology of Place in Hispanic Colorado*. Lincoln: University of Nebraska Press.

Comaroff, John L., and Jean Comaroff. 1991. *Christianity, Colonialism, and Consciousness in South Africa*. Of Revelation and Revolution, vol. 1. Chicago: University of Chicago Press.

Cordell, Linda S. 1991. "Durango to Durango: An Overview of the Southwest Heartland." In *Archaeological and Historical Perspectives on the Spanish Borderlands West*, Columbian Consequences, vol. 1, edited by David Hurst Thomas, 17–40. Washington, DC: Smithsonian Institution Press.

Creel, Darrell, and Charmion R. McKusick. 1994. "Prehistoric Macaws and Parrots in the Mimbres Area, New Mexico." *American Antiquity* 59 (3): 510–24. http://dx.doi.org/10.2307/282463.

Deagan, Kathleen A. 1995. *Puerto Real: The Archaeology of a Sixteenth-Century Spanish Town in Hispaniola*. Gainesville: University of Florida Press.

Deagan, Kathleen A. 1997. "Cross-Disciplinary Themes in the Recovery of the Colonial Middle Period." *Historical Archaeology* 31 (1): 4–8.

Deagan, Kathleen A. 2005. "Patterns South: The Evolution and Application of Pattern Recognition Tools in the Archaeology of the Spanish Colonies." In *In Praise of the Poet Archaeologist: Papers in Honor of Stanley South and His Five Decades of Historical Archaeology*, edited by Linda F. Carnes-McNaughton and Carl Steen, 30–36. South Carolina: Council of South Carolina Professional Archaeologists.

Deagan, Kathleen A., and Jane Landers. 1999. "Fort Mosé: Earliest Free African-American Town in the United States." In *"I, Too, Am America": Archaeological Studies of African-American Life*, edited by Theresa A. Singleton, 261–82. Charlottesville: University Press of Virginia.

Di Peso, Charles C. 1974. *Casas Grandes: A Fallen Trading Center of the Gran Chichimeca*, vols. 1–3. Amerind Foundation, Inc., Series No. 9. Dragoon, AZ: Amerind Foundation.

Dongoske, Kurt E., and Cindy K. Dongoske. 2002. "History in Stone: Evaluating Spanish Conversion Efforts through Hopi Rock Art." In *Archaeologies of the Pueblo Revolt: Identity, Meaning, and Renewal in the Pueblo World*, edited by Robert W. Preucel, 114–31. Albuquerque: University of New Mexico Press.

Donohue, J. Augustine. 1969. *After Kino: Jesuit Missions in Northwestern New Spain 1711–1767*. Rome: Jesuit Historical Institute.

Dozier, Edward P. 1983. *The Pueblo Indians of North America*. Prospect Heights, IL: Waveland Press.

Doyel, David E. 1989. "The Transition to History in Northern Pimería Alta." In *Archaeological and Historical Perspectives on the Spanish Borderlands West*, Columbian Consequences, vol. 1, edited by David Hurst Thomas, 139–58. Washington, DC: Smithsonian Institution Press.

Eggan, Fred. 1950. *Social Organization of the Western Pueblos*. Chicago: University of Chicago Press.

Eggan, Fred. 1979. "Pueblos: Introduction." In *Southwest*, edited by Alfonso Ortiz, Handbook of North American Indians, William C. Sturtevant, general editor, vol. 9: 224–35. Washington, DC: Smithsonian Institution Press.

Ewing, Russell C. 1934. "The Pima Uprising, 1751–1752: A Study in Spain's Indian Policy." PhD dissertation, Department of History, University of California, Berkeley.

Ezell, Paul H. 1961. *The Hispanic Acculturation of the Gila River Pima*. American Anthropological Association Memoir 90. Washington, DC: American Anthropological Association.

Ezell, Paul H. 1983. "History of the Pima." In *Handbook of North American Indians*, vol. 10, edited by Alfonzo Ortiz, 149–61. Washington, DC: Smithsonian Institution.

Ferris, Neal. 2009. *Native-Lived Colonialism: Challenging History in the Great Lakes*. Tucson: University of Arizona Press.

Flint, Richard. 2008. *No Settlement, No Conquest: A History of the Coronado Entrada*. Albuquerque: University of New Mexico Press.

Flint, Richard, and Shirley Cushing Flint. 2005. *Documents of the Coronado Expedition, 1539–1542: "They Were Not Familiar with His Majesty, nor Did They Wish to Be His Subjects*. Dallas: Southern Methodist University Press.

Fontana, Bernard. 1994. *Entrada: The Legacy of Spain and Mexico in the United States*. Tucson: Southwest Parks and Monuments Association.

Fontana, Bernard. 1996. "The O'odham." In *The Pimeria Alta Missions and More*, edited by James E. Officer, Mardith Schuetz-Miller, and Jorge Olvega, 19–28. Tucson: The Southwestern Mission Research Center.

Fox, Robin. 1967. *The Keresan Bridge: A Problem in Pueblo Ethnology*. New York: Humanities Press.

Frank, Ross. 1998. "Demographic, Social, and Economic Change in New Mexico." In *New Views of Borderlands History*, edited by Robert H. Jackson, 21–40. Albuquerque: University of New Mexico Press.

Frank, Ross. 2000. *From Settler to Citizen: New Mexican Development and the Creation of Vecino Society, 1750–1820*. Berkeley: University of California Press.

Galgano, Robert C. 2005. *Feast of Souls: Indians and Spaniards in the Seventeenth-Century Missions of Florida and New Mexico*. Albuquerque: University of New Mexico Press.

Gilman, Patricia, Marc Thompson, and Kristina C. Wyckoff. 2014. "Ritual Change and the Distant: Mesoamerican Iconography, Scarlet Macaws, and Great Kivas in the Mimbres Region of Southwestern New Mexico." *American Antiquity* 79 (1): 90–107. http://dx.doi.org/10.7183/0002-7316.79.1.90.

Gosden, Chris. 2004. *Archaeology and Colonialism: Cultural Contact from 5000 BC to the Present*. Cambridge: Cambridge University Press.

Gosden, Chris, and Chantal Knowles. 2001. *Collection Colonialism: Material Culture and Colonial Exchange*. Oxford: Berg.

Graves, William M. 2002. "Power, Autonomy, and Inequality in Rio Grande Puebloan Society, AD 1300–1672." PhD dissertation, Arizona State University, Tempe.

Gutiérrez, Ramón A. 1991. *When Jesus Came, the Corn Mothers Went Away: Marriage, Sexuality, and Power in New Mexico, 1500–1846*. Stanford: Stanford University Press.

Hackel, Steven W. 2005. *Children of Coyote, Missionaries of Saint Francis: Indian-Spanish Relations in Colonial California 1769–1850*. Chapel Hill: University of North Carolina Press.

Hackett, Charles W., and Charmion C. Shelby. 1942. *Revolt of the Pueblo Indians of New Mexico, and Otermin's Attempted Reconquest, 1680–1682*. Coronado Cuarto Centennial Publications, 1540–1949. 2 vols. Albuquerque: University of New Mexico Press.

Hadley, Diana, Thomas H. Naylor, and Mardith K. Schuetz-Miller, eds. 1997. *The Central Corridor and the Texas Corridor 1700–1765*, The Presidio and Militia on the Northern Frontier of New Spain, vol. 2, pt. 2. Tucson: University of Arizona Press.

Hale, Kenneth, and David Harris. 1979. "Historical Linguistics and Archeology." In Southwest, edited by Alfonso Ortiz, Handbook of North American Indians, William C. Sturtevant, general editor, vol. 9, 170–77. Washington, DC: Smithsonian Institution Press.

Haley, Brian D., and Larry R. Wilcoxon. 1997. "Anthropology and the Making of Chumash Tradition." *Current Anthropology* 38 (5): 761–94. http://dx.doi.org/10.1086/204667.

Haley, Brian D., and Larry R. Wilcoxon. 2005. "How Spaniards Became Chumash and Other Tales of Ethnogenesis." *American Anthropologist* 107 (3): 432–45. http://dx.doi.org/10.1525/aa.2005.107.3.432.

Hammond, George P., and Agapito Rey. 1940. *Narratives of the Coronado Expedition, 1540–1542*. Albuquerque: University of New Mexico Press.

Hammond, George P., and Agapito Rey. 1953. *Don Juan de Oñate: Colonizer of New Mexico, 1595–1628*. Albuquerque: University of New Mexico Press.

Hammond, George P., and Agapito Rey. 1966. *The Rediscovery of New Mexico, 1580–1954*. Albuquerque: University of New Mexico Press.

Harmon, Marcel J. 2006. "Religion and the Mesoamerican Ball Game in the Casas Grandes Region of Northern Mexico." In *Religion in the Prehispanic Southwest*, edited by C. S. VanPool, T. L. VanPool, and D. A. Phillips, Jr., 185–217. Lanham, MD: AltaMira Press.

Hart, Siobhan M. 2012. "Decolonizing through Heritage Work in the Pocumtuck Homeland of Northeastern North America." In *Decolonizing Indigenous Histories: Exploring Prehistoric/Colonial Transitions in Archaeology*, edited by Maxine Oland, Siobhan M. Hart, and Liam Frink, 86–109. Tucson: University of Arizona Press.

Hart, Siobhan M., Maxine Oland, and Liam Frink. 2012. "Finding Transition: Global Pathways to Decolonizing Indigenous Histories in Archaeology." In *Decolonizing Indigenous Histories: Exploring Prehistoric/Colonial Transitions in Archaeology*, edited by Maxine Oland, Siobhan M. Hart, and Liam Frink, 1–18. Tucson: University of Arizona Press.

Hartmann, William K. 2014. *Searching for Golden Empires: Epic Cultural Collisions in Sixteenth-Century America*. Tucson: University of Arizona Press.

Hayes, Alden C., Jon Nathan Young, and A. H. Warren. 1981. *Excavation of Mound 7, Gran Quivira National Monument, New Mexico. Publication in Archeology 16*. Washington, DC: National Park Service.

Hordes, Stanley. 2005. *To the End of the Earth: A History of the Crypto-Jews of New Mexico*. New York: Columbia University Press.

Hu, Di. 2013. "Approaches to the Archaeology of Ethnogenesis: Past and Emergent Perspectives." *Journal of Archaeological Research* 21 (4): 371–402. http://dx.doi.org/10.1007/s10814-013-9066-0.

Hull, Kathleen L. 2009. *Pestilence and Persistence: Yosemite Indian Demography and Culture in Colonial California*. Berkeley: University of California Press.

Jackson, Robert H. 1998. "Northwestern New Spain: The Pimería Alta and the Californias." In *New Views of Borderlands History*, edited by Robert H. Jackson, 41–72. Albuquerque: University of New Mexico Press.

Jackson, Robert H. 1999. *Race, Caste, and Status: Indians in Colonial Spanish America*. Albuquerque: University of New Mexico Press.

Johnson, John R., and Joseph G. Lorenz. 2010. "Genetics and the Castas of Colonial California." In *Alta California: Peoples in Motion, Identities in Formation, 1769–1850*, edited by Steven W. Hackel, 157–93. Berkeley: University of California Press.

Kessell, John L. 1970. *Mission of Sorrows: Jesuit Guevavi and The Pimas, 1691–1767*. Tucson: University of Arizona Press.

Kessell, John L. 1979. *Kiva, Cross, and Crown: The Pecos Indians and New Mexico, 1540–1840*. Albuquerque: University of New Mexico Press.

Kessell, John L., and Rick Hendricks, eds. 1992. *By Force of Arms: The Journals of Don Diego de Vargas, New Mexico, 1691–1693*. Albuquerque: University of New Mexico Press.

Kessell, John L., Rick Hendricks, and Meredith Dodge, eds. 1995. *To the Royal Crown Restored: The Journals of Don Diego de Vargas, New Mexico, 1692–1694*. Albuquerque: University of New Mexico Press.

Kessell, John L., Rick Hendricks, and Meredith Dodge, eds. 1998. *Blood on the Boulders: The Journals of Don Diego de Vargas, New Mexico, 1694–1697*. 2 vols. Albuquerque: University of New Mexico Press.

Kidder, Alfred V. 1936. *Phillips Academy Papers of the Southwestern Expedition No. 7. The Pottery of Pecos*, vol. 2. New Haven: Yale University Press.

King, Stacey. 2012. "Hidden Transcriptions, Contested Landscapes, and Long-Term Indigenous History in Oaxaca, Mexico." In *Decolonizing Indigenous Histories: Exploring Prehistoric/Colonial Transitions in Archaeology*, edited by Maxine Oland, Siobhan M. Hart, and Liam Frink, 230–66. Tucson: University of Arizona Press.

Knaut, Andrew L. 1995. *The Pueblo Revolt of 1680: Conquest and Resistance in Seventeenth Century New Mexico*. Norman: University of Oklahoma Press.

Lapham, Heather A. 2005. *Hunting for Hides: Deerskins, Status, and Cultural Change in the Protohistoric Appalachians*. Tuscaloosa: University of Alabama Press.

Larson, Daniel O., John R. Johnson, and Joel C. Michaelsen. 1994. "Missionization among the Coastal Chumash of Central California: A Study of Risk Minimalization Strategies." *American Anthropologist* 96 (2): 263–99. http://dx.doi.org/10.1525/aa.1994.96.2.02a00020.

Levy, Jerrold E. 1992. *Orayvi Revisited: Social Stratification in an "Egalitarian" Society*. Santa Fe: School of American Research Press.

Liebmann, Matthew J. 2002. "Signs of Power and Resistance: The (Re)Creation of Christian Imagery and Identities in the Pueblo Revolt Era." In *Archaeologies of the Pueblo Revolt: Identity, Meaning, and Renewal in the Pueblo World*, edited Robert W. Preucel, 132–46. Albuquerque: University of New Mexico Press.

Liebmann, Matthew J. 2010. "The Best of Times, the Worst of Times: Pueblo Resistance and Accommodation during the Spanish *Reconquista* of New Mexico." In *Enduring Conquests: Rethinking the Archaeology of Resistance in Spanish Colonialism in the Americas*, edited by Matthew Liebmann and Melissa S. Murphy, 199–222. School for Advanced Research Advanced Seminar Series. Santa Fe: School for Advanced Research.

Liebmann, Matthew J. 2012a. "The Rest is History: Devaluing the Recent Past in the Archaeology of the Pueblo Southwest." In *Decolonizing Indigenous Histories: Exploring Prehistoric/Colonial Transitions in Archaeology*, edited by Maxine Oland, Siobhan M. Hart, and Liam Frink, 19–44. Tucson: University of Arizona Press.

Liebmann, Matthew J. 2012b. *Revolt: An Archaeological History of Pueblo Resistance and Revitalization in 17th Century New Mexico.* Tucson: University of Arizona Press.

Liebmann, Matthew, and Melissa S. Murphy. 2010. *Enduring Conquests: Rethinking the Archaeology of Resistance in Spanish Colonialism in the Americas. School for Advanced Research Advanced Seminar Series.* Santa Fe: School for Advanced Research.

Liebmann, Matthew, and Uzma Z. Rizvi. 2008. *Archaeology and the Postcolonial Critique.* Lanham, MD: Altamira Press.

Lightfoot, Kent G. 2005. *Indians, Missionaries, and Merchants: The Legacy of Colonial Encounters on the California Frontiers.* Berkeley: University of California Press.

Lightfoot, Kent G. 2012. "Lost in Translation: A Retrospective." In *Decolonizing Indigenous Histories: Exploring Prehistoric/Colonial Transitions in Archaeology,* edited by Maxine Oland, Siobhan M. Hart, and Liam Frink, 282–98. Tucson: University of Arizona Press.

Lightfoot, Kent G., Antoinette Martinez, and Ann M. Schiff. 1998. "Daily Practice and Material Culture in Pluralistic Social Settings: An Archaeological Study of Cultural Change and Persistence from Fort Ross, California." *American Antiquity* 63 (2): 199–222. http://dx.doi.org/10.2307/2694694.

Lightfoot, Kent G., Lee M. Panich, Tsim D. Schneider, Sara L. Gonzalez, Matthew A. Russell, Darren Modzelewski, Theresa Molino, and Elliot H. Blair. 2013. "The Study of Indigenous Political Economies and Colonialism in Native California: Implications for Contemporary Tribal Groups and Federal Recognition." *American Antiquity* 78 (1): 89–103. http://dx.doi.org/10.7183/0002-7316.78.1.89.

Lomawaima, Hartman H. 1989. "Hopification: A Strategy for Cultural Preservation." In Archaeological and Historical Perspectives on the Spanish Borderlands *West*, Columbian Consequences, vol. 1,, edited by David Hurst Thomas, 93–99. Washington, DC: Smithsonian Institution Press.

Lydon, Jane. 2009. *Fantastic Dreaming: The Archaeology of an Aboriginal Mission.* Lanham: Alta Mira Press.

Lyons, Claire L., and John K. Papadopoulos, eds. 2002. *The Archaeology of Colonialism: Issues and Debates.* Los Angeles: Getty Research Institute.

Majewski, Teresita, and James E. Ayres. 1997. "Toward an Archaeology of Colonialism in the Greater Southwest." *Revista de Arqueología Americana* 12:55–86.

Mathers, Clay, Jeffrey M. Mitchem, and Charles M. Haecker, eds. 2013. *Native and Spanish New Worlds: Sixteenth-Century Entradas in the American Southwest and Southeast.* Amerind Studies in Anthropology, John Ware series editor. Tucson: University of Arizona Press.

Matthew, Laura E. 2000. "El nahuatl y la identidad Mexicana en la Guatemala colonial." *Mesoamerica (Antigua, Guatemala)* 40:41–68.

Matthew, Laura E. 2007. "Whose Conquest? Nahua, Zapoteca, and Mixteca Allies in the Conquest of Central America." In *Indian Conquistadors; Indigenous Allies in the*

Conquest of Mesoamerica, edited by Laura E. Matthew and Michel R. Oudijk, 102–26. Norman: University of Oklahoma Press.

Matthew, Laura E. 2012. *Memories of Conquest: Becoming Mexicano in Colonial Guatemala*. First Peoples: New Directions in Indigenous Studies Series. Chapel Hill: University of North Carolina Press.

McGuire, Randall H., and Maria Elisa Villalpando. 1989. "Prehistory and the Making of History in Sonora." In *Archaeological and Historical Perspectives on the Spanish Borderlands West*, Columbian Consequences, vol. 1, edited by David Hurst Thomas, 159–77. Washington, DC: Smithsonian Institution Press.

Mills, Barbara J. 2002. "Acts of Resistance: Zuni Ceramics, Social Identity, and the Pueblo Revolt." In *Archaeologies of the Pueblo Revolt: Identity, Meaning, and Renewal in the Pueblo World*, edited by Robert W. Preucel, 85–98. Albuquerque: University of New Mexico Press.

Mills, Barbara J. 2008. "Colonialism and Cuisine: Cultural Transmission, Domestic Practice, and Agency at Zuni Pueblo." In *Cultural Transmission and Material Culture: Breaking Down Boundaries*, edited by Lee Horne, Brenda Bowser, and Miriam Stark, 245–62. Tucson: University of Arizona Press.

Mirafuentes Galvan, José Luis. 1994. "Colonial Expansion and Indian Resistance in Sonora: The Seri Uprisings in 1748 and 1750." In *Violence, Resistance, and Survival in the Americas; Native Americans and the Legacy of Conquest*, edited by William B. Taylor and Franklin G.Y. Pease, 101–23. Washington, DC: Smithsonian Institution Press.

Mitchell, Mark D. 2013. *Crafting History in the Northern Plains: A Political Economy of the Heart River Region, 1400–1750*. Tucson: University of Arizona Press.

Mitchell, Mark D., and Laura L. Scheiber. 2010. "Crossing Divides: Archaeology as Long-Term History." In *Across the Great Divide: Continuity and Change in Native North American Societies, 1400–1900*, edited by Laura L. Scheiber and Mark D. Mitchell, 1–22. Tucson: University of Arizona Press.

Mobley-Tanaka, Jeannette. 2002. "Crossed Cultures, Crossed Meanings: The Manipulation of Ritual Imagery in Early Historic Pueblo Resistance." In *Archaeologies of the Pueblo Revolt: Identity, Meaning, and Renewal in the Pueblo World*, edited by Robert W. Preucel, 77–84. Albuquerque: University of New Mexico Press.

Naylor, Thomas H., and Charles W. Polzer. 1986. *The Presidio and Militia on the Northern Frontier of New Spain*. Tucson: University of Arizona Press.

Officer, James E. 1987. *Hispanic Arizona, 1536–1856*. Tucson: University of Arizona Press.

Oland, Maxine, Siobhan M. Hart, and Liam Frink. 2012. *Decolonizing Indigenous Histories: Exploring Prehistoric/Colonial Transitions in Archaeology*. Tucson: University of Arizona Press.

Oliver, Jeff. 2010. *Landscapes and Social Transformations on the Northwest Coast: Colonial Encounters in the Fraser Valley*. Tucson: University of Arizona Press.

Ortiz, Alfonso. 1969. *The Tewa World: Space, Time, Being, and Becoming in as Pueblo Society*. Chicago: University of Chicago Press.

Oudijk, Michel R., and Laura E. Matthew. 2007. "Mesoamerican Conquistadors in the Sixteenth Century." In *Indian Conquistadors: Indigenous Allies in the Conquest of Mesoamerica*, edited by Laura E. Matthew and Michel R. Oudijk, 28–63. Norman: University of Oklahoma Press.

Palka, Joel. 2005. *Unconquered Lacandon Maya: Ethnohistory and Archaeology of Indigenous Culture Change*. Gainesville: University Press of Florida.

Panich, Lee M. 2013. "Archaeologies of Persistence: Reconsidering the Legacies of Colonialism in Native North America." *American Antiquity* 78 (1): 105–22. http://dx.doi.org/10.7183/0002-7316.78.1.105.

Panich, Lee M., and Tsim D. Schneider. 2014. *Indigenous Landscapes and Spanish Missions: New Perspectives from Archaeology and Ethnohistory. The Archaeology of Colonialism and Native North American Series*. Tucson: University of Arizona Press.

Pauketat, Timothy. 2001. "Practice and History in Archaeology: An Emerging Paradigm." *Anthropological Theory* 1 (1): 73–98. http://dx.doi.org/10.1177/14634 990122228638.

Pauketat, Timothy. 2003. "Materiality and the Immaterial in Historical-Processual Archaeology." In *Essential Tensions in Archaeological Method and Theory*, edited by T. L. Van Pool and C. S. Van Pool, 41–53. Salt Lake City: University of Utah Press.

Pavao-Zuckerman, Barnet. 2011. "Rendering Economies: Native American Labor and Secondary Animal Products in the Eighteenth-Century Pimería Alta." *American Antiquity* 76 (1): 3–23. http://dx.doi.org/10.7183/0002-7316.76.1.3.

Polzer, Charles W., and Ernest J. Burrus. 1971. *Kino's Biography of Francisco Javier Saeta*. Rome: Jesuit Historical Institute.

Polzer, Charles W., and Thomas E. Sheridan. 1997. *The Californias and Sinaloa-Sonora, The Presidio and Militia on the Northern Frontier of New Spain*, vol. 2, pt. 1. Tucson: University of Arizona Press.

Preucel, Robert W., ed. 2002a. *Archaeologies of the Pueblo Revolt: Identity, Meaning, and Renewal in the Pueblo World*. Albuquerque: University of New Mexico Press.

Preucel, Robert W. 2002b. "Writing the Pueblo Revolt." In *Archaeologies of the Pueblo Revolt: Identity, Meaning, and Renewal in the Pueblo World*, edited by Robert W. Preucel, 3–29. Albuquerque: University of New Mexico Press.

Preucel, Robert W., Loa P. Traxler, and Michael V. Wilcox. 2002. "'Now the God of the Spaniards is Dead': Ethnogenesis and Community Formation in the Aftermath of the Pueblo Revolt of 1680." In *Traditions, Transitions and Technologies: Themes in Southwestern Archaeology, Proceedings of the 2000 Southwest Symposium*, edited by Sarah H. Schlanger, 71–93. Boulder: University Press of Colorado.

Pubols, Louise. 2010. "Becoming Californio: Jokes, Broadsides, and a Slap in the Face." In *Alta California: Peoples in Motion, Identities in Formation, 1769–1850*, edited by Steven W. Hackel, 131–55. Berkeley: University of California Press.

Ramenofsky, Ann F., and Jeremy Kulisheck. 2013. "Regarding Sixteenth-Century Native Population Change in the Northern Southwest." In *Native and Spanish New Worlds: Sixteenth-Century Entradas in the American Southwest and Southeast*, edited by Clay Mathews, Jeffery M. Mitchem, and Charles M. Haecker, 123–39. Amerind Studies in Anthropology, John Ware series editor. Tucson: University of Arizona Press.

Rice, Prudence, and Don Rice. 2005. "The Final Frontier of the Maya: Central Peten, Guatemala, 1450–1700 CE." In *Untaming the Frontier in Anthropology, Archaeology, and History*, edited by Bradley Parker and Lars Rodseth, 147–17. Tucson: University of Arizona Press.

Riley, Carroll L. 1999. *The Kachina and the Cross: Indians and Spaniards in the Early Southwest*. Salt Lake City: University of Utah Press.

Riley, Carroll L. 2001. "Spaniards in Aztlan." In *The Road to Aztlan: Art from a Mythic Homeland*, edited by Virginia M. Fields and Victor Zamudio-Taylor, 236–47. Los Angeles: Los Angeles County Museum of Art.

Rojo, Danna A. Levin. 2001. "The Road to Aztlan Ends in New Mexico." In *The Road to Aztlan: Art from a Mythic Homeland*, edited by Virginia M. Fields and Victor Zamudio-Taylor, 248–61. Los Angeles: Los Angeles County Museum of Art.

Sando, Joe S. 1992. *Pueblo Nations: Eight Centuries of Pueblo Indian History*. Santa Fe: Clear Light Publishers.

Schaafsma, Polly. 1999. "Tlalocs, Kachinas, Sacred Bundles, and Related Symbolism in the Southwest and Mesoamerica." In *The Casas Grandes World*, edited by C. F. Schaafsma and C. L. Riley, 164–92. Salt Lake City: University of Utah Press.

Scheiber, Laura L., and Mark D. Mitchell, eds. 2010. *Across the Great Divide; Continuity and Change in Native North American Societies, 1400–1900*. Tucson: University of Arizona Press.

Scholes, Francis V. 1944. "Juan Martínez de Montoya, Settler and Conquistador of New Mexico." *New Mexico Historical Review* 19 (3): 337–42.

Scheiber, Laura L., and Judson Byrd Finley. 2011. "Mobility as Resistance: Colonialism among Nomadic Hunter-Gatherers in the American West." In *Hunter-Gatherer Archaeology as Historical Process*, edited by Kenneth E. Sassaman and Donald H. Holly, Jr., 167–86. Amerind Studies in Archaeology, John Ware, series editor. Tucson: University of Arizona Press.

Schroeder, Albert H. 1979. "Pueblos Abandoned in Historic Times." In *Southwest*, edited by Alfonso Ortiz, Handbook of North American Indians, William C. Sturtevant, general editor, vol. 9, 236–254. Washington, DC: Smithsonian Institution Press.

Schroeder, Susan, ed. 2010. *The Conquest All over Again: Nahuas and Zapotecs Thinking, Writing, and Painting Spanish Colonialism*. Portland, OR: Sussex Academic Press.

Seymour, Deni J. 2011. *Where the Earth and Sky Are Sewn Together*. Salt Lake City: University of Utah Press.

Seymour, Deni J. 2012. "'Big Trips' and Historic Apache Movement and Interaction: Models for Early Athapaskan Migrations." In *From the Land of Ever Winter to the American Southwest: Athapaskan Migrations, Mobility, and Ethnogenesis*, edited by Deni J. Seymour, 377–409. Salt Lake City: University of Utah Press.

Shepard, Anna O. 1942. *Rio Grande Glaze Paint Ware*. Contributions to American Anthropology and History No. 39. Washington, DC: Carnegie Institution.

Sheridan, Thomas E. 1999. *Empire of Sand: The Seri Indians and the Struggle for Spanish Sonora 1645–1803*. Tucson: University of Arizona Press.

Silliman, Stephen W. 2005. "Culture Contact or Colonialism: Challenges in the Archaeology of Native North America." *American Antiquity* 70 (1): 55–74.

Silliman, Stephen W. 2009. "Change and Continuity, Practice and Memory: Native American Persistence in Colonial New England." *American Antiquity* 74 (2): 211–30.

Silliman, Stephen W. 2012. "Between the Longue Durée and the Short Purée: Postcolonial Archaeologies of Indigenous History in Colonial North America." In *Decolonizing Indigenous Histories: Exploring Prehistoric/Colonial Transitions in Archaeology*, edited by Maxine Oland, Siobhan M. Hart, and Liam Frink, 113–31. Tucson: University of Arizona Press.

Silverberg, Robert. 1970. *The Pueblo Revolt*. Lincoln: University of Nebraska Press.

Simmons, Marc. 1979. "History of Pueblo-Spanish Relations to 1821." In Southwest, edited by Alfonso Ortiz, Handbook of North American Indians, William C. Sturtevant, general editor, vol. 9, 178–93. Washington, DC: Smithsonian Institution Press.

Simmons, Marc. 1991. *The Last Conquistador: Juan De Oñate and the Settling of the Far Southwest*. Norman: University of Oklahoma Press.

Snow, David H. 1981. "Protohistoric Rio Grande Pueblo Economics: A Review of Trends." In *The Protohistoric Period on the North American Southwest, AD 1450–1700*, edited by David R. Wilcox and W. Bruce Masse, 354–77. Arizona State University Anthropological Research Papers No. 24. Tempe: Arizona State University.

Snow, David, H. 1998. *New Mexico's First Colonists: The 1597–1600 Enlistments for New Mexico under Juan Oñate, Adelantado and Gobernador*. Albuquerque: Hispanic Genealogical Research Center of New Mexico.

Snow, David H. 2010. "Down at the Shell-bead Water." In *All Trails Lead to Santa Fe*, 37–63. Santa Fe: Sunstone Press.

Somerville, Andrew D., Ben A. Nelson, and Kelly J. Knudson. 2010. "Isotopic Investigation of Pre-Hispanic Macaw Breeding in Northwest Mexico." *Journal of Anthropological Archaeology* 29 (1): 125–35.

Spicer, Edward H. 1962. *Cycles of Conquest: The Impact of Spain, Mexico, and the United States on the Indians of the Southwest, 1533–1960*. Tucson: University of Arizona Press.

Spielmann, Katherine A. 1989. "Colonist, Hunters, and Farmers: Plains-Pueblo Interaction in the Seventeenth Century." In *Archaeological and Historical Perspectives on the Spanish Borderlands West*, Columbian Consequences, vol. 1, edited by David Hurst Thomas, 101–14. Washington, DC: Smithsonian Institution Press.

Spielmann, Katherine A. 1991. *Interdependence in the Prehistoric Southwest: An Ecological Analysis of Plains-Pueblo Interaction*. New York: Garland.

Spielmann, Katherine A. 1998. "The Pueblo IV Period: History of Research." In *Migration and Reorganization: The Pueblo IV Period in the American Southwest*, edited by Katherine A. Spielmann, 1–30. Arizona State University Anthropological Research Papers No. 51. Tempe: Arizona State University.

Spielmann, Katherine A., Jeannette L. Mobley-Tanaka, and James M. Potter. 2006. "Style and Resistance in the Seventeenth-Century Salinas Province." *American Antiquity* 71 (4): 621–48.

Spielmann, Katherine A., Tiffany Clark, Diane Hawkey, Katharine Rainey, and Suzanne K. Fish. 2009. "'. . . being weary, they had rebelled': Pueblo Subsistence and Labor under Spanish Colonialism." *Journal of Anthropological Archaeology* 28 (1): 102–25.

Stein, Gil J. 2002. "Colonies without Colonialism: A Trade Diaspora Model of Fourth Millennium B.C. Mesopotamia Enclaves in Anatolia." In *The Archaeology of Colonialism*, edited by Claire Lyons and John K. Papadopoulos, 27–64. Los Angeles: Getty Research Institute.

Stein, Gil J., ed. 2005. *The Archaeology of Colonial Encounters: Comparative Perspectives*. Santa Fe: School of American Research.

Stojanowski, Christopher M. 2010. *Bioarchaeology of Ethnogenesis in the Colonial Southeast*. Gainesville: University Press of Florida.

Thomas, David Hurst, ed. 1989. *Archaeological and Historical Perspectives on the Spanish Borderlands West*. Columbian Consequences, vol. 1. Washington, DC: Smithsonian Institution Press.

Tiesler, Vera, Pilar Zabala, and Andrea Cucina. 2010. *Natives, Europeans, and Africans in Colonial Campeche: History and Archaeology*. Gainesville: University Press of Florida.

Trigg, Heather B. 2005. *From Household to Empire: Society and Economy in Early Colonial New Mexico*. Tucson: University of Arizona Press.

Van Buren, Mary. 2010. "The Archaeological Study of Spanish Colonialism in the Americas." *Journal of Archaeological Research* 18 (2): 151–201.

Voss, Barbara L. 2005. "From Casta to Californio: Social Identity and the Archaeology of Culture Contact." *American Anthropologist* 107 (3): 461–474.

Voss, Barbara L. 2008a. *The Archaeology of Ethnogenesis: Race and Sexuality in Colonial San Francisco*. Berkeley: University of California Press.

Voss, Barbara L. 2008b. "Poor People in Silk Shirts: Dress and Ethnogenesis in Spanish-Colonial San Francisco." *Journal of Social Archaeology* 8 (3): 404–32.

Wade, Maria F. 2008. *Missions, Missionaries, and Native Americans: Long-Term Processes and Daily Practices*. Gainesville: University Press of Florida.

Warren, A. Helene. 1969. "Tonque: One Pueblo's Glaze Pottery Industry Dominated Middle Rio Grande Commerce." *El Palacio* 76:36–42.

Warren, A. Helene. 1979. "The Glaze Paint Wares of the Upper Middle Rio Grande." In *Archaeological Investigations in Cochiti Reservoir, New Mexico, Volume 4: Adaptive Change in the Northern Rio Grande Valley*, edited by Jan V. Biella, and Richard C. Chapman, 187–216. Albuquerque: Office of Contract Archaeology, Department of Anthropology, University of New Mexico.

Whiteley, Peter M. 1988. *Deliberate Acts: Changing Hopi Culture through the Oraibi Split*. Tucson: University of Arizona Press.

Whiteley, Peter M. 2003. "Reconnoitering 'Pueblo' Ethnicity: The 1852 Tesuque Delegation to Washington." *Journal of the Southwest* 45 (3): 437–518.

Whittlesey, Stephanie M. 2004. "Mesoamerica, the Hohokam, and the Tucson Basin." In *Pots, Potters, and Models: Archaeological Investigations at the SRI Locus of the West Branch Site, Tucson, Arizona, Vol. 2: Synthesis and Interpretations*, edited by S. M. Whittlesey, 509–530. Technical Series No. 80. Tucson: Statistical Research.

Whittlesey, Stephanie M., and J. Jefferson Reid. 2013. "Macaw Symbolism and Ritual at Grasshopper Pueblo and Paquimé." *Journal of Arizona Archaeology* 2 (2): 178–95.

Wilcox, Michael V. 2009. *The Pueblo Revolt and the Mythology of Conquest: An Indigenous Archaeology of Contact*. Berkeley: University of California Press.

Wilshusen, Richard H. 2010. "The Dine at the Edge of History: Navajo Ethnogenesis in the Northern Southwest, 1500–1750." In *Across the Great Divide; Continuity and Change in Native North American Societies, 1400–1900*, edited by Laura L. Scheiber and Mark D. Mitchell, 192–211. Tucson: University of Arizona Press.

Wroth, William. 2010. "Barrio de Analco: Its Roots in Mexico and Its Role in Early Colonial Santa Fe, 1610–1780." In *All Trails Lead to Santa Fe*, 163–78. Santa Fe: Sunstone Press.

Yannakakis, Yanna. 2011. "Allies or Servants? The Journey of Indian Conquistadores in the Lienzo of Analco." *Ethnohistory (Columbus, Ohio)* 58 (4): 653–82.

Yetman, David. 1994. "Cows." *Journal of the Southwest* 36 (2): 148–58.

Yetman, David. 2012. *Conflict in Colonial Sonora; Indians, Priests, and Settlers*. Albuquerque: University of New Mexico Press.

PART 1

The New Mexico Colony

Native and Colonist Worlds Colliding

TWO

"The Peace That Was Granted Had Not Been Kept"

Coronado in the Tiguex Province, 1540–1542

MATTHEW F. SCHMADER

INTRODUCTION

In the sweep of history, instances of first contact between indigenous peoples and explorers from foreign lands form a dramatic and often tumultuous turning point in the lives and cultures of all participants. The "Age of Discovery," as characterized by European exploration and later by enterprises of colonial expansion, is strewn with many examples of intercultural collisions. Across the globe, from Africa to South Asia and later into Polynesia, native cultures were permanently and usually negatively impacted. Perhaps nowhere was this page of history more dramatically turned than in the events surrounding the exploration of the Fourth Part of the World (Lester 2009), or the "New World," as it came to be known.

Starting with Cristóbal Colón's first encounters with native Caribbean peoples, New World explorations based out of Spain and Portugal would unrelentingly range across the entire Western Hemisphere for all of the sixteenth century. Historian Richard Flint (2008:206) notes that over 130 Spanish-led expeditions were conducted between 1492 and 1598 in the Americas, a summary that

DOI: 10.5876/9781607325741.c002

does not include the Portuguese enterprises. Considering the massive effort and geography involved, native responses to European contact were by no means uniform or passive. Noting that the Taíno peoples had destroyed Colón's first colony of La Navidad with a total loss of Spanish settlers' lives, Matthew Liebmann and Melissa Murphy (Liebmann and Murphy 2010:3) state that "this was not an anomalous incident, but merely the first episode in a long pattern of native opposition to Spanish colonialism that spanned more than three centuries and ranged across two continents."

This chapter explores the texts and contexts of one of the most significant of the sixteenth-century Spanish explorations, the 1540–42 expedition into present-day northern Mexico and the American Southwest led by Francisco Vázquez de Coronado (see chapters by Thomas E. Sheridan and Stewart B. Koyiyumptewa [9], J. Andrew Darling and B. Sunday Eiselt [7], and Kelly L. Jenks [8], this volume, for discussion of later Spanish colonial texts). Expeditionary documents of the Coronado exploration will be reviewed in detail to discern the range of reactions and responses elicited by native peoples when confronted with first contact by foreigners. As Liebmann and Murphy (2010:4) observe, "Much of what we think we know about native negotiation of Spanish colonialism is founded upon modern readings of historical texts." They point out that there were filters and motivations of documentary writers that often underrepresented the "multitudes whose identities fell into the ambiguous interstices between Indian and Spaniard" (Liebmann and Murphy 2010:4). This chapter attempts to fill out that void by summarizing a variety of native tactics and strategies inferred from written eyewitness accounts of the Coronado expedition. By so doing, it affirms the conclusions of Liebmann and Murphy (2010:6) that "the colonial landscape was a patchwork of domination, resistance, accommodation, and negotiation as indigenous peoples exerted a variety of strategies" in response to colonizing efforts and that "armed confrontation [was] but one of an array of strategies employed by indigenous peoples in their interactions" with the Spanish (Liebmann and Murphy 2010:4).

This chapter will focus the material consequences of what is described in documents, attempting to more strongly bridge gaps that can exist between history and archaeology. As Liebmann and Murphy (2010:5) also note, "Archaeology complements historical studies of post-1492 life in the Americas . . . in many ways [more] . . . than that afforded by documents alone." They go on to observe that "many everyday acts of resistance leave no material signature" and that "those that do leave material traces are often equivocal at best" (Liebmann and Murphy 2010:6). Recognizing that documents do not account for much of what is contained in the archaeological record, this chapter draws a more direct connecting line between the inferential nature of native actions in contact situations and the specific material consequences of those actions. This will be done by examining the material record of one significant locality where first contact and ensuing conflict occurred in the American Southwest.

THE VÁZQUEZ DE CORONADO EXPEDITION

On February 22, 1540, one of the largest land-based explorations ever organized in the New World by the Spanish Crown (Schmader 2011:314–15; 2014:116) departed Compostela, then the provincial capital of Nueva Galicia, and began its fateful journey northward.[1] Competitive rights to conduct the expedition were granted to the viceroy of Nueva España, Antonio de Mendoza, and interest in the outcome was greatly anticipated (Hammond and Rey 1940:87). It had been just twenty years since Hernán Cortés vanquished the Aztec empire and fewer than ten years following the conquest of Peru by the Pizarro brothers in the early 1530s. The short span from 1519 to 1539 witnessed breathtaking results in Spanish imperial expansion, both in terms of huge land claims and physical wealth of gold, silver, and jewels to fill royal coffers. Expectation of finding another great civilization to the north of Nueva España, and a final route to the orient (Flint 2008:17–19), were piqued by reports of Álvar Núñez Cabeza de Vaca, whose odyssey of survival in the mid-1530s along the United States–Mexico border encountered evidence of settled lands (Goodwin 2008). In 1539, Viceroy Mendoza sent a small party under Fray Marcos de Niza north as far as Cíbola (now Zuni pueblo in New Mexico), and the outcome seemed encouraging that another great civilization lay ahead (see John G. Douglass and Graves, chapter 1 in this volume).

To lead the larger exploration, Mendoza chose his twenty-nine-year-old governor of the province of Nueva Galicia, Captain General Francisco Vázquez de Coronado y Luján (Hammond and Rey 1940:83–85). The expedition was not funded by the Spanish Crown but rather was a private enterprise that cost its investors nearly $20 million in present-day value of silver (Schmader 2011).[2] Three primary investors staked over $ $2 million each: Viceroy Mendoza, Vázquez de Coronado (mostly from his wife Beatriz Estrada's estate), and Aztec conquistador Pedro de Alvarado shortly before his death in 1541. The average cost in cash and goods for a captain was about $175,000 and the cost of an average foot soldier was $30,000 (S. Flint 2003:44–48). The assembled force grew in numbers as it proceeded northward from Compostela to Culiacán (Figure 2.1), eventually totaling 375 European men-at-arms. Several women vital to the expedition are named in the documents, and others, unnamed, surely went. Slaves and porters were important to the contingent, and many were attached to households (Flint 2008). Over 1,100 horses and several thousand head of livestock supported the expedition.

Importantly, the force included at least 1,300 native Mexican indigenous soldiers (*indios amigos* or *aliados*) of mixed Tarascan, Tenochca, Tlatelolca, and Mexica descent. It is possible that number could have been 2,000 or more (Flint

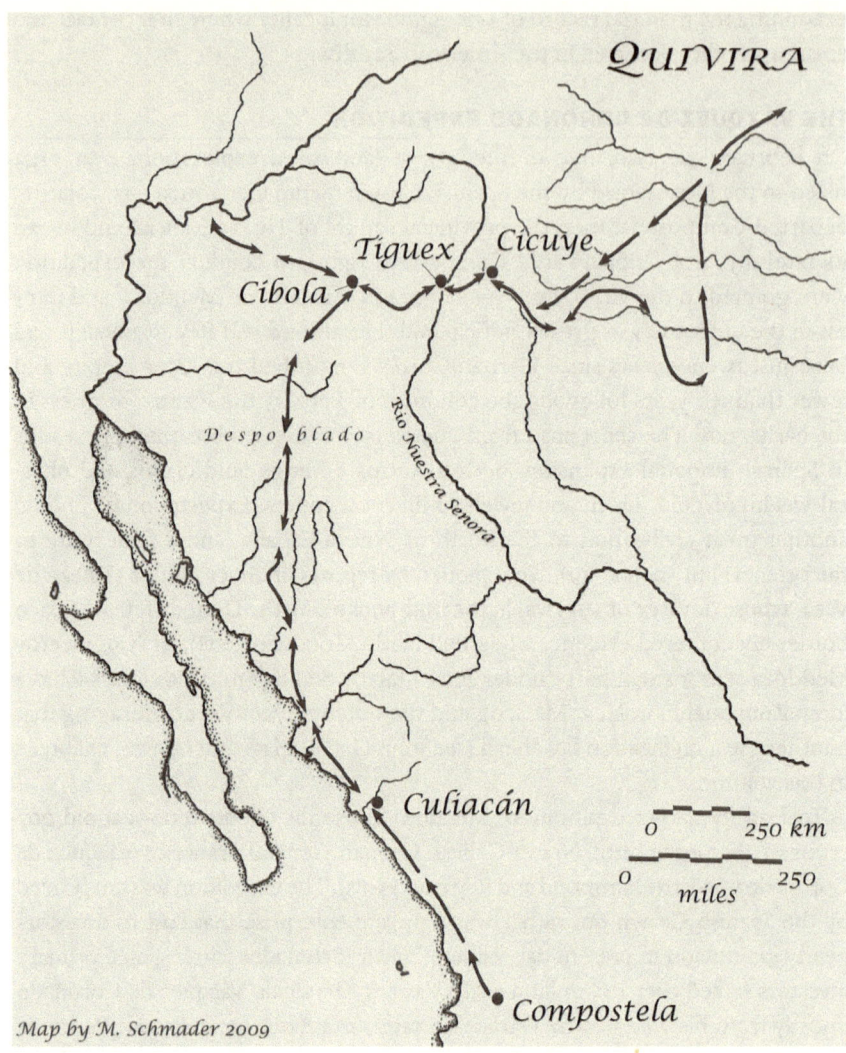

FIGURE 2.1. *Approximate route of the Francisco Vázquez de Coronado expedition, February 1540 to June 1542, showing place-names mentioned in the chapter. Map by author.*

2008:58–61). See chapter by Douglass and Graves, chapter 1 in this volume, on overall make-up of troops heading both north and south during this period from central Mexico). The salient fact is that three-fourths of the expedition were native to central and western Mexico, and were not Europeans. Much of the exploration's provisioning did not include modern weaponry: it was outfitted with just 21 crossbows, 25 *arquebuses* (primitive muskets), 60 swords, and 50 coats of chainmail (Aiton 1939). The majority of soldiers used native weapons and armor called *armas de tierra*, which "included cotton tunics, round shields, traditional feathered headgear, banners and other insignias; *macanas* (obsidian-edged swords) clubs, lances, slings, and bows and arrows" (Flint and Flint 2005:138; also see Flint 1997).

Numerous cultural groups were encountered as the expedition made its way along the western coast of Mexico and then on a path mostly due north following the route taken earlier by de Niza (see Figure 2.1). By the time Vázquez de Coronado reached Cíbola and the vicinity of Zuni, the pueblo people were prepared but could not be certain if Coronado and his forces were coming to avenge the killing of Estevan, de Niza's charismatic Moorish guide (Goodwin 2008). Coronado was intent on reaching his perceived goal of a promising civilization with exploitable resources; further, his forces were strained, tired, and hungry. Neither side accurately assessed the other and in the process of deteriorating communications, fighting broke out. This established a repeated pattern of interaction between the expedition and the peoples they were to encounter, as distrust would escalate into outright bloodshed numerous times in the ensuing two years.

The battle at the major Zuni pueblo of Hawikku was hard fought but brief. New European technologies, tactics, horses, and likely the indios amigos themselves, overcame the Zuni defenders. Coronado was badly wounded early in the conflict and had to be rescued by his captains, Hernando de Alvarado and Diego López de Cárdenas (Hammond and Rey 1940:169, 181). The first meeting between natives and nonnatives, on July 7, 1540, did not set a precedent for communication and diplomacy but instead had erupted into fighting and casualties.

The expedition rested and reprovisioned during the summer months of 1540 while an advance scouting party under Alvarado pushed east past Acoma Pueblo. By September 1540, Alvarado had led the first group of nonnatives to see the present-day Rio Grande: "The Nuestra Señora river flows through a broad valley planted with fields of maize. There are some cottonwood groves. There are twelve pueblos. The houses are made of mud, two stories high. The people seem good, more given to farming than to war" (Hammond and Rey 1940:183). This area was thereafter called the "Provincia de Tiguex" by Vázquez de Coronado (Figure 2.2). It is situated north of and includes part of the present-day city of Albuquerque, New Mexico.[3]

Alvarado continued eastward through the Galisteo Basin of New Mexico and to the pueblo of Cicuye (Pecos) before arriving at the edge of the Great Plains. There, he heard of possible riches even further east toward a land called Quivira but by then Alvarado had to rejoin López de Cárdenas, who had begun to set up winter quarters outside a major Tiguex village called Alcanfor (Hammond and Rey 1940:218–20). Coronado arrived in the Rio Grande Valley later by way of a

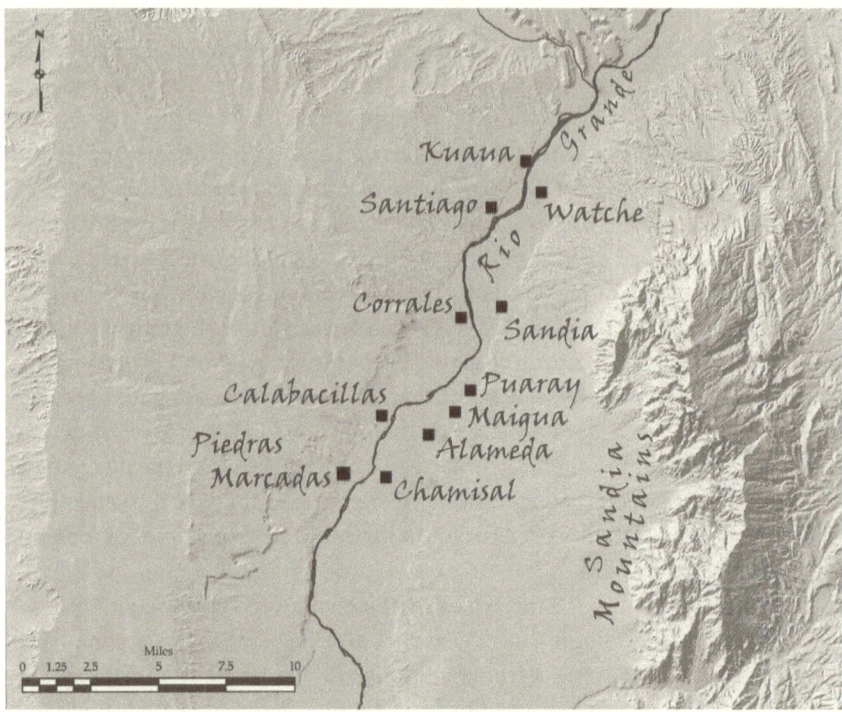

FIGURE 2.2. *Map of Vázquez de Coronado's "Tiguex Province" (middle Rio Grande valley) showing locations of known occupied pueblo villages at the time of contact in 1540. Illustrative map by author showing settlements fifteen miles upriver of Albuquerque. © 2016 Society for American Archaeology. Reprinted by permission from Advances in Archaeological Practice, volume 4, number 1.*

more southerly route (Sánchez 1988). By the time the entire force had reassembled, the especially harsh winter of 1540 had set in and the group was woefully unprepared. Cold and hunger forced them to take over Alcanfor (Hammond and Rey 1940:219).

Demands for food and clothing, imprisonment of native guides, and assaults on pueblo women worsened relations. In retaliation, the pueblos stole horses and killed several native Mexican guards. Tensions erupted into a battle at the Tiguex pueblo of Arenal, after which more than 100 pueblo men were burned at the stake. Any remaining Puebloan resistance consolidated at "the strongest" pueblo, called Moho, three to four leagues (13 to 16 kilometers, or 8 to 10 miles) away from Alcanfor. Vázquez de Coronado personally led the initial assault on Moho, but it took a siege of fifty to eighty days to finally overcome the village (Hammond and Rey 1940:360). Dozens more native people died in that prolonged series of skirmishes. Coronado was never able to control worsening tensions during the winter of 1540–41, and permanent damage to Spanish-Native relations had been done.

By the spring of 1541 Coronado hurriedly left the Tiguex Province for Pecos Pueblo. Spurred ever eastward by stories, trickery, and hopes of fortune, the expedition soon found itself on the edge of the Great Plains (Sánchez 1997:236). There they noted its vastness, many tribes, and massive herds of buffalo. Continuing on through the Texas panhandle, Coronado decided to send nearly all of the expedition back to Tiguex while he and thirty-five others rode on, possibly into Kansas before realizing they would never find Quivira (Sánchez 1997:244–48). Vázquez de Coronado was compelled to return for a second winter in the Tiguex Province in 1541–42 before retracing his steps back to Mexico (Hammond and Rey 1940:28). Coronado's return to Culiacán was not marked by triumph. He did deliver his force with few casualties, though he never fully recovered from a fall off his horse and died at the age of forty-four some dozen years later (Bolton 1949:405).

NATIVE RESPONSES DERIVED FROM EXPEDITIONARY DOCUMENTS

Surviving documents of the Coronado expedition contain abundant contemporaneous material to inform about many events that took place (see chapter by Sheridan and Koyiyumptewa, chapter 9 in this volume, for discussion of later Spanish texts describing events at Hopi Mesa). These documents have been transcribed in and translated into several forms and versions (e.g., Flint and Flint 2005; Hammond and Rey 1940; Winship 1896). Perhaps the most complete eyewitness account was provided by a literate member of the expedition, Pedro de Castañeda de Nájera, who wrote his recollections while in Spain twenty years later, during the 1560s. A careful reading of Castañeda's version of events reveals a wealth of information about interactions between the expeditionary forces and native peoples, and particularly about native responses to those fast-moving circumstances. His account will be used as a primary source to analyze several types of native responses to these rapidly changing situations. Other sources used will include Vázquez de Coronado himself, as well as captain Hernando de Alvarado and other anonymous texts from the time.

Long-Distance Information Exchange

At the time of European contact, native networks of information exchange appear to have been broad geographically, and knowledge of the expedition's movements was shared far ahead of its physical arrival. As Michael Wilcox (2009:103) points out, the "Pueblos . . . had individual historical experiences, protocols for communication, and trade relations with other ethnic groups in the surrounding areas." For example, Castañeda describes a delegation that came to Zuni from Pecos Pueblo, a distance of 190 miles away: "There came to Cíbola some Indians from a pueblo of the province called Cicuye [Pecos], distant seventy leagues to the east" (Hammond and Rey 1940:217). Information of Coronado's advance would have reached Pecos at least a week ahead to allow for the travel time from Pecos to Zuni. The delegation intended to stave off the eastward progress of the expedition, or at least befriend it ahead of time.

The residents of Cíbola made reference to "a settled area" thirty-five leagues (ninety miles) to the west, which was the Hopi pueblos (Flint and Flint 2005:498). Coronado describes a communication network made up of smoke signals to warn of his advance and arrival: "From time to time the Indians sent up their smoke clouds, which were answered from a distance with as much coordination as we would have known to do ourselves. Thus, they were notified that we were traveling and where we had reached" (Flint and Flint 2005: 257; Hammond and Rey 1940:167).

Another example of information networks is provided by Castañeda. When hostilities broke out later in the Rio Grande province of Tiguex, knowledge of it was widely shared: "These [men] spread the news throughout the land, telling how the peace that was granted them had not been kept. This resulted in great harm later" (Flint and Flint 2005; Hammond and Rey 1940).

Symbolic or Ritualized Behavior

Native reaction to foreigner interlopers sometimes translated into symbolic and ritualized behavior. Castañeda describes how "their most reliable peace pact consists in crossing their hands, and this peace they keep inviolable" and that "they answered their signs for peace by similar ones, which consisted of making a cross" (Hammond and Rey 1940:218; see also Flint and Flint 2005:399). When situations with the Coronado expedition became tense, the pueblo people pressed their point through symbolic acts. At Hopi, leaders took corn meal and "they drew lines and tried to prevent our men from crossing them" (Flint and Flint 2005:396; see also Hammond and Rey 1940:214).

Measurement and accounting of safe distances, in addition to lines not to be crossed, were also kept. Castañeda says that a pueblo man "shot an arrow, which landed at the foot of Don Lope's horse. Putting another arrow in his bow, he told him to leave or he would shoot to kill" and "when they saw that [Don Lope] was in a safe place, they began to shout and howl and to send a shower of arrows" (Hammond and Rey 1940:229–30; see also Flint and Flint 2005:405). The symbolic effect of shouting and physical posturing was used as tensions built in Tiguex: "Certain warriors . . . used to come out every morning to make a display to frighten our army in some way" (Castañeda, in Hammond and Rey 1940:230; see also Flint and Flint 2005:405).

The pueblo people also seem to have held that new and mysterious animal, the horse, with a sense of special power. At Zuni, Castañeda noted that "they made their peace ceremonies by approaching the horses, taking their sweat, and anointing themselves" (Hammond and Rey 1940:218; see also Flint and Flint 2005:399). Later, in the Tiguex Province, Puebloans targeted horses by stealing a number of them. When Captain Diego López de Cárdenas went to investigate at a nearby village, he "heard a great shouting inside, with horses running around as in a bull ring and the Indians shooting arrows at them" (Hammond and Rey 1940:225; see also Flint and Flint 2005:403).

Spanish officials used their own ritual symbolism when they announced their intentions to make the pueblo people vassals of the king of Spain. They read the *requerimiento*, a proclamation recounting the history of the world, Spain's rights to lands in the New World, an ultimatum to submit to the king, and a directive to learn the ways of Catholicism (Flint 2008:109; Liebmann and Murphy 2010). The requerimiento was delivered to the pueblo people in highly formalized Spanish with no basic interpretation. The ritual symbolism of reading the requerimiento prior to initiating any action must have seemed an odd device to the pueblo people in terms of the theatrics involved. They, in turn, responded with symbolism of their own: the Zunis "drew lines in front of [the friar], indicating that the army should not cross them [and] threw dirt in the air . . . They were never willing to come in peace . . . nor did they stop shooting arrows" (Castañeda, in Flint 2008:108–9).

Trust and Respect Systems

Systems of trust and mutual respect seem to have been important for communication across Puebloan linguistic boundaries and as a means of diplomacy (see Wilcox 2009:103–5). It is perhaps in this realm more than any other that Vázquez de Coronado failed to realize the importance of compromise and restraint: had he understood the significance of native respect systems, he might have avoided many of the problems he ultimately faced. This is evident during the expedition's initial stay during the winter of 1540–41 in the Tiguex Province of the Rio Grande Valley. The expedition was poorly prepared for the high desert cold, and was suffering from lack of food as well. Coronado was compelled to set up his main encampment at the village of Alcanfor, in the northern part of the Tiguex Province. It did not help that the pueblo's "ill feeling was aggravated by the general's desire to gather some clothing and distribute it among the soldiers" (Castañeda, in Hammond and Rey 1940:224; see also Flint and Flint 2005:402).

When Coronado instructed his men to go throughout the Tiguex Province rather than to put too great a burden on one village, it worsened the situation. "If they saw an Indian with a better [cloak] they exchanged it with him without any consideration or respect" and as Castañeda noted, "the Indians resented this very much." Another aggravating factor was the devastating effect that horses and livestock had on the pueblos' agricultural fields, which still had useful stubble (a winter fuel source) and possibly food at the end of the harvest season (Flint 2008; Wilcox 2009).

A crucial moment came when a pueblo man brought forth charges of an attempted rape on his wife at the Tiguex village of Arenal. When this appeal for justice went unheeded, "in the end he went away without getting any redress for what he had demanded" (Castañeda, in Hammond and Rey 1940:225; see also Flint and Flint 2005:403). In retaliation, the pueblo people then stole horses, an act of defiance that demanded Coronado's swift action. He called a council of his leaders, decided on a course of action, and read the requerimiento to the village chiefs. When this attempt to achieve submission failed, Arenal was attacked.

After a short fight, the pueblo men surrendered by making the sign of the cross. But the captives, believing they had surrendered in peace, were instead rounded up to be burned at the stake and further serious bloodshed ensued when they fought to save their lives. This series of horrendous events marked a permanent turning point in relations, for as Castañeda stated, "this was the beginning of the distrust the Indians had from then on for the word of peace." He goes on to state that "the Indians replied that they would not trust those who did not know how to keep the word they had pledged . . . and that they had not kept the peace" (Hammond and Rey 1940:227; see also Flint and Flint 2005:403). Several months later, at the final standoff and siege of Moho Pueblo, all attempts to ask for reconciliation went unheeded: "They paid no attention to the requisitions for peace made upon them, nor would they grant it" and "we were unable to induce them to make peace" With a sense of finality, Castañeda notes that "they did not want to trust people who did not keep their friendship or word they gave" (Hammond and Rey 1940:228; see also Flint and Flint 2005:403–4).

Defensive Tactics

Information about Puebloan defensive and offensive tactical organization is readily apparent in Castañeda's narrative. He describes a defensive tactic at Zuni, in which "these people waited in the open within sight of the pueblo, drawn up in squadrons." At Tiguex, the people had already begun to fortify their villages, as captain López de Cárdenas "found the pueblos enclosed by a palisade." Further, "Cárdenas could do nothing because they refused to come out into the field, and as the pueblos are strong, they could not be harmed" (Castañeda in Hammond and Rey 1940:225–26; see also Flint and Flint 2005:403). When the men who had surrendered at Arenal realized they were not prisoners but were in fact destined to be burned alive, "about one hundred who were in the tent began to offer resistance and defend themselves with stakes which they rushed out to seize." Following the battle at Arenal, the remaining populace in the Tiguex Province consolidated themselves at two villages in self-defense: "Most of the people of these pueblos had taken refuge in these two places," that is, the villages called Moho Pueblo and Pueblo de la Cruz by the Spanish (Flint and Flint 2005:404; see also Hammond and Rey 1940:228).

The critical confrontation occurred at the pueblo of Moho, where Coronado himself led the first assault on the village. But as Castañeda describes, the assault was repulsed, as "the enemy had been getting ready for many days and had so many stones to hurl upon our men" (Hammond and Rey 1940:228; see also Flint and Flint 2005:404). Coronado then elected to surround the pueblo and lay siege to it, which lasted a period of fifty to eighty days. During the standoff there were several skirmishes, but the provisioned village of Moho was caught short of a most precious resource: "What troubled the Indians most was their lack of water. Within the pueblo they dug a very deep well, but they were unable to obtain water" (Castañeda, in Hammond and Rey 1940:229; see also Flint and Flint 2005:404). Even the act of digging a well in the midst of a siege could be regarded as an act of self-defense.

The last acts of self-preservation occurred when "the Indians decided to abandon the pueblo during the night, and they did so. Placing their women in the middle, they set out." But the escapees were discovered, and after a fight "they fell back to the river, which was high and cold . . . few of the enemy escaped death or injury" (Castañeda, in Hammond and Rey 1940:230; see also Flint and Flint 2005:405). The siege had ended, yet "there were a few who remained in the pueblo, and who resisted in one of the sections, but they were overcome in a few days."

Offensive Tactics

The pueblo people acted not only in self-defense to situations imposed on them by the expedition, but they actively engaged in offensive tactics and strategies as well. Vázquez de Coronado describes the first fighting at Hawikku: "The people who were on the roof defending themselves had no difficulty at all inflicting the injury on us that they had power [to do]. With an infinity of large stones they hurled from the roof, they knocked me to the ground twice. If it had not been for the excellent helmet I wore, I think the result would have been grim for me" (Coronado, in Flint and Flint 2005:257).

Early in the expedition's stay at Tiguex, "the men in the pueblo came out to fight, shooting arrows and berating Alvarado, saying that he had broken his word and friendship." When the people of Arenal retaliated for the lack of justice sought in the attempted rape of a woman, a soldier "who was guarding the horses came bleeding and wounded, saying that the Indians of the land had killed one companion and were driving the horses before them to their pueblos" (Castañeda, in Hammond and Rey 1940:225; see also Flint and Flint 2005:403). When Coronado then attacked Arenal, Castañeda recounts that "the defenders wounded many of our men with arrows which they shot from the inside of their houses" (Flint and Flint 2005:403; Hammond and Rey 1940:226).

The later siege and battles at Moho began, as noted above, with an assault led by Coronado himself. But the initial attack did not go well for the expeditionary forces, because the pueblo people "had so many stones to hurl upon our men that they stretched many on the ground. They wounded close to one hundred men with arrows" (Castañeda, in Hammond and Rey 1940; see also Flint and Flint 2005). Other attempts were repulsed when Coronado's soldiers "could not harm the enemy . . . because of heavy showers of arrows that soon fell upon them" and because "they shot arrows from terraces with much shouting." The pueblos inflicted significant casualties on the expedition, as "many of our men came out badly wounded." During one skirmish, "the enemy fell upon them, killing a Spaniard and a horse and wounding others" (Hammond and Rey 1940:228–29; see also Flint and Flint 2005:404).

Capitulatory Behavior

A diplomatic tactic tried by several pueblos was to meet the strange newcomers with acts of capitulation. At Zuni, Castañeda notes that "the Indians gave them some presents of dressed skins, shields, and head pieces" and that "they presented a large number of turkey cocks, much bread, dressed deer skins, pinyon nuts, flour, and maize" (Hammond and Rey 1940:217; see also Flint and Flint 2005:398). When Alvarado reached Acuco (Acoma) on his way to explore the Rio Grande Valley, the residents, he noted, "came to us in peace, although they could have refused to do it . . . They gave us cotton mantas, [bison] and deer hides, turquoises, [turkeys], and the rest of the food[s] they have" (*Relación del Suceso* [anonymous text], in Flint and Flint 2005:499). When Alvarado reached Tiguex, he describes how "the *principales* and people came from twelve pueblos. [They came] in order, those from one [pueblo] behind the other. They walked around our tent playing a flute, and an old man [was] speaking. In this [same] way they came into the tent and presented me with food, mantas, and hides they were carrying" (Alvarado in Flint and Flint 2005:305).

Upon their arrival in the Tiguex Province, "the Indians all came out peacefully, seeing that men who were feared in all those provinces were coming with Bigotes," a chief of Pecos captured as an expeditionary guide. When Hernando de Alvarado's advance scouting party arrived at Pecos, "the people came out to meet him and their captain (Bigotes) with demonstrations of joy and took him into the pueblo with drums and fifes." When it became clear that the entire expeditionary force intended to overwinter in Tiguex, Castañeda states that "as the natives had to provide quarters for the Spaniards, they found themselves compelled to abandon a pueblo." Consequently, "they did not take along any belongings but their persons and clothing" (Hammond and Rey 1940:224; see also Flint and Flint 2005:402). Following the brief fight at Arenal, the pueblo warriors understood that they were better off surrendering than having the whole pueblo destroyed: "The natives soon laid down their arms and surrendered at their mercy." During the prolonged siege of Moho, "one day, before the pueblo was taken, they asked for a conference." Castañeda continues, "As they had learned we did not harm women and children, they wanted to give us theirs" (Hammond and Rey 1940:224; see also Flint and Flint 2005:402).

Deceptive Tactics

Native use of deception was another apparently widespread stratagem. At Moho, Castañeda describes how pueblo leaders "told [Cárdenas] that if he wanted to talk with them, he should dismount and they would approach him on foot to discuss peace." Then, "when [Cárdenas] was close to them, they said that they bore no weapons and that he should remove his" but as the pueblo chief Xauian "embraced [Cárdenas] while two other Indians who had accompanied him drew two maces, which they had concealed behind their backs. They struck [Cárdenas] two blows over the helmet so that they nearly stunned him" (Hammond and Rey 1940:227–28; see also Flint and Flint 2005:404).

More covert forms of deception were practiced in an attempt to lead the force away from the pueblo homeland. Vázquez de Coronado, in a letter to the king, stated that "while I was overseeing the subjugation and pacification of the natives of this provincial [of Tiguex], some native Indians from other provinces beyond these gave me a report that in their land were much grander towns and buildings . . . that there were lords who ruled them, that they ate out of golden dishes" (Coronado, in Flint and Flint 2005:319). Coronado had taken several captives who were forced to become guides. One of the captives, El Turco, often talked about gold and riches to be found further to the east in his native land called Quivira. El Turco "claimed that in his land there was a river . . . two leagues wide, with fish as large as horses and a great number of very large canoes with sails" (Castañeda, in Hammond and Rey 1940:236; see also Flint and Flint 2005:408). El Turco made numerous references to precious metals including golden jingle bells and table service of silver and gold plates in lands to the east. Ultimately, the Spaniards' impatience for that form of deception, which fruitlessly led them far onto the Great Plains, resulted in their killing El Turco out of spite.

Organizational Strategies

Native populations employed a broader strategy of organizational tactics in response to contact. The disruption of intervillage relations within the Tiguex Province forced groups to relocate: "They found themselves having to abandon a pueblo and seek lodging for themselves in the other pueblos of their friends" (Castañeda, in Hammond and Rey 1940:224; see also Flint and Flint 2005:402). After the battle at Arenal had been fought and the numerous casualties inflicted on that village, "most of the people of these pueblos had taken refuge in these two places," that is, the last remaining Tiguex villages called Moho and Pueblo de la Cruz.

During the occupation of the Tiguex Province, Coronado sought allies outside the area: "The general sent a captain to Zia, which had sent messages offering submissions" (Castañeda, in Hammond and Rey 1940:233; see also Flint and Flint 2005:407). That strategy on the part of Coronado may have helped obtain badly needed food, clothing, and supplies. But more important, it likely gained him geopolitical intelligence and added relief by not creating an adversary of every pueblo in the region. This informal allegiance with Zia may have also opened access to sources of obsidian in the Jemez Mountains, which would have been vital for provisioning native weaponry carried by the indios amigos. The Zias, in turn, may have gained assurance that conflicts occurring in Tiguex would not be repeated against them. In fact, the whole of the "Quirix Province" to the north, as Coronado called them (i.e., the Keres-speaking pueblos of Santa Ana, Zia, San Felipe, Santo Domingo, and Cochití), seems to have been politically united to appease, rather than oppose, the expedition.

Once the Tiguex stronghold of Moho fell, and the resistance was broken, the pueblo people had one last organizational choice to make: "The twelve pueblos of Tiguex were never resettled as long as the army remained in that region, no matter what assurances were given them" (Castañeda, in Hammond and Rey 1940:233–34; see also Flint and Flint 2005:407). The consequences of this decision were powerful and long lasting. Several hundred Pueblo people were casualties of direct hostilities in the Tiguex Province alone (Flint 2008). Each of the Tiguex towns reported by Alvarado and other chroniclers was burned and left in ruin. Moreover, the wrath unleashed upon the pueblo people by Coronado's soldiers left a deep scar of distrust and outright fear of the foreign invaders. In particular, the clash in belief systems between native and Christian religions and exposure to new European thoughts would resonate into the next several centuries (Preucel 2002; Wilcox 2009). Contributing factors such as disease and changes in subsistence brought about by exposure to Old World plants and animals would have a substantial and lasting effect.

PHYSICAL EVIDENCE OF FIRST CONTACT

Today, the Tiguex Province, as named by Vázquez de Coronado's expedition, occupies a stretch of about twenty miles along the Rio Grande floodplain northward from Albuquerque, New Mexico.

The "twelve villages" of Tiguex were evenly distributed on either side of the river (Figure 2.2), and when Coronado decided to spend the winter of 1540, he likely arrived at the north end of the province near Santiago Pueblo (opposite the present-day town of Bernalillo). The twelve contact-period villages have almost all been identified on the basis of ceramic evidence, but place-names from the Spanish expeditionary documents—Alcanfor, Alameda, Arenal, Pueblo de la Cruz, and Moho—have yet to be tied to specific sites with absolute certainty. For recent discussions of this topic, see Matthew Schmader (2011), Flint (2011), and William Mathers (2011).

Investigations have been conducted at the largest of the Tiwa village sites, called Piedras Marcadas Pueblo ("village of the marked rocks") since 2007 (Schmader 2011, 2014, 2016a). Surface ceramics indicate an occupation from AD 1300 until the early 1600s (Marshall 1987; Schmader 2011:347). Based on remote-sensing studies, Piedras Marcadas is estimated to contain at least 1,000 ground-floor adobe rooms and several hundred more second- and third-story rooms arranged in three apartment-like complexes or roomblocks (Schmader 2011, 2016a).

Electrical resistivity (ER) is the principal remote-sensing technique used at the site. Surveys using ER of one hectare (2.5 acres) in the central portion of the site reveal several hundred ground-floor rooms arranged in a rectangular layout, surrounding an open interior plaza (Schmader 2014). Possible passageways are found at the northwest and southeast corners of the plaza, along with a large above-ground kiva built into the northern section of the roomblock, and an underground kiva in the west-central part of the plaza.

Following ER studies, intensive metal detection conducted over a half-hectare area (1.25 acres) has identified more than 1,000 sixteenth-century metal artifacts, which are mapped in relation to subsurface adobe architecture. Metal artifacts include many iron and wire fragments, unshaped lead blobs, and pieces of copper alloy sheet. Hardware includes wrought iron nails (Figure 2.3a), horse shoe fragments, and pieces of chain. Personal items include clothing lace tags (aglets), clothing fasteners, buckles, belt loops, and decorative medallions (Figure 2.3b, 2.3c, 2.3d, 2.3e, and 2.3f respectively). Military-related objects include chainmail, lead musket balls, body armor, scabbard tip, copper crossbow arrow points called "boltheads," and the snapped end of a dagger (Figure 2.4a through 2.4h respectively). Characteristic facet-headed wrought iron nails, aglets, and the copper crossbow boltheads are precise diagnostics of the Coronado expedition (Flint 1992; Schmader 2011:316–18).

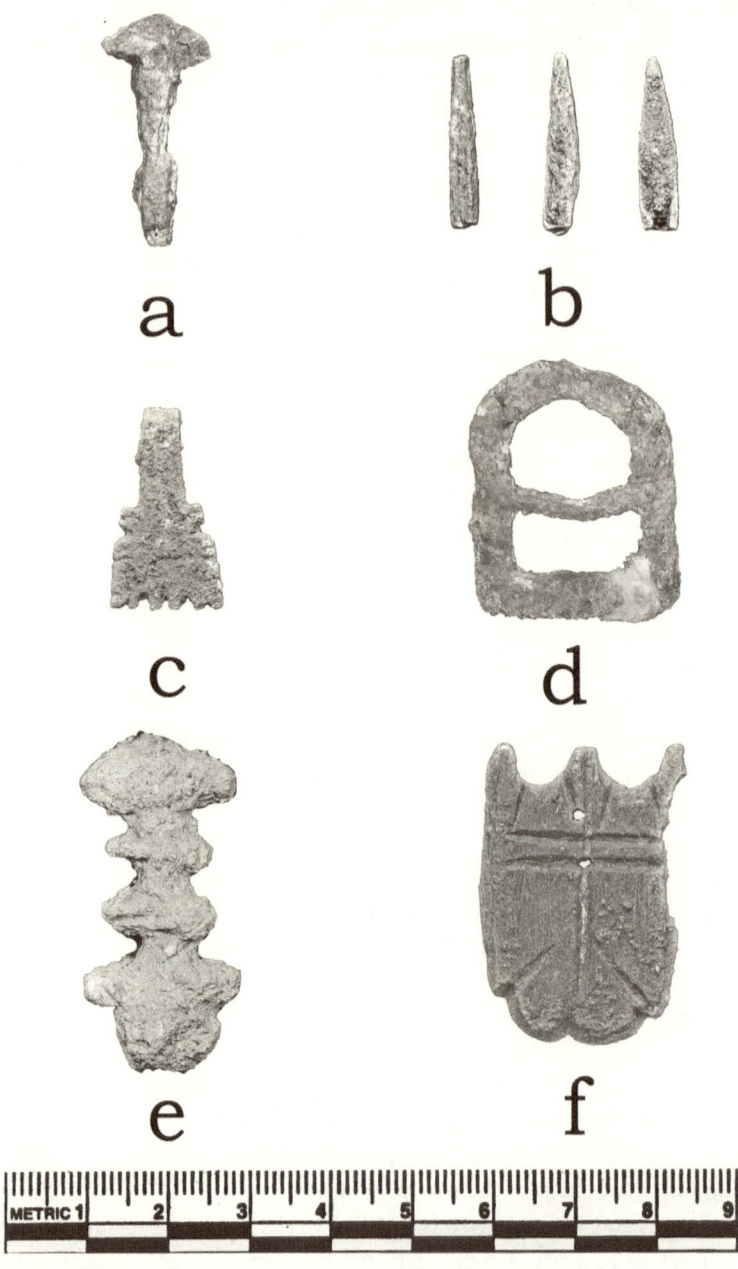

FIGURE 2.3. *Sample of sixteenth-century metal artifacts recovered from Piedras Marcadas pueblo: (a) wrought iron facet-headed nail, (b) copper alloy clothing lace tags ("aglets"), (c) copper alloy clothing fastener, (d) copper alloy belt buckle, (e) ornate copper alloy belt loop, (f) copper alloy medallion. Photograph by author.*

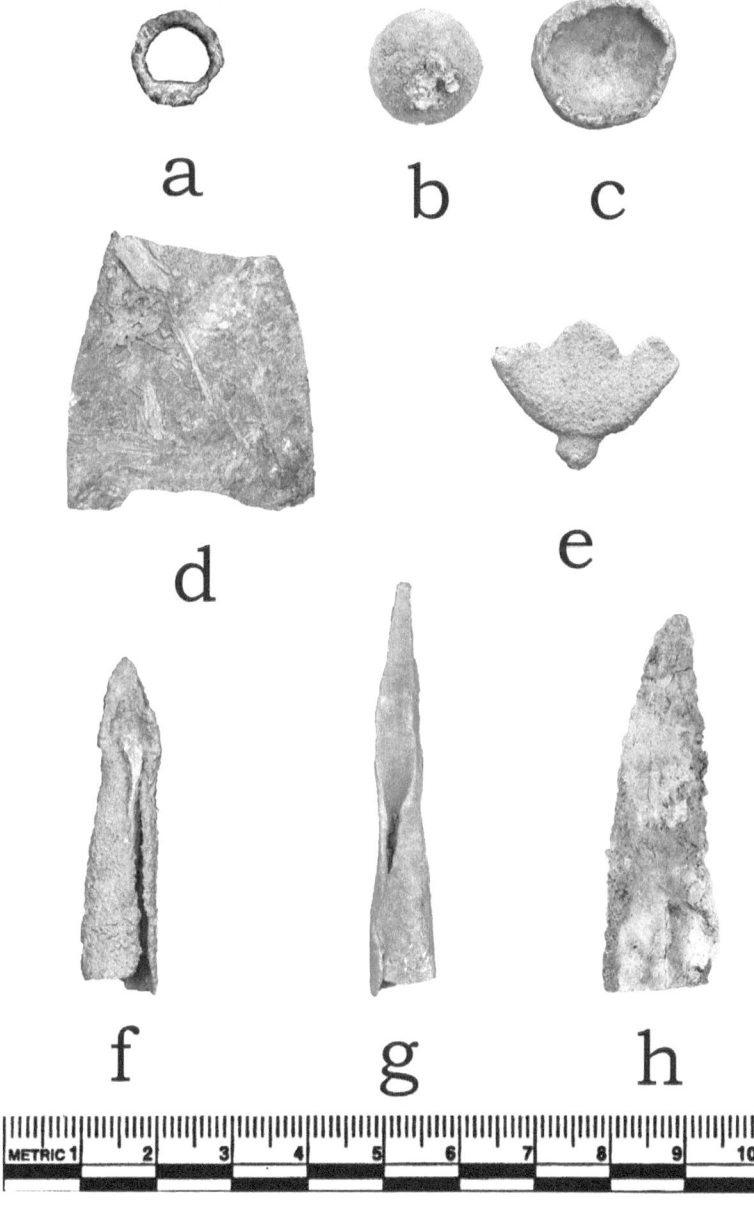

FIGURE 2.4. *Military-related metal sixteenth-century metal artifacts recovered from Piedras Marcadas Pueblo: (a) iron chainmail link, (b) lead ball, for use in a musket, or arquebus, (approximately .50 caliber), (c) lead musket ball, flattened from impact, (d) copper sheet, probably used as body armor from interior of vest (note preserved straw impressions), (e) copper alloy scabbard tip, (f, g) pure copper crossbow boltheads, (h) broken iron (or steel) dagger tip. Photograph by author.*

Metal fragmentation, heavy loss and breakage of personal gear, and abundance of armaments and munitions indicate that Piedras Marcadas was the scene of at least one or more intense fights between the pueblo's inhabitants and Coronado's forces (Schmader 2016a, 2016b). The majority of sixteenth-century artifacts are found three centimeters to eight centimeters below present-day ground surface; this shallow artifact depth indicates a relatively stable ground surface. The relationship between metal artifact distributions and adobe walls suggests several areas where fighting probably occurred (Schmader 2016a). For example, some locations adjacent to walls contain numerous broken horseshoe nails and lost personal items.

In turn, these site characteristics relate to descriptions found in the expeditionary documents. The documents describe how Coronado's initial attack used ladders to scale the walls, but that attempt was thrown back. Other areas fit the description of the pueblos as having been "palisaded," since normally open passages were likely blocked off where the expeditionary forces may have tried to gain access to the plaza. Exterior walls and passageways at Piedras Marcadas contain high concentrations of broken material. Areas within the plaza contained a higher number of items such as lead musket balls, crossbow boltheads, pieces of body armor and chainmail, and the broken dagger tip, which also indicates combat activity (Schmader 2011, 2016b).

Distributions of sixteenth-century metal artifacts may reflect Spanish military tactics of the period and of the expedition. Potential multiple lines of attack are consistent with some documentary descriptions, such as at Moho, where several skirmishes are described. The presence of broken horseshoe nails is consistent with the use of horses in many aspects of fighting. The abundance of broken items reflects the amount of high-energy activity, particularly fighting, that occurred at close quarters (Schmader 2016b).

The documentary record is scanty, however, when it comes to the intriguing topic of interactions or conflict between Mexican native indios amigos soldiers and indigenous pueblo groups (Flint 1997, 2008:58). The unique circumstances of the expedition represents one of the first significant contacts between so many different native people from such a broad geographic area. In events leading up to the battle of Arenal, the pueblo people killed fifty or sixty horse and pack animals, and they "clubbed and killed four or five Nahua Indians" who had been standing guard over the animals (Flint 2008:147). Castañeda notes that during the battle at Arenal, the "mounted men, along with many Indian allies from New Spain, built some heavy smudge fires in the basements [kivas] into which they had broken holes, so that the Indians were forced to sue for peace" (Hammond and Rey 1940:226; see also Flint and Flint 2005:402).

The site of Piedras Marcadas is significant because it contains material evidence of fighting between native Mexican soldiers and pueblo people. Small

Puebloan "bird points" are found on the surface in proximity to sixteenth-century metal fragments. Numerous surface obsidian flakes, particularly within the plaza, may be breakage debris from central Mexican *macanas* or *macahuitls* (flake-edged wooden clubs; Schmader 2011, 2014). Other projectile points found on the surface do not appear to have been made locally and could have been imports brought by indios amigos (see Medrano Enríquez 2012).

Slingstones (Figure 2.5) are found outside the north and south walls of the central roomblock and within the central plaza area. These stones range in diameter from forty millimeters to 80 millimeters and often exhibit grinding along their midlines, a characteristic that helps to distinguish them from ordinary river cobbles (Robert York, personal communication, 2012; see also York and York 2011). Some stones may have been thrown by Puebloan defenders, as described by "the many stones they had to hurl upon us," but other stones may have been thrown by indios amigos using more formal slings. It is unknown if pueblos used formal slings at the time of contact (Robert York, personal communication, 2012).

Coronado expeditionary sites are quite rare. Only a handful have been found in Arizona, New Mexico, and Texas. Extant assemblages large enough to be interpreted as battle sites include the Zuni pueblo of Hawikku (Damp 2005), and Piedras Marcadas (Schmader 2016a, 2016b). The Piedras Marcadas assemblage is the largest and most concentrated of the Coronado sites (Schmader 2011:322). Evidence found at the site suggests that it is a "ground zero" location of the first contact between native Puebloan peoples of the Southwest and a force of foreign explorers.

CONCLUSIONS

Events surrounding first cultural contacts and ensuing negotiations, accommodation, or conflict are complex and multifaceted. Present-day perceptions of contact may suggest simple, finite, and short-lived events. But as these complicated historical episodes are examined more closely, it becomes clear that all cultural contacts have causes, effects, consequences, and collateral impacts that can involve many thousands of people over several centuries. The story of first European and native Mexican contact with the peoples of the American Southwest is a profound case in point.

The Vázquez de Coronado expedition's political and economic failures were so deep that it would take the Spanish Crown a full forty years before considering renewed attempts at exploring Nuevo México. By then, the focus would shift from exploration to setting the foundation for eventual colonization (Hammond and Rey 1966). It was not until 1580 that the next expedition, a small group led by Francisco Chamuscado and Fray Augustín Rodriguez, would venture into the northlands. A follow-up expedition, a larger effort led by Antonio de Espejo

FIGURE 2.5. *Sample of slingstones recovered from surface context at Piedras Marcadas Pueblo (diameters range from forty-five to eighty millimeters).*

in late 1582, was intended to ensure the safety of two priests left behind at the Tiguex pueblo of Puaray by Chamuscado and Rodríguez. Upon reaching Puaray Pueblo, however, it was learned that the priests had been killed (Hammond and Rey 1966:221).

The largest expedition after Coronado's was organized by Gaspar Castaño de Sosa, who, in defiance of the orders of the new viceroy, Luis Velasco, assembled some 200 men and women in an attempt to establish Nuevo México's first colony in 1590 (Hammond and Rey 1966:245–95). These unsuccessful attempts cleared the way for sanctioning Juan de Oñate to establish the first real colony in Nuevo México. Oñate entered Nuevo México in 1598 with 130 families and 400 soldiers, the largest group to come north since Vázquez de Coronado nearly sixty years earlier. The new colony was established at Ohkay Owingeh (Yunque-Yunque, or San Juan Pueblo) and experienced so many difficulties that Oñate resigned his post by 1607. Despite its rocky early beginnings, colonization was by then set in place and events of the mid-seventeenth century would create strife and animosity culminating in the Pueblo Revolts of 1680–96 (see Liebmann and colleagues, chapter 5 in this volume).

The dramatic effects of exploration, colonization, and missionization on the native populations can be seen dramatically in the central Rio Grande Valley. Beginning in 1540, Vázquez de Coronado's Tiguex Province is described as having twelve towns. The estimated population at first contact may have been as high as 10,000 (Barrett 2002:12). In the Tiguex Province, the "twelve towns" appear to have persisted until 1602, and the period of most rapid decline began in the mid-1620s. By then, several of the larger Tiwa pueblos on the west side of the Rio Grande, including Piedras Marcadas, already appear to have been permanently unoccupied. Certainly by 1640, there appears to have been broadscale reorganization and abandonment of even more villages. Population estimates of about 7,000 for sixteen to eighteen villages in the greater middle Rio Grande Basin plummeted by 86 percent to 990 people at just five villages by 1641 (Barrett 2002:64).

Significantly, no major southern Tiwa settlements seem to have persisted on the west side of the river—a pattern that would continue until the Pueblo Revolt—and just three centers of occupation were on the east side of the Rio Grande: Sandia, Puaray, and Alameda. These three pueblos are mentioned consistently as the last, postcontact/prerevolt (AD 1598–80) villages disappeared in the former Tiguex Province. The population level may have dwindled to several hundred at the most. The final distribution of people took place as a diaspora from the central Rio Grande area to the western pueblos of Zuni and Hopi at the end of the seventeenth century.

There are numerous hypothesized factors for rapid population decline, including disease, famine, drought, raids, tribute labor, forced relocation, and disruption of trade and land relations. All likely contributed in some way to the dramatic declines seen in the earlier part of the 1600s. Note that Wilcox (2009) emphasizes site abandonment as a crucial social mechanism for self-preservation and cultural survival. The long-term success of that strategy is evident in the persistence and cultural resilience of the Pueblo peoples throughout the southwest.

Analysis of expeditionary period documents in this chapter suggests that precontact Puebloan peoples internally moderated and resolved conflicts through the same mechanisms of symbolic behavior or mutual respect systems that they tried on foreigners they encountered for the first time. They likely believed these time-tested strategies would work, but when they did not, Pueblo peoples could only resort to more intensified responses of defensive and offensive tactics, deception, and ultimately to broader-scale reorganization. European expeditionary tactics of pitting indigenous groups against each other were similarly unsuccessful when tried in the Puebloan world.

There is no general agreement among scholars as to the nature of interpueblo relations just prior to the first expeditions into the American Southwest. The emergence of warrior societies in the central Rio Grande Valley (Schaafsma 2002) suggests the institutionalized depth of social divisions among some Pueblo groups. However, there is little physical evidence of actual hostility among the pueblos during the time just before European contact. Architectural details show that while plazas were enclosed, they were not completely barricaded. Defensive locations were not constructed among the Rio Grande pueblos until the revolt period (Wilcox 2009).

It was into this context of negotiated tolerance and potential friction in the Pueblo world that the first expeditions arrived. The presence of a new "common enemy" may have served to overcome inter-Puebloan differences and provide a source of needed unity. The limits of that unity were tested to the greatest extent when hard choices arose: whether to come to the aid of other pueblos in need or under attack, or whether to acquiesce to the demands of foreigners rather than face the ultimate wrath of resistance.

In the middle Rio Grande Valley, few pueblos offered help to the besieged Tiguex settlements. This followed preexisting social (and ethnolinguistic) boundaries, particularly with Keres settlements to the north. Zia Pueblo elected to protect itself from Coronado's forces by offering aid and likely had little choice in the face of events occurring just miles away. Even within the Tiguex Province, villages seem to have been autonomous, resulting in nonprovision of aid to other nearby pueblos in times of conflict. The exception to this seems to have been when the remaining populace decided to assemble at the Tiguex village of Moho for a final last stand against Coronado in early 1541.

Likely, there were complex pueblo-specific and interpueblo dynamics to which each group had to respond individually or situationally. As suggested elsewhere in this chapter, it appears that mechanisms to moderate the severity of conflicts were socially and ritually institutionalized prior to the time of first contact with outsiders. The fact that these mechanisms were used by pueblo peoples against foreigners in the face of contact-related hostilities or conflict-laden circumstances is of great interest.

The seeds of the Pueblo Revolt were planted deeply and irreversibly by the actions and events of the first contact between natives and nonnatives in the American Southwest 140 years earlier. The initial breakdown in mutual respect, followed by the resentful treatment of the Pueblo people, the destruction of their villages, and the casualties suffered left scars that carried well past 1540. Those deep scars were reopened by explorations in the latter part of the 1500s and were certainly not healed by the many difficulties that came to pass throughout the seventeenth century. When the Pueblo Revolt did occur in 1680, it was in many senses the inevitable outcome of forces set in motion during the first contact with nonnative peoples on the Vázquez de Coronado expedition.

NOTES

1. The definitiveness of this statement should be clarified in several ways. The only other land-based expedition of comparable size from the time period was led by Gonzalo Pizarro, who was sent by his half-brother Francisco Pizarro from Ecuador into the Amazon Basin to find the "land of cinnamon." Gonzalo Pizarro left Ecuador in 1541 with 220 Spaniards and about 4,000 Indian allies but within months, two-thirds or more of the expeditionary forces had died. Rather than continue on, he left completion of the exploration to Francisco de Orellana, who then got credit as the "discoverer" of the Amazon River.

Other large expeditions that took place *north* of South America were all launched by sea or were smaller. Thus, Coronado's remains the largest land-based expedition with the exception of the Pizarro-Orellana exploration, which was also not organized by the Spanish Crown but rather by Francisco Pizarro himself (for a discussion of the 136 New World expeditions that occurred in the sixteenth century, see R. Flint 2008:205–18).

2. Estimating current monetary values from the variety of medieval currencies is notoriously difficult. Some estimates are based on the values of commodities, such as the cost of a horse, while others are tied to salaries for certain jobs. The cost estimate for the Coronado expedition is based on information compiled by Shirley Flint (2003), who estimated a value of 574,000 sixteenth-century silver pesos. Each silver peso weighed an ounce, and so the base market value in precious metal is 574,000 times the spot price per ounce of silver (which ranges from thirty dollars in early 2013 to twenty dollars in early 2016).

This would generate a precious-metal cost value of the expedition at nearly $20 million, not adjusted for inflation. Inflationary costs over several centuries may drive the actual value of the goods and services assembled and paid for on the expedition into the hundreds of millions of dollars in today's currency. As S. Flint (2003:52) points out, the sum of 574,000 silver pesos was enormous: at nearly nineteen tons, it was almost three times the amount taken by Cortés from his conquest of Tenochtitlan, and more than Francisco Pizarro's share of the legendary treasure ransom paid by the Inca emperor Atahualpa.

3. The twelfth pueblo is likely Isleta, located twenty-three miles south of Piedras Marcadas.

REFERENCES CITED

Aiton, Arthur S. 1939. "Documents: Coronado's Muster Roll." *American Historical Review* 44 (3): 556–70. http://dx.doi.org/10.2307/1839903.

Barrett, Elinore M. 2002. *Conquest and Catastrophe: Changing Rio Grande Pueblo Settlement Patterns in the Sixteenth and Seventeenth Centuries*. Albuquerque: University of New Mexico Press.

Bolton, Herbert E. 1949. *Coronado, Knight of Pueblos and Plains*. Albuquerque: University of New Mexico Press.

Damp, Jonathan E. 2005. *The Battle of Hawikku: Archaeological Investigations of the Zuni-Coronado Encounter at Hawikku*. Zuni Cultural Enterprise Research Series No. 13. Zuni, NM: Zuni Cultural Enterprise.

Flint, Richard. 1992. The Pattern of Coronado Expedition Material Culture. Master's thesis, Department of Behavioral Sciences, New Mexico Highlands University, Las Vegas, NM.

Flint, Richard. 1997. "Armas de la Tierra: The Mexican Indian Component of Coronado Expedition Culture." In *The Coronado Expedition to Tierra Nueva*, edited by Richard Flint and Shirley C. Flint, 47–60. Boulder: University Press of Colorado.

Flint, Richard. 2008. *No Settlement, No Conquest: A History of the Coronado Entrada*. Albuquerque: University of New Mexico Press.

Flint, Richard. 2011. "Moho and the Tiguex War." In *The Latest Word from 1540: People, Places, and Portrayals of the Coronado Expedition*, edited by Richard and Shirley Flint, 348–66. Albuquerque: University of New Mexico Press.

Flint, Richard, and Shirley C. Flint, eds. 2005. *Documents of the Coronado Expedition, 1539–1542*. Dallas: Southern Methodist University.

Flint, Shirley. 2003. "The Financing and Provisioning of the Coronado Expedition." In *The Coronado Expedition from the Distance of 460 Years*, edited by Richard and Shirley Flint, 42–56. Albuquerque: University of New Mexico Press.

Goodwin, Robert. 2008. *Crossing the Continent, 1527–1540*. New York: Harper Books.

Hammond, George P., and Agapito Rey. 1940. *Narratives of the Coronado Expedition, 1540–1542*. Albuquerque: University of New Mexico Press.

Hammond, George P., and Agapito Rey. 1966. *The Rediscovery of New Mexico*. Albuquerque: University of New Mexico Press.

Lester, Toby. 2009. *The Fourth Part of the World*. New York: Simon and Schuster.

Liebmann, Matthew, and Melissa Murphy. 2010. "Rethinking the Archaeology of 'Rebels, Backsliders, and Idolaters'." In *Enduring Conquests*, edited by Matthew Liebmann and Melissa Murphy, 3–18. Santa Fe: School for Advanced Research.

Marshall, Michael P. 1987. *An Archaeological Survey of the Mann-Zuris Pueblo Complex (LA 290): A Southern Tiwan Settlement of the Middle Rio Grande District*. Corrales, NM: Cibola Research Consultants.

Mathers, William. 2011. "Tangled Threads, Loose Ends, and Knotty Problems: The Place of Moho in Tiguex Archaeology, Geography, and History." In *The Latest Word from 1540: People, Places, and Portrayals of the Coronado Expedition*, edited by Richard and Shirley Flint, 367–397. Albuquerque: University of New Mexico Press.

Medrano Enríquez, Angélica María. 2012. *Arqueología del conflicto: La Guerra del Mixtón (1541–1542) vista a través del Peñol de Nochistlán*. Guadalajara: La Taberna Literaria Editores.

Preucel, Robert W. 2002. *Archaeologies of the Pueblo Revolt*. Albuquerque: University of New Mexico Press.

Sánchez, Joseph P. 1988. *The Rio Abajo Frontier, 1540–1692: A History of Early Colonial New Mexico. History Monograph Series*. Albuquerque: Albuquerque Museum.

Sánchez, Joseph P. 1997. "A Historiography of the Route of the Expedition of Francisco Vazquez de Coronado: Río de Cicuye to Quivira." In *The Coronado Expedition to Tierra Nueva. The 1540–1542 Route across the Southwest*, edited by Richard Flint and Shirley C. Flint, 235–51. Boulder: University Press of Colorado.

Schaafsma, Polly. 2002. *Warrior, Shield, and Star: Imagery and Ideology of Pueblo Warfare*. Santa Fe: Western Edge Press.

Schmader, Matthew F. 2011. "Thundersticks and Coats of Iron: Recent Discoveries at Piedras Marcadas Pueblo, NM." In *The Latest Word from 1540: People, Places, and Portrayals of the Coronado Expedition*, edited by Richard and Shirley Flint, 308–347. Albuquerque: University of New Mexico Press.

Schmader, Matthew F. 2014. "New Light on the Francisco Vázquez de Coronado Expedition of 1540–1540." In *Building Transnational Archaeologies: The 11th Southwest Symposium*, edited by Elisa Villalpando and Randall H. McGuire, 111–132. Arizona State Museum Technical Series No. 209. Tucson: Arizona State Museum.

Schmader, Matthew F. 2016a. "How Tribal Consultation and Non-Invasive Techniques Led to a Better Understanding of Vázquez de Coronado's Expedition of 1540–1542." *Advances in Archaeological Practice* 4 (1): 1–16. http://dx.doi.org/10.7183/2326-3768.4.1.1.

Schmader, Matthew F. 2016b. "The Slingstones and Arrows of Unfortunate Outrage: Vázquez de Coronado and the "Tiguex War" of 1540." In *Preserving Fields of Conflict: Papers from the 2014 Fields of Conflict Conference and Preservation Workshop*, edited by Steven D. Smith, 51–57. Columbia: University of South Carolina.

Wilcox, Michael V. 2009. *The Pueblo Revolt and the Mythology of Conquest*. Berkeley: University of California Press.

Winship, George Parker. 1896. *The Coronado Expedition, 1540–1542*. Fourteenth Annual Report of the U.S. Bureau of American Ethnology, 1892–93, Part I. Washington, DC: US Government Printing Office.

York, Robert, and Gigi York. 2011. *Slings and Slingstones: The Forgotten Weapons of Oceania and the Americas*. Kent, OH: Kent State University Press.

THREE

Meeting in Places

Seventeenth-Century Puebloan and Spanish Landscapes

PHILLIP O. LECKMAN

INTRODUCTION

> *[New Mexico] lies more than twelve hundred miles northward from Old Mexico, and six hundred of these are desert, inhabited by innumerable Indians so barbarous and savage that they are naked and have no houses or agriculture . . . But upon reaching the settlements of New Mexico, there are people who wear clothes and shoes and who are excellent farmers.*
> —Fray Alonso de Benavides, *Revised Memorial of 1634* (Hodge et al. 1945)

Beginning with the first Spanish entradas into New Mexico in the middle and late sixteenth centuries (see Matthew E. Schmader, chapter 2 in this volume), encounters with the Puebloan peoples of the northern Rio Grande Valley presented Spanish explorers and colonizers with many seemingly familiar elements. The chronicler of early expeditions and the correspondence of the colonial administrators that followed them repeatedly remark on what their authors perceived to be the civilized aspects of sixteenth- and early seventeenth-century Pueblo society, comparing them favorably to the communities of less settled peoples they encountered elsewhere. They provide effusive discussions

DOI: 10.5876/9781607325741.c003

of the "attractive" masonry and adobe Puebloan villages, "their streets and plazas well-planned and strong" (Hodge et al. 1945:47; Jojola 1997:180), which early expeditions nicknamed after Spanish and Mesoamerican towns they felt resembled them: Valladolid, Galisteo (Barrett 2002; Hammond and Rey 1966). Beyond the villages themselves, the Spanish expressed awe for Puebloan irrigation systems, repeatedly remarking upon well-made canals and ditches "built as if by Spaniards" (Hammond and Rey 1966:182, cited in Anschuetz 2003:1). At a regional scale, Spanish accounts ordered the numerous villages and settlements of the Puebloan world into "provinces" by language and geography, noting their "capitals" and once again contrasting these settled regions with the domains of less sedentary peoples beyond the borders of the New Mexico "kingdom" (Hammond and Rey 1966; Morrow 1996).

But while plazas, irrigated fields, and ordered provinces resonated strongly with seventeenth-century Iberian notions of community and landscape, the perceived points of tangency described in early Spanish accounts were in many respects based on fundamental misrecognitions (Lycett 2014). The manifestations of these phenomena in the Puebloan Southwest were in fact rooted in very different understandings of land use, landscape, and meaning, drawing on equally extensive, but quite distinct, cultural and historical roots. The impacts of this misperceived, partial tangency on land use and landscape in seventeenth-century New Mexico were far reaching, informing colonial Spanish policies and reactions at all levels. In some circumstances, the gaps in understanding between Spanish and Puebloan concepts of plazas, towns, and other outwardly shared phenomena provided a space for individual actors or groups to define themselves in opposition to colonial religious and civil authority, or to redefine traditional Puebloan landscape practices to accommodate a changing world. Frequently, however, the differences between Spanish and Puebloan concepts of space, land use, and community imposed unintentional hardships, as misperceptions of Puebloan landscapes based on their ostensible Iberian analogues contributed to painful ongoing processes of culture contact and change and aggravated existing pressures on Nuevo Mexico's Puebloan populations.

The interplay between Puebloan and Spanish concepts of space and landscape operates at a multitude of social and physical scales. The discussion that follows is therefore multiscalar as well, structured in terms analogous to the now-familiar Puebloan notion of nested spatial tetrads described by Alfonso Ortiz (1969). As described by Ortiz and elaborated by others (Anschuetz 1998; Fowles 2004, 2009; Snead and Preucel 1999; Tilley 1994), this four-part division of the physical, ideological, and ceremonial landscape entails a series of "nested, but interrelated regions" (Snead and Preucel 1999:176) converging inward from the sacred mountains conceptually bounding the Puebloan world to sequentially encompass the broader Puebloan landscape—the fields, shrines and community lands of a particular village, the conceptual borders of the village itself, and, finally, the enshrined central spaces within the village, centered on its plazas (Greene and Leckman 2011; Ortiz 1969; Snead and Preucel 1999). This nested landscape is dotted with shrines delineating each set of conceptual boundaries, as well as a series of sacred hills, caves, lakes, pools, and other features specific to each village.

While lacking the explicit ceremonial geography that bounds Puebloan plazas, villages, and communities via shrines, sacred mountains, and other ceremonially resonant features, colonial Iberian conceptions of space were imbued with a broadly analogous set of nested geographies. Idealized Iberian communities were imagined as finite, formally constituted civic spaces, centered on a plaza and its church (Crouch et al. 1982) and set within a bounded landscape of communal fields and pastures (Vassberg 1984; Melville 1997) that was in turn nested within a series of broader geopolitical divisions: the province, the region, and ultimately the larger colonial polity itself (Trigg 2005).

The obvious similarities between Puebloan and colonial Iberian conceptual landscapes, the equally significant differences and discontinuities these external resemblances concealed and complicated, and the implications of both similarities and differences for understanding the rapidly changing New Mexico landscape of the seventeenth century are at the root of the discussion that follows. Drawing on data and analysis derived from recent fieldwork conducted by the University of Chicago under the direction of Mark Lycett (1997, 2002a, 2002b, 2004, 2005, 2014), the remainder of this chapter explores the interplay between Puebloan and Spanish conceptions of landscape and their potential impacts on the early New Mexico Colony through a consideration of seventeenth-century spatial organization and land use practices at LA 162, a large village and *visita*—or mission site without a resident priest—also known as Paako, or San Pedro, located on the eastern flanks of the Sandia Mountains (Lycett 2002a). Following the nested systems of community scale endemic to both Puebloan and Spanish notions of space and place, the structure of social space within Paako itself is considered first, with a particular emphasis on the changing structure and function of the village's plazas and other community spaces. Next, I address changing land use and landscape practices in the immediate vicinity of the village, defined and occupied by community fields, outlying farm camps, shrines, and other small structures. Finally, I consider the Paako community in terms of its broader regional setting, as defined by the mutual conceptual world shared among Puebloan communities of the northern Rio Grande Valley and, later, as formally delineated as the Spanish colony of New Mexico.

NATURAL SETTING

Paako is located in an upland setting along the eastern margins of both the colonial and pre-Hispanic Pueblo worlds, along the eastern flanks of the Sandia Mountains (Figure 3.1) rising east of present-day Albuquerque (Kelley 1982). While the range's dramatic, craggy western face dominates the middle Rio Grande Valley skyline, forming a significant physical and cultural landmark visible for many miles across the northern Rio Grande region (Greene and Leckman 2011; Ortiz 1969:19), the eastern face is smoother and more gently sloping and supports large, continuous stands of relatively lush pine forest (Kelley 1982:5). This area is watered by a series of drainages that, while initially radiating out from the base of the mountains in all directions, ultimately drain west to the Rio Grande (Anschuetz 1984:120). The two largest of these eastern drainages are Tijeras Creek, which runs south along the southern portion of the eastern Sandias, then cuts west, delineating the range's southern edge before emptying into the Rio Grande near present-day Isleta Pueblo, and the Arroyo San Pedro, which drains the north-central portion of the Sandias, running north to merge with the Arroyo Tonque some eighteen kilometers north of Paako near the important precontact pueblo of Tunque, which gives the drainage its name. From Tunque, this drainage system flows northwest, ultimately draining into the Rio Grande at present-day San Felipe Pueblo. Paako is situated on the upper reaches of the Arroyo San Pedro watershed, approximately seven kilometers north of the forested divide separating it from the Tijeras drainage (Figure 3.2).

The site's upland setting likely presented both challenges and opportunities to its inhabitants. Elevations in the mountains ringing Paako range from 2,804 to 3,255 meters (9,200 to 10,678 feet) along the crest of the Sandias to 2,259 meters (7,411 feet) at Monte Largo, the highest peak in the southern San Pedro Mountains to the east of the site. Within the Arroyo San Pedro watershed, the topography slopes gradually northward, with elevations ranging from approximately 2,175 meters (7,136 feet) along the divide with the Tijeras Arroyo watershed to 1,675 meters (5,495 feet) at the Arroyo San Pedro's confluence with the Arroyo Tonque (Figure 3.3). Paako itself is located at an elevation of approximately 1,980 meters (6,496 feet).

National Weather Service climate data compiled for a rolling series of thirty-year averages between 1961 and 2010 at the weather station at Sandia Park, the nearest recording station to Paako, indicate an average frost-free period ranging between 190 and 202 days, a sufficient period to accommodate most historically and ethnographically documented southwestern planting regimes (e.g., Muenchrath et al. 2002). Average Corn Growing Degree Day (CGDD) heat units accumulated at Sandia Park over the same period for a typical Puebloan growing season range between roughly 1,900 and 2,175, well short of the average CGDD total required from planting to maturity by 123

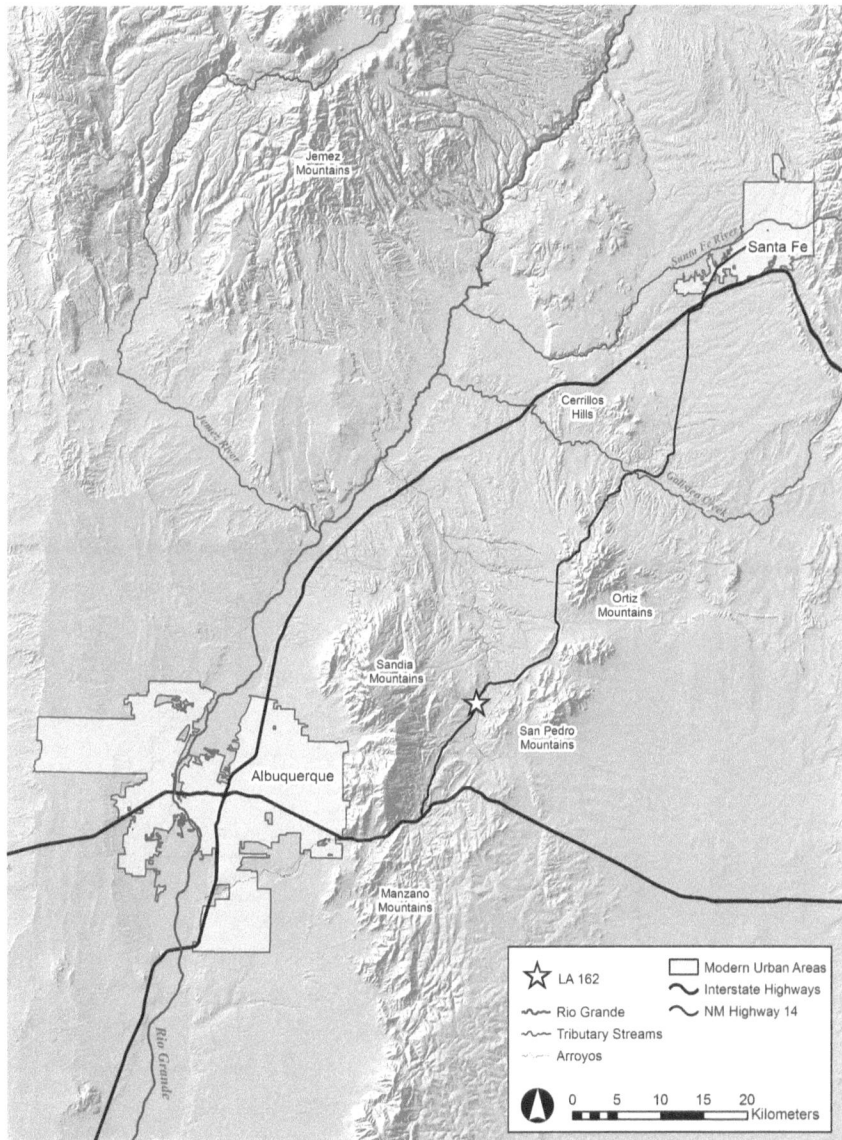

FIGURE 3.1. *LA 162's location in the Middle Rio Grande Valley.*

historical-period maize varieties grown out by archaeobotanist Karen Adams and her colleagues (K. Adams et al. 2006:54) in a 2004–5 experimental study (Van West and Cordell 2013). According to a recent climate study at Tijeras Pueblo, however (Van West and Cordell 2013), Adams believes that some indigenous varieties of maize could, in fact, mature with only 1,900 to 2,100 CGDD

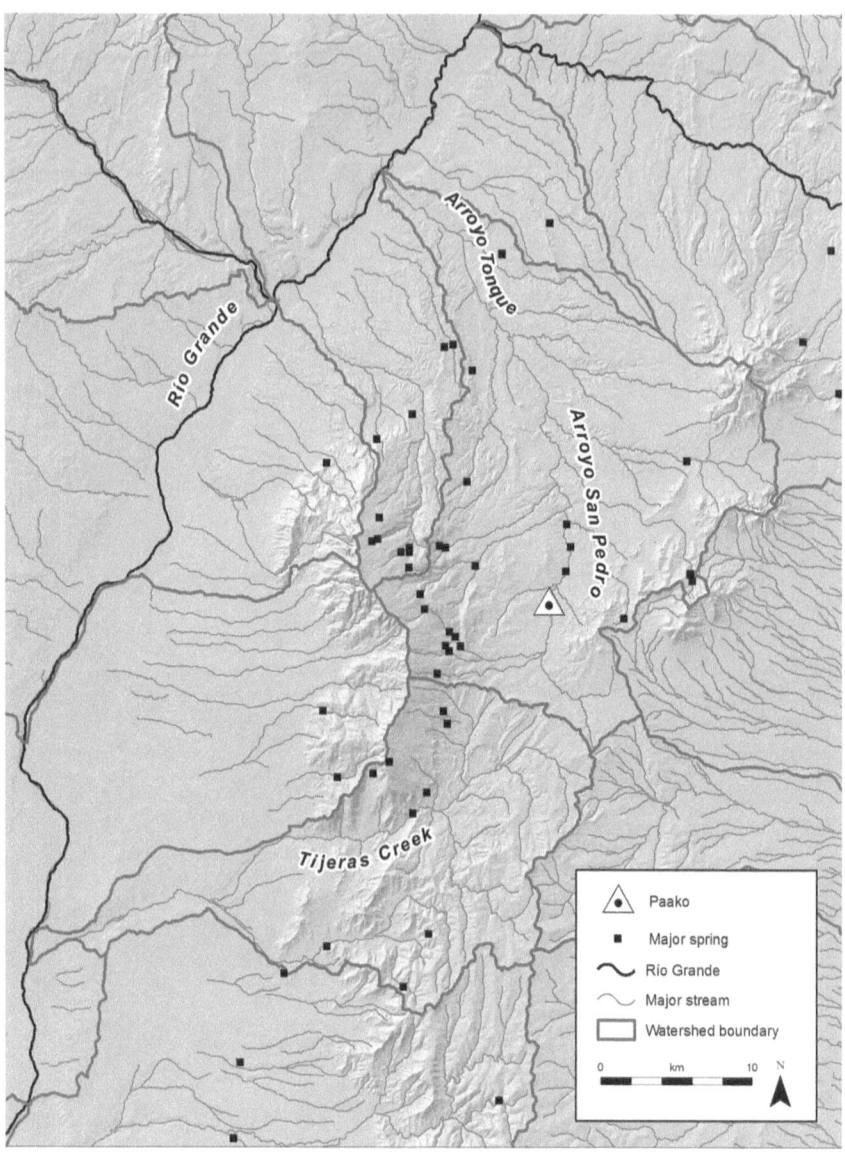

FIGURE 3.2. *Local watersheds and drainage systems in the vicinity of LA 162.*

heat units, a total well within the possible range at Paako. However, considerable annual variation exists, and the growing period in some years was likely inadequate for crop production (Lycett 1997:13): according to Kurt Anschuetz (1984:123), the shortest recorded period between killing frosts on record at Sandia Park is only 87 days, in 1945.

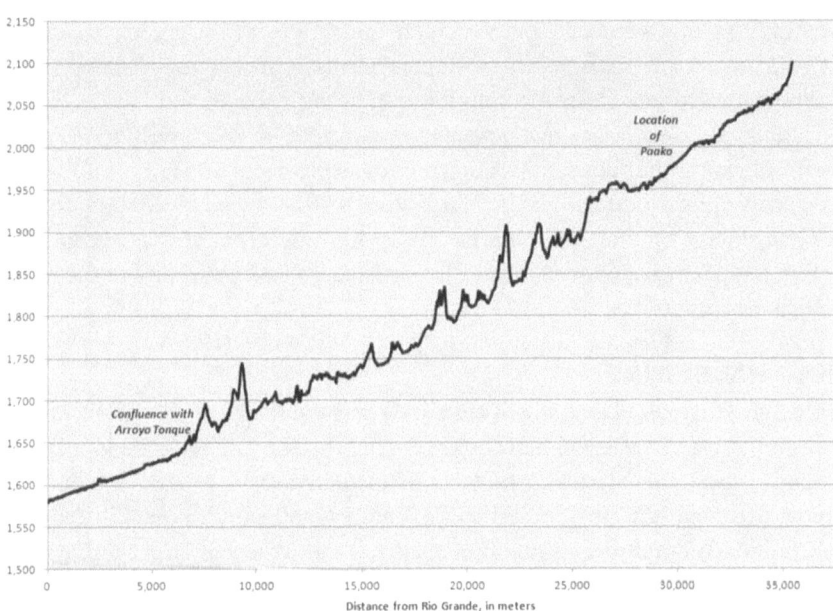

FIGURE 3.3. *North-south elevation profile of the Arroyo San Pedro watershed.*

On the other hand, annual precipitation in the area averages roughly twenty to thirty centimeters higher than average annual precipitation observed in the Rio Grande Valley to the west. Likewise, the Arroyo San Pedro floodplain in the immediate vicinity of the site is the largest expanse of relatively level quaternary floodplain soils in the overall East Mountain area, and one of the largest such areas within the entire Arroyo Tonque watershed (Anderson et al. 1997). Although the East Mountain region as a whole is characterized by soils considered marginal by modern agricultural standards (Anschuetz 1984:127–29), floodplain soils in the vicinity of Paako exhibit the best mix of characteristics among these (Hacker 1977; Hacker and Banet 2008). This is especially true for the soil types along the San Pedro drainage in the immediate vicinity of Paako, surrounding the Arroyo's confluence with a large intermittent drainage approximately 1.25 kilometers north of the pueblo.

Finally, the San Pedro Spring, some 165 meters southeast of Paako, represents one of the most reliable and highest-volume water sources in the area, allowing a spring-fed segment of the Arroyo San Pedro to run perennially for distances ranging from 3.5 to 6.6 kilometers depending on runoff or local precipitation (Campbell Corporation 2000). According to available hydrological data (US Geological Survey 2012), this represents one of the only perennial drainages in a level, relatively low-elevation setting in the entire East Mountain region, and the longest expanse of perennial stream—and one of only two total—in the entire

Arroyo Tonque watershed. Together, then, the region in the immediate vicinity of Paako combines many of the attributes necessary for the establishment and maintenance of a successful community on both Puebloan and Iberian terms, including relatively large, gently sloping expanses of comparatively fertile soils and a reliable water source with significant, dependable outflows. And while Puebloan agricultural camps and farmsteads of all periods were situated to take advantage of these affordances, the small settlements of the seventeenth century appear to have been located in particularly close proximity to the most advantageous settings.

CULTURAL SETTING

Although settlement along the eastern and southern flanks of the Sandia Mountains on at least a seasonal basis began during the Rio Grande Developmental Period (AD 600–900) or earlier, the Arroyo San Pedro around Paako was relatively thinly occupied until the late thirteenth century and early fourteenth century, when a marked increase in site frequency and the advent of larger multiroom pueblos may mark the first year-round settlement of the area (Anschuetz 1984; Cordell 1979, 1980; Lycett 1997).

Certainly, site frequencies in the vicinity of Paako increase dramatically during the early Rio Grande Classic Period (ca. AD 1310–1450), jumping from only six sites with Rio Grande Coalition Period (ca. AD 1215–1310) materials to 105 sites with evidence for Early Classic occupations (Gossett and Gossett 1990; Walley 2006). Paako itself was initially settled at this time, as were the two other large, aggregated settlements in the East Mountain area, Tijeras Pueblo (LA 581) and San Antonio Pueblo (LA 24), both of which were located within the Tijeras Arroyo watershed, some 15 and 12.5 kilometers southwest of Paako respectively (Figure 3.4). Paako was the largest of these Early Classic Period communities, with at least twenty-six roomblocks constructed and occupied between AD 1300 and 1425 (Lambert 1954; Lycett 1997, 2002a) and perhaps a thousand or more rooms (Eckert and Cordell 2004). Early Classic Paako was organized into two architectural divisions separated by a small intermittent drainage, with at least eleven primarily adobe roomblocks located in the H-shaped southern division around an enclosed central plaza and several adjacent plazas, and fourteen masonry, adobe and mixed masonry-and-adobe roomblocks in four adjoined plaza groups making up the northern division (Figure 3.5) (Lambert 1954; Lycett 1997). The extensive Early Classic occupation at Paako came to an end during the early fifteenth century, followed by an apparent occupational hiatus (Lambert 1954; Lycett 1997). This period saw a decline throughout the East Mountain area: Tijeras Pueblo was also abandoned as a residential site during the first quarter of the fifteenth century, with only San Antonio consistently occupied throughout the Classic Period (Akins 2004; Anschuetz 1984; Cordell 1980; Dart 1980; Lycett 1997).

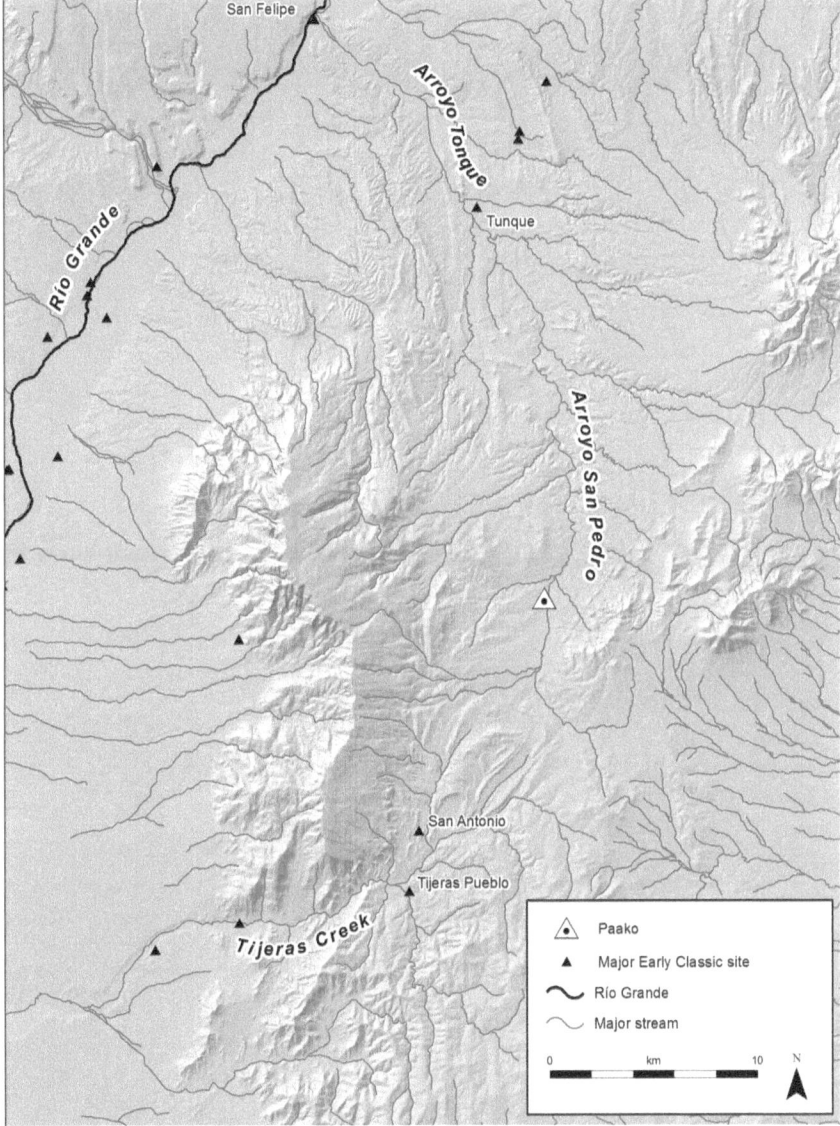

FIGURE 3.4. *Major Early Classic–period sites in the East Mountains.*

After a hiatus of perhaps a century or less, a much smaller population returned to Paako at the close of the sixteenth century or perhaps the earliest years of the seventeenth. This occupation, which is associated with a decorated assemblage dominated by Glaze E and F types, had a much smaller footprint as well, focused on a group of four masonry roomblocks surrounding a single plaza in

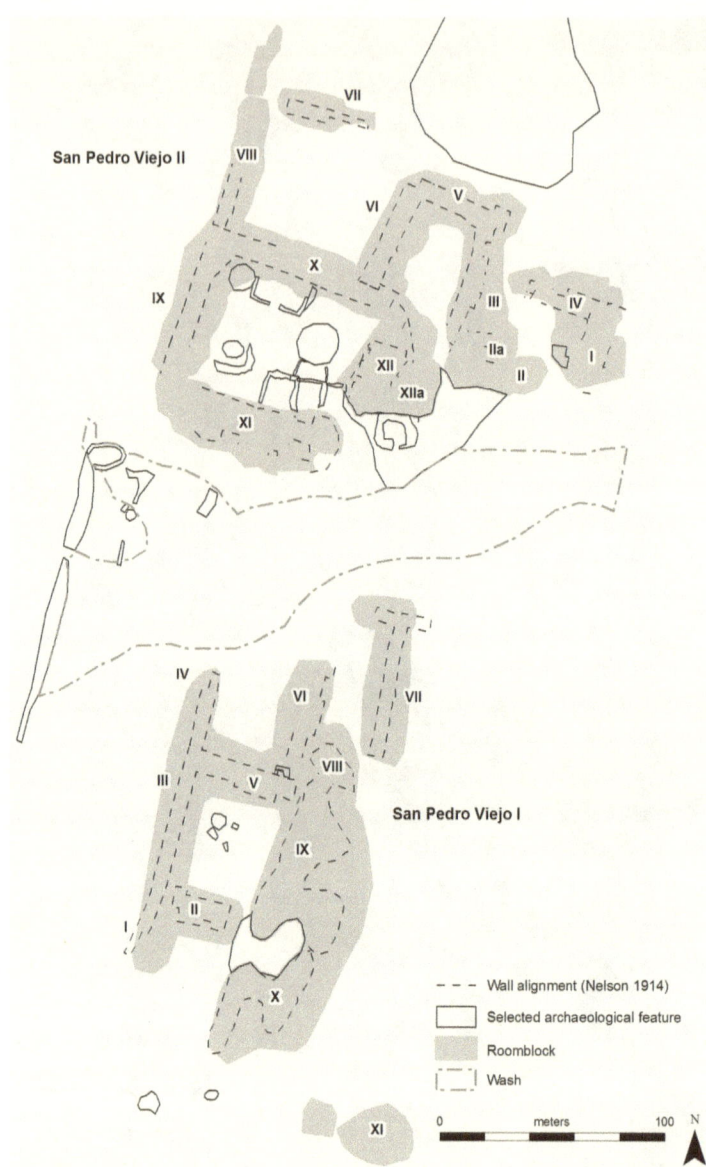

FIGURE 3.5. *Site map of LA 162 illustrating major divisions and roomblocks identified by Nels Nelson (1914).*

the pueblo's northern division (Figure 3.6) (Lycett 1997, 2002a). Although the documentary record surrounding LA 162 is sparse and somewhat ambiguous, a sizeable pueblo located in approximately the correct geographic position was repeatedly visited by sixteenth-century expeditions (Barrett 2002; Lambert 1954;

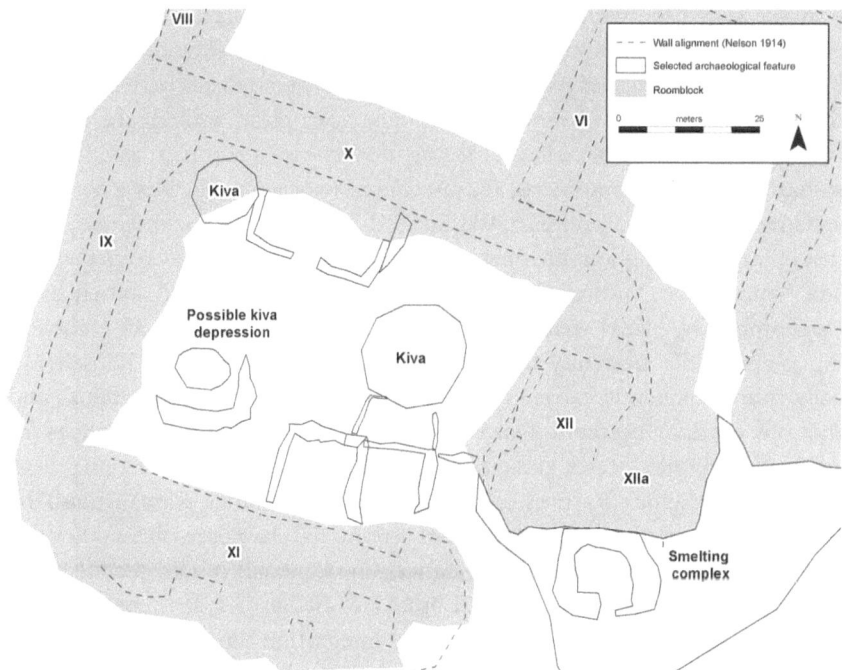

FIGURE 3.6. *Map of the seventeenth-century plaza group at LA 162.*

Lycett 1997). The name Paako appears in a list of East Mountain–area villages paying tribute to Oñate in 1598 (Lambert 1954; Lycett 1997, 2002b), the basis by which Adolph Bandelier, Marjorie Lambert, and other investigators attributed it to LA 162. Colonial records from the early and mid-seventeenth century refer to the establishment of a visita at a site called San Pedro, the granting of an *encomienda* at this location, and its subsequent abandonment and resettlement by mid-century (Lambert 1954:6). According to Lycett (2002b:68), no documentary evidence for residential occupation at San Pedro exists after the early 1660s. However, this place-name remained associated with LA 162 through the seventeenth and eighteenth centuries (e.g., Eidenbach 2012:52–53), was applied to Hispanic communities founded in the area beginning in the mid-nineteenth century (Cordell 1980; Lycett 1997), and was the name used by Bandelier when he visited the site in 1892 (Lange and Riley 1966:380–81).

VILLAGE SPACES: PAAKO AND ITS PLAZA

Within both Puebloan and Iberian settlements of the seventeenth century, space and place were conceptually and physically centered on open public plazas constituting important communal, extramural spaces, and venues for activities both economic and sacred. Among the pueblos, as discussed above, public plazas were the sacred and symbolic centers of both the pueblo itself, the broader community lands encompassing it, and, ultimately, the cosmos. Physically embodied by the earth navel shrines typically found at their centers, plazas were—and are—the conceptual "center of centers" or "middle-heart-place" evoking the place of emergence, concepts of male and female duality, and a complex, multilayered system of dualities, oppositions, and directional associations (Fowles 2009; Snead and Preucel 1999; Swentzell 2011; Wilson 2011). In the large, plaza-oriented towns that emerged throughout the Puebloan region around AD 1275–1300 (Graves and Van Keuren 2011), with one or more central plazas surrounded and enclosed by roomblocks, plazas were also a primary focus of economic life, functioning as a shared community activity area, with many aspects of a household's daily round frequently carried out on the plazas themselves or on the shared rooftops overlooking them. Plazas were and are also the primary venues for dances, ceremonies, feasts, and other large-scale ritual performances integral to community religious practices. In many pueblo communities, plazas are also the locations of kivas, the semisubterranean ceremonial chambers where other rituals are conducted, often before an audience consisting only of initiated members of religious societies privy to special ritual knowledge (Triadan 2006). As such, plazas serve both to promote community integration through economic and ceremonial activities shared among the village as a whole, and to serve as venues for more restricted activities that enforce and reiterate community power relations and social norms (Graves and Van Keuren 2011; Triadan 2006).

Colonial Spanish rules for town planning, as codified by the 1573 Laws of the Indies (Crouch et al. 1982), afforded plazas a similarly central role within an idealized colonial community. Drawn ultimately from Greek and Roman antecedents as much as conventions of medieval Iberian town-building, these regulations specify the plaza as the center of town life, "the point at which civic identity was expressed" (Crouch et al. 1982:42), and the proper venue for a range of community activities, from fiestas and religious processions to markets and trade fairs. Spanish plazas, like their Puebloan counterparts, were spaces intended for the display and reinforcement of exemplary civic conduct. Unlike Pueblo plazas, however, plazas laid out in accordance with colonial Spanish ideals were designed to highlight the civic and ceremonial trappings of the imperial state. With building space along plaza edges designated for administrative structures and the residences of the elite citizenry, the idealized Spanish plaza was above all oriented around and toward the community church, prominently sited on the plaza in a location selected for maximum visibility and authority (Crouch et al. 1982; Wilson 2011:21–22).

In seventeenth-century New Mexico, however, the idealized concepts of Iberian town planning stipulated in the Laws of the Indies were formally enacted only at Santa Fe, the colonial capital, and then only in an incomplete, attenuated sense (Crouch et al. 1982; Wilson 2011). Elsewhere in New Mexico the small population of secular Spanish settlers resided primarily in dispersed *estancias* often occupied by fewer than twenty inhabitants including servants (Trigg 2005:90–91). Like the similar farmsteads operated by Franciscan missionaries (Ivey 2005, 2006), these dispersed settlements were typically situated adjacent to existing Puebloan population centers and relied upon both the *encomienda* labor of pueblo inhabitants and the economic, agricultural, and social infrastructure afforded by the pueblos and the Franciscan missions and residential/administrative complexes, or *conventos*, that were constructed in the vicinity of many major villages by the early 1630s (Ivey 2005, 2006; Lycett 2014; Trigg 2005). As many as twenty mission complexes occupied by resident friars were established, with another ten settlements served by smaller, periodically visited visitas, and another nine fluctuating from one status to the other (Lycett 2004, 2014).

In the absence of planned Spanish towns, pueblos and mission conventos both became primary focuses for Spanish notions of civic structure and organization (Wilson 2011). The array of domestic, industrial, and religious structures composing the convento were major centers of economic production as well as religious and social indoctrination, "the single most important location of colonial and indigenous contact" (Lycett 2002a:63). Even beyond the massive, relatively lofty fortress-churches at their centers, the extensive, planned architectural complexes established at major mission sites such as Nuestra Senora de los Angeles de Pecos (Ivey 2005) were monumental constructions at a scale unprecedented in the Puebloan world, representing a mobilization of raw material, labor, and time that in and of itself must have constituted a fundamental reshaping of Puebloan society (Lycett 2004:371–72). As elsewhere in New Spain, seventeenth-century mission churches themselves were built for maximum effect on their audiences, exploiting local topography (Lycett 2004) and natural light (Wilson 2011:22) to imbue church buildings with imposing power and divine inspiration (Liebmann 2015).

In most cases, the large seventeenth-century convento complexes established at major Puebloan population centers were placed at the margins of existing pueblo communities, rather than within them (Ferguson 1996; Ivey 1988, 2005; Jojola 1997:180–82; Lycett 2002a, 2004). Several authors have suggested that the relatively isolated situation of such complexes illustrates the "contested nature of the missionary enterprise" (Lycett 2004:371), with Puebloan leaders perhaps offering resistance to the physical intrusion of mission infrastructure into more integral village spaces (Ferguson 1996:117; Kubler 1940). Over time, however, the economic, social, and political importance of major mission centers frequently drew the indigenous communities surrounding them more tightly into their orbits. The subsequent architectural histories of communities associated with major mission complexes are diverse and complex, but in many communities an occupational shift occurred as some pueblo inhabitants relocated their dwellings away from traditional village plazas and into closer proximity to the mission and convento (Ivey 1988, 2005; Jojola 1997). The resurgence of extremely traditional, archetypal forms of plaza-centered spatial organization in pueblo communities established in the wake of the Revolt of 1680 may be seen in this context as an effort to reclaim Puebloan understandings of plaza and village space from the influences imposed by eighty years of mission-centered interaction (Liebmann 2006, 2012; Liebmann et al. 2005). Similarly, many villages reestablished by colonial authorities after the Spanish Reconquest were organized around church-centered plazas, imposing at least a physical accordance with Spanish concepts of community space (Jojola 1997:181; Liebmann 2012:215–16).

Beyond the Rio Grande Valley and the network of the missionized major village that were the primary focus of Spanish colonization and settlement, efforts to impose religious architecture and other trappings of Spanish community organization onto existing Puebloan public and community spaces were more varied and met with mixed success. At Paako, the village layout that emerged during the village's initial fourteenth-century occupation exhibits most of the hallmarks of other plaza-centered Pueblo towns of the period. Between the site's major north and south divisions, twenty-two roomblocks surrounded at least eight or nine enclosed plazas. Where tested archaeologically, the plazas display features and artifacts suggesting their intensive use for a range of domestic and public activities (Lycett 2002a, 2002b). Although the only kivas associated with the early occupation identified to date are located within roomblocks rather than at a subterranean level (Lambert 1954), available evidence suggests public spaces were organized in accordance with Puebloan norms: at least one potential plaza shrine, a group of large boulders located in the central plaza of the south division's main roomblock, was noted by Bandelier in the early 1880s (Lange and Riley 1966), and may remain partially visible today.

As mentioned, the site's seventeenth-century occupation had a much smaller footprint than its predecessor, presumably reflecting a much-reduced local population. A single plaza in the site's northern division was the focus of activity during the period. Multiple test excavations conducted between 1996 and 2005 during University of Chicago investigations at Paako indicate its intensive use and reuse during the colonial period, with multiple well-maintained plaza surfaces associated with late glazeware ceramics and faunal evidence for goats, sheep, horses, and other European domesticated animals (Lycett 2002a; Morrison, Cole, and Lycett 2002). Features documented by excavations include possible jacal structures, hearths, and small pits, indicating the continued economic use of at least portions of the plaza in a manner consistent with earlier periods (Morrison, Cole, and Lycett 2002). The persistence of traditional Puebloan ceremonial uses of the plaza during at least the early portion of the colonial period is indicated

FIGURE 3.7. *Rectilinear structure constructed in the southwest corner of Paako's seventeenth-century plaza.*

by the presence of at least two and probably three subterranean plaza kivas, each apparently associated with late glaze artifacts and other historical-period evidence (Lambert 1954).

As the colonial period progressed, however, evidence suggests the plaza's function changed. As recounted by Mark Lycett (2002a, 2004), a probable kiva in the southwestern corner of the plaza was demolished, filled, and leveled, and a rectangular, east-southeast-oriented structure measuring approximately fifteen meters by eight meters was constructed atop the resulting small elevated mound (Figure 3.7). In its dimensions, placement, orientation, and construction, this structure is consistent with small seventeenth-century visitas from the Zuni area, the Tompiro region, and elsewhere (Johansen 2002; Lycett 2002a). If this structure, which was associated with late glaze ceramics including a candlestick fragment, is in fact the remnant foundations of a visita chapel, its construction atop a probable kiva and its imposition into the center of Paako's main plaza suggests an attempt at a clear symbolic replacement of the architectural elements of one ceremonial system with another (see chapters by John G. Douglass and William M. Graves [1], and David Hurst Thomas [15], this volume).

Its placement also suggests that it was an attempt to subdivide and reconfigure this public space akin to the similarly sited visita constructed at the Zuni pueblo of Kechiba:wa, which Thomas Ferguson suggests was situated in the middle of the site's main plaza as part of an effort to supplant plaza-based ceremonial activities (Ferguson 1996:118). If chapel construction at Paako did represent an effort to transform a Puebloan ritual and public space into one organized along Spanish lines, however, it seems to have been largely unsuccessful: the chapel structure may never have been completed, and in any event its use seems to have been short lived. Eventually, it may have been partially dismantled and incorporated into the postresidential corral network that ultimately consumed much of the plaza (Lycett 2002a).

As efforts to reconfigure Paako's plaza as a public and ceremonial space organized along Spanish norms began and faltered, probably as the village's resident population declined (Lycett 2002a), an ultimately more comprehensive transformation of the plaza in conjunction with novel Iberian economic and subsistence activities proceeded alongside it. Artifact assemblages dominated by seventeenth-century ceramics in association with animal dung and other evidence for animal husbandry, as well as a paucity of artifactual evidence from later time periods, suggest that the repurposing of plaza space for animal penning apparently began relatively early in the colonial period. Along the southern edge of the plaza, data from test excavations includes evidence for the construction of a series of enclosures associated with large deposits of animal dung, indicating the use of this area for animal penning. Excavation evidence suggests the corral network increased in size over time, perhaps as adjacent roomblocks ceased to be residentially occupied as residential structures (Lycett 2002a; Morrison, Cole, and Lycett 2002; Seddon 2002). Finally, a network of stone enclosures was built that eventually incorporated as much as 40 percent of the total plaza for animal pens, including the entire frontage of the plaza's southern roomblock (Figure 3.8). As this stone corral complex was constructed at the very end of Paako's occupational sequence, Lycett (2002a) suggests it may indicate the site's postresidential use as a logistical herding camp.

Simultaneous with the subdivision of Paako's plaza by an expanding corral network, a group of roomblocks at the southeastern corner of the plaza was developed into a large, intensively used metal-smelting and metallurgical facility, with evidence for a diverse range of activities, including charcoal production, the preparation, smelting and assay of copper and lead ores, and the production of copper ornaments, again within a broader artifact assemblage dominated by seventeenth-century ceramics (Thomas 2008). In addition to requiring fairly intensive labor and large quantities of wood to feed the production of charcoal fuels, the production of precious metals at the smelting complex also involved intense heat and the incorporation or production of numerous noxious

FIGURE 3.8. *Corrals erected within Paako's seventeenth-century plaza.*

substances such as sulfur, copper sulfide, and lead slag (Thomas 2008). While less extensive than the corral network, the presence of the smelting facility at the heart of seventeenth-century Paako's residential, social, and ceremonial spaces was in many respects an even greater impact on the ability of these spaces to function in accordance with Puebloan principals of village organization and public space.

In summary, while Puebloan and Spanish attitudes toward village organization and public space in the vicinity of larger villages were focused on the interplay between traditional Puebloan plazas and emerging public spaces focused around the Spanish church and convento, changes within the historically occupied plaza at Paako over the course of the seventeenth century indicate that efforts to transform it into a public space ordered around Spanish religious architecture ultimately faltered. Instead, Paako's plaza saw a transition from an open, domestically, and ceremonially focused space into an economically focused one, subdivided into discrete zones of industrial and pastoral activity. Such a transformation is not unusual: many ancestral sites residentially abandoned during the sixteenth and seventeenth centuries were eventually reconfigured into sporadically occupied herding camps for sheep and goats (Ferguson 1996; Lycett 1995;

2002a) (see Laurie D. Webster, chapter 4 in this volume), and anecdotal and ethnographic evidence indicates the presence of Puebloan herders in residentially abandoned areas of the Galisteo Basin into at least the early twentieth century (Lycett 2002a).

COMMUNITY SPACES

Just as they overemphasized the similarities between Spanish and Puebloan systems of community and public space within pueblos, Spanish accounts from the sixteenth and seventeenth centuries likewise overemphasize and misrecognize evidence for canal irrigation in the lands surrounding northern Rio Grande communities (e.g. Anschuetz 1998, 2003; Cordell 1979; Levine and Anschuetz 1998; Lycett 2004, 2005, 2014; Wozniak 1987), reflecting the central role played by acequia systems within Iberian concepts of agriculture and land use (e.g., Crouch et al. 1982; Rivera and Glick 2010; Vassberg 1984). Similarly, while Iberian agriculture certainly incorporated dry-farming technologies alongside acequia irrigation, Spanish documentary sources uniformly suffer from an apparent inability to fully recognize other elements of Puebloan agriculture, particularly the extensive, dispersed systems of water-harvesting features designed to maximize the diversity of ecological and topographical settings exploited for subsistence purposes, thereby minimizing and spreading out the risk of precipitation or crop failure in any particular setting. Even when discussed, Puebloan agricultural systems not tied to canal irrigation are frequently attributed to the "natural" fertility of the land (Anschuetz 2003), while failure to engage in the kind of intensive irrigation agriculture familiar to the Spanish is seen as evidence for fundamental Puebloan shiftlessness (Hackett 1937; Hodge et al. 1945).

The notion of "community" and community lands superficially shared between Puebloan and Iberian populations likewise masked extremely different understandings of the appropriate structure and use of these communal spaces. Spanish concepts of communal land use during the colonial period make a clear distinction between fields and lands intended for grazing, emphasizing shared pasturage, mobile herds, and the use of "fallow"—that is, untended—field systems for forage (Crouch et al. 1982; Melville 1997; Vassberg 1984). It is not clear to what extent this land use system was implemented within Puebloan communities wholly or partially integrated into the seventeenth-century colonial system. However, fragmentary documentary evidence indicates that both missionaries and civil colonists maintained large herds of sheep, goats, and cattle by the middle decades of the seventeenth century, and that this rapidly expanding economy was accompanied by disputes between civil and religious authorities over the use of Puebloan labor (Baxter 1987; Hackett 1937; Hodge et al. 1945). In any case, it is easy to see potential conflicts between Iberian notions of land use based largely on the combination of livestock and acequia irrigation and Puebloan land use concepts based on extensive, dispersed agricultural systems, and to envision some of the potential negative effects of such a conflict upon the latter.

On the whole, evidence suggests the economic and social landscape of the community of field houses and agricultural camps surrounding seventeenth-century Paako was, like the occupation of the seventeenth-century pueblo itself, substantially smaller and less intensively occupied than the precontact antecedent whose footprint it occupied. In general, outlying sites and structures with evidence for seventeenth-century occupation or use were much closer and much more tied physically to Paako on the one hand and the reliable water and relatively optimal soils afforded by the Arroyo San Pedro and its floodplain on the other. While structures and camps associated with the late thirteenth-century to early fifteenth-century Arroyo San Pedro community stretched out along the Arroyo floodplain, its tributaries, and adjacent slopes to distances of five kilometers or more, seventeenth-century settlement contracted to areas that were to an almost complete extent no more than 1.5 kilometers from either the perennial segment of the Arroyo San Pedro or from Paako itself (Figure 3.9). While this settlement pattern represents a literal reoccupation of the core of the precontact Arroyo San Pedro community, with nearly all field structures either located in immediate proximity to or remodeled from their fourteenth-century antecedents, artifact patterns suggest this was likewise contracted, with a considerably smaller spatial extent and a reduced occupational intensity.

As a spring-fed, perennial drainage with relatively regular, predictable flows (Campbell Corporation 2000), the Arroyo San Pedro represents a setting where the canal irrigation technologies available to Puebloan farmers during the precontact period might have been effective (Anschuetz 1998, 2003; Cordell 1979; Eckert and Cordell 2004; Ford 1972). No direct evidence for such a system along the Arroyo San Pedro has been documented to date, however, and given the heavily downcut nature of the contemporary drainage and the rather impermanent, ephemeral nature of ditches, headgates, and most of the other archaeological trappings of such a system, none seems likely to be forthcoming (e.g., Anschuetz 1998; Arbolino 2001). Neither is direct evidence available for any intensification of irrigation or other agricultural technologies during the seventeenth century, though several colonial-period features at Paako itself (Figure 3.10)—including large berms erected across several intermittent drainages that cross the site, and a relatively large reservoir adjacent to and potentially fed by runoff redirected by the berms—could be interpreted as the remnants of a system for redirecting and storing water to benefit agricultural fields located along several gentle slopes adjacent to the pueblo (Lycett 1997).

However, evidence for domesticated European crops in Paako's macrobotanical and pollen records is to date almost absent (Morrison, Arendt, and Barger 2002; Rozo 2012), suggesting agricultural production during the seventeenth

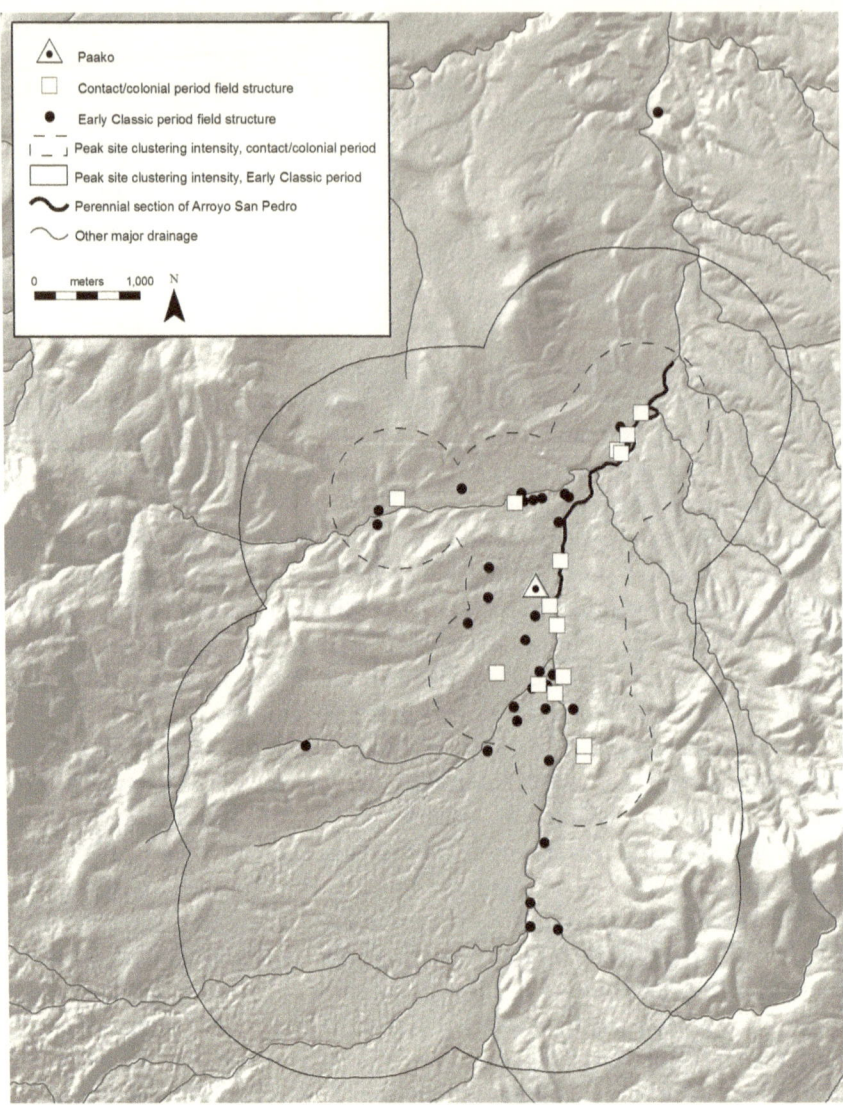

FIGURE 3.9. *Precontact- and contact-period Arroyo San Pedro community settlement patterns.*

century remained focused on the same species for which precontact Puebloan agricultural systems were developed. The best indirect evidence for irrigation along the Arroyo San Pedro during either the precontact or seventeenth-century occupations at Paako may therefore be the settlement patterns evident for the Arroyo San Pedro community itself: although the slopes and side drainages that the distribution of sites and agricultural camps suggests were part of the subsistence landscape of precontact community likely represent a broader, more

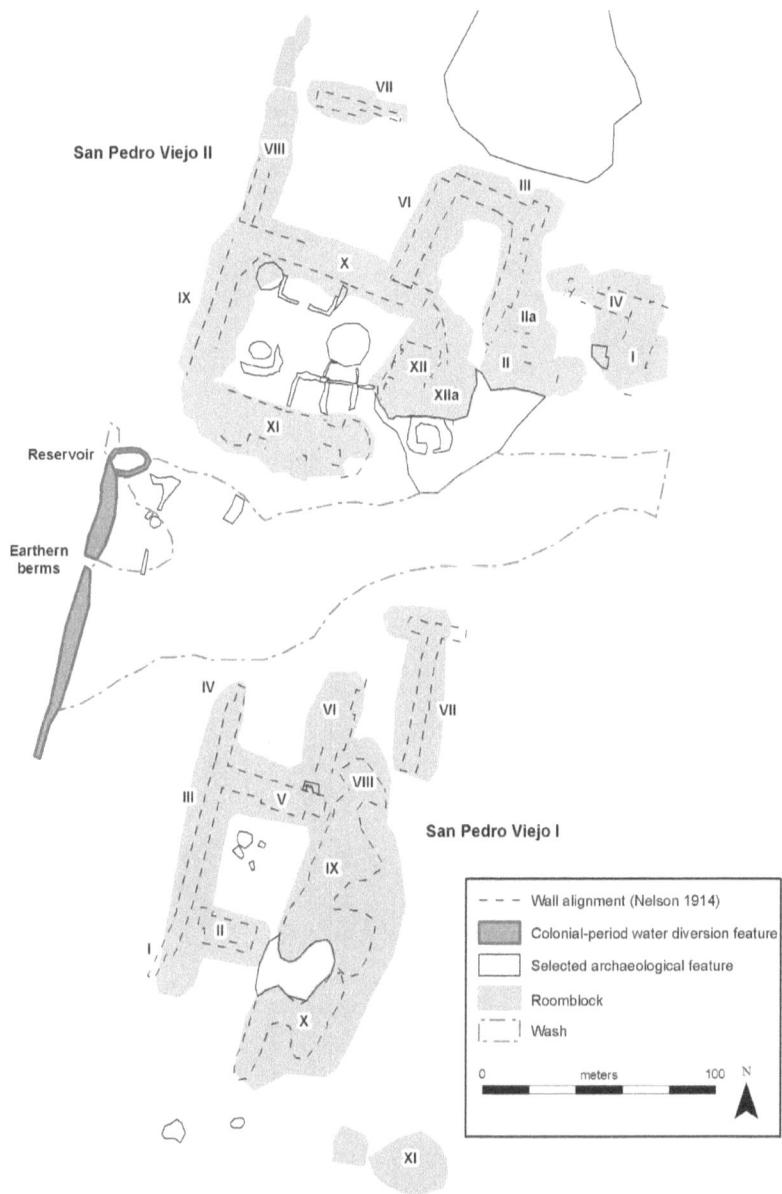

FIGURE 3.10. *Colonial-period water-management features at Paako.*

diversified agricultural base than that attested to by seventeenth-century evidence, the perennial arroyo banks where seventeenth-century land use is focused appear to have been used to an equally intensive degree during the fourteenth and early fifteenth centuries as well (Figure 3.11 and Figure 3.12).

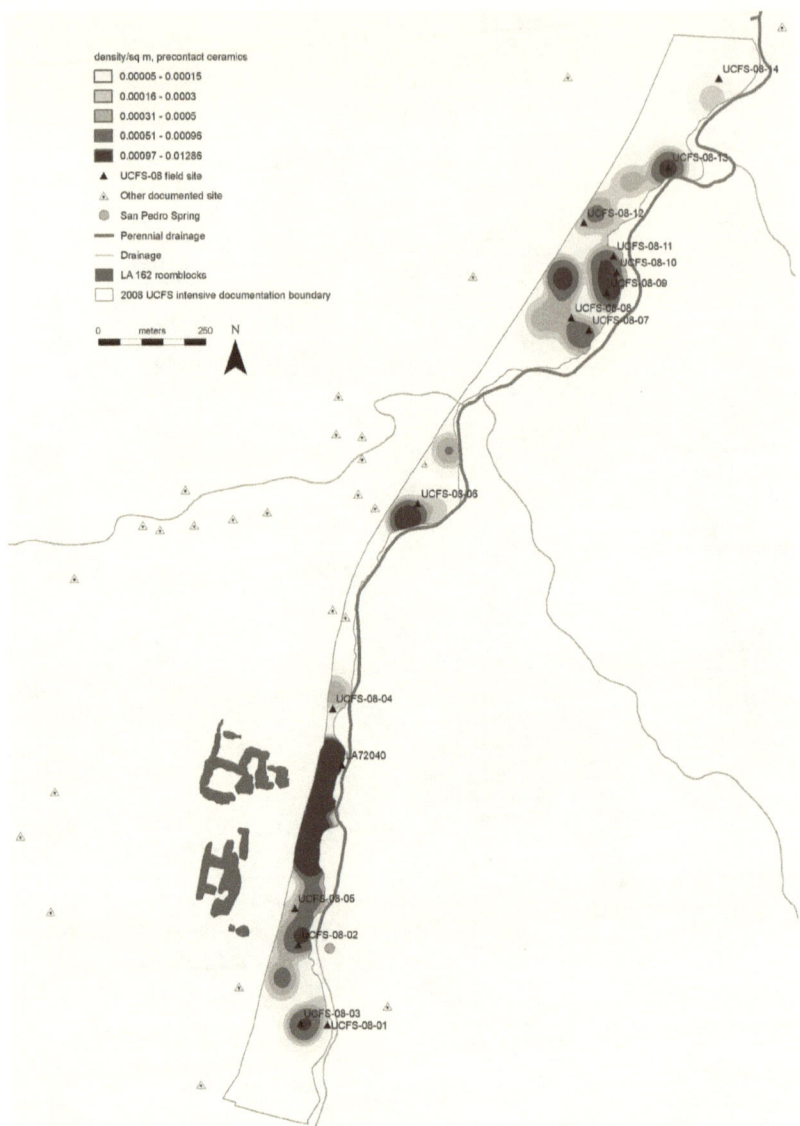

FIGURE 3.11. *Estimated precontact-period ceramic density along the Arroyo San Pedro floodplain, based on intensive survey and point location of all artifacts within the indicated survey area.*

As discussed above, faunal evidence exists for the relatively vigorous adoption of European fauna by Paako's indigenous population (e.g. Sunseri and Gifford-Gonzalez 2002), including horses and sheep but consisting primarily of goats. In contrast to the very limited evidence for the use and adoption of European food

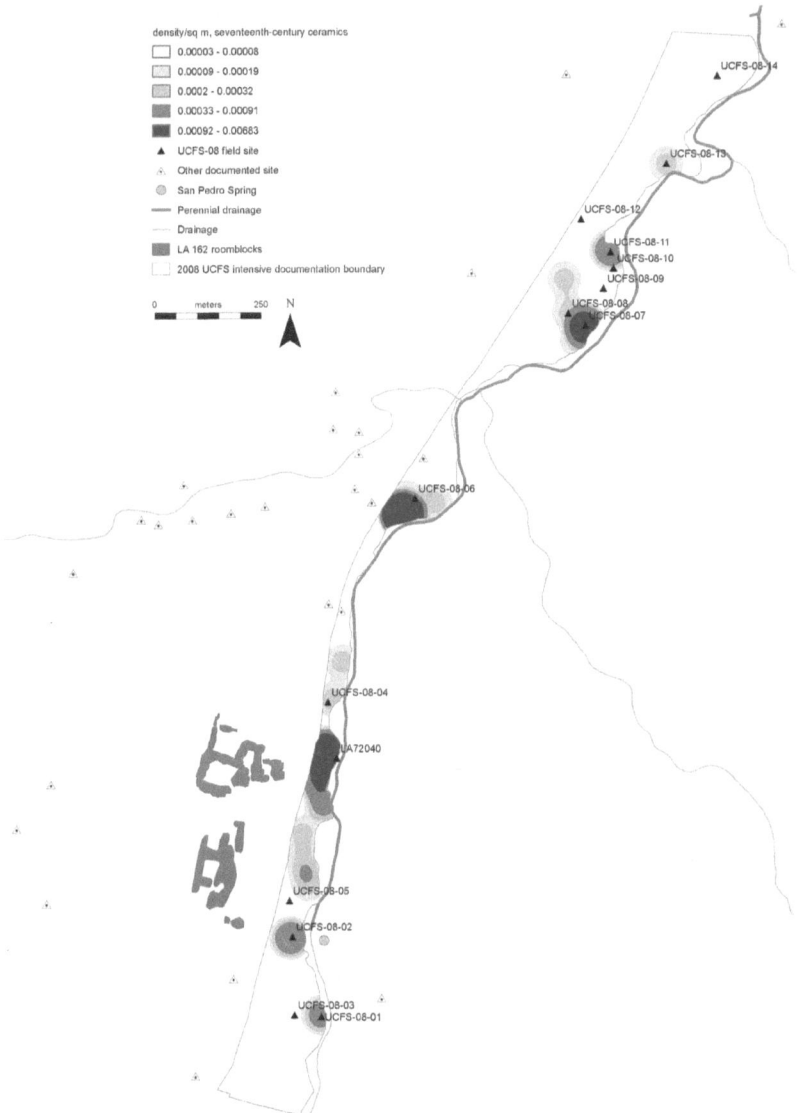

FIGURE 3.12. *Estimated contact-period ceramic density along the Arroyo San Pedro floodplain, based on intensive survey and point location of all artifacts within the indicated survey area*

plants, European animal domesticates are fairly common within seventeenth-century assemblages from Paako (Lycett 1997, 2002a, 2004, 2005, Sunseri and Gifford-Gonzalez 2002). Limited evidence also exists to suggest environmental change in the vicinity of Paako during the seventeenth century that potentially relates to the impacts of livestock, including increased erosion and the appearance of Old World weedy taxa in the site's pollen record (Morrison, Arendt, and Barger 2002; Rozo 2012). These pressures may have disrupted dispersed agricultural systems reliant on water harvesting, adding to the factors influencing the upper Arroyo San Pedro's residents to refocus their agricultural and economic activities on the best available agricultural lands and most reliable water sources.

However, it may also reflect the beginnings of a refocused subsistence strategy among Paako's residents in which the diversification of subsistence risk and investment previously reflected in extensive water-harvesting strategies and the exploitation of dispersed, diverse ecological, and topographic settings was gradually superseded by a dual risk-management strategy on the Iberian model, pairing the use of novel technologies for agricultural intensification, such as acequia irrigation, with mobile subsistence resources in the form of goats or sheep. To some extent, patterns present within archaeofaunal data at Paako suggest that livestock at the site were primarily managed and used by Puebloan, rather than Iberian populations, with butchering patterns and cooking strategies seemingly a continuation of pre-contact practices (Sunseri and Gifford-Gonzalez 2002). A similar pattern has also been noted at missionized villages in the southern Tompiro region (Spielmann et al. 2009).

The refocus of seventeenth-century agricultural land use along the Arroyo San Pedro on easily accessible—and controllable, protectable, or fenceable—floodplain lands located within minutes of the central pueblo may therefore reflect the beginning of a changing system of landscape use and land tenure that may ultimately have culminated in the abandonment of the settlement and its postoccupational reuse as a sheepherding camp (Lycett 2002a; Seddon 2002; Morrison, Cole, and Lycett 2002), as seen elsewhere in the Pueblo world as discussed above. Throughout the New Mexico Colony, sheepherding and the use of remote sheep camps eventually developed into a parallel, but similarly motivated system of maintaining land tenure over valuable resources—such as the San Pedro Arroyo and Spring—with similar goals and functions to the systems of rotating sedentism discussed extensively by Anschuetz (1998, 2003, 2006) for the Tewa Basin. While seventeenth-century herds were typically owned by missions or *encomenderos* rather than Pueblos, the mobility afforded by sheepherding may have provided a vehicle for continuing patterns of circulation and dispersed resource use within a Spanish colonial system that was otherwise suspicious of Puebloan mobility and at least occasionally acted to constrain the movement of Pueblo peoples beyond their villages (Hackett 1937:108, 111; Hodge et al. 1945:170). If the sheep camp at Paako was in fact used by Puebloan herders after its residential occupation ceased, this perhaps served as a means of maintaining traditional access to local resources in the face of a transformed land use system (Ferguson 1996; Lycett 2002a; Morrison, Cole, and Lycett 2002; Murrell et al. 2010) akin to similar patterns of focused reoccupation seen in prehistory on the Pajarito Plateau and elsewhere (Kohler 1992; Van Zandt 1999).

While the dual influences of livestock grazing on the one hand and acequia irrigation on the other may have contributed to changing uses and conceptions of space and landscape within the seventeenth-century Arroyo San Pedro community, colonial Spanish attitudes toward sedentism, population mobility, and the appropriate behavior of a missionized population may also have played a role in the transformation of the community landscape. As Lycett (2004:364) notes, the Franciscan mission system sought to "impose control over time, labor, language, and learning," introducing new rhythms and patterns of work as well as a new series of economic activities linked to the mission economy and intended to indoctrinate the mission's charges into colonial systems of production. The presence of such attitudes and beliefs among New Mexico's religious and civil administrators likely discouraged traditional dispersed farming of the sort discussed by Robert Preucel (1988), with farmers in residence at remote camps for weeks or months. On a more local scale, they may also have encouraged a land use pattern focused on the day use of nearby agricultural camps, with populations returning daily to residences in the pueblo (e.g., Bayer and Montoya 1994). Certainly, the kind of precolonial land use pattern suggested for at least some areas in the Arroyo San Pedro community, in which field houses seem to have been the center of a full range of domestic and social activities that ultimately included burial, does not seem consistent with the demands and goals of a missionized landscape. Although Paako's incorporation into the mission system was apparently limited and temporally discontinuous, the close proximity of seventeenth-century agricultural camps to Paako and the relatively sparse, spatially constricted ceramic assemblages associated with these camps may suggest the presence of some of these pressures.

THE NORTHERN RIO GRANDE WORLD

Just as Spanish perceptions of Puebloan plazas, villages, and shared community lands assumed broad tangency between Spanish and Puebloan notions of these phenomena, problematically overlooking the numerous functional and conceptual differences separating them, so too did Spanish attitudes toward the organization of the northern Rio Grande Pueblo world as a whole. Spanish misperceptions of Pueblo sedentism—specifically, the failure to recognize the importance of movement and migration as a land use strategy and as a process for temporarily leaving stressed or unproductive areas to let them recover (Anschuetz 2003, 2006)—has already been discussed above. To Spanish religious and civil authorities, the short- or long-term abandonment of large, seemingly permanent residential sites was seen on the one hand as fearful flight or escape from colonial control (Hackett 1937; Hodge et al. 1945) and, on the other, as a cessation of occupation and forfeiture of land rights, aggravating existing grievances and land disputes between Pueblo farmers and colonists (Hodge et al. 1945:172).

Likewise, rather than understanding the various Puebloan-occupied areas of New Mexico as a patchwork of numerous autonomous communities and groups of communities, each roughly equivalent to its neighbors and relying on similar mix of ecological zones and agricultural/gathering practices for sustenance, Spanish explorers and administrators in New Mexico emphasized linguistic and geographic boundaries to conceive of the Puebloan world as a series of finite, bounded "provinces" (e.g., Flint and Flint 2005; Hammond and Rey 1966; Hodge et al. 1945) that could be readily joined as a single political entity under Spanish rule. Within this Kingdom of New Mexico, colonial administrators focused their efforts on defensible, more densely populated areas suitable for a narrower range of subsistence strategies and centered on a finite network of missions intended as focal points for population movement and economic activity. Missionized communities also served as dispersal centers for new ideas and technologies such as domesticated livestock or irrigation methods (Ivey 2005, 2006). Franciscan stores built up to guard against drought, crop failure, or uncertainty (e.g. Hodge et al. 1945; Trigg 2005) also attracted immigrants from outlying zones. Emphasis of the Spanish colony on borders and defense and the resulting focus on Rio Grande Valley areas suitable for intensive irrigation aggravated this shift. With population movement into these areas accompanied by a general apparent population decline (e.g., Lycett 1995), the shrinking number of communities located in outlying areas became increasingly isolated.

If site densities are estimated among both major Early Classic (Figure 3.13) and contact-period and colonial (Figure 3.14) Pueblo sites (Adams and Duff 2004; Adler 1996; Barrett 2002), it is clear that Paako was always somewhat isolated from nearby pueblos compared to sites in the Rio Grande valley to the west or the Manzano Mountain and Tompiro areas to the south. No other major villages are located within twelve kilometers of Paako during either period, as compared to an mean nearest-neighbor distance of approximately eight kilometers among major Early Classic pueblos, and only eleven kilometers even among the more sparsely distributed pueblos occupied during the seventeenth century. That said, at the beginning of its late Classic occupation, Paako was still bordered by the major ceramic-producing village of Tunque roughly 18 kilometers to the north and the still-occupied pueblo at San Antonio roughly 12.5 kilometers to the south. At the beginning of the contact period, Paako remained at a crossroads of sorts, lying adjacent to several major routes between regions—from the Rio Grande Valley to the plains, from the Santo Domingo Basin and Galisteo Basin to the southern Albuquerque Basin / Isleta area via the San Pedro, San Antonio, and Tijeras Arroyos, or from the Santo Domingo Basin and Galisteo Basin to Tajique, Chilili, Quarai, and other pueblos along the eastern and southern margins of

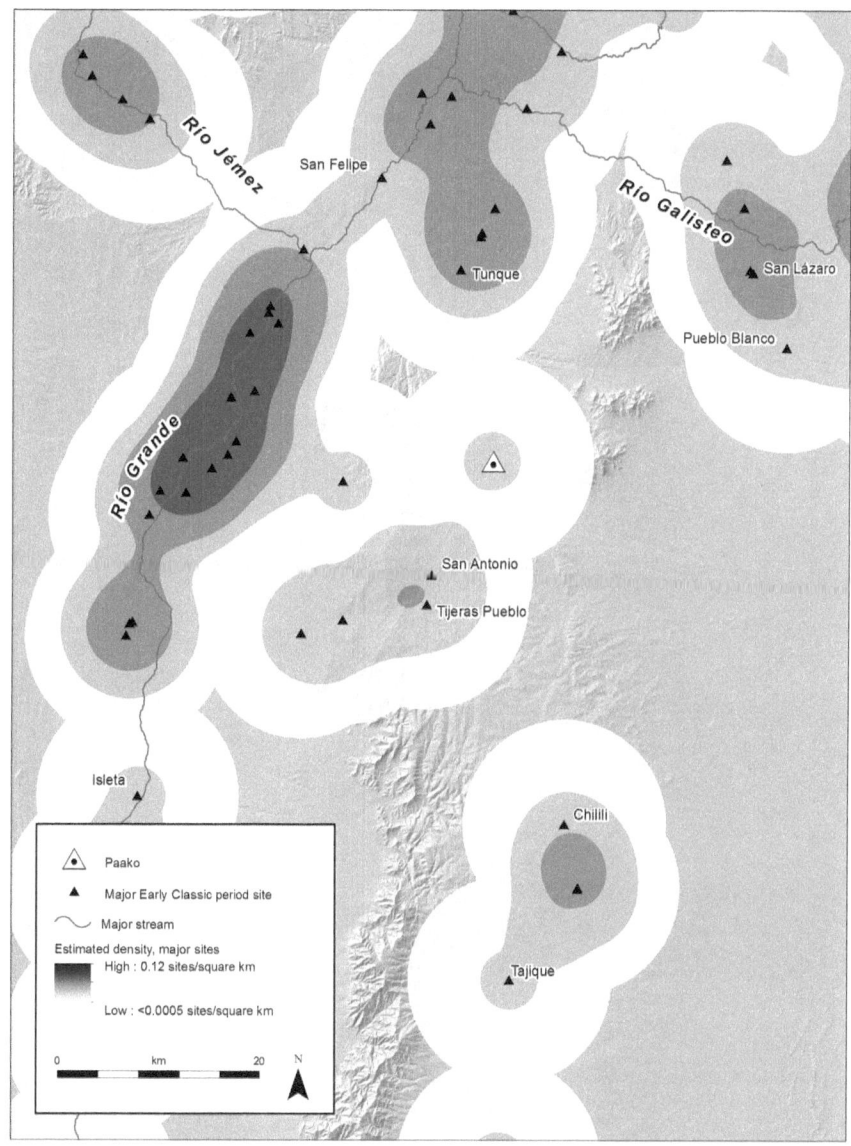

FIGURE 3.13. *Density of major Middle Rio Grande pueblo sites during the Early Classic Period.*

the Manzano Mountains (Figure 3.15). By the mid- to late 1600s, however, Paako lay far outside the major centers of occupation and corridors of movement, as many Manzano and Tompiro sites and outlying Galisteo and Santo Domingo Basin sites ceased to be occupied by residential populations. By the middle years of the seventeenth century, the nearest occupied communities to Paako were

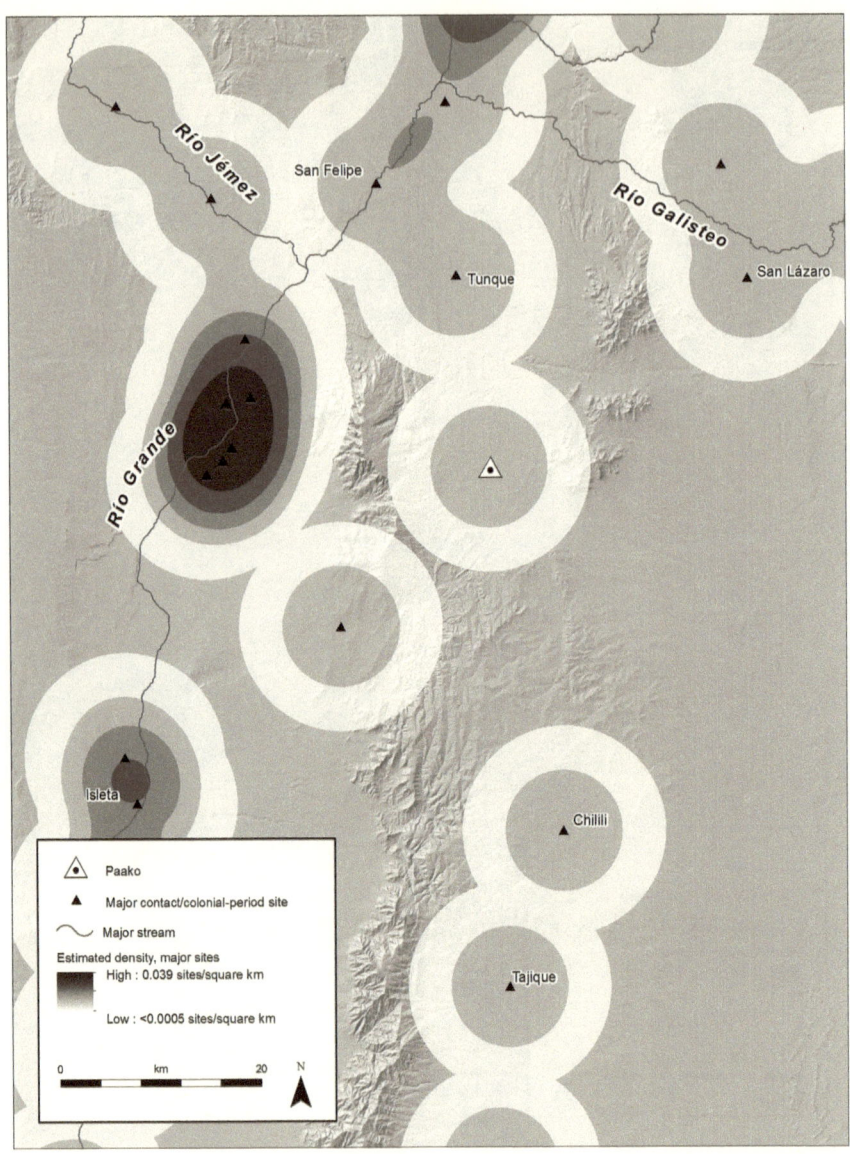

FIGURE 3.14. *Density of major Middle Rio Grande pueblo sites during the contact and colonial periods.*

apparently San Felipe, some thirty-two kilometers to the north and Isleta to the southwest along the Rio Grande, at a distance of more than fifty kilometers along likely travel routes (Figure 3.16). To the northeast, the nearest occupied village in the Galisteo Basin after the contact-period abandonment of Pueblo Blanco was San Lázaro, some thirty-five kilometers distant along likely routes.

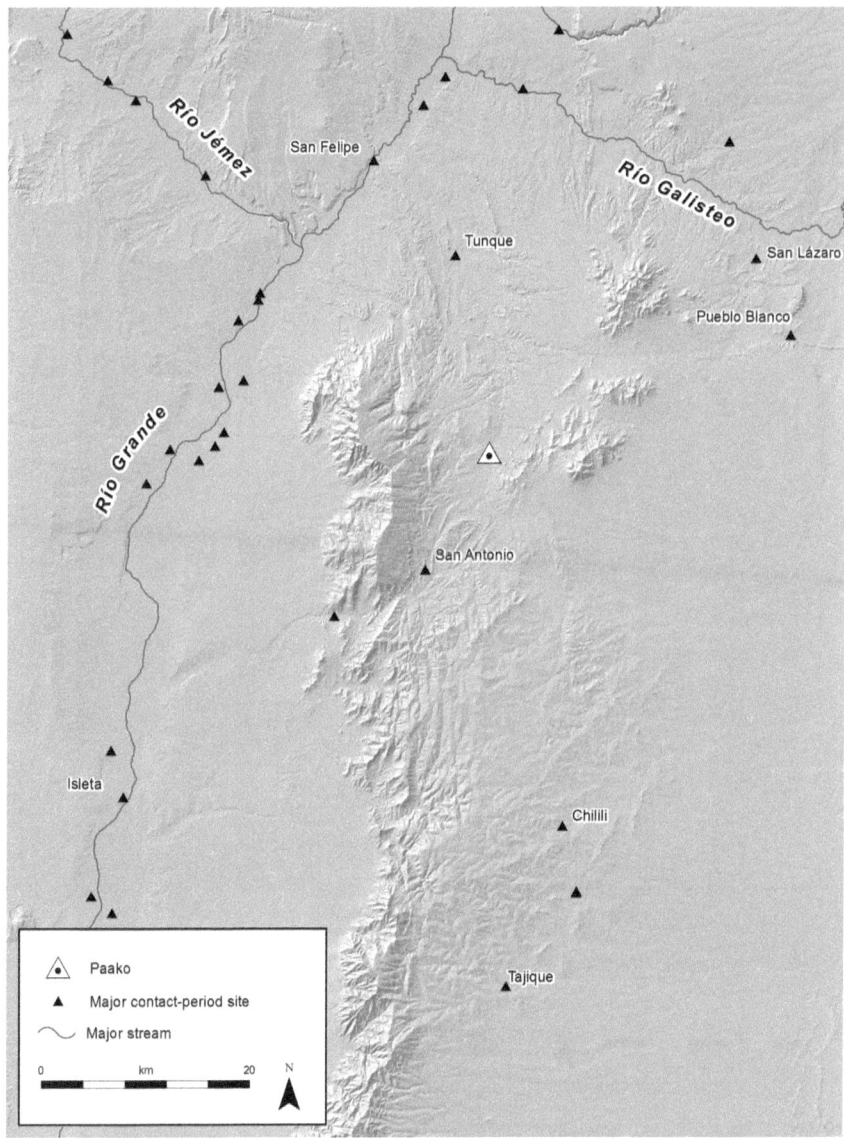

FIGURE 3.15. *Paako and neighboring communities at the beginning of the contact.*

PERIOD

This new isolation was aggravated by changing relationships with non-Puebloan nomadic groups sparked by Spanish notions of bounded states and policies toward "uncivilized" groups, especially in areas of cultural contact such as Paako. On seventeenth- and eighteenth-century European maps (Eidenbach

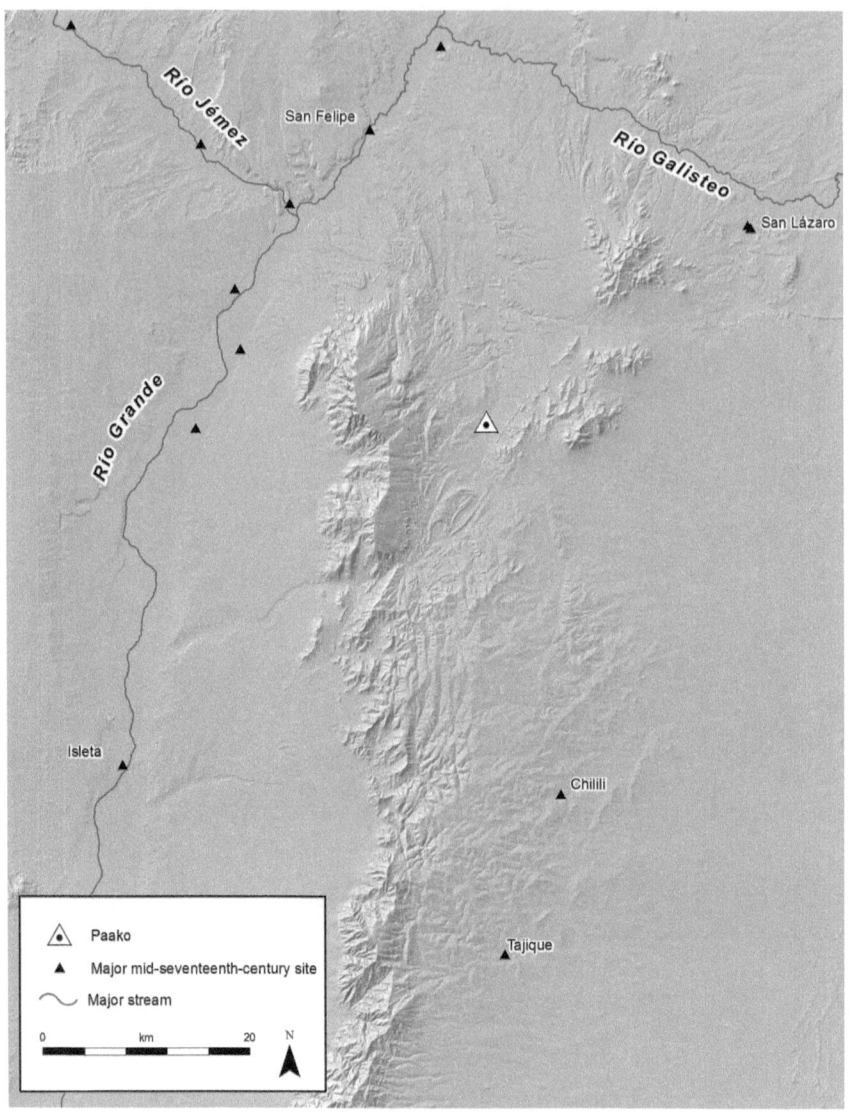

FIGURE 3.16. *Paako and neighboring communities in the mid-seventeenth century.*

2012), the East Mountain region sits upon a literal frontier, straddling the dense mountain ranges separating the named, mapped settlements and missions of the Kingdom of New Mexico from the surrounding tribal names of outlying, unconquered *indios bárbaros*. According to site records maintained by the New Mexico Cultural Resource Information System, four sites identified as Plains Apache are located within sixteen kilometers of Paako, including one potential Apachean site on the San Pedro floodplain within three kilometers of Paako

(Walley 2006). Available documentation suggests these sites were more ephemeral and contained less material culture than adjacent Puebloan field houses, attributes typical of sites associated with mobile groups (Seymour 2015, 2016).

The considerable differences in attitude toward Apachean groups and other non-Puebloan nomads between Puebloans and the Spanish are well documented. Prior to the arrival of the Spanish, the social and physical boundaries between Pueblos and nomads were shifting, permeable, and contingent, with beneficial trade relationships sealed by kin ties playing as large a role as violent raids (Brooks 2002; Forbes 1994; Hickerson 1994; Kelley 1986; Seymour 2015, 2016). With the onset of Spanish rule, civil and religious colonial administrators attempted to firmly delineate social and physical borders between Puebloans perceived as settled and sedentary and indios bárbaros in outlying zones (Brooks 2002; Forbes 1994; Weber 2005). While Franciscans such as Alonso Benavides attempted conversions among nomadic groups on several occasions (Hodge et al. 1945), Apacheans and other non-Pueblo nomads were more typically seen as a significant threat, both in terms of the potential for raids and military conflict as well as their possible appeal as a refuge for backsliders among or incitement to newly missionized Puebloans (Forbes 1994). Policies intended to restrict potentially harmful contacts thus exacerbated tensions between the New Mexico villages and their former trading partners. The resulting conflicts were extremely difficult for places such as Paako, and intensified pressures to either relocate toward better-protected, better-supplied mission communities along the Rio Grande, on the one hand, or abandon the northern Rio Grande region entirely on the other (Brooks 2002).

From this perspective, the residential shifts of the later seventeenth century from areas under environmental and economic stress and threats of violence to locations with access to intensified agricultural methods, reliable stores, and better and more numerous social and economic connections were probably somewhat less negative within the mobile, shifting settlement framework of the Pueblos (e.g., Anschuetz 2006) than they were within the sedentism-focused paradigm employed by Spanish friars and colonial administrators and indeed, by many modern authors. As discussed above, the new subsistence strategies enabled by introduced technologies and domesticates—with intensified irrigation agriculture along the Rio Grande and other major streams coupled with the socially acceptable mobility afforded by sheepherding in the traditional Spanish mode—in many respects enabled continued ties to "abandoned" areas outside the Rio Grande Valley.

CONCLUSIONS

By 1776, when an expedition led by the Franciscan emissary Fray Francisco Atanasio Domínguez made its way across New Mexico en route to California, the landscape Domínguez traversed was in many respects profoundly different from that explored by the entradas of two centuries earlier. The account of Domínguez's journey details a greatly reduced number of Pueblo settlements, each with its mission church and array of nearby irrigated fields (Domínguez 1956). Villages with access to good water for irrigation are described as larger and more prosperous, their canal networks discussed in glowing terms. Conversely, outlying communities without such resources, such as Zia, are described as small and relatively poor. Pecos and Galisteo, the two remnant communities still hanging on in outlying areas to the east of the Rio Grande Valley, are portrayed in the direst terms, with dwindling populations living in constant fear of raids from Comanches and other nomads and contemplating abandonment.

If the world described by Domínguez is in many respects one ordered in accordance with Spanish attitudes and ideals on the colonial frontier, however, numerous traces of older Puebloan traditions are also apparent. While villages along the Rio Grande and other major streams are described as entirely dedicated to irrigation, for instance, the subsistence base for outlying communities such as Jemez, Santa Ana, Acoma, or Zia are also said to include *milpas* fed by floods or rainwater alone. In communities located sufficiently far from areas of major Spanish settlement to retain a large land base free of major encroachments—such as Acoma, Jemez, or Zuni—Domínguez also describes remote fields and outlying settlements, occupied seasonally to take advantage of opportune agricultural settings. Finally, despite the churches and missions he describes in each community along his path, Domínguez describes Pueblo culture in general in a way that makes clear both the lack of penetration of Spanish religious beliefs and customs even by the late eighteenth century and the relative resignation of Domínguez and other church leaders toward the persistence of pueblo dances and other customs.

In the New Mexico Colony described by Domínguez, the misapprehensions and misrecognitions of the early colonial period are perhaps not entirely resolved in favor of one perspective or other, but joined and layered such that the forms and attitudes of colonial Spanish culture are continually subject to reinterpretation in ways that retain space for Puebloan attitudes. On the one hand, for instance, plazas and villages in many communities are reordered along a Spanish model focused on prominent community churches, but these spaces also remain central to Puebloan rituals and worldviews (Scully 1989; Swentzell 2011). If the gaps in understanding between ostensibly similar aspects of Spanish and Pueblo worlds aggravated the painful, often violent imposition of colonial values and practices on seventeenth-century New Mexico, they also sometimes opened routes for synthesis and experimentation, enabling the creation of spaces within which Puebloan culture could survive and revitalize.

ACKNOWLEDGMENTS

Above all, I would like to thank the University of Chicago Field Studies Program under Mark Lycett and Kathleen Morrison for providing me the opportunity for research and fieldwork at Paako, and to the Campbell Corporation for the opportunity to conduct archaeological survey and testing on the Arroyo San Pedro floodplain. I am deeply indebted to Dr. Lycett and Dr. Morrison for their years of encouragement and mentorship and their generosity in sharing their own insights into the archaeology of seventeenth-century New Mexico. Thanks are also due to my many colleagues at Paako over the years, especially Noah Thomas, Jennifer Rozo, Peter Johansen, Sandy Morrison, Kelly Jenks, and Jun Sunseri, and to my colleagues and mentors at Statistical Research, including Robert Heckman, Brad Vierra, John Douglass, Billy Graves, Monica Murrell, and Teresita Majewski. I am also grateful for the support and mentorship of Paul and Suzanne Fish and Gary Christopherson at the University of Arizona; to James Snead, Mark Allen, and Heather Atherton; and to Emily Jones, Kurt Anschuetz, and Deni Seymour for conversations and scholarship that offered valuable insight.

REFERENCES CITED

Adams, E. Charles, and Andrew I. Duff, eds. 2004. *The Protohistoric Pueblo World, A.D. 1275–1600*. Tucson: University of Arizona Press.

Adams, Karen R., Cathryn M. Meegan, Scott G. Ortman, R. Emerson Howell, Lindsay C. Werth, Deborah A. Muenchrath, Michael K. O'Neill, and Candice A. D. Gardner. 2006. *MAIS (Maize of American Indigenous Societies) Southwest: Ear Descriptions and Traits that Distinguish 27 Morphologically Distinct Groups of 123 Historic USDA Maize (Zea mays L. spp. Mays) Accessions and Data Relevant to Archeological Subsistence Model. Manuscript on file*. Cortez, CO: Crow Canyon Archaeological Center.

Adler, Michael A., ed. 1996. *The Prehistoric Pueblo World, AD 1150–1350*. Tucson: University of Arizona Press.

Akins, Nancy J. 2004. *Excavations at San Antonio de Padua (LA 24), NM 14, Bernalillo County, New Mexico. Archaeology Notes No. 293*. Santa Fe: Office of Archaeological Studies, Museum of New Mexico.

Anderson, Orin J., Glen E. Jones, and Gregory N. Green. 1997. *Geological Map of New Mexico*. USGS Open-File Report OF-97-52. Washington, DC: USGS, Department of the Interior.

Anschuetz, Kurt F. 1984. "Prehistoric Change in Tijeras Canyon, New Mexico." MA thesis, Department of Anthropology, University of New Mexico.

Anschuetz, Kurt F. 1998. Not Waiting for the Rain: Integrated Systems of Water Management for Intensive Agricultural Production in North-Central New Mexico. PhD dissertation, Department of Anthropology, University of Michigan, Ann Arbor.

Anschuetz, Kurt F. 2003. "The Reflection of European History on Pueblo Water Uses: A Refraction of Indigenous Cultural-Historical Process." Manuscript in possession of author.

Anschuetz, Kurt F. 2006. "Tewa Fields, Tewa Traditions." In *Canyon Gardens: The Ancient Pueblo Landscape of the American Southwest*, edited by V. B. Price and B. H. Morrow, 57–76. Albuquerque: University of New Mexico Press.

Arbolino, Rina D. 2001. "Agricultural Strategies and Labor Organization: An Ethnohistoric Approach to the Study of Prehistoric Farming Systems in the Taos Area of Northern New Mexico." PhD dissertation, Southern Methodist University.

Barrett, Elinore M. 2002. *Conquest and Catastrophe: Changing Rio Grande Pueblo Settlement Patterns in the Sixteenth and Seventeenth Centuries*. Albuquerque: University of New Mexico Press.

Baxter, John O. 1987. *Las Carneradas: Sheep Trade in New Mexico 1700–1860*. Albuquerque: University of New Mexico Press.

Bayer, Laura, and Floyd Montoya. 1994. *Santa Ana: The People, the Pueblo, and the History of Tamaya*. Albuquerque: University of New Mexico Press.

Brooks, James F. 2002. *Captives and Cousins: Slavery, Kinship, and Community in the Southwest Borderlands*. Published for the Omohundro Institute of Early American History and Culture, Williamsburg, Virginia. Chapel Hill: University of North Carolina Press.

Campbell Corporation. 2000. *Campbell Ranch Master Plan. Report submitted to Bernalillo County, New Mexico, May 2000*. Albuquerque: Campbell Corporation.

Cordell, Linda S. 1979. *Cultural Resources Overview: Middle Rio Grande Valley, New Mexico*. Albuquerque, Santa Fe: USDA Forest Service, Southwestern Region, and Bureau of Land Management, New Mexico State Office.

Cordell, Linda S. 1980. *Tijeras Canyon: Analyses of the Past*. Albuquerque: University of New Mexico Press.

Crouch, Dora P., Daniel J. Garr, and Axel I. Mundigo. 1982. *Spanish City Planning in North America*. Cambridge, MA: MIT Press.

Dart, Al. 1980. *Archaeological Investigations at San Antonio de Padua, LA 24, Bernalillo County, New Mexico. Laboratory of Anthropology Note No. 167*. Santa Fe: Office of Archaeological Studies, Museum of New Mexico.

Domínguez, Francisco A. 1956. *The Missions of New Mexico, 1776: A Description by Fray Francisco Atanasio Dominguez with Other Contemporary Documents*. Translated by E. B. Adams and F. A. Chavez. Albuquerque: University of New Mexico Press.

Eckert, Suzanne L., and Linda S. Cordell. 2004. "Pueblo IV Community Formation in the Central Rio Grande Valley: The Albuquerque, Cochiti, and Lower Rio Puerco Districts." In *The Protohistoric Pueblo World, A.D. 1275–1600*, edited by E. Charles. Adams and Andrew. I. Duff, 35–42. Tucson: University of Arizona Press.

Eidenbach, Peter L. 2012. *An Atlas of Historic New Mexico Maps, 1550–1941*. Albuquerque: University of New Mexico Press.

Ferguson, Thomas J. 1996. *Historic Zuni Architecture and Society: An Archaeological Application of Space Syntax*. Anthropological Papers of the University of Arizona 60. Tucson: University of Arizona Press.

Flint, Richard, and Shirley C. Flint. 2005. *Documents of the Coronado Expedition, 1539–1542*. Dallas: Southern Methodist University Press.

Forbes, Jack D. 1994. *Apache, Navaho, and Spaniard*. 2nd ed. Norman: University of Oklahoma Press.

Ford, Richard I. 1972. "An Ecological Perspective on the Eastern Pueblos." In *New Perspectives on the Pueblos*, ed. A. Ortiz, 1–18. Albuquerque: University of New Mexico Press.

Fowles, Severin M. 2004. "The Making of Made People: The Prehistoric Evolution of Hierocracy among the Northern Tiwa of New Mexico." PhD dissertation, Department of Anthropology, University of Michigan, Ann Arbor.

Fowles, Severin M. 2009. "The Enshrined Pueblo: Villagescape and Cosmos in the Northern Rio Grande." *American Antiquity* 74 (3): 448–66.

Gossett, William J., and Cye W. Gossett. 1990. *Archaeological Inventory of 2,100 Acres near San Antonito, New Mexico, Bernalillo County for ABQ Development Campbell Ranch*. Report Submitted to ABQ Development and New Mexico State Historic Preservation Division. Albuquerque, NM: Rio Abajo Archaeological Services.

Graves, William M., and Scott Van Keuren. 2011. "Ancestral Pueblo Villages and the Panoptic Gaze of the Commune." *Cambridge Archaeological Journal* 21 (2): 263–82. http://dx.doi.org/10.1017/S0959774311000278.

Greene, Gregory, and Phillip O. Leckman. 2011. "The Burnt Corn Landscape." In *Burnt Corn Pueblo: Conflict and Conflagration in the Galisteo Basin, AD 1250–1325*, edited by J. E. Snead and M. W. Allen, 70–93. Anthropological Papers of the University of Arizona No. 74. Tucson: University of Arizona Press.

Hacker, Leroy W. 1977. *Soil Survey of Bernalillo County and Parts of Sandoval and Valencia Counties, New Mexico*. United States Department of Agriculture, Natural Resources Conservation Service. Washington, DC: US Government Printing Office.

Hacker, Leroy W., and Christopher Banet. 2008. *Soil Survey of Sandoval County Area, New Mexico: Parts of Los Alamos, Sandoval, and Rio Arriba Counties*. United States Department of Agriculture, Natural Resources Conservation Service. Washington, DC: US Government Printing Office.

Hackett, Charles W. 1937. *Historical Documents Relating to New Mexico, Nueva Vizcaya, and Approaches Thereto, to 1773*. Vol. 3, collected by A. F. Bandelier and F. R. Bandelier. Publication No. 330. Washington, DC: Carnegie Institution of Washington.

Hammond, George P., and Agapito Rey, eds. 1966. *The Rediscovery of New Mexico, 1580–1594: The Explorations of Chamuscado, Espejo, Castaño de Sosa, Morlete, and Leyva* de Bonilla and Humaña. *Coronado Cuarto Centennial Publication*. Vol. 3. Albuquerque: University of New Mexico Press.

Hickerson, Nancy P. 1994. *The Jumanos: Hunters and Traders of the South Plains*. Austin: University of Texas Press.

Hodge, Frederick W., George P. Hammond, and Agapito Rey. 1945. *Fray Alonso de Benavides' Revised Memorial of 1634*. Albuquerque: University of New Mexico Press.

Ivey, James E. 1988. *In the Midst of a Loneliness: The Architectural History of the Salinas Missions. Southwest Cultural Resources Center, Professional Papers no. 15*. Santa Fe: National Park Service.

Ivey, James E. 2005. *The Spanish Colonial Architecture of Pecos Pueblo, New Mexico: Archaeological Excavations and Architectural History of the Spanish Colonial Churches and Related Buildings at Pecos National Historical Park, 1617–1995. Professional paper / History Program, Division of Cultural Resources Management, Intermountain Region, National Park Service; no. 59*. Santa Fe, NM: History Program, Division of Cultural Resources Management, Intermountain Region, National Park Service, Dept. of the Interior.

Ivey, James E. 2006. "The Estancia: The New Mexican Hacienda." In *Canyon Gardens: The Ancient Pueblo Landscape of the American Southwest*, edited by V. B. Price and Baker H. Morrow, 75–86. Albuquerque: University of New Mexico Press.

Johansen, Peter G. 2002. *The Lost Church of Paako?* Poster Presented at the 67th Annual Meetings of the Society for American Archaeology, Denver, CO.

Jojola, Theodore S. 1997. "Pueblo Indian and Spanish Town Planning in New Mexico: The Pueblo of Isleta." In *Anasazi Architecture and American Design*, edited by V. B. Price and Baker. H. Morrow, 171–85. Albuquerque: University of New Mexico Press.

Kelley, Vincent C. 1982. *Albuquerque: Its Mountains, Valley, Water, and Volcanoes*. 3rd ed. Scenic Trips to the Geologic Past, No. 9. Socorro, NM: New Mexico Bureau of Geology and Mineral Resources, New Mexico Institute of Mining and Technology.

Kelley, J. Charles. 1986. *Jumano and Patarabueye: Relations at La Junta de los Rios*. Ann Arbor: University of Michigan Museum.

Kohler, Timothy A. 1992. "Field Houses, Villages, and the Tragedy of the Commons in the Early Northern Anasazi Southwest." *American Antiquity* 57 (4): 617–35. http://dx.doi.org/10.2307/280826.

Kubler, George. 1940. *The Religious Architecture of New Mexico in the Colonial Period and since the American Occupation*. Albuquerque: University of New Mexico Press.

Lambert, Marjorie F. 1954. *Paa-ko: Archaeological Chronicle of an Indian Village in North Central New Mexico. Monograph No. 19*. Santa Fe: School of American Research.

Lange, Charles H., and Carroll L. Riley, eds. 1966. *The Southwestern Journals of Adolph F. Bandelier, 1880–1882*. Albuquerque: University of New Mexico Press.

Levine, Frances, and Kurt F. Anschuetz. 1998. *Adjusting our Scale of Analysis: Observations of Protohistoric Change in Pueblo Land Use*. Paper presented at the 63rd Annual Meeting of the Society for American Archaeology, Seattle, WA.

Liebmann, Matthew J. 2006. "'Burn the Churches, Break Up the Bells: The Archaeology of the Pueblo Revolt Revitalization Movement in New Mexico, A.D. 1680–1696." PhD dissertation, Department of Anthropology, University of Pennsylvania, Philadelphia.

Liebmann, Matthew J. 2012. *Revolt: An Archaeological History of Pueblo Resistance and Revitalization in 17th Century New Mexico*. Tucson: University of Arizona Press.

Liebmann, Matthew J. 2015. "At the Mouth of the Wolf: The Archaeology of Seventeenth-Century Franciscans in the Jemez Valley of New Mexico." In *Franciscan Evangelization in the Spanish Borderlands II*, edited Timothy J. Johnson and Gert Melville, 1–18. Oceanside, CA: Academy of American Franciscan History.

Liebmann, Matthew J., Thomas J. Ferguson, and Robert W. Preucel. 2005. "Pueblo Settlement, Architecture, and Social Change in the Pueblo Revolt Era, A.D. 1680 to 1696." *Journal of Field Archaeology* 30 (1): 45–60. http://dx.doi.org/10.1179/009346 905791072459.

Lycett, Mark T. 1995. "Archaeological Implications of European Contact: Demography, Settlement and Land Use in the Middle Rio Grande Valley, New Mexico." PhD dissertation, Department of Anthropology, University of New Mexico, Albuquerque.

Lycett, Mark T. 1997. *Preliminary Report of Archaeological Surface Documentation and Test Excavations at LA 162, Bernalillo County, New Mexico, conducted by Northwestern University Archaeological Field Studies Program, between 17 June and 8 August, 1996, under Permit SP–269. Report Submitted to New Mexico Cultural Properties Review Committee and Richard C. Chapman, Chair, University of New Mexico Board of Archaeologists*. Santa Fe: Department of Anthropology, University of Chicago.

Lycett, Mark T. 2002a. *Report of Archaeological Excavations at LA 162, Bernalillo County, New Mexico, Conducted by the University of Chicago Archaeological Field Studies Program, between June 18 and August 5, 2001. Report Submitted to New Mexico Cultural Properties Review Committee and Richard C. Chapman, Chair, University of New Mexico Board of Archaeologists*. Santa Fe: Department of Anthropology, University of Chicago.

Lycett, Mark T. 2002b. "Transformations of Place: Occupational History and Differential Persistence in 17th Century New Mexico." In *Archaeologies of the Pueblo Revolt: Identity, Meaning, and Renewal in the Pueblo World*, edited by R. W. Preucel, 61–74. Albuquerque: University of New Mexico Press.

Lycett, Mark T. 2004. "Archaeology under the Bell: The Mission as Situated History in 17th Century New Mexico." *Missionalia* 32:357–79.

Lycett, Mark T. 2005. "On the Margins of Peripheries: The Consequences of Differential Incorporation in the Colonial Southwest." In *The Late Postclassic to Spanish-Era Transition in Mesoamerica: Archaeological Perspectives*, edited by S. Kepecs and R. Alexander, 97–116. Albuquerque: University of New Mexico Press.

Lycett, Mark T. 2014. "Towards an Historical Ecology of the Mission in Seventeenth Century New Mexico." In *Indigenous Landscapes and Spanish Missions: New Perspectives from Archaeology and Ethnohistory*, edited by T. Schneider and L. Panich, 172–90. Tucson: University of Arizona Press.

Melville, Elinor G. K. 1997. *A Plague of Sheep: Environmental Consequences of the Conquest of Mexico*. Cambridge: Cambridge University Press. http://dx.doi.org/10.1017/CBO9780511571091.

Morrison, Kathleen D., Nicole Arendt, and Nicole Barger. 2002. *Vegetation History of the San Pedro Valley: Pollen Evidence for Anthropogenic Change.* Poster session presented at the 67th Annual Meeting of the Society for American Archaeology, Denver, CO.

Morrison, Sandra L., Melissa M. Cole, and Mark T. Lycett. 2002. "Comparatively barren, tho several layers of ash and charcoal are to be noted": Variability and Occupational History in 17th Century Plaza Contexts at LA 162. Poster Session Presented at the 67th Annual Meeting of the Society for American Archaeology, Denver, CO.

Morrow, Baker H. 1996. *A Harvest of Reluctant Souls: The Memorial of Fray Alonso de Benavides, 1630.* Niwot: University Press of Colorado.

Muenchrath, Deborah A., Maya Kuratomi, Jonathan A. Sandor, and Jeffrey A. Homburg. 2002. "Observational Study of Maize Production Systems of Zuni Farmers in Semiarid Zuni, New Mexico." *Journal of Ethnobiology* 22 (1): 1–33.

Murrell, Monica L., Phillip O. Leckman, and David T. Unruh. 2010. "Summary and Recommendations." In *A Cultural Resource Inventory of 2,050 Acres of the Jemez Canyon Reservoir, Maximum Pool, Sandoval County, New Mexico*, edited by M. L. Murrell and P. O. Leckman. vol. Contract No. DACW09-03-D-0005. Task order 16. Draft prepared for U.S. Army Corps of Engineers, Albuquerque District, Albuquerque, New Mexico. Technical Report No. 10-104. Tucson: Statistical Research.

Nelson, Nels. 1914. Unpublished field maps. New York: American Museum of Natural History.

Ortiz, Alfonso. 1969. *The Tewa World: Space, Time, Being and Becoming in a Pueblo Society.* Chicago: University of Chicago Press.

Preucel, Robert W. 1988. "Seasonal Agricultural Circulation and Residential Mobility: A Prehistoric Example from the Pajarito Plateau, New Mexico." PhD dissertation, Department of Anthropology, University of California, Los Angeles.

Rivera, Jose A., and Thomas F. Glick. 2010. *The Iberian Origins of New Mexico's Community Acequias.* Paper presented at the 2010 Conference of the Alliance for Historic Landscape Preservation, Albuquerque, NM.

Rozo, Jennifer L. 2012. "Transforming Landscapes, Transforming Lives: People, Plants, Livestock, and the Landscape of Production in Spanish Colonial New Mexico." Unpublished dissertation research proposal, University of Chicago.

Scully, Vincent. 1989. *Pueblo: Mountain, Village, Dance.* 2nd ed. Chicago: University of Chicago Press.

Seddon, Matthew T. 2002. *The Colonization of the Plaza: Transformations in Public Space at Paako (LA 162)*. Poster session presented at the 67th Annual Meetings of the Society for American Archaeology, Denver, CO.

Seymour, Deni J. 2015. "Mobile Visitors to the Eastern Frontier Pueblos: An Archaeological Example from Tabirá." *Plains Anthropologist* 60 (233): 4–39. http://dx.doi.org/10.1179/2052546X13Y.0000000005.

Seymour, Deni J. 2016. "Conceptualizing Mobility in the Pueblo Areas: Evidence in Images." In *Fierce and Indomitable: The Protohistoric Non-Pueblo World*, edited by Deni J. Seymour, 39–63. Salt Lake City: University of Utah Press.

Snead, James E., and Robert W. Preucel. 1999. "The Ideology of Settlement: Ancestral Keres Landscapes in the Northern Rio Grande." In *Archaeologies of Landscape: Contemporary Perspectives*, edited by W. Ashmore and A. K. Knapp, 169–200. Oxford: Blackwell.

Spielmann, Katherine A., Tiffany Clark, Diane Hawkey, Katharine Rainey, and Suzanne K. Fish. 2009. "'. . . being weary, they had rebelled': Pueblo Subsistence and Labor under Spanish Colonialism." *Journal of Anthropological Archaeology* 28 (1): 102–25. http://dx.doi.org/10.1016/j.jaa.2008.10.002.

Sunseri, Jun, and Diane Gifford-Gonzalez. 2002. *The Paa-ko Archaeofauna: Evidence for Creolization in Animal Use*. Poster Session Presented at the 67th Annual Meetings of the Society for American Archaeology, Denver, CO.

Swentzell, Rina. 2011. "Bupingeh: The Middle-Heart-Place." In *The Plazas of New Mexico*, edited by C. Wilson and S. Polyzoides, 63–68. San Antonio: Trinity University Press.

Thomas, Noah H. 2008. "Seventeenth Century Metallurgy on the Spanish Colonial Frontier: Transformations of Technology, Value and Identity." PhD dissertation, Department of Anthropology, University of Arizona, Tucson.

Tilley, Christopher. 1994. *A Phenomenology of Landscape: Places, Paths and Monuments*. Oxford: Berg.

Triadan, Daniela. 2006. "Dancing Gods: Ritual, Performance, and Political Organization in the Prehistoric Southwest." In *Archaeology of Performance: Theaters of Power, Community, and Politics*, edited by T. Inomata and L. S. Coben, 159–86. New York: Alta Mira Press.

Trigg, Heather B. 2005. *From Household to Empire: Society and Economy in Early Colonial New Mexico*. Tucson: University of Arizona Press.

US Geological Survey. 2012. National Hydrography Dataset for HUC1302, New Mexico. Accessed 15 January 2012. https://nhd.usgs.gov/data.html.

Van West, Carla R., and Linda S. Cordell. 2013. "Using Tree-Ring Data to Explore Community Formation in Fourteenth-Century Central New Mexico." Unpublished manuscript in possession of the author.

Van Zandt, Tineke. 1999. "Architecture and Site Structure." In *The Bandelier Archaeological Survey*, vol. 2, edited by R. P. Powers and J. D. Orcutt, 309–88. Santa Fe:

Intermountain Cultural Resources Management Archaeology Program, National Park Service.

Vassberg, David E. 1984. *Land and Society in Golden Age Castile.* Cambridge: Cambridge University Press.

Walley, Scott. 2006. *Cultural Resource Survey for 525 Acres on the Campbell Ranch Residential Development, Village 2, Unit 2, Bernalillo County, New Mexico. Report Submitted to Campbell Corporation and New Mexico State Historic Preservation Division.* Albuquerque, NM: Lone Mountain Archaeological Services.

Weber, David J. 2005. *Bárbaros: Spaniards and Their Savages in the Age of Enlightenment.* New Haven: Yale University Press.

Wilson, Christopher. 2011. "Center Place, Plaza, Square: Three Traditions of Place Making." In *The Plazas of New Mexico*, edited by C. Wilson and S. Polyzoides, 9–52. San Antonio: Trinity University Press.

Wozniak, Frank E. 1987. *Irrigation in the Rio Grande Valley, New Mexico: A Study of the Development of Irrigation Systems Before 1945.* Santa Fe: New Mexico Historic Preservation Division.

FOUR

Hopi Weaving and the Colonial Encounter

A Study of Persistence through Change

LAURIE D. WEBSTER

INTRODUCTION

The Spanish colonization of New Mexico initiated numerous changes in the production of indigenous textiles and the use of native dress in Pueblo communities. In Pueblo communities in and around the Rio Grande Valley, Spanish tribute demands and the diversion of Pueblo labor and land to colonial projects led to changes in the sexual division of weaving labor, the contexts and scheduling of textile production, and regional patterns of textile exchange (Webster 1997, 2000, 2001). Far to the west of Spanish settlement, people in the remote Hopi villages were also impacted by colonial tribute and labor demands, but they were able to maintain their traditional organization of textile production and manufacture and use of precontact styles of clothing through the colonial period and into modern times.

What historical and social processes account for the persistence of Hopi weaving during the turbulent years of the Spanish colonial period? How did Hopi people negotiate the adversities and opportunities of colonialism to ensure the production of textiles into the postcolonial era? As noted by Leo Panich

DOI: 10.5876/9781607325741.c004

(2013:105) in his discussion of "archaeologies of persistence," processes of continuity and change are not only entwined in many postcontact indigenous histories, but often the social changes that arose from colonial interactions are what enabled or facilitated continuity, resulting in what Neal Ferris (2009) and Stephen Silliman (2009) refer to as "changing continuities," or processes of continuity through change.

In this chapter, I use multiple lines of evidence from archaeological data, Spanish documentary accounts, and Hopi narratives to explore the trajectory of Hopi weaving during the Spanish colonial period and how it was reinterpreted and transformed, even as it was perpetuated (Panich 2013:106–7). After providing an overview of the major Spanish colonial impacts on Pueblo weaving in general, and on Hopi weaving in particular, I explore the major changes and continuities in Hopi textile production in the wake of Spanish contact and the ways in which Hopi resistance, cultural practices, and cultural values contributed to the persistence of this ancient craft. Archaeological data from the Hopi villages of Awat'ovi and Wàlpi serve as the main source of archaeological information for this study (Figure 4.1). Located at the eastern edge of the Hopi Mesas on Antelope Mesa, Awat'ovi was the largest of the Hopi villages at the time of European contact and a trade and communications portal with the outside world (Dongoske and Dongoske 2002:116; see also Thomas E. Sheridan and Stewart B. Koyiyumptewa, chapter 9 in this volume). After the establishment of the Awat'ovi Mission in 1629, Awat'ovi was also the base of Franciscan operations at Hopi (Montgomery et al. 1949). Originally situated at the base of First Mesa, Wàlpi village was the site of a *visita* during the mission period. After the Pueblo Revolt of 1680, it was relocated to the top of First Mesa for increased security. The documentary evidence used in this study comes primarily from published Spanish colonial narratives and records (e.g., Hackett 1937; Kessell 1979; Scholes 1930, 1935, 1937, 1942), but because these data strongly privilege the colonial viewpoint, I also consider more recent Hopi accounts derived from oral tradition (Courlander 1971; Preucel 2002:7; Wiget 1982; Yava 1978; see also chapter by Sheridan and Koyiyumptewa [4], this volume).

COLONIAL IMPACTS ON PUEBLO WEAVING LABOR: A BRIEF OVERVIEW

When the first Spaniards arrived in the northern Southwest, Pueblo weaving was a rich and flourishing craft tradition. Precontact Southwestern weaving is well represented by an extensive and diverse archaeological textile record (Kent 1983a; Teague 1998). These textiles are supplemented by fourteenth- through seventeenth-century kiva murals that illustrate the use of similar garments in ceremonies (Dutton 1963; Hibben 1975; Smith 1952; Webster 2007). Early Spanish accounts from the period 1540–1610 describe the Piro and Tiguex (Tiwa) villages

FIGURE 4.1. *Map of Hopi Reservation. From* Hopi Basket Weaving: Artistry in Natural Fibers *by Helga Teiwes (1996). © 1996 The Arizona Board of Regents. Reprinted by permission of the University of Arizona Press.*

in the Rio Grande Valley and the Hopi villages to the west as the major producers of cotton fiber and textiles among the Pueblos (Bolton [1908] 1963:146–47; Hammond and Rey 1953:1014; Winship 1896:587). They also describe the spinning and weaving of cotton textiles in kivas, identify Pueblo men as the principal loom-weavers, and discuss the winter months, or the agricultural off-season, as the time of year when most weaving activities took place (Hammond and Rey 1953:610, 627, 636, 645, 660; 1966:82–83; Winship 1896:521, 575).

After Spanish colonization, the *encomienda* and *repartimiento* systems (colonial systems of forced tribute and labor) were imposed upon the Pueblos, as in other parts of New Spain, to channel tribute and labor to colonial purposes (see John G. Douglass and William M. Graves, chapter 1 in this volume). Under the encomienda, Pueblo households were forced to make twice-yearly payments of woven cotton *mantas* (blankets), hides, or corn to their *encomenderos* (Hackett 1937:120; Snow 1983:350–351). Colonial governors also forced Pueblo people living in and near the Rio Grande Valley to produce large quantities of woven and knitted textiles on their behalf (Kessell 1979:156; Scholes 1937:106). The vast majority of these textiles were shipped south to markets in New Spain in exchange for imported goods. During the late 1630s, one governor, Luis de Rosas, operated an *obraje*, or weaving workshop, in Santa Fe staffed with Indian and Spanish labor (Scholes 1937:117, 143–44, n. 6). A surviving 1638 trade invoice from this workshop documents the shipment of more than 500 textiles to the mining and economic center of Parral in southern Chihuahua, Mexico (Bloom 1935). The invoice lists many types of fabrics, including nineteen pieces of *sayal* (coarse woolen sackcloth), each a hundred *varas* (approximately one yard) long, that could only have been produced on the European treadle loom.[1]

Another governor, Bernardo López de Mendizábal, collected large quantities of woven blankets and hand-knitted stockings, an estimated 1,400 pairs in 1661 alone, from the eastern Pueblos for export (Hackett 1937:153; Kessell 1979:177; Scholes 1942:48). Assisted by his *alcaldes mayors* (provincial magistrates), Mendizábal distributed woolen fleeces from his flocks to various Rio Grande Pueblo villages, returning within a specified period of time for the finished goods, Most of this "production on demand" was scheduled to coincide with the spring and fall shearing of the governor's sheep (Kessell 1979:178; Webster 1997:153). Unlike precontact Pueblo textile production, which was performed primarily by men in extramural kivas during the winter, at least some of this tribute textile production was conducted by women, and probably children, within households during the warmer months.[2] The use of the upright loom technology by women for tribute blanket production, if this was the apparatus used, would have required not only a shift in male attitudes toward the use of this technology by women, but also changes in the settings of this work and the scheduling of female labor.

Similar forced labor practices were engaged in by some Franciscan missionaries, who shipped Pueblo-made textiles south to Mexico in exchange for new furnishings for their missions (Scholes 1930, 1935). By 1660, if not before, missionaries were exporting Pueblo-woven blankets and knitted stockings to Parral, with much of the spinning, weaving, and knitting of these textiles performed by Pueblo women (Bloom 1927:229). Pueblo men were also involved in these activities, and in at least one mission (Isleta), were engaged in producing long lengths of yardage on European treadle looms in weaving workshops (Hackett 1937:144, 213).

Although Pueblo people tended large flocks of sheep for the missionaries prior to the Pueblo Revolt (see Phillip O. Leckman, chapter 3 in this volume), these sheep were considered mission property, and their wool was doled out sparingly (Hackett 1937:113, 191). Some Pueblo converts wore woolen cloth made in the missions, but most mission-made woolen fabrics were intended for export. All this changed after the Pueblo Revolt, when the Pueblos appropriated large numbers of Spanish sheep, and their use of wool skyrocketed (Webster 1997). Although Pueblo people increased their personal flocks after the reconquest, they were also once again forced to produce textiles for the missions and the Spanish civil authorities without compensation (Hackett 1937:448; Kelly 1941:66–67). Only the Hopi villages, which permanently expelled Spanish authority in 1700, were exempt from these pressures (see chapters by Matthew Liebmann and colleagues [5], this volume). Most of this eighteenth-century tribute production occurred at Acoma, Laguna, Zuni, Jemez, and in the southern Tiwa and Rio Grande Keres villages in the southern and western portion of the New Mexico Colony, where sheep and cotton were most plentiful (Hackett 1937:427, 471; Kelly 1941:76).[3] Except for in a few middle Rio Grande Pueblo villages, weaving for internal use dramatically declined among the eastern Pueblos by the mid-1700s, and by the early 1800s many Rio Grande Pueblo people were wearing woolen clothing imported from Acoma, Laguna, Zuni, and Hopi (Minge [1976] 1991:36; Kessell 1980:246). Of all the Pueblos, only the Hopi villages were entirely self-sufficient in their use of both cotton and woolen textiles and producing both types of fabrics for exchange by this time (Webster 1997:637–39).

COLONIAL IMPACTS ON HOPI WEAVING

Although the remote Hopi villages were shielded from many seventeenth-century Spanish colonial pressures, they were not exempt from tribute demands on weaving labor. In 1629, a church and convent were established at Awat'ovi and a visita was constructed at Wàlpi. Soon after, additional churches and convents were built at Oraibi and Shongopovi and another visita at Mishongnovi. By the mid-1630s, the missionized Hopi villages had been given in encomienda and were subject to the same textile tribute demands as Pueblo villages farther east. For example, a 1664 document describes the collection of an unspecified number of mantas from Awat'ovi by its *encomendera*, Elena Gómez (Hackett 1937:243).

Another Spanish account describes the forced production of textiles for one Hopi missionary during the 1650s. In a 1655 complaint registered by several Hopi individuals before the *custodián* Antonio de Ibargaray, the administrative leader (prelate) of the New Mexico Franciscan mission program, the *guardián* at Jongopabí (Shongopovi), Salvador de Guerra, the guardian at Jongopabi (Shongopovi), was charged with forcing residents to weave mantas of cotton and wool and demanding "a stipulated number of finished pieces, regardless of whether he gave them sufficient raw material, and stated that failure to produce the required number within a certain time was punished by whipping" (Scholes 1942:12). Although Guerra subsequently admitted to using Hopi labor for the weaving of mantas, he claimed not to have known that the quantities of raw materials were inadequate, blaming "those who apportion it." He also denied setting time limits for the completion of the weavings. In a 1663 document, the *alcalde mayor* of the Salinas Province, Nicolás de Aguilar, who had spent some time at the Hopi Mesas, supported the Hopi claims, adding that the Hopi individuals who had lodged the complaint had been severely punished, one later dying from his wounds (Hackett 1937:141). This testimony reveals that at least one friar at Hopi requisitioned textiles from Hopi workers, imposed short-term quotas on the completion of the finished textiles, and had mission representatives working on his behalf to distribute the raw materials, a strategy reminiscent of that used by Governor Mendizábal and some Franciscan missionaries among the Rio Grande Pueblo villages. The Guerra testimony also indicates that at least some fiber supplies (i.e., those that were apportioned) were under the control of mission personnel. It is reasonable to assume that if this activity was occurring at one Hopi mission, it probably occurred at others. This testimony fails to specify what kinds of looms were being used to make these tribute mantas, but no documentary or archaeological evidence has come to light to indicate the use of European treadle looms at the Hopi missions.

The level of tribute textile production at Hopi probably was not constant, but ebbed during lulls in missionary activity. For example, missionary activity is known to have waned during the 1630s in response to violent uprisings and to have relaxed again during the 1670s as a result of the drought, disease, famine, and civil unrest that plagued most of the colony (Scholes and Adams 1952:28). In 1680, the Hopi villages joined with other Pueblo communities in a regionwide revolt that resulted in the local destruction of the Hopi missions and the death of the resident Franciscan priests and some converts (see chapter by Liebmann and colleagues, this volume, for discussion of the Puebloan perspective on its aftermath in other portions of the eastern Pueblo communities). Subsequent Spanish attempts to reestablish the mission at Awat'ovi led to the destruction of the village in 1700–1701 by neighboring communities with the tacit support of a traditional Awat'ovi faction (Whiteley 2002; Yava 1978:91–93). After this time, the Hopi villages were free of direct Spanish administrative and religious control (but see chapter by Sheridan and Koyiyumptewa [4], this volume) and any additional Spanish tribute demands.

CONTINUITY AND CHANGE IN HOPI TEXTILE PRODUCTION

I now examine the major changes and continuities in Hopi textile production during the first century of colonization, from the establishment of the missions in 1629 through the early decades of the post–Pueblo Revolt period. The major changes were the adoption of wool, the knitting technique, and one or two imported dyes; the adoption or expansion of embroidery; and shifts in the organization of weaving labor for tribute production, whereas the major continuities were the continued production of cotton textiles and the use of traditional styles of dress, and the perpetuation of a traditional organization of production for the manufacture of native textiles (Webster 1997).

Most of the information about Hopi weaving for this period derives from the archaeological excavations conducted at Awat'ovi and Wàlpi Villages (E. C. Adams 1982; Montgomery et al. 1949; Smith 1972). The Awat'ovi data provide information for the Franciscan, Pueblo Revolt, and early postrevolt periods (1629–1700), the Wàlpi data for the eighteenth century (1700–1790). Awat'ovi and its mission establishment were extensively excavated by the Peabody Museum of Harvard in the 1930s (Montgomery et al. 1949; Smith 1952, 1972). Four decades later, excavations were conducted in several closed-off rooms at present-day Wàlpi Village (E. C. Adams 1982). Both excavations yielded abundant evidence of textiles and other weaving-related information in the form of loom holes, weaving tools, and sheep faunal remains (J. Adams and Larson 1979; Kent 1979; Olsen 1978; Webster 1997, 2000; Wheeler 1978). The adobe bricks used to build the 1630s Awat'ovi Mission were another important source of information about the early use of introduced fibers and dyes. Dissolved and then analyzed, the bricks were found to contain cotton seeds, plant and animal fibers, cordage, and other perishable materials that had been incorporated into the bricks as a binder (Jones 1939; see also Webster 1997:270–71, appendix D).

The Adoption of Wool

The Hopi probably regarded wool as a precious commodity from the start. Not only is it easier to raise a flock of sheep then to cultivate a cotton field, but wool is easier to process, has greater warmth, and has a stronger affinity for dyes than cotton. It also occurs in a variety of natural shades. Sheep were introduced to the Hopi Mesas in 1629 with the establishment of the missions (Scholes 1930:100).

When the Hopi missions were actively staffed, the mission sheep and their wool probably came under Franciscan authority. But during those rare periods when mission activity waned and the friars were absent, the Hopi would have had direct access to these resources. Although the leaders of the Pueblo Revolt urged their followers to reject all Spanish introductions after the Pueblo Revolt, the Hopi, as well as all of the other Pueblos, seized control of the sheep left behind after the expulsion of the Spaniards and never let go. Sheep raising was an important economic activity at Hopi after the revolt and into the following centuries (E. C. Adams 1989:87; E. B. Adams and Chavez 1956:303; Bolton 1950:246; Coues 1900:361).

The main archaeological sources of information about the use of sheep and wool at Hopi all come from Awat'ovi: Stanley Olsen's (1978) faunal study of the domestic sheep and goat remains (difficult to distinguish) in the Hopi village and Franciscan mission complex, my reanalysis of the fibers in the mission bricks that were used to construct the main church during the 1630s, and my analysis of the textiles from the mission burials, which largely postdate the Pueblo Revolt, though some could have been casualties of that conflict (Montgomery et al. 1949:97; Webster 1997). Domestic sheep/goat bones were recovered in significant quantities from both mission and village contexts. Olsen identified 17 percent of the faunal bone from the Awat'ovi Village as sheep or goat, much of it butchered, and interpreted this to mean that, with the Franciscans' permission, the Hopis were able to supplement their native diet with the meat of these animals. In contrast, sheep/goat were found to constitute almost 40 percent of the faunal bone from postrevolt contexts in the mission, which suggested to Olsen that the Hopi's use of these animals more than doubled after the Pueblo Revolt (Olsen 1978:29–30). Elsewhere, I have argued that Olsen's interpretation of the use of sheep/goat within the Awat'ovi Village prior to the revolt may be inflated because most of the butchered sheep/goat bone from the seventeenth-century Hopi village came from the uppermost levels of fill and thus could also be postrevolt in age (Webster 1997:330–32).

Although cotton was more common than wool fiber in the mission bricks, three were found to contain evidence of sheep manure or wool fiber, documenting the early presence of sheep at Awat'ovi (Webster 1997:317, appendix D). Of the probable 27 native burials in the church, most of which are thought to date to or postdate the Pueblo Revolt, 19 were associated with woolen plain-weave cloth, warp-faced or warp-float belts, 2/2 (over 2, under 2) twill fabric, or embroidery (Webster 1997:278–305, appendix C; 2000). Wool blankets served as the customary burial shrouds. In contrast, excavations in the seventeenth-century Awat'ovi Village yielded only one example of a wool textile, a knitted legging, from a structure that probably burned during the destruction of the village in 1700–1701 (Webster 1997:201). Because conditions in the burned sections of the village favored the preservation of cotton (which carbonizes when burned), and conditions in the unburned mission favored the preservation of wool (which survives better in open, unburned contexts than does cotton), it is not possible to compare the use of wool and cotton in the village and mission during the colonial period from these data alone.

Several conclusions can be drawn about the use of wool at Awat'ovi from the mission burials, however. First, by the time of the Pueblo Revolt, the people of Awat'ovi were already using wool to produce traditional styles of garments. Second, these woolen garments were being made by the same spinning and weaving techniques used to weave cotton. Third, based on the diverse range of woolen textiles recovered from the postrevolt burials, the Awat'ovi inhabitants had probably been using wool for some time to meet their clothing needs.

The archaeological textile evidence from Wàlpi further corroborates the extensive use of wool at Hopi during the postrevolt period. Most eighteenth-century native textiles from Wàlpi are also made of wool. They include such precontact types of fabrics as plain weaves, diagonal and twill weaves, and plaids, and such precontact styles of garments as blankets, kilts, mantas, and warp-faced belts, as well as at least one Spanish-introduced style, weft-faced blankets (Kent 1979). These patterns led Kate Peck Kent (1979:16, 38) to conclude that by the early eighteenth century, wool had largely replaced cotton for textile use at Hopi and was used for most articles of every dress, with cotton reserved primarily for articles of ceremonial significance.

The Adoption of New Dyes

At least one and possibly two new imported dyes, both associated with the use of wool, were used at Awat'ovi during the seventeenth century. A bright blue wool yarn probably dyed with indigo was recovered from a postrevolt mission burial, and an orange wool yarn possibly dyed with brazilwood was recovered from one of the mission bricks (Webster 1997:288–89). Whereas the blue yarn is almost certainly indigo-dyed, the source of the orange dye is more questionable. (The dyes have not been chemically tested.) The fact that both yarns are z-spun (slant from upper right to lower left like the middle of the letter Z) and appear to have been spun with a native stick-and-whorl spindle suggests that the people of Awat'ovi had direct access to the dyestuffs used to color them, even though no archaeological evidence of preprocessed lump indigo or brazilwood sticks were found. Because most of the woven textiles from Awat'ovi have discolored to a deteriorated brown or a carbonized black, it is unknown whether any of these fabrics were originally dyed.

Indigo and brazilwood were traded north from Mexico and brought to the Southwest as part of the Spanish wool-weaving tradition, where they were widely used by New Mexican Hispanic blanket weavers. Reportedly, indigo was the most common dyestuff imported into the colony, followed by brazilwood (Bowen and Spillman 1979:208–9). Both dyes were used almost exclusively on wool fiber (Webster 1997:576, 585–86). The earliest reference I have found to their presence in New Mexico relates to Governor Mendizábal's importation of indigo and brazilwood for his commissioned weavers during the 1660s (Hackett 1937:254). It is reasonable to assume, however, that indigo was brought north decades earlier by early colonists or via the mission supply service for coloring the wool of Spanish sheep.

Although brazilwood is not known to have played an important role in Hopi weaving, indigo was considered by the Hopi to be their most precious dye for producing the symbolically important colors of blue and green (Colton 1965:50). By the early 1700s, indigo was being regularly imported into the New Mexico Colony (e.g., Ahlborn 1983:39, 47). By then, it was probably also traded to Hopi via the Rio Grande Pueblos, a practice that continued into the early twentieth century (e.g., Parsons 1936:1015). Eighteenth-century woolen fabrics from Wàlpi indicate the extensive use of indigo by Hopi weavers by the early 1700s (Kent 1979:5). Cochineal, the important and expensive red dye derived from insects, was apparently never used by the Pueblos to dye cloth. Instead, most Pueblo use of cochineal involved the unraveling of commercially dyed imported wool fabrics to acquire red yarns for embroidery or woven blankets (Kent 1983b:29). No raveled red yarns were identified in the Awat'ovi or Wàlpi assemblages.

The Adoption of Knitting

Knitting is the only Spanish-introduced textile technique, with the possible exception of embroidery, which is known to have replaced a precontact technique. Before Spanish contact, the Pueblos made their leggings by a process known as looping. The transfer of knitting to the Pueblos is undocumented, but it was most likely introduced by the missionaries or other Spanish authorities early on during the colonial period for the purpose of tribute production. By the mid-1600s, Pueblo-made knitted wool stockings were among the most common tribute products exacted from the Pueblos. By the time of the Pueblo Revolt, knitting had largely replaced looping for the Pueblos' own needs as well, with most Pueblo leggings now made of wool rather than cotton (Webster 1997:611–12).

The Awat'ovi excavations yielded two examples of woolen knitting, both probably the remains of leggings, one from a probable postrevolt funerary context in the mission and the other from a late seventeenth-century room in the Awat'ovi Village that also yielded an example of cotton looping (Webster 1997:301). The recovery of cotton looping and wool knitting from the same late seventeenth-century context suggests that the Hopi initially maintained strict fiber associations with these techniques, working the introduced technique of knitting with the introduced fiber of wool and the precontact technique of looping with the precontact fiber of cotton. All eighteenth-century leggings from Wàlpi are knitted and made of wool (Kent 1979:32).

The Adoption or Expansion of Embroidery

The timing of the appearance of embroidery in the Southwest is still open to question. Embroidery involves the application of decorative yarns, usually through the use of a needle, to a finished piece of cloth. Although Kent (1983a:183–91) considered some late prehistoric textiles to be embroidered, others have argued that these fabrics were decorated by a supplementary-weft technique ("brocade") in which decorative yarns were added during the weaving process (Teague 1998:87–88; Webster 2000:194–200). If Kent's scenario is correct, then cotton embroidery was largely replaced by wool embroidery sometime during the seventeenth century. If the other scenario is correct, then embroidery was probably introduced by the Spaniards through the missions, and replaced supplementary weft early on as a method for decorating the borders of native ceremonial textiles. Regardless of its origins, wool embroidery was practiced by the Pueblos during the seventeenth century, and it soon became the most important technique for expressing Pueblo iconography on cloth (Kent 1983b) (Figure 4.2).

The archaeological remains of embroidered textiles were recovered from seventeenth-century mission burials at Awat'ovi, Zuni, and Jemez (Webster 1997:601–2; 2000:194–95, 198–200). All examples consist of the remains of woolen embroidery yarns, sometimes associated with deteriorated background fabrics. The garments are very fragmentary but probably represent the remains of embroidered kilts or mantas. At Awat'ovi, the remains of embroidered textiles were recovered from four mission burials (Webster 1997:290–92, appendix C; 2000:194–95). Now a deteriorated brown color that may not represent their original shade, the woolen embroidery yarns consist of parallel strands worked back and forth in a running stitch, some retaining the crimp of their original geometric designs. In all cases, the background fabrics to which these embroidery yarns were applied either are highly degraded or have completely disintegrated, making it impossible to determine whether the embroidery was inserted parallel to the warp or the weft.[4] Microscopic examination of fiber samples from the creases of the embroidery yarns suggests that most of these ground fabrics were cotton, though at least one may have been wool. At Wàlpi, a well-preserved example of brown wool embroidery on a white wool fabric was recovered from an eighteenth-century context, indicating that white wool was sometimes

FIGURE 4.2. *Excerpt of map by Don Bernardo de Miera y Pacheco, ca. 1760, illustrating the "Dress and Dance of the Indians of New Mexico." Situated on map near Zuni and "Moqui" (Hopi), this illustration appears to show women wearing embroidered manta dresses and men in embroidered shirts and kilts. From John Kessell,* Kiva, Cross, and Crown: The Pecos Indians and New Mexico 1540–1840, *National Park Service, US. Department of the Interior, Washington, DC, 1979.*

substituted for white cotton as a background for early embroidered Hopi textiles. Other eighteenth-century examples of wool embroidery from Wàlpi were applied to cotton cloth (Kent 1979:9–12, 17).

Mission-period Hopi textiles exhibit none of the Spanish stylistic changes reported for some other types of material culture, such as pottery (E. C. Adams 1989:85; Mills 2008:256–57). While poor textile preservation undoubtedly provides an incomplete picture, seventeenth-century Awat'ovi textiles appear to be devoid of Spanish symbols, designs, or forms. The embroidery examples are too deteriorated to determine their specific designs, but they are clearly geometric, not curvilinear or naturalistic like most mission-period Spanish designs (e.g., Montgomery et al. 1949:figs. 59–62). The floral motifs found on some later Acoma and Zuni women's embroidered wool mantas were never used on Hopi embroidered fabrics (Kent 1983b:pls. 12–15). The triangle-and-hook motif embroidered on an eighteenth-century fabric from Wàlpi (Kent 1979:9–10) is the exact same motif used to decorate kilt borders in the late precontact Awat'ovi murals (Smith 1952:fig. 25) and used on Hopi kilts and mantas today (Webster and Loma'omvaya 2004:84–87). Closely tied to rain, clouds, and fertility in Hopi cosmology, the symbolism of these embroidered designs may have gone unrecognized by the missionaries and other Spaniards, who may have viewed them only as pleasant geometric decorations.

Changes in the Tools and Organization of Textile Production

Except for two minor additions—knitting needles and metal sewing needles—the Pueblo loom and tool kit remained unchanged throughout the Spanish period. Two possible metal knitting needles were identified in the Awat'ovi assemblage, but the high value and relative scarcity of metal during the mission period suggests that most knitting needles used by the Pueblos were made of wood (Webster 1997:313, 696). The only eyed metal (copper) needle found at Awat'ovi, associated with a mission burial, bore traces of wool cloth or yarn on its corroded surface, suggesting its use for wool embroidery (Webster 1997:313, 695). Despite the presence of metal needles at Awat'ovi, nearly all eyed needles recovered at Awat'ovi, as well as Wàlpi, were made of bone (J. Adams and Larson 1979:8; Wheeler 1978:56).

Spanish documentary sources do not address the organization of textile production at Hopi during the mission period, but I suggest that several changes occurred, the first supported by archaeological evidence, the others inferred. The first involves the transfer or expansion of traditional weaving practices from kivas to houseblock religious rooms during the seventeenth century. Excavations at Awat'ovi revealed the presence of loom holes in the paved floors of five Pueblo V–period kivas (Smith 1972). One was immediately decommissioned when the church was built over it, leaving four known kivas where weaving could have taken place at Awat'ovi during the mission period. The extent to which these kivas were in use during the mission period is still debated, however. Watson Smith (1972:67, 75) suggested they were abandoned between 1630 and 1680 under missionary pressure, whereas Hopi oral traditions indicate their continued use (Courlander 1971:160). Although two of these kivas were in use when the village was destroyed in 1700–1701, this could represent postrevolt reoccupation (Smith 1972:70, 75).

At this point, it is not possible to demonstrate the practice of weaving in kivas during the mission period. However, loom holes were also identified in two nonkiva settings at seventeenth-century Awat'ovi: Room 611, a large interior houseblock room with a paved floor in the seventeenth-century Hopi village, and Room 463, a Hopi room within the mission complex that is considered to postdate the revolt.[5] Other than kivas, Room 611 is the only nonkiva context at Awat'ovi where loom holes and pairs of loom blocks cooccurred.[6] Elsewhere, I have suggested that this room may have functioned as a religious room analogous to a kiva where communal activities, including weaving, were practiced after missionary pressures forced the transfer of such activities from kivas to less visible areas of the village (Webster 1997:310–11, 321–24). Two similar rooms were identified at Hawikuh (Webster 1997:246, 310–11, 324). The presence of loom holes with intact loom anchors in Hopi Room 463 in the postrevolt mission indicates that weaving was also being performed in nonkiva settings at Hopi by this time. At Wàlpi, loom anchors set into the floors of eighteenth-century religious rooms further substantiate that loom weaving was not confined to kivas after the revolt, but was being performed in both kivas and other ritual settings (J. Adams and Larson 1979:43–53).

The inferred changes in textile production during the mission period relate to the production of textiles for tribute purposes. Elsewhere I have argued that tribute production required changes in the gender composition of the weaving labor pool and the settings of textile production (Webster 1997). Given the lack of strong evidence for the use of the upright loom in houseblock rooms (except for aforementioned Room 611) during the mission period, or in the mission complex except after the revolt, the most parsimonious interpretation for the production of tribute textiles on upright looms is that these fabrics were being woven in kivas, if their use was permitted by the missionaries, in outdoor settings such as plazas, or both. If most loom weaving for tribute production occurred in kivas, then men may have been the primary weavers of tribute textiles at Hopi. If this production was also occurring in households or outside, then any or all members of the household could have been involved, and women may have played a greater role in their production. Since most tribute production in colonial New Mexico reportedly took place during the warmer months after the spring shearing (Kessell 1979:178; Webster 1997:153, 616), weaving easily could have been performed in outdoor settings, where looms would leave little archaeological trace. Other aspects of tribute textile production, including the processing of wool fleeces into yarn and the knitting of stockings, were probably performed by all household members, working outdoors or in households. Such activities also would have left few archaeological traces.

Continuity in Weaving and Spinning Practices

Precontact weaving and spinning technologies appear to have been maintained at Hopi throughout the mission period. Only a few weaving tools survived at

Awat'ovi, but they include a long weaving batten probably associated with the use of the traditional upright loom, and several bone weaving tools, including the serrated rib from a Spanish-introduced mule that could have served as a batten for a narrow loom (Webster 1997:311–12; Wheeler 1978:57, fig. 16a). No tools associated with the use of European spinning wheels or treadle looms were identified in the Awat'ovi or Wàlpi assemblages.

Excavations in eighteenth-century religious rooms at Wàlpi yielded a wide assortment of weaving tools, including wooden battens, weaving combs, temples, and shuttles associated with the use of the traditional upright loom (J. Adams and Larson 1979:43–53). The assemblage also produced several spindle whorls, including a wooden whorl still attached to a spindle. All of these tools show continuity with precontact Pueblo weaving and spinning practices as well as those employed by more recent Hopi weavers (Kent 1983b:27–29).

Continuity in Cotton Cultivation

Although the cultivation and weaving of cotton declined throughout the Pueblo world during the Spanish period (Webster 1997), it managed to persist at Hopi. Early Spanish visitors to Hopi emphasized the intensive cultivation of cotton in the Hopi villages and the extensive production of cotton textiles (Hammond and Rey 1940:286; 1953:327, 1014; 1966:137, 190–93, 226). Fray Perea, writing in 1629, observed that the Hopi "harvested much cotton" (Hodge et al. 1945:217), and his observation is corroborated by the considerable quantities of cotton lint, fiber, and seeds incorporated into the Awat'ovi mission bricks during the 1630s (Webster 1997:345). As elsewhere in the Pueblo world, cotton cultivation probably declined at Hopi during the seventeenth century as a result of tribute production, the diversion of labor, and drought and crop failures (Webster 1997:565–68). Yet, the archaeological record from Awat'ovi and Wàlpi confirms the continued production of cotton textiles at Hopi during the mission period.

Preservation issues make it impossible to quantitatively determine the extent to which cotton was woven into textiles at Awat'ovi during the mission period. Cotton and wool tend to preserve under very different conditions at open sites (burned conditions favoring cotton, unburned conditions favoring wool), so the cotton and wool data are irreparably skewed. Because preservation conditions in the unburned mission strongly favored the preservation of wool, even if cotton were present with the mission burials, it was unlikely to be preserved. Indeed, microscopic cotton fibers were identified in the creases of several woolen embroidery yarns, suggesting the use of cotton for the base fabrics, but the cotton textiles themselves did not survive. Only two unburned cotton textiles were recovered from the mission, both associated with metallic pigments. Because metal acts as a fungicide on cellulosic materials, these pigments were directly responsible for the cotton preservation.

The most diverse assortment of cotton textiles and raw materials from Awat'ovi—carbonized plain-weave and looped fabrics as well as two dozen carbonized cotton seeds—came from the still-occupied eastern section of the Hopi village (Test 46, Rooms 1 and 3), believed to have burned during the destruction of Awat'ovi (Webster 1997:296–302, 316, 347–48, 691–92, 698).[7] Although the use of cotton and wool at Awat'ovi cannot be directly compared, this important late seventeenth-century assemblage reveals the continued use of cotton textiles at Awat'ovi seven decades after the introduction of sheep and wool (Webster 1997:347).

In contrast to conditions at Awat'ovi, most of the Wàlpi textile assemblage was recovered from the innermost, dry rooms of the village where cotton, wool, and other perishable materials were equally likely to survive. Therefore, it is highly significant that only a few cotton cloth fragments were identified in the entire eighteenth-century Wàlpi assemblage (Kent 1979), and only eleven cotton seeds were recovered from pre-1840 contexts (Gasser and Scott 1981:130). Most native textiles and yarns from eighteenth-century contexts at Wàlpi were made of wool. Even though cotton continued to be grown and woven at Hopi during the seventeenth, eighteenth, and nineteenth centuries, Hopi cultivation of the crop began its decline in the 1600s (Bolton 1950:246; Brooks 1944; Thomas 1932:151). With this decline came the reservation of cotton for ceremonial textiles, with wool becoming the primary fiber for everyday Hopi dress.

Continuity in the Organization of Textile Production for Native Consumption

As discussed at the beginning of this chapter, early Spanish chroniclers writing during the sixteenth and early seventeenth centuries identified Pueblo men as the primary weavers and spinners in Pueblo society and reported that most of this work took place in kivas during the winter months (Hammond and Rey 1953:610, 627, 636, 645, 660; 1966:82–83; Winship 1896:521, 575). Although Hopi women undoubtedly played a role in tribute textile production during the mission period, the strong cooccurrence of loom holes with what are assumed to be male-related ritual settings (kivas, religious rooms) at Awat'ovi and Wàlpi suggests that Hopi men resumed their highly gendered system of textile production after the Pueblo Revolt, if it had ever changed at all.[8] After that time, Hopi men continued to dominate all aspects of textile production at Hopi except for the manufacture of rabbit-fur blankets (Kent 1983b:90).

Archaeological loom-hole distributions at sites near the Hopi Mesas indicate that loom weaving was primarily a kiva-based activity prior to European contact (Hargrave 1931; Smith 1972). A similar coassociation of loom holes with

FIGURE 4.3. *Wàlpi kiva interior showing Hopi man weaving on a traditional upright Pueblo loom, 1899. Photo by H. S. Poley. Courtesy, Denver Public Library, Western History Collection, call number P-99.*

kivas is found at sites in the Rio Grande Valley and on the eastern periphery of the Pueblo world after AD 1300. Archaeological and ethnological data suggest that this close association of loom holes with kivas persisted only at Hopi and perhaps Pecos Pueblo after the Pueblo Revolt (Webster 1997). When the first Anglo-Americans visited the Hopi villages in the nineteenth century, kivas were still the focus of most cotton spinning, embroidery, and weaving activities, and most of these activities were being performed by men during the winter months (Parsons 1936:372, 515, 967; see also Beaglehole 1937:23–31). This organization of textile production persisted well into the twentieth century at Hopi and is still practiced today with some modifications (Figure 4.3).

Continuity in the Demand for Hopi Textiles and the Intensification of Exchange

A demand for Hopi-made textiles was perpetuated during the mission period in a number of ways. Both Hopi oral traditions and Spanish accounts relate that the Hopi performed their native dances periodically during the mission period. Although the Franciscans apparently suppressed the kiva religion for a time, Hopi oral traditions indicate the continued practice of kiva-based ceremonies intermittently during this period (Courlander 1971:160). An undated comment by France Scholes in the J. O. Brew papers at the Peabody Museum relates that Diego Romero testified that the people of Awat'ovi were still openly performing their ceremonial dances at the time of his visit with Governor Peñalosa, which, according to Ross Montgomery et al. (1949:187), occurred in the spring of 1662. Presumably, these ceremonies included the use of ritual regalia, which would have maintained the demand for ceremonial textiles and encouraged their continued production.

Furthermore, the Awat'ovi mortuary evidence indicates that traditional burial practices, which included the placing of feathered prayer sticks, food, and native baskets with the deceased, continued to be observed during this period. Native-woven textiles were the customary shrouds for most of the mission burials, and at least four individuals were buried in decorated embroidered clothing, possibly their ceremonial kilts or mantas (Webster 1997:344). By removing these items from active use, the inclusion of these native textiles in mortuary practice contributed to their continued demand (Webster 1997:548-49). Although Hopi men adopted Western styles of daily dress earlier than women, especially when away from their villages, traditional handwoven clothing derived from precontact garment styles was worn on a daily basis by both Hopi men and women well into the late nineteenth century and early twentieth century and is still worn in traditional ceremonies today (Kent 1983b; Webster 1997:534).

After the Spaniards were expelled and tribute demands lifted, Hopi weavers were free to produce textiles not only for local consumers but for trade to outside communities. Much of this production was accomplished through the use of newly controlled supplies of wool. After the reconquest, Hopi woolen textiles—and to a lesser extent, cotton ones—probably began entering the New Mexico Pueblo villages in greater quantities. The Hopi also resumed the trade of textiles to their nomadic neighbors (Beaglehole 1937:84). By the mid-nineteenth century, Hopi was the principal supplier of cotton textiles and women's woolen manta dresses to the Rio Grande Pueblos, and by the end of the century, to Zuni and Acoma as well (Webster 1997:639-43). This intensification of textile production ensured Hopi not only a pivotal place in the Rio Grande economic sphere, but also regular access to desirable imports such as trade cloth and indigo dye that entered New Mexico via the Camino Real and the Santa Fe Trail, as well as imported goods from other pueblos, which served to maintain contacts in times of stress (see also Lomawaima 1989:93).

DISCUSSION

The geographical remoteness and marginal environment of the Hopi Mesas played a pivotal role in shielding the Hopi people from many of the Spanish labor demands experienced by Pueblo villages closer to the Rio Grande Valley. Because of its considerable distance from the Rio Grande, Hopi was relatively free of mission activity until 1629. The threat of Navajo and Apache raids in the region further buffered the Hopi villages from frequent long-term contacts with Spaniards (E. B. Adams 1954:4). Because the Hopi people, as a whole, were never subject to major population relocations, forced to work on Spanish farms, or encroached upon by Spanish settlements, they were able to maintain their traditional territory and residence patterns, critical factors for the maintenance of native identities during the colonial era (Gasco 2005:104; Lightfoot 2005:214; Spicer 1962:576–77; Van Buren 2010:178).

The changes and continuities in Hopi weaving after European contact provide insights into some of the dynamic social processes through which the Hopi negotiated the constraints and opportunities of the colonial period to insure the persistence of this ancient craft (see Panich 2013). Like other Pueblo villagers, The Hopi were not merely passive observers to the social disruptions and labor demands wrought by Spanish colonization (see Liebmann 2010:200; Preucel 2002:22), but employed various actions and strategies, offensive and defensive, to resist and ameliorate these conditions. Many of these responses directly affected the trajectory of Hopi weaving during the Spanish period.

For example, documentary sources indicate that in 1655, several Hopi individuals made the long-distance journey to the provincial capital in Santa Fe to lodge a formal complaint before the then-head of the New Mexico Franciscan program, Custodian Ibargaray, in regards to the forced textile labor practices of Fray Guerra at Shongopovi discussed earlier in this chapter. This Hopi action led to the removal of Guerra from his position later that year (Scholes 1942). Presumably, it also resulted in a lessening of textile tribute demands at Hopi, at least for a time.

Two other offensive actions—the Pueblo Revolt and the destruction of Awat'ovi—influenced the trajectory of Hopi weaving by returning autonomy to the Hopi people and inaugurating a period of cultural revival (Whiteley 2002). By essentially terminating the Franciscan mission program at Hopi, the Pueblo Revolt gave the Hopi people unrestricted access to mission sheep and wool for their weaving. Two decades later, the destruction of Awat'ovi brought an end to Spanish authority at Hopi, and, as Whiteley (2002:161) has argued, issued in "a full-blown revitalization and transformation of Hopi society," which would have included a renewed interest in the visible symbols of Hopi social identity, including daily and ritual dress.

Less violent strategies such as passive resistance and skilled diplomacy were used by the Hopi and other Pueblo people to avoid direct confrontation with the missionaries and other Spanish authorities (E. C. Adams 1989; Mobley-Tanaka 2002). For example, the feigning of conversion would have enabled Pueblo people to mask their secret observance of traditional rites and to conceal their ritual paraphernalia (Knaut 1995). Participation in the mission program also provided native people with regular access to favorable material goods—such as metal needles, wool, and imported dyes—and the information needed to process them.

By taking a flexible approach toward Spanish material introductions, Hopi weavers were able to integrate advantageous new raw materials, such as wool and imported indigo dye, into the traditional textile repertoire without compromising ancient textile traditions or Hopi cultural values. Through a process that Hartman Lomawaima (1989:97) has called "Hopification," Hopi weavers incorporated advantageous Spanish introductions into Hopi life, imbued them with Hopi values, and made them Hopi while maintaining the foundational elements of Hopi weaving practice, just one way in which Hopi people used existing cultural values to negotiate the challenges of the Spanish colonial period (see further discussion of the concepts of Hopification [Lomawaima 1989] and Pueblofication [Brown 2013] in the chapter by Douglass and Graves, chapter 1 in this volume).

CONCLUSIONS

The primary changes to Hopi weaving during the mission period were the adoption of wool and the knitting technique. There is no evidence in the Awat'ovi assemblage for the use of introduced garment forms or the incorporation of Spanish decorative symbols, except for the imported ecclesiastical garments used by the friars and other church leaders. The Awat'ovi assemblage indicates that by the time of the Pueblo Revolt, most weave structures and garments made of cotton prior to Spanish contact were now made primarily of wool.

Sometime during the 1700s, Spanish-style weft-faced woolen blankets appeared in the Wàlpi archaeological record (Kent 1979:13–14). Emulating a Spanish long, narrow, banded blanket made on a European treadle loom, these Hopi-made versions were woven on the traditional Pueblo upright loom and continued to be made in this way into the twentieth century (Kent 1983b:42–44). All other native-woven textiles in the eighteenth-century Wàlpi assemblage perpetuate weave structures and clothing styles popular in the northern Southwest prior to European contact. Similar textiles were made by Hopi weavers well into the twentieth century, and many of these garments are still woven at Hopi for ceremonial use today.

Men are still the primary weavers in Hopi society, though women have begun to play a greater role. Today, much of the weaving at Hopi takes place not in kivas, but in households, classrooms, or other nonritual settings. No longer an integral part of the Hopi male role, weaving is now practiced by fewer men, some of whom specialize in the production of traditional textiles for sale to other Hopis or to people in other Pueblo communities. These changes in Hopi weaving were not imposed from the outside, but are internal changes that began in the early twentieth century as more men became involved in outside wage work and, more recently, as young people have moved to the cities for educational and employment opportunities.

Despite these changes in the organization of textile production at Hopi, locally made textiles continue to be woven and to play a critical role in the performance of religious ceremonies, in the fulfillment of social obligations, and for marking rites of passage such as initiations and weddings (Webster and Loma'omvaya 2004). Hopi weavers still use the same weaving technologies and weaving tools developed a millennium ago by their ancestors. Because the raw materials have changed and certain styles are no longer produced, the products now look a bit different, but the process has endured. The trajectory of Hopi weaving after European contact is a prime example of "changing continuities," the persistence of a native craft through the negotiation, reinterpretation, and integration of cultural knowledge and outside introductions to ensure the survival of an ancient craft tradition.

NOTES

1. The treadle loom is an industrial weaving machine capable of producing very long lengths of fabric. During the sixteenth and early seventeenth centuries, it was introduced to many areas of New Spain, including Peru, Ecuador, Guatemala, Mexico, New Mexico, and California, for the purpose of providing cloth for the Spanish colonies, much of it supplied through tribute. Equipped with reed heddles, wide shedding devices (harnesses), foot pedals (treadles), and a rigid horizontal frame, the treadle loom is typically wound with long lengths of warp, enabling weavers to produce significant lengths of cloth within a relatively short period of time (Fisher 1979). In contrast, the traditional Pueblo loom produces fabrics of a relatively short, fixed length, and its string-heddle apparatus requires the expenditure of considerable time and effort (Kent 1983b:fig. 19).

2. In contrast to textile production in the Valley of Mexico during the Aztec and early colonial periods, where women were the principal weavers of loom-woven textiles in households for both domestic and tribute production (Brumfiel 1991), men are considered to have been the primary loom weavers in late pre-Hispanic times and at the time of European contact on the Colorado Plateau, based on the ritual nature of many loom-woven fabrics, the presence of loom holes in ritual structures (kivas), and early Spanish accounts about Pueblo male loom weavers.

3. For a revealing account of how these woolen textiles were requisitioned by the governors and the impact of these activities on the Pueblos, see Charles Hackett 1937:484.

4. If the embroidery yarns were inserted parallel to the warp, as in more recent Pueblo embroidered textiles, we could rule out any historical connection to the supplementary-weft technique.

5. Information about these rooms comes from the artifact and room cards in the Awat'ovi archives at the Peabody Museum, Harvard University.

6. The only settings at Awat'ovi where loom holes were identified were kivas, Room 611 in the Hopi village, and Room 463 in the mission. Another archaeological correlate of weaving on the upright loom, the loom block (sometimes referred to as a warping block), is a large stone block equipped with a hole or socket for accommodating a wooden bar. Historically, loom blocks were used in groups of two or four to prepare the warp for weaving or to frame-braid a sash. Therefore, at least two are required for textile production (Woodbury 1954:155–157). Loom blocks have a wider distribution at Awat'ovi than loom holes, recovered from seventeen postcontact settings in the village and mission (Webster 1997:308–11). Most of these features contained only one loom block, suggesting their secondary use as seats or for other nonweaving purposes. Multiple loom blocks were confined to seven seventeenth-century settings at Awat'ovi: three kivas and three nonkiva rooms in the seventeenth-century Hopi village, the kiva under Church 2, and a postrevolt room in the mission. All of the kivas that contained loom blocks also contained loom holes in their paved floors. In addition, Room 611 also contained both loom blocks and loom holes. In contrast, none of the nonkiva domestic rooms that contained two or more loom blocks also contained loom holes. Although Richard Woodbury (1954:55) suggested that most loom blocks found in storage or living rooms at Awat'ovi represented a secondary use of these objects, the possibility cannot be ruled out that the single and multiple occurrences of loom blocks in domestic rooms of the seventeenth-century Hopi village were related to the preparation of warp for textile production, including the production of tribute textiles.

7. Jesse Walter Fewkes (1898:606, 619) and Smith (1972:69–73) suggest that these eastern rooms burned during the destruction of Awat'ovi. The Awat'ovi room cards at the Peabody Museum indicate that the rooms that yielded the burned cotton remains (Test 46, Rooms 1 and 3) were domestic rooms.

8. My interpretation of Hopi kivas and religious rooms as male-related extrahousehold ritual settings for textile production is based on early ethnographic accounts that describe such settings as the focus of most communal cotton spinning, embroidery, weaving, and ceremonial preparation activities by Hopi men (e.g., Brooks 1944; Parsons 1936).

REFERENCES CITED

Adams, E. Charles. 1982. *Wàlpi Archaeological Project: Synthesis and Interpretation.* Flagstaff: Museum of Northern Arizona.

Adams, E. Charles. 1989. "Passive Resistance: Hopi Responses to Spanish Contact and Conquest." In *Columbian Consequences*, edited by David Hurst Thomas, 77–91. Washington, DC: Smithsonian Institution.

Adams, Eleanor B. 1954. *Bishop Tamarón's Visitation of New Mexico, 1760. Historical Society of New Mexico Publications in History.* Vol. 15. Albuquerque: Historical Society of New Mexico.

Adams, Eleanor B., and Fray Angelico Chavez, translators and annotators. 1956. *The Missions of New Mexico, 1776: A Description by Fray Francisco Atanasio Dominguez, with Other Contemporary Documents.* Albuquerque: University of New Mexico Press.

Adams, Jenny L., and Robert E. Larson. 1979 *Perishable Artifacts of Floral and Faunal Material. Wàlpi Archaeological Project, Phase II.* Vol. 5. Flagstaff: Museum of Northern Arizona.

Ahlborn, Richard E. 1983. "Frontier Possessions: The Evidence from Colonial Documents." In *Colonial Frontiers*, edited by Christine Mathers, 35–57. Santa Fe: Ancient City Press.

Beaglehole, Ernest. 1937. *Notes on Hopi Economic Life.* Yale University Publications in Anthropology 15. New Haven: Yale University.

Bloom, Lansing B. 1927. "Early Weaving in New Mexico." *New Mexico Historical Review* 2 (3): 228–38.

Bloom, Lansing B. 1935. "A Trade Invoice of 1638 for Goods Shipped by Governor Rosas from Santa Fe." *New Mexico Historical Review* 10 (3): 242–48.

Bolton, Herbert E. 1950. *Pageant in the Wilderness: The Story of the Escalante Expedition to the Interior Basin, 1776.* Salt Lake City: Utah State Historical Society.

Bolton, Herbert E. [1908] 1963. *Spanish Exploration in the Southwest, 1542–1706.* New York: Barnes and Noble.

Bowen, Dorothy B., and Trish Spillman. 1979. "Appendix B: Natural and Synthetic Dyes." In *Spanish Textile Tradition of New Mexico and Colorado*, edited by Nora Fisher, 207–11. Santa Fe: Museum of International Folk Art.

Brooks, Juanita. 1944. "Journal of Thales H. Haskell." *Utah Historical Quarterly* 12 (1–2): 68–98.

Brown, Tracy L. 2013. *Pueblo Indians and Spanish Colonial Authority in Eighteenth Century New Mexico.* Tucson: University of Arizona Press.

Brumfiel, Elizabeth. 1991. "Weaving and Cooking: Women's Production in Aztec Mexico." In *Engendering Archaeology: Women and Prehistory*, edited by Joan M. Gero and Margaret W. Conkey, 224–51. Oxford: Basil Blackwell.

Colton, Mary Russell Ferrell. 1965. *Hopi Dyes.* Flagstaff: Museum of Northern Arizona Press.

Coues, Elliott. 1900. *On the Trail of a Spanish Pioneer: The Diary and Itinerary of Francisco Garcés, 1775–1776.* New York: Francis P. Harper.

Courlander, Harold. 1971. *The Fourth World of the Hopis.* New York: Crown.

Dongoske, Kurt E., and Cindy K. Dongoske. 2002. "History in Stone: Evaluating Spanish Conversion Efforts through Hopi Rock Art." In *Archaeologies of the Pueblo Revolt: Identity, Meaning, and Renewal in the Pueblo World*, edited by Robert W. Preucel, 114–31. Albuquerque: University of New Mexico Press.

Dutton, Bertha P. 1963. *Sun Father's Way: The Kiva Murals of Kuaua, A Pueblo Ruin, Coronado State Monument, New Mexico.* Albuquerque: University of New Mexico Press.

Ferris, Neal. 2009. *Native-Lived Colonialism: Challenging History in the Great Lakes*. Tucson: University of Arizona Press.

Fewkes, Jesse Walter. 1898. *Archaeological Expedition into Arizona in 1895*. Annual Report no. 17, 519–742. Washington, DC: Bureau of American Ethnology.

Fisher, Nora. 1979. "Appendix A: The Treadle Loom." In *Spanish Textile Tradition of New Mexico and Colorado*, edited by Nora Fisher, 192–95. Santa Fe: Museum of International Folk Art.

Gasco, Janine L. 2005. "Spanish Colonialism and Processes of Social Change in Mesoamerica." In *The Archaeology of Colonial Encounters*, edited by Gil J. Stein, 69–108. Santa Fe: School of American Research Press.

Gasser, Robert E., and Linda J. Scott. 1981. "Archaeobotanical Materials." *Wàlpi Archaeological Project, Phase II*. Vol. 7. Flagstaff: Museum of Northern Arizona.

Hackett, Charles W. 1937. *Carnegie Institution of Washington Publication 330*. Vol. 3. Historical Documents Relating to New Mexico, Nueva Vizcaya, and Approaches Thereto, to 1773. Washington, DC: Carnegie Institution of Washington.

Hammond, George P., and Agapito Rey. 1940. *Narratives of the Coronado Expedition, 1540–1542*. Albuquerque: University of New Mexico Press.

Hammond, George P., and Agapito Rey. 1953. *Don Juan de Oñate, Colonizer of New Mexico, 1595–1628*. 2 vols. Coronado Cuarto Centennial Publication. Albuquerque: University of New Mexico Press.

Hammond, George P., and Agapito Rey. 1966. *The Rediscovery of New Mexico, 1580–1594*. Albuquerque: University of New Mexico Press.

Hargrave, Lyndon L. 1931. "Excavations at Kin Tiel and Kokopnyama." In *Recently Dated Pueblo Ruins in Arizona*, by Emil W. Haury and Lyndon L. Hargrave, 80–120. Smithsonian Miscellaneous Collections No. 82, No. 11. Washington, DC: Smithsonian.

Hibben, Frank C. 1975. *Kiva Art of the Anasazi at Pottery Mound*. Las Vegas: KC Publications.

Hodge, Frederick W., George P. Hammond, and Agapito Rey, eds. 1945. *Fray Alonso de Benavides' Revised Memorial of 1634*. Albuquerque: University of New Mexico Press.

Jones, Volney. 1939. *Plant Materials from Bricks from Awat'ovi Mission*. Manuscript on file, J.O. Brew Papers, Peabody Museum Archives. Cambridge, MA: Harvard University.

Kelly, Henry W. 1941. *Franciscan Missions of New Mexico, 1740–1760*. Historical Society of New Mexico Publications in History X. Albuquerque: University of New Mexico Press.

Kent, Kate Peck. 1979. *An Analysis of Textile Material from Wàlpi Pueblo*. Wàlpi Archaeological Project, Phase II. Vol. 6. Flagstaff: Museum of Northern Arizona.

Kent, Kate Peck. 1983a. *Prehistoric Textiles of the Southwest*. Santa Fe: School of American Research Press.

Kent, Kate Peck. 1983b. *Pueblo Indian Textiles*. Santa Fe: School of American Research Press.

Kessell, John L. 1979. *Kiva, Cross, and Crown: The Pecos Indians and New Mexico, 1540–1840*. Washington, DC: National Park Service, U.S. Department of the Interior.

Kessell, John L. 1980. *The Missions of New Mexico since 1776*. Albuquerque: University of New Mexico Press.

Knaut, Andrew L. 1995. *The Pueblo Revolt of 1680: Conquest and Resistance in Seventeenth Century New Mexico*. Norman: University of Oklahoma Press.

Liebmann, Matthew J. 2010. "The Best of Times, the Worst of Times: Pueblo Resistance and Accommodation during the Spanish *Reconquista* of New Mexico." In *Enduring Conquests: Rethinking the Archaeology of Resistance in Spanish Colonialism in the Americas*, edited by Matthew Liebmann and Melissa S. Murphy, 199–222. School for Advanced Research Advanced Seminar Series. Santa Fe: School for Advanced Research.

Lightfoot, Kent G. 2005. *Indians, Missionaries, and Merchants: The Legacy of Colonial Encounters on the California Frontiers*. Berkeley: University of California Press.

Lomawaima, Hartman H. 1989. "Hopification: A Strategy for Cultural Preservation." In *Archaeological and Historical Perspectives on the Spanish Borderlands West*. Columbian Consequences, vol. 1, edited by David Hurst Thomas, 93–99. Washington, DC: Smithsonian Institution Press.

Mills, Barbara J. 2008. "Colonialism and Cuisine: Cultural Transmission, Domestic Practice, and Agency at Zuni Pueblo." In *Cultural Transmission and Material Culture: Breaking Down Boundaries*, edited by Lee Horne, Brenda Bowser, and Miriam Stark, 245–62. Tucson: University of Arizona Press.

Minge, Ward A. [1976] 1991. *Acoma: Pueblo in the Sky*. Acoma: Pueblo of Acoma.

Mobley-Tanaka, Jeannette. 2002. "Crossed Cultures, Crossed Meanings: The Manipulation of Ritual Imagery in Early Historic Pueblo Resistance." In *Archaeologies of the Pueblo Revolt: Identity, Meaning, and Renewal in the Pueblo World*, edited by Robert W. Preucel, 77–84. Albuquerque: University of New Mexico Press.

Montgomery, Ross G., Watson Smith, and John O. Brew. 1949. *Franciscan Awat'ovi. Reports of the Awat'ovi Expedition, No. 3*. Peabody Museum of American Archaeology and Ethnology. Vol. 36. Cambridge, MA: Harvard University.

Olsen, Stanley J. 1978. "The Faunal Analysis." In *Bones from Awat'ovi*, by Stanley J. Olsen and Richard P. Wheeler, vi–34. Reports of the Awat'ovi Expedition No. 11. Papers of the Peabody Museum of American Anthropology and Ethnology, Vol. 70, Nos. 1 and 2. Cambridge, MA: Harvard University.

Panich, Lee M. 2013. "Archaeologies of Persistence: Reconsidering the Legacies of Colonialism in Native North America." *American Antiquity* 78 (1): 105–22. http://dx.doi.org/10.7183/0002-7316.78.1.105.

Parsons, Elsie C. 1936. *Hopi Journal of Alexander M. Stephen*. 2 vols. New York: Columbia University Press.

Preucel, Robert W. 2002. "Writing the Pueblo Revolt." In *Archaeologies of the Pueblo Revolt: Identity, Meaning, and Renewal in the Pueblo World*, edited by Robert W. Preucel, 3–29. Albuquerque: University of New Mexico Press.

Scholes, France V. 1930. "The Mission Supply Service of the New Mexico Missions in the Seventeenth Century." *New Mexico Historical Review* 5 (1,2,4): 186–210, 386–404.

Scholes, France V. 1935. "Civil Government and Society in New Mexico in the Seventeenth Century." *New Mexico Historical Review* 10 (2): 71–111.

Scholes, France V. 1937. *Church and State in New Mexico, 1610–1650*. Historical Society of New Mexico Publications in History 7. Albuquerque: University of New Mexico Press.

Scholes, France V. 1942. *Troublous Times in New Mexico, 1659–1670*. Historical Society of New Mexico Publications in History 11. Albuquerque: University of New Mexico Press.

Scholes, France V., and Eleanor B. Adams. 1952. "Inventories of Church Furnishings in Some of the New Mexico Missions, 1672." *Dargan Historical Essays*, 27–38. Albuquerque: University of New Mexico Press.

Silliman, Stephen W. 2009. "Change and Continuity, Practice and Memory: Native American Persistence in Colonial New England." *American Antiquity* 74 (2): 211–30.

Smith, Watson. 1952. *Kiva Mural Decorations at Awat'ovi and Kawaika-a. Reports of the Awat'ovi Expedition No. 5. Papers of the Peabody Museum of American Anthropology and Ethnology.* Vol. 37. Cambridge, MA: Harvard University.

Smith, Watson. 1972. No. 1. vol. 39. *Prehistoric Kivas of Antelope Mesa, Northeastern Arizona.* Reports of the Awat'ovi Expedition No. 9. Papers of the Peabody Museum of American Anthropology and Ethnology. Cambridge, MA: Harvard University.

Snow, David H. 1983. "A Note on Encomienda Economics in Seventeenth-Century New Mexico." In *Hispanic Arts and Ethnohistory*, edited by Marta Weigle, 347–57. Santa Fe: Ancient City Press.

Spicer, Edward H. 1962. *Cycles of Conquest*. Tucson: University of Arizona Press.

Teague, Lynn S. 1998. *Textiles in Southwestern Prehistory*. Albuquerque: University of New Mexico Press.

Teiwes, Helga. 1996. *Hopi Basket Weaving: Artistry in Natural Fibers*. Tucson: University of Arizona Press.

Thomas, Alfred B. 1932. *Forgotten Frontiers: A Study of the Spanish Indian Policy of Don Juan Bautista de Anza, Governor of New Mexico, 1777–1787*. Norman: University of Oklahoma Press.

Van Buren, Mary. 2010. "The Archaeological Study of Spanish Colonialism in the Americas." *Journal of Archaeological Research* 18 (2): 151–201. http://dx.doi.org/10.1007/s10814-009-9036-8.

Webster, Laurie D. 1997. *Effects of European Contact on Textile Production and Exchange in the North American Southwest: A Pueblo Case Study*. PhD dissertation, Department of Anthropology, University of Arizona, Tucson. Ann Arbor: University Microfilms.

Webster, Laurie D. 2000. "The Economics of Pueblo Textile Production and Exchange in Colonial New Mexico." In *Beyond Cloth and Cordage: Archaeological Textile Research in the Americas*, edited by Penelope Ballard Drooker and Laurie D. Webster, 179–204. Salt Lake City: University of Utah Press.

Webster, Laurie D. 2001. "An Unbroken Thread: The Persistence of Pueblo Textile Traditions in the Postcolonial Era." In *The Road to Aztlan: Art from a Mythic Homeland*, by Virginia M. Fields and Victor Zamudio-Taylor, 174–289. Los Angeles: Los Angeles County Museum of Art.

Webster, Laurie D. 2007. "Ritual Costuming at Pottery Mound: The Pottery Mound Textiles in Regional Perspective." In *New Perspectives on Pottery Mound*, edited by Polly Schaafsma, 167–206. Albuquerque: University of New Mexico Press.

Webster, Laurie D., and Micah Loma'omvaya. 2004. "Textiles, Baskets, and Hopi Cultural Identity." In *Identity, Feasting, and the Archaeology of the Greater Southwest: Proceedings of the 2002 Southwest Symposium*, edited by Barbara J. Mills, 74–92. Boulder: University Press of Colorado.

Wheeler, Richard P. 1978. "Bone and Antler Artifacts." In *Bones from Awat'ovi* by Stanley J. Olsen and Richard P. Wheeler, 35–74. Reports of the Awat'ovi Expedition No. 11. Papers of the Peabody Museum of American Anthropology and Ethnology, Vol. 70, No. 1 and 2. Cambridge, MA: Harvard University.

Whiteley, Peter. 2002. "Re-imagining Awat'ovi." In *Archaeologies of the Pueblo Revolt: Identity, Meaning, and Renewal in the Pueblo World*, edited by Robert W. Preucel, 147–66. Albuquerque: University of New Mexico Press.

Wiget, Andrew O. 1982. "Truth and the Hopi: An Historiographic Study of Documented Oral Tradition Concerning the Coming of the Spanish." *Ethnohistory (Columbus, Ohio)* 29 (3): 181–99. http://dx.doi.org/10.2307/481183.

Winship, George P. 1896. *The Coronado Expedition, 1540–1542*. Annual Report of the Bureau of American Ethnology No. 14, Pt. 1. Washington, DC: Bureau of American Ethnology.

Woodbury, Richard B. 1954. *Prehistoric Stone Implements of Northeastern Arizona*. Reports of the Awatovi Expedition No. 6. Papers of the Peabody Museum of American Anthropology and Ethnology, Vol. 34. Cambridge, MA: Harvard University.

Yava, Albert. 1978. *Big Falling Snow: A Tewa-Hopi Indian's Life and Times and the History and Traditions of His People*, edited and annotated by Harold Courlander. New York: Crown Publishers.

FIVE

The Pueblo World Transformed

Alliances, Factionalism, and Animosities in the Northern Rio Grande, 1680–1700

MATTHEW LIEBMANN, ROBERT PREUCEL, AND JOSEPH AGUILAR

INTRODUCTION

Nine years after the famous Pueblo Revolt of 1680, a Zia war captain named Bartolomé de Ojeda gave his Spanish colonial captors a rare glimpse into the indigenous politics of New Mexico. "The Keres, Taos, and Pecos fought against the Tewas and Tanos," reported Ojeda, while "the Keres and Jemez finished off the Piros and Tiwas." The pueblo of Acoma had split into factions. The Zunis battled the Hopis. Apaches "inflicted all the damage they could" at the pueblos of their enemies. And the Utes "waged unceasing war upon the Jemez, Taos, and Picuris, and with even greater vigor upon the Tewas" (Liebmann 2012:169; Twitchell 1914, 2:276–77). In stark contrast with the unity that had characterized the 1680 uprising, the pan-Pueblo alliance had fallen into disarray by the end of the decade. The Pueblos were at war with one another as well as with their Ute and Athapaskan neighbors. The former colony of New Mexico was in chaos. Ojeda's testimony emboldened the exiled Spaniards and set the stage for Don Diego de Vargas's reconquest campaign of 1692.

DOI: 10.5876/9781607325741.c005

More than three centuries later, Ojeda's testament still raises intriguing questions regarding the events that occurred in New Mexico after the Pueblo Revolt. What happened to the pan-Pueblo alliance that facilitated the revolt? How did the independent Native communities interact in the absence of a foreign colonial government? Was Ojeda's testimony accurate? And how did the Native political alliances, animosities, and factions forged during this period affect the outcome of the Spaniards' *reconquista*?

Historical documents relating to the postrevolt period in New Mexico are murky at best. Texts produced by colonial officials (who were exiled in El Paso del Norte, 300 miles south of Santa Fe) provide only a few meager details regarding the events that occurred among the Pueblos during the dozen years between the Pueblo Revolt and the Spanish Reconquest. The testimonies of Pueblo captives suggest that the organizer of the 1680 Revolt, the charismatic prophet and holy man from Ohkay Owingeh (San Juan Pueblo) known as Po'pay, was deposed in 1681 because of his autocratic behavior (Hackett and Shelby 1942:2:274, 296; Sanchez 1983; Liebmann 2012:79). Following the Spaniards' ouster, Po'pay had reportedly toured the pueblos in the manner of a Spanish governor and even exacted tribute from his followers (Twitchell 1914:2:272; Kessell 1979:238). An alliance of Keres, Taos, and Pecos Indians deposed Po'pay and installed Luis Tupatú of Picuris as leader. But by 1688, Tupatú was also overthrown. Po'pay regained power, only to die shortly thereafter and be replaced once again by Tupatú (Twitchell 1914:2:276). Apparently leadership of the Pueblos was contested and particularly volatile during the dozen years of Pueblo independence that followed the revolt.

Beyond these few scant details, however, historical texts are largely silent regarding the years between 1680 and 1692 in New Mexico. After the Spaniards' retreat, the documentary record concerning events in the Pueblo world is frustratingly mute. And for the most part, Native oral traditions regarding this era have not been shared with outsiders (see Thomas E. Sheridan and Stewart B. Koyiyumptewa, chapter 9 in this volume). Fortunately, the events that occurred during this period left an indelible mark in the archaeological record. The things Pueblo people designed, made, lived in, broke, and threw away provide a window into the dozen years between 1680 and the reconquista of the 1690s in New Mexico, telling us what happened to the pan-Pueblo alliance that facilitated the Revolt of 1680. In what follows, we examine changing relations within and among six of the new, postrevolt Pueblo villages established in the wake of the 1680 uprising. We are particularly interested in the "social lives" of these communities. Who founded and lived at these villages? Who were their allies? Who were their enemies? And how did the residents of each village choose to negotiate the Spaniards' return in the 1690s? We develop this archaeological history by combining information from Spanish colonial documents with the archaeological record—particularly data from ceramics and lithics—to discover concordances and reveal contradictions. In the process, we demonstrate the ways that material culture challenges and augments traditional historical accounts, ultimately providing a more detailed and nuanced understanding of the Pueblo Revolt period.

THE MESA VILLAGES

Postrevolt Pueblo Indians' settlement patterns consisted of an extended network of mission villages founded prior to 1680, mesatop redoubts and refugee communities (both newly constructed and reoccupations of older settlements), and appropriated former Spanish colonial settlements. In the northern Rio Grande, people constantly flowed back and forth between these different loci. Some eastern Pueblo individuals took refuge among the western villages of Acoma, Hopi, and Zuni. Still others joined with the Apache and Navajo. These dislocations mark an important moment in Pueblo Indian history, as they gave rise to new social formations that continue to structure Pueblo Indian communities as we know them today (Liebmann and Preucel 2007).

After taking ritual possession of Santa Fe in 1692, Vargas visited each of the Pueblo villages to secure their allegiance (Kessell and Hendricks 1992:509). He began with Cochiti Pueblo because it was the place where Antonio de Otermín's 1681 abortive attempt at reconquest was turned back. Vargas relates: "It was an established opinion that the surrender of the pueblo [Cochiti] would be a victory of greater consequence and triumph than even that of the villa [of Santa Fe]" (Kessell and Hendricks 1992:382–83). For this reason, the general was disturbed to find many villages, including Cochiti, abandoned and their inhabitants living in new mesa-top communities overlooking the Rio Grande Valley.

Over the past decade, the Rio Grande mesa villages have become the subject of intensive archaeological investigations (Liebmann 2012; Liebmann et al. 2005; Preucel 2000, 2002). We are currently analyzing ceramic and lithic data from six of these villages, including Kotyiti (LA 295), Cerro Colorado (LA 2048), Patokwa (LA 96), Astialakwa (LA 1825), Boletsakwa (LA 136), and Tunyo (LA 23). Ceramic data is particularly important because it has the potential to reveal population movements as well as trade and exchange relationships. Similarly, the lithic data (primarily elemental signatures of obsidian attained through XRF analysis) can indicate movements across the landscape and changes in lithic procurement strategies. Here we provide results of our ceramic and lithic analyses from Kotyiti, Patokwa, Boletsakwa, Cerro Colorado, and Astialakwa.

Alliances Revealed through Ceramics

Our ceramic analyses seek to distinguish between pottery brought by the migrants joining these new communities, the production of new pottery by these migrants at these communities, and the trade of pottery between communities. Patricia Capone's petrographic analysis of ceramics from Kotyiti identified five different tempering materials in the Kotyiti glazewares: devitrified tuff, crystalline basalt, igneous porphyritic felsite, vitric tuff, and latite (Capone and Preucel 2002). The largest group, at 59 percent, is devitrified tuff. This result is consistent with other studies (e.g., Warren 1976:B117, 1979:239) and almost certainly indexes ceramics that were locally produced at Kotyiti by Cochiti potters. The second largest group, at 17 percent, is crystalline basalt. This material has been called "Zia basalt" in the literature, and archaeologists generally assume this to have been produced in the Zia district (Warren 1979). Two other materials, igneous porphyritic felsite and vitric tuff, account for about 10 percent each of the Kotyiti glazeware assemblage. The latter may be locally produced. The smallest group, at 3 percent, is represented by latite temper, which is characteristic of San Marcos Pueblo in the Galisteo Basin (Warren 1976:B132). San Marcos people may have brought these ceramics to Kotyiti after the abandonment of their village. Helene Warren (1979:239) found similar results when she examined a sample from Kotyiti, which she interpreted as evidence for Galisteo refugees.

The ceramic assemblage at Kotyiti also contains significant information regarding the local production of pottery by Tewa refugees. Capone's analysis of the Tewa wares identified only two kinds of temper: ash and devitrified tuff. The dominant temper, at 65 percent, is ash. This material is not available in the immediate vicinity of Kotyiti and likely derives from deposits in the Española Valley. It is the dominant tempering material of the Tewa wares from Tunyo (Black Mesa). However, a significant number of Tewa ware sherds from Kotyiti (35 percent) contained devitrified tuff. As noted above, this material is locally available and is widely distributed across the Pajarito Plateau. Given that this is the dominant tempering material for the Kotyiti glazewares, this raises the intriguing possibility that Tewa refugees lived at Kotyiti and made their own pottery using the local tempering materials. Vargas's journals mention reports of Tewa warriors convening at Kotyiti in 1693 (Kessell et al. 1995:410). The presence of tuff-tempered Tewa wares suggests that their presence was not fleeting, but in fact that Tewa people lived alongside their Cochiti hosts at Kotyiti.

After 1680, trade among many of the Pueblos increased. Villages that formerly maintained a calculated social distance from one another now exchanged ceramics regularly. This shift in exchange networks is most clearly exemplified in the ceramic assemblages of the ancestral Jemez villages of Patokwa (founded in 1681) and Boletsakwa (founded in 1683), which document dramatic changes in trade with the neighboring Tewa-speaking Pueblos located to the northeast (Liebmann 2012:150–51).

Prior to the 1680s the Jemez appear to have been a fairly xenophobic lot, at least in terms of ceramic trade—and particularly in their relations with Tewa pueblos. Nonlocal ceramics appear in relatively meager amounts at prerevolt ancestral

Jemez villages, with Tewa wares comprising just .1 percent of the ceramic assemblages from 1300 to 1680 (Elliott 1991:80; Liebmann 2012:156; Reiter 1938:189–92). Stylistic studies of Jemez and Tewa wares support the notion that the Jemez had remarkably little interaction with neighboring regions before 1680 (Graves and Eckert 1998:276; Morley 2002:237–39). The few interactions that did occur were probably bellicose. Relations between the Tewas and Jemez were reportedly so hostile prior to the Pueblo Revolt that in 1634, one Jemez leader proudly wore around his neck a string of human ears from the Tewa warriors he had killed (Hodge et al. 1945:70). After 1680, however, the icy relations among Jemez and Tewa peoples seems to have thawed. The number of Tewa wares increased dramatically in the assemblages of the Jemez pueblos (rising to 5.3 percent overall). In fact, Tewa wares outnumber Jemez Black-on-white at Patokwa and Boletsakwa (a result of the contemporaneous cessation of production of Jemez Black-on-white following the 1680 Revolt, see Liebmann 2012:129–33, 149).

These patterns suggest that Jemez and Tewa people forged new relationships in the wake of the revolt, presumably as a result of Po'pay's unification of the Pueblos in 1680. The Tewa Pueblos were uncompromising in their resistance throughout the revolt and reconquest eras, maintaining stalwart ties with other likeminded tribes during the Spanish interregnum (including the Jemez and the Keres of Kotyiti). The Jemez people appear to have fostered an alliance with the Tewas that was stronger in the sixteen years following the revolt than it had been for three centuries prior to 1680. Thus the ceramic record calls into question the notion that the Jemez were at war with the Tewas during the Spanish interregnum, as suggested by historical accounts (Kessell and Hendricks 1992:26). In fact, in 1694 a coalition of Jemez and Tewa warriors attacked the Zias, demonstrating that the strength of the Jemez-Tewa partnership endured nearly fourteen years after Po'pay's initial uprising (Kessell et al. 1998:320, 798).

The Jemez extended their alliances to other groups in addition to the Tewas during this period as well. Vargas's journals clearly state that Boletsakwa was a multiethnic community, with the Jemez living there alongside allies from Kewa (Santo Domingo Pueblo) (Kessell et al. 1995:416, 445; 1998:403, 406, 586). "Apaches" (probably ancestral Navajo persons) were also lodged at Patokwa alongside their Jemez brethren in 1692–93 (Kessell and Hendricks 1992:521–22). And the population of Kotyiti comprised residents originally from Cochiti, San Felipe, San Marcos, and (as noted above) likely some Tewa allies as well (Capone and Preucel 2002).

Alliances Revealed through Lithics

Ceramic production and trade weren't the only change that occurred among the Pueblos in the wake of 1680. X-ray fluorescence analyses of the obsidian

TABLE 5.1. XRF provenience of obsidian artifacts found at revolt-era sites of the Jemez Valley. Numerals represent number of artifacts recovered from each site traced to that source.

LA No.	Site Name	Cerro del Medio source	Cerro Toledo source	Paliza Canyon source	Bear Springs Peak source	El Rechuelos source	Source Unknown	N (Total)
96	Patokwa (1681–1716)	28	6	4	3	1	0	42
136	Boletsakwa (1683–95)	24	10	14	6	0	0	54
2048	Cerro Colorado (1689–93)	31	6	2	7	0	0	46
1825	Astialakwa (1693–94)	14	3	2	2	0	18	39

artifacts from Astialakwa, Patokwa, Boletsakwa, and Cerro Colorado document concurrent shifts in patterns of lithic procurement during the era of Pueblo independence that allude to the enduring bonds formed during this period as well (Table 5.1). Most conspicuous is the lithic assemblage from Astialakwa, which differs substantially from that of thirty-four other sites in the Jemez region, including Patokwa, Boletsakwa, and Cerro Colorado. From the earliest pre-Hispanic times through the 1680s, Jemez peoples obtained nearly all of their obsidian from four local sources, with obsidian from the Cerro del Medio source being the most prevalent in the assemblages of Patokwa, Boletsakwa, and Cerro Colorado, and eighteen other ancestral Jemez sites.

However, after the return of the Spaniards in 1692 this pattern shifts. At Astialakwa (founded and occupied between November 1693 and July 1694, see Liebmann 2012:191), a substantial number of obsidian artifacts originated from an unknown source that may be located in the Bearhead Peak area to the east of the Jemez Province, a source not previously used by ancestral Jemez peoples (Shackley 2005, 2012). At Astialakwa, 46 percent of the obsidian artifacts (n = 18) were manufactured out of this previously unknown source. Bearhead Peak is an area sacred to the people of Cochiti, and this obsidian source is not only the closest to Kotyiti, but it is farther from Astialakwa than any of the four primary obsidian sources that the Jemez used prior to the 1690s (specifically, the Cerro del Medio, Cerro Toledo, Paliza Canyon, and Bear Springs Peak sources). The most parsimonious explanation for the appearance of this new obsidian at Astialakwa is that people migrating between Astialakwa and Kotyiti procured it as they traveled between these villages. The most likely scenarios involve Jemez warriors obtaining the this previously unused obsidian while traveling to aid in the defense of Kotyiti when it was attacked in April of 1694, Kotyiti warriors bringing it to Astialakwa as they aided in the defense of that village when it was attacked in July of that same year, or both. Either way, this conspicuous shift in obsidian procurement is a material index of the alliances forged between the Jemez of Astialakwa and the Keres of Kotyiti during the Pueblo Revolt era.

ON PUEBLO FACTIONALISM

Bartolomé de Ojeda's testimony suggests that the Pueblo world was not one of unvarying alliances during the Spanish interregnum, however. Numerous lines of evidence, from both documentary and archaeological data, suggest that factionalism was endemic to Pueblo communities between 1680 and 1694. Indeed, Tewa anthropologist Ed Dozier notes that factionalism is a persistent condition among contemporary Pueblo tribes. He links this phenomenon to the "authoritarian, totalitarian characteristics" of Pueblo societies, noting that "opposition to the compulsory dictates of the Pueblo authorities . . . [has] resulted in frequent factional disputes" from pre-Hispanic through modern times (Dozier 1966:175).

The study of Pueblo factionalism has a long history in Southwestern anthropology. Numerous scholars have reported on the prevalence of factionalism in different Pueblo communities (Dozier 1966; Fenton 1957; Fox 1961; French 1949; Pandey 1967; Whitman 1940, 1947). This research was part of a broader focus on the adaptive role of temporary political conflicts on the survival of cultural groups. Commenting on the increasing importance of factionalism as an anthropological concept in the late 1950s, Ted Lewellen (2003:104) noted, "It was evident that in certain circumstances factions could be more adaptive than could conventional politics in organizing and channeling political conflict, especially during periods of rapid social change." In some ways, this work can be seen as a corrective to Ruth Benedict's (1934) "culture and personality" thesis of Pueblo people as "Apollonian," passive, and peaceful.

More recently, scholars have reconceptualized factionalism as a dynamic social process (Levy and Pepper 1992; Norcini 2005; Whiteley 1983, 1988). These studies hold that factions are contingent political groupings centered on specific social issues and based upon competition over new resources. Significantly, these scholars emphasize the agency of Pueblo people in assessing local political conditions and charting their own futures. For example, Peter Whiteley (1983:41–44) has shown that both of the factions associated with the famous Orayvi split sought to resist oppression and acculturation by Americans. Similarly, Marilyn Norcini (2005) has studied the political process resulting in the adoption of the 1935 Santa Clara Constitution. She suggests that indigenous strategies have been underrepresented in the literature because of the neglect of local significance and meanings.

Archaeological studies have documented the existence of Pueblo factionalism in pre-Hispanic and historical contexts alike (Herr and Clark 1997; Mills 2004).

Van Dyke (2008:344) suggests that there were several decades of competition between ritual leaders in Chaco Canyon that resulted in some moving to Aztec to establish a new ritual center. Similarly, Wendy Ashmore (2007:194) speculates that the collapse of Chaco was instigated by factionalism within a corporate leadership organization. David Brugge (1969:191) links this pattern of factionalism to the historic period, arguing that "the effects of conquest, including forced conversion and subjugation to white rule, did not ameliorate the condition in any way, but supplied new issues around which the old factions could rally."

From our perspective, the Pueblo Revolt period is a critical historical context, ripe for the study of factionalism. While there is no question that factionalism is endemic to many small-scale societies, we believe that there are important differences in the factionalism that emerged in precolonial and colonial situations. To put it more clearly, Spanish colonialism raised the ante. As a complex system that rapidly incorporated non-state actors into state-level societies, Spanish colonialism engendered new kinds of factions in its colonies in the Americas and beyond. In the Southwest, it produced a variety of crosscutting social and political networks linking Pueblo and non-Pueblo, and Native and non-Native peoples.

Historical sources make clear the fact that Po'pay behaved increasingly despotically in the year following the famed Pueblo uprising (Liebmann 2012:77–79). Such despotism is a factor specifically cited by Dozier in the fomenting of Pueblo factionalism. It is easy to imagine other Pueblo leaders following Po'pay's lead during this period, as many of these leaders were likely part of his retinue before he was deposed. At Patokwa, for example, a rift seems to have formed in the community between 1681 and 1683. Ultimately the community split in two as a result of this factionalism, with one group leaving Patokwa. This splinter group traveled approximately ten kilometers to the east where its members founded the new village of Boletsakwa. Tree-ring dates collected from the roof beams of Boletsakwa confirm that the site was constructed in 1683 (Robinson et al. 1972:45).

The Jemez were not the only Pueblo group to split into factions in the wake of the 1680 uprising. Factionalism seems to have characterized Isleta and Kewa during this period as well (Hackett and Shelby 1942:2:357; Kessell et al. 1995:113, 416, 445). The divided nature of postrevolt Pueblos was most clearly evident at Pecos, where a pro-Spanish faction had opposed a group of anticolonialists since the time of Coronado in the 1540s. By the mid-seventeenth century the rift had cleaved the residents of Pecos into two distinct settlements, with the Christian contingent perching in the shadow of the mission church and the more conservative, "traditional" bloc remaining in the old north section of the village. During the revolt the Christian citizens of Pecos smuggled the resident friar out of harm's way, while the "traditionalist" faction killed a second priest. Even with their colonizers gone after the Revolt of 1680, Pecos remained a pueblo divided (Kidder 1917, 1958:108; Kessell 1979:7, 26, 232–46).

The factionalized nature of the Pueblos during the Spanish interregnum was perhaps best summed up by a Tewa man from Tesuque Pueblo whom the Spaniards captured in late 1681. When asked about the Pueblo peoples' attitudes regarding the possible return of their former colonizers, he confided that "they were of different minds regarding it, because some said that if the Spaniards should come [the Pueblos] would have to fight to the death, and others said that in the end [the Spaniards] must come and gain the kingdom because they were sons of the land and had grown up with the natives" (Hackett and Shelby 1942:2:235). Initially this incipient factionalism was based around pro- and anti-Spanish contingents. But as time passed, these communal rifts were exacerbated by the raids of Utes, Navajos, and Apaches (Liebmann 2012:95–98). As the testimony of another *indio ladino* (a Spanish-speaking Native who had been educated in a mission by Franciscan friars) indicated to the Spaniards in the early 1680s: "He said that it is true that there are various opinions among them, most of them believing that they would have to fight to the death with the said Spaniards, keeping them out. Others, who were not so guilty, said, 'We are not to blame, and we must await [the Spaniards] in our pueblos.' And he said that when the hostile Apaches came they denounced the leaders of the rebellion, saying that when the Spaniards were among them they lived in security and quiet, and afterwards with much uneasiness" (Hackett and Shelby 1942:2:240). Such seems to have been the case at the Jemez village of Patokwa, where tensions came to a head in 1683. Ultimately the community of Patokwa cleaved in two, with one group leaving to form the new settlement of Boletsakwa. The process of one village splitting into two (termed "schismatic factionalism") appears to have been a particularly common response to intra-Pueblo dissent in pre-Hispanic times, when migration and settlement were unencumbered by the shackles of colonialism (Dozier 1966:172; Siegel and Beals 1960:394). Still, schismatic factionalism has persisted among the Pueblos into modern times, exemplified in the famous Orayvi split of 1906 at Hopi (Cameron 1999; Whiteley 1988, 2008). This pattern was reestablished in the 1680s, when the dissident group from Patokwa split off to found Boletsakwa.

Animosities

The factionalism that was so prevalent within Pueblo communities in the wake of the revolt was detrimental to the maintenance of the pan-Pueblo alliance forged by Po'pay in 1680. Yet it paled in comparison with the disruptions caused by the outright hostilities that developed between some of the Pueblos at this time. Maybe the biggest rift formed between the Keres-speaking Zias and Santa Anas with their Tewa neighbors to the north. Again, ceramics provide insight into the relations among these groups both before and after 1680. The Zias seem to have maintained steady if not voluminous trade relations with the Tewas prior the revolt, with Tewa wares comprising between 2 and 4 percent of prerevolt Zia ceramic assemblages (Ellis 1966:807–10). After 1680, however, this trade ceased. While Tewa wares increased dramatically in the assemblages of the nearby Jemez pueblos, at the Zia-Santa Ana refuge of Cerro Colorado, Tewa ceramics are virtually nonexistent, composing just .1 percent (one sherd) of the total ceramic assemblage.

Ceramic and documentary evidence suggests that the Zias and Santa Anas became alienated from the Tewas by the late 1680s. Although we do not have ceramic data to assess the relationship between these groups during the early years of the revolt period (from 1680 to 1689), it appears that by the time the Zias and Santa Anas were living at Cerro Colorado (1689–94) they were no longer in regular contact with the Tewas, as evidenced by the nearly complete lack of Tewa pottery found there. The cause of this rift is unknown, though it is tempting to speculate that the Zias' lackluster participation in the 1680 uprising and subsequent reluctance to follow Po'pay's commands in the wake of the revolt (leaving their church intact and not killing the priest) may have earned their reprobation from the Tewas (Liebmann 2011:206–11). In fact, the Zias reportedly offered their prospective obedience to the Spaniards just a year after the revolt, in the event that the Spaniards would have been successful in reconquering the region in 1681 (Hackett and Shelby 1942:2:387). This course of action would have earned Po'pay's reproach and was likely the origin of the rift between the Tewas and the Zia and Santa Ana residents of Cerro Colorado.

CONCLUSIONS

Spanish historical documents indicate that factionalism and hostilities erupted among the Pueblos during the postrevolt period. However, our results reveal that an enduring alliance existed among the Tewa, Jemez, and Keres of Kotyiti. Much of the Tewa pottery at Kotyiti was likely made by Tewa refugees, some of whom may have come with Juan Griego, a leader from Ohkay Owingeh. The increase in Tewa pottery at the Jemez sites of Astialakwa, Patokwa, and Boletsakwa indicates more frequent interactions between Jemez and Tewa people, if not the presence of actual Tewa people at those villages. Vargas learned of this alliance during his siege at Tunyo. This coalition-of-the-unwilling also included people from Kewa, and several accounts refer to Kewa people living with the Jemez on the mesas (at Boletsakwa). These findings seem to contradict Ojeda's statements that "the Keres" were at war with "the Tewas" during the late seventeenth century. Ojeda's homogenization of linguistic-ethnic groups as unitary federations glosses over the subtleties and nuances of these disputes. It is true that friction, if not outright conflict, existed between the Tewas and *some* Keres people—notably the Zias and Santa Anas. But the Keres of Kotyiti, as well as those living in the Jemez Province, were allies of the Tewas during this period. While this superficial glossing could have resulted from Ojeda's limited purview, more likely it reflects the less-nuanced ear of a Spanish scribe who recorded the gist of his testimony but omitted important caveats.

Other pueblos appear to have joined and left this coalition at various times throughout the 1680s–90s. The Tano pueblos of San Lázaro and San Cristóbal left the Ohkay (San Juan) people at Embudo to join the main Tewa force at Tunyo. However, the San Felipe people at Kotyiti fell out with the Cochiti leadership and left the community to build their own mesa village. Strong ties persisted among many of the other Keres groups. Vargas was particularly worried that the Keres of Cochiti would succeed in enlisting the support of the Keres of Zia, San Felipe, and Santa Ana (Kessell et al. 1998:138). Thus although there was some inter-Pueblo conflict during the revolt era, the core of resistance—the Tewa/Jemez/Kotyiti alliance—appears to have persisted throughout the Spanish interregnum.

To return to our original question, why did the pan-Pueblo alliance break down after the Pueblo Revolt? In truth, the alliance didn't so much break down after 1680 as it was continually renegotiated by Pueblo leaders in response to changing needs within each postrevolt community. The instability of centralized leadership is understandable since there was no Pueblo tradition of a single supreme leader (Beninato 1990). The characterization of Po'pay as the primary instigator served the Spaniards' purpose of identifying a scapegoat, but it also neglects the agency of other important leaders, such as Alonso Catiti, El Zepe, Luis Cunixu, and Antonio Malacate. These individuals played key roles in the planning and execution of the revolt. Significantly, these leaders made their own decisions to ally with or oppose the Spanish colonizers during the reconquest. Ultimately, those decisions shaped the course of the Spanish-Pueblo relations for the next century and beyond.

REFERENCES CITED

Ashmore, Wendy. 2007. "Building Social History at Pueblo Bonito: Footnotes to a Biography of Place." In *The Architecture of Chaco Canyon, New Mexico*, edited by Steven Lekson, 179–98. Salt Lake City: University of Utah Press.

Benedict, Ruth. 1934. *Patterns of Culture*. New York: Routledge and Kegan Paul.

Beninato, Stefanie. 1990. "Popé, Pose-yemu, and Naranjo: A New Look at Leadership in the Pueblo Revolt. of 1680." *New Mexico Historical Review* 65 (4): 417–35.

Brugge, David M. 1969. "Pueblo Factionalism and External Relations." *Ethnohistory (Columbus, Ohio)* 16 (2): 191–200. http://dx.doi.org/10.2307/481305.

Cameron, Catherine M. 1999. *Hopi Dwellings: Architectural Change at Orayvi*. Tucson: University of Arizona Press.

Capone, Patricia, and Robert W. Preucel. 2002. "Ceramic Semiotics: Women, Pottery, and Social Meanings at Kotyiti Pueblo." In *Archaeologies of the Pueblo Revolt: Identity, Meaning and Renewal in the Pueblo World*, edited by Robert W. Preucel, 99–113. Albuquerque: University of New Mexico Press.

Dozier, Edward P. 1966. *Hano, a Tewa Indian Community in Arizona*. New York: Holt, Rinehart and Winston.

Elliott, Michael L. 1991. "Pueblo at the Hot Place: Archaeological Excavations at Giusewa Pueblo and San Jose de los Jemez Mission, Jemez State Monument, Jemez Springs, New. Mexico." Ms. on file. Santa Fe: New Mexico State Monuments.

Ellis, Florence H. 1966. "The Immediate History of Zia Pueblo as Derived from Excavation in Refuse. Deposits." *American Antiquity* 31 (6): 806–11. http://dx.doi.org/10.2307/2694453.

Fenton, W. N. 1957. *Factionalism at Taos Pueblo, New Mexico*. Washington, DC: US Government Printing Office.

Fox, J. R. 1961. "Veterans and Factions in Pueblo Society." *Man* 61 (9): 173–76. http://dx.doi.org/10.2307/2797406.

French, David H. 1949. *Factionalism in Isleta Pueblo*. Seattle: University of Washington Press.

Graves, William M., and Suzanne L. Eckert. 1998. "Decorated Ceramic Distributions and Ideological Developments in the Northern and Central Rio Grande Valley, New Mexico." In *Migration and Reorganization: The Pueblo IV Period in the American Southwest*, edited by Katherine A. Spielmann, 263–84. Arizona State University Anthropological Research Papers No. 51. Tempe: Arizona State University.

Hackett, Charles W., ed. and Charmion C. Shelby, trans. 1942. *Revolt of the Pueblo Indians of New Mexico, and Otermin's Attempted Reconquest, 1680–1682*. 2 vols. Coronado Cuarto Centennial Publications, 1540–1949. Albuquerque: University of New Mexico Press.

Herr, Sarah, and Jeffery J. Clark. 1997. "Patterns in the Pathways: Early Historic Migrations in the Rio Grande Pueblos." *Kiva* 62 (4): 365–89. http://dx.doi.org/10.1080/00231940.1997.11758341.

Hodge, Frederick W., George P. Hammond, and Agapito Rey, eds. 1945. *Fray Alonso de Benavides' Revised Memorial of 1634*. Albuquerque: University of New Mexico Press.

Kessell, John R. 1979. *Kiva, Cross, and Crown: The Pecos Indians and New Mexico 1540–1840*. Albuquerque: University of New Mexico Press.

Kessell, John R., and Rick Hendricks, eds. 1992. *By Force of Arms: The Journals of don Diego de Vargas, 1691–1693*. Albuquerque: University of New Mexico Press.

Kessell, John R., Rick Hendricks, and Meredith D. Dodge, eds. 1995. *To the Royal Crown Restored: The Journals of Don Diego de Vargas, New. Mexico 1692–1694*. Albuquerque: University of New Mexico Press.

Kessell, John R., Rick Hendricks, and Meredith D. Dodge, eds. 1998. *Blood on the Boulders: The Journals of Don Diego de Vargas, New Mexico, 1694 1697*. 2 vols. Albuquerque: University of New Mexico Press.

Kidder, Alfred V. 1917. *The Old North Pueblo of Pecos: The Condition of the Main Pecos Ruin.* Papers of the School of American Archaeology, No. 38. Santa Fe: Archaeological Institute of America.

Kidder, Alfred V. 1958. *Pecos, New Mexico: Archaeological Notes.* Papers of the Robert S. Peabody Foundation for Archaeology, No. 5. New Haven: Phillips Academy.

Levy, Jerrold E., and Barbara Pepper. 1992. *Orayvi Revisited: Social Stratification in an "Egalitarian" Society.* Santa Fe: School of American Research Press.

Lewellen, Ted C. 2003. *Political Anthropology: An Introduction.* New York: Praeger Publishers.

Liebmann, Matthew. 2011. "The Best of Times, the Worst of Times: Pueblo Resistance and Accommodation. during the Spanish Reconquista of New Mexico." In *Enduring Conquests. Rethinking the Archaeology of Resistance to Spanish Colonialism in the Americas*, edited by Matthew Liebmann and Melissa S. Murphy, 199–221. Santa Fe: School of Advanced Research Press.

Liebmann, Matthew. 2012. *Revolt: An Archaeological History of Pueblo Resistance and Revitalization in 17th Century New Mexico.* Tucson: University of Arizona Press.

Liebmann, Matthew, T. J. Ferguson, and Robert W Preucel. 2005. "Pueblo Settlement, Architecture, and Social Change in the Pueblo Revolt Era, A.D. 1680–1696." *Journal of Field Archaeology* 30 (1): 45–60. http://dx.doi.org/10.1179/009346905791072459.

Liebmann, Matthew, and Robert W. Preucel. 2007. "The Archaeology of the Pueblo Revolt and the Formation of the Modern Pueblo World." *Kiva* 73 (2): 195–217. http://dx.doi.org/10.1179/kiv.2007.73.2.006.

Mills, Barbara J. 2004. "The Establishment and Defeat of Hierarchy: Inalienable Possession and the History of Collective Prestige Structures in the Pueblo Southwest." *American Anthropologist* 106 (2): 238–51. http://dx.doi.org/10.1525/aa.2004.106.2.238.

Morley, Selma E. 2002. "Stylistic Variation and Group Self-Identity: Evidence from the Rio Grande. Pueblos." PhD dissertation, Department of Anthropology, University of California, Los Angeles.

Norcini, Marilyn. 2005. "The Political Process of Factionalism and Self-Governance at Santa Clara, Pueblo, New Mexico." *Proceedings of the American Philosophical Society* 149 (4): 544–90.

Pandey, Triloki N. 1967. *Factionalism in a Southwestern Pueblo.* PhD dissertation, Department of Anthropology, University of Chicago.

Preucel, Robert W. 2000. "Living on the Mesa: Hanat Kotyiti, a Post-Revolt Cochiti Community in the Northern Rio Grande." *Expedition* 42 (1): 8–17.

Preucel, Robert W., ed. 2002. *Archaeologies of the Pueblo Revolt: Identity, Meaning and Renewal in the Pueblo World.* Albuquerque: University of New Mexico Press.

Reiter, Paul. 1938. *The Jemez Pueblo of Unshagi, New Mexico, with Notes on the Earlier. Excavations at "Amoxiumqua" and Giusewa.* Monographs of the School of American

Research No. 6. Santa Fe: University of New Mexico and the School of American Research.

Robinson, William J., John W. Hannah, and Bruce G. Harrill. 1972. *Tree-Ring Dates from New Mexico I, O, U: Central Rio Grande Area*. Tucson: Laboratory of Tree-Ring Research, University of Arizona.

Sanchez, Jane C. 1983. "Spanish-Indian Relations during the Otermín Administration, 1677–1683." *New Mexico Historical Review* 58 (2): 133–51.

Shackley, M. Steven. 2005. *Obsidian: Geology and Archaeology in the North American Southwest*. Tucson: University of Arizona Press.

Shackley, M. Steven. 2012. "Source Provenience of Obsidian Artifacts from Astialakwa (LA 1825) Jemez. Valley, New Mexico." Unpublished manuscript in possession of the authors.

Siegel, Bernard J, and Alan R Beals. 1960. "Pervasive Factionalism." *American Anthropologist* 62 (3): 394–417. http://dx.doi.org/10.1525/aa.1960.62.3.02a00020.

Twitchell, Ralph Emerson. 1914. *The Spanish Archives of New Mexico*. 2 vols. Cedar Rapids: Torch Press.

Van Dyke, Ruth M. 2008. *The Chaco Experience: Landscape and Ideology at the Center Place*. Santa Fe: School of American Research Press.

Warren, A. Helene. 1976. "The Ceramics and Mineral Resources of LA 70 and the Cochiti Area." In *Archaeological Excavations at Pueblo del Encierro, LA 70, Cochiti Dam Salvage. Project, Cochiti, New Mexico, Final Report: 1954–1965 Field Seasons*, edited by D. H. Snow, B1–184. Santa Fe: Laboratory of Anthropology Notes, Museum of New Mexico.

Warren, A. Helene. 1979. "Historic Pottery of the Cochiti Reservoir Area." In *Adaptive Change in the Northern Rio Grande Valley*. Archaeological Investigations. in the Cochiti Reservoir, New Mexico, vol. 4, , edited by J. Biella and R. Chapman, 235–45. Albuquerque: University of New Mexico.

Whiteley, Peter M. 1983. *Third Mesa Hopi Social Structural Dynamics and Sociocultural Change: The View from Bacavi*. PhD dissertation, Department of Anthropology, University of New Mexico, Albuquerque.

Whiteley, Peter M. 1988. *Bacavi: Journey to Reed Springs*. Flagstaff: Northland Press.

Whiteley, Peter M. 2008. *The Orayvi Split: A Hopi Transformation. Anthropological Papers of the American Museum of Natural History, No. 87*. New York: American Museum of Natural History.

Whitman, William. 1940. *The San Ildefonso of New Mexico*. New York: D. Appleton-Century.

Whitman, William. 1947. *The Pueblo Indians of San Ildefonso: A Changing Culture*. New York: Columbia University Press.

SIX

Comanche New Mexico

The Eighteenth Century

SEVERIN FOWLES, JIMMY ARTERBERRY,
LINDSAY MONTGOMERY, AND HEATHER ATHERTON

INTRODUCTION

Traditional accounts of the eighteenth-century world in the American Southwest often make reference to "Spanish New Mexico." Spaniards may have been wildly outnumbered by the surrounding indigenous communities, and their political control may have been patchy and tenuous. But this rarely prevents scholars from drawing a circle around the region and labeling it Spanish. A European colony, it is assumed, is still a European colony, even if it is a very small and powerless one.

Increasingly, however, this position is coming under fire. Some of the strongest critiques have emerged within Pueblo communities, many of which now openly reject the language of "Spanish conquest." Europeans, they observe, may have invaded the Southwest at the end of the sixteenth century—and then again at the end of the seventeenth century following the Pueblo Revolt— but they never "conquered" the region in any meaningful sense of the term. With respect to the eighteenth century in particular, some Pueblo commentators are quick to point out that Spaniards were economically and militarily

DOI: 10.5876/9781607325741.c006

dependent on indigenous communities, with little actual power to impose their will (see John G. Douglass and William M. Graves, chapter 1 in this volume). Certainly the metal-clad immigrants from the south rattled their sabers, made proclamations, and founded settlements (many of which, during the mid-eighteenth century, remained so weak as to be periodically abandoned), but asserting dominance is not the same thing as achieving dominance. An aspirational colonialism is merely that. From this perspective, we are still looking at a "Pueblo New Mexico" in which Europeans participated but as neither the sole nor even the primary authors. Pueblo critics, in other words, are challenging us to reimagine the eighteenth century as a time of indigenous history-making, the goal being to rewrite this early chapter of the "Historic period" as a veritable "Pueblo V period," that much neglected extension of the Pecos Classification recently championed by Matthew Liebmann (2012a).[1] Indeed, the new trend among the Rio Grande Pueblos to formally reinstate indigenous toponyms—to take down signs for "San Juan Pueblo," for instance, and replace them with signs for "Ohkay Owingeh"—might be interpreted as contributions to this reimagining.

Historians, for their part, have also sought alternatives to Eurocentric accounts of the colonial Southwest. Since the 1970s, contributors to the so-called New Indian History have cast a spotlight on the perspectives and political agendas of native actors in the tug-and-pull of colonial power struggles, redressing a long-standing tendency to typecast American Indian societies as anachronistic obstacles to Euro-American progress whose primary discursive role was to stand in for a primordial wildness that had no choice but to succumb to the inexorable advance of civilization.[2] Indeed, old myths of the vanishing Indian—however much they still circulate in popular White discourse—are themselves vanishing from much academic writing. And even if the narrative forms and framing categories within the New Indian History remain decidedly Euro-American in their overall orientation (see Mihesuah 1998), there can be little question that the attention to native protagonists offers an important rejoinder to earlier accounts.

Nowhere is this more spectacularly evident than in contemporary commentary on the political history of the Comanches, that most notoriously militant of Native American tribes. The Comanche past is extraordinary: at the start of the colonial era, their ancestors were Shoshonean hunter-gatherers living in small camps dispersed throughout northern Colorado and Wyoming; during the final decade of the seventeenth century, they acquired horses and quickly remade themselves into the most skilled equestrian warriors and long-distance traders in North America; by the mid-eighteenth century, they had ousted the Apache from the Southern Plains and emerged as a continental power; and into the mid-nineteenth century, they were key players in an expanding regional economy of horses, slaves, hides, and guns that eventually extended from the Canadian Plains deep into northern Mexico (see John 1996; Kavanagh 1996). Unlike many other native groups, then, the Comanches have always been seen as agents of Southwestern history in the nonnative imagination. However, until quite recently their agency was inevitably written about as a wild barbarism bent on destruction. Most historical commentary, that is, has portrayed the tribe as possessing a *negative* agency that didn't so much pursue goals as frustrate those of others—foiling the northern expansion of Spain in the eighteenth century, upending the lives of Apaches and other native occupants of the Southern Plains, and delaying the westward expansion of the United States well into the nineteenth century. As the title of one early work put it, historians studied "The Comanche Barrier to South Plains Settlement" (Richardson 1933).

The older specter of negative agency hasn't gone away. On the contrary, the most widely read recent history of the tribe is S. C. Gwynne's *Empire of the Summer Moon*, a New York Times best seller that recounts Comanche history with all the dark zeal for primitive violence that one finds in mid-twentieth century Westerns such as *The Searchers* (1956, directed by John Ford). In Gwynne's pen, the Comanches transformed the Southwest into a veritable war zone, "an open and bleeding wound, a smoking ruin littered with corpses and charred chimneys, a place where anarchy and torture killings had replaced the rule of law, where Indians and especially Comanches raided at will" (Gwynne 2010:3). No doubt this remains the White public's dominant image. But within contemporary academic scholarship, the look of Comanche history is changing rapidly, primarily due to the efforts of Pekka Hämäläinen, whose *The Comanche Empire* presents us with a bold new vision of the Southwest in which the dominant actors were neither Hispano nor Pueblo, but Comanche. "When Comanches subjected Texas and New Mexico to systematic raiding of horses, mules, and captives, draining wide sectors of those productive resources, they in effect turned the [European] colonies into [Native American] imperial possessions," he suggests. "That Spanish Texas and New Mexico remained unconquered by Comanches is not a historical fact; it is a matter of perspective" (Hämäläinen 2008:5).

What are we to make of the fact that some historians now write of an eighteenth-century Comanche conquest of New Mexico—of a "Comanche New Mexico," as it were, rather than a Spanish or Pueblo New Mexico? How, in particular, are we to understand Hämäläinen's provocative notion of a reversed colonialism in which European colonists suddenly found *themselves* in the position of the colonized? And how, in the end, are we, as archaeologists, to respond to the new vision of a veritable Comanche empire in the Southwest? How indeed, when a century of research on the archaeology of colonial New Mexico still hasn't produced a single published example of a "Comanche" site in the region?[3] Could it be that we've simply missed the archaeological traces of an entire Native American empire that has been there all along, unacknowledged, just beneath our nose?

There are many issues to deal with here, not least the notion of "empire" itself. A number of historians have written loosely about a Comanche empire in the Southwest, but Hämäläinen takes this idea seriously, and he does so for at least three reasons. First, to speak of a Comanche imperial project is to radicalize the question of native agency, pushing the agenda of the New Indian History to its furthest extent. It is not just that Native Americans were actors who pursued their own local goals in the face of European colonialism; now we are encouraged to imagine far bolder Native American actors with geopolitical aspirations and strategies that rivaled and sometimes eclipsed those of Europeans.

Second, the notion of a Comanche empire further challenges us to expand our understanding of "empire" as a cross-cultural analytical category. Clearly, the Comanches were not attempting to build a regional polity following Roman or Incan models. They were not, in other words, interested in conquering foreign territories so as to turn them into Comanche provinces ruled by Comanche governors. "Their aim," proposes Hämäläinen (2008:4–5), "was not to conquer and colonize, but to coexist, control, and exploit. Whereas more traditional imperial powers ruled by making things rigid and predictable, Comanches ruled by keeping them fluid and malleable." If the Comanches can be said to have ruled an empire, then it was more of an economic than a political empire. Thousands of mounted Comanche soldiers regularly maneuvered throughout the Plains, New Mexico, Texas, and northern Mexico to engage in a complicated and ever-shifting combination of diplomacy and warfare. But their goal was to extract resources and maintain access to markets, rather than to obtain political subjugation. In this sense, one might draw a parallel with the so-called Mongolian shadow empires of the Eurasian steppe (Barfield 2001), though Hämäläinen's central point seems to be that we should seek to understand the alterity of Comanche political organization on its own terms, without reducing it to existing anthropological or historical models derived from other cultural traditions.

Third, and perhaps most important, the notion of a Comanche empire pushes back against the persistent tendency to portray American westward expansion during the nineteenth century as a civilizing process whereby order was introduced into an organizational void. Indeed, Hämäläinen argues that the regional might of the Comanches was actively forgotten precisely in order to legitimize the American takeover of the West. The result was an insidious form of national amnesia that began to set in on the heels of the Treaty of Guadalupe Hidalgo in 1848 and then, more deeply, after the Comanches finally surrendered to the US military at Fort Sill in 1875. "Comanches ruled the Southwest for well over a century," concludes Hämäläinen, "but they left behind no marks of their dominance. There were no deserted fortresses or decaying monuments to remind the [American] newcomers of the complex imperial history they were displacing. Envisioning a new kind of empire, one of cities, railroads, agricultural hinterlands, and real estate, Americans set out to tame, commodify, and carve up the land . . . With each new layer of American progress, the memory of the Comanches and their former power grew dimmer" (Hämäläinen 2008:342). Again, his suggestion is that this erasure of Comanche history has been an implicit part of America's own imperialistic project (see also DeLay 2008). Thus, by rereading colonial archives to bring this indigenous empire to light, revisionist historians could be said to participate in a broader postcolonial critique.

TOWARD AN ARCHAEOLOGY OF COMANCHE NEW MEXICO

Our goal in this chapter is to explore how archaeology might contribute to this revisionist effort. Whether or not one is willing to take the notion of a Comanche empire seriously, there is no question that the tribe exerted a strong influence on both native and nonnative communities across an impressive swath of North America during the eighteenth and early nineteenth centuries. And while historians' reliance on written colonial archives may lead them to conclude that the Comanches "left behind no marks of their dominance," we take this apparent invisibility as a beginning point for research—as an archaeological challenge to uncover whatever material traces may still exist.

We are particularly interested in the Comanche presence in New Mexico during the early eighteenth century, at a time when the tribe was still developing its equestrian adaptation and readying itself for a takeover of the Southern Plains, which would become its base of operations for more than a century beginning in the 1740s. During this formative period in the emergence of Comanche identity, the tribe's relationship with the northern Rio Grande Pueblo communities was vital. The Taos region, in particular, could be said to stand at the heart of Comanche ethnogenesis. This was a region with extensive pasturage for large herds of Spanish horses, which the Comanches' relatives, the Utes, were poised to acquire after the Pueblos drove the Spanish out in 1680. As the horse made its way north through native trade networks into Comanche hands, new economic and military potentials were unleashed. Within a generation, the distribution of power in the northern Rio Grande was profoundly transformed. Returning to the region at the end of the seventeenth century, the Spanish discovered that both they and the Pueblo communities now had to contend with the repeated invasions of a new kind of *indios bárbaros*: mounted nomads who could strike with great speed and military agility over long distances.

The first potential written references to the Comanche appear on French maps from the 1680s, during the period of Spanish exile. The French regularly reported the presence of a group known as the Padouca at the northeastern edge of New

Mexico, often in the vicinity of the headwaters of the Arkansas River, not far from Taos. In later mid-eighteenth century documents, Padouca was clearly used by the French as a term for Comanche—or perhaps for a particular Comanche band—but historians have long disagreed over whether the earliest mentions of "Padouca" might have instead referred to an Apache band or simply to those living in the Arkansas headwaters region, regardless of language and culture (see Secoy 1951). We consider this as an open question, complicated of course by two of the central facts of the colonial period: first, many indigenous identities were undergoing substantial transformation and, second, colonial authorities often knew almost nothing about indigenous groups, particularly about the highly nomadic groups whose home territories were far from colonial settlements.[4]

Some ancestral Comanches surely began to visit northern New Mexico during the late seventeenth century, most likely in the company of the Ute, whose long history of occupation immediately northwest of Taos would have given them both an intimate knowledge of the landscape and established access to Pueblo trade networks. The subsequent ethnic divisions between various Numic-speaking tribes (Ute, Paiute, Shoshone, Comanche, etc.) would have then just been emerging, as the return of the Spanish to the New Mexico and the spread of European technologies impacted native worlds throughout the region. Indeed, while some archaeologists have sought to naturalize Comanche military aggression—presenting it as a deeply precolonial pattern that was merely accentuated by the adoption of the horse (Sutton 1986)—Blackhawk (2007) makes a compelling argument that Comanche ethnogenesis must be understood as a complex response to a new landscape of colonial violence that rippled out from Spanish New Mexico, creating new possibilities and economic rationales for raiding and captive-taking.

Be that as it may, the greater Taos area was clearly a key locus of self-fashioning for the Comanches at the start of the eighteenth century. The tribe's early horse herds were primarily obtained from this region. In fact, local Hispano oral traditions still include stories about how the initial Comanche herds were built up through raids on settlements a short distance south of the modern town of Taos. Insofar as the tribe's historic identity is inseparable from an equestrian lifestyle, one might say that Taos was where the Comanches truly became "Comanche."

Full-blown Comanche militarism also saw its beginnings in the Taos region. In 1706, en route to El Cuartelejo to retrieve the remnants of the Picuris Tribe, Juan de Ulibarri stopped at Taos Pueblo and learned from the local leaders that the threat of Ute and Comanche aggression was palpably felt. "They were very certain that the infidel enemies of the Ute and Comanche tribe were about to come to make an attack upon this pueblo," Ulibarri wrote (Thomas 1935:61). Marching a short distance northeast of Taos, Ulibarri also learned that combined Ute and Comanche attacks had taken a heavy toll on Apache settlements (*rancherías*). This marked the beginning of a drawn-out competition between the Comanche and the Apache that would eventually lead to the latter's retreat from the Southern Plains.

Comanchería proper was more or less established during the 1740s. The confederated Comanche bands, greatly enlarged by the influx of captives and refugees, secured control of the Southern Plains' vast grasslands, which became the ecological foundation for the two cornerstones of the Comanche economy: buffalos and horses (see Hämäläinen 2010). By mid-century, the Comanche had split with their former Ute allies and assumed a position of dominance across a large region from Wyoming down into northern Mexico. Taos continued to serve as a strategic center for Comanche economic and political ambitions, however, both as a major market—during the 1700s, the Taos trade fairs were rivaled only by those at Pecos Pueblo—and as a target for continued raids. "Whether they are at peace or at war," wrote Fray Francisco Atanasio Domínguez (1956:112) in 1776, "the Comanches always carry off all they want, by purchase in peace and by theft in war." The Comanches were so comfortable navigating the Taos landscape during this period that they sometimes brought over a thousand horses from their herd to feed on the lush grassy meadows near Taos Pueblo when the dry season limited pasturage on the Plains (Domínguez 1956:111). In contrast, the *vecinos* living in the region were notably constrained in their use of the landscape and its resources; throughout much of the mid-eighteenth century, few had horses at all and the threat of Comanche raiding forced most of the colonists to live within the walls of Taos Pueblo for protection (Jenkins 1966:98).

There is no question that the Comanches were regular visitors to the Taos region during the critical period when they were emerging as a militarized equestrian society with regional economic ambitions. Hämäläinen (2008:83) goes so far as to write of eighteenth-century Taos Pueblo as "a virtual Comanche satellite," whose loyalties most frequently lay not with the Spanish officials but with the powerful and wealthy Comanches who dominated trade in slaves, horses, bison meat, and hides. If one is to talk of an emergent Comanche empire, then Taos, it seems, should be viewed as a kind of imperial outpost. And yet, prior to the research reported herein, no Comanche sites had been identified in the Taos region despite many decades of archaeological survey.

Compare this situation with the great many Jicarilla Apache sites that dot the Taos landscape (see Eiselt 2009, 2012, 2013; Girard 1986; Johnson et al. 2009; Woosley and Olinger 1990). The Jicarilla's presence is indeed strong and archaeologically visible. On the one hand, the Jicarilla's heightened visibility is itself linked to the influence of the Comanches, for it was only after the Comanches' militarized thrust into the Southern Plains that the Jicarilla were forced to seek permanent refuge in the northern Rio Grande. On the other hand, the Jicarilla displayed remarkable resilience. As Eiselt (2013) has carefully documented, they developed a distinctive enclave economy focused on exchange of micaceous pottery and upland resources, which served as important supplements to the agricultural products of lowland Hispano and Pueblo communities. Reduced mobility and the relatively liberal use of durable remains such as pottery, chipped stone, and metal, as well as a strategic willingness to accept Christianity and to appear in Catholic baptismal records—all of this enhances our archaeological perception of the Jicarilla presence.

The Comanches, in contrast, have traditionally been viewed as the destroyers rather than the creators of sites. In fact, beyond their regular appearance at Taos trade fairs, the most memorable Comanche incident in the region is surely the 1760 attack on Taos Pueblo and its surrounding ranches, including the Villalpando compound, the largest Hispano settlement near Taos. Shortly afterward, Bishop Tamarón offered a brief report, observing that nearly 3,000 Comanches had besieged Taos, killing many, taking fifty-six women and children as captives, and leaving smoldering structures in ruin (Adams 1954:58; Hämäläinen 2008:51–52). The large-scale attack was in response to a direct insult: some months earlier, Taos had flaunted Comanche scalps in front of a Comanche audience at one of the pueblo's scalp dances (John 1996:330). Nevertheless, these sorts of incidents have left us with the impression that the archaeological signature of the Comanches in the Taos region—were one to go looking for such a thing—would primarily be found in the charred remains of destroyed Hispano, Pueblo, and Jicarilla Apache sites. As in other parts of New Mexico, "Comanche archaeology" continues to be understood primarily in negative terms.

TESTIMONY OF THE RIO GRANDE GORGE

Recent surveys in the Rio Grande Gorge, just west of Taos, are beginning to change this impression, however, bringing to light a previously unknown diversity of Comanche sites. The Rio Grande Gorge (Figure 6.1) is a rugged rift valley filled with talus ridges, scree slopes, and cliffs that cut down sharply into the Taos plateau. As such, it has remained largely unsettled, posing a major barrier to movement in the region. But the gorge does have the advantage of being a hidden subterranean space with occasional sediment-filled basins that are today covered with weedy sagebrush but that prior to the ravages of late nineteenth-century sheepherding would have been filled with grasses suitable for equestrian camps. Indeed, anyone on horseback looking for a hideout while planning trading or raiding expeditions would have found a number of excellent options in the gorge.

This is particularly true in the vicinity of the confluence of the Rio Grande and the Rio Pueblo, where the gorge broadens somewhat and includes a great

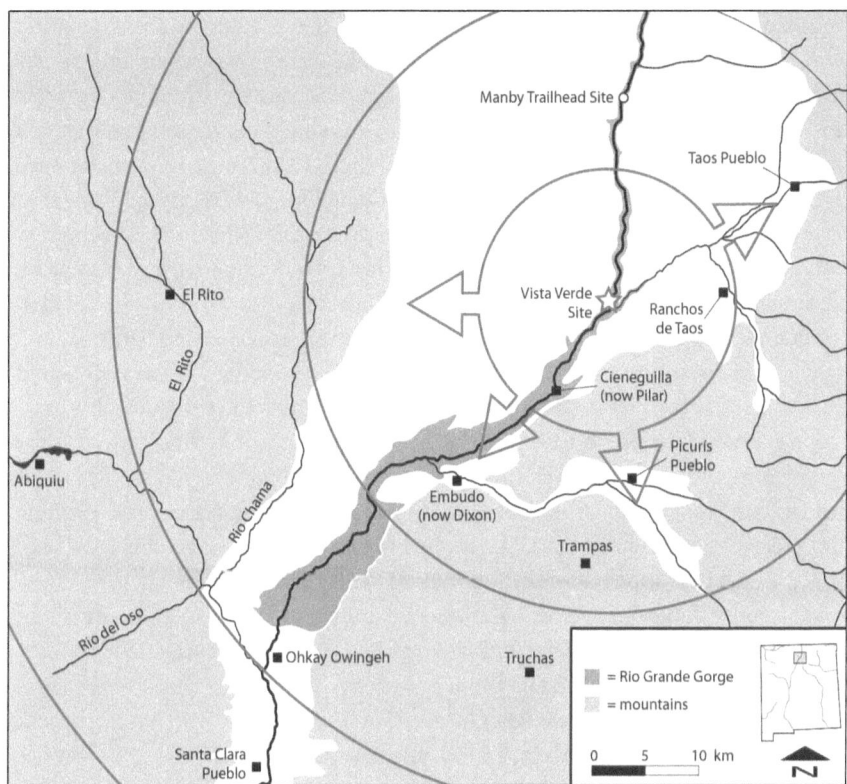

FIGURE 6.1. *The Vista Verde Site (LA 75747), located within Rio Grande Gorge at the confluence of the Rio Grande and the Rio Pueblo—in easy striking distance of a number of eighteenth-century Native American and European settlements.*

series of secluded and easily defensible basins accessible via old trails that had likely been in use for many millennia. During the eighteenth century, the Rio Grande–Rio Pueblo confluence was also roughly equidistant from a number of key communities in northern New Mexico—Taos Pueblo, Picuris Pueblo, Ohkay Owingeh Pueblo, Embudo (present-day Dixon), Abiquiú—each of which could be reached within a half day's horse ride. What had previously been a kind of interstitial no-man's land between pueblo centers would have offered, during the colonial era, a strategic location for mounted traders and raiders. As discussed below, it is precisely in this location that the strongest evidence of a Comanche presence has been found.

The first mounted tribes to camp in the Rio Grande Gorge appear to have been the Jicarilla and Ute, both of whom were early converts to an equestrian lifestyle. Jicarilla sites dating from the seventeenth century through the mid-nineteenth century are relatively easily identified by the presence of thin micaceous pottery and a light distribution of metal artifacts in association with small tipi rings (2–2.5 meters diameter). Jicarilla rock art remains poorly defined, but our research has suggested that it can be broadly characterized as lightly pecked with a frequent focus on shield-bearers, morning stars, Mountain Spirit headdresses, horses, and the like (Figure 6.2). In fact, the earliest images of equestrian battles in the Rio Grande Gorge were probably created by Athapaskan groups during the seventeenth century when the Apache and Navajo posed the most significant military threat to both native and nonnative communities. At the Lightning Arrow Site near the Rio Grande–Rio Pueblo confluence, for instance, we have documented numerous pecked battle scenes; most warriors are on foot, but there is at least one mounted warrior depicted astride a "boat form" horse (Figure 6.2A), which James Keyser (1987) argues is among the earliest horse forms in the Plains Biographic Tradition of rock art. Significantly, three Jicarilla micaceous pot drops and one probable tipi clearing were located in close association with the pecked rock art at the Lightning Arrow Site, strengthening the claim for Jicarilla affiliation. Indeed, this Apachean rock art tradition appears to have continued well into the nineteenth century, as evidenced by additional pecked battle scene images at another site in the gorge, just to the south, that was explicitly identified as having a Jicarilla affiliation by tribal consultants (Figure 6.2C).

The Ute occupation of the Rio Grande Gorge is more difficult to document, though this is surely due to a lack of research attention rather than the absence of Ute sites in the region (but see Montgomery 2015, in press). We know that at the onset of Spanish colonialism, the Ute already had deep historical roots in southern Colorado and northern New Mexico, a fact that is still commented on at Taos Pueblo, where a long history of relations and intermarriage with the Ute is quickly acknowledged. The nearest Ancestral Ute sites that have been identified with confidence, however, are at the northern edge of the Taos region, near the Rio Grande–Rio Hondo confluence, where pecked and abraded rock art panels with distinctive iconography (e.g., oversized bears and elks, pluralities of small quadrupeds, and almost Fremont-like anthropomorphs) are found in direct association with brownware pottery (Figure 6.3).[5]

These traces of a late pre-Hispanic Ute presence are significant insofar as it was the Ute's familiarity with the Taos region that facilitated the Comanches' entrance. Not only did the Comanches probably receive their first horses from their Ute cousins, whose proximity to liberated Spanish herds during the Pueblo Revolt era led them to be key middlemen in the early horse trade; the Ute are also known to have regularly enlisted Comanche muscle in their raids on northern New Mexico during the early eighteenth century. The Comanches' perception of the New Mexican landscape, in this sense, would have been initially guided, quite literally, by the Ute.

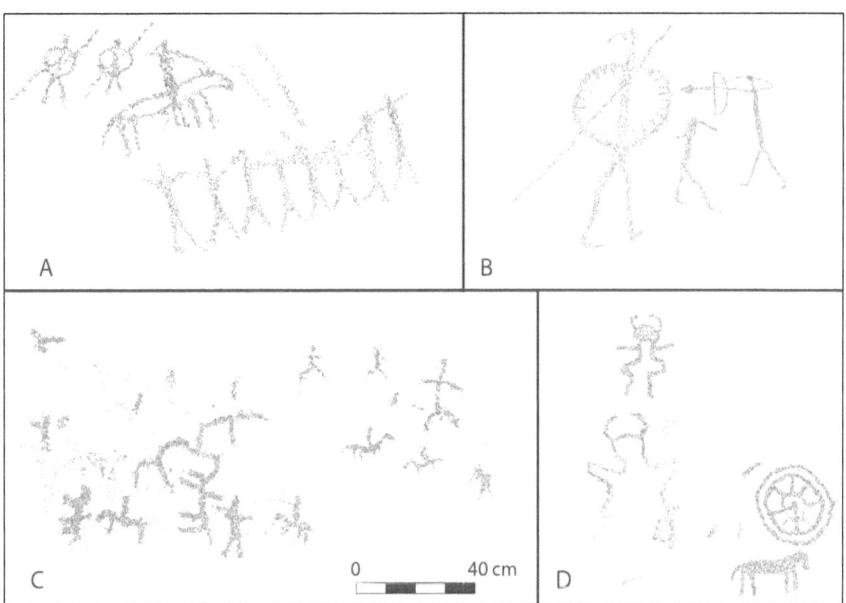

FIGURE 6.2. *Probable Jicarilla Apache rock art from the Rio Grande Gorge: A and B: lightly pecked rock art at the Lightning Arrow Site, near the confluence of the Rio Grande and the Rio Pueblo (probably late seventeenth century); C and D: pecked rock art at the Pilar Morada Site (LA 55948), near the confluence of the Rio Grande and the Arroyo Cieneguilla (probably late eighteenth or early nineteenth century).*

FIGURE 6.3. *Lightly abraded and pecked rock art at the Manby Trailhead Site (LA 102341). This panel and a cluster of others were found in association with brownware pottery, and are likely affiliated with the ancestral Ute occupation of the Taos region.*

One gets a good sense of this at the most impressive of the eighteenth-century sites in the gorge: the Vista Verde Site (LA 75747) (Figures 6.1 and 6.4), located directly opposite of the Rio Grande–Rio Pueblo confluence, quite close to the Apachean material at the Lightning Arrow Site, discussed above. The Vista Verde Site has been a focus of sustained research since 2008; it is the largest site in the Rio Grande Gorge, with a striking density of rock art panels encircling a large flat basin bounded by rugged basalt talus ridges. Archaic and Ancestral Pueblo individuals visited the area for millennia, at least to a limited extent, as evidenced by rock art and isolated projectile points. Extensive use of the Vista Verde Site, however, appears to have only begun during the early colonial period. In the course of a magnetic gradiometer survey of the central basin in 2009, for instance, a large buried feature (roughly twenty by fifteen meters) resembling a horseshoe-shaped dance ground was located. The feature exhibits a clear opening to the southeast and three pronounced dipole anomalies along its northwestern edge that may represent bonfires, as well as evidence of at least one large tipi ring in direct association a few meters away (Goodmaster 2011). Subsequent conversations with consultants from the Ute Mountain nation have suggested that this buried archaeological complex may be an early Bear Dance ground, which the ancestral Ute are known to have constructed in the region during the early colonial period (Terry Knight, personal communication, 2010).

If the Vista Verde Site was indeed an established gathering place in the Rio Grande Gorge for the Ute, it makes sense that it would have been selected as a base camp for combined forces of Ute and Comanche raiders during the early eighteenth century. Surface mapping within the central basin immediately north of the buried dance ground revealed the presence of a large encampment composed of two dozen or more tipi rings. The absence of micaceous pottery in association with the tipi rings makes a Jicarilla affiliation unlikely, despite the Jicarilla's strong archaeological presence in neighboring portions of the gorge. In fact, essentially no cultural artifacts—beyond the tipi rings themselves—seem to have been left on the surface of the site; not even hearths were constructed within the tipis, suggesting that this was a "cold camp," similar to those created by Plains warriors in advance of a raid.

Unlike the relatively ambiguous architectural and artifactual evidence at the site, the hundreds of rock art panels that surround the tipi compound offer a world of interpretive possibilities, insofar as those who camped there seem to have been compelled to document their presence, often in extraordinary detail. The rock art is unusual and diverges in both its technology and iconographic content from prior traditions in the region. Almost all other local rock art is pecked, for instance, the artists having used stone and, later, metal tools to break through the dark patina of basalt boulders to expose the light interior. Indeed, pecking characterizes all known Archaic, Pueblo, Jicarilla Apache, Ute, and

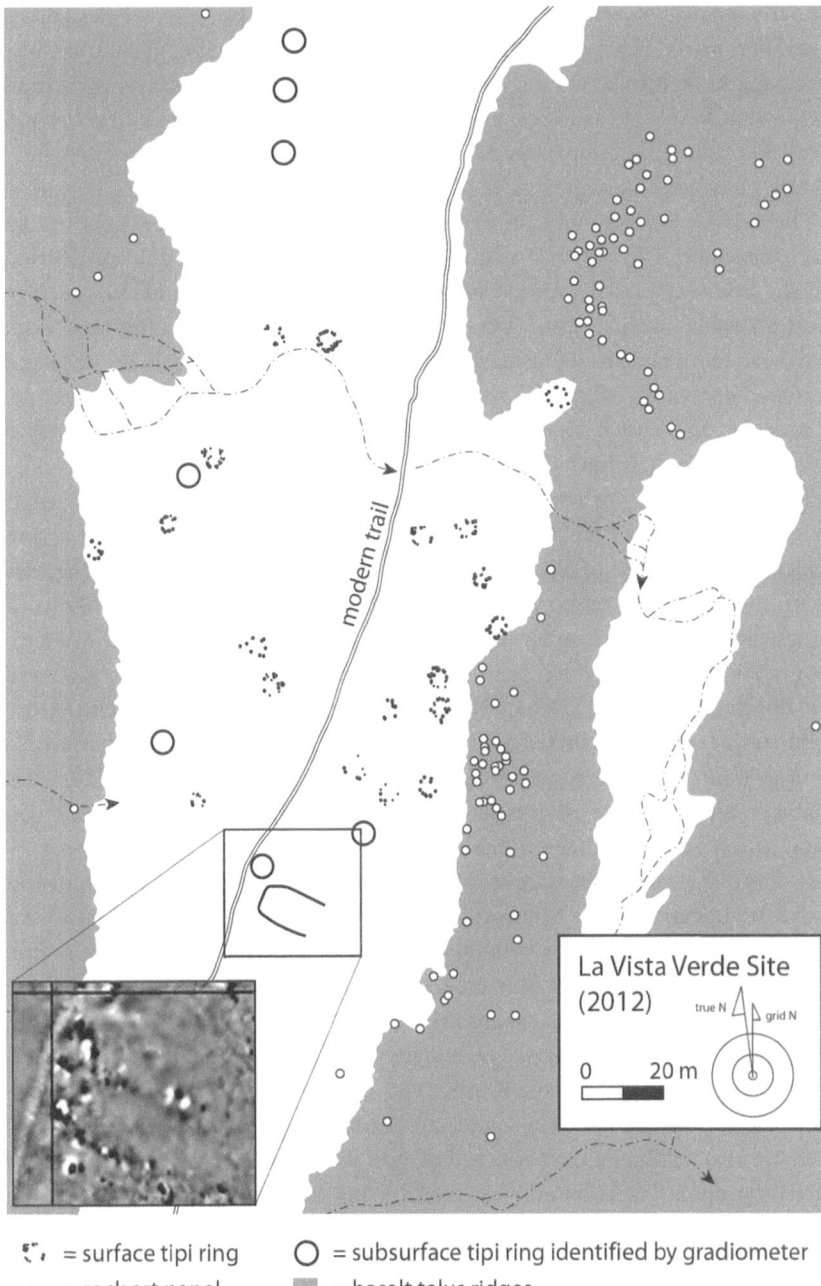

° = surface tipi ring   ◯ = subsurface tipi ring identified by gradiometer
∘ = rock art panel   ▨ = basalt talus ridges

FIGURE 6.4. *Map of the central tipi encampment (Area 6) at the Vista Verde Site. The highlighted area presents the magnetic gradiometer detail highlighting the possible dance ground and tipi complex at the southern edge of the encampment.*

Hispano petroglyph traditions in this part of the Southwest (e.g., see Schaafsma 1992; Slifer 1998). The dominant rock art of the Vista Verde Site, in contrast, was produced by lightly scratching and abrading with metal tools, leaving behind glyphs that barely (if at all) break through the patina of the rock. The overall result has little visual impact and is often impossible to see in direct sunlight, a fact that has led the imagery to be overlooked by past researchers.

The relative inscrutability of the scratched rock art, however, provides an important clue. Clearly, this is a technological tradition that did not develop locally; it is very poorly adapted to hard basalt of the Rio Grande Gorge. The most plausible interpretation is that it evolved in an area with softer rock, such as the extensive sandstones of northern Colorado and Wyoming in the ancestral Comanche territory, where the same artistic gesture using the same tools results in a deeper and much more visible glyph: an "incised" rather than merely a "scratched" icon, in other words.

The iconographic content of the images supports this interpretation nicely. As should be evident in Figures 6.5–6.11, the rock art at the Vista Verde Site depicts a wide range of Plains-style imagery including tipis, mounted horses, battle scenes, horse raids, warriors, shields, parfleches, and more. Many of the glyphs find parallels in Keyser's (1987, 2004; see also Loendorf 2008) Plains Biographic Tradition, which originated in the ancestral Comanche region and was dominated by incised imagery on sandstone cliff faces. By the end of the eighteenth century the Plains Biographic Tradition had spread across much of central North America, from northern Mexico to southern Alberta—effectively characterizing the area of regular Comanche incursions following their conquest of the Southern Plains in the 1740s.

Part of what makes the rock art of the Vista Verde Site so intriguing, however, is that it appears to have been produced very early on in the development of the Biographic Tradition by mounted warriors who were just beginning their expansionist push into New Mexico. Rock art is notoriously difficult to position temporally, but in this case we are assisted by two key details. First, the imagery includes abundant evidence of indigenous equestrianism, indicating that it dates to a time after the Pueblo Revolt (1680–92), when Spanish horses first made their way into native hands in significant numbers. Second, the Vista Verde Site rock art also exhibits a near absence of gun icons, which is notable insofar as later Biographic Tradition imagery typically displays guns prominently. During the 1740s, French guns began to be widely traded among Plains tribes, and colonial correspondence discussing the situation at Taos reported that visiting Comanches were well supplied during this period (Twitchell 1911:440). Had guns been present at the Vista Verde Site, we assume they would have been regularly depicted, as was indeed the case in most subsequent Biographic Tradition imagery. This, then, provides us with a reasonable *terminus ante quem*.

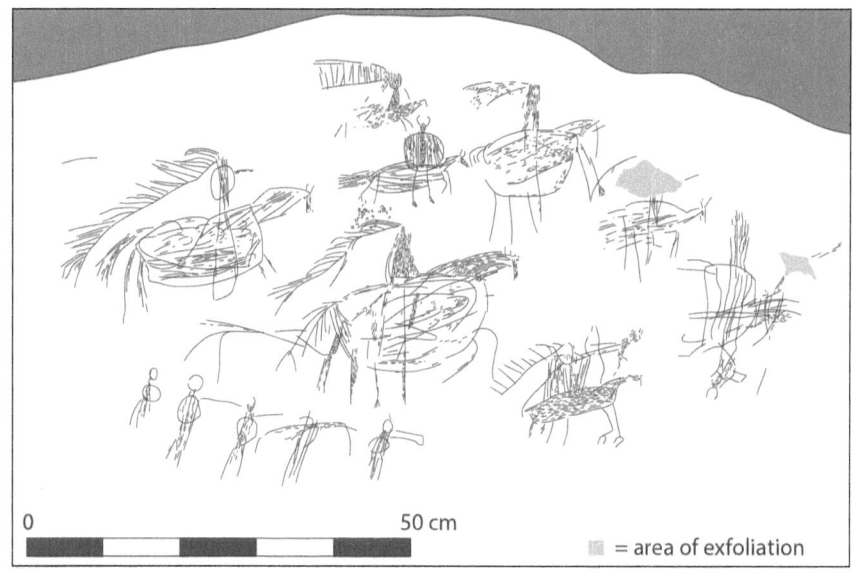

FIGURE 6.5. *Scratched and abraded rock art from the Vista Verde Site (detail of Panel 2014-009A).*

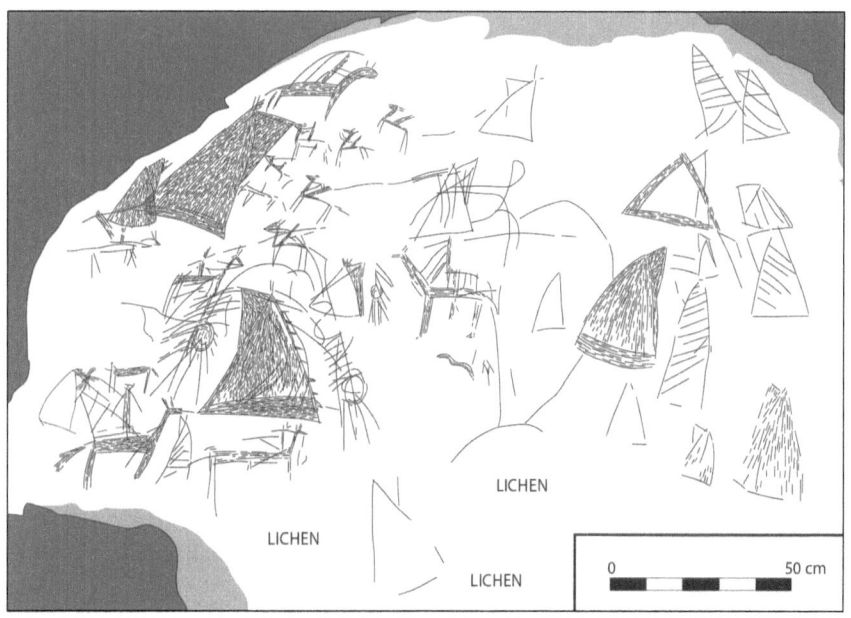

FIGURE 6.6. *Scratched and abraded rock art from the Vista Verde Site (Panel 2008-353).*

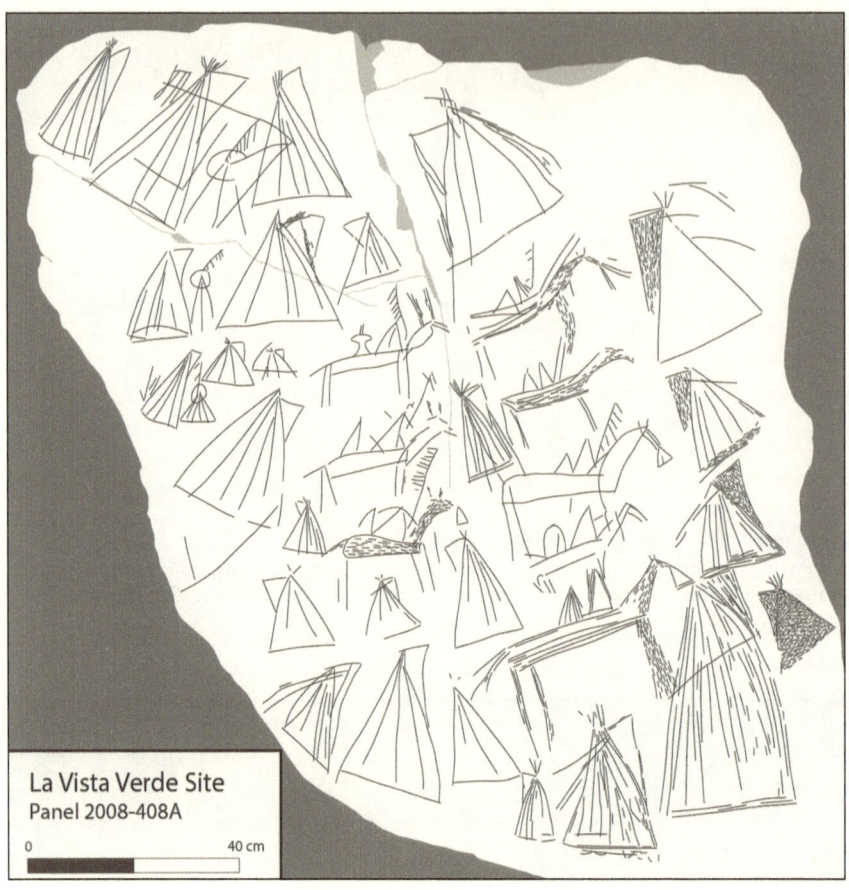

FIGURE 6.7. *Scratched and abraded rock art from the Vista Verde Site (Panel 2008-408A).*

This conclusion is broadly supported by details from the panels that the Comanche did create. Figure 6.5, for instance, is a detail from one panel at the Vista Verde Site depicting a classic Plains scene: a group of mounted and pedestrian warriors are pursing three bison, just outside the detail in the lower right of the panel. Seven of the warriors ride horses, their status being signified by long flowing war bonnets. One of the mounted warriors is depicted with a shield and buffalo horn headdress, a signature element of Comanche regalia. Below them are five additional pedestrian warriors; each has his shield, one holds a club, and three seem to wield lances. The combination of mounted and pedestrian warriors might itself point to an early eighteenth-century date, but so too does the most notable detail in this panel, namely, the body covering that shields a number of the horses. Depictions of horse body armor have been previously found in rock art at a handful of sites to the north of Taos in the ancestral

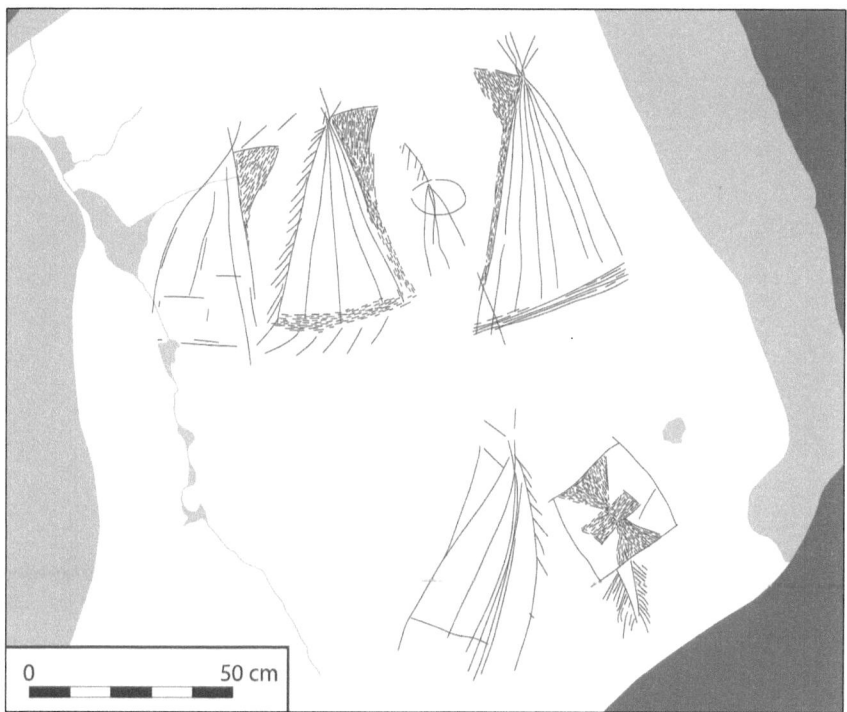

FIGURE 6.8. *Scratched and abraded rock art from the Vista Verde Site (Panel 2008-374B, overlying graffiti removed).*

Comanche territory of Colorado and Wyoming (Mitchell 2004), and this imagery speaks both to a Comanche affiliation (the Comanche were one of the few tribes to armor their horses) and to the chronology of the Vista Verde Site generally. The Comanche produced and used thick sheets of bison hide as armor only during the first half of the eighteenth century, mimicking the Spanish use of metal horse armor. The last archival reference to this practice was in 1751 (Secoy 1951:532), after which the widespread availability of guns rendered the cumbersome hide armor an ineffective strategy of defense.

The chronological outlines we are left with—roughly AD 1700–50—effectively bracket the early period of combined Comanche and Ute raiding in the northern Rio Grande valley.[6] And as we have suggested, the influence of both tribes might be read into the site: the location, perhaps, was selected by the Ute, while the imagery bears strong Comanche influence. This, we think, is a reasonable interpretation that is consistent with colonial records and local oral histories, as well as with many details within the rock art itself.

Regarding the latter, it is worth highlighting one rock art panel (Figure 6.6) at the Vista Verde Site in which certain noteworthy details lend additional support to

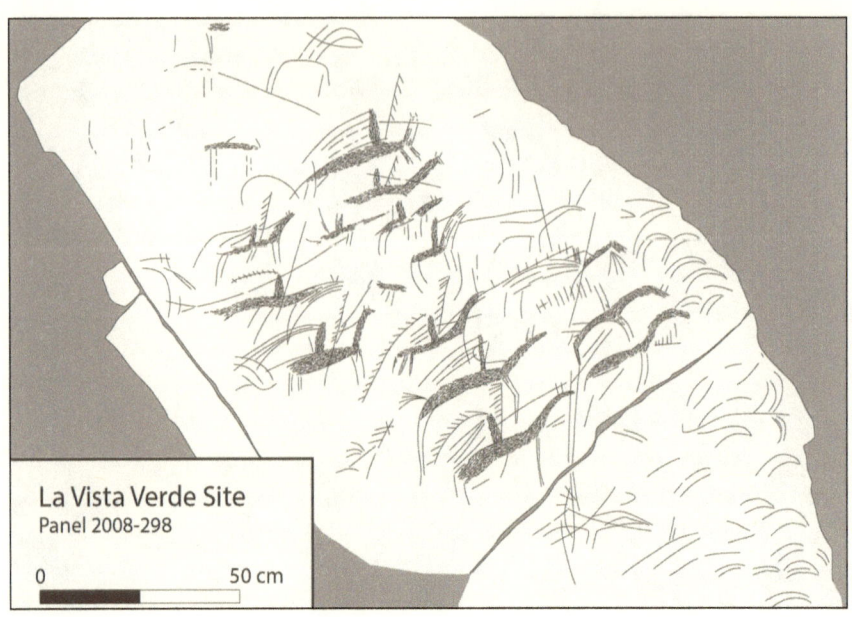

FIGURE 6.9. *Scratched and abraded rock art from the Vista Verde Site (Panel 2008-298).*

FIGURE 6.10. *Scratched and abraded rock art from the Vista Verde Site (Panel 2008-059, overlying graffiti removed).*

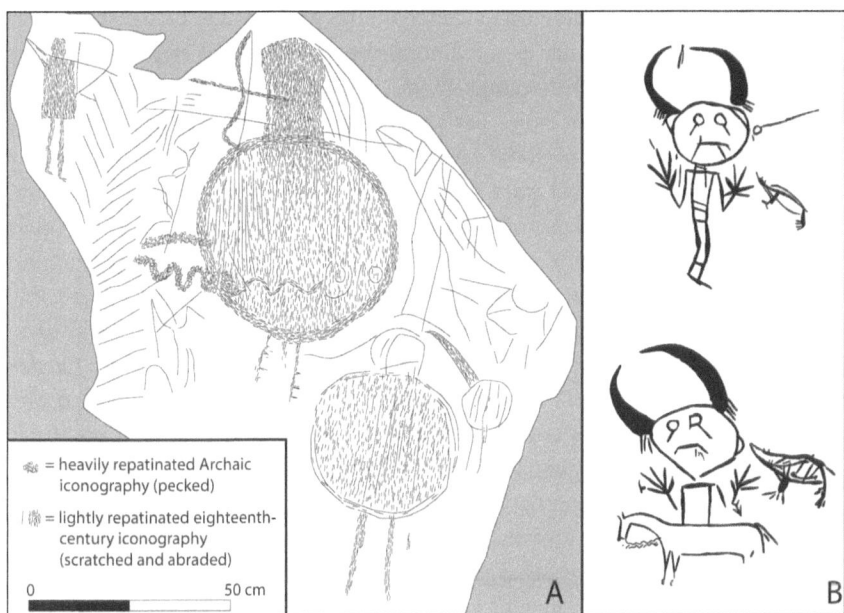

FIGURE 6.11. *A. Panel 2009-234 at the Vista Verde Site (overlying graffiti removed). B. Rock art details from the Tolar Site, Wyoming (based upon Loendorf and Olsen 2003).*

a specifically Comanche affiliation. The panel illustrates a tipi encampment under attack. One can clearly identify a cluster of sixteen tipis as well the many mounted warriors of the camp, all facing left. The aggressors are facing right, and among them is a dominant warrior, leaping over a tipi at the top of the panel, his long war bonnet flowing behind him. While we cannot identify the cultural affiliation of the right-facing warriors, there are good grounds for identifying the aggressed camp as Comanche. This is evident in certain subtle details, such as the way the poles extended off the top of the tipi in two clusters—a distinctively Comanche architectural pattern (Jimmy Arterberry, personal communication, 2011)—as well as the inclusion of a snake glyph in the lower center of the panel. Within the Plains Sign Language system, the Comanches were known as the "Snakes"[7] (Wallace and Hoebel [1952] 1986:5), and here it seems the rock artist was making an explicit effort to assert that the settlement under attack was specifically a Comanche camp. The snake glyph, in this sense, served as a kind of signature.

THE ONSET OF COMANCHE IMPERIALISM IN NEW MEXICO

Accepting the interpretation of the Vista Verde Site as one of perhaps many sites left behind by the Comanche during their period of early eighteenth-century raiding, we stand in a strong position to explore the deeper logics behind the emergence of Comanche "imperialism" in New Mexico, as proposed by

Hämäläinen. The archaeological evidence on the ground may be paltry indeed; this is to be expected insofar as the Comanche traveled light and purposefully left behind few traces of their camps, in part to elude potential pursuers. But for a brief period in the Taos region—early on in the tribe's experiments with equestrianism, militarism, and regional economic involvement—rock art appears to have served as a key cultural space where new identities were being worked out.

At a basic level, the rock art of the Vista Verde Site reflects a desire to archive and assert the local visits of Comanche bands. Many hundreds of tipi glyphs were scratched onto the rocks surrounding the central camp. In some cases, the glyphs are simple triangles; a tipi with its smoke flap open might be all that was represented, as if the artist was simply acknowledging his or her participation in an expedition to the northern Rio Grande Valley and nothing more. In other cases, whole tipi encampments were depicted, giving us a potential sense of the scale and organization of the expedition. One panel, for instance, depicts twenty-five tipis (perhaps 150–200 people) organized into a broadly circular arrangement with mounted horses in the center (Figure 6.7). Interestingly, this panel is positioned on the edge of the central basin of the Vista Verde Site, where we have found evidence of a circular compound with roughly the same number of tipi rings.

The tipi depictions reveal much more than simply the scale of encampments. Many of the tipi glyphs are accompanied by images of tripods supporting shields and feathered lances (Figure 6.8), signaling that an important warrior occupied the tipi and was preparing for an impending battle. Within Comanche society, shields were regularly hung outside warriors' doorways to absorb the sun's powerful medicine, thereby making them more effective on the battlefield (Wallace and Hoebel [1952] 1986:251). The lance displayed its potency by the number of feathers or scalps hanging from it, which served as a tally of the military accomplishments of its owner. Honorable Comanche warriors were obligated to fight with a lance rather than a bow and arrow or a gun, for the lance necessitated intimate contact with one's opponent and, hence, greater bravery (Kavanagh 2008:267). Similar displays took place once the battle or raid was over. "A warrior returning from a successful raiding party," recalled Comanche informants in the 1930s, "set his lance upright before the door of his lodge with the scalps of his victims dangling from it. No one except the owner could remove the trophies. As in the case of the shield, tradition records that some lances had power, and the lance carried by the leaders was a characteristic sign of office" (Wallace and Hoebel [1952] 1986:111). We might go so far as to imagine that the depictions of shields and lances in Comanche rock art followed a sympathetic logic: beyond their role as signs of office for those residing in the tipis pitched nearby, the images plausibly also functioned as iconographic extensions of the warrior's weaponry. Scratched onto the south-facing surfaces of dark black basalt boulders, the images of shields and lances would have absorbed the sun's potency on behalf of their prototypes all day long.

Militarism and the desire for public acknowledgment of bravery clearly preoccupied those camping at the Vista Verde Site. Tallies, seemingly archiving particular warriors' accomplishments, were added to the sides of both human figures and their tipis; panels depicting horse raids offered records of the number of stolen horses; parfleche glyphs appear to have served as a means both of identifying participants in a military expedition and of acknowledging the power of the medicine bundles stored within them; and mounted warriors were illustrated with long flowing war bonnets, headwear adorning only those Comanche men "whose military achievements entitled them to wear it" (Wallace and Hoebel [1952] 1986:213) (see Figures 6.8–6.11).

One rock art image highlights this pattern with special clarity. Figure 6.11A depicts a military engagement between two warriors, each probably serving as a representative of a military group. On the left, a diminutive warrior in Pueblo attire is perched with a simple D-shaped bow. A far more impressive Comanche warrior with a headdress, recurved bow, and large body shield occupies the center of the panel. In the lower right, another warrior (possibly two) seems to be covering the central warrior's back. This much can be readily identified. When viewed from within the Comanche iconographic tradition, however, a number of additional details become significant (Jimmy Arterberry, personal communication, 2011). The herringbone pattern between the two warriors, for instance, emerges as another tally, quite likely of the number of successful arrows each side shot in the altercation. Twenty-five arrows of the dominant warrior's group seem to have hit and killed an opponent; only seven such arrows are tallied for his adversary—little question, then, which side was victorious. Indeed, the Comanche's success was further indexed by the tangle of scratched lines falling away from the dominant warrior's bow, which can be read as signifiers of the many bows that were broken by the Comanche in the course of the battle. Moreover, in the faintly scratched lines at the upper right of the panel, we can now squint and see the image of a bear—that most powerful of species—lending its spiritual assistance to the central warrior. The vague and sketchy rendering of the bear was probably an intentional iconographic strategy of depicting the bear's spiritual status (again, Arterberry, personal communication, 2011), but later rock art gives us a sense of what was intended. Two probable Comanche panels at the Tolar Site in Wyoming, for example, offer more detailed renderings of individuals with similarly positioned bear glyphs (Figure 6.11B) (Loendorf and Olsen 2003). The bear glyph in the Vista Verde panel may be largely illegible by comparison, but there is no ambiguity regarding its link to the central warrior, for the artist has scratched a line connecting the warrior's shoulder and the bear's head. Indeed, five lines in the panel were included to establish biographic connections in this way: each warrior is connected to his arrow tally, and the central warrior—in addition to being connected with his spirit bear—has lines linking him to his allied shield-bearer as well as to his tally of broken bows (see Figure 6.11A).

Other rock art panels depict the fray of battle much more vividly as a swirl of gestural lines. Figure 6.12 is the tracing of a panel a short distance north of the Vista Verde Site. Here we encounter a chaotic tangle of traces, within which as many as seven stylized horses can be identified. The riders of some are missing or indistinct, but others clearly include riders bearing shields and wielding lances or clubs. Lines extend out from each warrior to touch or strike combatants. In the case of the warrior just above the center of the image, two lines extend down to touch a combatant in the lower right of the panel, and additional lines extend out from his lance or club to strike the figure in the upper right, the latter of whom almost seems to have exploded from the blow. The image, in this sense, anticipates the well-known Plains tradition of counting coup, in which one of the most prestigious acts of bravery involved confronting and touching an opponent on the battlefield (Lowie [1954] 1982; Mishkin 1940). Such acts were the raw material out of which leaders were made within historic Comanche society. Indeed, the Comanches typically counted coup before going into war (Wallace and Hoebel 1986:252), which may explain why so many rock art panels were created at the Vista Verde Site. Gestural images likely provided important complements to the oral narration of acts of military bravery (Fowles and Arterberry 2013).

What is perhaps most remarkable about the images at the Vista Verde Site, then, is that they collectively point to the presence of a highly developed military culture at an early date. Again, the images were probably created during the first half of the eighteenth century, only a generation or two after the Comanches had acquired the horse. And yet, the tribe was already committed to the new world of indigenous imperialism that would characterize Comanche life on the Plains for over a century beginning in the mid-eighteenth century.

There is a sense in which the encampment at the Vista Verde Site even anticipated the spatial strategies the Comanches would so effectively deploy at the height of their regional ambitions. As many have observed, the special genius of Comanche geopolitics stemmed from the tribe's ability to transform a former periphery—the Southern Plains—into an interregional center place, shifting the political and economic gravity toward the intersection of various European and Native American polities. In doing so, the Comanches benefited immensely from the colonial rivalries between the Spanish and French, just as they profited from their ability to extract the resources of Texas and northern Mexico for trade in the markets of New Mexico and the Northern Plains. The Comanches were, in this sense, self-fashioned arbiters of in-between places.

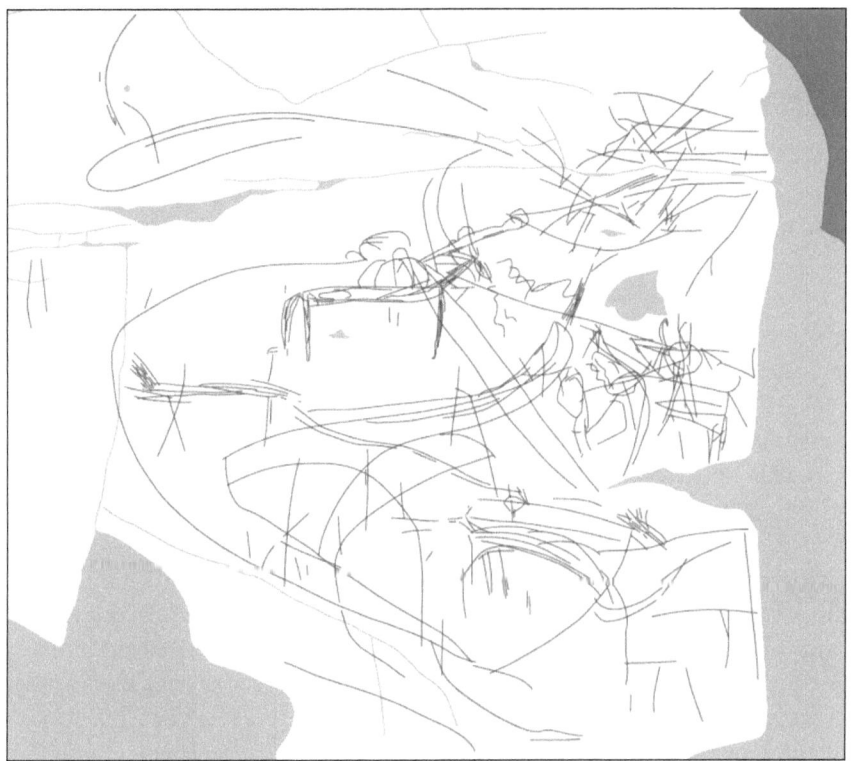

FIGURE 6.12. *Scratched and abraded rock art from the Rio Grande Gorge, just north of the Vista Verde Site (Panel 2009-209).*

At the Vista Verde Site, a similar spatial logic prevailed. Tucked away within the Rio Grande Gorge, the site occupies a rugged landscape that was peripheral to Pueblo and Hispano centers in the region. In fact, our surveys have suggested that the site was situated in a transitional area where shifts in late pre-Columbian rock art and a local concentration of Pueblo shield-bearers mark the presence of an ethnic boundary—a "no man's land" of sorts—between the traditional territories of Taos Pueblo to the northeast and the Tewa pueblos to the southwest. The Comanche appear to have inserted themselves precisely into this interstitial space during the early eighteenth century. From there, they were well poised to engage multiple local communities: trading with some, simultaneously raiding others, and all the while remaining hidden away in a subterranean canyon. The occupants of the Vista Verde Site, then, were playing out in microcosm what would become a truly continental strategy following the Comanches' takeover of the southern Plains.

CONCLUSION

The study of Comanche archaeology—in New Mexico but also throughout the American West—remains in its infancy with its most exciting days still to come; of this, we are quite convinced. Intellectually, we find ourselves in a moment when historians have recently awakened to the remarkable scope and savvy of Comanche politics, offering bold new visions of the tribe's regional influence that archaeologists have not yet even attempted to trace on the ground as a material phenomenon. How are we to respond? What are we to do when historians write of an entire indigenous empire in the middle of North America that has completely escaped archaeological detection?

Quibbling over definitions of what an empire is—and whether the Comanches should be considered one—would be a narrow and unproductive response, we suggest. Indeed, the traditional understanding of Comanche history has been hamstrung precisely by the tendency to impose preconceived notions of what an expansionist polity "should" look like, as well as by our heavy reliance on colonial documents authored by the Comanches' European or Euro-American opponents. As recent work by Hämäläinen and others has so ably demonstrated, much can still be accomplished through revisionist study of the existing historical archives, but archaeologists have a great deal to contribute as well, particularly insofar as they offer the possibility of building new archives composed of evidence authored by the ancestral Comanches themselves. Alternative archives of this sort have always been a core commitment of historical archaeology, and our research at the Vista Verde Site follows closely in this tradition. The scratched images of Comanche militarism in the Rio Grande Gorge offer a rare glimpse of what the early eighteenth-century social and political landscape looked like from an indigenous perspective. They provide us an opportunity to imagine a *Comanche New Mexico*, counterbalancing dominant accounts of Spanish colonial New Mexico. We hope it goes without saying that this in no way denies the necessity of continuing to imagine yet other New Mexicos: Pueblo, Apache, Navajo, Ute, Genizaro, Mestizo, and so forth. The goal is to proliferate such perspectives, rather than limit them.

Regarding Comanche history in particular, three principal conclusions have emerged from our study. First, the rock art imagery clearly reveals that the reorganization of Comanche society around equestrianism and the new logics of tallying military honors occurred with remarkable speed. Within a generation of acquiring the horse, the Comanches had developed elaborate new cultural norms for building social prestige—which is to say that the Comanches were unquestionably a "hot" society, fully aware that they were making history. As the Comanche cultural critic Paul Chaat Smith has put it, "Contrary to what most people (Indian and non-Indian alike) now believe, our true history is one of constant change, technological innovation, and intense curiosity about the world.

How else do you explain our instantaneous adaptation to horses, rifles, flour, and knives?" (Smith 2009:4). We expect other archaeological sites to emerge that demonstrate an even older stage of development, but to our knowledge, the imagery at the Vista Verde site currently provides some of the earliest archaeological evidence of counting coup (broadly conceived) in North America, most other documented examples having been dated to the period after AD 1750 (e.g., Keyser 1979; Parsons 1987).

Second, new systems of prestige appear to have gone hand in hand with new strategies regarding how to maneuver at a regional level. We know a good deal about Comanche movements during the late eighteenth and the nineteenth centuries following the tribe's conquest of the Southern Plains, based upon both oral history and written colonial documents. Again, the Comanches were infamous arbiters of intermediary zones, playing various nations off one another to great economic and political effect. Our evidence from the Vista Verde Site suggests that such tactics did not emerge out of the blue, however. On the contrary, the Comanches were already developing their basic geopolitical strategies in the northern Rio Grande during the early eighteenth century.

Finally, we take it as quite significant that despite having documented hundreds of scratched rock art panels at the Vista Verde site, including dozens of images of military conflicts, only one panel thus far includes an image of a European. When battle scenes were depicted, they inevitably featured altercations between opposed Native American warriors instead. Bearing this in mind, one might speculate that the main occupation of the site was actually somewhat earlier than we have proposed—perhaps during the Pueblo Revolt period itself, when the Spanish were in exile—rather than shortly after the reconquest. We interpret the absence of nonnative subjects in the Vista Verde rock art differently, however. It provides, we suggest, a useful reminder that while our written histories privilege interactions between Europeans and Native Americans, the truly consequential political relations for most communities in the colonial Southwest were between indigenous nations. And it is in this sense that we might look to a time and place like the northern Rio Grande during the eighteenth century and begin to imagine a very different sort of colonial setting, one in which the Comanches stood in the position of the expansionistic polity and in which local residents—native and nonnative alike—were forced to adapt to the politics of these powerful interlopers.

NOTES

1. For other archaeological efforts to foreground native agency in accounts of the eighteenth century, see Sunday Eiselt's (2012) study of the Jicarilla Apache settlement of the northern Rio Grande Valley, as well as Michael Wilcox's (2009) and Matthew Liebmann's (2012b) studies of Pueblo reinvention during the Spanish colonial period.

2. For critical discussions of the New Indian History, see Ned Blackhawk (2005), William T. Hagan (1997), and Daniel K. Richter (1993). For exemplary recent examples of such historical revisionism in the American Southwest, see Blackhawk (2006), James Brooks (2002), Brian DeLay (2008), Ramón Gutiérrez (1991), and Pekka Hämäläinen (2008).

3. The published literature on Comanche archaeology is minimal. No monograph-length studies exist, and only a few articles (notably, Mitchell 2004 and Newton 2011) explicitly address Comanche sites.

4. "Komántcia" as an ethnonym appears to have originated as a Ute term, referring to "anyone who wants to fight me all the time" (Opler 1943:156). While the Ute often collaborated with the Comanches during the early eighteenth century, the relationship was clearly fraught and broke down entirely in the 1740s. Spanish use of the term "Comanche" to describe the Eastern Shoshone groups who had migrated onto the Southern Plains was probably inherited from the Ute.

5. Dennis Slifer (1998) notes that ancestral Ute rock art in southern Colorado, immediately to the north, was frequently executed in red pigment, but no such pictographs have been located during our survey of the Rio Grande Gorge.

6. It also precludes the possibility that other Plains groups—notably the Kiowa and Pawnee—were the authors the Vista Verde rock art. The Kiowa and Pawnee both have a long historical presence in the Rio Grande Valley. A Pawnee individual was baptized in New Mexico as early as 1702; an elderly Kiowa woman was buried at Isleta in 1727; and after 1730, dozens of individuals from both tribes came to be baptized by Spanish missionaries in New Mexico. These, however, were all individuals who entered New Mexican society as captives, victims of the eighteenth-century wars in which the Comanche played a defining role. In contrast, the first church burial records documenting deaths at the hands of either Kiowa or Pawnee raiders in the Spanish colony itself do not appear until the start of the nineteenth century (Brugge 1965), well after the Vista Verde rock art was produced.

7. The Comanche were one of a number of Shoshonean groups referred to as the "Snakes"; however of those groups, only the Comanches were known to have been regular visitors to the Taos region during the early eighteenth century.

REFERENCES CITED

Adams, Eleanor B., ed. 1954. *Bishop Tamaron's Visitation of New Mexico, 1760*. Albuquerque: University of New Mexico Press.

Barfield, Thomas. 2001. "The Shadow Empires: Imperial State Formation along the Chinese-nomad Frontier." In *Empires: Perspectives from Archaeology and History*, edited by Susan E. Alcock, Terence N. D'Altroy, Kathleen D. Morrison, and Carla M. Sinopoli, 10–41. Cambridge: Cambridge University Press.

Blackhawk, Ned. 2005. "Look How Far We've Come: How American Indian History Changed the Study of American History in the 1990s." *OAH Magazine of History* 19 (6): 13–17. http://dx.doi.org/10.1093/maghis/19.6.13.

Blackhawk, Ned. 2006. *Violence over the Land: Indians and Empires in the Early American West*. Cambridge, MA: Harvard University Press.

Blackhawk, Ned. 2007. "The Displacement of Violence: Ute Diplomacy and the Making of New Mexico's Eighteenth-Century Northern Borderlands." *Ethnohistory (Columbus, Ohio)* 54 (4): 723–55. http://dx.doi.org/10.1215/00141801-2007-028.

Brooks, James F. 2002. *Captives and Cousins: Slavery, Kinship, and Community in the Southwest Borderlands*. Chapel Hill: University of North Carolina Press.

Brugge, David M. 1965. "Some Plains Indians in the Church Records of New Mexico." *Plains Anthropologist* 10 (29): 181–89.

DeLay, Brian. 2008. *War of a Thousand Deserts: Indian Raids and the U.S.-Mexican War*. New Haven: Yale University Press.

Domínguez, Francisco Atanasio. 1956. *The Missions of New Mexico, 1776: A Description by Fray Francisco Atanasio Dominguez, with Other Contemporary Documents*. Editor and translator Eleanor B. Adams and Fray Angelico Chavez. Albuquerque: University of New Mexico Press.

Eiselt, B. Sunday. 2009. "The Jicarilla Apaches and the Archaeology of the Taos Region." In *Between the Mountains—Beyond the Mountains: Papers in Honor of Paul R. Williams*, edited by Emily Brown, Karen Armstrong, David M. Brugge, and Carol Condie. Papers of the Archaeological Society of New Mexico, vol. 35. Albuquerque: Archaeological Society of New Mexico.

Eiselt, B. Sunday. 2012. *Becoming White Clay: A History and Archaeology of Jicarilla Apache Enclavement*. Salt Lake City: University of Utah Press.

Eiselt, B. Sunday. 2013. "Upland-Lowland Corridors and Historic Jicarilla Apache Settlement in the Northern Rio Grande." In *From Mountaintop to Valley Bottom: Understanding Past Land Use in the Northern Rio Grande Valley, New Mexico*, edited by Bradley J. Vierra. Salt Lake City: University of Utah Press.

Fowles, Severin, and Jimmy Arterberry. 2013. "Gesture and Performance in Comanche Rock Art." *World Art* 3 (1): 67–82. http://dx.doi.org/10.1080/21500894.2013.773937.

Girard, Jeffrey S. 1986. "SMU Archaeological Field School Survey." Manuscript on file, Fort Burgwin Research Center, Ranchos de Taos, NM. *Summary (Indianapolis, Ind.)*:1986.

Goodmaster, Christopher. 2011. *Geophysical Survey Results: Area 6 of the La Vista Verde Site, Orilla Verde Recreation Area, New Mexico*. Report in possession of the senior author.

Gutiérrez, Ramón A. 1991. *When Jesus Came, the Corn Mothers Went Away: Marriage, Sexuality, and Power in New Mexico, 1500–1846*. Palo Alto, CA: Stanford University Press.

Gwynne, S. C. 2010. *Empire of the Summer Moon: Quanah Parker and the Rise and Fall of the Comanches, the Most Powerful Indian Tribe in American History*. New York: Scribner.

Hagan, William T. 1997. "The New Indian History." In *Rethinking American Indian History*, edited by Donald L. Fixico, 29–42. Albuquerque: University of New Mexico Press.

Hämäläinen, Pekka. 2008. *The Comanche Empire*. New Haven: Yale University Press.

Hämäläinen, Pekka. 2010. "The Politics of Grass: European Expansion, Ecological Change, and Indigenous Power in the Southwest Borderlands." *William and Mary Quarterly* 67 (2): 173–208. http://dx.doi.org/10.5309/willmaryquar.67.2.173.

Jenkins, Myra Ellen. 1966. "Taos Pueblo and Its Neighbors: 1540–1847." *New Mexico Historical Review* 41 (2): 85–114.

John, Elizabeth A. H. 1996. *Storms Brewed in Other Men's Worlds: The Confrontation of Indians, Spanish, and French in the Southwest, 1540–1795*. Norman: University of Oklahoma Press.

Johnson, David M., Chris Adams, Charles Hawk, and Skip Keith Miller. 2009. *Final Report on the Battle of Cieneguilla: A Jicarilla Apache Victory over the U.S. Dragoons March 30, 1854*. Report No. 20. United States Forest Service, Southwestern Region, Department of Agriculture.

Kavanagh, Thomas W. 1996. *The Comanches: A History, 1706–1875*. Lincoln: University of Nebraska Press.

Kavanagh, Thomas W., ed. 2008. *Comanche Ethnography: Field Notes of E. Adamson Hoebel, Waldo R. Wedel, Gustav G. Carlson, and Robert H. Lowie*. Lincoln: University of Nebraska Press.

Keyser, James D. 1979. "The Plains Indian War Complex and the Rock Art of Writing-on-Stone, Alberta, Canada." *Journal of Field Archaeology* 6 (1): 41–48.

Keyser, James D. 1987. "A Lexicon for Historic Plains Indian Rock Art: Increasing Interpretive Potential." *Plains Anthropologist* 32 (115): 53–71.

Keyser, James D. 2004. *Art of the Warriors: Rock Art of the American Plains*. Salt Lake City: University of Utah Press.

Liebmann, Matthew. 2012a. "The Rest Is History: Devaluing the Recent Past in the Archaeology of the Pueblo Southwest." In *Decolonizing Indigenous Histories: Exploring Prehistoric/Colonial Transitions in Archaeology*, edited by Siobhan M. Hart, Maxine Oland, and Liam Frink, 19–44. Tucson: University of Arizona Press.

Liebmann, Matthew. 2012b. *Revolt: An Archaeological History of Pueblo Resistance and Revitalization in 17th Century New Mexico*. Tucson: University of Arizona Press.

Loendorf, Lawrence L. 2008. *Thunder and Herds: Rock Art of the High Plains*. Walnut Creek, CA: Left Coast Press.

Loendorf, Lawrence L., and Linda Olsen. 2003. "The Tolar Petroglyph Site." *American Indian Rock Art* 29:1–10.

Lowie, Robert H. [1954] 1982. *Indians of the Plains*. Lincoln: University of Nebraska Press.

Mihesuah, Devon A., ed. 1998. *Natives and Academics: Researching and Writing about American Indians*. Lincoln: University of Nebraska Press.

Mishkin, Bernard. 1940. *Rank and Warfare among the Plains Indians*. Monographs of the American Ethnological Society III. New York: J. J. Augustin.

Mitchell, Mark D. 2004. "Tracing Comanche History: Eighteenth-Century Rock Art Depictions of Leather-Armoured Horses from the Arkansas River Basin, South-Eastern Colorado, USA." *Antiquity* 78 (299): 115–26.

Montgomery, Lindsay. 2015. "Yndios Barberos: Nomadic Archaeologies of Spanish New Mexico." PhD dissertation. Department of Anthropology, Stanford University, Palo Alto, CA.

Montgomery, Lindsay. In press. "When the Mountain People Came to Taos: Ute Archaeology in the Northern Rio Grande." In *Current and Future Research in Numic Archaeology, Ethnohistory, and Ethnography of the American West*, edited by Robert Brunswig and David Hill. Boulder: University Press of Colorado.

Newton, Cody. 2011. "Towards a Context for Late Precontact Culture Change: Comanche Movement Prior to the Eighteenth Century Spanish Documentation." *Plains Anthropologist* 56 (217): 53–69. http://dx.doi.org/10.1179/pan.2011.006.

Opler, Marvin K. 1943. "The Origins of Comanche and Ute." *American Anthropologist* 45 (1): 155–58. http://dx.doi.org/10.1525/aa.1943.45.1.02a00250.

Parsons, Mark L. 1987. "Plains Indian Portable Art as a Key to Two Texas Historic Rock Art Sites." *Plains Anthropologist* 32 (117): 257–74.

Richardson, Rupert Norval. 1933. *The Comanche Barrier to South Plains Settlement: A Century and a Half of Savage Resistance to the Advancing White Frontier*. Glendale, CA: Arthur H. Clark Company.

Richter, Daniel K. 1993. "Whose Indian History?" *William and Mary Quarterly* 50 (2): 379–93. http://dx.doi.org/10.2307/2947082.

Schaafsma, Polly. 1992. *Rock Art in New Mexico*. Santa Fe: Museum of New Mexico Press.

Secoy, Frank R. 1951. "The Identity of the 'Paduca': An Ethnohistorical Analysis." *American Anthropologist* 53 (4): 525–42. http://dx.doi.org/10.1525/aa.1951.53.4.02a00060.

Slifer, Dennis. 1998. *Signs of Life: Rock Art of the Upper Rio Grande*. Santa Fe: Ancient City Press.

Smith, Paul Chaat. 2009. *Everything You Know about Indians Is Wrong*. Minneapolis: University of Minnesota Press.

Sutton, Mark Q. 1986. "Warfare and Expansion: An Ethnohistoric Perspective on the Numic Spread." *Journal of California and Great Basin Anthropology* 8 (1): 65–82.

Thomas, Alfred Barnaby. 1935. "The Diary of Juan de Ulibarri to El Cuartelejo, 1706." In *After Coronado: Spanish Exploration Northeast of New Mexico, 1696–1727*, edited by Alfred Barnaby, 59–77. Norman: University of Oklahoma Press.

Twitchell, Ralph Emerson. 1911. *The Leading Facts of New Mexican History*. Vol. 1. Grand Rapids, IA: Torch Press.

Wallace, Ernest, and E. Adamson Hoebel. [1952] 1986. *The Comanches: Lords of the South Plains*. Norman: University of Oklahoma Press.

Wilcox, Michael. 2009. *The Pueblo Revolt and the Mythology of Conquest: An Indigenous Archaeology of Contact*. Berkeley: University of California Press.

Woosley, Anne I., and Bart Olinger. 1990. "Ethnicity and the Production of Micaceous Ware in the Taos Valley." *Archaeological Society of New Mexico Papers* 16:351–73.

SEVEN

Aquí Me Quedo

Vecino Origins and the Settlement Archaeology
of the Río del Oso Grant, New Mexico

J. ANDREW DARLING AND B. SUNDAY EISELT

Yo me quedo a cantar con los obreros en esta nueva historia y geografía
(Here I stay to sing with the workers in this new history and geography)
—Pablo Neruda, Victor Jara, and Patricio Castillo (1974),
from the song "Aquí Me Quedo" (authors' translation)

INTRODUCTION

For some historians, the fascination with Hispano culture in New Mexico begins with the simple, demographic proposition that these communities constitute a unique cultural group, formed from centuries of isolation on Spain's northern frontier (Nostrand 1970, 1975, 1980). Richard Nostrand based his interpretation of Hispano exceptionalism on cultural traits and demographic data, identifying in the process a geographic culture area he called the "Hispano Homeland," a concept that drew immediate criticism from borderlands scholars. Appropriately called the Hispano-Homeland debate, scholarly discourse focused on the twin issues of ethnicity and frontier isolation in the cultural emergence of New Mexican Spanish-speaking populations (Frank 1996; Rodríguez 1986). For Nostrand's detractors, the Hispano Homeland was a fabrication; a myth of Spanish purity spun from the threads of American ethnoclass interests (Blaut and Ríos-Bustamante 1984; Hansen 1981). For his supporters, the unique demographic and historical trajectories of New Mexican populations and the benefits of the Homeland thesis for comparative and analytical research were significant (Hall 1984; Meinig 1984; Simmons et al. 1984). The debate ultimately reached an impasse, leaving a new generation of scholars to reframe it altogether. Following the prevailing interactionist view of ethnicity at the time, Sylvia Rodríguez (1986) argued that the Hispano-Chicano identity of New Mexico was produced, not through isolation, but through its many entanglements with outsiders past and present. Ross Frank presented a combined historical and economic perspective, locating the genesis of the distinctive vernacular expression of Vecinos and Vecino culture under the colonial, socioeconomic policies of the Bourbon monarchy in Spain (Frank 1996). John Van Ness (1987b) argued that the rural agropastoral village tradition contributed decisively to the evolving contemporary Hispano identity of the region.[1]

"Homeland" evokes a political concept of shared mother country, native land, land of birth, and, by implication, a certain priority of place or possession. "Ethnogenesis" refers to the appearance of new ethnic groups (or group identities), based on a recognizable, coherent system of shared beliefs, practices, and material systems, in an area where they did not exist before. Both concepts are cited in discussions of Vecino origins in the northern Rio Grande region, but they mostly refer to shifting states defined by new frontier boundaries and political borders or configurations of material culture and social practice. While the value of these ideas should not be downplayed, they may not prove entirely satisfactory for archaeologists who seek to understand social change as a process.

"Aquí me quedo"—"here I stay" or "here I remain"—is a phrase heard throughout Latin America (and frequently seen on restaurant marquees and hotel billboards) that offers a different perspective. Immortalized as a Chilean protest anthem in the 1970s, the phrase evokes a sense of belonging and a defiant attachment to place.[2] As a construct or metaphor of the Hispano Homeland in New Mexico, it speaks to the transformation of the Spanish colonial population into an endemic one, a decolonization, but only after its initial expulsion during the Revolt of 1680 and the subsequent Reconquest in 1692. In the eighteenth century, the reconstituted Spanish colony encompassing the northern Rio Grande above Santa Fe was reestablished on a slate that for the most part had been wiped clean by the Pueblo Revolt. A new administration moved quickly to consolidate its frontiers, to establish and protect new settlements from warring Plains nomads, and to make the colonies economically viable. It took nearly a century to achieve. However, with independence looming, an era of postcolonial decolonization was about to begin.

"Aquí me quedo" is a sentiment that contemporary Hispano New Mexicans can relate to, as the descendants of Spanish colonists and Native and *genízaro* ancestors.[3] For the purposes of the following discussion, the phrase also serves to contextualize an archaeological consideration of the origin of New Mexican Vecino society, specifically in the northern Rio Grande, in ways that help to elucidate and explain the transformation of this late colonial society into an endemic community decades before Mexican independence in 1821.

WHO WERE THE VECINOS?

Prior to reconquest, the term *vecino* referred to a person's racial status in the institutionalized Spanish *regimen de castas*, a system well suited to perpetuating the separation of colonizer and colonized or conqueror and conquered. However, after the 1790s, being vecino conferred civic status under Spanish law regardless of racial background or heritage (Jenks 2011, and chapter 8 in this volume). One simply had to own land, which was a significant issue in establishing an individual's *calidad*, or status in legal proceedings (such as marriage declarations and property exchange). The qualities of being a Spanish citizen no longer served as the legal means of racial *segregation* for the purposes of regulating marriage (miscegenation) and position relative to the Spanish Crown. Instead, it became an instrument of social *integration* within communities of vecinos, and a framework for emergent, corporate landholding that promoted endogamous unions among property owners of mixed heritage (Eiselt and Darling 2014).

The sharp rise in the vecino population beginning in the late eighteenth century was an obvious measure of the prosperity wrought by the Bourbon reforms. However, few archaeological treatments have focused on the materials and settlement changes that must have accompanied the transformation of late Spanish colonial society into the Hispano social formation known as Vecino (but see Jenks, chapter 8 in this volume). This chapter describes the emergence of the Vecino cultural pattern from the 1730s to the 1830s using archaeological and ethnohistoric materials from the Rio del Oso Valley above Española (Figure 7.1). The Rio del Oso grant was settled by the first generation of reconquest *españoles* in 1734 and again in the 1810s by some of their ethnically mixed descendants. Archaeological components are distinctive and mark the shift from a late colonial (postreconquest) settlement pattern to Vecino as it appears in the northern Rio Grande. This analysis suggests that shifting relations between vecino families through marriage and filial ties with property—not status or race—conditioned endogamous unions among Vecinos in the settlement of new lands and ultimately contributed to the decolonization of the region.

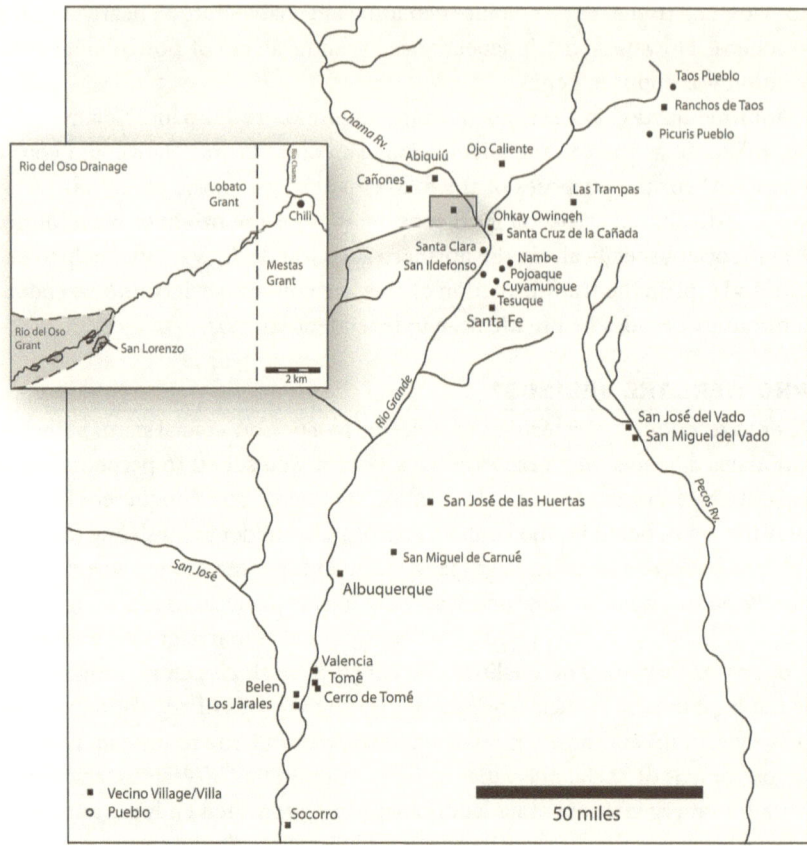

FIGURE 7.1. *Villages mentioned in the text.*

THE DEMOGRAPHIC RISE OF VECINOS

Ross Frank (2000) and others (Bustamante 1982; González 1969; Swadesh 1974) relate the economic ascendancy of Hispano villages in Spanish Colonial New Mexico to an emergent self-identity that increasingly differentiated vecino "citizens" from their Indian neighbors.[4] Economic advancement was stimulated even further with the establishment of the Bourbon monarchy in Spain during the early 1700s, whose economic reforms rippled throughout the Spanish colonies. In New Mexico, the Bourbon reforms helped to secure the province from warring Plains tribes and provided a market structure that could circulate wealth and capital throughout the colonies while generating taxes owed to the Spanish Crown (Frank 2000). Some of this wealth went directly into Vecino households, but it also provided many opportunities for New Mexican settlers and local heads of household to become legally recognized as Vecino. In addition to receiving land and money for military service, Vecino families provided livestock, meat, agricultural produce, salt, tobacco, and textiles for distribution to pacified tribes. Government purchases greatly stimulated the growth of vibrant cottage industries in weaving, carpentry, and blacksmithing that by the 1790s quickly became hallmarks of a distinctive Vecino material culture and lifeway (Dickey 1949; Frank 2000).

But the reforms did more than that. They laid the foundations for a demographic rise that was unparalleled in the American Southwest. A close examination of the years prior to the nineteenth century reveals the dynamic cycles of growth and decline leading up to this steady and rapid rise in population, and calculated growth rates put these apparent fluctuations into perspective (Figure 7.2). The New Mexico settlements experienced the greatest rate of population growth in the 1750s, rising to 7 percent. This type of growth far exceeds the biological capacities of settled agricultural communities (Chamberlain 2006), but can be attributed to a colonial pattern in which cycles of growth and decline are tied to enslavement (as a means for augmenting population), raiding, and disease. Oscillating demographic rise and decline reached a low point in the 1760s, when the colonial population actually fell by 2.6 percent, only to recover at a paltry 0.2 percent during the following decade.

After the 1790s, this trend reversed. The annual population growth rate stabilized and began to rise steadily between 2.3 and 1.8 percent per annum over the next 100 years. Unlike the marked fluctuations that characterized most of the eighteenth century, the post-1790s growth rate is consistent with natural population growth in stable agricultural communities (Chamberlain 2006). More important, the 1790 census marks the first time that the settler and *casta* (ethnically mixed and detribalized) populations turned the demographic corner, rising sharply from 14,416 in 1790 to 56,223 by 1850 (almost tripling in sixty years). This inflection coincides with the initiation of what may be called a Vecino phase of material culture and settlement in the northern Rio Grande (Eiselt and Darling 2014).[5]

NEW LANDS, NEW LAND GRANTS

Population change is reflected in the expansion and contraction of Vecino territory through time, a reflection not only of demographics but also geopolitics and raiding. During the first forty years after the reconquest, settlers were distributed in only three villages—Santa Fé, Albuquerque, and Santa Cruz de la Cañada—with individual *estancias* and ranches lining the low-lying farmlands of the Rio Grande. The sharp rise in annual population growth in the 1740s necessitated the first wave of settlement expansion. Overcrowding and poverty among the colony's freed and enslaved population compelled Spanish authorities to establish eleven new community grants from 1740 to 1765, providing land ownership and

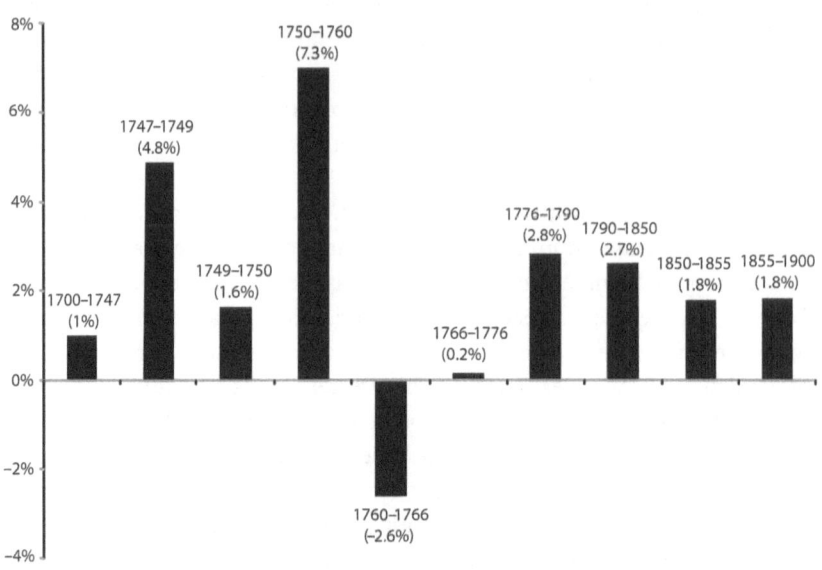

Census Interval	Beginning Population	Ending Population	Interval in Yrs.	Growth Rate
1700–1747	3,000	4,791	47	1.0%
1747–1749	4,791	5,278	2	4.8%
1749–1750	5,278	5,365	1	1.6%
1750–1760	5,365	11,194	10	7.3%
1760–1766	11,194	9,580	6	-2.6%
1766–1776	9,580	9,742	10	0.2%
1776–1790	9,742	14,416	14	2.8%
1790–1850	11,416	56,223	60	2.7%
1850–1855	56,223	61,547	5	1.8%
1855–1900	61,547	139,550	45	1.8%

FIGURE 7.2. *Changes in population growth rate from 1700 to 1900 using the formula for exponential population growth: $P(t) = P_0 e^{rt}$; where $P(t) =$ the amount of population at time t, $P_0 =$ initial amount of population at time $t = 0$, $r =$ growth rate, and $t =$ time.*

access to legal vecino status and social mobility to hundreds of *genízaros*. The ancestral make-up of these villages and grants was highly diverse, demonstrating the polyethnic roots of Vecino society (Brooks 2002).

The sharp drop in the population during the 1760s and 1770s at the hands of Comanche and Athapaskan raiders forced the abandonment of many of these settlements and a corresponding decline in land ownership over the same period. Some villages, such as San José de las Huertas and San Miguel de Carnué, were never reoccupied. In other cases—as in Abiquiú, Ranchos de Taos, and Las Trampas—settlers sought temporary protection in the larger villas or nearby

Pueblos. Land ownership expanded again on a grand scale following the execution of Spanish treaties with the Comanche, Jicarilla, Navajo, and Ute tribes in the late 1780s, leading to the establishment of the highly integrated multi-community settlement pattern described by John Van Ness (1991) and others (Kutsche and Van Ness 1981; Quintana 1991; Snow 1979; Weber 1979).

Land requests show a comparable pattern over the same period (Snow 1979). Roughly 20 to 25 requests were made every decade from 1699 to about 1775, followed by less than 10 requests per decade from 1775 to 1819, indicative of early eighteenth-century attempts by colonial residents to subjugate and occupy new territory but with little success due to raiding and disease. In contrast, the Mexican territorial period (1821 to 1849) witnessed a dramatic increase, including fifty applications for lands in unoccupied locations during the 1820s alone.[6] Nostrand (1970, 1975, 1980) mapped the Vecino homeland in the northern Rio Grande using census data from the 1850s and 1900s, demonstrating the dramatic expansion of villages and corporate land holdings to the north, south, east, and west from a central core area of population (Figure 7.3). Kenneth Weber (1979) also identifies a "splinter-diffusion" or "hiving off" pattern of internal colonization as new lands became available for settlement.

VECINO SETTLEMENT PATTERN

The settlement pattern and cultural ecology of land grants demonstrate the transformation from the late colonial (settler) to Vecino period. Prior to the 1790s, private (noncommunity) grants were awarded almost exclusively for the purposes of grazing livestock. These were large, 10,000 to 30,000 acre parcels, comparable in size and purpose to the *peonias*, or foot soldier grants, given to settlers or colonists to occupy new lands. Such large allotments were generally made when intensive development of a region was not possible due to low population densities and tribal raiding. Historical documents indicate that many of these *mercedes* were not occupied on a permanent basis, even though they might contain log cabins and corrals built by the settlers or their servants (Van Ness 1987a:162). The owners of the grant or their representatives used the land through transhumant grazing practices to fulfill the minimal requirements of legal ownership. An important consideration in awarding a grant was the ability of the petitioners to occupy and hold frontier lands against hostile tribes (Van Ness 1987a:166). To accomplish this, they had to have access to resources and personnel. Consequently, most grants were awarded to the leading citizens of the region, many of whom were the settlers of the reconquest or their children. Tenure rights were vested in kindred families that were usually (but not always) represented by male heads in whose name the grant was made. The extended family units of the grant (including the servants) constituted the basic corporate, social, and economic units for livelihood and inheritance (Van Ness 1987a:166–67).

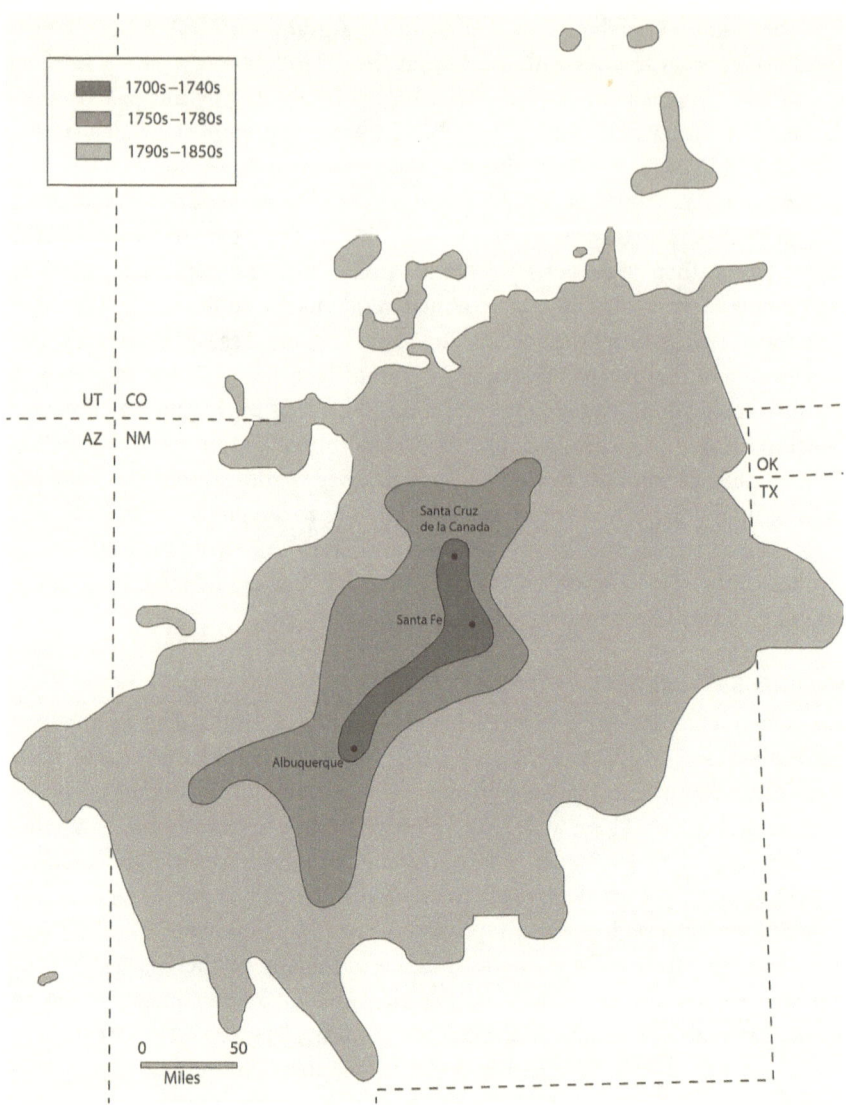

FIGURE 7.3. *The expansion of the Vecino Homeland after Nostrand (1970, 1975, 1980). The 1700s to 1780s boundaries are approximated from historical documents.*

Fifty or sixty years after the reconquest, colonial populations fell back into more defensible communities, and large areas of land and certain land grants appropriated on the return of the Spanish were abandoned. Populations declined dramatically, and, teetering on the brink of survival, they concentrated in a few remaining fortified settlements. This trend reversed itself in the later part of the eighteenth century. Populations rebounded, year-round settlements appeared along tributary streams, and land grant cooperatives adopted mixed economies that relied on stock raising, farming, and trade (Van Ness 1991).

The *rancho* was the most prevalent settlement pattern at this time. In its general usage, the term *rancho* implies a small rural property managed by individual families or groups of coresident families for the purpose of subsistence-level farming or ranching, but in its more specific usage refers to the area of settlement within the grant rather than the entire grant. Rancho households within grants typically consisted of the members of an extended kin network who resided in clustered structures, located within or among individual farm lots (called *lineas*). Household facilities and buildings included mud-and-thatch (*jacal*) structures and adobe houses. Dried foods were stored in ceramic vessels, adobe bins, or wooden bins that were placed in a *dispensa*, or storage shed, attached to the main residence. Grain, farm implements, and fodder were stored in a *fuerte*, or thick-walled stone structure (Wozniak et al. 1992:153). Other storage facilities included subterranean *soterranos* and raised platforms (*tapeistes*). Together these closely spaced domestic structures comprised an extended family household compound.

The typical land grant of the later period delineated an area in which the residents selected parcels of irrigable land (the *lineas*, or long lots) that were privately owned and could be sold after a period of occupation (Westphall 1983). The occupants managed a shared ditch system and were required to act as stewards of the watershed commons (Crawford 1988; Rivera 1998; Swadesh 1974:32). The commonwealth or shared portions of the grant, typically situated above the acequias and cultivated bottomland, were communally owned and managed for hunting, herding, and wild plant and timber harvesting. The acequia and long-lot agricultural complex promoted and protected regional biodiversity by creating a patchwork of habitats linked by crosscutting irrigation corridors (Peña 1999). Farming in this context did not end at the edge of the field. Rather, the farm was part of an ecological system that was embedded in a larger nexus of cultural and biological interactions that promoted regional biodiversity (Eiselt 2013).

THE DOCUMENTARY HISTORY OF THE RIO DEL OSO GRANT

Archaeological demography provides some of the best evidence for the emergence of an endemic growth pattern in Vecino populations. Our example comes from the Rio del Oso Valley above Española (see Figure 7.1). Spanish settlers first occupied the valley soon after the Spanish reconquest. Juan Manuel de Herrera, and Rosalía Valdez (with her two sons Juan Valdez and Ignacio Valdez), and several other petitioners were granted a tract of land encompassing approximately 10,000 acres in 1734.[7] Soon after, Roque Jacinto Jaramillo also joined the grant. Herrera was Jaramillo's contemporary and father-in-law; Jaramillo married

Herrera's second daughter, Juana. These individuals were the children of the reconquest, inhabitants of Santa Cruz de la Cañada who had come with their parents from Mexico City, Zacatecas, and the El Paso exile colony to resettle New Mexico. Vargas recruited Jaramillo's father, a brick mason, in 1693 from the largely Spanish artisan class in Mexico City (Kessell et al. 1998:223). Roque was around eleven years old at the time of the trip (Kessell et al. 1998:247). Rosalía's father, José Ruiz, was born in Oviedo, Spain. Accompanied by his wife and two children, he traveled with the original colonists in 1696 and became the Sargento Mayor (Sargent Major) at Santa Cruz where Rosalía was born around 1700, but he was later killed at the Zuni Mission while singing a hymn in the church after mass. Juan Manuel de Herrera's mother and stepfather, likewise, lost both of their spouses in the Pueblo Revolt, but joined their families in marriage, after retreating to the El Paso exile colony (Kessell et al. 1998:1144; 1995:43).

The settlement of El Paraje Rio Oso, as it was then known, was small in its early stages. The 1744 census by Fray Miguel de Menchero indicates that together the Rancho de Chama and Rio del Oso settlements maintained only eleven to seventeen families (Hackett 1937:399; Jones 1979:123), not enough to ward off a devastating attack by the Utes that occurred in 1736. Nearly all of the settlers abandoned their ranches, but Jaramillo and Herrera stayed, reaffirming their interest in the grant in 1746, and possibly moving their headquarters downstream. Further depredations by the Comanche and Utes in 1747 prompted most of the early settlers of the Abiquiú area to flee once again. Nevertheless, Jaramillo persisted, purchasing shares from the others who abandoned the grant citing the lack of sufficient water and farmland. Shortfalls in water and real estate may only be partly true. Jaramillo used the Rio del Oso as pasturage for his cattle, and his children built structures and were farming in the valley in 1762; but, their presence also was short lived. Jaramillo lost his claim to the grant soon thereafter, having become entangled in an unrelated dispute over the adjoining Vallecitos grant. The Rio del Oso grant reverted to public domain in 1763 and was held in trust by Juan José Lobato, *alcalde mayor* (municipal magistrate) of Santa Cruz de la Cañada, for the next fifty years.[8]

On October 5, 1810, José Antonio Valdez along with ten other heads of household requested a new grant in the valley.[9] Some thirty years later this grant was reaffirmed by the alcalde of Santa Cruz de la Cañada in 1840. José Ramón Vijil (justice of the peace for the district of Santa Clara) surveyed the area in August to put the settlers in possession of the land. Vijil's 1840 report provides the only existing description of the Rio del Oso grant and its inhabitants during the nineteenth century.[10] By the 1870s, the settlement had acquired a name. An 1877 map drafted by G. M. Wheeler of the US Army Corps of Engineers shows the village of San Lorenzo and related houses midway up the valley (Wheeler 1877).

GENEALOGY OF THE RIO DEL OSO GRANT

The US Court of Private Land Claims extinguished the title to the Rio del Oso grant in 1893 (Swadesh 1974:212), effectively ending the historic occupation, but leaving us with a number of unanswered questions. Were any of the later grant occupants related to the first settlers? If so, then how did kinship condition occupancy and ownership of the Rio del Oso lands? Are phases of occupation (the first of which is clearly derived from the reconquest) reflected in the archaeological record of the valley and, if so, how did they change through time? Using land grant documents and baptism, marriage, and death records, we reconstructed the genealogy of the grant and traced the family histories of eight out of eleven of the nineteenth-century petitioners.

Figure 7.4 renders the grant genealogy in simplified terms beginning with the first settlers of the de Vargas reconquest on the left. These individuals were the parents of the eighteenth-century Rio del Oso grant residents or owners. José Antonio Valdez, the main petitioner on the 1840s grant, was the third son of Juan Bautista Valdez (Van Ness 1980:11). The parents of Juan Bautista are currently unknown, but he appears to have grown up in the Rosalía Valdez household, after she left the Rio del Oso and took up residence at the Plaza Colorada near Abiquiú. Juan Bautista founded the community of Cañones to the west of the Rio del Oso grant in 1807. Jose Antonio's sister, Antonia Rosa Valdez, in turn married José María Ortega. He and his brother San Juan (both petitioners on the grant) were born in Chili to the east, at the mouth of the Rio del Oso. The parents of the Ortega's maternal grandmother are currently unknown. Cristóbal and Juan Pedro Herrera were brothers as well and were related to Juan Manuel Herrera, Roque Jaramillo's partner and son-in-law. Juan Manuel was Cristobal and Juan Pedro's great-uncle on their father's side. The great-grandfather of Juan Cristobal and Polito Lobato, also brothers, was Juan José Lobato, the alcalde mayor who exterminated the Herrera-Jaramillo holding in 1763. Their mother also is currently unknown.

The grant genealogy is revealing with respect to marriage patterns and land acquisition. First, the Rio del Oso grant was resettled in 1810 by sets of siblings, either brothers or brothers and sisters, who could claim lineal descent from one of the original landowners (Herrera, Jaramillo, or Valdez). The sisters drew spouses from families that were unrelated to the original three lines (the Vijils and Ortegas), but the lands where they grew up bordered or were in close proximity to the Rio del Oso grant. The Ortegas could claim ties to the adjoining Mestas grant to the east (which encompassed the neighboring settlements of Chili and La Cuchilla at the mouth of the Rio del Oso), and the Valdez family occupied the Cañones region to the west. These ties would have facilitated innumerable resources and cooperation across the boundaries of the grant for social events, trade, and herd management.

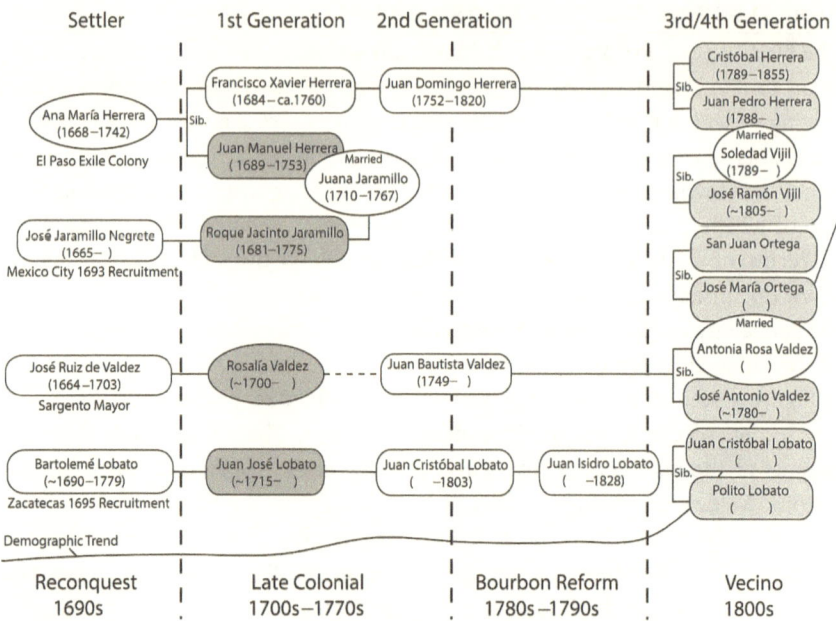

FIGURE 7.4. *Rio del Oso grant genealogy. Rounded rectangles represent the males, and the ovals represent the females in lines of descent. Marriage is indicated by overlap in polygons of different shapes, and siblings are marked in the nodes of branches labeled "Sib." Shaded polygons indicate the residents or owners of the Rio del Oso grant during the late colonial and Vecino periods. The demographic rise of Vecino populations are graphed relative to the genealogy of the grant.*

What remains to be fully deciphered, however, is the occupational hiatus of the Rio del Oso Valley between 1760 and 1810, effectively skipping the second generation after the reconquest from the terminal late colonial through the Bourbon reform period. The presumed grandchildren or great-grandchildren (third and fourth generations) of the original reconquest settlers reestablished the Rio del Oso Valley settlement by the early 1800s. This reoccupation is consistent with the population boom that marks the appearance of Vecino settlements throughout the northern Rio Grande. However, little is known of the parents and grandparents of these sibling sets that reoccupied the Rio del Oso during the Vecino period.

One possible explanation lies in the high frequency of captives and Indian adoptions in the reconquest households of the 1740s, especially on rural land grants, where the availability of labor was key to survival.[11] The gaps in the Rio del Oso lineages may suggest the incorporation of unidentified Indian children and/or children of mixed heritage into Spanish households. Nevertheless, the anonymity of these individuals, particularly by comparison with the record of the preceding generation of reconquest *españoles* and subsequent generations of Vecinos, seems particularly telling.

Indian or mixed-blood adoptions could undermine subsequent claims to lands or grants based solely on direct lineal descent. However, complementary or advantageous marriages among siblings during the expansion of the Vecino homeland also could bolster land claims and serve to consolidate corporate landholdings and kinship alliances that crosscut grant (and family) boundaries. Such alliances provided a clear mechanism for the hiving-off process or pattern of splinter-diffusion described by Weber (1979:81) by which daughter villages were created from mother villages, thereby expanding Vecino occupation into neighboring grants in outlying areas. This is easily recognizable in the archaeological evidence produced by a full coverage survey conducted in the Rio del Oso, as follows.

THE ARCHAEOLOGICAL RECORD OF THE RIO DEL OSO GRANT

Archaeological research on ranchos involves a survey of the entire grant so that contemporary features can be identified and settlement patterns and household organization can be reconstructed (Church 2002; Galindo 2004:195). Survey coverage of the Rio del Oso meets these requirements. The combined efforts of multiple researchers have documented nearly the entire Rio del Oso grant and the lower reaches of the Rio del Oso Valley watershed (Anschuetz 1993, 1995; Gadd 1988, 1989a, 1989b; Jeançon 1911, 1912; Vierra 1980). Research also has identified a large Jicarilla Apache presence in the valley dating to the mid-1800s (Eiselt 2012).

Two occupations define the Spanish and subsequent Vecino record. The early component pertains to the Jaramillo-Herrera grant and consists of three household complexes surrounded by hundreds of meters of rock walls on the south side of the drainage. Two of the household complexes are located at the village of Pesede'uinge (a Classic Period Pueblo site), and the third is positioned upstream in an area used previously for late prehistoric farming. Settlers built the extensive network of walled terraces from rock scavenged from Puebloan structures and features. This includes prehistoric grinding stones, grinding slicks, and cupule boulders. The walls are substantial, one meter in width at the base by fifty centimeters in height in many places, and are constructed of large boulders that would have required draft animal transport. Most of the walled areas are located on the second and third terraces above the valley floor, in areas that would have required rainwater farming to be productive, further supporting the contention that they likely served as enclosed pastures. The total area includes nearly seventy acres of walled terraces.

The household complexes of this early period of historic occupation are simple, consisting of a single linear room block associated with an *horno* (earthen oven) and *torreón* (guard tower), a plan that is repeated at all three sites. Figure 7.5 (top) illustrates the typical roomblock arrangement. Prehistoric groundstone and cobble clusters or scatters also are common in the vicinity of structures, but artifacts are rare. Occasional historic plain or micaceous sherds are all that remains. Horno foundations are rounded to subrounded in outline and are approximately one to two meters in diameter and two to three cobble courses in height. The stonework for the structural foundations is, however, distinctive, being made with carefully laid masonry composed of locally acquired angular rock with well-dressed (flat) interior and exterior facing. While no rubble core is evident between the parallel rows, the presence of possible adobe melt toward interiors of structures suggest that the walls built above the foundation were composed of either adobe brick or jacal, consisting of small posts and thatch covered with an adobe plaster. The quality of the masonry is distinctive for the late colonial period and is clearly distinguishable from the later Vecino structures that feature loosely laid stone foundations with aboveground, post-and-adobe construction. The lack of structural mounds suggests that building materials were removed and reutilized after abandonment. Structures range in size from 7 to 10 meters in length by 4 to 5 meters in width and show evidence of an interior wall that divides the building into two rooms. Their locations on the edges of valley terraces overlooking the Rio del Oso provide for easy access to live water sources below, adjacent flat-top mesas, and vistas up and down the valley.

The proximity of these late colonial occupations to late Pueblo (possibly revolt period) settlements also suggests that their placement was strategic. This includes not only the symbolic reoccupation of Puebloan settlements but also the availability of ready-made construction materials and preexisting structures that could be reused by the Spanish settlers. This pattern of occupation and reuse has been documented elsewhere in the northern Rio Grande (Snow 1976) and can include the modification of existing prehistoric structural mounds for animal pens, habitation, cultivation or grazing.

Torreones also may have been refurbished from Puebloan structures, kivas, or circular stone shrines. The largest of these at Pesede'uinge measures seven meters in diameter at the base. Jeançon (1912:29–30) noted the lack of apparent kivas at Pesede'uinge, and argued that the *torreón* seemed to be built up from the foundation of a kiva with cobbles held in place by adobe cement. The structure stood approximately two meters high in 1912 and still contained several vigas in the roof.

The nineteenth-century occupation of the valley is very different. This occupation consists of one large, multidwelling settlement, identified as San Lorenzo on historic maps, and three additional household complexes located at some distance including structures, livestock pens, and early-component rock-lined fields. San Lorenzo household complexes display a "classic" nineteenth-century

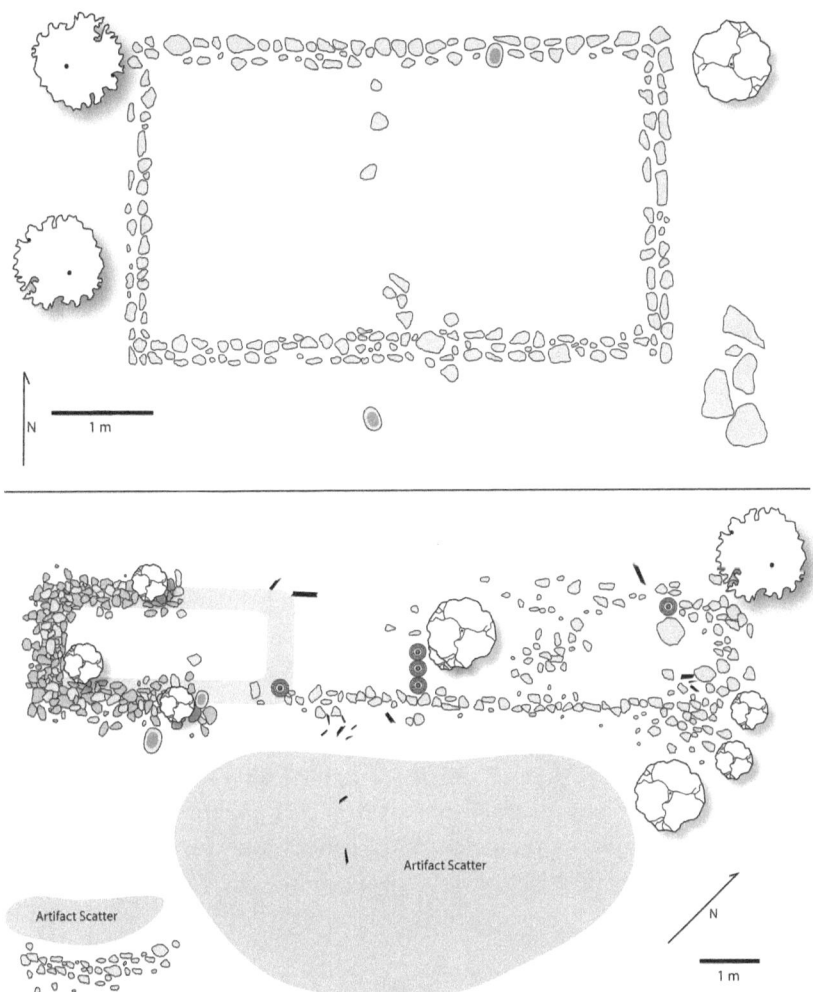

FIGURE 7.5. *Early and late component structures in the Rio del Oso Valley. Top: eighteenth-century structure from LA 299 (Pesede'uinge). Bottom: nineteenth-century household complex from LA 90870.*

structure described in ethnohistoric documents as a small linear or L-shaped roomblock adjoining a substantial stone *fuerte* (storage facility) and surrounded by a rock-lined courtyard with external trash accumulations (Wozniak et al. 1992) (see Figure 7.5). The concentrated accumulation of artifacts at the site in middens associated with structures suggests permanent, year-round occupation. Structures are smaller and less substantial jacales with expedient stone foundations. Unlike the earlier occupation, sites are located on both sides of

Vecino Origins and the Settlement Archaeology of the Rio del Oso Grant | **201**

the drainage in areas relatively devoid of prehistoric Pueblo architecture (none of the nineteenth-century occupations are situated on top of Pesede'uinge or prehistoric habitation sites).

The later occupants also made greater use of the valley as evidenced by isolated sheep herder structures, wagon roads, trails, and Hispanic rock art downstream. *Torreones* and *hornos* are not part of this record, and sites are not situated on strategic overlooks. Moreover, artifacts show the integration of Native American material culture into men's and women's activities. This includes evidence for small amounts of plain (grayware) and micaceous ceramic production;[12] the use of expedient stone tools for cutting and as gunflints; the utilization of milling equipment scavenged from Puebloan sites; and the production of tinworks including frames, *nichos* (household alters), and cone tinklers, or ornaments that Jicarilla women used to decorate their clothes. Additional evidence for regular trade with Indian people includes Tewa plainware and decorated ceramics, Jicarilla micaceous cookware, and metal arrow points also obtained from the Jicarilla.

Unlike the earlier residents, whose settlements were positioned to defend against Ute and Comanche attacks, the residents of San Lorenzo carried on a brisk trade in metals and ceramics with the *Saitinde* band of the *Ollero*, a subdivision of the Jicarilla Apache, who also occupied the valley starting in the mid-1800s (Eiselt 2012; Eiselt and Darling 2012). Jicarilla encampments are located on the north side of the valley and overlap the boundaries of the grant. These settlements represent several extended families of around forty to fifty people. The *Gojia*, an annual Jicarilla gathering and foot race, was celebrated at the mouth of the Rio del Oso prior to the fall hunt in the Jemez Mountains, which brought additional families and neighboring Tewa people from Ohkay Owingeh to trade (Eiselt 2012).

LATE SPANISH COLONIAL AND VECINO SETTLEMENT PATTERN IN THE RIO DEL OSO VALLEY

In summary, the settlement pattern of the early and late occupational components of the valley reveal a marked archaeological contrast (Table 7.1). Created by the children of españoles from Mexico City, Zacatecas, and the El Paso exile colony, the late Spanish colonial occupation exhibits a settlement pattern that is quasi-military or defensive in nature, situated on top of Pueblo archaeological sites, and focused on exploitation of the valley for large-scale livestock management and farming. Settlement was equally strategic and expedient, taking advantage of the readily available building material provided by recently (and perhaps forcefully) abandoned Tewa structures, as well as preexisting field and irrigation systems, which when left fallow would have sustained ample forage for the grazing of livestock.

TABLE 7.1. Comparison of late colonial and Vecino occupations in the Rio del Oso.

Settlement index	Late colonial (settler)	Vecino
Occupation	Defensive and exploitive	Integrated and interactive
Location	On top of prehistoric Pueblos and on strategic overlooks	Scavenging from prehistoric Pueblos, strategic access to resources
Architecture	Walled terraces, torreones, and hornos	Courtyards, storage, corral, and herding facilities
Artifacts	Low surface-artifact densities, short-term superficial occupation	High artifact densities, long-term highly integrated occupation
Interactions	No evidence for Native American materials and practices.	Ample evidence for Native American trade materials and practices.

The early eighteenth-century Spanish colonial occupation was short lived, and the valley remained unoccupied for nearly fifty years due to Ute and Comanche raiding, though use of the Rio del Oso Valley as a pilgrimage route and travel corridor by Tewa and Athapaskan populations likely continued. In the final decades of the eighteenth century, the new Vecino population that emerged reestablished and occupied former Spanish land grants prior to expansion into previously unoccupied areas. The new settlement pattern lacks the defensive posture and is more fully integrated into the surrounding landscape and engaged with Indian neighbors, including the semisettled *Saitinde* band of the Jicarilla Apache. The later grant emphasized an integrated subsistence-settlement economy with significant Indian input into technology and trade, and unlike the earlier colonial occupation, the Vecino settlement of San Lorenzo was located away from the late prehistoric or early historic Pueblo archaeological sites. While even the settlement of San Lorenzo did not survive, other Vecino settlements persist until the present day and have done so since the initial expansion of Vecino population beginning in the late eighteenth century.

"AQUÍ ME QUEDO"

This chapter proposes that the permanent, "Hispanic" occupation of the Rio del Oso Valley and many other areas like it in northern New Mexico was the result of Vecino population growth and settlement expansion beginning approximately 100 years after the Spanish reconquest. This was accompanied by material and sociocultural practices visible in the historical and archaeological records. "Aquí me quedo" provides the metaphor for the transformation of a people who were formerly citizens of Spain into a cohesive, endemic society that was increasingly less dependent on the administrative and religious apparatus embodied by the Spanish Crown. The *penitente*, who assumed responsibility for maintaining the rituals and beliefs of the secularized and disenfranchised

Catholic Church in colonial New Mexico, offers an obvious example of the decolonization process that signaled a break with Spanish authority decades before Mexican independence. However, this was not the only institution. The system of *mayordomos*, acequia associations, and other religious, political, and even quasi-military organizations also served to establish the Vecino community and to assume local authority.

Genealogical reconstruction speaks to the gradual decolonization of the northern Rio Grande region, in particular the transformation of the Spanish colonial status system from one that intentionally segregated Spanish reconquest settlers from nonlanded *genízaros* and Indians to the more inclusive system in which all individual landholders were considered Vecinos regardless of, or perhaps in spite of, family bloodline.

The temporary abandonment of the Rio del Oso Valley from the 1760s to the early 1800s by Spanish settlers is an especially critical time in the transformation of colonial society. It may also serve as a prime example of a broader pattern of partial abandonment of lands during Ute and Comanche hostilities, and the concentration of survivors in defensible towns and settlements. This set the stage for the initial breakdown in Spanish institutions including the arcane and untenable *regimen de castas*, after it became necessary to replace lost family members with adopted captives or individuals of mixed ancestry.

The land negotiations that led to the Vecino reoccupation of the Rio del Oso after 1810 also suggest that genealogical reckoning by Vecinos purposely emphasized descent from late Spanish colonial land grant founders, while simultaneously suppressing Native or *genízaro* ancestry. This had little to do with matters of race or denial of certain details of descent. Instead, it was necessary for new marriages to perpetuate the family and consolidate existing landholdings on the basis of ancestral ties to original landholders and grant recipients. Historians recognize this but the implications have not been appreciated sufficiently in archaeological investigations. Current chronologies, for example, still use historical events, such as Mexican independence in 1821 or the American invasion of the 1840s, as benchmarks for culture change. However it is clear that many of the sociocultural transformations indicative of the new Vecino community in the northern Rio Grande precede these events by years or even decades.

THE HOMELAND REVISITED

We have characterized the Spanish Colonial to Vecino transition as a "decolonization" with certain implications for population dynamics and the occupation of new lands. Slavery and miscegenation were driving forces in the population dynamics of the late colonial period along with disease and deaths due to raiding. Frontier violence along with customs of marriage and inheritance that segregated populations limited the stability and longevity of land holdings. This is reflected not only in the abandonment of villages and land grants, but also in the occupations themselves—the locations, structure, and content of archaeological sites that were defensive, quasi-militaristic, and that appropriated the Puebloan landscape.

After 1790, Vecino status shifted from the strictly legal definition that existed nearly 100 years earlier. The demographic collapse of the eighteenth century that followed the Comanche raids and a series of epidemics generally undermined local, colonial systems of class and status that served to distinguish Vecinos from *naturales*. The Bourbon reforms stimulated a significant increase in endogamous marriages among property-owning Vecinos of mixed heritage, which in turn, served to concentrate wealth and property within a new ethnic group. By the early 1800s, Vecinos were marrying within landholding groups in order to extend control over territory and integrate the economies of neighboring grants. Filial ties with property conditioned the emergence and consolidation of an endemic Vecino population with connections to a deeper Indian heritage. When viewed demographically, the need for favorable endogamous unions to consolidate and hold property promoted the process of Vecino decolonization. The archaeological record reflects this process and the material connections to Indian neighbors that resulted.

In short, the Rio del Oso Valley provides a compelling case study, demonstrating an important but overlooked body of data (kinship) and the demographic processes responsible for changes in land tenure and the hiving-off of new settlements. Hispanic settlement of the Rio del Oso includes late Spanish colonial and Vecino occupations that are clearly discernable in the archaeological record, and the genealogy of the grant demonstrates the connections between them.

Richard Nostrand's Homeland Thesis was a milestone in studies of Southwestern cultures, sparking a debate that still influences borderlands scholars today. Efforts to locate the source and nature of New Mexico's Spanish-speaking population have identified two axes of interest—cultural interactions and connections to the land—both emphasizing place-based, civic identities that are unique to New Mexican Hispanos. However, it is also understood generally that historical efforts of the Bourbon state to make the colony economically viable also contributed to its transformation.

"Aquí me quedo," or "here I stay," is more than a simple reference to a protest song made famous throughout Latin America. It is a metaphor through which Vecino origins in northern New Mexico may be better understood. "Here I stay" appeals to the notion of a people and a homeland that was quickly subsumed by the American invasion following Mexican independence but only after Vecino society emerged as a persistent indigenous community.

NOTES

1. For editorial consistency we use the term "Hispano" rather than "Hispanic" following Adrian Bustamante 1982; Charles Carrillo 1997; Richard Nostrand 1980, 1992; Rodríguez 1986; Van Ness 1987b, 1991. We acknowledge that the terms "Hispanic" and "Hispano" are not interchangeable but refer the reader to these authors for further nuanced discussion of the differences.

2. Chilean poet, Pablo Neruda, memorialized the phrase in the song, "Aquí Me Quedo," the music for which was composed by Victor Jara (with Patricio Castillo). It was recorded in 1973 and was released in 1974 on the album *Manifiesto* following the deaths of Neruda and Jara.

3. *Genízaro* was a specialized ethnic term used by the Spanish to designate the mixed progeny of Indian captives, who were born free but, having been raised in the Spanish milieu, had lost their tribal identity, customs, and language (Chávez 1979:198).

4. In early eighteenth-century parlance the term *vecinos* referred to Spanish neighbors as opposed to *naturales*, who were "uncivilized," presumably unbaptized, Pueblo Indians. In its most basic form, a Vecino was a tithes-paying settler with an established household and the legal right to marry other settlers. For non-Vecinos, becoming Vecino required a change in legal status that was based on land ownership and economic achievement. Eligibility also was determined by adherence to the Catholic faith and by behaving like fellow colonials. After reconquest, the system became more relaxed. Indian, ethnically mixed, and *genízaro* individuals could achieve Vecino status through Plains Indian trade and warfare, which brought them the necessary economic success, independent of their position in the local expression of the *regimen de castas* (Bustamante 1991).

5. See Sunday Eiselt and Andrew Darling (Eiselt and Darling 2014) for additional analysis of this demographic pattern.

6. Land ownership was also facilitated by the 1822 Plan of Iguala, which extended Mexican citizenship to all individuals regardless of their ethnic or economic consequences. The new administration, eager to secure the loyalties of the population under Mexican rule, further undertook a broad program of reaffirming titles to grants during the 1840s.

7. Vincento Jirón and Joseph Gomes were additional associates. Jirón and Ignacio Valdez likely never settled on the grant.

8. Frances Swadesh (1974:212) points out that as the ranking civil servant of this district, Lobato frequently took possession of lands that were forfeited by settlers during Indian raids, and later placed settlers in possession of lands that were claimed in his name. Although it is unclear whether Lobato actually occupied this grant (as required by Spanish law), he did sell portions to neighboring landowners. A certain amount of land speculation therefore clouds the history of the Rio del Oso valley and its relation to the larger Lobato grant that encompassed it.

9. Spanish Archives of New Mexico, Vol. 1, SG 59 Roll 31, Case File 112, State Record Center and Archives, Santa Fe.

10. An excerpt: "proceeding to divide them from east to west in the area of the houses to some with a greater number of varas than others so that the width of land is not equal and to each is as follows: Cristoval Herrera 287, José Antonio Valdez 287, Cristoval Lobato 115, Seberino Valerio 115, Miguel Mariano Chavez 115, Jose Ramon Vijil 115 (a short piece given in this intermediate area without owner since it is considered unusable), and follows Jose Maria Ortega 115, San Juan Ortega 230, Francisco Gallego, 115, Juan Pedro Herrera 115, Polito Lobato 230. The uplands of this grant being left without division as far as where one cannot see the source of water for the main acequia [canal], for from there all that is irrigated they divide in equal parts as if they were legitimate heirs of that site, being preferred in distributing without title the said Valdez and the rest who make primary use with these and others that the ditch provides, and who work in maintaining the entire said acequia. They agree unanimously that some of the said donors [shareholders or associates] would do their part for whatever reason, this being the primary title of the aforementioned Valdez. The boundaries of this land being distinguished on the north by the canyon of the Almagre, on the south by the upland adjacent to the river, on the east where the arroyo of the Almagre empties, and on the west the rim of Ute Mesa." Translation by J. Andrew Darling; for the original Spanish, see Eiselt (2012).

11. The Mestas grant provides an example. Juan de Mestas established the settlement of La Cuchilla at the mouth of the Rio del Oso in the early 1730s (Swadesh 1974:33). In 1808 Manuel Mestas, a famous genízaro who had served the Abiquiú settlers as a Ute interpreter, was a private landowner at La Cuchilla. Several other residents of the same surname were listed at Abiquiú, including Guadalupe Mestas, who was married to José el Apache in the 1780s. Swadesh (1974:43) states that these families may have been relatives of Manuel Mestas, or they all may have acquired the surname through service to the Mestas family of La Cuchilla. Given that 73 percent of the captives during the early to mid-1700s were Apache (Brugge 1985), the likelihood that at least some of the Vecino residents of the lower Chama (including the Rio del Oso) during the nineteenth century had Athapaskan or Ute blood cannot be discounted.

12. See discussions of Vecino micaceous ceramic production in Carrillo (1997) and in Eiselt and Darling (2012).

REFERENCES CITED

Anschuetz, Kurt F. 1993 (Submitted to). "Preliminary Report for the 1992 Field Season: The University of Michigan Río del Oso Archaeological Survey, Española Ranger District." Española Ranger District, Santa Fe National Forest, Española. Manuscript on file, US Department of Agriculture, US Forest Service, Southwestern Region, Santa Fe National Forest, Santa Fe. *Santa Fe National Forest.*

Anschuetz, Kurt F. 1995. Preliminary Report for the 1993 Field Season: The University of Michigan Río del Oso Archaeological Survey, Española Ranger District, Santa Fe National Forest. Manuscript on file, US Department of Agriculture, US Forest Service, Southwestern Region, Santa Fe National Forest, Santa Fe.

Blaut, James M., and Antonio Ríos-Bustamante. 1984. "Commentary on Nostrand's 'Hispanos' and their 'Homeland.'" *Annals of the Association of American Geographers* 74 (1): 157–64. http://dx.doi.org/10.1111/j.1467-8306.1984.tb01441.x.

Brooks, James F. 2002. *Captives and Cousins: Slavery, Kinship, and Community in the Southwest Borderlands*. Chapel Hill: University of North Carolina Press.

Brugge, David M. 1985. *Navajos in the Catholic Church Records of New Mexico, 1694–1875*. Tsaile, AZ: Navajo Community College Press.

Bustamante, Adrian H. 1982. "Los Hispanos: Ethnicity and Social Change in New Mexico." PhD dissertation, Department of American Studies, University of New Mexico, Albuquerque.

Bustamante, Adrian H. 1991. "'The Matter Was Never Resolved': The Casta System in Colonial New Mexico, 1693–1823." *New Mexico Historical Review* 66 (2): 143–63.

Carrillo, Charles M. 1997. *Hispanic New Mexican Pottery: Evidence of Craft Specialization 1790–1890*. Albuquerque: LPD Press.

Chamberlain, Andrew T. 2006. *Demography in Archaeology*. Cambridge: Cambridge University Press. http://dx.doi.org/10.1017/CBO9780511607165.

Chávez, Angélico. 1979. "Genízaros." In *Southwest*, edited by Alfonso Ortiz, 467–73. Handbook of North American Indians, Vol. 9, William C. Sturtevant, general editor. Washington, DC: Smithsonian Institution.

Church, Minette. 2002. "The Grant and the Grid: Homestead Landscapes in the Late Nineteenth-Century Borderlands of Southern Colorado." *Journal of Social Archaeology* 2 (2): 220–44.

Crawford, Stanley. 1988. *Mayordomo: Chronicle of an Acequia in Northern New Mexico*. Albuquerque: University of New Mexico Press.

Dickey, Roland F. 1949. *New Mexico Village Arts*. Albuquerque: University of New Mexico Press.

Eiselt, B. Sunday. 2012. *Becoming White Clay: A History and Archaeology of Jicarilla Apache Enclavement*. Salt Lake City: University of Utah Press.

Eiselt, B. Sunday. 2013. "Upland-Lowland Corridors and Historic Jicarilla Apache Settlement in the Northern Rio Grande." In *From Mountain Top to Valley Bottom: Understanding Past Land Use in the Northern Rio Grande Valley, New Mexico*, edited by Bradley J. Vierra, 131–44. Salt Lake City: University of Utah Press.

Eiselt, B. Sunday, and J. Andrew Darling. 2012. "Vecino Economics: Gendered Economy and Micaceous Pottery Consumption in Nineteenth-Century Northern New Mexico." *American Antiquity* 77 (3): 424–48. http://dx.doi.org/10.7183/0002-7316.77.3.424.

Eiselt, B. Sunday, and J. Andrew Darling. 2014. "Ethnogenesis and Demography in Southwest Vecino Society." In *"Archaeology and History: Integrating Cause across Historical Ecology, Demography, and Movement,"* edited by Ann F. Ramenofsky and

L. Cynthia Herhahn. Manuscript on file, Department of Anthropology, Southern Methodist University, Dallas, Texas.

Frank, Ross. 1996. "Economic Growth and the Creation of the Vecino Homeland in New Mexico, 1780–1820." *Revista de Indias* 56 (208): 743–82. http://dx.doi.org/10.3989/revindias.1996.i208.805.

Frank, Ross. 2000. *From Settler to Citizen: New Mexican Economic Development and the Creation of Vecino Society, 1750–1820*. Berkeley: University of California Press.

Gadd, Powys. 1988. "Río del Oso / Palacio Arroyo Erosion Allotment, Cultural Resource Survey, Española Ranger District, Santa Fe National Forest, New Mexico." Forest Service Clearance Report 1988-10-037. Manuscript on file, US Department of Agriculture, US Forest Service, Southwest Region, Albuquerque, New Mexico.

Gadd, Powys. 1989a. "Non-Project Cultural Resource Survey, Río del Oso, Española Ranger District, Santa Fe National Forest, New Mexico." Forest Service Clearance Report 1989-10-008. Manuscript on file, US Department of Agriculture, US Forest Service, Southwest Region, Albuquerque, New Mexico.

Gadd, Powys. 1989b. "Río del Oso Electric Fence, Cultural Resource Survey, Rio Arriba County, New Mexico, Española Ranger District, Santa Fe National Forest, New Mexico." Forest Service Clearance Report 1989-10-086. Manuscript on file, US Department of Agriculture, US Forest Service, Southwest Region, Albuquerque, New Mexico.

Galindo, Mary Jo. 2004. "The Ethnohistory and Archaeology of Nuevo Santander *Rancho* Households." In *Household Chores and Household Choices: Theorizing the Domestic Sphere in Historical Archaeology*, edited by Kerri S. Barille and Jamie C. Brandon, 179–96. Tuscaloosa: University of Alabama Press.

González, Nancie. 1969. *The Spanish-Americans of New Mexico: A Heritage of Pride*. Albuquerque: University of New Mexico Press.

Hackett, Charles W. 1937. *Historical Documents Relating to New Mexico, Nueva Vizcaya, and Approaches Thereto, to 1773*. Vol. 3. Washington, DC: Carnegie Institution.

Hall, Thomas D. 1984. "Commentary." *Annals of the Association of American Geographers* 74 (1): 171.

Hansen, Niles. 1981. "Commentary on the Hispano Homeland in 1900." *Annals of the Association of American Geographers* 71 (2): 280–82. http://dx.doi.org/10.1111/j.1467-8306.1981.tb01355.x.

Jeançon, Jean A. 1911. "Explorations in Chama Basin, New Mexico." In *Records of the Past: Volume X*, edited by Frederick B. Wright, 92–108. Washington, DC: Records of the Past Exploration Society.

Jeançon, Jean A. 1912. "Ruins at Pesedeuinge." In *Records of the Past: Volume XI*, edited by Frederick B. Wright, 38–37. Washington, DC: Records of the Past Exploration Society.

Jenks, Kelly L. 2011. "Vecinos en la Frontera: Interaction, Adaptation, and Identity at San Miguel del Vado, New Mexico." PhD dissertation, School of Anthropology, University of Arizona, Tucson.

Jones, Oakah L. 1979. *Los Paisanos: Spanish Settlers on the Northern Frontier of New Spain.* Norman: University of Oklahoma Press.

Kessell, John L., Rick Hendricks, and Meredith D. Dodge. 1995. *To the Royal Crown Restored (The Journals of Don Diego de Vargas).* Albuquerque: University of New Mexico Press.

Kessell, John L., Rick Hendricks, and Meredith D. Dodge. 1998. *Blood on the Boulders: The Journals of Don Diego de Vargas, 1694–1697.* Albuquerque: University of New Mexico Press.

Kutsche, Paul, and John R. Van Ness. 1981. *Cañones: Values, Crisis, and Survival in a Northern New Mexico Village.* Salem, WI: Sheffield Publishing Company.

Meinig, Donald W. 1984. "Commentary." *Annals of the Association of American Geographers* 74 (1): 172.

Neruda, Pablo, Victor Jara, and Patricio Castillo. 1974. "Aqui me Quedo." In *Manifesto Chile September 1973.* United Kingdom: Label XTRA 1143.

Nostrand, Richard L. 1970. "The Hispanic-American Borderland: Delimitation of an American Culture Region." *Annals of the Association of American Geographers* 60 (4): 638–61. http://dx.doi.org/10.1111/j.1467-8306.1970.tb00751.x.

Nostrand, Richard L. 1975. "Mexican Americans Circa 1850." *Annals of the Association of American Geographers* 65 (3): 378–90. http://dx.doi.org/10.1111/j.1467-8306.1975.tb01046.x.

Nostrand, Richard L. 1980. "The Hispano Homeland in 1900." *Annals of the Association of American Geographers* 70 (3): 382–96. http://dx.doi.org/10.1111/j.1467-8306.1980.tb01321.x.

Nostrand, Richard L. 1992. *The Hispano Homeland.* Norman: University of Oklahoma Press.

Peña, Devon G. 1999. "Cultural Landscapes and Biodiversity." In *Ethnoecology: Situated Knowledge, Located Lives,* edited by Virginia D. Nazarea, 107–32. Tucson: University of Arizona Press.

Quintana, Frances L. 1991. *Pobladores: Hispanic Americans of the Ute Frontier.* Aztec, NM: Frances Leon Quintana.

Rivera, José A. 1998. *Acequia Culture: Water, Land, and Community in the Southwest.* Albuquerque: University of New Mexico Press.

Rodríguez, Sylvia. 1986. *The Hispano Homeland Debate.* Working Paper Series No. 17. Palo Alto, CA: Stanford Center for Chicano Research, Stanford University.

Simmons, Marc, Fray Angelico Chavez, D. W. Meinig, and Thomas D. Hall. 1984. "Rejoinder." *Annals of the Association of American Geographers* 74 (1): 169–71. http://dx.doi.org/10.1111/j.1467-8306.1984.tb01443.x.

Snow, David H. 1976. *Archaeological Excavations at Pueblo del Encierro, LA 70, Cochiti Dam Salvage Project, Cochiti, New Mexico: Final Report 1965–1965 Field Seasons*. Laboratory of Anthropology Notes 98. Santa Fe: Museum of New Mexico.

Snow, David H. 1979. "Rural Hispanic Community Organization in Northern New Mexico: An Historical Perspective." In *The Survival of Spanish American Villages*, edited by Paul Kutsche, 45–52. Colorado College Studies 15. Colorado Springs: Colorado College.

Swadesh, Frances L. 1974. *Los Primeros Pobladores: Hispanic Americans of the Ute Frontier*. Notre Dame, IN: University of Notre Dame Press.

Van Ness, John R. 1980. "The Juan Bautista Valdez Grant: Was It a Community Land Grant?" *Journal of the West* 19:107–16.

Van Ness, John R. 1987a. "Hispanic Land Grants: Ecology and Subsistence in the Uplands of Northern New Mexico and Southern Colorado." In *Land, Water, and Culture: New Perspectives on Hispanic Land Grants*, edited by Charles L. Briggs and John R. Van Ness, 141–216. New Mexico Land Grant Series. Albuquerque: University of New Mexico.

Van Ness, John R. 1987b. *Hispanos: Ethnic Identity in Cañones*. Working Paper Series No. 20. Palo Alto, CA: Stanford Center for Chicano Research, Stanford University.

Van Ness, John R. 1991. *Hispanos in Northern New Mexico: The Development of Corporate Community and Multicommunity*. New York: AMS Press.

Vierra, Bradley J. 1980. "Cultural Resources Report: An Archaeological Survey of Pesedeuinge (AR 03-10-08-390) and the Surrounding Area." Manuscript on file, US Department of Agriculture, US Forest Service, Southwest Region, Santa Fe National Forest, Albuquerque, New Mexico.

Weber, Kenneth R. 1979. "Rural Hispanic Village Viability from an Economic and Historic Perspective." In *The Survival of Spanish American Villages*, edited by Paul Kutsche, 79–90. Colorado College Studies 15. Colorado Springs: Colorado College.

Westphall, Victor. 1983. *Mercedes Reales: Hispanic Land Grants of the Upper Rio Grande Region*. Albuquerque: University of New Mexico Press.

Wheeler, George M. 1877. "Parts of Southern Colorado and Northern New Mexico." Atlas Sheet No. 69. US Geographical Surveys West of the 100th Meridian. Corps of Engineers, US Army. Washington, DC: Government Printing Office.

Wozniak, Frank J., Meade F. Kemrer, and Charles M. Carrillo. 1992. "History and Ethnohistory along the Río Chama." Manuscript on file. Albuquerque, New Mexico: US Army Corps of Engineers, Albuquerque District.

EIGHT

Becoming Vecinos

Civic Identities in Late Colonial New Mexico

KELLY L. JENKS

INTRODUCTION

The New Mexico Colony, founded in 1598, is both the oldest and arguably the most remote Spanish colony in the American Southwest, factors that likely contributed to the emergence of a distinctly New Mexican cultural identity during the late colonial period (1692–1821). Throughout its long history, generations of colonists from New Spain—many of whom were of mixed ethnic heritage (Snow 1996)—interacted closely and constantly with a variety of indigenous groups residing within and around the colony (Brooks 2002; Swadesh 1979; Trigg 2003; Trigg and Gold 2005). These colonists adopted elements of indigenous architectural traditions (Boyd 1973; Bunting 1976; Kubler 1990), subsistence practices (Dunmire 2004; Trigg 2005), and craft technologies (Dick 1968; Moore 1992), and exploited existing indigenous trade networks to supplement their supplies of food, cooking ware, clothing and bedding material, and domestic labor (Eiselt 2006; F. Levine 1991; Snow 1983). Pigs did not fare well in the harsh climate, thus, sheep and to a lesser extent goats and cattle formed the basis of an emergent herding economy (Baxter 1987; Dunmire 2013). Relationships

DOI: 10.5876/9781607325741.c008

between male colonists and local, indigenous women were exceedingly common, and while these relationships ranged in character from brutal enslavement and rape to church-sanctioned marriage, most unions produced children of mixed ancestry and variable legal status. Thus, by the late eighteenth century, New Mexico's Spanish colonial population could be characterized as a multi-ethnic "menagerie of frontier peoples" (C. Carrillo 1997:25), many of whom had little or no Spanish ancestry.

Between circa 1785 and 1810, the New Mexico colony experienced rapid economic and population growth culminating in what many scholars have come to view as a cultural fluorescence (Boyd 1974; Brooks 2002; C. Carrillo 1997; L. Frank and Miller 2001a, 2001b, 2001c; R. Frank 1991, 2000; Swadesh 1974). In order to expand and protect its territory, colonial authorities granted lands along the frontier to groups of applicants, many of whom were of indigenous or mixed heritage and lacked the wealth or status to purchase lands nearer to the colonial core. These settlers pushed the boundaries of the colony beyond the middle Rio Grande Valley by establishing numerous rural villages far north and south along the Rio Grande, northwest along the Chama River, and east along the Pecos River. In order to obtain the supplies and protection necessary to survive in these peripheral spaces, the colonists sought out and established trading relationships with members of neighboring indigenous groups—especially the Comanches, Apaches, Navajos, and Utes (C. Carrillo 1997; Eiselt and Darling 2012; R. Frank 2000; Kutsche et al. 1976; Swadesh 1974; Van Ness 1979). Blending local and imported traditions, colonists developed unique forms of craft production, syncretic religious practices, and a distinctive regional dialect. Within this context, colonists increasingly identified themselves in legal documents as Vecinos (literally, "neighbors"), employing a term that "denoted both a cultural and civic identity, rather than caste or race" (Nieto-Phillips 2008:38). Their strong preference for this term suggests that the most salient aspect of Spanish colonial identity in late colonial New Mexico was not Spanish ethnicity but one's residence and accepted membership in a Spanish colonial community. This chapter explores the significance of Vecino identity in New Mexico and considers how it was manifested in the spatial organization and material remains of village sites during the late eighteenth and nineteenth centuries.

UNDERSTANDING AND DEFINING CIVIC IDENTITY IN COLONIAL NEW MEXICO

Vecino derives from *vecindad*, a Castilian term dating to the medieval period when Christians began to reconquer and resettle lands previously occupied by the Moors. Within this context, *vecindad* referred to the various rights and responsibilities shared by members of these new Christian communities, which often included rights to common lands and natural resources and obligations to construct, occupy, govern, and protect the settlement (Herzog 2003). This concept accompanied Spanish colonists into the Americas and eventually into New Spain's northern frontier, where the derivative term *vecino* was used to identify colonial citizens who inhabited, maintained, and defended colonial settlements and, thus, were entitled to exercise their rights to grants of property and access to common lands (Guerrero 2010; Gutiérrez 1991; Herzog 2003).

The use of Vecino as an identifier in legal records in colonial New Mexico increased in the late eighteenth century and early nineteenth, eventually superseding the use of the *casta*, or racial categories, that dominated records earlier in the colony's history (R. Frank 2000; Gutiérrez 1991:191–94). This same period also witnessed an expansion of colonial efforts to establish settlements in the north and east, a task that royal authorities achieved by issuing grants of land along these frontiers to applicants of varied ethnic backgrounds, many of whom lacked the social or economic capital to purchase lands in more desirable locations within the colony. Granting lands (and the civic rights and obligations reserved for landowners) to individuals of primarily indigenous ancestry transformed these "Indians" into Spanish colonial citizens and likewise transformed colonial citizenship into something a little less "Spanish." Thus, as the colony became increasingly dominated by and dependent on multiethnic settlements along the frontier, New Mexicans began to recognize civic status and practice as more important than ethnic heritage (Jenks 2013b). And, this emphasis on and expression of Vecino identity would continue to grow even during the Mexican period (1821–46) (Gutiérrez 1991:table 5.1), encouraged by further expansion of the colony through communal land grants and by the new government's legal abolition of racial categories.

This growing emphasis on civic identity also is evident in other parts of New Spain during the late eighteenth century and early nineteenth, though the context and specific character of these identities vary by region. The terms *vecino, vecinos de razón*, and *gente de razón* were used in the colonial settlements of Arizona and California to describe individuals mostly of non-European ancestry who were subjects of the Spanish Crown (Guerrero 2010:5–7). Many of these individuals were (or were closely related to) presidio soldiers, and by highlighting their civic status these terms served to distinguish them from neighboring populations with similar ethnic backgrounds but dissimilar loyalties and lifestyles (Guerrero 2010:7, 12; Jenks 2013a). At the presidio of San Francisco in northern California, Barbara Voss and others have examined archival and archaeological evidence of the creation of another civic identity—Californio—that united a small but diverse group of colonists and soldiers by emphasizing their shared affiliation with the colony, which set them apart from the local Native population (Smith-Lintner 2007; Voss 2005, 2008). Both of these examples differ somewhat from Vecino identity in New Mexico, which developed among farmers rather than soldiers and thus emphasized the village over the colony (Jenks 2011a). Nevertheless, the proliferation of these civic identities during this period seems to reflect a wider shift in identity politics in New Spain.

Civic identity was an important organizing principle for the colonists, and it is equally important to contemporary archaeologists as we attempt to understand what constituted a "Spanish" way of life in colonial settlements that were occupied extensively—sometimes exclusively—by individuals of mixed and indigenous ancestry. In investigating this specific kind of civic identity, it is important to understand that, during this period, Vecino identity was thought of less as a legally ascribed status than as a process and performance—an identity that was earned through displays of commitment to the community and enacted in daily practices associated with Vecino identity. As Tamar Herzog (2003:42) says of vecindad in eighteenth-century Castile, "People are citizens by virtue of their activities, and they lose their condition as citizens if they fail to enact the citizen role. Status is thus socially negotiated and socially recognized." This explanation of Vecino identity lends itself to interpretation through the archaeological theory of practice, which borrows from Pierre Bourdieu (1977) and Anthony Giddens (1979) in viewing routine activities within a structured space as simultaneously constructing and expressing underlying cultural values (e.g., Clark 2005; Lightfoot et al. 1998), including those associated with notions of "good" and "bad" citizenship. Viewed through this lens, continuity or change in these daily practices may be seen as evidence of the evolution of these cultural values in response to internal or external stimuli.

I draw on practice theory to identify and interpret evidence of Vecino identity at a sample of excavated Hispanic New Mexican sites occupied at various times, and in various places, in the former Spanish colony. The term "Vecino" expresses close physical proximity to other persons, typically in the form of shared residence within a neighborhood. Thus, the spatial organization of Hispanic villages structured Vecino identity in both a literal and figurative sense. Similarly, Vecino identity was expressed through the act of being a vecino of a particular community—participating in the routines and rituals of daily life within that village. Because Vecino identity was defined by one's residence and participation in a New Mexican Hispanic village, analyses of the historical, material, and spatial records of village life at Hispanic New Mexican sites dating to the late colonial period can be used to derive, inductively, the processes involved in the construction and expression of that identity.

Finally, social identities gain meaning and shape through comparison and contradiction with "others," and Vecino identity is no exception. Civic identity peaked in importance in New Mexico during a period of regular interactions between an increasingly rural Hispanic village population and various neighboring nomadic tribes, and was sustained as relations with these tribes were gradually supplanted by relations with American traders, soldiers, and ranchers. The significance of community membership and residence for Vecinos, therefore, likely derived in part from the absence or relative unimportance of village life for nomadic Indians and early American populations, who at various times were the enemies or economic allies of Vecino communities. In this way, an examination of Vecino identity requires some consideration of the social and economic context of these communities, and an appreciation of how the identity was shaped not only by what villagers did, but also by what they chose *not* to do. The remainder of this chapter explores, through the comparison of archaeological assemblages from Hispanic New Mexican sites, what it *meant* to be a Vecino within this Spanish colony, how this civic identity varied across space, and how it evolved over time.

EXCAVATING VECINDAD: IDENTIFYING AND EXPLORING REGIONAL PATTERNS

I reviewed and compared archaeological data from twenty-five New Mexican Hispanic sites in order to identify broad patterns of behavior shared by Vecinos and to interpret apparent variations in these patterns (Table 8.1 and Figure 8.1). I have organized these sites by region and present them in roughly chronological order, with the expectation that much of the variation between sites can be understood as the result of shared environmental context and settlement history. Most of the regional categories are self-explanatory, though it is worth explaining that Rio Arriba, Rio Medio, and Rio Abajo are local terms that refer to the upper, middle, and lower portions of the Rio Grande Valley, and divisions between the three are marked by the mouths of the Jemez and Puerco Rivers.

It would be difficult, if not impossible, to compare data from all of these sites using quantitative measures, as different archaeologists focused on different attributes and too many variables and categories are involved. Therefore, these comparisons are largely qualitative, focusing on observed differences in the patterns of archaeological data. I include plaza communities and isolated ranch sites in the sample, but have excluded colonial-period cities (Santa Fe, Albuquerque, Santa Cruz, and El Paso) because data from these sites are likely to be anomalous. There is some bias toward sites in the Rio Arriba, owing to the relative abundance of cultural resource management (CRM) projects conducted in this region and the ready availability of contract reports produced by the Office of Archeological Studies. Likewise, sites located in present-day Colorado are likely underrepresented, as site reports are more difficult to obtain.

TABLE 8.1. Sample of Hispanic New Mexican sites.

County	Site Name(s)	Date Range	Source
Rio Medio and Rio Abajo Regions			
Valencia	Valencia (LA 67321)	1700–ca. 1850	(Akins 2001; Brown and Vierra 1997; Mensel 1996; Wiseman 1988)
Bernalillo	San Antonio de Los Poblanos (LA 46635)	1710–1830	(Rudecoff 1987a; Rudecoff and Carrillo 1987)
Bernalillo	Tijeras Arroyo Hacienda Site (LA 140040)	1720–1846	(Hurt et al. 1980)
Bernalillo	San José de Los Ranchos (LA 46638)	1730–1904	(Condie 2007; Rudecoff 1987b; Sargeant 1985)
Sandoval	San José de las Huertas (LA 25674)	1764–1838	(Atherton and Rothschild 2008; Brody and Colberg 1966; Crane and Wenzel 1991; Ferg 1984; Rothschild and Atherton 2004)
Sandoval	Ideal Site (LA 8671)	1835–65	(Brody and Colberg 1966; Crane and Wenzel 1991; Ferg 1984)
Sandoval	Rio Puerco Site (ENM 198)	1800s	(Haeker 1976)
Socorro	Paraje de Fra Cristóbal (LA 1124)	1857–1924	(Boyd 1986)
Rio Arriba Region			
Santa Fe	Trujillo-Romero Site (LA 6579)	1750–1821	(Maxwell et al. 1998; Wiseman 1996)
Santa Fe	Santa Fe River Site 16/4 (LA 16769)	1750–1850	(Crane and Wenzel 1991; F. Levine et al. 1985; Payne 1999; Toll 1985)
Taos	Ranchos de Taos (LA 8976)	1770s–present	(Eiselt and Darling 2012; Gonzalez 2007)
Rio Arriba	Los Luceros / La Soledad (LA 37549)	1775–1912	(Snow 1999)
Santa Fe	Vicente Valdez Site (LA 4968)	1830–70	(Boyer et al. 2001; Moore 2000)
Rio Arriba	Parker Borrego	1830–80	(Eiselt and Darling 2012; Peles 2010)
Chama River Region			
Rio Arriba	Santa Rosa de Lima de Abiquiú (LA 806, LA 6602)	1700–early 1900s	(C. Carrillo 1978; Eiselt and Darling 2012; Moore et al. 2004)
Rio Arriba	La Puente (LA 54313)	1700–early 1900s	(Betram 1990; Boyer 1992; Moore et al. 2004)
Rio Arriba	Las Casitas (LA 917)	1750–1870	(Eiselt and Darling 2012; Quintana and Snow 1980; Sunseri 2009)

continued on next page

TABLE 8.1.—*continued*

County	Site Name(s)	Date Range	Source
Rio Arriba	Trujillo House (LA 59658)	1840–94	(Betram 1990; Betram et al. 1989; Moore et al. 2004)
Rio Arriba	San Lorenzo Ranch Sites (LA 12272, LA 90870, AR-03-10-06-1573, AR-02-10-06-1574)	1800s	(Eiselt 2006; Eiselt and Darling 2012)
PECOS RIVER REGION			
San Miguel	San Miguel del Vado (LA 2734)	1790s–present	(Hurt 2002; Jenks 2011b, 2011b, 2013b; Neasham 1940)
San Miguel	El Cerrito (LA 101030, LA 84318)	1820–early 1900s	(Boyd 1971; Hannaford and Severts 1996; Townsend 2004; Windes 2011; Windes and Bagwell 2004)
San Miguel	José María Martínez Site (LA 99029)	1850–1970	(Moore 2003)
Guadalupe	Los Ojitos (LA 98907)	1860s–1940	(Gray and O'Mack 2008; Hanson et al. 2010; Jenks 2009; O'Mack 2006)
Chaves	Ontiberos Site (LA 27573)	1903–8	(Oakes 1983)
PURGATOIRE RIVER REGION (COLORADO)			
Las Animas	La Placita (5LA6104)	1880s–90s	(Clark 2003, 2005, 2012; Clark and Corbett 2006; Clark and Wilkie 2006)

Rio Medio and Rio Abajo Regions

Archaeologists have conducted excavations at a number of Hispanic sites in the Middle and Lower Rio Grande Valley area, including the plaza communities of Valencia, San Antonio de Los Poblanos, San José de Los Ranchos, and San José de las Huertas; a small hamlet that developed around the Paraje de Fra Cristobal; and three isolated *ranchos* (see references in Table 8.1). The site of Valencia is situated south of Albuquerque and east of the Rio Grande along the Camino Real. Colonists settled the neighboring plaza communities of Los Poblanos and Los Ranchos in the early eighteenth century on the east bank of the Rio Grande just north of Albuquerque. Frequent floods caused most residents to abandon these plazas by the early twentieth century. The site of Las Huertas is located just north of Las Huertas Creek (a tributary of the Rio Grande) near the present-day town of Placitas. The ranch sites are spread across the region: one east of Albuquerque along the Tijeras Arroyo, one south of Las Huertas on the Las Huertas Creek, and one on the Rio Puerco in Navajo territory in the west. The last and latest of the sites in this sample, Paraje de Fra Cristobal, was settled in the mid-nineteenth century east of the Rio Grande and about seven miles downstream from the ruins of Fort Craig.

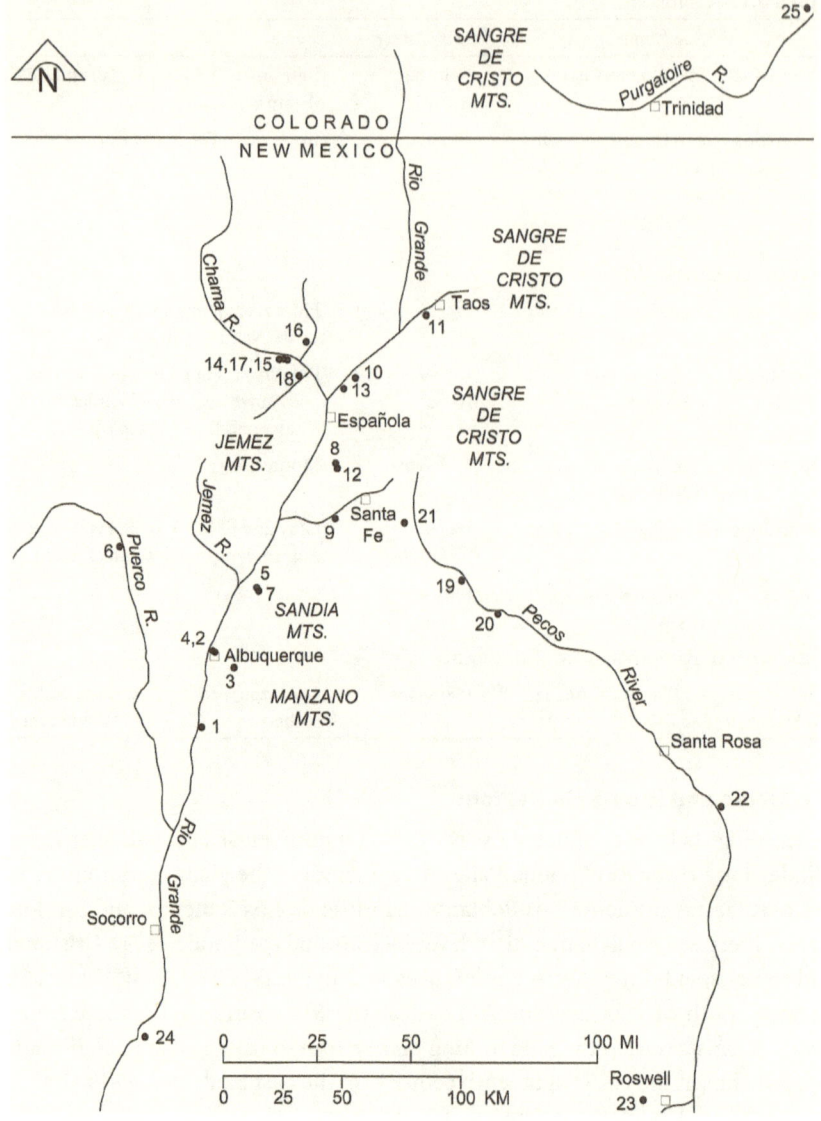

FIGURE 8.1. *Sample of twenty-five excavated Hispanic sites: (1) Valencia, (2) Los Poblanos, (3) Tijeras Arroyo, (4) Los Ranchos, (5) San José de las Huertas, (6) ENM 198, (7) Ideal Site, (8) Trujillo-Romero, (9) Santa Fe River Site 16/4, (10) Los Luceros, (11) Ranchos de Taos, (12) Vicente Valdez, (13) Parker Borrego, (14) La Puente, (15) Santa Rosa de Lima, (16) Las Casitas, (17) Trujillo House, (18) San Lorenzo Ranch Sites, (19) San Miguel del Vado, (20) El Cerrito, (21) José María Martínez, (22) Los Ojitos, (23) Ontiberos, (24) Paraje de Fra Cristóbal (25) La Placita. (The tables are organized by area and date, while the map numbers are assigned based on proximity.)*

Most of these sites produced numerous faunal remains, with sheep/goat bone dominating the collections followed by cow, pig, and chicken. Eggshells were identified at several sites, as were examples of wild game species (especially mule deer). Paraje de Fra Cristobal in the south was the only site in this sample to produce rabbit bones (Boyd 1986). Butchery marks were observed at several sites, most often on sheep/goat bone, and archaeologists interpreted these marks as evidence that these animals were raised and butchered at those sites (Boyd 1986; Rudecoff and Carrillo 1987). New Mexican ceramics also were abundant, often being dominated by locally made utility wares such as Carnue Plain and Plain Black. Decorated wares included Isleta Red-on-tan; Tewa Series Polychrome; Puname-area polychromes; Ranchitos and Santa Ana Polychrome; and a few decorated wares from Acoma, Laguna, Zuni, and Hopi. The most abundant wares were typically those produced by nearby Pueblos, thus wares produced by Northern Tewa potters (e.g., Tewa Polychrome) were more common in the north while wares produced by Keresan potters—especially those in the Puname region—were more common in the middle (Figure 8.2). New Mexican ceramics were least common at Paraje de Fra Cristobal, which, in addition to being occupied later than the other sites, also was located some considerable distance from Pueblo potting communities (Boyd 1986).

All of the sites in this sample produced some historical-period artifacts, though these were most abundant in sites with twentieth-century components (e.g., Los Ranchos and Paraje de Fra Cristobal). Mexican majolica and Euro-American white-bodied tableware sherds were present at most sites, and porcelain was present at a few. Lithic artifacts were relatively rare, often consisting of expedient tools, gunflints, strike-a-lights, and a few groundstone artifacts. Botanical remains identified included maize, beans, peaches, and melon, as well as wood charcoal fragments mostly from riparian and low-elevation species.

Rio Arriba Region

Excavated Hispanic sites in the Upper Rio Grande region include the plaza communities of Ranchos de Taos and La Soledad, a small hamlet identified as the Vicente Valdez Site, and three *ranchos* (see Table 8.1). Ranchos de Taos, which was founded in the eighteenth century and is still occupied today, is located south of Taos along the Rio Grande del Rancho River. The remains of La Soledad are situated along the Rio Grande underneath a rural hamlet near the town of Alcalde. The Vicente Valdez Site is a loose cluster of eight colonial-period structures situated on the east bank of the Rio Tesuque. Once again, the ranch sites are spread across the region, with one located north of San Juan Pueblo on the Rio Grande, one just north of the Vicente Valdez Site on the Rio Tesuque (north

FIGURE 8.2. *Pueblo potting areas.*

of Cuyamungue Pueblo), and one on the east bank of the Santa Fe River west of the city of Santa Fe.

In contrast to the Rio Medio, the most abundant artifacts from Hispanic sites in the Rio Arriba appear to be New Mexican ceramics, which often outnumber materials from other material categories. Utility and decorated wares (likely produced by Northern Tewa potters) and micaceous wares (likely produced by Jicarilla Apache potters) dominate these ceramic collections. Common utility wares include Plain (Kapo) Black, Plain Red, Tewa Micaceous, and Sangre de Cristo Micaceous, while decorated wares include Tewa Polychrome Series, Red Mesa Black-on-white, and a little Puname Polychrome. Once again, the type and distribution of New Mexican ceramics seem to reflect local market availability. Faunal remains are the second most common artifact, and while fewer of these collections have been analyzed, the most commonly identified species are sheep/goat and cow. Ax-cut butchering marks were observed at two sites, one of which also produced bones with saw marks (Peles 2010). Many sites produced small quantities of Mexican majolica sherds, while Euro-American white-bodied wares were recovered from sites occupied after the opening of the Santa Fe Trail in 1821. Lithic artifacts were relatively rare. Botanical remains identified at these sites include maize, peach, and beans, as well as watermelon, piñon, pistachio, plantain, wheat, orange, lentil, plum, and pepper.

Chama Region

Archaeologists have conducted excavations at several Hispanic sites in the Chama River region (west of Rio Arriba), including the plaza communities of Las Casitas, La Puente, and Santa Rosa de Lima de Abiquiú, as well as a few small ranch sites (see Table 8.1). Las Casitas was a fortified, plaza-centered settlement occupied primarily by *genízaros*, a term commonly used to describe the free descendants of Native American captives. The settlement was established above El Rito, a tributary of the Chama River. The site of Santa Rosa de Lima is situated immediately south of the Chama River just east of Abiquiú, while La Puente, located several miles east, probably represents an earlier incarnation of that community. Sunday Eiselt has identified and investigated several small ranch sites associated with the old community of San Lorenzo, all located along the Rio del Oso, another tributary of the Chama River (J. Andrew Darling and B. Sunday Eiselt, chapter 7 in this volume; Eiselt 2006). Contract excavations also have been conducted at the Trujillo House site located just west of Santa Rosa de Lima (Betram 1990; Betram et al. 1989; Moore et al. 2004).

Analyses of faunal bone recovered from these sites identify the remains of sheep/goat (dominant in the Mexican and American periods); cow (more common in the Spanish period); and smaller numbers of equid, pig, dog, and chicken bones. Several sites produced mule deer bones, and small numbers of bear, rabbit, bison, antelope, turkey, cougar, and badger bone were recovered from either Las Casitas (Quintana and Snow 1980; Sunseri 2009) or La Puente (Betram 1990; Boyer 1992; Moore et al. 2004). Chop marks were observed on most of the domestic animals (including horse) and on most of the large game at Las Casitas. Eggshell, likely from chicken eggs, also was recorded at La Puente. New Mexican ceramics were abundant at all sites, and most seemed to include a mix of utility wares produced by Northern Tewa, Jicarilla Apache, and Hispanic potters (Eiselt and Darling 2012). Common utility wares include Plain Black (Tewa and Hispanic), micaceous wares (Tewa and Jicarilla Apache), and Plain Red (Tewa). Decorated wares include Tewa Polychrome Series, Casitas Red-on-brown, San Juan Red-on-tan, and a few Puname-area Polychromes.

Lithic artifacts are surprisingly common at Hispanic sites in the Chama region, and include debitage (byproducts of stone tool production), expedient tools, groundstone, ceramic polishing stones, and strike-a-lights, most produced using locally available materials. Historical-period artifacts recovered from these sites are diverse, and include Euro-American white-bodied tableware fragments, clothing fasteners, and comb fragments. Only the site of La Puente produced majolica (a few dozen fragments [Moore et al. 2004]), and tin tinklers and tin scraps (suggesting tinworking) were found at the ranch sites around old San Lorenzo (Eiselt 2006; see also Darling and Eiselt, chapter 7 this volume). Botanical remains include maize, peach, squash, apricot, and chili pepper, as well as wood charcoal produced from riparian and lower-elevation species (especially piñon and juniper).

Pecos and Purgatoire River Regions

Relatively less archaeological work has been done at Hispanic sites located east of the Rio Grande Valley. Hispanic settlements in the east were established relatively late, mostly in the nineteenth century and early twentieth century, in territories previously explored by New Mexican bison hunters (*cíboleros*), participants in the Plains trade (*comancheros*), and shepherds. Archaeologists have conducted test excavations at the late Spanish colonial plaza communities of San Miguel del Vado and El Cerrito, the American-period hamlets of Los Ojitos and La Placita, and a couple of isolated ranch sites (see Table 8.1). The late eighteenth-century village of San Miguel was established just west of a natural ford (*vado*) in the Upper Pecos River as it flows out of the Sangre de Cristo Mountains and onto the plains. El Cerrito was a later, smaller settlement located about thirteen miles downstream from San Miguel on the same Spanish colonial land grant. Hispanic homesteaders founded Los Ojitos in the 1860s and 1870s south of Puerta de Luna along a bend in the Pecos River. Archaeologists have investigated several Hispanic sites along the Purgatoire River in present-day Colorado (e.g., R. Carrillo et al. 2003; Church 2001, 2002); however, only the site of La Placita, an illegal plaza settlement dating to the late nineteenth century, is included in this sample. Finally, test excavations have been conducted in a midden associated with the José María Martínez Site—a ranch located along the Pecos River upstream from San Miguel—and at the Ontiberos site—an early nineteenth-century Hispanic ranch house and dugout located west of Roswell in southeastern New Mexico.

Faunal remains recovered from the eastern sites exhibit considerable variation, with more sheep/goat bone recorded for the earlier settlements of the Upper/Middle Pecos and more cow bone identified in the later sites in the north (La Placita) and south (Ontiberos). Small quantities of pig, equid, chicken, and dog bones were identified, along with wild species including mule deer, elk, bison, turkey, and fish. Eggshell, likely from chickens, was recorded at several sites. La Placita and Ontiberos produced butchered remains of cottontail rabbits and jackrabbits, suggesting that these animals were either raised or captured and then butchered at the site (Clark 2003, 2012; Oakes 1983). Saw marks appear more frequently on cow bones, suggesting that some of these derive from cheap stew cuts of meat purchased by the residents, whereas chop marks identified on sheep/goat bone likely resulted from butchering the animal at home. New Mexican ceramics were relatively abundant in sites near the Sangre de Cristo Mountains, where the most commonly identified types were Sangre de Cristo Micaceous, Plain Black, Plain Red, and Tewa Polychrome Series, though a few Puname-area Polychromes also were recorded. New Mexican ceramics were less common along the Middle Pecos and wholly absent at La Placita and Ontiberos—later sites located far from any indigenous potting communities. Historical-period artifacts commonly recovered from these sites include sewing equipment, clothing fasteners, and Euro-American white-bodied tableware fragments. Canning jars were present at sites established during the American period (Los Ojitos, Ontiberos, and La Placita), but are conspicuously absent from the assemblages of sites established during the Spanish or Mexican periods. Lithic artifacts were rare, consisting mostly of debitage and expedient tools produced using local materials. Analyses of macrobotanical remains recovered from the New Mexican sites reported maize, beans, peach, cherry, squash, and apricot. La Placita, in contrast, produced only wild plants such as piñon and Chenopodium seeds.

What Does It Mean to Be Vecino?

Certain characteristics are shared by most or all of the Vecino sites described above. Not all villages were laid out in the same manner, but most contained a Catholic church or chapel in a central location, and some Catholic materials or features are documented at most sites. Domestic architecture typically consisted of a hybrid of Spanish and Pueblo traditions, made up of linear arrangements of habitation, storage, and animal rooms/corrals often clustered together or organized around a central patio. Structure walls could be any combination of adobe and stone, though high stone foundations were more common in flood-prone areas. Most structures had flat, Pueblo-style roofs and dirt/puddled-adobe floors, sometimes covered with linoleum or milled lumber as these materials became available. Rooms were multipurpose with few interior features (corner fireplaces, niches, storage pits) and could be readily altered to serve the needs of the season or to accommodate new goods, animals, or family members.

Archaeological evidence of the raising of sheep and goats for their wool, milk, and meat is extremely common. It is also evident that cattle ranching, while less common, was practiced in all regions and time periods. Smaller numbers of animals often were kept for subsistence purposes, such as pigs and chickens (mostly for their eggs), and equines were used for agricultural labor and transportation. Most Vecinos grew garden vegetables, fruit trees, and some crops—especially in the productive floodplains of the Rio Grande—and common cultigens included maize, peaches, squash, chilies, and beans. Wheat and corn were staple crops, according to records of that time, though most of the archaeological evidence for these crops is indirect, consisting of ovens (*hornos*) for cooking wheat bread and *manos* and metates (especially in the northwest) for grinding corn. Grist mills (*molinos*) constructed along the acequias ground the wheat harvested by community members into usable flour (e.g., Gritzner 1974). Unfortunately, these features have received less study than the communities themselves. Wild animals were sometimes hunted, probably as much for the hides as for their meat; however, in most cases it appears that they were hunted opportunistically to supplement local supplies, and wild resources seldom appear in contexts where they would have been difficult to obtain.

Stock animals frequently were butchered at the household level, often through use of metal axes to produce roast or stew-sized cuts and breaking open the cranium to harvest the tongue and brain. Meat could be prepared in pit roasts or stewed in earthenware pots with chilies or other vegetables. Surplus meat and plant food were commonly preserved through drying, even after the introduction of American canning technology, and part of the popularity of stews in New Mexico probably derives from a tradition of working with dried food. Groundstone and griddles, while sometimes present, were less common in Vecino assemblages than expected. It may be that cornmeal products (tortillas, atole) were less fundamental to Vecino cuisine than they were to the diets of their Pueblo neighbors and/or that corn was more often used as animal fodder.

Artifacts relating to the manufacture and maintenance of cloth/clothing are present at all of these sites, and evidence of limited metallurgy is common as well. The leather clothing and commercial exports described in historical accounts are not especially apparent in the material record, perhaps because these items were generally obtained in trade from nomadic Indian groups or perhaps because the material correlates that I seek (metal and lithic scrapers) are not the best or only correlates of this activity. Evidence from all sites indicates that Vecinos were active participants in local trade networks, regularly bartering with neighboring indigenous communities and occasionally traveling to regional trade centers (e.g., Santa Fe) in order to reach a broader market for their goods. The church also likely facilitated social and economic interactions, drawing rural settlers to the nearest parish church for religious holidays, and inviting neighboring communities to enjoy food and entertainment at the annual feast day celebration.

Regional Variants and Change over Time

While Vecino sites have much in common, some general differences can be observed between sites located in different regions or occupied at different times (see Darling and Eiselt, chapter 7 in this volume). A variety of social and economic factors influenced village layout, and some settlements—especially along the Chama River and the Middle Pecos—appear to have been more dispersed. Frances Swadesh (1974) suggested that this pattern in the Chama River area was deliberate, making it easier for settlers to conduct illicit trade with indigenous neighbors and making their properties less appealing to potential Indian raiders. Environmental conditions also may have played a role—especially for the Middle Pecos settlements—as the narrow, flood-prone river valley and difficult terrain would have made it particularly difficult for residents to travel back and forth from a central village to their allotted agricultural lands.

Faunal assemblages were surprisingly small in the Las Huertas grant sites (San José de las Huertas and the Ideal Site). Documentary and oral history indicate that these settlers raised sheep and goats (Atherton and Rothschild 2008; Rebolledo and Márquez 2000), so the lack of faunal bone may simply be a product of excavations focusing on interior spaces. Rabbits appear in the faunal assemblages of several sites, but only contributed significantly to the local diet at La Placita (in southeastern Colorado), which also is the only village that appears not to have cultivated crops. A greater diversity of crops (including sugar cane) could grow in the lower latitudes of the Rio Medio and Rio Abajo; however, this diversity is not readily apparent in the botanical remains described above. Many more lithic artifacts have been recovered from sites in the Chama River area than in any other region, and include greater numbers of expedient tools, gunflints or strike-a-lights, and groundstone. This region also has more evidence suggesting local craft production, both in the form of tinworking (Brown et al. 1978:138; Darling and Eiselt, chapter 7 in this volume; Eiselt 2006) and ceramic manufacture (Brown et al. 1978:58–59; Eiselt 2006; D. Levine 1990, 2004; Olinger 2004).

The most obvious differences between Vecino sites are found in patterns of nonlocal goods, reflecting the approximate areas of different local and regional trade networks that existed within New Mexico. Local trade networks are most apparent in the assemblages of New Mexican ceramics. The New Mexican ceramic assemblage from the single Vecino site in the Rio Abajo region was dominated by wares likely produced by Southern Tiwa potters at Isleta or Isleta del Sur (see Figure 8.2). Decorated/polished wares produced by Keresan potters at Santa Ana and Zia and Western Keres potters at Acoma and Laguna occurred most frequently in Vecino sites in the Rio Medio region. Vecino sites in the north were supplied mostly with decorated/polished wares produced by Northern Tewa potters and micaceous utility wares produced in and around the Sangre de Cristo Mountains (mostly by Jicarilla Apache potters). In addition, sites in the northwest (Chama River area) contained greater numbers of locally produced polished black wares, and sites in the far north (Taos) and far east (Pecos River) contained greater numbers of Apachean micaceous ceramics. Vecino sites located far away from Pueblo or Apache communities—that is, the Ontiberos Site and La Placita—did not possess New Mexican ceramics.

Regional trade networks are most apparent in the assemblages of historical-period artifacts. Majolica and Mexican glaze ware ceramics are the most obvious Mexican imports, and these items appear consistently—if not in great numbers—at sites along the Camino Real. Fewer (if any) majolica/Mexican glaze ware sherds were recovered from sites outside of the Rio Grande Valley, including at relatively populous sites like San Miguel del Vado. The purchase and resulting presence of majolica ceramics could indicate greater wealth or social status, or a desire to project a more Spanish identity (see Snow 1993). However, it is unlikely that the absence of these ceramics outside of the Rio Grande Valley reflected differences in ethnicity or class (with genízaro buffer settlements being excluded from the Mexican trade), as San José de Las Huertas began as a genízaro buffer settlement and produced dozens of Mexican ceramics. In most cases, differences in the prevalence of Mexican imports within the Vecino assemblages likely reflect differences in access to the Camino Real trade. American imports seem to have penetrated more deeply into the countryside, appearing in the assemblages of most sites occupied after 1821. Unfortunately, it is difficult to determine how the distribution of American goods might have changed over the course of the territorial period, as the date ranges for sites often are based on the prevalence of American imports. (Thus, there is a fair amount of circular reasoning involved in making the observation that American imports are available everywhere after the train arrived in 1880.)

As the previous statement suggests, some of the differences between the assemblages of Vecino sites may reflect change over time rather than (or in addition to) regional differences. Animal husbandry practices are remarkably consistent; however, the introduction of American cattle from the Central and Southern Plains and the growth of the cattle industry around Las Vegas do appear to have influenced sites along the Pecos River. Horticulture likely was similarly affected, as the demand for fodder increased and the availability of cheap grain imports—especially wheat—made it easier to change crops. Bone saws first appear during this period, and the rise of a butchering industry likely responded more to the demands of an Anglo market (including soldiers) than to the needs of Vecinos, though some this saw-cut meat did make it into Vecino homes. Band saws also changed the timber industry, bringing more milled lumber into Vecino villages and homes.

Clothing manufacture and maintenance remained important throughout time; however, in earlier sites this may be expressed more in wool shears, weaving equipment, awls, and leather-working tools (scrapers), with later assemblages more likely to include scissors, needles, buttons, and beads. Flaked glass items may be more abundant than flaked stones in the later assemblages, especially in areas where the local stone is not as sharp or easily modified as glass (e.g., San Miguel del Vado and Los Ojitos). Finally, American land-use laws restricted the landholdings of older communities while the new Homestead Acts influenced the arrangement of new settlements. In most cases, the loss of the common lands drove members of older land grant communities into the labor force to compensate for the loss of grazing lands and timber. Those who sought to establish new communities were forced to deal with an American public land grant system that used an arbitrary grid to measure out equal sections of land that, because they ignored local geography, varied tremendously in available resources and agricultural productivity (see Church 2002).

In sum, Vecino identity drew on a common set of beliefs and routine practices, many of which emphasized social integration and economic interdependence. These values are apparent in the corporate structure of the villages and in the spiritual, familial, and economic ties between community members and between communities. At a regional level, the emphasis on economic interdependence linked Vecinos to neighboring Native communities, whose differing values and practices influenced the development of Vecino identity in those regions, thus creating interesting regional variants.

CONCLUSIONS

The concept of Vecino identity—a civic identity defined by one's residence and accepted membership in a Spanish colonial community—is intriguing, particularly for those studying cross-cultural interaction and identity formation. Historical archaeologists are often frustrated by their inability to distinguish ethnic groups along cultural frontiers because these groups often shared overlapping territories, performed many of the same tasks, and used materials that were produced by or circulated among all of them. To further complicate matters, these groups often intermixed and intermarried, raising children of mixed heritage (e.g., Cordell and Yannie 1991). The conscious adoption of Vecino identity by New Mexican colonists moved the focus away from ethnic divisions and toward shared practices, allowing us to recognize the creation of this new civic and cultural identity (Nieto-Phillips 2008:38) and investigate how vecindad helped to integrate a multiethnic, multicultural population.

Archaeologists working in culture-contact zones tend to fixate on the ethnic component of these relations, deriving "ethnicities" from historical-period notions of race or caste, and expecting that cross-cultural interactions would have led to an exaggeration of ethnic differences (Barth 1969), some of which will be visible in the archaeological record as "ethnic markers." Often times, this is the case. Ethnicity, however, is not the only axis of social identification, and sometimes—especially along colonial or national frontiers—civic identity becomes the more important organizing principle of a population. Amidst the many studies of creolization (e.g., Cusick 2000; Dawdy 2000; Deagan 1973; Worth 2012) and ethnogenesis (e.g., Anderson 1999; Hill 1996; Lightfoot 2005; Voss 2008) along colonial frontiers, this examination of Vecino identity serves as a reminder that diverse frontier populations often came together as communities, and membership in a community could be just as—or more—important than affiliation with an ethnic group. Thus, there is something valuable to be learned from focusing less on the attributes that divided colonial populations and more on the practices that united them.

REFERENCES CITED

Akins, Nancy J. 2001. *Valencia: A Spanish Colonial and Mexican-Period Site along NM 47 in Valencia County, New Mexico*. Archaeology Notes No. 267. Santa Fe: Office of Archaeological Studies, Museum of New Mexico.

Anderson, Gary C. 1999. *The Indian Southwest, 1580–1830: Ethnogenesis and Reinvention*. Norman: University of Oklahoma Press.

Atherton, Heather N., and Nan A. Rothschild. 2008. "Colonialism, Past and Present, in New Mexico." *Archaeologies* 4 (2): 250–63. http://dx.doi.org/10.1007/s11759-008-9056-x.

Barth, Fredrik. 1969. "Ethnic Groups and Boundaries." In *Ethnic Groups and Boundaries*, 294–325. London: Allen and Unwin.

Baxter, John O. 1987. *Las Carneradas: Sheep Trade in New Mexico 1700–1860*. Albuquerque: University of New Mexico Press.

Betram, Jack B. 1990. "Archaeofaunal Analysis of Samples from Casa Trujillo (LA 59658) and La Puente de Abiquiú (LA 54313), Rio Arriba County, New Mexico." Manuscript on file, Office of Archaeological Studies, Museum of New Mexico, Santa Fe.

Betram, Jack B., Jeanne A. Schutt, Steve L. Kuhn, Amy C. Earls, W. Nicholas Trierweiler, Christopher R. Lintz, John C. Acklen, Charles M. Carrillo, and Janette Elyea. 1989. *Report of Surface Collection and Testing at 18 Sites near Abiquiu Reservoir, Northern New Mexico*. Albuquerque: Mariah Associates.

Bourdieu, Pierre. 1977. *Outline of a Theory of Practice*. Cambridge: Cambridge University Press. http://dx.doi.org/10.1017/CBO9780511812507.

Boyd, Douglas Kevin. 1986. "Paraje (de Fra Cristobal): Investigations of a Territorial Period Hispanic Village Site in Southern New Mexico." MA thesis, Department of Anthropology, Texas A&M University, College Station.

Boyd, E. 1971. "The Plaza of San Miguel del Vado." *El Palacio* 77 (4): 17–26.

Boyd, E. 1973. "Domestic Architecture in New Mexico." *El Palacio* 79 (3): 12–29.

Boyd, E. 1974. *Popular Arts of Spanish New Mexico*. Santa Fe: Museum of New Mexico Press.

Boyer, Jeffrey L. 1992. "La Puente: Eighteenth-Century Hispanic Village Life on the Rio Chama Frontier." In *Current Research on the Late Prehistory and Early History of New Mexico*, edited by Bradley J. Vierra and Clara Gualtieri, 227–37. Albuquerque: New Mexico Archaeological Council.

Boyer, Jeffrey L., James L. Moore, and Steven A. Lakatos. 2001. *US 84/285 Santa Fe to Pojoaque Corridor: Preliminary Results of Data Recovery Investigations at Five Sites near Cuyamungue, Santa Fe County, New Mexico. Archaeology Notes 296*. Santa Fe: Office of Archaeological Studies, Museum of New Mexico.

Brody, J. J. and Anne Colberg. 1966. "A Spanish-American Homestead Near Placitas, New Mexico." *El Palacio* 73 (2): 11–20.

Brooks, James F. 2002. *Captives and Cousins: Slavery, Kinship, and Community in the Southwest Borderlands*. Chapel Hill: University of North Carolina Press.

Brown, Kenneth L., and Bradley J. Vierra. 1997. *Excavations at Valencia Pueblo (LA 953) and a Nearby Hispanic Settlement (LA 67321)*. Albuquerque: Office of Contract Archeology, University of New Mexico.

Brown, Lorin W., Charles L. Briggs, and Marta Weigle. 1978. *Hispano Folklife of New Mexico: The Lorin W. Brown Federal Writers' Project Manuscripts*. 1st ed. Albuquerque: University of New Mexico Press.

Bunting, Bainbridge. 1976. *Early Architecture in New Mexico*. Albuquerque: University of New Mexico Press.

Carrillo, Charles M. 1978. *Archaeological Assessment and Recommendation for the Spanish Colonial Village of Santa Rosa de Lima de Abiquiú*. Washington, DC: Report submitted to the National Endowment of the Arts.

Carrillo, Charles M. 1997. *Hispanic New Mexican Pottery: Evidence of Craft Specialization 1790–1890*. Albuquerque: LPD Press.

Carrillo, Richard F., Constance La Lena, and Diane Benavides Mason, eds. 2003. *Context Study of the Hispanic Cultural Landscape of the Purgatoire/Apishapa, Las Animas County, Colorado: An Interdisciplinary Approach to the History, Architecture, Oral History, and Historical Archaeology*. Prepared for the Trinidad Historical Society, Trinidad, CO. Funded, in part, by a Colorado Historical Society State Historical Fund Grant, Las Animas County Commissioners, Evergreen Resources, and members of the Trinidad Historical Society.

Church, Minette. 2001. "Homesteads on the Purgatoire: Frontiers of Culture Contact in 19th Century Colorado." PhD dissertation, Department of Anthropology, University of Pennsylvania. Ann Arbor, MI: University Microfilms.

Church, Minette. 2002. "The Grant and the Grid: Homestead Landscapes in the Late Nineteenth-Century Borderlands of Southern Colorado." *Journal of Social Archaeology* 2 (2): 220–44.

Clark, Bonnie J. 2003. "On the Edge of Purgatory: An Archaeology of Ethnicity and Gender in Hispanic Colorado." PhD dissertation, Department of Anthropology, University of California, Berkeley. Ann Arbor, MI: University Microfilms.

Clark, Bonnie J. 2005. "Lived Ethnicity: Archaeology and Identity in Mexicano America." *World Archaeology* 37 (3): 440–52. http://dx.doi.org/10.1080/00438240500168525.

Clark, Bonnie J. 2012. *On the Edge of Purgatory: An Archaeology of Place in Hispanic Colorado*. Lincoln: University of Nebraska Press.

Clark, Bonnie J., and Kathleen Corbett. 2006. "Finding Common Ground in Common Places: Interdisciplinary Methods for Analyzing Historic Architecture on Archaeological Sites." In *Between Dirt and Discussion: Methods, Methodology, and Interpretation in Historical Archaeology*, edited by Steven Archer and Kevin Bartoy 151–67. New York: Springer. http://dx.doi.org/10.1007/978-0-387-34219-1_8.

Clark, Bonnie J., and Laurie A. Wilkie. 2006. "The Prism of Self: Gender and Personhood." In *Handbook of Gender in Archaeology*, edited by Sarah M. Nelson, 1–32. Lanham, MD: AltaMira Press.

Condie, Carol J., ed. 2007. *Los Ranchos Plaza (LA 46638): Test Excavations at a Spanish Colonial Settlement in Bernalillo County, New Mexico, 1996–1997*. Albuquerque: Maxwell Museum of Anthropology, University of New Mexico.

Cordell, Linda S., and Vincent J. Yannie. 1991. "Ethnicity, Ethnogenesis, and the Individual: A Processual Approach toward Dialogue." In *Processual and Postprocessual Archaeologies: Multiple Ways of Knowing the Past*, edited by R. W. Preucel. Occasional Paper no. 10. Carbondale: Center for Archaeological Investigations, Southern Illinois University.

Crane, Susan, and Kristen Wenzel. 1991. "A Study of Material Culture in 18th Century and Early 19th Century Spanish Colonial Domestic and Mission Sites in New Mexico: Comparisons Using Archival and Archaeological Records (Lecture Presented to AN 313: Archeology and Ethnohistory of the Southwest, The Colorado College, July 5, 1991. Department of Anthropology, The Colorado College, Colorado Springs)." Manuscript on file at Archaeological Records Management System (ARMS), Museum of New Mexico, Santa Fe.

Cusick, James G. 2000. "Creolization and the Borderlands." *Historical Archaeology* 34 (3): 46–55.

Dawdy, Shannon Lee. 2000. "Understanding Cultural Change through the Vernacular: Creolization in Louisiana." *Historical Archaeology* 34 (3): 107–23.

Deagan, Kathleen A. 1973. "Mestizaje in Colonial St. Augustine." *Ethnohistory* 20 (1): 55–65. http://dx.doi.org/10.2307/481426.

Dick, Herbert W. 1968. "Six Prehistoric Pottery Types from Spanish Sites in New Mexico." In *Collected Papers in Honor of Lyndon Lane Hargrave*, edited by Albert H. Schroeder, 77–94. Albuquerque: Archaeological Society of New Mexico.

Dunmire, William W. 2004. *Gardens of New Spain: How Mediterranean Plants and Foods Changed America*. Austin: University of Texas Press.

Dunmire, William W. 2013. *New Mexico's Spanish Livestock Heritage: Four Centuries of Animals, Land, and People*. Albuquerque: University of New Mexico Press.

Eiselt, B. Sunday. 2006. "The Emergence of Jicarilla Apache Enclave Economy during the 19th Century in Northern New Mexico." PhD dissertation, Department of Anthropology, University of Michigan, Ann Arbor. Ann Arbor, MI: University Microfilms.

Eiselt, B. Sunday, and J. Andrew Darling. 2012. "Vecino Economics: Gendered Economy and Micaceous Pottery Consumption in Nineteenth Century Northern New Mexico." *American Antiquity* 77 (3): 424–48. http://dx.doi.org/10.7183/0002-7316.77.3.424.

Ferg, Alan. 1984. *Historic Archaeology on the San Antonio de Las Huertas Grant, Sandoval County, New Mexico*. CASA Papers 3. Cortez, CO: Complete Archaeological Service Associates.

Frank, Larry, and Skip Keith Miller. 2001a. *Religious Art of New Mexico, 1780–1907*. 1st ed. A Land So Remote, vol. 1. Santa Fe: Red Crane Books.

Frank, Larry, and Skip Keith Miller. 2001b. *Religious Art of New Mexico, 1780 1907*. 1st ed. A Land So Remote, vol. 2. Santa Fe: Red Crane Books.

Frank, Larry, and Skip Keith Miller. 2001c. *Wooden Artifacts of Frontier New Mexico, 1700s–1900s*. 1st ed. A Land So Remote, vol. 3. Santa Fe: Red Crane Books.

Frank, Ross Harold. 1991. "The Changing Pueblo Indian Pottery Tradition: The Underside of Economic Development in Late Colonial New Mexico, 1750–1820." *Journal of the Southwest* 33 (3): 282–381.

Frank, Ross Harold. 2000. *From Settler to Citizen: New Mexican Economic Development and the Creation of Vecino Society, 1750–1820*. Berkeley: University of California Press.

Giddens, Anthony. 1979. *Central Problems in Social Theory: Action, Structure, and Contradiction in Social Analysis*. Berkeley: University of California Press. http://dx.doi.org/10.1007/978-1-349-16161-4.

Gonzalez, Albert D. 2007. "The History and Archaeology of the Eighteenth-Century Community at Ranchos de Taos, New Mexico." Master's thesis, Department of Anthropology, University of Texas, Dallas.

Gray, Marlesa, and Scott O'Mack. 2008. "Work Plan for Archaeological Testing of the Los Ojitos Site, LA 98907, Guadalupe County, New Mexico." Submitted to US Department of the Interior, Bureau of Reclamation, Upper Colorado Region, Albuquerque Area Office. Copies available from US Department of the Interior, Bureau of Reclamation, Upper Colorado Region, Albuquerque Area Office.

Gritzner, Charles. 1974. "Hispano Gristmills in New Mexico." *Annals of the Association of American Geographers* 64 (4): 514–24. http://dx.doi.org/10.1111/j.1467-8306.1974.tb01000.x.

Guerrero, Vladimir. 2010. "Caste, Race, and Class in Spanish California." *Southern California Quarterly* 92 (1): 1–18. http://dx.doi.org/10.2307/41172505.

Gutiérrez, Ramón A. 1991. *When Jesus Came, the Corn Mothers Went Away: Marriage, Sexuality, and Power in New Mexico, 1500–1846*. Stanford, CA: Stanford University Press.

Haeker, Charles M. 1976. "Modes of Subsistence and Level of Technology of the Eighteenth-Century Spanish Settlers on the Rio Puerco." Master's thesis, Department of Anthropology, Eastern New Mexico University, Portales.

Hannaford, Charles A., and Patrick H. Severts. 1996. *Archaeological Investigations at a Well in San Miguel del Vado, San Miguel County, New Mexico. Archaeology Notes 156*. Santa Fe: Office of Archaeological Studies, Museum of New Mexico.

Hanson, Jeffery R., Karen K. Swope, Kelly L. Jenks, David T. Unruh, and Brandon M. McIntosh. 2010. *Archaeological Testing at Locus B of the Los Ojitos Site, LA 98907, Guadalupe County, New Mexico*. Technical Report 10-87. Albuquerque: Statistical Research.

Herzog, Tamar. 2003. *Defining Nations: Immigrants and Citizens in Early Modern Spain and Spanish America*. New Haven: Yale University Press. http://dx.doi.org/10.12987/yale/9780300092530.001.0001.

Hill, Jonathan D., ed. 1996. *History, Power, and Identity: Ethnogenesis in the Americas, 1492–1992*. Iowa City: University of Iowa Press.

Hurt, Teresa D. 2002. *Class III Cultural Resource Survey of 221 Acres for ENMR Plateau Telecommunications El Valle Fiber Optic Cable Route, San Miguel County, New Mexico*. Lone Mountain Report No. 682B. Albuquerque: Lone Mountain Archaeological Services.

Hurt, Wesley R., Herbert W. Dick, and Carrol W. Burroughs. 1980. "The Tijeras Arroyo Site: A Report on the 1939 Excavation Project." Manuscript on file at Archaeological Records Management System (ARMS), Museum of New Mexico, Santa Fe.

Jenks, Kelly L. 2009. *Archaeological Testing of the Los Ojitos Site, LA 98907, Guadalupe County, New Mexico*. Technical Report 09-34. Statistical Research, Albuquerque, New Mexico.

Jenks, Kelly L. 2011a. "Vecinos en la Frontera: Colonial History and Archaeology at San Miguel del Vado, New Mexico." *SMRC Revista* 45 (166–169): 15–25.

Jenks, Kelly L. 2011b. "Vecinos en la Frontera: Interaction, Adaptation, and Identity at San Miguel del Vado, New Mexico." PhD dissertation, School of Anthropology University of Arizona, Tucson. Ann Arbor, MI: UMI-Proquest.

Jenks, Kelly L. 2013a. "An Analysis of Majolica Ceramics from the Hispanic Presidio Community at Tubac, Santa Cruz County, Arizona." *Journal of Arizona Archaeology* 2 (2): 117–39.

Jenks, Kelly L. 2013b. "Building Community: Exploring Civic Identity in Hispanic New Mexico." *Journal of Social Archaeology* 13 (3): 371–93. http://dx.doi.org/10.1177/1469605313494288.

Kubler, George. 1990. *The Religious Architecture of New Mexico in the Colonial Period and since the American Occupation*. Albuquerque: University of New Mexico Press.

Kutsche, Paul, John R. Van Ness, and Andrew T. Smith. 1976. "A Unified Approach to the Anthropology of Hispanic New Mexico: Historical Archaeology, Ethnohistory, and Ethnography." *Historical Archaeology* 10:1–16.

Levine, Daisy F. 1990. "Tewa or Hispanic Manufacture? Pottery from Eighteenth and Nineteenth Century Spanish Sites near Abiquiu." In *Clues to the Past: Papers in Honor of William M. Sundt*, edited by Meliha S. Duran and David T. Kirkpatrick, 173–83. Papers of the Archaeological Society of New Mexico 16. Albuquerque: Archaeological Society of New Mexico.

Levine, Daisy F. 2004. "Native Ceramic Analysis and Interpretation." In *Adaptations on the Anasazi and Spanish Frontiers: Excavations at Five Sites near Abiquiu, Rio Arriba County, New Mexico*, edited by James L. Moore, Jeffrey L. Boyer and Daisy F. Levine, 147–68. Archaeology Notes 187. Santa Fe: Office of Archaeological Studies, Museum of New Mexico.

Levine, Frances E. 1991. "Economic Perspectives on the Comanchero Trade." In *Farmers, Hunters, and Colonists: Interaction between the Southwest and the Southern Plains*, edited by Katherine A. Spielmann, 155–69. Tucson: University of Arizona Press.

Levine, Frances E., John C. Acklen, Jack B. Bertram, Stephen C. Lent, and Gale McPherson. 1985. *Archeological Test Excavations at LA 16769*. PNM Archeological Report No. 5. Albuquerque: Public Service Company of New Mexico.

Lightfoot, Kent G. 2005. *Indians, Missionaries, and Merchants: The Legacy of Colonial Encounters on the Californian Frontiers*. Berkeley: University of California Press.

Lightfoot, Kent G., Antoinette Martinez, and Ann M. Schiff. 1998. "Daily Practice and Material Culture in Pluralistic Social Settings: An Archaeological Study of Culture Change and Persistence from Fort Ross, California." *American Antiquity* 63 (2): 199–222. http://dx.doi.org/10.2307/2694694.

Maxwell, Timothy D., Jeffrey L. Boyer, Steven A. Lakatos, and Janet Spivey. 1998. *Letter Report: Excavations at 3 Sites (LA 835, 6579, and 101410) for the US 285-Pojoaque South Project*. Santa Fe: Office of Archaeological Studies, Museum of New Mexico.

Mensel, Macy. 1996. *Archaeological Investigations along NM 47 and a Data Recovery Plan for LA 67321, Valencia County, New Mexico*. Archaeology Notes 181. Santa Fe: Office of Archaeological Studies, Museum of New Mexico.

Moore, James L. 1992. "Spanish Colonial Stone Tool Use." In *Current Research on the Late Prehistory and Early History of New Mexico*, edited by Bradley J. Vierra and Clara Gualtieri, 239–44. Albuquerque: New Mexico Archaeological Council.

Moore, James L. 2000. *Archaeological Testing Report and Data Recovery Plan for Two Historic Spanish Sites along U.S. 84/285 between Santa Fe and Pojaque, Santa Fe County, New Mexico*. Archaeology Notes 268. Santa Fe: Office of Archaeological Studies, Museum of New Mexico.

Moore, James L. 2003. *Occupation of the Glorieta Valley in the Seventeenth and Nineteenth Centuries. Archaeology Notes 262*. Santa Fe: Office of Archaeological Studies, Museum of New Mexico.

Moore, James L., Jeffrey L. Boyer, and Daisy F. Levine, eds. 2004. *Adaptations on the Anasazi and Spanish Frontiers: Excavations at Five Sites near Abiquiú, Rio Arriba County, New Mexico. Archaeology Notes 187*. Santa Fe: Office of Archaeological Studies, Museum of New Mexico.

Neasham, Aubrey. 1940. "Special Report on the Proposed National Historic Site of San Miguel del Vado (Submitted to Region III, National Park Service, Department of the Interior; located in the LA 2734 site file)." Manuscript on file, Archaeological Records Management System (ARMS), Museum of New Mexico, Santa Fe.

Nieto-Phillips, John M. 2008. *The Language of Blood: The Making of Spanish-American Identity in New Mexico, 1880s–1930s*. Albuquerque: University of New Mexico Press.

O'Mack, Scott. 2006. *Draft Nomination to the National Register of Historic Places for the Los Ojitos Archaeological District*. Submitted to US Department of the Interior, Bureau of Reclamation, Upper Colorado Region, Albuquerque Area Office. Copies available from US Department of the Interior, Bureau of Reclamation, Upper Colorado Region, Albuquerque Area Office.

Oakes, Yvonne R. 1983. *The Ontiberos Site: A Hispanic Homestead near Roswell, New Mexico. Laboratory of Anthropology Notes 311*. Santa Fe: Office of Archaeological Studies, Museum of New Mexico.

Olinger, Bart. 2004. "X-ray Fluorescence Analysis of Pottery from La Puente and the Trujillo House." In *Adaptations on the Anasazi and Spanish Frontiers: Excavations at Five Sites near Abiquiu, Rio Arriba County, New Mexico*, edited by James L. Moore, Jeffrey L. Boyer and Daisy F. Levine, 147–68. Archaeology Notes 187. Santa Fe: Office of Archaeological Studies, Museum of New Mexico.

Payne, Melissa. 1999. "Valley of Faith: Historical Archaeology in the Upper Santa Fe River Basin." PhD dissertation, Department of Anthropology, University of New Mexico Albuquerque. Ann Arbor, MI: University Microfilms.

Peles, Ashley A. 2010. "Production and Consumption on a 19th-century Spanish New Mexican Homestead: Exploring Daily Life through Faunal and Floral Analyses." Master's thesis, Department of Anthropology, University of Massachusetts, Boston. Ann Arbor, MI: University Microfilms.

Quintana, Frances L., and David H. Snow. 1980. "Historical Archaeology of the Rito Colorado Valley, New Mexico." *Journal of the West* 19 (3): 40–50.

Rebolledo, Tey Diana, and María Teresa Márquez. 2000. *Women's Tales from the New Mexico WPA: La Diabla a Pie*. Houston: Arte Público Press.

Rothschild, Nan A., and Heather N. Atherton. 2004. "Current Research at San Jose de las Huertas, New Mexico." *Maxwell Center for Anthropological Research Newsletter* (2):8–10.

Rudecoff, Christine A. 1987a. *Archaeological Testing at LA 46635 (San Antonio de los Poblanos), Bernalillo County, New Mexico. Laboratory of Anthropology Notes 311*. Santa Fe: Laboratory of Anthropology, Museum of New Mexico.

Rudecoff, Christine A. 1987b. *Archaeological Testing in the Paseo del Norte Right-of-Way, Los Ranchos de Albuquerque, Bernalillo County, New Mexico. Laboratory of Anthropology Notes 387*. Santa Fe: Laboratory of Anthropology, Museum of New Mexico.

Rudecoff, Christine A., and Charles M. Carrillo. 1987. "Test Excavations at Los Poblanos: A Spanish Colonial Community on the Middle Rio Grande." In *Secrets of a City: Papers on Albuquerque Area Archaeology, in Honor of Richard A. Bice*, edited by Anne V. Poor and John Montgomery, 48–56. Papers of the Archaeological Society of New Mexico 13. Albuquerque: Archaeological Society of New Mexico.

Sargeant, Kathryn. 1985. "An Archaeological and Historical Survey of the Village of Los Ranchos." Manuscript on file, Archaeological Records Management System (ARMS), Museum of New Mexico, Santa Fe.

Smith-Lintner, Cheryl Ann. 2007. "Becoming Californio: Archaeology of Communities, Animals, and Identity in Colonial California." PhD dissertation, University of California, Berkeley. Ann Arbor, MI: University Microfilms.

Snow, David H. 1983. "A Note on Encomienda Economics in Seventeenth-Century New Mexico." In *Hispanic Arts and Ethnohistory in the Southwest: New Papers Inspired by the Work of E. Boyd*, edited by Marta Weigle, 347–58. Santa Fe: Ancient City Press.

Snow, David H. 1993. "Purchased in Chihuahua for Feasts." In *El Camino Real de Tierra Adentro*, edited by J.-e. Piper and L. Jacobson, 133–46. Cultural Resources Series No. 11. Santa Fe: New Mexico Bureau of Land Management.

Snow, David H. 1996. *New Mexico's First Colonists: The 1597–1600 Enlistments for New Mexico under Juan de Oñate, Adelante and Gobernador*. Albuquerque: Hispanic Genealogical Research Center of New Mexico.

Snow, David H. 1999. *Archeological Monitoring of Backhoe Trenches, The Main House: Los Luceros, New Mexico*. Albuquerque: Cross-Cultural Research Systems.

Sunseri, Jun U. 2009. *Nowhere to Run, Everywhere to Hide: Multi-Scalar Identity Practices at Casitas Viejas*. PhD dissertation, Department of Anthropology, University of California, Santa Cruz. Ann Arbor: UMI-Proquest.

Swadesh, Frances Leon. 1974. *Los Primeros Pobladores: Hispanic Americans of the Ute Frontier*. Notre Dame, IN: University of Notre Dame Press.

Swadesh, Frances Leon. 1979. "Structure of Hispanic-Indian Relations in New Mexico." In *The Survival of Spanish American Villages*, edited by Paul Kutsche, 53–61. Colorado College Studies 15. Colorado Springs: Colorado College.

Toll, Mollie S. 1985. *Flotation at a Spanish Colonial Farm (LA 16769) along the Santa Fe River, New Mexico. Technical Series 137*. Albuquerque: Castetter Laboratory for Ethnobotanical Studies, University of New Mexico.

Townsend, Stephen. 2004. *A Class III Cultural Resource Inventory for Proposed Upgrades to the San Miguel del Bado MDWCA Domestic Water Delivery System, San Miguel del Bado, San Miguel County, New Mexico*. Report 2003-30, Townsend Archaeological Consultants Las Vegas, New Mexico.

Trigg, Heather B. 2003. "The Ties That Bind: Economic and Social Interactions in Early-Colonial New Mexico, A.D. 1598–1680." *Historical Archaeology* 37 (2): 65–84.

Trigg, Heather B. 2005. *From Household to Empire: Society and Economy in Early Colonial New Mexico*. Tucson: University of Arizona Press.

Trigg, Heather, and Debra Gold. 2005. "Cultural Identity and Mestizaje in Seventeenth Century New Mexico." Paper presented at the 70th Annual Meeting of the Society for American Archaeology, Salt Lake City, UT.

Van Ness, John R. 1979. "Hispanic Village Organization in Northern New Mexico: Corporate Community Structure in Historical and Comparative Perspective." In *The Survival of Spanish American Villages*, edited by Paul Kutsche, 21–44. Colorado College Studies 15. Colorado Springs: Colorado College.

Voss, Barbara L. 2005. "From *Casta* to *Californio*: Social Identity and the Archaeology of Culture Contact." *American Anthropologist* 107 (3): 461–74. http://dx.doi.org/10.1525/aa.2005.107.3.461.

Voss, Barbara L. 2008. *The Archaeology of Ethnogenesis: Race and Sexuality in Colonial San Francisco*. Berkeley: University of California Press.

Windes, Thomas C. 2011. "A Dendrochronological Study of Nineteenth-Century San Miguel del Vado and San José del Vado in Northeastern New Mexico." *New Mexico Historical Review* 86 (4): 461–89.

Windes, Thomas C., and Elizabeth A. Bagwell. 2004. "A Village on the Edge: San Miguel del Vado, New Mexico." Paper presented at the 69th Annual Meeting of the Society for American Archaeology, Montreal, Quebec, Canada.

Wiseman, Regge N. 1988. *The Valencia Project: A Proposal for Data Recovery*. Laboratory of Anthropology Note 446. Santa Fe: Laboratory of Anthropology, Museum of New Mexico.

Wiseman, Regge N. 1996. *Testing Report and Data Recovery Plan for the U.S. 285 Pojoaque South Project*. Archaeology Note 186. Santa Fe: Office of Archaeological Studies, Museum of New Mexico.

Worth, John E. 2012. "Creolization in Southwest Florida: Cuban Fishermen and 'Spanish Indians,' ca. 1766–1841." *Historical Archaeology* 46 (1): 142–60.

NINE

Moquis, Kastiilam, and the Trauma of History

Hopi Oral Traditions of Seventeenth-Century Franciscan Missionary Abuses

THOMAS E. SHERIDAN AND STEWART B. KOYIYUMPTEWA

INTRODUCTION

On November 7, 2002, soon after *Moquis and Kastiilam:* The Hopi History Project began,[1] Stewart B. Koyiyumptewa of the Hopi Cultural Preservation Office interviewed vice-chairman of the Hopi Tribe, Elgean Joshevama, in his office in Kykotsmovi, Arizona. Stewart was there to record Hopi oral traditions Vice-Chairman Joshevama had heard about the Kastiilam, the Spaniards who conquered and missionized the Hopis between 1629 and the Pueblo Revolt in 1680. "The information that I heard about came from not a lot of discussions, because apparently this was an issue that was very difficult to talk about, and so people were not very willing to even say too much about what happened then," Vice-Chairman Joshevama responded. "But I sense that it was an important time to Hopi because of the disruption of our lives and how it later on impacted our lives. And even today, I think, we're still struggling with some of those issues that, that the Spaniards inflicted on us."

As the interview proceeded, Vice-Chairman Joshevama reflected on his work at the Hopi Guidance Center with Hopi children who had been sexually abused.

DOI: 10.5876/9781607325741.c009

"And, and as I was working with them I was curious to see how these victims of abuse had a lot of feelings. And, these feelings included anger," he continued. "A lot of feelings of being sad, sometimes some signs of depression, some signs of helplessness, guilt." Vice-Chairman Joshevama went on to say:

> And, and the more I worked with them trying to help get them past these kinds of feelings, trying to help with what they had been going through, to get them to a point where they might now be able to talk about it easier, the more I began to think that these children were showing me, and showing us who were working with them, to me were similar to the way that we in the villages were behaving too.
>
> We had a lot of suspicions of each other. We were angry at each other. We weren't very happy. We were sad sometimes and a lot of times these kinds of feelings of anger, sadness, would come out in different ways in our villages. And, then I recalled this part of our history that something happened to us a long time ago, and in particular, that period between about 1630 and 1680 when the Spanish were here and from the stories that we learned, they forced our people to do things that was against our way of doing things. (Sheridan et al. 2015:236)

Spanish conquest and missionization were profoundly traumatic for the Hopis, shaking the very foundations of Hopi society and provoking Hopis to carry out acts of violence that still haunt them today. The Franciscans never asked, "Could we be your guests here," Vice-Chairman Joshevama observed:

> They just simply intruded into Hopi lives and then enslaved us, slaved our people, and then subjected Hopi to a very foreign way of life. But Hopi, all this time, had already had its own way of life. We had our own initiations, we had our own rituals, we had our own ceremonies, we had own spiritual beings that we would talk to and pray to those. And, then here comes a foreign intruder and totally tells us that that's not right. This is the way your life has to be lived. And, so they forced that kind of idea or that concept on us. And, when any time anybody does that to somebody, it's, it's going to create a lot of feelings. It's going to create anger but at the same time fear because what can you do about it when these people have the might of the weapon, the modern weapon at the time, and that they could kill you without any kind of respect given to whether you agree with them or not.
>
> See they, they just took completely away our freedom to live the kind of life that we had up to that point. So, those were the things that I thought about when I saw the similarities between the victims of sexual abuse of children, and then when I look at our villages and how they were behaving, and that behavior was pretty much the same as what these children were showing as victims of abuse. And, I concluded then that we, we must have been victims of abuse at some point, and that's when I thought back on our history and I thought of that period. That's when this abuse happened to us. (Sheridan et al. 2015:237)

ABUSIVE GUESTS: FRANCISCAN MISSIONARIES ON THE HOPI MESAS

Like the other Pueblo peoples in southwestern North America, the Hopi Indians first encountered Europeans in 1540, when Francisco Vázquez de Coronado's expedition passed through the region like a brief but brutal plague. Spanish accounts of this initial contact between Kastiilam and Moquis, the latter the term the Spaniards used for Hopis, paint a relatively benign picture of the interactions. More than four centuries of Hopi oral traditions, in contrast, report that Coronado's soldiers destroyed a Hopi village (Sheridan et al. 2013; Sheridan et al. 2015). For the next nine decades, contact between Hopis and Spaniards was intermittent, but in 1629, the governor of New Mexico led six Franciscans and thirty soldiers to establish missions among the Ácomas, Zunis, and Hopis. The leader of the Franciscans, custodio Padre Fray Esteban de Perea, claimed that the Ácomas and Zunis welcomed the Spaniards. But the Hopis at Awat'ovi, the easternmost Hopi pueblo on Antelope Mesa, received them "with some coolness" because an "apostate Indian of the Christian pueblos" had told them that the Spaniards "were coming to burn their pueblos, rob their haciendas, and behead their children." The Franciscans later accused Hopis at Awat'ovi of poisoning their first missionary, Padre Fray Francisco de Porras, in 1632.[2]

Despite Hopi resistance, however, Franciscan missionization proceeded. Missionaries established *cabeceras* (headquarters) with resident priests at Awat'ovi on Antelope Mesa, Songòopavi on Second Mesa, and Orayvi on Third Mesa, with *visitas* (subsidiary churches) at Wàlpi on First Mesa and Musangnuvi on Second Mesa. The primary purpose of the religious mission in New Spain was to convert Native peoples to Roman Catholicism and transform them into vassals of the Spanish Crown. This usually involved prohibiting people from practicing their own religious ceremonies and beliefs. At Awat'ovi, for example, the sanctuary of the mission church—that most sacred of Catholic ritual spaces—was constructed on top of a perfectly preserved kiva (Montgomery et al. 1949). Building the church above one of the Hopis' sacred underground chambers proclaimed that the Christian God was superior to Hopi gods, that Christian sacred spaces were submerging Hopi sacred spaces.

Conquest and colonization took an unrelenting material toll on the Hopis and other Pueblo peoples during the seventeenth century as well. Demands for labor and tribute under both missions and the *encomienda* system, which granted prominent Spaniards the right to extract foodstuffs and textiles from Pueblo households, increasingly burdened the Pueblos as their populations plummeted because of Old World diseases. At the beginning of the seventeenth century, when Juan de Oñate's expedition was establishing the colony of Nuevo México, Elinore Barrett (2002:64) estimates, there were about eighty-one occupied pueblos along the Rio Grande and its tributaries. That number had plummeted to about thirty-one when the revolt broke out eight decades later. Her figures do not include either Zuni or Hopi communities. Population figures are more difficult to calculate because not all rooms in a pueblo may have been inhabited at any one time. Spanish observers provided population figures, but those were no more than educated guesses, colored by where the Spaniards went and for whom they were writing. Barrett (2002:65) speculates that there may have been perhaps 60,000 Pueblo inhabitants when Oñate arrived. By 1678, that number had dropped to 17,000. She argues that the greatest losses of both pueblos and people took place in the late 1630s and early 1640s, when smallpox decimated the Pueblo world (Barrett 2002:78). More recent studies contend that even greater declines occurred after 1650, with another wave of disease ravaging the Pueblos in 1671 (Liebmann 2012:40).

Climate change compounded epidemics. In the mid-1660s, the third worst drought between AD 622 and 1994 seared the northern Southwest (Grissino-Mayer et al. 1997; Grissino-Mayer et al. 2002; Parks et al. 2006). It was a cold drought, with cooler temperatures reducing the growing season for corn, the staple of Pueblo peoples. In the words of Carla Van West and her colleagues, "These harsh conditions initiated around 1664 and continued, almost unbroken, through 1678" (Van West et al. 2013:8). For three straight years—1667, 1668, and 1669—summer monsoons failed to moisten the parched fields of the Salinas pueblos, forcing their abandonment over the next decade. The Piro pueblos of the southern Rio Grande Basin also drained away. The smallpox epidemic of the early 1640s had savaged the southern Pueblos most, causing the abandonment of eleven of 14 Piro pueblos and five of 11 Salinas pueblos (Barrett 2002). Drought provided the coup de grâce three decades later.

The same drought that afflicted the Pueblo World in New Mexico withered crops on the Hopi Mesas. From 1650 to 1680, the Palmer Drought Severity Index (PDSI) for the Southwest was negative, indicating poor conditions for agriculture for all years except seven; between 1664 and 1670, the drought was particularly harsh, with negative PDSI ranging from –1.632 in 1666 to –3.303 in 1668 (Cook 2000).

An even more sensitive indicator of agricultural conditions on the Hopi Mesas is the PDSI for the month of June, when the all-important spring crops were ripening. Between 1660 and 1679, June PDSI was negative for fourteen of twenty years; from 1666 to 1670, June PDSIs reveal why famine stalked the Hopi pueblos as one dry year slid into another: 1666 (–2.232), 1667 (–3.407), 1668 (–3.542), 1669 (–1.095), 1670 (–4.954).[3] What little household surpluses were left after the demands of missionaries and *encomenderos* had been met would have been quickly exhausted.

The final blow may have been a hard freeze during the growing season in the summer of 1680, as evidenced by a "frost ring" in the tree-ring chronology for the San Francisco Peaks and other sites in western North America. "Given that bristlecone pines in the Rocky Mountain region put on new growth from late June to late August or early September (Salzer 2000:92), we suspect that this destructive frost took place at a point in the corn-growing season when it was too late to replant at lower elevations," Van West et al. (2013:9; italics original) surmise. "The frost-damaged section of the SFP ring of 1680 is located within or near the latewood rather than the early wood. It is likely that this destructive freeze took place in early August during a year *and* a multiyear interval of exceptional cold. Our guess is that this 'event' was a contributing factor in the timing of the revolt."

It is a truism in the social sciences that there are no "natural disasters." Mission and encomienda exacerbated cold and drought, grinding the Hopis and their Pueblo neighbors down. During these decades when famine and abuse haunted the Hopi mesas, many Hopis who may have converted to Christianity returned to the beliefs of their ancestors. Similar patterns of nativistic resistance and rebellion aggravated by drought wracked colonial Sonora in the mid-eighteenth century as well (Brenneman 2004; Sheridan 1999). Hopis and other Pueblo peoples were forced to carry out their religious ceremonies in secret, far from the prying eyes of missionaries. "Whose religion had been taken away? Whose ceremonies had been stamped down?" Vice-Chairman Joshevama asked rhetorically. "It's no wonder that we understand that in order for a Hopi person, or a Hopi people to do something that would bring back those kinds of things that had been important to them, that they had to steal themselves away in secrecy" (Sheridan et al. 2015:238). Later in the interview, he added, "So that they would not forget. So that they could maybe teach the younger ones who might have been there with them those kinds of things that they needed to have them remember" (Sheridan et al. 2015:239).

THE INVESTIGATION OF PADRE FRAY SALVADOR DE GUERRA

When we began the Hopi History Project, Hopi colleagues, teachers, and elders expressed a great deal of interest in how Spanish colonial officials and missionaries portrayed colonial abuses. They wanted to see how those representations articulated with, or silenced, the Hopi people's long memory of missionary abuses during the seventeenth century prior to the Pueblo Revolt. One case in particular captured their attention because of its horrific details.

In 1655, a Hopi named Juan Xiveni appeared before Padre Fray Antonio de Ybargaray, the *custodio* of New Mexico. As custodio, Ybargaray was the highest-ranking Franciscan in charge of New Mexico's missions. Xiveni represented the Spanish-appointed Hopi *gobernador* (governor) of Orayvi and its *naturales*, or native inhabitants. They sent him to lodge a formal complaint against Padre Fray Salvador de Guerra, missionary in the pueblo of Orayvi on Third Mesa, "because of the terrible and inhuman punishments that [Guerra] has given to some natives, whipping them extremely cruelly in all parts and limbs of their bodies, and afterwards scalding them and anointing them with boiling turpentine." Ybargaray, Guerra's superior, took the charges seriously enough to travel to the Second Mesa village of Songòopavi and conduct a formal investigation, which is how and why the case made its way into the Spanish colonial record (see Sheridan et al. 2015).[4]

Guerra's worst abuse involved a Hopi named Juan Cuna, whom Guerra had caught in an unspecified "idolatry." During the first stage of the investigation, Ybargaray heard the testimonies of three Hopis from Orayvi—Joseph Ocheguene, a *fiscal* (native official who carried out the policies of the gobernador) and two *capitanes de guerra* (war captains) from Orayvi: Francisco Quera and Juan Cocpi. All three confirmed that Guerra kicked and punched Juan Cuna just outside the door to Orayvi's mission church until he was "bathed in blood." Then, inside the church, Guerra tied Cuna to a ladder and whipped him severely "on the back, belly, and all of the other parts of his body." Finally, the Franciscan "scalded him from head to foot with a large lump of turpentine, and he burned him with it." After these grisly punishments, Cuna and "other idolaters" were dispatched to Awat'ovi under the charge of Joseph Ocheguene and other Hopi fiscales. Cuna died, "unconscious and speechless," along the trail between Orayvi and Songòopavi.

Guerra denied that he kicked or punched Cuna, stating that he only gave him a slap on the face from which "six or seven drops of blood came out of his nose." He admitted to having Cuna tied up and whipped, but claimed that he did not do the lashing, that "the lashes did not exceed twenty, and he gave him no lashes on the belly." As for the turpentine, "seeing that [Cuna] was old and sick, he had thrown on him no more than ten or twelve drops, and not all [over] his body, as the witnesses state." Guerra then accused fiscal Joseph Ocheguene of whipping Cuna to death because he "did not want to walk."

In light of Guerra's testimony, Ybargaray ordered Ocheguene, Quera, and Cocpi to ratify their statements. Ocheguene could not be located because Franciscan lay brother Fray Pedro Moreno, who "loved him well," had told Ocheguene to hide because of Guerra's counteraccusations. So Ybargaray took Moreno's testimony. Moreno stated that Ocheguene only hit Cuna "with a switch or branch on the legs so that he would move along." Quera and Cocpi swore that their original statements were true and also testified that Ocheguene did no harm to Cuna.

While at Songòopavi in June, Ybargaray also investigated other charges against Guerra brought by Hopi leaders from Orayvi, Songòopavi, and Musangnuvi. The Hopis said that Guerra "compelled them to make many cotton mantas, for which the aforesaid father would give them half the cotton that was necessary to finish them. And the harshness of the aforesaid father obliged them to finish [the mantas] with cotton they had in their homes within eight days. Because of this rush, they could not plant their cotton [fields] or cultivate their milpas [corn fields]." As to his "harshness," the Hopi officials accused Guerra of "whipping them terribly and giving them up to forty and fifty lashes, and scalding and smearing them with burning-hot turpentine." Ybargaray took the testimonies of nine Hopis who confirmed those charges. Guerra denied them. Ybargaray called the Hopis back in again, and they all ratified their original charges. They also declared that Guerra was only entitled to less than a third of the mantas he demanded of them.

Mission Indians were supposed to supply their missionaries with food, cloth, and other basics. These provisions were in addition to the annual stipend the missionary received from the Spanish Crown. But missions were not parishes, and the Franciscans were not secular clergy who could own property or receive benefices. Nor could they charge mission Indians for administering the sacraments to them (Farriss 1968; Taylor 1999). Franciscans such as Guerra tried to justify the extraction of mantas from their neophytes by claiming that it was in the support of the mission, not the missionary. But Guerra clearly violated the moral economy of the Hopis by forcing them to produce an excessive amount of mantas at a time when they needed to plant their fields.

The investigation then moved to Santo Domingo, where, in July, Ybargaray and five other Franciscans found Guerra guilty of killing Cuna and the other charges. Clearly shocked by his behavior, they concluded that Guerra not only had to be removed from Orayvi but sent to Mexico City as well. Ybargaray and the others therefore sentenced Guerra to seclusion in the *convento*, or priests' residence, at the mission of Quarai until he could be deported to Mexico City for punishment by Franciscan superiors of the Provincia de Santo Evangelio. Guerra was also prohibited from saying mass or administering the sacraments.

But Guerra may never have traveled to Mexico City. In 1659–60, he was stationed at Taos. A year later, he was posted to Isleta. In 1661, he served at Ácoma and then at Jemez, where he was notary to Fray Alonso de Posada, comisario of the Holy Office of the Inquisition (Scholes 1945). During the 1660s, Guerra was Posada's right-hand man during his crusade against governors Bernardo López de Mendizábal and Diego de Peñalosa (Scholes 1942). Guerra remained at Jémez at least until 1668, when he described himself as "preacher, difinidor actual, commissary of the Santa Concordia, secretary of the Holy Custodia of the Conversion of San Pablo of New Mexico, and minister-guardian of the congregation of San Diego de los Jemez" (translated by Scholes 1929:196). In 1672, he was in charge of the supply train itself (Bloom and Mitchell 1938). Guerra's fall from grace was short indeed.

THE TORTURE AND DEATH OF SITKOYMA

Most Hopi oral traditions of missionary abuses are generalized accounts. The most common concern having to haul beams for mission churches from distant mountains or of priests abusing Hopi women, often after sending their husbands away to fetch water from distant springs. Occasionally, however, precise details emerge. One afternoon in October 2009, during a three-day workshop with members of the Hopi Tribe's Cultural Resources Advisory Task Team (CRATT; Figure 9.1), Leigh Kuwanwisiwma, director of the Hopi Cultural Preservation Office, led a field trip to a natural amphitheater in the mountains south of Third Mesa known as Katsina Buttes. There, while talking about how Hopis had to hold their ceremonies in secret during the mission period, Kuwanwisiwma gave another version of what may have been Juan Cuna's punishment. Four years later, on October 19, 2012, Stewart B. Koyiyumptewa recorded Kuwanwisiwma's narrative of the incident at greater length (see Sheridan et al. 2015).

After discussing the "pretty systematic . . . suppression of Hopi religion," including the burning of Hopi paraphernalia and altars "necessary to conduct ceremonies and initiate members," Kuwanwisiwma talked about how the missionaries were called away from the Hopi missions to attend a meeting in Santa Fe:

> So one individual by the name of Sitkoyma from Orayvi thought about quickly sponsoring a katsina Home Dance—we call it *Nimàntikive*—and that was because his son had recently married and had gone through the Hopi wedding ceremony so I guess you would think that at least those kinds of ceremonies were not forbidden by the church.
>
> And as he looked throughout the village of Orayvi and other villages, he knew that other traditional weddings had also been completed. But because the katsina ceremonies were never completed, they could never conduct the Home Dance, which is a really major part of the Hopi wedding ceremony. There's many things that occur between both sets of the family and, particularly—and of the ceremony—there's an exchanging of different kinds of personal vows between the bride and husband. And, you know, of course, because the katsinas were forbidden, none of the brides that had gone through—over a period of years—never completed that part of the Hopi wedding ceremony. So, he thought that maybe he could take advantage of the absence of the priest, the church and the military to quickly conduct—sponsor and conduct—a katsina ceremony, Home Dance, so that that last piece of the ceremony would be offered to the couple and then subsequently work towards concluding the Hopi ceremony.
>
> So he probably sought advice and got support, and they say that it was out of season—the katsina season had ended—but he took that opportunity to quickly call together some people. Men and I'm sure women, and said this is what I want to do. And that was to hold a katsina ceremony and Home Dance for his new bride, his new daughter in law. So they said that they quickly convened out of season—and yes, they still remembered the Home Dance songs—so they quickly put together their own types of paraphernalia and then because they really didn't want to have a big, big public show because they were afraid that would be very well be immediately known by the Spanish priest and the military, they took

FIGURE 9.1. *Hopi History Project Workshop with the Cultural Resources Advisory Task Team (CRATT) of the Hopi Cultural Preservation Office, Kykotsmovi, Arizona, October 21, 2009. Photograph by T. J. Ferguson).*

FIGURE 9.2. *Katsina Buttes (Kaktsintuyqa), where Hopis performed ceremonies in secret during the Franciscan mission period. Photograph: by T. Sheridan.*

refuge in what we now call Katsina Buttes or *Kaktsintuyqa*. So that's where the men practiced the katsina Home Dance and then when they were ready then they announced it and Sitkoyma, Sitkoyma was the guy in charge of it (figure 9.2).

And so he invited other villages that if in fact they were able and willing. He invited all the brides that had gone through the ceremony to go there so that they could conclude a part, and part of the last parts of the Hopi wedding ceremonies. So they say that brides from throughout the mesas, they'd accept the invitations, so the dance was held. And we now call it over in the Hopi Buttes area about maybe half an hour away from Old Orayvi due east, we call it now that whole landscape *Kaktsintuyqa* but we also call this one alcove that they used as a plaza we call it *Tipkya* and *Tipkya* is a very important place in a village and that's where the final Home Dances are danced—where the bride is shown publically to everybody, the audience. So that's what happened. They danced the Home Dance and then towards the evening, all the brides were dressed up in their robes and then they were presented to the people witnessing it and then of course to the katsinas, the katsina spirits. So that's what happened and of course everybody I'm sure with that happening and then ending successfully, everybody liked all of our dances, was pretty happy about it.

After returning from Santa Fe, however, the priest at Orayvi found out about Sitkoyma's sponsorship of the forbidden Home Dance. Hopis referred to that missionary in particular, and missionaries in general, as Tota'tsi: Kuwanwisiwma defined Tota'tsi as "a spiritual person that you can never ever please and if you don't please him, *Tota'tsi* will do whatever it can to get its way." The missionary ordered Sitkoyma to be arrested and interrogated. Then, in Kuwanwisiwma's words:

> The Tota'tsi told the military to announce and also make sure that on a particular day he wanted all of Orayvi to converge on the plaza. So that's what happened. It was announced that on a certain day no one would be allowed [to leave] the village and the military of course I'm sure, made sure of that. I'm sure they had units watching the village outside the village, making sure. And what the Tota'tsi now had decided was that because he [Sitkoyma] was convicted of violating this decree of the ban on Hopi ceremonies that he had to be publically punished and that was the intent of having the whole village come to the Orayvi plaza where when Sitkoyma got there, the posts had already been put into the plaza there and he was led there and then tied there with his frontal body tied, strapped. Hands were tied. And then he was tied to this post. So the priest, they say, who was fluent in Hopi, then announced the charges, the conviction and now the punishment. So the punishment was flogging by horsewhip. So that's what happened with the whole village present there. The priest and the military commander ordered the whipping of Sitkoyma.
>
> So he received some initial slashes they say and of course quite literally the horsewhip with the amount of force landing on human skin simply cut it open. And there were more slashes they say until Sitkoyma, because of the amount of whipping he took, was literally covered in blood from throughout his body and they say he was screaming. The point was that if there were any further violations of different kinds of decree, such as the one that Sitkoyma and others violated, this would be the kind of punishment that they would receive.
>
> So while Sitkoyma was still strapped there, still alive, then Tota'tsi then ordered the military, I guess, to show Sitkoyma and the village really what he meant when he said you will suffer the consequences if you dare violate church and military decrees. So what he ordered then was to have the military people pour turpentine on Sitkoyma, on his wounds. And you can imagine what Sitkoyma was going through. So based on the turpentine and everything else that happened, they say that Sitkoyma died there in Orayvi plaza still strapped you know to the post that was there in the village. And so when you look back to that incident you can see probably the kind of horrific trauma the whole village witnessed and suffered. And also what Sitkoyma also went through. (Sheridan et al. 2015:173–74)

THE PUEBLO REVOLT AND THE DESTRUCTION OF AWAT'OVI

The torture and death of Sitkoyma, may have been one of the tipping points that pushed the Hopis to rebel. Kuwanwisiwma continued:

So one Hopi informant said that was what Sitkoyma went through—what he did and was killed there—the decision on whether to join the Pueblos in the revolt was being debated and the Hopis being pacifist people, against the taking of life, were not really wanting to participate in the Pueblo Revolt that the Pueblos were planning. But they say that when the Hopi chiefs and leaders witnessed this thing of Sitkoyma, that's when Orayvi said, "We will participate in the Pueblo Revolt. We just simply need to get rid of the church and the military." And when Orayvi decided to do that then because it was one of the biggest ceremonial centers, largest in population, very influential, then that's where other Hopi villages, particularly Songòopavi, Musangnuvi, Wàlpi, and Awat'ovi, decided to join Orayvi in the Pueblo Revolt (Sheridan et al. 2015:178–79)

We do not know if the torture and death of Sitkoyma were the same incident as that of Juan Cuna. Some of the details are different, particularly the location of Sitkoyma's death in the Orayvi plaza. Juan Cuna supposedly died on the trail to Awat'ovi. The possibility that more than one Hopi individual was killed by whipping and scalding with turpentine would only strengthen our contention that missionary abuses profoundly traumatized the Hopis and drove them to rebellion. If Sitkoyma and Juan Cuna were one and the same, however, Hopis waited twenty-five years to throw off the Spanish yoke.

What we do know is that rebellion was simmering throughout the Pueblo world long before the coordinated uprising of August 10, 1680. After the revolt erupted, Sargento Mayor Diego López Sambrano stated that he had witnessed sorcery, rebellion, and punishment for "more than forty years" since the administration of Governor Fernando de Argüello (1644–47), "who hanged, and lashed, and imprisoned more than forty Indians" (Hackett and Shelby 1942:2:298–99). Pueblo peoples, including the Hopis, clearly had been contemplating rebellion for a very long time.

During the early days of the revolt, the Hopis killed the three missionaries stationed among them. In Fray Padre Silvestre Vélez de Escalante's "Extracto de Noticias," written nearly a century after the revolt, the Franciscan chronicler includes the interrogation of a Pueblo rebel named Bartolomé de Ojeda, who was captured during Governor Domingo Jironza Pétriz de Cruzate's siege of the pueblo of Zia in 1689. Ojeda provided an account of the missionaries' execution:

> This fatal news [the murder of Padre Fray Agustín de Santa María by the Zunis] reached Moqui, and the Moquinos immediately undertook to kill the friars who administered them. And they were Father Fray José de Espeleta (he had been a missionary for 40 years), Fray José Trujillo, and Fray José de Figueras. An Indian named Francisco, also a Moquino, whom Father Espeleta had reared, defended them. And seeing this, the apostate rebels said to him: "Now you must kill them yourself, and if not, we must kill you." In order to save his life, although against his

will, he gave up the charitable office of advocate for the three blameless priests, and agreed to be their executioner. They placed the three friars together as a target (for their rage) and Francisco, impelled by fear, went on shooting at them with a musket until all three died of the bullet wounds. Then some compassion entered them, which could also have been a horrible manifestation of such execrable evil at seeing the three bodies stretched out, and they carried them to a church and burned them in it. The same Moquino Francisco related this long afterwards to this witness, Bartolomé de Ojeda, with tears in his eyes. (In Sheridan et al. in prep.)

Francisco was the same Francisco Espeleta who served as chief spokesperson for the Hopis who refused to allow the Franciscans to return in 1700. He also may have organized, if not masterminded, the destruction of Awat'ovi in late November of that same year. If Bartolomé de Ojeda's account of young Francisco's reluctance to kill his namesake is accurate, Espeleta must have had a radical change of heart over the next two decades of Hopi independence. Taught to read and write by his namesake, Fray Padre Espeleta, whom he killed during the Pueblo Revolt, Espeleta emerges from Spanish pages as the foremost opponent to the Franciscans. Wily, intransigent, and fluent in Spanish, he embodies Hopi resistance to the Spaniards.

During his reconquest of the Pueblo world, Diego de Vargas visited Awat'ovi, Wàlpi, Musangnuvi, and Songòopavi, where the Hopis appeared to "reconcile" themselves to God and king (see Sigüenza y Góngora 1693). But that was just an example of one Hopi strategy: to tell the Spaniards what they wanted to hear so they would go away. When the Franciscans returned to stay, Hopi resistance hardened. The rejection of the missionaries appears unequivocal everywhere except Awat'ovi in José Narvaez y Valverde's account, written in 1730 (see Sheridan et al. in prep.).

The standard interpretation of the destruction of Awat'ovi is that Espeleta and other Hopi leaders razed the pueblo and killed its men because its inhabitants had invited the Franciscans to return (Figure 9.3). Adolph Bandelier (1892:372) provides one of the first and most detailed published accounts of it—an account that largely shaped subsequent non-Hopi understandings of the event: "In the meantime, Ahua-tuyba [Awat'ovi] had virtually become again a Christianized pueblo. In the last days of the year 1700, or in the beginning of 1701, the Moquis of the other pueblos fell upon the unsuspecting village at night. The men were mostly killed, stifled in their estufas [kivas], it is said; the women and children were dragged into captivity, and the houses were burnt."

Hopi accounts paint a much more complex picture, one in which leaders of important ceremonial societies at Awat'ovi were spared in order to keep those societies from dying out. There were also accusations of witchcraft and disorder (*koyaanisqatsi*) at Awat'ovi and a desire to wrest control of important

FIGURE 9.3. *Ruins of mission church at Awat'ovi on Antelope Mesa. Photograph by T. Sheridan.*

initiation societies such as the Wuwtsim, which originated there, from Hopis who were considered to be corrupt (Curtis 1922; Courlander 1982; Malotki et al. 2002; Sheridan et al. in prep.; Whiteley 2002). Anthropologist Peter Whiteley (2002) argues that the Hopis in 1700 were engaged in a cultural revitalization movement that was redefining what it meant to be Hopi. Like other Pueblo peoples, the Hopis had endured decades of forced labor and religious persecution. Some may have converted to Christianity; others were compelled to attend mass and allow their children to be baptized. But the Spaniard's God had not brought them prosperity. Instead, pestilence and drought stalked the land. Hopis conspired with the other Pueblos to kill their missionaries and drive the Spaniards from their homelands. When the Spaniards returned to Nuevo México, many Tewas, Tiwas, Tanos, Jemez, and Keresans sought refuge on their mesas. Those desperate, uprooted people must have stiffened Hopi resistance. Never again, they may have told one another as they revived their ceremonies. Never again would the katsinam or the corn mothers be driven away by the gray-robed Franciscans.

Whatever their motivations, however, the destruction of one of their own communities and the killing of their own people still sear Hopi memories today. The covenant that the Hisatsinom (Hopi ancestors) made with Màasaw, Guardian of the Fourth World, required them to be a humble, peaceful people.

As Vice-Chairman Joshevama explained, "We have this basic value of respecting all forms of life. Human life is respected. Animal life is respected. The spiritual life, the plant life. All of these are respected. And, that's what our ceremonial events are based on" (Sheridan et al. 239). The forced labor, the suppression of their religion, the sexual exploitation of their women, and the shocking brutality of a Padre Fray Salvador de la Guerra—all drove the Hopis to kill their missionaries during the 1680 Pueblo Revolt and then, twenty years later, to destroy the village of Awat'ovi itself to prevent the missionaries from returning. "But what they left us though was with the consequence," Vice-Chairman Joshevama observed. "They left us with us having to deal with the guilt of destroying our own people. And, then the anger we have to deal with of those who survived it, the survivors of Awatovi probably felt a lot of anger. And, what do they do with that anger? A lot of it is suppressed" (Sheridan et al. 2015:242).

HISTORICAL TRAUMA, SOCIAL MEMORY, AND HEALING THE SOUL WOUND

Vice-Chairman Joshevama was expressing what a growing number of researchers and clinicians have observed among American Indian and Alaskan Native (AIAN) peoples: "historical" or "intergenerational" trauma (Duran and Duran 1995; Brave Heart–Jordan 1995, Brave Heart 1999a, 1999b, 2000; Brave Heart and DeBruyn 1998; Duran, Duran, and Brave Heart 1998). Maria Yellow Horse Brave Heart, a pioneer in the identification and treatment of historical trauma, defines it as the "cumulative emotional and psychological wounding, over the lifespan and across generations, emanating from massive group trauma experiences" (Brave Heart 2003:7). Examples of historical trauma experienced by AIAN peoples include "community massacres, genocidal policies, pandemics from the introduction of new diseases, forced relocation, forcible removal of children through Indian boarding school policies and the prohibition of spiritual practices" (Begay 2012:11). For the Hopis, those systematic assaults began in 1540 when, according to Hopi oral traditions, Coronado's soldiers destroyed a Hopi village on Antelope Mesa (Sheridan et al. 2013; Sheridan et al. 2015).

Substance abuse is one of a "constellation of features" Brave Heart describes as "historical trauma response (HTR)." Others self-destructive behaviors include "suicidal thoughts and gestures, depression, anxiety, low self-esteem, anger, and difficulty recognizing and expressing emotions" (Brave Heart 2003:7). One of the consequences of such trauma—a consequence Vice-Chairman Joshevama himself acknowledged—is "historical unresolved grief," which may be "impaired, delayed, fixated, and/or disenfranchised" (Brave Heart 2003:7). Unlike posttraumatic stress disorder (PTSD), historical trauma is collective rather than individual, passed down from one generation to another. Research on survivors of the Jewish Holocaust (Fogelman 1988, 1991; Yehuda 1999; Kidron 2003),

African Americans (Cross 1998; Eyerman 2002), and Cambodian refugees (Sack et al. 1995) identify similar patterns of what many Native Americans call the "soul wound."

The two volumes of Moquis and Kastiilam: The Hopi History Project tell the story of that trauma, and the Hopis' resistance to it, from both Hopi and Spanish points of view. For nearly 500 years, the story has been overwhelmingly one-sided. Historians and anthropologists have relied upon documents written by representatives of the Spanish Empire. Hopi voices have been silenced, ignored, or relegated to "myth." Those of us on the project have attempted to restore a balance to the historical record by presenting not only Spanish documents about the Hopis but interviews with Hopi elders about the Spaniards carried out by members of the Hopi Cultural Preservation Office. We argue that these Hopi oral traditions are living records of the past that have just as much, if not more, scholarly validity as the letters, court records, and reports of Spanish officials and Franciscan missionaries. Both are lines of evidence—"texts" in the parlance of literary and cultural criticism—that need to be interrogated. Both have their strengths and limitations that need to be understood.

The testimony of the Vice-Chairman Joshevama offers a historical memory distinct from colonial documentary representations in content, form, and voice. As noted at the beginning of this chapter, the abuses of the missionaries were "very difficult to talk about, and so people were not very willing to even say too much about what happened then." In other words, the Spanish presence in the Hopi pueblos was still a sensitive subject more than 300 years later.

The vice-chairman's testimony also reveals that some Hopi memories of trauma are grounded in a generalized identity of descent; no particularities are mentioned. Instead, Hopis are referred to as a single group who suffered and were abused by Spaniards. Other narratives such as Leigh Kuwanwisiwma's narrative about Sitkoyma reference specific persons, places, events, landscape features, or supernatural beings (Whiteley 1988, 1998), often foregrounding clans or villages rather than the Hopi Tribe, which in many respects was a creation of the Indian Reorganization Act of 1934. The juxtaposition of Kuwanwisiwma's very specific account with more general stories of missionary abuse suggest the depth, richness, and diversity of Hopi narratives about the past. There is no single Hopi oral tradition about the Kastiilam. On the contrary, Hopi chronicles about the past are like underground rivers that flow together and break apart, surfacing only when the moral topography of speaker and audience comes together and the narratives issue forth as small springs.

Accounts such as that of Vice-Chairman Joshevama also meld past and present together in a way that fosters an "imagined community" based on the intergenerational memory of colonial trauma. A frequent use of "we," "our people," and "our way of life" reflects this sense in the vice-chairman's testimony. Moreover, this generalized identity of descent emphasizes, and is reinforced by, disruption and interruption. In the words of Vice-Chairman Joshevama, the missionaries "didn't ask, 'Could we be your guests here?' They didn't ask if they could build the churches or their missions in our villages." On the contrary, "They just simply intruded into Hopi lives and then enslaved us, slaved our people, and then subjected Hopi to a very foreign way of life. But Hopi, all this time, had already had its own way of life." The disruption and interruption of the "Hopi way of life," then, is remembered as more than simple transgressions or individual acts of violence on the part of the colonizers. On the contrary, the Spaniards attempted to destroy or transform many domains central to the social reproduction of the Hopi people: their subsistence activities, their spiritual practices, their gender relationships, and their political organization. "And, when any time anybody does that to somebody, it's, it's going to create a lot of feelings," Vice-Chairman Joshevama noted. "It's going to create anger but at the same time fear because what can you do about it when these people have the might of the weapon, the modern weapon at the time, and that they could kill you without any kind of respect given to whether you agree with them or not" (Sheridan et al. 2015:237).

Along with anger and fear, an even more powerful trope of guilt also emerges. Although the Hopis rebelled by carrying out their rituals in secret, and by participating in the Pueblo Revolt, they had to destroy the village of Awat'ovi to keep the missionaries from reestablishing missions among the Hopi and suppressing the Hopi way of life once again. "They never returned to have that, have that influence again. But what they left us though was the consequence. They left us having to deal with the guilt of destroying our own people. And, then the anger we have to deal with of those who survived it, the survivors of Awat'ovi probably felt a lot of anger. And, what do they do with that anger? A lot of it is suppressed" (Sheridan et al. 2015:242). Past injustices continue to cause contemporary ills.

Missionary abuses during the 1600s and the destruction of Awat'ovi in 1700 remain open wounds among the Hopis today. The enduring experience of these emotive memories accounts for the Hopi Tribe's response to a formal apology for past abuses issued by the Diocese of Gallup. When Bishop Donald Pelotte, a Native American whose father was of the Abenaki/Algonquin Nation, met with Hope Tribe members in 2000, he reported, "They are still cautious and uncertain about efforts at reconciliation. Nonetheless, they are open to allow[ing] us to prove that we are indeed serious about healing the past by asking us for support of their efforts to have justice regarding treaty rights, land and water rights, education, housing, health care, social services, training in jobs, and the use of sacred lands" (Pelotte 2000). The Hopi Tribe also replaced Columbus Day with

Hopi Independence Day—August 10, the anniversary of the outbreak of the Pueblo Revolt—as a paid tribal holiday.

Nevertheless, Hopis still debate whether or not those memories should be exhumed. Perhaps because of his experience dealing with sexually abused children, Vice-Chairman Joshevama believes that the traumatic past has to be confronted:

> How can we do a healing from that event, from those events? How can we heal?
>
> So, what they did, what the Hopi did, start doing from that point is they just took those kinds of feelings and put them under here, stash it away somewhere else, but you know what happens when you stash something, you hide it. At some point it starts to creep back out and it surfaces. And that, that's what happens. And that's what's happening even to this day. And then the younger people would learn from this, they carry it on. And it's like telling our children that this is the way you're going to have to be because this is what somebody did to your family a long time ago instead of saying, "We need to talk about this and let's, let's try to find a way to resolve it so that we don't carry it onto the next generation." To me, that's the step we need to take. And that's what I have been hoping can happen, that people can understand and, and not practice that kind of generational abuse. (Sheridan et al 2015:243)

NOTES

1. The Hopi History Project is a formal collaboration between the University of Arizona (UA) and the Hopi Tribe. Its goals are to tell the story of relations between Hopis and Spaniards during the period when the Spanish Empire was attempting to incorporate the Hopi people into its colony of New Mexico. Researchers at the UA's Southwest Center, School of Anthropology, and Arizona State Museum have selected, transcribed, translated, and annotated Spanish documents about the Hopis, whom the Spaniards called Moquis. The Hopi Cultural Preservation Office of the Hopi Tribe has interviewed Hopi elders to gather their oral traditions about the Kastiilam, the Hopi term for Spaniards. The results will be published in two volumes by the University of Arizona Press. The project has been partially funded by a series of grants from the National Historic Publications and Records Commission (NHPRC) and a Collaborative Research Grant from the National Endowment for the Humanities.

2. Padre Fray Estevan de Perea's Account of the Grand Conversion of New Mexico, 1632 (Sheridan et al. 2015), Real Academia de la Historia, Madrid, Papeles de Jesuitas, Tomo 86, fol. 578. Our translation is from a transcript by historian Herbert Eugene Bolton. Charles Lummis published an English translation in *Land of Sunshine*, November and December, 1901. Lansing Bloom made slight revisions and published his version in *New Mexico Historical Review* 8:211–35, 1933. A third translation appeared in Hodge et al. 1945:210–221).

3. Southwest Paleoclimate Project, June PDSI, Hopi Mesas, AZ. Courtesy of Dr. Jeffrey Dean, Laboratory of Tree-Ring Research, University of Arizona.

4. Archivo Histórico-Nacional, Inquisición 1729, exp. 2, n. 3, ff. 34–38, 44–51. Madrid, Spain.

REFERENCES CITED

Bandelier, Adolph. 1892. *Final Report of Investigations among the Indians of the Southwestern United States, Carried on Mainly in the Years from 1880 to 1885, Part II*. Cambridge, MA: John Wilson and Son University Press.

Barrett, Elinore M. 2002. *Conquest and Catastrophe: Changing Rio Grande Pueblo Settlement Patterns in the Sixteenth and Seventeenth Centuries*. Albuquerque: University of New Mexico Press.

Begay, Tommie. 2012. "Toxic Stress: Linking Historical Trauma to the Contemporary Health of American Indians and Alaskan Natives." PhD dissertation, Department of Teaching, Learning and Sociocultural Studies, University of Arizona, Tucson.

Bloom, Lansing, and Lynn Mitchell. 1938. "The Chapter Elections in 1672." *New Mexico Historical Review* 13 (1): 85–115.

Brave Heart, Maria Yellow Horse. 1999a. "Gender Differences in the Historical Trauma Response among the Lakota." *Journal of Health and Social Policy* 10 (4): 1–21. http://dx.doi.org/10.1300/J045v10n04_01.

Brave Heart, Maria Yellow Horse. 1999b. "Oyate Ptaleya: Rebuilding the Lakota Nation through Addressing Historical Trauma among Lakota Parents." *Journal of Human Behavior in the Social Environment* 2 (1–2): 109–26. http://dx.doi.org/10.1300/J137v02n01_08.

Brave Heart, Maria Yellow Horse. 2000. "Wakiksuyapi: Carrying the Historical Trauma of the Lakota." *Tulane Studies in Social Welfare* 21–22 (2): 245–66.

Brave Heart, Maria Yellow Horse. 2003. "The Historical Trauma Response among Natives and Its Relationship with Substance Abuse: A Lakota Illustration." *Journal of Psychoactive Drugs* 35 (1): 7–13. http://dx.doi.org/10.1080/02791072.2003.10399988.

Brave Heart, Maria Yellow Horse, and L. M. DeBruyn. 1998. "The American Indian Holocaust: Healing Historical Unresolved Grief." *American Indian and Alaska Native Mental Health Research* 8 (2): 56–78.

Brave Heart–Jordan, Maria Yellow Horse. 1995. "The Return to the Sacred Path: Healing from Historical Trauma and Historical Unresolved Grief among the Lakota." PhD dissertation, Smith College for Social Work, Northampton, MA.

Brenneman, Dale. 2004. "Climate of Rebellion: The Relationship between Climate Variability and Indigenous Uprisings in Mid-Eighteenth-Century Sonora." PhD dissertation, Department of Anthropology, University of Arizona, Tucson.

Cook, E. R. 2000. *Southwestern USA Drought Index Reconstruction*. International Tree-Ring Data Bank. IGBP PAGES/World Data Center for Paleoclimatology Data

Contribution Series #2000-053. Boulder, CO: NOAA/NGDC Paleoclimatology Program.

Courlander, Harold, ed. 1982. *Hopi Voices: Recollections, Traditions, and Narratives of the Hopi Indians. Recorded, transcribed, and annotated by Harold Courlander*. Albuquerque: University of New Mexico Press.

Cross, William E. 1998. "Black Psychological Functioning and the Legacy of Slavery." In *International Handbook of Multigenerational Legacies of Trauma*, edited by Y. Danieli, 387–400. New York: Plenum Press. http://dx.doi.org/10.1007/978-1-4757-5567-1_25.

Curtis, Edward. 1922. *The Hopi*. The North American Indian, vol. 12. Norwood, MA: Plimpton Press.

Danieli, Yael, ed. 1998. *International Handbook of Multigenerational Legacies of Trauma*. New York: Plenum Press. http://dx.doi.org/10.1007/978-1-4757-5567-1.

Duran, Bonnie, Eduardo Duran, and Maria Yellow Horse Brave Heart. 1998. "Native Americans and the Trauma of History." In *Studying Native America: Problems and Prospects*, edited by Russell Thornton, 60–76. Madison: University of Wisconsin Press.

Duran, Eduardo, and Bonnie Duran. 1995. *Native American Postcolonial Psychology*. Albany: State University of New York Press.

Eyerman, Ron. 2002. *Cultural Trauma: Slavery and the Formation of African American Identity*. Cambridge: Cambridge University Press.

Farriss, Nancy. 1968. *Crown and Clergy in Colonial Mexico, 1759–1821*. London: Athlone Press.

Fogelman, Eva. 1988. "Intergenerational Group Therapy: Child Survivors of the Holocaust and Offspring of Survivors." *Psychoanalytic Review* 75 (4): 621–40.

Fogelman, Eva. 1991. "Mourning without Graves." In *Storms and Rainbows: The Many Faces of Death*, edited by A. Medvene, 25–43. Washington, DC: Lewis Press.

Grissino-Mayer, Henri D., Christopher H. Baisan, Kiyomi A. Morino, and Thomas W. Swetnam. 2002. *Multi-Year Trends in Past Climate for the Middle Rio Grande Basin*, AD 622–1992. Final Report Submitted to the USDA Forest Service, Rocky Mountain Research Station, Albuquerque. Laboratory of Tree-Ring Research Report 2000/6. Tucson: Laboratory of Tree-Ring Research, University of Arizona.

Grissino-Mayer, Henri D., Christopher H. Baisan, and Thomas W. Swetnam. 1997. *A 1,373-Year Reconstruction of Annual Precipitation for the Southern Rio Grande Basin*. Final report submitted to the Legacy Program of Defense, El Paso, Texas. Tucson: Laboratory of Tree-Ring Research, University of Arizona. A 1:374.

Hackett, Charles, and Charmion C. Shelby. 1942. *Revolt of the Pueblo Indians of New México and Otermin's Attempted Reconquest 1680–1682, Part 1*. Coronado Historical Series, vol. 8. Coronado Cuarto Centennial Publications, 1540–1940, edited by George P. Hammond. Albuquerque: University of New Mexico Press.

Hodge, Frederick Webb, George P. Hammond, and Agapito Rey. 1945. *Fray Alonso de Benavides' Revised Memorial of 1634*. Vol. 4 of *Coronado Cuarto Centennial Publications*,

1540–1940, edited by George P. Hammond. Coronado Historical Series. Albuquerque: University of New Mexico Press.

Kidron, Carol. 2003. "Surviving a Distant Past: A Case Study of the Cultural Construction of Trauma Descendant Identity." *Ethos* (Berkeley, Calif.) 31 (4): 513–44. http://dx.doi.org/10.1525/eth.2003.31.4.513.

Liebmann, Matthew. 2012. *Revolt: An Archaeological History of Pueblo Resistance and Revitalization in Seventeenth-Century New Mexico*. Tucson: University of Arizona Press.

Malotki, Ekkehart, Michael Lomatuway'ma, Lorena Lomatuway'ma, and Sidney Namingha Jr. 2002. *Hopi Tales of Destruction*. Lincoln: University of Nebraska Press.

Montgomery, Ross Gordon, Watson Smith, and John Otis Brew. 1949. *Franciscan Awatovi: The Excavation and Conjectural Reconstruction of a 17th- Century Spanish Mission Establishment at a Hopi Indian Town in Northeastern Arizona*, vol. 36. Papers of the Peabody Museum of American Archaeology and Ethnology, Harvard University. Reports of the Awatovi Expedition, Peabody Museum, Harvard University, No. 3. Cambridge, MA: Peabody Museum.

Parks, J. A., Dean, Jeffrey S., and Betancourt, J. L. 2006. "Tree Rings, Drought, and the Pueblo Abandonment of South-Central New Mexico in the 1670s." In *Environmental Change and Human Adaptation in the Ancient American Southwest*, edited by David E. Doyel and Jeffrey S. Dean, 214–27. Salt Lake City: University of Utah Press.

Pelotte, Donald. 2000. "Seeking Forgiveness, Building Communion: A Time for Atoning and Reconciling." *Encuentro 2000*. United States Conference of Catholic Bishops, July 6, 2000.

Sack, William, Gregory Clarke, and John Seeley. 1995. "Post-Traumatic Stress Disorder across Two Generations of Cambodian Refugees." *Journal of the American Academy of Child and Adolescent Psychiatry* 34 (9): 1160–66. http://dx.doi.org/10.1097/00004583-199509000-00013.

Salzer, Mathew. 2000. "Dendroclimatology in the San Francisco Peaks Region of Northern Arizona, USA." PhD dissertation, Department of Geosciences, University of Arizona, Tucson.

Scholes, France. 1929. "Documents for New Mexico Missions." *New Mexico Historical Review* 4 (2): 195–201.

Scholes, France. 1942. *Troublous Times in New Mexico 1659–1670*. Albuquerque: University of New Mexico Press.

Scholes, France. 1945. "Friar Personnel and Mission Chronology, 1598–1629." *New Mexico Historical Review* 20 (1): 58–82.

Sheridan, Thomas. 1999. *Empire of Sand: The Seri Indians and the Struggle for Spanish Sonora, 1645–1803*. Tucson: University of Arizona Press.

Sheridan, Thomas, Stewart Koyiyumptewa, Anton Daughters, T. J. Ferguson, Leigh Kuwanwisiwma, Dale Brenneman, and LeeWayne Lomayestewa. 2015. *Moquis and Kastiilam: Hopis, Spaniards, and the Trauma of History, Volume I, 1540–1679*.

Sheridan, Thomas, Stewart B. Koyiyumptewa, Anton Daughters, T. J. Ferguson, Leigh Kuwanwisiwma, Dale Brenneman, and Lee Wayne Lomayestewa. 2013. "Moquis and Kastiilam: Coronado and the Hopis." *Journal of the Southwest* 55 (4): 377–434. http://dx.doi.org/10.1353/jsw.2013.0009.

Sheridan, Thomas, Stewart Koyiyumptewa, Anton Daughters, T. J. Ferguson, Leigh Kuwanwisiwma, Dale Brenneman, and LeeWayne Lomayestewa. In prep. 1680–1780. *Moquis and Kastiilam: Hopis, Spaniards, and the Trauma of History*, vol. 1, 1540–1679. Ms. to be submitted to University of Arizona Press.

Sigüenza y Góngora, Carlos de. 1693. *Mercurio Volante, con al noticia de la recuperación de las provincias del nuevo méxico*. México: Antuerpia. An English translation can be found in *Mercurio Volante of Don Carlos de Sigüenza y Góngora: An Account of the First Expedition of Don Diego de Vargas into New Mexico in 1692*. Trans. with an Introduction by Irving Leonard. Los Angeles: Quivira Society, 1932.

Taylor, William. 1999. *Magistrates of the Sacred: Priests and Parishioners in Eighteenth-Century Mexico*. Palo Alto: Stanford University Press.

Van West, Carla R., Thomas C. Windes, Frances Levine, Henri D. Grissino-Mayer, and Matthew W. Salzer. 2013. "The Role of Climate in Early Spanish-Native American Interactions in the US Southwest." In *Native and Spanish New Worlds: Sixteenth-Century Entradas in the American Southwest and Southeast*, edited by Clay Mathers, Jeffrey M. Mitchem, and Charles M. Haecker, 81–98. Amerind Studies in Anthropology, John Ware, series editor. Tucson: University of Arizona Press.

Whiteley, Peter. 1988. *Deliberate Acts: Changing Hopi Culture through the Oraibi Split*. Tucson: University of Arizona Press.

Whiteley, Peter. 1998. *Rethinking Hopi Ethnography*. Washington, DC: Smithsonian Institution.

Whiteley, Peter. 2002. "Re-Imagining Awat'ovi." In *Archaeologies of the Pueblo Revolt: Identity, Meaning, and Renewal in the Pueblo World*, edited by Robert Preucel, 147–66. Albuquerque: University of New Mexico Press.

Whiteley, Peter. 2008. "Explanation vs. Sensation: The Discourse of Cannibalism at Awat'ovi." In *Social Violence in the Prehispanic American Southwest*, edited by Deborah L. Nichols and Patricia L. Crown, 184–215. Tucson: University of Arizona Press.

Yehuda, R. 1999. *Risk Factors for Posttraumatic Stress Disorder*. Washington, DC: American Psychiatric Press.

PART 2

Divergent Histories and Experiences in the Pimería Alta, Southern Arizona

TEN

Population Dynamics in the Pimería Alta, AD 1650–1750

LAUREN E. JELINEK AND DALE S. BRENNEMAN

INTRODUCTION

The demographic landscape of the Pimería Alta—the Spanish term for the Northern Pimas, or O'odham, and their collective territory during the sixteenth, seventeenth, and eighteenth centuries—has been widely debated by historians and archaeologists alike. Published histories have primarily focused on the processes and consequences of Spanish colonialism, drawing few conclusions about the relationships among distinct groups outside of the colonial sphere of influence (e.g., Bannon 1955; Bolton 1908, 1919, 1921, 1930, 1936, 1990; Dobyns 1959; Kessell 1970, 1974, 1976; Manje 1954; McCarty 1976, 1997; Nentvig 1951; Pfefferkorn 1949; Polzer 1971, 1976; Smith et al. 1966). Archaeological interpretations have likewise emphasized Spanish installations, such as missions and presidios, and indigenous acculturation rather than native population diversity and interaction (e.g., Barnes 1971, 1983; Barton et al. 1981; Beaubien 1937; Chambers 1955; Cheek 1974; Ciolek-Torrello and Brew 1976; DeLong and Miller 1936; Elson and Doelle 1987; Fratt 1981, 1986; Haury and Fathauer 1974; Horton 1998; Huckell and Huckell 1982; Olson 1985; Pinkley 1936; Robinson 1963; Robinson and Barnes

DOI: 10.5876/9781607325741.c010

1976; Shenk et al. 1975; Sugnet and Reid 1994). Compared with most current interpretations of available archaeological data for the Spanish contact and colonial periods, the documentary record paints a much more dynamic picture of populations constituting or bordering the Pimería Alta.

Reports of Jesuit missionaries and Spanish authorities describe ethnically diverse groups with shifting alliances and a far-reaching exchange system, whereas past analyses of archaeological data have provided few indications of population differentiation. To examine the complex relationships among neighboring groups during this volatile period, we have adopted an ethnohistoric approach, wherein multiple lines of evidence are evaluated and compared to construct a regionally specific historical narrative (W. Wood 1990). New research among seventeenth- and eighteenth-century documents, combined with a reanalysis of archaeological data, provides fresh insights into the dynamics of this social landscape during a time when the ancestral boundaries and interrelationships of modern tribes were in constant flux.

THE PIMERÍA ALTA, ARCHAEOLOGICAL TRADITIONS, AND A HISTORY OF EARLY SPANISH CONTACT

The geographic land base of the Pimería Alta, situated mostly within the northern Sonoran Desert, extends across the present-day international border between southern Arizona and northwestern Sonora. Stretching westward from the margins of the Sierra Madre foothills to the Gulf of California, and northward from the Río Magdalena-Concepción drainage to the Gila River (Figure 10.1), it spans multiple biotic subregions, as north-south-trending mountain ranges separated by basins and through-flowing drainages descend and become more widely spaced in the east-west transition from semiarid desert uplands to arid coastal plain. The range in elevation and intermittent nature of river stretches and arroyos create distinct ecological settings with considerable differences in temperature, rainfall, stream flow, soils, plants, and wildlife, offering a remarkable diversity of resources available for food, shelter, medicine, and fiber, with the greatest abundance and widest variety in the higher elevations to the east (Dimmitt 2000). Differential access to these resources shaped patterns of foraging, planting, and settlement among the peoples of the region and influenced their interactions (Brenneman 2004).

Prior to AD 1450, during the fourteenth century and early fifteenth, this geographic expanse was both a borderland and a heartland for several distinct, widespread archaeological traditions, including the Patayan, Trincheras, and Hohokam. The Patayan complex overlapped the western third of the region, with boundaries extending west into the California deserts and north to the Grand Canyon. This complex is primarily defined by a paddle-and-anvil buff ware ceramic tradition with distinctive rim forms (McGuire and Schiffer 1982; Rogers

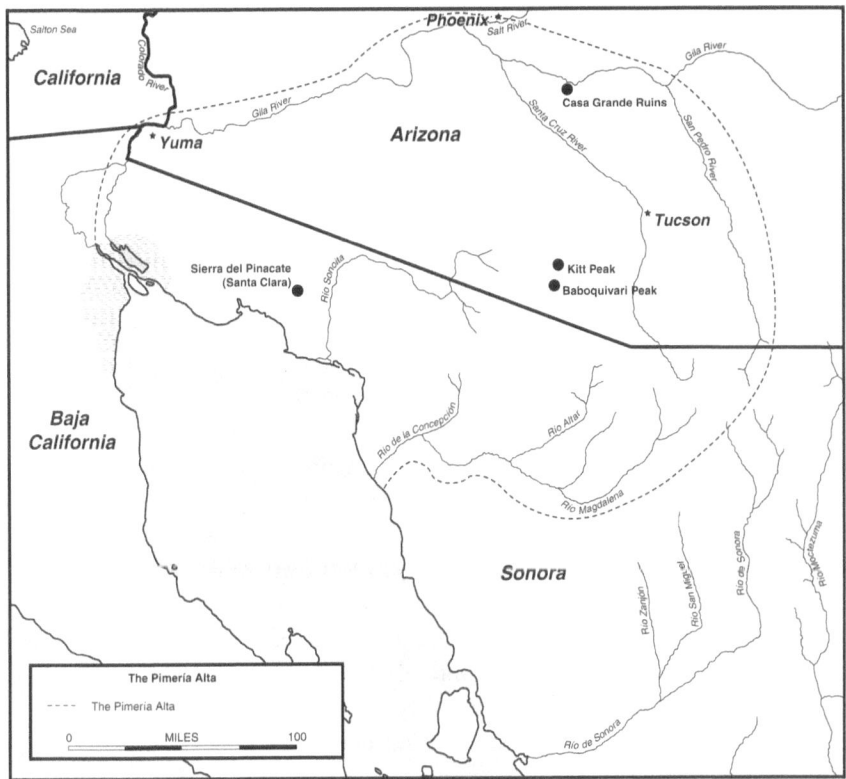

FIGURE 10.1. *The Pimería Alta.*

1928, 1936, 1945; Schroeder 1952, 1957, 1958; Waters 1982). Bordering the Patayan area on the south was the Trincheras tradition, which encompassed the entire Río Concepción-Magdalena drainage and extended to the Río Sonora in the east. It is characterized by decorated Trincheras Purple-on-red specular ceramic types and terraced hillside sites known as *cerros de trincheras* (Bowen 1976; Downum 2007; Downum et al. 1993; Fish et al. 2007; Gallaga and Newell 2004; McGuire and Villalpando 1993; Villalpando and McGuire 2009). The northern boundary of the Trincheras region overlapped with the Hohokam tradition, which extended east toward New Mexico and north along the Verde River. Red-on-buff and red-on-brown decorated ceramics, irrigation agriculture, and participation in the long-distance exchange of shell and turquoise are indicative of this widespread archaeological tradition (Dean 1991; Downum 1993; Doyel 1987; Doyel et al. 2000; Doyel and Plog 1980; Fish and Fish 2002; Fish et al. 1984; Fish et al. 1992; Harry 2003). The last phase of the Hohokam sequence was punctuated by a shift in mortuary practices, population aggregation into larger settlements, construction of platform mounds, and the introduction of polychrome ceramics classified as Roosevelt redwares. The spread of this ceramic tradition, especially Salado polychromes, occurred throughout the Southwest (Clark 2001; Dean 2000; Loendorf 2001; J. Wood 2000).

European explorers and missionaries during the sixteenth and seventeenth centuries found the region inhabited by scattered groups of O'odham speakers who interacted with each other and with several other linguistic groups living at the region's margins. Much of our information about the distribution of peoples in and around the Pimería Alta, as well as their interrelationships, derives from accounts of missionaries who took up residence and explored among the O'odham beginning in the late seventeenth century. Earlier encounters between northern O'odham and Spaniards were sporadic and yielded few descriptions. The 1539–42 expeditions of Fray Marcos de Niza and Francisco Vázquez de Coronado brought Spaniards no closer than the southeastern fringes of O'odham territory and produced accounts with ambiguous information regarding ethnic identifications and precise locations (Bolton 1990; Flint 2008; Flint and Flint 1997, 2005; Hartmann 2011; Hartmann and Hartmann 2011; Reff 1991). More useful are the chronicles from the Colorado River explorations of Hernando de Alarcón in 1540 (Flint and Flint 2005) and Juan de Oñate y Salazar in 1604–5 (Hammond and Rey 1953; Sheridan et al. 2015), which provide descriptions of several groups whose names correlate with historically known River Yuman tribes, and possibly an O'odham community living on the Gila River near its confluence with the Colorado. Populations living along this western margin of the Pimería Alta were described in greater detail, as were the complicated political alliances among each group that had resulted in substantial population movements prior to the arrival of these expeditions.

As the northernmost frontier of Sonora, the Pimería Alta was on the periphery of Spanish colonial settlement in the Americas until the end of the seventeenth century. Missionary efforts and Spanish colonization began in northeastern Sonora during the 1640s and involved limited contact with northern O'odham until the 1670s–80s, when mining discoveries drew settlers northward, near the southeastern fringe of O'odham territory. By the mid-1680s, enterprising ranchers were running cattle as far north as the southern slopes of the Huachuca Mountains and as far west as the upper Santa Cruz River. Documents from this period provide our first glimpses of the easternmost O'odham, but it was not until the 1687 arrival of the Jesuit missionary, Father Eusebio Francisco Kino, that a more complete picture of the Pimería Alta began to emerge (Bannon 1955; Burrus 1971; Kessell 1970, 2002). Kino set out to expand the Jesuit mission among the O'odham and by 1700 had systematically traversed the entire region, founding twenty-five mission communities in the south and east and traveling along all major drainages to the Colorado River and Gulf of Mexico (Bolton 1919; Burrus 1971; Manje 1954). For two decades following his death in 1711, however, a shortage of missionaries confined evangelical efforts to the southern portion of the Pimería Alta. Spanish colonial settlement in the region began in the 1720s, with families arriving to occupy the fertile San Luis Valley along the bend of the Santa Cruz. Isolated mining camps were soon established in the uplands to the west, and the extraordinary discovery of silver chunks and slabs southwest of present-day Nogales in 1736 drew many more *gente de razón* (literally, "people of reason") with the promise of quick wealth. By the Pima Revolt of 1751, indigenous populations of the broader region had been acquiring European trade goods, encountering ranchers and miners, and exposed to epidemic diseases for some time, with Spaniards residing as far north as Guevavi and Tubac, northwest in the Arivaca Valley, and west along the Río Magdalena and the Río Altar (Hadley and Sheridan 1995; Kessell 1970, Officer 1987).

Kino and his frequent traveling companion, Captain Juan Mateo Manje, identified several groups of O'odham-speakers: Pimas, who inhabited the upland watersheds of the Sonora, San Miguel, Magdalena, Altar, Santa Cruz, and San Pedro Rivers; Sobaipuris, who occupied the middle Santa Cruz and middle to lower San Pedro River Valleys; Gila Pimas (or Gileños), along the Gila River; Sobas, who farmed along the lower Río Altar at Oquitoa and downstream along the Río Asunción, as well as ranging the desert regions to the south, west, and northwest of the Asunción; and Papagos, in the desert interior regions west of the Santa Cruz and south of the Gila (Archivo General de la Nación, Mexico [AGN], Favores Celestiales de Jesús y de María SS.^{ma} y del Gloriosíssimo Apostol de las Indias San Francisco Xavier, Misiones, legajo 27, ff. 1–433; AGN, Segunda Parte, Luz de Tierra Incógnita . . . desde Fines del Año de 1693 hasta el de 1721, Historia, legajo 393, ff. 47–95v) (Figure 10.2). In addition, numerous other populations inhabited the peripheries of the Pimería Alta, including Ópatas, Janos, Jocomes, and Apaches to the east, and various Yuman groups to the west. The basis upon which chroniclers distinguished among O'odham groups is not clear, though it seems likely that dialect and self-identification were factors. Manner of subsistence apparently was not, as members of the same group might reside in large, permanent or semipermanent settlements and practice agriculture, or range as small, mobile *rancherías* to forage the region's diverse plant and animal resources.

RESEARCH METHODOLOGY

Examining population interaction and demographic change among the populations in and bordering the Pimería Alta during the sixteenth, seventeenth, and eighteenth centuries requires an ethnohistoric approach from a regional perspective. New research among Spanish colonial documents has centered on texts containing information about the O'odham and their neighbors, with preference given to eyewitness observations penned by individuals possessing firsthand experience of the region. The selection of documents includes histories, letters,

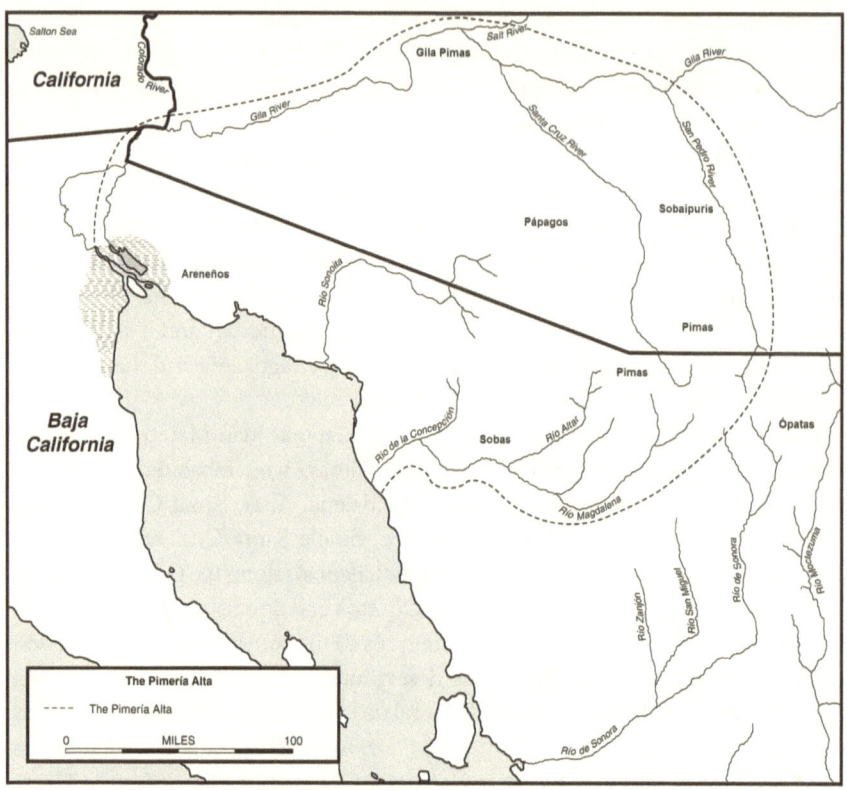

FIGURE 10.2. *O'odham distribution in the Pimería Alta as reported by Kino and Manje.*

reports, maps, and testimonies (Spanish and indigenous) prepared by missionaries, military officers, and civil authorities. Most inform the published secondary works—narrative histories and ethnohistories—also used in this study and several have been published as transcriptions or in English translation, but many others have not yet been published. Care has been taken to work from microfilm or photographic copies of Spanish archival originals whenever possible. Despite the valuable insight into indigenous population dynamics that contemporary colonial documents provide, however, they allow partial views at best, filtered through the often distorted lens of European perspectives.

The archaeological record offers an important, additional source of data to help expand our view. Archaeological remains dating to the sixteenth, seventeenth, and eighteenth centuries were reexamined to identify spheres of interaction between distinct groups. Research primarily focused on attributes associated with projectile point and ceramic manufacture and style, specifically rim construction, rim thickness, and neck height. Absolute dating of sites from this period is imprecise, due to pronounced de Vries effects on the radiocarbon curve beginning around

AD 1450. De Vries effects refer to short term, high-frequency variations in radiocarbon activity that are measured in tree rings. These radiocarbon anomalies appear as wiggles on the radiocarbon curve, resulting in multiple possible intercepts and a wider date range. Nevertheless, many sites have been assigned relative dates based on the presence of Spanish trade goods or specific artifact types. A reanalysis of archaeological data demonstrates that groups living in the heart of the Pimería Alta had a lengthy history of interaction with peoples inhabiting the eastern and western peripheries. The following is a summary of the ethnohistorical and archaeological evidence of these interactions.

PIMERÍA ALTA: EASTERN SPHERE

Ethnohistoric Evidence

Documents from the 1640s offer the earliest references to the O'odham of the Pimería Alta, calling them Hímeris—a term derived from the site of Ímuris in the upper Río Magdalena Valley, where Spaniards probably first encountered them (Archivo Histórico de Hacienda, México [AHH], Carta de Cornelio Guillereagh al Padre Visitador Alvara Flores de Sierra, 30 de marzo, 1673, Temporalidades, legajo 278, exp. 13; Biblioteca Nacional de México [BNM], Memorial de Fray Thomás Manso, Año 1646, 05–08). This name was also initially applied to O'odham living near Bacoachi, in the area near the headwaters of the Río Sonora (AGN, Carta Anua de 1653, Misiones, legajo 26, f. 153v) (Figure 10.3). By the 1680s, however, "Hímeris" fell from use and was replaced with "Pimas" with reference to the rancherías of Cananea and Huachuca,[1] near the headwaters of the San Pedro River, as well as those occupying the upper watersheds of the Río Magdalena and the Santa Cruz River as far north as Guevavi (AHH, Certificación de Joseph Romo de Vivar, Temporalidades, legajo 278, exp. 22; Archivo de Hidalgo del Parral, Chihuahua [AHP], Causa Criminal contra un India llamado Canito, microfilm 1686B, exp. 19). Sobaipuris enter the written record as "Pimas of Quíburi," identified as such in the 1686 criminal trial case against a Pima leader known as Canito. As yet unfamiliar to settlers, these Pimas were regarded as a group apart, more closely associated with the place of Quíburi on the middle San Pedro than with the other Pimas. Four years later, Sonora's chief magistrate, Captain Blas del Castillo, distinguished Sobaipuris by that name from Pimas and Sobas (AGN, Carta al Gobernador Isidro Pardiñas Villar de Francos, Junio 15, Provincias Internas, vol. 30, ff. 267–75), and in 1692, Kino linked the Sobaipuris with the Río "de Quíburi" (San Pedro River). His reference in 1699 to two of the Gileño villages as Sobaipuri signals a possible connection between the two groups (AGN, Favores Celestiales, Misiones, legajo 27, ff. 14, 33).

The ease with which O'odham messengers moved throughout the region as they carried word about Kino's comings and goings suggests friendly interaction among most groups. For example, Kino was at the Pima village of Tucubavia,

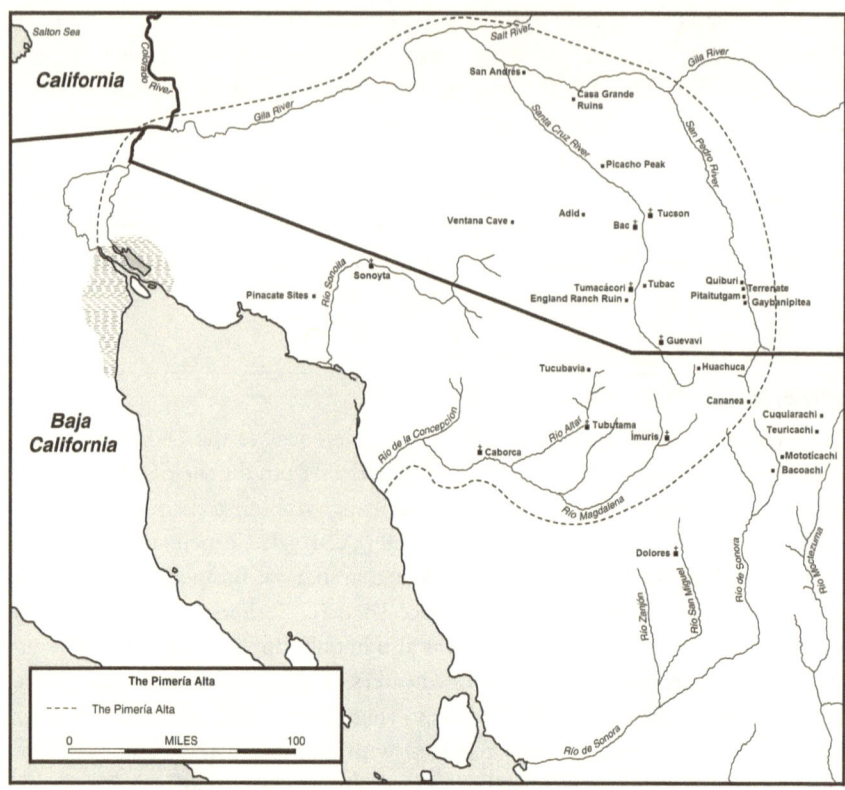

FIGURE 10.3. *Pimería Alta sites and landmarks (some sites are plotted according to their locations on historic maps because they have not been relocated).*

on the upper Río Altar, when Sobaipuri and Pima messengers from Bac and Tumacácori, respectively, arrived to invite him to visit their rancherías on the Santa Cruz River in 1691 (AGN, Favores Celestiales, Misiones, legajo 27, f. 9). In 1698, the leader of the Sobas in the Caborca region sent word to Kino at San Andrés, a Gileño village near the confluence of the Gila River with the Santa Cruz, that he would meet him and guide him through all the coastal rancherías (Archivo General de Indias, Seville [AGI], Diario por el Capp.ⁿ Diego Carrazco, Audiencia de Guadalajara, legajo 134, ff. 13–26v). Similarly, while at San Marcelo de Sonoyta (just below the present-day international border) in 1700, Kino received a cross sent by a Gila Pima leader near Casa Grande (AGN, Favores Celestiales, Misiones, legajo 27, f. 59).

Not all interactions were amicable, however. The Sobas were traditional enemies of the eastern Pimas, tenuously reconciling with them only through the efforts of Kino. Several years prior to the priest's 1687 arrival, some Sobas had killed the leader of Cosari (Dolores), on the upper Río San Miguel (AGN,

Favores Celestiales, Misiones, legajo 27, ff. 14–14v). In 1695, a Pima governor from the ranchería of Tucubavia, at the headwaters of the Río Altar, affirmed that the Sobas downstream, though O'odham, had always been enemies (AHP, Testimonio de autos de guerras fechos por los capitanes Juan Fernández de la Fuente, Don Domingo Terán de los Ríos y Don Domingo Jironza Petriz de Cruzate ... Año de 1695, microfilm 1695, ff. 111v–112). Sobas appear to have been more closely affiliated with Areneños (Sand Papagos, or Hia Ced O'odham) to the north and northwest, and with coastal Pimas Bajos to the south, who, Kino observed, came to help harvest crops at Caborca (AGN, Favores Celestiales, Misiones, legajo 27, ff. 12v, 15, 175–175v). Tensions also appear to have existed among the Sobaipuris, according to Manje, who in 1697 was told by the Sobaipuri leader of Quíburi that his people had recently abandoned several villages a few leagues north because a falling out with their more northerly relatives farther downstream had led to some deaths (Bancroft Library [BL], Photostat of the Linga Manuscript, Bolton Papers I, item 203). There are some indications this rift may have resulted from Spanish colonial influences, however (AHP, Autos de guerra, microfilm 1695, ff. 28–31v).

Relationships between eastern O'odham and Ópatan groups to the south and east, though obscured by Spanish colonial influences, appear to have varied by river valley. The first colonial encounter with Hímeris took place in 1645, in the vicinity of the upper Río Magdalena rather than along the Río San Miguel, where settlers had already taken up residence (BNM, Manso Memorial, 05–08; Yetman 2012). This suggests that the Río Magdalena Pimas, at least, maintained a prudent distance from their Eudeve neighbors until missionaries persuaded a ranchería to relocate to the San Miguel five years later, in 1650 (AGN, Carta Anua, Misiones, legajo 26, f. 134v).[2] Near the headwaters of the Río Sonora, however, Hímeris were reportedly allied with the northern Ópatas of Bacoachi as they resisted Jesuit entry into that village in 1649 (AHP, Autos fhos en razon de la entrada de Cucuribasca y Buchibacuachi, en la Provincia de Sonora ..., Microfilm 1649A, exp. 14; Yetman 2012). Four years later, a Hímeris ranchería was settled at Bacoachi, likely drawn southward by the Jesuit mission established there, and the Pima village of Mototícachi was reported as a few leagues north of the Ópata settlement in 1684 (AGN, Carta Anua, Misiones, legajo 26, f. 135v; AHH, Certificación de Joseph Romo de Vivar, Temporalidades, legajo 278, exp. 22). In 1686, a Pima leader nicknamed Canito, from that same general region, confessed to inciting Janos, Jocomes, and Sumas to attack and raid Christian villages, both Ópata and Spanish, in the neighboring Teuricachi Valley to the east, an act pointing toward existing tensions between the easternmost Pimas and Ópatas of that valley and perhaps linked to long-standing hostilities among the Ópata groups themselves (AHP, Canito, microfilm 1686B, exp. 19; Bannon 1955). Two years later, Ópatas stoked Spanish fears of Indian revolt by accusing seven Pimas from Mototícachi of having previously attacked the Teuricachi Valley and planning yet another attack; their allegations led to the destruction of Mototícachi (AHP, Causa criminal contra Nicolás de Higuera por homicidios perpetrado en las personas de algunos indios de Nación Pima, microfilm 1688C, exp. 130). In 1695, Pima resentment of the Ópata overseer at Tubutama and his harsh treatment of the Pima residents resulted in the death of that overseer as well as two other Ópatas, triggering an uprising along the Río Altar-Concepción drainage (BNM, Inocente, Apostólica y Gloriosa Muerte de V. P^e Francisco Xavier Saeta de la Compañía de Jesús, ms. 1118, ff. 155v, 156–157r).

The documentary record suggests an amicable relationship existed between Sobaipuris and several hunter-gatherer groups to their east prior to direct Spanish influence. Canito alleged in his 1686 confession that the Pimas of Quíburi lived in great friendship with the Janos and Jocomes, having relocated to Quíburi from the area of Cuquiárachi, northwest of the Teuricachi Valley (AHP, Canito, Microfilm 1686B, exp. 19). In 1692, Captain Francisco Ramírez de Salazar led a party of settlers to the San Pedro River Valley in pursuit of horses purportedly stolen by Sobaipuris in the company of Janos and Jocomes. He did not find the horses, but ended up taking several Sobaipuris to meet Kino, who visited their valley soon after in response (AHP, Testimonio de Autos que se remite al Gov.^{or} y Cap.^{n} gl. del Parral . . . Año de 1692, Microfilm 1692A, no. 1). This episode apparently marked a turning point in the Sobaipuri relationship with their eastern neighbors, for in 1695, General Juan Fernández de la Fuente learned from a Chinarra captive that an alliance of Janos, Jocomes, Sumas, Mansos, and Chinarras was friendly with the Apaches inhabiting the northern side of the Pinaleño Mountains, and that all had become hostile to the Pimas because the Pimas fought against them as auxiliaries of Spanish forces in the Teuricachi Valley. The alliance was also "in a state of hostility" with the Sobaipuris, who had sided with the Pimas (AHP, Autos de guerras, microfilm 1695, ff. 28–31v).

Archaeological Evidence

The suite of diagnostic artifacts associated with Sobaipuris was first formally articulated by Di Peso (1953) in his monograph on excavations at Santa Cruz de Terrenate (AZ EE:4:11[ASM]) and Santa Cruz del Pitaitutgam (AZ EE:8:15[ASM]). Di Peso argued that he had relocated the protohistoric Sobaipuri rancherías of Quíburi (AZ EE:4:11[ASM]) and Santa Cruz de Gaybanipitea (AZ EE:8:15 [ASM]). Subsequent evaluation of his claims has demonstrated that whereas he did locate and excavate the ruins of the presidio of Santa Cruz de Terrenate, it was not the location of the Sobaipuri settlement of Quíburi (Gerald 1968; Lyons 2004; Seymour 1989; Sugnet and Reid 1994). It has also been suggested that Di Peso mistook Santa Cruz del Pitaitutgam for Santa Cruz de Gaybanipitea (Seymour 1989, 2011; Vint 2007).

Di Peso identified two ceramic types that he associated with Sobaipuris (Di Peso 1953). He defined the first, Sobaipuri Plain, as a thick-walled plainware exhibiting a rim coil and a carbon core. Di Peso considered this ware similar to Papago Plain and argued that it was probably manufactured after 1700. Stephanie Whittlesey (1994) has argued that the Sobaipuri Plain vessels identified at Terrenate may have been manufactured by presidial soldiers rather than Sobaipuris. Whetstone Plain, the second type defined by Di Peso, was found in significantly lower quantities than Sobaipuri Plain at both Terrenate and Pitaitutgam. Whetstone Plain ceramics were manufactured with the paddle-and-anvil technique and are characterized by mixed angular and rounded sand inclusions without a carbon core. They exhibit a hand-smoothed surface lacking striation marks or polishing. Di Peso noted that the temper may contain a few mica particles. Whetstone Plain vessel forms are dominated by globular jars with straight or recurved rims, but bowls exhibiting straight or slightly recurved rims are also present. These ceramics lack a rim coil and range in thickness from 0.20 to 1.30 cm, with an average of 0.30 cm.

Subsequent refinements of the Whetstone typology by W. Bruce Masse (1981:37) describe Whetstone Plain as characterized by a bumpy appearance and a sandy finish caused by paddle-and-anvil thinning and hand finishing. The sherds range in color from reddish to grayish brown, and carbon streaks are rare. Vessel walls average from four to six millimeters thick, and common vessel forms include globular or ellipsoidal jars with slightly outflaring rims and vertical necks and small bowls with outflaring rims. Deni Seymour (2011) provides the most recent description of Whetstone Plain, defining it as a fine-pasted ware with minor voids from the unintentional inclusion of minor fragments of vegetable material. These ceramics lack a carbon streak but may have gray cores. Paste color ranges from tan to brown, and sherds are usually not fire clouded. Vessels are often thin walled, though some fragments of storage vessels and jars can be thicker. Jars are the most common vessel form, but bowls are also present. Based upon surface treatment, Seymour suggests that Whetstone Plain can be subdivided into four varieties, including matte, smoothed, wiped, and slightly polished. She has argued that the Whetstone Plain typology is too inclusive and incorporates a wide range of ceramic types (Seymour 2011:216). Whetstone Plain has been identified at numerous sites in the San Pedro and Santa Cruz River Valleys, the traditionally accepted Sobaipuri territory, but it has also been reported as far north as Picacho Peak and as far south as the Altar River Valley, and as such, may not necessarily be a diagnostic Sobaipuri artifact type (e.g., Dart 1989; Heilen and Reid 2006; McGuire and Villalpando 1993; Wallace and Homlund 1986).

In order to establish a baseline for comparisons with other assemblages, eight reconstructed vessels and fifteen rim sherds were reexamined from the Terrenate assemblage, while seven rim sherds were examined from Pitaitutgam (for additional information on the following analyses see Jelinek 2012). Material from Terrenate was predominately sand tempered, but one rim sherd contained a combination of sand and sherd temper. Three sherds contained carbon streaks and one specimen exhibited a rim coil; it is possible these sherds were merely mislabeled, however, because they more closely resembled Sobaipuri Plain. Rim thickness ranged from 0.46 to 0.99 cm, with an average of 0.68 cm. Material from Pitaitutgam was sparse. Of the seven rim sherds present in the assemblage from this site, one was a Roosevelt Redware and two exhibited such a large quantity of micaceous schist that they closely resembled Gila Plain, a Hohokam plainware. The four remaining plainware sherds were sand tempered and lacked a carbon core. One sherd exhibited a rim coil and rim thickness ranged from 0.51 to 0.87 cm, with an average of 0.61 cm.

A survey conducted along the middle Río Altar in Sonora resulted in the identification of several sites associated with O'odham groups during the seventeenth and eighteenth centuries. The ceramic assemblages recorded at these sites fit within the acceptable range of variation to thickness, color, rim morphology, vessel form, and surface treatment associated with Whetstone Plain, though they exhibited a greater degree of mica in the temper than samples from the comparative collections. Randall McGuire and María Elisa Villalpando Canchola (McGuire and Villalpando 1993) suggested that the Altar Valley ceramic assemblages fall within the larger category of Whetstone Plain, the ceramic type largely associated with Sobaipuris, but further analysis may identify different varieties.

An Upper Piman assemblage in the eastern Pimería Alta exhibits some similarities with materials from the Río Sonora, which was occupied primarily by Ópatas. Excavations at England Ranch Ruin (AZ DD:8:129 [ASM]), an Upper Piman site along the middle Santa Cruz River, yielded two types of plainware. The first was identified as Trincheras Plain based on the presence of pronounced incised wiping striations. The second, more common type was a relatively thick plainware with coarse temper and minor wiping striations. David Doyel (1977) concluded that this assemblage cannot be reasonably equated with either Sobaipuri Plain or Whetstone Plain, two types usually associated with Sobaipuris; W. Bruce Masse (1981), however, suggested that both types in this assemblage are similar to sherds found near Mission San José de Baviácora, along the Río Sonora.

Much of the evidence for interaction between Sobaipuris and the nomadic groups that dotted the eastern frontier of the Pimería Alta—including the Jocomes, Janos, Mansos, Sumas, and Apaches—derives from documents. Archaeological evidence of mobile groups is often difficult to identify because of the ephemeral nature of their habitations; however, Seymour (2009) has begun examining these sites in the eastern Southwest. Western Apache material culture is better known and documented in Arizona (Ferg 1987, 1992), though not necessarily at Sobaipuri and Upper Piman sites. Recent research at Santa Cruz de Gaybanipitea, the ranchería where the Sobaipuris defeated the Apaches and their allies in a contest between chosen warriors, may shed more light on this issue (Seymour 2014).

PIMERÍA ALTA: WESTERN SPHERE

Ethnohistoric Evidence

Kino's explorations revealed various connections between O'odham and Yuman speakers to the west. Among the Gileños near the Gila–Santa Cruz river confluence, in 1694, he learned of Cocomaricopas and Opas living downstream, and he talked with Pimas who spoke both languages well enough to allow him to construct a vocabulary (AGN, Favores Celestiales, Misiones, legajo 27, f. 13). In subsequent visits to the Gila River, Kino and Manje observed that Cocomaricopas were related by marriage with Pimas, with several rancherías below Gila Bend inhabited by both peoples, many of whom knew both languages (AGN, Favores Celestiales, Misiones, legajo 27, ff. 29, 31, 53; Biblioteca Nacional, Madrid [BN], Relación ytineraria del nuevo descubrimiento . . . a descubrir las nuevas naciones Cocopas, Yumas, y Pimas desde 7 de febrero hasta 14 de marzo deste presente año de 1699, ms. 3165, ff. 182–195v). Pimas may have resided even farther downstream almost 100 years earlier, judging from the Oñate expedition's encounter with four or five Oseca/Osera/Osara rancherías on the Gila side of the Gila-Colorado River confluence. There, inhabitants spoke a language similar to Tepehuan, part of the Tepiman family of languages that included O'odham (AGI, Relación de Fray Francisco de Escobar, 1605, Audiencia de México, legajo 20). Fashioning mantas of cotton and wearing their hair in the same fashion as the Gila River Pimas described by Russell (1975:158–59) in the early twentieth century, they may have been Gileños, Papagos, or Areneños (Akimel, Tohono, or Hia Ced O'odham, respectively). Population movements in the lower Colorado and Gila River Valleys appear to have been influenced by several factors, including shifts in the Colorado River delta and resulting cycles of water infill and recession of Lake Cahuilla over several centuries, the decline of Hohokam civilization and dispersal of formerly aggregated settlements, and the spread of European diseases (Sheridan et al. 2015:103). These movements probably triggered the hostilities among Yuman speakers remarked upon by Alarcón and Escobar, which continued into the mid-nineteenth century and frequently involved O'odham (Flint and Flint 2005; AGI, Escobar Relación, México, legajo 20). Kino observed that the Pimas and Cocomaricopas had a history of warfare with the Yumas (Quechan) farther downstream (AGN, Favores Celestiales, Misiones, legajo 27, f. 31v).

That the connection between O'odham and Cocomaricopas also extended southward is indicated by Manje's observation that Pimas at San Marcelo de Sonoyta had detailed information concerning waterholes and the route northward to the Gila River Cocomaricopas (BN, Relación itineraria 1699, Ms. 3165, f. 185v), and Father Juan María Salvatierra commented upon Cocomaricopas "mixed with" the Pimas at Sonoyta when he traveled there with Kino and Manje two years later (AGN, Relación itineraria de Juan María Salvatierra, 1701, Historia, legajo 21, f. 123v). Four Cocomaricopas traveled southward to the O'odham village Kino called San Francisco del Adid, in the Papaguería west of Bac, to see and speak with Kino in 1699 (AGN, Favores Celestiales, Misiones, legajo 27, f. 34v). More than forty years afterward, Father Jacobo Sedelmayr confirmed that Cocomaricopas were related by marriage with Pimas, whom they called Papagos, and that many Pimas lived among the Cocomaricopas, fluent in both languages. By this time, according to Sedelmayr, the Cocomaricopa nation had extended its reach eastward to just beyond the confluence of the Salt and Gila Rivers (AHH, Carta al reverendo padre provincial Mateo Ansaldo, Octubre 25, 1742, Temporalidades, legajo 17, exp. 42).

Another O'odham-Yuman relationship was observed between the Pimas of the westernmost desert—probably Areneños—and Quíquimas (Halyikwamai or possibly Cócopas) of the Colorado delta. Salvatierra reported that the coastal area south of the delta was populated by Pimas mixed with a branch of the Quíquimas, and that the Pimas who lived in that dry desert region just east of the coast were familiar with the Quíquimas and their lands (AGN, Relación itineraria, Historia, legajo 21, f. 128v). This relationship had some longevity, as indicated by Alarcón's comment that his interpreter—likely a Uto-Aztecan speaker from farther south in Mexico—could understand the language spoken by some people among the "Quicamas" (Flint and Flint 2005:197). The connection did not extend to the Pimas of Sonoyta, who had been at war with the Quíquimas, according to Salvatierra, and who tried to impede Spanish communication with them (AGN, Relación itineraria, Historia, legajo 21, f. 125).

Archaeological Evidence

The western portion of the Pimería Alta has long been considered a borderland between both Patayan and Hohokam archaeological traditions and Yuman and O'odham speakers. Excavations at Ventana Cave (AZ Z:12:5[ASM]), a large rock-shelter situated in the Castle Mountains in the Papaguería (a Papago subregion in the west-central part of the Pimería Alta), yielded one of the longest records of habitation in the Southwest (Haury 1950). Assemblages recovered from the upper levels at Ventana Cave were characterized by triangular projectile points with concave bases; Papago plain and Papago redware manufactured during the eighteenth and nineteenth centuries; and a few nonmicaceous, well-smoothed, thin-walled ceramics manufactured using the paddle-and-anvil technique. These nonmicaceous wares exhibited attributes consistent with both Lowland Patayan and Upper Piman manufacturing strategies, suggesting frequent interaction between these groups. Given this region's history as a contact zone for Yuman and O'odham speakers, it is not surprising that ceramics from this area would exhibit a mixture of attributes consistent with two different groups.

In the Sierra Pinacate, a volcanic region in northwest Sonora characterized by sparse vegetation and an extremely arid climate, several assemblages dating to the sixteenth and seventeenth centuries exhibit a mix of Lowland Patayan and Upper Piman material culture. Ceramic assemblages are predominately characterized by Lowland Patayan buffwares; however, projectile point styles mirror those used by O'odham speakers, specifically Sobaipuris who occupied territory farther east. Julian Hayden (1967) and Paul Ezell (1955, 1963a) argued that the Pinacate was likely occupied by Areneños who spoke an O'odham dialect, but acquired and used Lowland Patayan ceramics.

A mixture of Lowland Patayan and Upper Piman ceramic attributes was noted in several ceramic concentrations found associated with talus pits in the Tucson Basin (Madsen 1993). Although these ceramic assemblages shared more similarities with Papago plainwares, the long chimney-style necks and partially obliterated rim coils are reminiscent of attributes associated with Lowland Patayan ceramics along the Gila and Colorado Rivers. The lack of carbon streaking and associated European material culture suggests that these ceramics roughly date to 1450–1775.

Ceramic assemblages recovered from lands belonging to the Ak-Chin Indian Community, dating from 1400 to 1850, share similarities with both Lowland Patayan and Upper Piman assemblages. The initial analysis by William Deaver (1990) identified two ceramic complexes: Complex I contained ceramics with folded rims, stucco finish, and Red-on-Buff decoration, whereas Complex II lacked these attributes. A reanalysis of this typology by John Cable (1990) suggests that Complex I, which exhibits folded rims and decorated ceramics, was the earliest to appear. Cable's findings did not support the stringent division in ceramic complexes proposed by Deaver, however. He encountered folded rims and a stucco finish in both Complex I and II assemblages, implying that the largest qualitative difference between these two types lay in the presence of decorated ceramics. Cable (1990) concluded that the ceramic chronology demonstrated a progression away from Lowland Patayan attributes, characterized by a decrease in folded rims and the discontinued use of painted decoration. After these attributes were discontinued, the ceramics more closely resembled wares found among Sobaipuris and Upper Pimas.

SYNTHESIS AND CONCLUSIONS

As the above discussion illustrates, different groups inhabiting and bordering the Pimería Alta interacted with each other to a considerable degree. O'odham and Cocomaricopa messengers reportedly traveled widely and freely throughout the Pimería Alta (AGN, Favores Celestiales, Misiones, legajo 27, ff. 1–433). Pima knowledge of travel routes and water-holes in Cocomaricopa territory, the presence of Cocomaricopas among the Pimas of Sonoyta, and the probable presence of Pima rancherías near the Colorado-Gila confluence all serve as testimony to the long-standing relationship between these two peoples (BN, Relación itineraria 1699, Ms. 3165, ff. 182–195v; AGN, Relación itineraria, Historia, legajo 21, f. 123v; AGI, Escobar Relación, México, legajo 20). These interrelationships are also visible in the archaeological record. The presence of ceramic attributes associated with both Lowland Patayan and Upper Piman styles on the same vessel, exemplified in assemblages recovered from both the Tucson Basin (Madsen 1993) and Ventana Cave (Haury 1950), provides additional evidence of these ties. To the south and east, the identification of Whetstone Plain ceramics—a type generally associated with Sobaipuris—at Upper Piman sites in the Altar Valley may indicate that Pimas and Sobaipuris interacted with each other through either the exchange of vessels or intermarriage, wherein spouses introduced distinct ceramic-manufacturing practices to their community (McGuire and Villalpando 1993). Likewise, the similarity between ceramics found at England Ranch Ruin on the Santa Cruz River and those found at sites in the Río Sonora may indicate the movement of populations or trade items between these two regions (Doyel 1977; Masse 1980).

Social alliances between groups inhabiting the Pimería Alta are well established in the documentary record. Pimas living along the Gila River intermarried with the Cocomaricopas, and several rancherías below Gila Bend were multi-ethnic communities in which inhabitants spoke both O'odham and Yuman languages (AGN, Favores Celestiales, Misiones, legajo 27, ff. 1–433; BN, Relación itineraria 1699, Ms. 3165, ff. 182–195v; AHH, Carta 1742, Temporalidades, legajo 17, exp. 42). The Areneños and Quíqimas engaged in a similarly close and long-standing alliance in the Colorado delta region (AGN, Relación itineraria, Historia, legajo 21, ff. 105–135; Flint and Flint 2005). The mixture of Yuman (ceramics) and O'odham (projectile points) material culture found at archaeological sites in the Sierra Pinacate (Ezell 1955, 1963a, 1963b; Hayden 1967) reinforces the extent and nature of alliances described in the documentary record.

Although colonial chroniclers—especially Kino—generally described the Pimas as peaceful, social conflicts among these groups were remarked upon as well. Hostilities among the populations living along the Colorado River were frequent. Pimas, in their alliance with Cocomaricopas, had a history of warfare with Quechans. The Pimas of Sonoyta had a contentious relationship with the Quíquimas, to whom the Areneños were closely connected, and attempted to impede Spanish contact with them. Sobas, though O'odham speakers, were the traditional enemies of eastern Pimas, and appear to have been more closely linked with Areneños and with coastal Pimas Bajos (AGN, Favores Celestiales, Misiones, legajo 27, ff. 1–433; AGN, Relación itineraria, Historia, legajo 21, ff. 105–135; AHP, Autos de guerra, microfilm 1695, ff. 28–31v).

As with the Sobas discussed above, the conflicts documented between groups in the Pimería Alta were complicated, varied, and rarely clear cut. Relationships between eastern O'odham and Ópatan groups appear to have varied by river valley. Pimas and Ópatas were reportedly involved in an alliance resisting Jesuit entry into Bacoachi in 1649, but Pimas and Ópatas on the Río Magdelena avoided each other until 1650 (AHP, Autos, microfilm 1649A, exp. 14; AGN, Carta Anua, Misiones, legajo 26). Pima raiding of Ópata and Spanish colonial villages in the Teuricachi Valley (AHP, Higuera, microfilm 1688C, exp. 130) was one of several events that increased tensions among these groups, and Pima-Ópata antagonisms contributed to the death of three Ópatas at Tubutama in 1695 (BNM, Muerte de Saeta, ms. 1118, ff. 155v, 156–157r). Relationships between Sobaipuris and the Janos and Jocomes to the east appear to have initially been amicable (AHP, Canito, microfilm 1686B, exp. 19), but were radically altered when Ramírez de Salazar took several southern Sobaipuris to meet Kino (AHP, Autos de guerra, microfilm 1692A, no. 1). The ensuing alliance between Spaniards and southern Sobaipuris may have been the root of tensions with Sobaipuri communities to the north (AHP, Autos de guerra, microfilm 1695, ff. 28–31v; BL, Linga Ms., Bolton Papers I, item 203), as southern rancherías gained easier access to valuable Spanish goods and attracted raids from their former allies.

O'odham-speaking populations commonly interacted among each other and with multiple non-O'odham groups during the sixteenth, seventeenth, and eighteenth centuries. Documentary, archaeological, and oral historical data bear testimony to the dynamic interplay of alliances, conflicts, and interactions among these groups over time. The distribution of ceramic attributes accords with documentary reports that O'odham coresided with Yuman-speaking populations along the northern and western boundaries. There also appears to have been considerable interaction among O'odham groups of the San Pedro, Santa Cruz, and Altar River Valleys given that Whetstone Plain has been found at sites throughout much of the Pimería Alta. Archaeological evidence of possibly amicable interaction between O'odham along the Santa Cruz River and Ópatas near the Río Sonora accords with ethnohistorical evidence for early alliances between easternmost O'odham and Ópatas at the Sonora's upper reaches, though documents suggest that other interactions between O'odham and Ópatas were often quite hostile. Further ethnohistorical research using multiple lines of evidence to re-create shared historical narratives will help to clarify the variability in relations among these groups over time.

NOTES

1. Although Herbert Bolton (1936:269) believed Huachuca to be situated on Babocómari Creek, Kino's maps place the village farther south, near the headwaters of the San Pedro River (Burrus 1965).

2. Linguist David Shaul (in Yetman 2010) has suggested that the Eudeve language represents a Pima adaptation to Ópata, which implies an earlier pattern of coresidence and/or intermarriage among Pimas and Ópatans along the upper Río San Miguel and the lower Río Moctezuma. The Pimas involved were likely Nébomes, or Pimas Bajos (Pennington 1980).

REFERENCES CITED

Bannon, John Francis. 1955. *The Mission Frontier in Sonora, 1620–1687*. New York: United States Catholic Historical Society.

Barnes, Mark R. 1971. "Majolica from Excavations at San Xavier del Bac, 1968–1969." *Kiva* 37 (1): 61–4. http://dx.doi.org/10.1080/00231940.1971.11757752.

Barnes, Mark R. 1983. "Tucson: Development of a Community." PhD diss., School of Arts and Sciences, Catholic University of America, Washington DC.

Barton, C. Michael, Kay Simpson, and Lee Fratt. 1981. *Tumacacori Excavations, 1979/1980: Historical Archaeology at Tumacacori National Monument, Arizona. Publications in Anthropology 17*. Tucson, AZ: Western Archaeological and Conservation Center, National Park Service.

Beaubien, Paul. 1937. *Excavations at Tumacacori, 1934. Southwestern Monuments Special Report 15*. Washington, DC: National Park Service.

Bolton, Herbert Eugene. 1908. *Spanish Exploration in the Southwest, 1542–1706*. New York: Barnes and Noble.

Bolton, Herbert Eugene. 1919. *Kino's Historical Memoir of Pimería Alta: A Contemporary Account of the Beginnings of California, Sonora, and Arizona, By Father Eusebio Francisco Kino, S.J., Pioneer, Missionary, Explorer, Cartographer, and Ranchman, 1683–1711*. Cleveland: Arthur H. Clark Company.

Bolton, Herbert Eugene. 1921. *The Spanish Borderlands: A Chronicle of Old Florida and the Southwest*. New Haven, CT: Yale University Press.

Bolton, Herbert Eugene. 1930. *Anza's California Expeditions*. Berkeley: University of California Press.

Bolton, Herbert Eugene. 1936. *Rim of Christendom: A Biography of Eusebio Francisco Kino, Pacific Coast Pioneer*. New York: Russell and Russell.

Bolton, Herbert Eugene. 1990. *Coronado: Knight of Pueblos and Plains*. 4th ed. Albuquerque: University of New Mexico Press.

Bowen, Thomas. 1976. "Esquema de la historia de la cultura Trincheras." In *Sonora: Antropología del desierto*, edited by Beatrice Braniff and Richard S. Felger, 347–63.

Colección Científica 27. Mexico City: Instituto Nacional de Antropología e Historia, Secretaría de Educación Pública.

Brenneman, Dale S. 2004. "Climate of Rebellion: The Relationship between Climate Variability and Indigenous Uprisings in Mid-Eighteenth-Century Sonora." PhD dissertation, Department of Anthropology, University of Arizona, Tucson.

Burrus, Ernest J. 1965. *Kino and the Cartography of Northwestern New Spain*. Tucson: Arizona Pioneers' Historical Society.

Burrus, Ernest J. 1971. *Kino and Manje, Explorers of Sonora and Arizona: Their Vision of the Future*. Rome: Jesuit Historical Institute.

Cable, John S. 1990. "Who Were the Protohistoric Occupants of Ak-Chin?: A Study Concerning the Relationship between Ethnicity and Ceramic Style." In *Archaeology of the Ak-Chin Indian Community West Side Farms Project: Subsistence Studies and Synthesis Interrelations*, vol. 5, edited by Robert E. Gasser, Christine K. Robinson and Cory Dale Breternitz, 23.21–23.65. Soil Systems Publications in Archaeology 9. Phoenix: Soil Systems.

Chambers, George W. 1955. "The Old Presidio of Tucson." *Kiva* 20 (2–3): 15–6.

Cheek, Annetta L. 1974. "Evidence for Acculturation in Artifacts: Indians and Non-Indians at San Xavier del Bac, Arizona." PhD dissertation, Department of Anthropology, University of Arizona, Tucson.

Ciolek-Torrello, Richard, and Susan A. Brew. 1976. *Archaeological Test Excavations at the San Xavier Bicentennial Plaza Site*. Archaeological Series 102. Tucson: Arizona State Museum.

Clark, Jeffery J. 2001. *Tracking Prehistoric Migration: Pueblo Settlers among the Tonto Basin Hohokam*. Anthropological Papers of the University of Arizona 65. Tucson: University of Arizona Press.

Dart, Allen, ed. 1989. *The Gunsight Mountain Archaeological Survey: Archaeological Sites in the Northern Sierrita Mountains near the Junction of the Altar and Avra Valleys Southwest of Tucson, Arizona*. Tucson: Center for Desert Archaeology.

Dean, Jeffrey S. 1991. "Thoughts on Hohokam Chronology." In *Exploring the Hohokam: Prehistoric Desert Peoples of the American Southwest*, edited by George J. Gumerman, 61–149. Dragoon, AZ: Amerind Foundation.

Dean, Jeffrey S. 2000. "Introduction." In *Salado*, edited by Jeffrey S. Dean, 3–16. Dragoon, AZ: Amerind Foundation.

Deaver, William. 1990. "Native American Ceramics." In *Archaeology of the Ak-Chin Indian Community West Side Farms Project: Material Culture and Human Remains*, vol. 4, edited by Robert E. Gasser, Christine K. Robinson, and Cory Dale Breternitz, 15.11–15.35. Soil Systems Publications in Archaeology 9. Phoenix: Soil Systems.

DeLong, Scofield, and Leffler B. Miller. 1936. *Architecture of the Sonoran Missions: Sonora Expedition, Oct. 12–29*. Washington, DC: National Park Service.

Di Peso, Charles C. 1953. *The Sobaipuri Indians of the Upper San Pedro River Valley, Southeastern Arizona. Amerind Foundation Series 6.* Dragoon, AZ: Amerind Foundation.

Dimmitt, Mark A. 2000. "Biomes and Communities of the Sonoran Desert Region." In *A Natural History of the Sonoran Desert*, edited by Steven J. Phillips and Patricia Wentworth Comus, 3–18. Berkeley: University of California Press.

Dobyns, Henry F. 1959. "Tubac through Four Centuries: A Historical Resume and Analysis." Manuscript on file. Tucson: Arizona State Museum.

Downum, Christian E., ed. 1993. *Between Desert and River: Hohokam Settlement and Land Use in the Los Robles Community. Anthropological Papers of the University of Arizona 57.* Tucson: University of Arizona.

Downum, Christian E. 2007. "Cerros de Trincheras in Southern Arizona: Review and Current Status of the Debate." In *Trincheras Sites in Time, Space, and Society*, edited by Suzanne K. Fish, Paul R. Fish and María Elisa Villalpando, 101–36. Amerind Studies in Archaeology, vol. 1. Tucson: University of Arizona Press.

Downum, Christian E., John E. Douglas, and Douglas B. Craig. 1993. "The Cerro Prieto Site." In *Between Desert and River: Hohokam Settlement and Land Use in the Los Robles Community*, edited by Christian E. Downum, 53–95. Anthropological Papers of the University of Arizona 57. Tucson: University of Arizona Press.

Doyel, David E. 1977. *Excavations in the Middle Santa Cruz Valley, Southeastern Arizona. Contributions to Highway Salvage Archaeology 44. Arizona State Museum.* Tucson: University of Arizona.

Doyel, David E. 1987. "The Hohokam Village." In *The Hohokam Village: Site Structure and Organization*, edited by David E. Doyel, 1–20. Glenwood Springs, CO: Southwestern and Rocky Mountain Division of the American Association for the Advancement of Science.

Doyel, David E., Suzanne K. Fish, and Paul R. Fish, eds. 2000. *The Hohokam Village Revisited.* Fort Collins, CO: Southwestern and Rocky Mountain Division of the American Association for the Advancement of Science.

Doyel, David E., and Fred Plog, eds. 1980. *Current Issues in Hohokam Prehistory: Proceedings of a Symposium.* Arizona State University Anthropological Research Papers 23. Tempe: Arizona State University.

Elson, Mark D., and William H. Doelle. 1987. *Archaeological Assessment of the Mission Road Extension: Testing at AZ BB:13:6 (ASM).* Technical Report No. 87–86. Tucson: Institute for American Research.

Ezell, Paul H. 1955. "The Archaeological Delineation of a Cultural Boundary in Papaguería." *American Antiquity* 20 (4): 367–74. http://dx.doi.org/10.2307/277070.

Ezell, Paul H. 1963a. "Is There a Hohokam-Pima Culture Continuum?" *American Antiquity* 29 (1): 61–66. http://dx.doi.org/10.2307/278632.

Ezell, Paul H. 1963b. *The Maricopas: An Identification from Documentary Sources. Anthropological Papers 6.* Tucson: University of Arizona Press.

Ferg, Alan, ed. 1987. *Western Apache Material Culture: The Goodwin and Guenther Collections*. Tucson: University of Arizona Press.

Ferg, Alan. 1992. "Western Apache and Yavapai Pottery Features from the Rye Creek Projects." In *Synthesis and Conclusions. The Rye Creek Project: Archaeology in the Upper Tonto, Basin, vol. 3,*, edited by Mark D. Elson and Douglas B. Craig, 3–27. Tucson: Center for Desert Archaeology.

Fish, Paul R., and Suzanne K. Fish. 2002. "Looking South from Arizona: Changing Views of Interaction." In *Boundaries and Territories: Prehistory of the U.S. Southwest and Northern Mexico*, edited by María Elisa Villalpando, 155–163. Arizona State University Anthropological Research Papers 54. Tempe: Arizona State University.

Fish, Suzanne K., Paul R. Fish, and Christian E. Downum. 1984. "Hohokam Terraces and Agricultural Production in the Tucson Basin." In *Prehistoric Agricultural Strategies in the Tucson Basin*, edited by Suzanne K. Fish and Paul R. Fish, 55–72. Arizona State University Anthropological Research Papers 33. Tempe: Arizona State University.

Fish, Suzanne K., Paul R. Fish, and John H. Madsen, eds. 1992. *The Marana Community in the Hohokam World. Anthropological Papers of the University of Arizona 56*. Tucson: University of Arizona Press.

Fish, Suzanne K., Paul R. Fish, and María Elisa Villalpando, eds. 2007. *Trincheras Sites in Time, Space, and Society*. Amerind Studies in Archaeology, vol. 1. Tucson: University of Arizona Press.

Flint, Richard. 2008. *No Settlement, No Conquest: A History of the Coronado Entrada*. Albuquerque: University of New Mexico Press.

Flint, Richard, and Shirley Cushing Flint, eds. 1997. *The Coronado Expedition to Tierra Nueva: The 1540–1542 Route across the Southwest*. University Press of Colorado, Niwot.

Flint, Richard, and Shirley Cushing Flint, eds. 2005. *Documents of the Coronado Expedition, 1539–1542: "They Were Not Familiar with His Majesty, nor Did They Wish to Be His Subjects*. Dallas: Southern Methodist University Press.

Fratt, Lee. 1981. *Tumacacori Plaza Excavation, 1979: Historical Archaeology at Tumacacori National Monument, Arizona*. Publications in Anthropology 16. Tucson: Western Archeological and Conservation Center, National Park Service.

Fratt, Lee. 1986. "Tumacacori National Monument: Archaeological Assessment and Management Recommendations." In *Miscellaneous Historic Period Archaeological Projects in the Western Region*, edited by Martyn D. Tagg, 43–74. Publications in Anthropology 37. Tucson: Western Archeological and Conservation Center, National Park Service.

Gallaga, Emiliano, and Gillian E. Newell. 2004. "Introduction." In *Surveying the Archaeology of Northwest Mexico*, edited by Gillian E. Newell and Emiliano Gallaga, 1–23. Salt Lake City: University of Utah Press.

Gerald, Rex E. 1968. *Spanish Presidios of the Late Eighteenth Century in Northern New Spain*. Research Records 7. Santa Fe: Museum of New Mexico.

Hadley, Diana, and Thomas E. Sheridan. 1995. *Land Use History of the San Rafael Valley, Arizona (1540–1960)*. Fort Collins, CO: Rocky Mountain Forest and Range Experiment Station, US Department of Agriculture.

Hammond, George P., and Agapito Rey. 1953. *Don Juan de Oñate: Colonizer of New Mexico, 1595–1628*. Vol. 2. Albuquerque: University of New Mexico Press.

Harry, Karen. 2003. *Economic Organization and Settlement Hierarchies: Ceramic Production and Exchange among the Hohokam*. Westport, CT: Praeger.

Hartmann, William K. 2011. "The Mystery of the 'Port of Chichilticale'." In *The Latest Word from 1540: People, Places, and Portrayals of the Coronado Expedition*, edited by Richard Flint and Shirley Cushing Flint, 194–213. Albuquerque: University of New Mexico Press.

Hartmann, William K., and Gayle Harrison Hartmann. 2011. "Locating the Lost Coronado Garrisons of San Gerónimo I, II, and III." In *The Latest Word from 1540: People, Places, and Portrayals of the Coronado Expedition*, edited by Richard Flint and Shirley Cushing Flint, 117–53. Albuquerque: University of New Mexico Press.

Haury, Emil W. 1950. *The Stratigraphy and Archaeology of Ventana Cave*. Tucson: University of Arizona Press.

Haury, Emil W., and Isabel Fathauer. 1974. *Tucson, from Pithouse to Skyscraper*. Tucson: Tucson Historical Committee.

Hayden, Julian D. 1967. "A Summary Prehistory and History of the Sierra Pinacate, Sonora." *American Antiquity* 32 (3): 335–44. http://dx.doi.org/10.2307/2694662.

Heilen, Michael P., and J. Jefferson Reid, eds. 2006. *"Class III Cultural Resources Survey of Ironwood Forest National Monument." Manuscript on file*. Tucson: School of Anthropology, University of Arizona.

Horton, Tonia W. 1998. *"Tumacacori National Historical Park Cultural Landscape Documentation Study." Manuscript on file*. Tumacacori, Arizona: Tumacacori National Historical Park.

Huckell, Bruce B., and Lisa W. Huckell. 1982. "Archaeological Test Excavations at Tubac State Park." In *Archaeological Test Excavations in Southern Arizona*, edited by Susan A. Brew, 64–102. Archaeological Series 174. Tucson: Arizona State Museum.

Jelinek, Lauren E. 2012. "The Protohistoric Period in the Pimería Alta." PhD dissertation, School of Anthropology, University of Arizona, Tucson.

Kessell, John L. 1970. *Mission of Sorrows: Jesuit Guevavi and the Pimas, 1691–1767*. Tucson: University of Arizona Press.

Kessell, John L. 1974. "Friars versus Bureaucrats: The Mission as a Threatened Institution on the Arizona-Sonora Frontier, 1767–1842." *Western Historical Quarterly* 5 (2): 151–62. http://dx.doi.org/10.2307/967034.

Kessell, John L. 1976. *Friars, Soldiers, and Reformers: Hispanic Arizona and the Sonora Mission Frontier, 1767–1856*. Tucson: University of Arizona Press.

Kessell, John L. 2002. *Spain in the Southwest: A Narrative History of Colonial New Mexico, Arizona, Texas, and California.* Norman: University of Oklahoma Press.

Loendorf, Chris. 2001. "Salado Burial Practices." In *Ancient Burial Practices in the American Southwest: Archaeology, Physical Anthropology, and Native American Perspectives*, edited by Douglas R. Mitchell and Judy L. Brunson-Hadley, 123–48. Albuquerque: University of New Mexico Press.

Lyons, Patrick D. 2004. "José Solas Ruin." *Kiva* 70 (2): 143–81. http://dx.doi.org/10.1179/kiv.2004.70.2.003.

Madsen, John H. 1993. "Rock Cairn and Talus Pit Features in the Los Robles Community." In *Between Desert and River: Hohokam Settlement and Land Use in the Los Robles Community*, edited by Christian E. Downum, 96–106. Anthropological Papers of the University of Arizona 57. Tucson: University of Arizona Press.

Manje, Juan Mateo. 1954. *Luz de Tierra Incognita.* Translated by Harry J. Karns. Tucson: Arizona Silhouettes.

Masse, W. Bruce. 1980. *"The Peppersauce Wash Project: Excavations at Three Multicomponent Sites in the Lower San Pedro Valley, Arizona."* Contributions to Highway Salvage Archaeology in Arizona 53. Manuscript on file. Tucson: Arizona State Museum.

Masse, W. Bruce. 1981. "A Reappraisal of the Protohistoric Sobaipuri Indians of Southeastern Arizona." In *The Protohistoric Period in the North American Southwest, A.D. 1450–1700*, edited by David R. Wilcox and W. Bruce Masse, 28–56. Anthropological Research Papers 24. Tempe: Arizona State University.

McCarty, Kieran. 1976. *Desert Documentary: The Spanish Years, 1767–1821.* Tucson: Arizona Historical Society.

McCarty, Kieran. 1997. *A Frontier Documentary: Sonora and Tucson, 1821–1848.* Tucson: University of Arizona Press.

McGuire, Randall H., and Michael B. Schiffer, eds. 1982. *Hohokam and Patayan: Prehistory of Southwestern Arizona.* New York: Academic Press.

McGuire, Randall H., and María Elisa Villalpando, eds. 1993. *An Archaeological Survey of the Altar Valley, Sonora, Mexico.* Archeological Series 184. Tucson: Arizona State Museum.

Nentvig, Juan. 1951. *Rudo Ensayo.* Tucson: Arizona Silhouettes.

Officer, James E. 1987. *Hispanic Arizona, 1536–1856.* Tempe: University of Arizona Press.

Olson, Alan P. 1985. "Archaeology at the Presidio of Tucson." *Kiva* 50 (4): 251–70. http://dx.doi.org/10.1080/00231940.1985.11758041.

Pennington, Campbell W. 1980. *The Material Culture.* The Pima Bajo of Central Sonora, Mexico, vol. 1. Salt Lake City: University of Utah Press.

Pfefferkorn, Ignaz. 1949. *Sonora, A Description of the Province.* Translated by Theodore E. Treutlein. Albuquerque: University of New Mexico Press.

Pinkley, Frank. 1936. "Repair and Restoration of Tumacacori, 1921." *Southwestern Monuments Special Report* 10:261–84.

Polzer, Charles W. 1971. *Kino's Biography of Francisco Javier Saeta, S. J. Sources and Studies for the History of the Americas*. Vol. 9. St. Louis: Jesuit Historical Institute.

Polzer, Charles W. 1976. *Rules and Precepts of the Missions of Northwestern New Spain*. Tucson: University of Arizona Press.

Reff, Daniel T. 1991. "Anthropological Analysis of Exploration Texts: Cultural Discourse and the Ethnological Import of Fray Marcos de Niza's Journey to Cibola." *American Anthropologist* 93 (3): 636–55. http://dx.doi.org/10.1525/aa.1991.93.3.02a00060.

Robinson, William J. 1963. "Excavations at San Xavier del Bac, 1958." *Kiva* 29 (2): 35–57. http://dx.doi.org/10.1080/00231940.1963.11757651.

Robinson, William J., and Mark R. Barnes. 1976. "Mission Guevavi: Excavations in the Convento." *Kiva* 42 (2): 135–75. http://dx.doi.org/10.1080/00231940.1976.11757872.

Rogers, Malcolm J. 1928. "Remarks on the Archaeology of the Gila River Drainage." *Arizona Museum Journal* 1 (1): 21–24.

Rogers, Malcolm J. 1936. *Yuman Pottery Making. San Diego Museum Papers* 2. San Diego: San Diego Museum.

Rogers, Malcolm J. 1945. "An Outline of Yuman Prehistory." *Southwestern Journal of Anthropology* 1 (2): 167–98. http://dx.doi.org/10.1086/soutjanth.1.2.3628758.

Russell, Frank. 1975. *The Pima Indians*. Tucson: University of Arizona Press.

Schroeder, Albert H. 1952. "A Brief Survey of the Lower Colorado River from Davis Dam to the International Border." Manuscript on file. Boulder City, NV: Bureau of Reclamation, Region Three Office.

Schroeder, Albert H. 1957. "The Hakataya Cultural Tradition." *American Antiquity* 23 (2): 176–78. http://dx.doi.org/10.2307/276447.

Schroeder, Albert H. 1958. "Lower Colorado Buffware: A Descriptive Revision." In *Pottery Types of the Southwest*, edited by Harold S. Colton. Museum of Northern Arizona Ceramic Series 3D. Flagstaff: Northern Arizona Society of Science and Art.

Seymour, Deni J. 1989. "The Dynamics of Sobaipuri Settlement in the Eastern Pimería Alta." *Journal of the Southwest* 31 (2): 205–22.

Seymour, Deni J. 2009. "The Canutillo Complex: Evidence of Protohistoric Mobile Occupants in the Southern Southwest." *Kiva* 74 (4): 421–46. http://dx.doi.org/10.1179/kiv.2009.74.4.003.

Seymour, Deni J. 2011. *Where the Earth and Sky Are Sewn Together: Sobaipuri-O'odham Contexts of Contact and Colonialism*. Salt Lake City: University of Utah Press.

Seymour, Deni J. 2014. *A Fateful Day in 1698: Archaeological Insights into the Remarkable Sobaipuri-O'odham Victory over the Apache and their Allies*. Salt Lake City: University of Utah Press.

Shenk, Lynette O., George A. Teague, and James M. Hewitt. 1975. *Excavations at the Tubac Presidio. Archaeological Series 85*. Tucson: Arizona State Museum.

Sheridan, Thomas E., Stuart B. Koyiyumtewa, and Anton Daughters, T. J. Ferguson, Leigh Kuwanwisiwma, Dale S. Brenneman, and LeeWayne Lomayestewa, eds. 2015. *Moquis and Kastiilam: Hopis, Spaniards, and the Trauma of History*. Vol. 1. Tucson: University of Arizona Press.

Smith, Fay Jackson, John L. Kessell, and Francis J. S. J. Fox. 1966. *Father Kino in Arizona*. Phoenix: Arizona Historical Foundation.

Sugnet, Christopher L., and J. Jefferson Reid, eds. 1994. "The Surface of Presidio Santa Cruz de Terrenate. Partnership Education Cooperative Agreement, Grant A040-A30005." Manuscript on file. Tucson, AZ: Bureau of Land Management.

Villalpando, María Elisa, and Randall H. McGuire, eds. 2009. *Entre muros de piedra: La arqueología del Cerro de Trincheras*. Hermosillo, Sonora, Mexico: Centro Instituto Nacional de Antropología e Historia Sonora.

Vint, James M. 2007. *Report on Mapping and Data Collection of Six Sites along the San Pedro River in the Vicinity of Fairbank, San Pedro National Riparian Conservation Area, Cochise County, Southeastern Arizona*. Technical Report 2007-104. Tucson: Center for Desert Archaeology.

Wallace, Henry D., and James P. Homlund, eds. 1986. *Petroglyphs of the Picacho Mountains, South Central Arizona*. Goleta, CA: Institute for American Research.

Waters, Michael R. 1982. "The Lowland Patayan Ceramic Tradition." In *Hohokam and Patayan: Prehistory of Southwestern Arizona*, edited by Randall H. McGuire and Michael Brian Schiffer, 275–97. New York: Academic Press.

Whittlesey, Stephanie M. 1994. "Three Centuries of Pottery Across the Pimería Alta." Paper Presented at the 1994 Arizona Archaeological Council Fall Conference, Tucson, AZ.

Wood, J. Scott. 2000. "Vale of Tiers Palimpsest: Salado Settlement and Internal Relationships in the Tonto Basin Area." In *Salado*, edited by Jeffrey S. Dean, 107–41. Dragoon, AZ: Amerind Foundation.

Wood, W. Raymond. 1990. "Ethnohistory and Historical Method." In *Archaeological Method and Theory* Vol. 2, edited by Michael B. Schiffer, 81–110. Tucson: University of Arizona Press.

Yetman, David A. 2010. *The Ópatas: In Search of a Sonoran People*. Tucson: University of Arizona Press.

Yetman, David A. 2012. *Conflict in Colonial Sonora: Indians, Priests, and Settlers*. Albuquerque: University of New Mexico Press.

ELEVEN

Missions, Livestock, and Economic Transformations in the Pimería Alta

BARNET PAVAO-ZUCKERMAN

INTRODUCTION

Among the changes wrought by the arrival of Europeans in the Americas, the impact of introduced Eurasian livestock stands out as particularly far-reaching in space and time. The introduction of Eurasian domesticated animals was transformative for the environments, economies, sociopolitical interactions, cuisine, technology, and many other aspects of the daily life of Native Americans. And, the success or failure of domesticated livestock shaped the unfolding of the European colonial process throughout North America (Pavao-Zuckerman 2000; Pavao-Zuckerman and Reitz 2006:52). While not universally successful, Eurasian livestock in the southwestern region of North America paved the way for successful Spanish colonialism, and eventually formed the foundation of several important economic interactions in the region.

In the Southwest, Spanish colonial missions most often served as the vehicle for the introduction of livestock and for the transformation of Native American daily life. All Spanish colonial entities—secular, military, and religious—sought to

DOI: 10.5876/9781607325741.c011

establish economies based on animal husbandry and the exploitation of domesticated animals; however, missions were particularly well suited to the ranching enterprise. Spanish policies of *reducción*, or the physical resettlement of Native American communities at missions, served both to provide a captive audience for efficient proselytizing and amassed a large labor pool in support of various mission economic enterprises, including livestock ranching. Native American labor was co-opted by missionaries into European-styled intensive agriculture and animal husbandry with the goal of establishing and maintaining self-supporting agrarian communities (Radding 1997; Sheridan 1988). Agricultural surpluses were expected to fulfill the needs of the missions and to provide material support to nascent Spanish secular and military settlements in the region. While grains, particularly wheat, were usually the most important commodities, missions also served as important sources of livestock and livestock products. This was particularly the case in the Pimería Alta (Figure 11.1), the region encompassing present-day northern Sonora (Mexico) and southern Arizona (United States), where warm and dry environments could support large herds of cattle and sheep (Pavao-Zuckerman 2000; Pavao-Zuckerman and Reitz 2006).

MISSIONIZATION AND THE INTRODUCTION OF LIVESTOCK IN THE PIMERÍA ALTA

Missionization of the O'odham people in the Pimería Alta began in the late seventeenth century with the travels of Father Eusebio Francisco Kino, the Italian Jesuit missionary (see Lauren E. Jelinek and Dale S. Brenneman, chapter 10 in this volume). Kino embarked on his missionization efforts among the O'odham in the 1680s; however, Spanish settlement and proselytization among the Ópatas and the "Pimas Bajas" was unfolding at the southern border of the Pimería Alta from the early seventeenth century, particularly in association with mining activities (Spicer 1962). And Spanish colonialism in the Puebloan region of the northern Southwest was long underway by the time Kino arrived in the Pimería Alta.

At the time of missionization, the O'odham were seminomadic horticulturalists. While the O'odham developed sophisticated irrigated-agricultural systems, it is estimated that 80 percent of their yearly diet was contributed by wild resources collected during seasonal movements across the landscape (Radding 1997:49–50). During the winter months, O'odham farmers moved to aggregated upland camps near permanent water sources where they hunted and gathered wild foods. Communities dispersed somewhat during the summer agricultural season, as households moved into desert lowlands to take advantage of floodwater irrigation brought on by the summer rains. O'odham children were tasked with guarding crops from animal thieves, and no doubt honed their hunting skills by picking off would-be crop-stealers for dinner (Radding 1997). "Garden

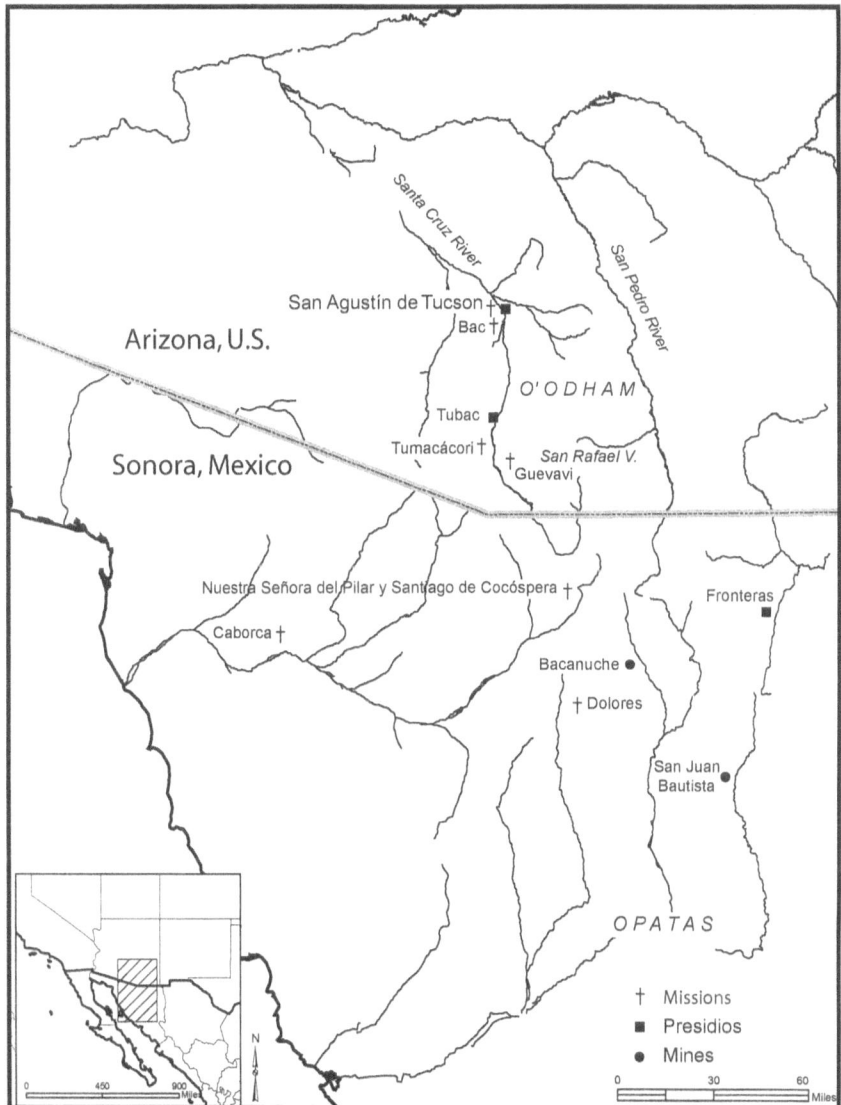

FIGURE 11.1. *Map of the Pimería Alta in the eighteenth century.*

hunting" by O'odham children (or adults) was likely an important source of protein during the summer months. This practice was very common among Hohokam farmers who lived in the region until around AD 1450 (Dean 2005, 2007; Szuter 1991), and no doubt continued with the O'odham. The seasonal movements of the O'odham people were largely structured by the availability water, a limited resource in the Sonoran Desert (Dobyns 1976:9). Winter settlements were placed near perennial streams or springs, and summer agricultural settlements were located near arroyos that could, when flooded by rainwater, be manipulated with ditches and brush fences to irrigate agricultural fields. Seasonal mobility, and the fluctuations in community size, also served to insulate O'odham communities against hostilities by other indigenous groups.

Missionization and Spanish colonialism were ultimately transformative of O'odham lifeways, but this transformation was patchwork, gradual, and reciprocal. The earliest impacts of European colonialism felt in the region were no doubt biological—the introduction of zoonotic epidemic diseases and Eurasian domesticated plants and animals. While very little direct evidence exists for the impact of epidemic diseases on O'odham people prior to the arrival of missionaries and written documents, several smallpox epidemics affected the southwestern region of North America prior to the mission period, including in 1520–24, 1592–93, 1602, 1646–48, and 1662–63 (Dobyns 1983:15). Other diseases also swept through the region, including measles, influenza, bubonic plague, diphtheria, typhus, and possibly cholera (Dobyns 1983). These epidemics continued in the mission period, with records of burials in church documents often exceeding the numbers of baptisms. Although Kino established missions at existing O'odham villages, these populations quickly dwindled as a result of disease, and outlying Native American communities were often resettled at struggling missions to bolster neophyte populations. Despite these resettlement efforts, indigenous populations at missions throughout the Pimería Alta continued to see precipitous declines throughout the eighteenth century (Dobyns 1963), a testament to O'odham cultural resilience.

While diseases likely impacted O'odham ancestral communities prior to the arrival of missionaries, most Eurasian animals and crops were unknown in the region until the mission period. Indeed, the region was devoid of domesticated animals throughout the pre-Hispanic period, with the exception of domesticated dogs and, briefly, turkeys. The history of ranching in the Pimería Alta begins with the sixteenth-century Spanish *entradas* by Coronado and Oñate. These entradas may have accidentally introduced one or more Eurasian animals to the region, but it is unlikely that any escapees survived Native hunters or the southwestern climate for very long.

The first intentional introduction of Eurasian livestock in the Pimería Alta occurred in the 1680s with the journeys of Father Kino. Kino, however, was preceded by horses, which appear to have spread from settlements to the south or possibly from the Spanish colony in New Mexico prior to his arrival. Captain Juan Matheo Manje, who accompanied Kino, noted that horse raiding was already a problem for the Native American communities they encountered (Burrus 1971; Sheridan 1988). Horses, apparently, spread independently and in advance of the spread of European colonialism.

As he traveled throughout the region, nominally establishing missions, Kino left behind wheat, cattle, and other small livestock, presumably with some instructions on what to do with the alien creatures and crops. Winter wheat had an almost immediate impact on indigenous life in the region—it was adopted by O'odham farmers soon after its introduction by Kino. The crop yielded a harvest of grain during spring, a traditionally lean time of the year, and was therefore an attractive addition to the traditional O'odham agricultural regime (Sheridan 1988).

The fate of the Eurasian animals deposited in the upper reaches of the Pimería Alta by Kino was less rosy. It is difficult to imagine that Kino was able to provide enough instruction during his brief visits for Native peoples to take up husbandry—particularly given that animal husbandry of large hooved animals was entirely unknown in North America. In some areas, cattle and other livestock were successfully introduced (Radding 1997; Sheridan 2006), but Eurasian livestock introduced into the northern reaches of the Pimería Alta around the late seventeenth and early eighteenth centuries were probably hunted more than husbanded, and disappeared soon after Kino departed (Spicer 1962:546). It was not until the establishment of permanent missions with resident priests that sustained herds of livestock were present on the landscape. Priests were resident at some missions by the second quarter of the eighteenth century, but some missions did not see a permanent presence until the late eighteenth century. Even when resident priests moved in, however, efforts to introduce livestock and co-opt Native labor for their care were not always successful. Livestock were not universally welcomed by Native people, and indigenous perceptions of livestock were often quite negative. The sharp-hooved, hungry, and thirsty animals represented a threat to both drinking water and agricultural fields and they scared off wild game. Documentary records indicate that Native peoples complained vociferously about the deleterious effects of the alien animals (Dobyns 1976; Radding 1997:171, 252, 254). The negative effects of cattle ranching were similarly felt in Alta California, where the loss of traditional hunting and gathering lands to livestock grazing forced many Native Californians onto the missions in search of food (Hackel 2005:71; Lightfoot 2005:86–87). It is not surprising, then, that attempts to expunge Europeans from the region by Native groups were often accompanied by the slaughter of livestock. During the Pima Revolt in 1751, the priest at Mission San Xavier del Bac reported that mission property including livestock was destroyed (Dobyns 1976:6, 14).

The establishment of European-style agriculture and animal husbandry was not possible without the co-option of Native lands, and Native labor. Land under the control of missions was technically the property of the affiliated Native community, an arrangement that reinforced the transitional nature of missions (Weber 2005:107). Missions were never intended to be permanent entities, but were a means to establish European-styled (but still self-sufficient) Native

American agricultural communities that were then converted from missions to secular parishes. Until that time, a portion of mission land was planted under the direction of the priest, and the remaining lands were distributed among Native households.

Native American converts provided all labor for mission lands—and mission agricultural yields were the product of Native labor. Missionaries employed several strategies to amass labor at missions in the region. Missions were usually established within O'odham communities to take advantage of the proximity to existing labor. As local populations dwindled from diseases, Spanish policies of reduccíon resettled more distant Native American populations at the mission. Neophyte communities were intended to be permanently settled, year-round agrarian communities, and missionaries discouraged Native people from leaving the mission for any reason. Prohibitions on seasonal movements to exploit wild resources kept labor, and souls, close by. Mission labor systems were generally structured so that all adult males worked three days on mission crops and animals, and three days on their own flocks and fields (Sheridan 1988). For their labor, Native laborers received rations from the mission's crops and stores. Mission surplus was used as insurance against famine, as well as to support non-Indian mission personnel. Surplus was also used to generate income though trade with other colonial entities, such as presidios, mining communities, and other secular colonies (Radding 1997:67–68).

Pimería Alta missions did not exist in a vacuum. By the time Kino established his first missions in the late seventeenth century, Spanish colonial influence was already well established among the Ópata and other groups in the Pimería Baja, and several mining communities and secular ranches were operating at the southern edge of the Pimería Alta, within traveling distance of O'odham communities. Missionization unfolded almost simultaneously with secular colonization and militarization in the northern Pimería Alta. By the mid-eighteenth century, missions comprised merely one part of a complex network of colonial settlements, including privately owned ranches, mining camps, presidios, and secular communities.

All of these entities created opportunities for the sale of mission goods, including husbandry and agricultural surplus. Livestock emerged as an important link connecting the missions to a regional and emerging global economy. The ultimate success of livestock in the region is due in great part to the co-option of O'odham labor and to a climate that is amenable to Eurasian livestock; however, the growth of ranching also occurred in response to the development of other colonial industries.

The growth of herds also had unintended consequences, including the creation of "24-hour, one-stop shops" for Native groups who adopted raiding as a strategy for economic survival during the colonial period. Large, permanent communities with growing herds of livestock were attractive targets for raiding. Mission livestock supported not only the colonial regime, but provided a handy and predictable resource for many raiding parties.

By the late eighteenth century, livestock was the foundation of three key economic processes in the region: ranching, rendering, and raiding. Livestock ranching became a primary economic strategy for the self-sufficiency of Spanish colonial missions, and in support of future colonialism. Rendering of mission livestock created animal products for a regional market in support of other colonial enterprises, including mining. And mission herds were a primary target of raiding that supported an entirely separate, illicit, regional economy. In concert with documentary evidence, zooarchaeological data from two Pimería Alta missions—San Agustín de Tucson (Pavao-Zuckerman 2010, 2011b; Pavao-Zuckerman and LaMotta 2007; Thiel and Mabry 2006) and Nuestra Señora del Pilar y Santiago de Cocóspera (Kessell 1970; Martínez 2005; Pavao-Zuckerman 2008, 2011b)—can illuminate the role of introduced Eurasian livestock and O'odham labor in these three primary economic interactions: ranching, rendering, and raiding.

PIMERÍA ALTA ZOOARCHAEOLOGY

Excavations at Mission San Agustín de Tucson were carried out by Desert Archaeology, Inc. as part of the City of Tucson's downtown revitalization project (Thiel and Mabry 2006). These excavations yielded a large assemblage of zooarchaeological remains from seven features dating to between 1795 and 1820 (Cameron et al. 2006; Pavao-Zuckerman and LaMotta 2007). Father Kino established the San Agustín Mission in the 1690s within an existing community of O'odham farmers living along the Santa Cruz River in what is now downtown Tucson, Arizona (Dobyns 1976:4). For much of the eighteenth century, San Agustín was a *visita*, serviced by the priest at the nearby head mission (*cabecera*) of San Xavier del Bac. San Agustín became a full-fledged mission with its own resident priest only after the expulsion of the Jesuits (and the arrival of the Franciscans) in 1767. It was only after the arrival of Franciscan missionaries that livestock herds took off—under the intermittent Jesuit presence, herds were slow to grow. The arrival of the Spanish garrison to Tucson in 1776, less than a decade after the arrival of the Franciscans, introduced a new market for livestock. Mission herds were large enough at that time to furnish the newly established presidio with livestock (see J. Homer Thiel, chapter 12 in this volume). By the turn of the nineteenth century, documentary records indicate that livestock herds were thriving (Dobyns 1976).

Excavations at Mission Nuestra Señora del Pilar y Santiago de Cocóspera were carried by the Instituto Nacional de Antropología e Historia (Sonora, Mexico) (Martínez 2005). Like San Agustín, Cocóspera was established by Kino among a group of O'odham *ranchería* settlements. It was initially established as a visita in the 1690s and was serviced by the clergy at a nearby head mission. Below, I use the general term "mission" to refer to both San Agustín and Cocóspera, although they are more accurately described as *visitas*, for at least most of their history. Livestock were more successful at Cocóspera than at San Agustín, and herds grew faster—at the turn of the eighteenth century, the neophytes at Cocóspera maintained around 500 head of cattle (Pickens 1993:43). Unfortunately, as a result of this success, the mission was frequently a target of livestock raiding.

In the zooarchaeological analyses below, three quantitative indices common to zooarchaeological analyses are employed. The first, NISP, or the number of identified specimens, is a count of the number of bone fragments, exclusive of mending pieces. This index is highly influenced by fragmentation, which is especially problematic for large-bodied taxa, whose skeletons tend to break into more fragments. In highly fragmented assemblages, larger-bodied taxa may appear more common in the archaeological assemblage than they were in the "death assemblage." The second, MNI, or the minimum number of individuals, is in part used to overcome some of the biases inherent in NISP. This method estimates the minimum number of individual animals that must have contributed a zooarchaeological assemblage, and is based on paired elements, portions, and age, when possible. The measure tends to inflate the importance of rarer and smaller-bodied taxa, particularly in smaller assemblages. Like NISP, MNI is also affected by fragmentation. A high rate of fragmentation tends to lower estimates of MNI. Third, biomass, which is based on bone weight, can be used in concert with NISP and MNI to overcome some of the problems encountered with fragmentation rates. Biomass is an estimate of the meat that may have been contributed by a given taxa. It is based on established ratios of bone-to-meat weights derived from modern experimental studies on animal carcasses (Reitz et al. 1987). While all of these indices are problematic when used on their own, together they provide a more complete and accurate depiction of animal use in the past.

RANCHING

Although Kino's initial attempts at introducing livestock met with mixed success, documentary records indicate that by 1701 the five missions established by Kino collectively held approximately 4,200 head of cattle (Jordan 1993:142). As Kino's brief visits were replaced by permanent missionaries, livestock continued to gain a foothold in the region, despite continued conflicts between Native farmers and the introduced animals. During the 1751 Pima Revolt, and the many smaller uprisings that preceded it, livestock were slaughtered alongside priests and in the company of the destruction of Catholic ritual objects, no doubt because the animals were viewed as symbols of Spanish oppression (Perez 2003).

Despite, or perhaps because of, this resistance, the growth of herds was patchy: at some missions herds grew quickly; at others, herds remained small until the late eighteenth century. This growth contrasts somewhat with that of ranching in Alta California. Missionization in the latter region was later, beginning in 1769, but introduced Eurasian livestock (and plants) exploded on the landscape (Hackel 2005:68–70; Lightfoot 2005). California missions maintained *ranchos* in the hinterlands, where cattle, horses, sheep, goats, and pigs were raised (Lightfoot 2005:57). Although the growth of herds was uneven across the Pimería Alta, mission inventories indicate that livestock holdings increased markedly at most missions throughout the eighteenth century (Table 11.1). Mission herds consisted predominantly of cattle (*Bos taurus*) and sheep (*Ovis aries*); many missions also maintained much smaller herds of goats (*Capra hircus*) (Dobyns 1976; Kessell 1970; McCarty 1976). Documentary records suggest that the ratio of cattle to sheep declined through the eighteenth century. In 1737, cattle outnumbered sheep 3 to 2 at Missions Guevavi and Bac, while in the 1760s, the animals occurred in roughly equal numbers at Guevavi, and sheep outnumbered cattle at the Bac Mission (Kessell 1970:197, 199, 200–201, 204).

Zooarchaeological evidence from Mission San Agustín and Mission Cocóspera confirms that ranching was a predominant economic activity at both missions, with primary reliance on cattle (Figures 11.2 and 11.3) (Pavao-Zuckerman 2010, 2011a, 2011b; Pavao-Zuckerman and LaMotta 2007).

At Mission San Agustín, the NISP and biomass of cattle remains far exceed all other taxa combined, and exceed those values for caprines (sheep and goats) by 3 to 1. At Mission Cocóspera, cattle dominate both by measures of NISP and biomass, although equal minimum numbers of caprine and cattle individuals are estimated. It should be noted that while sheep and goat skeletons are notoriously difficult to distinguish, the documentary record suggests that sheep were more numerous than goats, and the latter were not always present in mission flocks. In 1737, herds at Missions Guevavi and Bac each boasted approximately 150 sheep and 50 goats. By 1761, goats were absent from both missions (Kessell 1970:197, 200–201). And, while very few caprine specimens in the zooarchaeological assemblages are identifiable to species, most identifiable caprines are attributed to sheep. Given these observations, it is safe to assume that a majority of the remains identified only as inclusive in the subfamily Caprinae are, in fact, sheep.

While the data do suggest that the mission ranching strategies were focused primarily on cattle, there are several reasons why the data likely overemphasize the role of cattle relative to sheep. The large discrepancy between cattle and caprine in terms of biomass is largely attributable to the greater body size (and, therefore, bone weight) of cattle versus caprines. In addition, because cattle

TABLE 11.1. Inventories of livestock holdings at Pimería Alta missions and presidios.

Mission/ presidio, year	Cattle (%)		Sheep		
	N	%	N	%	Total
MISSION GUEVAVI					
1737	248	62.3%	150	37.7%	398
1761	890	55.2%	723	44.8%	1,613
MISSION BAC					
1737	240	61.5%	150	38.5%	390
1765	487	47.6%	536	52.4%	1,023
MISSIONS BAC AND TUCSON					
1819	5,700	89.1%	700	10.9%	6,400
TUCSON PRESIDIO					
1804	3,500	57.4%	2,600	42.6%	6,100
TUBAC PRESIDIO					
1804	1,000	16.7%	5,000	83.3%	6,000

Source: from Dobyns (1976), Kessell (1970), and McCarty (1976).

bones are larger than caprine remains, the former tend to break into more fragments, resulting in an inflated NISP.

Finally, sheep were raised for wool, meaning that many animals lived well into adulthood. Cattle, on the other hand, were exploited primarily for butchery products such as meat, hide, and tallow (Pavao-Zuckerman 2011b). The discrepancy between herd sizes as reported in written documents and the proportions of these animals in the zooarchaeological assemblages likely reflects a reduced life expectancy for cattle—cattle were killed younger, and in greater numbers, resulting in a much larger archaeological population than actually lived on the landscape at any given time.

Mission ranching strategies may have served to complement the ranching strategies of other nearby colonial enterprises, including presidios. Research by Dan Broockmann (2007) on zooarchaeological remains from the Tucson Presidio, located across the river from Mission San Agustín, suggests that caprines, including sheep, were more common at the presidio than at the mission. And, an 1819 census of the missions at Bac and Tucson indicates that cattle outnumbered sheep and goats by 9 to 1 (Dobyns 1976:51), while at the Tucson Presidio, the proportion of sheep to cattle was roughly equal, with cattle contributing only a slight majority (McCarty 1976:90). At the Tubac Presidio, located about forty-five miles to the south, sheep outnumbered cattle 5 to 1 on the 1804 inventory (McCarty 1976:85), indicating an even stronger emphasis on sheepherding at the presidio. Tubac was located just three miles from the closest mission, at

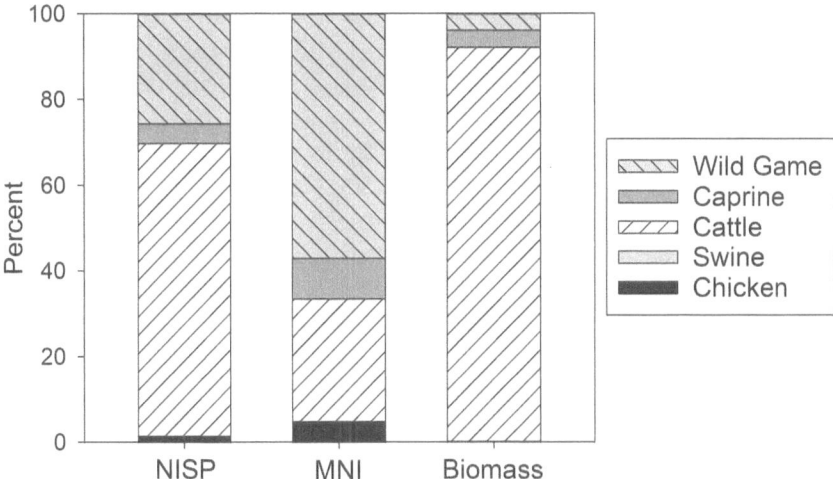

FIGURE 11.2. *Summary of zooarchaeological remains from Mission San Agustín.*

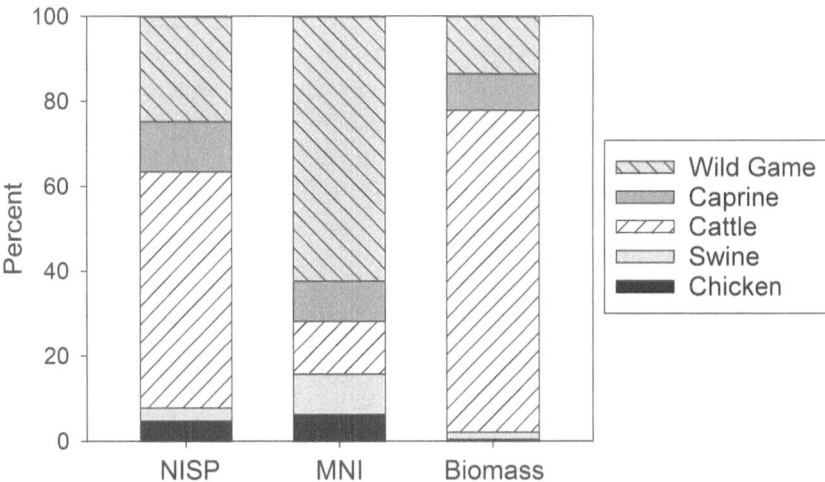

FIGURE 11.3. *Summary of zooarchaeological remains from Mission Cocóspera.*

Tumacácori. Given close proximity and interaction, it is possible that presidios and missions opted for complementary specialization of husbandry strategies in terms of the proportion of cattle versus sheep.

Documentary evidence suggests that cattle herds were not closely managed—the animals were probably primarily free-ranged and perhaps semiferal (Dobyns 1976; Jordan 1993; Radding 1997). A 1761 inventory at Mission Guevavi, located about sixty miles south of Mission San Agustín reported that over 800 head of cattle were "on the range," while less than 60 were housed in branding pens (Kessell 1970:200).

Age at death data within the zooarchaeological assemblages suggest that a typically "optimized" husbandry strategy was practiced at both missions. Zooarchaeological evidence indicates that a majority of cattle were slaughtered when they were between the ages of two and four (Pavao-Zuckerman 2010; Pavao-Zuckerman and LaMotta 2007). At this age, cattle reach adult size, and additional inputs into the animal do not result in additional consumable meat or animal byproducts (Dahl and Hjort 1976). A few animals at both missions, however, were allowed to reach an older age—these were perhaps animals used for traction (such as oxen), breeding, or dairying. While evidence for age at death in the caprine assemblages is scarce, it is telling that only a single caprine specimen in either assemblage was juvenile at the time of death. These animals were likely kept longer for their wool.

Documentary evidence suggests that cattle slaughter was a seasonal activity that took place in October or November when cooler temperatures meant that meat could be preserved by drying before spoiling (Pfefferkorn [1795] 1949:99). The Jesuit priest Ignaz Pfefferkorn recorded that meat from the fall slaughter was dried and served as a staple protein, often rehydrated in soups (Pfefferkorn [1795] 1949:100). Fresh meat was probably only seasonally available at the missions. In 1758, the priest (with limited medical training) at nearby San Ignacio recorded the death of a neophyte who died, he concluded, of an intestinal blockage from overindulgence of fresh beef during the fall slaughter (Stiger 1758). For the sin of gluttony, she was denied the sacraments of death.

RENDERING

Although mission herds were clearly an important source of meat (in dried form) that fed the neophyte community throughout the year, zooarchaeological and documentary evidence also suggest that mission herds were managed for the extraction of nonmeat products, such as hide and tallow, as was common in Alta California (Dallas 1955; Gust 1982; Hackel 2005; Lightfoot 2005; Pavao-Zuckerman 2011b).

Zooarchaeological assemblages from both Mission San Agustín and Mission Cocóspera are highly fragmented (Pavao-Zuckerman 2011b). Roughly 90 percent of medium and large mammal specimens from both missions were broken into fragments of less than four centimeters—a degree of fracturing that is not typical when carcasses are butchered solely for meat. And, it appears that much of this breakage at both missions occurred perimortem—in other words, when the bones were still fresh (Pavao-Zuckerman 2011b).

This pattern of bone breakage is consistent with other zooarchaeological assemblages believed to have been rendered for tallow or bone grease (Binford

1978; Mateos 2005; Outram 2001, 2002). While this pattern is cross-cultural (Binford 1978; Logan 1998; Manne and Bicho 2009; Mateos 2005; Munro and Bar-Oz 2005; Peale 1871; Reitz 1986; Yellen 1977; Zierhut 1967), the written record provides a local description of tallow rendering in the Pimería Alta during the mid-eighteenth century:

> Now the animal is skinned, the fat and tallow removed ... Fat is melted and preserved in bladders, the largest intestines of cattle, or in earthen pots. ... Those who slaughter several cattle at one time throw all the bones and marrow into a kettle full of water, cook them, and skim off the fat floating on top ... Tallow is either kneaded together after all fibres have been separated from it by much pounding, or it is melted. In this condition it is kept until candles are made or soap is boiled. (Pfefferkorn [1795] 1949)

As has been the practice in human societies for millennia (Burnham 1978), the bones from the butchered carcass are placed in boiling water and the fat (tallow) is skimmed off the top. However, Pferfferkorn's ([1795] 1949) description of tallow rendering omits the critical step of bone fracturing, a stage in tallow rendering that is abundantly visible in the archaeological record at both of the Pimería Alta mission sites discussed here.

Historically, tallow was used in the manufacture of food-grade greases, soaps, candles, and industrial lubricants (Burnham 1978; West 1949). While these materials were important for household and mission use, candles and industrial lubricants were particularly important to the mining industries in the southern reaches of the Pimería Alta. Tallow candles were the only source of illumination available to the mines, and tallow was the only widely available industrial grease (Bloom 1935; Sheridan 1988; West 1949:64–65). In the mid-eighteenth century, tallow was in such high demand that rendered grease from cattle carcasses was worth more than the living animal, and the price of tallow was highest near the mines (Pfefferkorn [1795] 1949:198–200). Documentary evidence from colonial-period New Mexico indicates that Spanish laws regulating intercolony trade were relaxed to permit the free flow of tallow candles to the region's mines (Trigg 2005; West 1949). Cattle hide was also in high demand by the mines, as it was used to make bags for hauling mineral ore. Unfortunately, any skinning marks are obscured by the high degree of fragmentation (Pavao-Zuckerman 2011b).

The importance of animal products in the Pimería Alta economy is not unique. In Alta California, mission ranchos served as vast factories on the hoof for the production of hide and tallow. So much tallow and hide was rendered from Alta California herds that the meat from the slaughtered carcasses was often just left to rot (Dallas 1955:25–26). Tallow and hides from California were shipped to Mexico City where they were redistributed for various uses, including for mining. In Alta California, hide processing is archaeologically visible in the presence of tanning vats, as well as hide scrapers (beamers) made from segments of cattle ribs (Deetz 1978). No such architectural or artifactual evidence from the Pimería Alta is known to support the hypothesis that tallow and hide were important trade commodities in this region. It is possible that the scale of hide processing was much greater in Alta California than in the Pimería Alta; however, archaeological investigations in the Pimería Alta have focused primarily on central mission compounds, rather than the surrounding landscapes, where evidence for rendering and hide processing are most likely to be found. In the Pimería Alta, missions and mines were located in close proximity, a unique situation in North America (West 1993:60). Mining communities were largely dependent upon local production of foodstuffs and materials, particularly hide and tallow, resulting in a strong economic link between mines and livestock ranching. Pimería Alta missions, with established herds and a captive labor force, were particularly well positioned to take advantage of this market. Many of the economic strategies employed by missions were no doubt influenced by their economic relationship with the mines, and missions ramped up production of agricultural surplus and livestock products to meet mining demands.

RAIDING

The introduction of livestock provided additional sources of food and raw materials that supported a well-developed "official" regional economy, but the herds also quickly became targets of Apache raiding, leaving the O'odham people, missionized or not, vulnerable. It is argued that livestock raiding was "the most significant economic catalyst for cultural interaction in the post-contact Southwest" (Record 2008:74). The "unofficial" raiding economy in many ways dwarfed the impact of sanctioned economic interactions in the region. Raiding, and the threat of raiding, was truly transformative of Native American and Spanish colonial life. Indeed, Apache raiding may have more significantly altered the daily life of the O'odham people than Spanish colonialism itself (Record 2008:84).

Apache raiding, generally in response to food shortages (Basso 1971:16), began in earnest in the mid-1600s, and spread with Spanish colonialism and Eurasian livestock. By the mid-eighteenth century, Apache raiding intensified to the point that the region was in chaos (Record 2008:79), and it continued throughout the latter half of the eighteenth century (Jordan 1993:143). Intense raiding lead to the abandonment of many cattle ranches, and livestock herds shrunk considerably in the wake of raids. The expulsion of the Jesuits in 1767 furthered this decline, and it was not until the 1790s that herds regained their numbers.

Although more study is needed, documentary evidence suggests that missions modified their ranching strategies in response to intensified raiding, particularly by shifting the species composition of mission herds. While sheep and cattle were usually introduced in roughly equal numbers, the proportion of sheep in the Pimería Alta generally declined (Jordan 1993). By the 1760s, sheep were rare in many parts of Sonora, both because shepherding is labor intensive compared to cattle ranching, and because the fluffy animals are more easily caught in the thorny Sonoran Desert scrub (Jordan 1993:142). In New Mexico, however, sheep were often preferred by secular colonists because the animals were more difficult for raiding groups to run off than cattle (Merrill 1994:137; Weber 1992:310). Wool was no doubt an important resource for local consumption in the Pimería Alta, but a wool-based textile industry never developed to the extent that it did in the Puebloan region—Sonoran herds were small, and wool textile production occurred primarily for household consumption, not for export (Pfefferkorn [1795] 1949: 102–3).

While sheep may have declined in some parts of Sonora, inventories of livestock holdings at various missions in the Pimería Alta (see Table 11.1) suggest that the proportion of sheep actually *increased* from the 1730s to the 1760s, just as raiding intensified (Dobyns 1976; Kessell 1970; McCarty 1976). The presence of thriving cattle herds at Mission Cocóspera made the community the target of raiding by hostile Native American groups, and the mission was attacked repeatedly throughout its occupation (Martínez 2005). Interestingly, sheep were more common at Mission Cocóspera than at Mission San Agustín. This may have been an adaptive response to managing risk during a volatile period in the mission's history.

In contrast, the cattle-dominant zooarchaeological assemblage from Mission San Agustín dates to the turn of the nineteenth century, during a hiatus in intensive raiding activity (Record 2008:81). Data from an 1819 inventory of livestock in the combined herds at Mission San Agustín and the nearby Mission San Xavier del Bac indicate that cattle outnumbered sheep by 9 to 1. During peaceful times, it may have been possible for missions to intensify cattle ranching and reduce investment in the more labor-intensive husbandry of sheep.

CONCLUSIONS

Throughout North America, European colonialism was predicated on the successful introduction of Eurasian livestock that had the potential to transform the daily life, economies, and environments of Native peoples. This was particularly the case at Spanish missions, where clergy were responsible for establishing and maintaining self-supporting agrarian communities by co-opting Native American labor into European-styled intensive agriculture and animal husbandry. Native laborers were also expected to produce a surplus that could fulfill the needs of the missions, and provide material support to nascent Spanish secular and military settlements. Pimería Alta missions were particularly well suited to the ranching enterprise; they were located in an environment that was amenable to livestock ranching, among Native communities who ultimately provided the labor for ranching and in proximity to other colonial entities with demands for both domesticated animals and livestock products. In concert with documentary evidence, zooarchaeological data from Mission San Agustín de Tucson and Mission Nuestra Señora del Pilar y Santiago de Cocóspera indicate that introduced Eurasian livestock, particularly cattle, served as the foundation for several central regional economic interactions, including ranching, rendering, and raiding.

Mission ranching activities were supported on the backs of Native laborers. The co-option of Native labor by missions had profound effects on the daily life of the O'odham at missions. Policies of permanent residency, reduccíon, and the three-day labor (plus one day of worship) requirement conflicted with traditional practices of seasonal mobility to exploit wild resources. The introduction of domesticated livestock, the labor demands of ranching, and restrictions on traditional hunting practices no doubt all came with implications not just for workloads, but the division of labor within O'odham communities.

Wild game was not entirely abandoned, however, as wild species are found in both zooarchaeological assemblages. Many of these species may have been caught in agricultural fields, perhaps by young hunters sent into the fields to protect crops from hungry pests. However, some game animals, such as deer, were no doubt captured some distance from the missions. In writing, priests disapproved of hunting trips that took neophytes away from the missions (and therefore away from their influence) (Dobyns 1976:24), but wild game remains were found within the mission compounds at both sites, suggesting that priests derived some benefits from these activities, including access to fresh meat and a wider variety of foods than was otherwise available. Mission priests in Alta California were equally disproving of traditional hunting pursuits by Native converts, but were also equally happy to partake of the fruits of neophyte fishing expeditions, particularly on Fridays (Lightfoot 2005:98). Ironically, the involvement of O'odham people in livestock ranching may have decreased their access to fresh meat, except through what was captured through "garden hunting." Cattle were primarily free-ranged, and rounded up by Native laborers usually only once or twice a year, particularly in the fall, for slaughter. This may have been the only time that fresh beef was available, as most was dried for later consumption. O'odham children, who protected crops from animal pests, may have contributed more fresh meat to the diet than the vast mission herds.

Native labor also supported not just production of meat protein for local consumption, but also the rendering of tallow for candles and industrial lubricants that fed the demands of nearby mining enterprises. The impact of this additional labor demand on O'odham daily life and division of labor is not fully understood, but it was no doubt substantial. Paradoxically, while missions and mining enterprises were often in competition for Native labor and colonial resources, the mining communities in the southern Pimería Alta were dependent upon the local production of foodstuffs as well as raw materials, including hide and tallow. Mines were an important source of wealth for the Spanish Crown, so much so that normal restrictions on intercolony trade were lifted so that missions could fulfill the material needs of the mines (West 1949). However, this aspect of the relationship between missions and mines in the region is illuminated only by the zooarchaeological record (Pavao-Zuckerman 2011b), as written documents are relatively silent on the role of animal products in intracolony trade (West 1949). As a result of this relationship, the co-option of Native labor at missions ultimately supported a regional economic system that enriched the colonial regime.

Thriving herds made missions the target of livestock raiding by hostile groups, and the zooarchaeological and written records give some insight into how missions may have managed herds in response to the stresses of livestock raiding. Ranching strategies were always diversified, but the documentary record suggests that under normal conditions, cattle were the preferred ranch animal in the Pimería Alta, as they were less labor intensive and easier to manage in the Sonoran thorn scrub. During times of intensified raiding, however, it appears that sheep, which were more resistant to raiding, and easier to corral, took on greater importance.

Zooarchaeological and documentary evidence demonstrate that introduced Eurasian livestock not only transformed Native environments and daily life, but served as the catalyst for social and economic interactions in the Pimería Alta. Eurasian livestock and Native labor connected missions to a broader regional and global economy, both sanctioned and illicit, and ultimately supported the Spanish colonial endeavor. Far from isolated frontier outposts, missions were surprisingly interconnected to regional and global colonial enterprises, and responded dynamically to economic opportunity, and economic stresses.

ACKNOWLEDGMENTS

The research presented above was carried out primarily in the Stanley J. Olsen Laboratory of Zooarchaeology, Arizona State Museum, University of Arizona, where the author served on the faculty until shortly before the publication of this contribution. Identification and analysis of zooarchaeological remains from Mission San Agustín were completed by Vincent LaMotta and the author, and were funded by Desert Archaeology, Inc. Many thanks to Desert Archaeology, Inc., Homer Thiel, and Jonathan Mabry for the opportunity to examine these materials, and to Vin for his hard work on this project. The author is also very grateful to Júpiter Martínez (INAH-Sonora) for access to the zooarchaeological materials from Mission Cocóspera—identification and analysis of these materials was carried out by the author. Dale Brenneman (Office of Ethnohistorical Research, Arizona State Museum) provided much appreciated assistance in navigating the ethnohistorical literature. Figure 11.1 was drafted by Ashley Blythe and modified by the author. Additional support for the analysis of zooarchaeological materials was provided by Marilyn Malone, Fran Hodgins, Rachel Diaz de Valdez, and Felicia Durso. A version of this paper was presented at the 2012 Annual Meeting of the Society for American Archaeology. Many thanks to three anonymous reviewers for their helpful comments on the edited volume.

REFERENCES CITED

Basso, Keith H., ed. 1971. *Western Apache Raiding and Warfare: From the Notes of Grenville Goodwin*. Tucson: University of Arizona Press.

Binford, Lewis R. 1978. *Nunamiut Ethnoarchaeology*. New York: Academic Press.

Bloom, Lansing B. 1935. "A Trade-Invoice of 1638." *New Mexico Historical Review* 10 (3): 242–48.

Broockmann, Daniel D. 2007. "A Little on the Wooly Side: Zooarchaeology at the Tucson Presidio." Master's thesis, School of Anthropology, University of Arizona, Tucson.

Burnham, Frank. 1978. *Rendering: The Invisible Industry*. Fallbrook, CA: Aero Publishers.

Burrus, Ernest J. 1971. *Kino and Manje: Explorers of Sonora and Arizona, Their Vision of the Future*. St. Louis, MO: Jesuit Historical Institute.

Cameron, Judi L., Jennifer A. Waters, Barnet Pavao-Zuckerman, Vincent M. LaMotta, and Peter D. Schulz. 2006. "Faunal Remains." In *Rio Nuevo Archaeology, 2000–2003: Investigations at the San Agustín Mission and Mission Gardens, Tucson Presidio, Tucson Pressed Brick Company, and Clearwater Site*, edited by J. Homer Thiel and Jonathan B. Mabry, 13.1–13.51. Technical Report No. 2004-11. Tucson, AZ: Desert Archaeology.

Dahl, Gudrun, and Anders Hjort. 1976. *Having Herds: Pastoral Herd Growth and Household Economy*. Stockholm Studies in Social Anthropology 2. Stockholm, Sweden: Department of Social Anthropology, University of Stockholm.

Dallas, Sherman Forbes. 1955. "The Hide and Tallow Trade in Alta California, 1822–1846." PhD dissertation, Department of Economics, Indiana University, Bloomington.

Dean, Rebecca M. 2005. "Site-Use Intensity, Cultural Modification of the Environment, and the Development of Agricultural Communities in Southern Arizona." *American Antiquity* 70 (3): 403–31. http://dx.doi.org/10.2307/40035307.

Dean, Rebecca M. 2007. "Hunting Intensification and the Hohokam 'Collapse.'" *Journal of Anthropological Archaeology* 26 (1): 109–32. http://dx.doi.org/10.1016/j.jaa.2006.03.010.

Deetz, James F. 1978. "Archaeological Investigations at La Purísima Mission." In *Historical Archaeology: A Guide to Substantive and Theoretical Contributions*, edited by Robert L. Schuyler, 160–90. Farmingdale, NY: Baywood Publishing Company.

Dobyns, Henry F. 1963. "Indian Extinction in the Middle Santa Cruz River Valley, Arizona." *New Mexico Historical Review* 38 (2): 163–81.

Dobyns, Henry F. 1976. *Spanish Colonial Tucson*. Tucson: University of Arizona Press.

Dobyns, Henry F. 1983. *Their Number Become Thinned: Native American Population Dynamics in Eastern North America*. Knoxville: University of Tennessee Press.

Gust, Sherri M. 1982. "Faunal Analysis and Butchering." In *The Ontiveros Adobe: Early Rancho Life in Alta California*, edited by Jay D. Frierman, 101–79. Report prepared for the Redevelopment Agency, City of Santa Fe Springs, CA, by Greenwood and Associates, Pacific Palisades, CA. Copies available from the Redevelopment Agency, City of Santa Fe Springs, CA.

Hackel, Steven W. 2005. *Children of Coyote, Missionaries of Saint Francis: Indian-Spanish Relations in Colonial California, 1769–1850*. Chapel Hill: University of North Carolina Press.

Jordan, Terry G. 1993. *North American Cattle-Ranching Frontiers*. Albuquerque: University of New Mexico Press.

Kessell, John L. 1970. *Mission of Sorrows: Jesuit Guevavi and the Pimas, 1691–1767*. Tucson: University of Arizona Press.

Lightfoot, Kent G. 2005. *Indians, Missionaries, and Merchants: The Legacy of Colonial Encounters on the California Frontiers*. Berkeley: University of California Press.

Logan, Brad. 1998. "The Fat of the Land: White Rock Phase Bison Hunting and Grease Production." *Plains Anthropologist* 43 (166): 349–66.

Manne, Tiina H., and Nuno F. Bicho. 2009. "Vale Boi: Rendering New Understandings of Resource Intensification & Diversification in Southwestern Iberia." *Before Farming* [online version] 2009/2 article 1:1–21. http://dx.doi.org/10.3828/bfarm.2009.2.1.

Martínez, Júpiter. 2005. "Valle de Cocóspera Archaeological Project: Recent Finds." *Manuscript on file*. Hermosillo, Sonora, Mexico: Instituto Nacional de Antropología e Historia.

Mateos, Ana. 2005. "Meat and Fat: Intensive Exploitation Strategies in the Upper Palaeolithic Approached from Bone Fracturing Analysis." In *The Zooarchaeology of Fats and Oils*, edited by Jacqui Mulville and Alan K. Outram, 150–59. Oxford: Oxbow Books.

McCarty, O. F. M. Kieran, 1976. *Desert Documentary: The Spanish Years, 1767–1821*. Tucson: University of Arizona Press.

Merrill, William L. 1994. "Cultural Creativity and Raiding Bands in Eighteenth-Century Northern New Spain." In *Violence, Resistance, and Survival in the Americas*, edited by William B. Taylor and Franklin G. Y. Pease, 124–52. Washington, DC: Smithsonian Institution Press.

Munro, Natalie D., and Guy Bar-Oz. 2005. "Gazelle Bone Fat Processing in the Levantine Epipalaeolithic." *Journal of Archaeological Science* 32 (2): 223–39. http://dx.doi.org/10.1016/j.jas.2004.08.007.

Outram, Alan K. 2001. "A New Approach to Identifying Bone Marrow and Grease Exploitation: Why the "Indeterminate" Fragments Should Not be Ignored." *Journal of Archaeological Science* 28 (4): 401–10. http://dx.doi.org/10.1006/jasc.2000.0619.

Outram, Alan K. 2002. "Bone Fracture and Within-Bone Nutrients: An Experimentally Based Method for Investigating Levels of Marrow Extraction." In *Consuming Passions and Patterns of Consumption*, edited by Preston Miracle and Nicky Milner, 51–63. Cambridge: McDonald Institute for Archaeological Research.

Pavao-Zuckerman, Barnet. 2000. "Vertebrate Subsistence in the Mississippian-Historic Period Transition." *Southeastern Archaeology* 19 (2): 135–44.

Pavao-Zuckerman, Barnet. 2008. "Introduction and Practice of Animal Husbandry at Pimería Alta Missions." *Journal of the West* 47 (3): 32–39.

Pavao-Zuckerman, Barnet. 2010. "Animal Husbandry at Pimería Alta Missions: El Ganado en el Sudoeste de Norteamérica." In *Anthropological Approaches to Zooarchaeology: Colonialism, Complexity and Animal Transformations*, edited by Douglas V. Campana, Pam J. Crabtree, Susan D. deFrance, Justin Lev-Tov, and Alice M. Choyke, 150–58. Oxford: Oxbow Books.

Pavao-Zuckerman, Barnet. 2011a. "Landscape Use at San Agustín." In *Contemporary Archaeologies of the Southwest*, edited by William H. Walker and Kathryn Venzor, 227–44. Boulder: University Press of Colorado.

Pavao-Zuckerman, Barnet. 2011b. "Rendering Economies: Native American Labor and Secondary Animal Products in the Eighteenth-Century Pimería Alta." *American Antiquity* 76 (1): 3–23. http://dx.doi.org/10.7183/0002-7316.76.1.3.

Pavao-Zuckerman, Barnet, and Vincent M. LaMotta. 2007. "Missionization and Economic Change in the Pimería Alta: The Zooarchaeology of San Agustín de Tucson." *International Journal of Historical Archaeology* 11 (3): 241–68. http://dx.doi.org/10.1007/s10761-007-0030-x.

Pavao-Zuckerman, Barnet, and Elizabeth J. Reitz. 2006. "Introduction and Adoption of Animals from Europe." In *Environment, Origins, and Population*, edited by Douglas Ubelaker, 485–491. Handbook of North American Indians, vol. 3, William C. Sturtevant, general editor, Washington, DC: Smithsonian Institution Press.

Peale, Titian R. 1871. "On the Uses of the Brain and Marrow of Animals among the Indians of North America." *Annual Report of the Board of Regents of the Smithsonian Institution* 1870:390–91.

Perez, Robert Cristian. 2003. "Indian Rebellions in Northwestern New Spain: A Comparative Analysis, 1695–1750's." PhD dissertation, Department of History, University of California, Riverside. Ann Arbor, Michigan: ProQuest.

Pfefferkorn, Ignaz. [1795] 1949. *Sonora: A Description of the Province*. Translated by Theodore E. Trautlen. Albuquerque: University of New Mexico Press.

Pickens, Buford. 1993. *The Missions of Northern Sonora: A 1935 Field Documentation*. Tucson: University of Arizona Press.

Radding, Cynthia. 1997. *Wandering Peoples: Colonialism, Ethnic Spaces, and Ecological Frontiers in Northwestern Mexico, 1700–1850*. Durham, NC: Duke University Press.

Record, Ian W. 2008. *Big Sycamore Stands Alone: The Western Apaches, Aravaipa, and the Struggle for Place. New Directions in Native American Studies*. Norman: University of Oklahoma Press.

Reitz, Elizabeth J. 1986. "Vertebrate Fauna from Locus 39, Puerto Real, Haiti." *Journal of Field Archaeology* 13 (3): 317–28.

Reitz, Elizabeth J., Irvy R. Quitmyer, H. Stephen Hale, Sylvia J. Scudder, and Elizabeth S. Wing. 1987. "Application of Allometry to Zooarchaeology." *American Antiquity* 52 (2): 304–17. http://dx.doi.org/10.2307/281782.

Sheridan, Thomas E. 1988. "Kino's Unforeseen Legacy: The Material Consequences of Missionization among the Northern Piman Indians of Arizona and Sonora." *Smoke Signal* (49/50): 151–67.

Sheridan, Thomas E. 2006. *Landscapes of Fraud: Mission Tumacácori, the Baca Float, and the Betrayal of the O'odham*. Tucson: University of Arizona Press.

Spicer, Edward Holland. 1962. *Cycles of Conquest: The Impact of Spain, Mexico, and the United States on the Indians of the Southwest, 1533–1960*. Tucson: The University of Arizona Press.

Stiger, Gaspar. 1758. "Mission Register." In *The Bancroft Collection, Latin Americana*. Berkeley, CA: Bancroft Library.

Szuter, Christine R. 1991. *Hunting by Prehistoric Horticulturalists in the American Southwest*. New York: Garland Publishing.

Thiel, J. Homer, and Jonathan B. Mabry, eds. 2006. *Rio Nuevo Archaeology, 2000–2003: Investigations at the San Agustín Mission and Mission Gardens, Tucson Presidio, Tucson Pressed Brick Company, and Clearwater Site*. Technical Report No. 2004-11. Tucson: Desert Archaeology.

Trigg, Heather B. 2005. *From Household to Empire: Society and Economy in Early Colonial New Mexico*. Tucson: University of Arizona Press.

Weber, David J. 1992. *The Spanish Frontier in North America*. New Haven, CT: Yale University Press.

Weber, David J. 2005. *Bárbaros: Spaniards and Their Savages in the Age of Enlightenment*. New Haven, CT: Yale University Press.

West, Robert C. 1949. *The Mining Community in Northern New Spain: The Parral Mining District*. Colección iberoamericana 30. Berkeley, CA: Editorial Iberoamericana.

West, Robert C. 1993. *Sonora: Its Geographical Personality*. Austin: University of Texas Press.

Yellen, John E. 1977. "Cultural Patterning in Faunal Remains: Evidence from the !Kung Bushmen." In *Experimental Archeology*, edited by Daniel Ingersoll, John E. Yellen, and William MacDonald, 271–331. New York: Columbia University Press.

Zierhut, Norman W. 1967. "Bone Breaking Activities of the Calling Lake Cree." *Alberta Anthropologist* 1 (3): 33–36.

TWELVE

Life in Tucson, on the Northern Frontier of the Pimería Alta

J. HOMER THIEL

INTRODUCTION

In 1879, Francisco Solano León was called to testify at a trial by lawyers seeking to understand whether a land grant was valid. He was asked, "Do you know what became of the archives of the Mexican Justice of the Peace of Tucson?" and answered, "They were taken to Imuris, in the District of Magdalena, Sonora, Mexico, and thereafter I do not know what became of them" (United States Court of Private Land Claims, 1879, 4:117–121, Special Collections, University of Arizona, Tucson). This and other losses of military, civil, and church archives of Tucson has hindered modern Tucsonans from understanding many aspects of their community's rich history. Today, many residents know little of the city's Spanish mission and presidio past.

Archaeological research, conducted in the last twenty years by Desert Archaeology, Inc., and the nonprofit Archaeology Southwest (formerly the Center for Desert Archaeology), has helped fill in some of the gaps in our knowledge of Tucson's early history (Thiel 1996, 2004, 2005, 2008a, 2008b; Thiel et al. 1995; Thiel and Mabry 2006). Excavation work has uncovered architectural remains

DOI: 10.5876/9781607325741.c012

along with a number of trash-filled pits and middens that have yielded artifacts and food materials. Documentary research has uncovered new information in archives in Spain, Mexico, California, and Arizona. As a result of this research, the biographies of several hundred Tucson Presidio families have been compiled, the northeast corner of the presidio and the mission gardens have been re-created for a historical parks, and a better understanding of daily life within the presidio has been developed.

THE PIMERÍA ALTA

The Pimería Alta was the northern lands of the Spanish Empire in what is now northern Mexico and the American Southwest (Figure 12.1). The region is mountainous in places, mostly desert, with occasional oases where water can be obtained close to the surface. In the seventeenth century, the region was sparsely occupied by Native Americans living in small settlements called *rancherías*. Pima or O'odham residents practiced subsistence agriculture while continuing to hunt wild game and collect wild plants (Officer et al. 1996).

Father Eusebio Francisco Kino, a Jesuit priest, was the first European to extensively explore the Pimería Alta (see chapter by Lauren E. Jelinek and Dale S. Brenneman, chapter 10 in this volume). He was tasked with establishing missions and *visitas*, or smaller satellite churches. Native Americans were expected to settle permanently at the missions, convert to Catholicism, and become productive members of the new society—raising crops, providing labor, and helping protect the missions against other hostile Native Americans (Polzer 1998).

Kino's endeavors resulted in the establishment of over twenty missions at existing Native American settlements before his death in 1711. The missions were slow to develop: the distance from Mexico City and the lack of rich natural resources resulted in little attention being given by the Spanish government. The Jesuit mission church at San Xavier del Bac was finally completed in the 1750s, only to see the Pima Revolt of 1751 empty the area of Spaniards. When they returned they constructed a presidio fortress at the village of Tubac, situated north of the Mission of Tumacacori and south of Bac. The presence of Spanish soldiers allowed for the return of Catholic clergy to Bac, and afterward the Spaniards had a relatively good relationship with the local O'odham and Pima (Officer 1989).

THE SAN AGUSTÍN MISSION

Father Kino visited the O'odham village of S-cuk Son in the late 1690s. The village name, roughly translates to "at the base of the black," the black referring to the volcanic mountain immediately west of the village. The bedrock of the mountain forced the Santa Cruz River to the surface, and the residents of the village ran small irrigation ditches to fields of maize, beans, and squash.

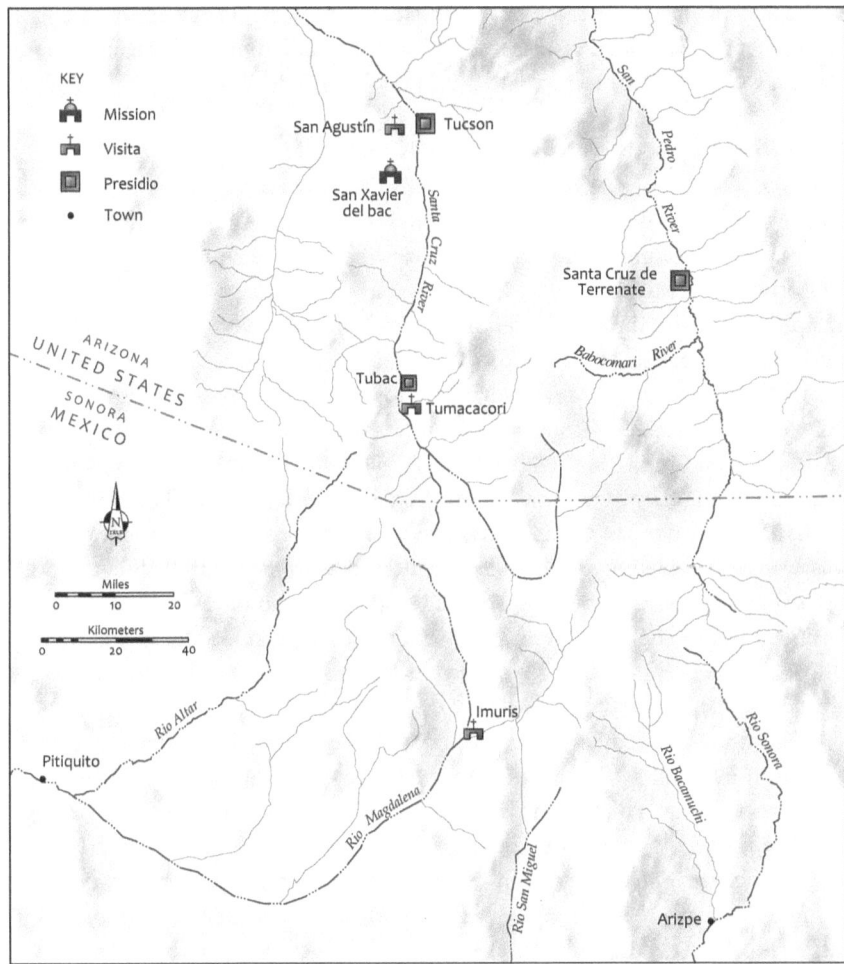

FIGURE 12.1. *Map of the Pimería Alta (prepared by Catherine Gilman, Desert Archaeology, Inc.).*

Kino brought Old World crops, including wheat and fruit trees, as well as cattle, horses, and sheep, to the villagers (Polzer 1998).

Kino selected the village to be a visita of Bac, to the south. The missionaries also planned on opening a trade school to teach the local O'odham crafts, including tanning leather and pottery making, though these endeavors apparently never panned out. The village was occasionally visited by the Spanish priest, but it was not until 1771 that a church, San Agustín, was constructed there, fulfilling the promise made decades earlier by Kino (Dobyns 1976). Throughout the course of its occupation, the San Agustín Mission had problems maintaining a stable population. Contemporary missions throughout the Pimería Alta and

Alta California faced the same problem, a result of periodic epidemics of smallpox and other European diseases, as well as high child mortality (Jackson 1998). Malaria was also a problem in Tucson (Mabry and Thiel 1995).

THE PRESIDIO SAN AGUSTÍN DEL TUCSON

In August 1775, an Irishman named Hugo O'Conor, a captain in the Spanish military, selected the location of the new Presidio San Agustín del Tucson on a terrace overlooking the Santa Cruz River floodplain, a short distance east of the San Agustín Mission. He had been tasked to examine the physical locations of the line of presidio forts extending from Louisiana westward to California, studying each existing fortress to identify deficiencies in its construction and location. Some forts were selected by him for closure, and new locations for presidios were identified. O'Conor's mission was to define the northern boundaries of the Spanish Empire in the New World at a time when other colonial powers were expanding their territorial claims. In the Pimería Alta, conflicts with indigenous Native American groups had to be addressed, and the placement of forts was crucial to providing protection for settlements to the south (Santiago 1994).

During O'Conor's travels, he stopped at the Presidio of Tubac. He found a fortified captain's house surrounded by other dwellings, storehouses, and stables. O'Conor was skeptical that it was defensible against hostile Native American attacks (Santiago 1994).

In the 1770s, the Spaniards were allied with the peaceable O'odham speakers, who lived in small settlements along the Santa Cruz and San Pedro Rivers in southern Arizona. The Spaniards and O'odham were allied against the Apache, who lived primarily in the mountains to the north and regularly traveled south to raid their neighbors in search of livestock, foodstuffs, goods, and captives (Officer et al. 1996). The Apache were heading south, deeper into Sonora, raiding missions, ranches, and mining communities occupied by the Spanish and their Native allies.

O'Conor decided to move the garrison at Tubac. In 1776, sixty soldiers and their families arrived in Tucson from Tubac and built a wooden palisade. Only a handful of these soldiers had been born in Spain; the rest were second- or third-generation (or more) residents of communities along the northern Spanish frontier. The men enlisted for ten-year intervals, often reenlisting at the end of their service since work as a soldier was the only occupation in the region that came with regular pay. Some of the men rose through the ranks, either from family connections or through demonstrated ability, while others served as foot soldiers, spending their spare time raising crops on the Santa Cruz River floodplain. Surviving records indicate that many of the men participated in dozens of expeditions against the Apache. Some would eventually receive invalid pensions as a result of wounds received during these raids. Most would remain in the community after retiring from the military, and in the coming years, their sons would in turn enlist in the military (Thiel 2008c).

The basic outline of early Tucson history can be assembled from surviving records. However, these records fail to provide other kinds of information that can be derived from archaeological excavations. In the remainder of this chapter, I examine both documentary and archaeological evidence of the early presidio and mission history of Tucson. What was life like for the soldiers and civilians who lived at the Presidio San Agustín del Tucson? How did the residents of Tucson cope with their isolation and obtain the items that they needed to negotiate day-to-day existence? Research conducted over the last twenty years can begin to answer these and many other questions about daily life in early Tucson.

BUILDING A FORTRESS

O'Conor's placement of a fortress within the Tucson Basin helped close off the route along the Santa Cruz River used by Apache raiders and protected travelers heading north to the Gila River, while providing an easy base for excursions out into Apache territory. A secondary purpose was to solidify the Spanish claim to the region as British and Russian explorers journeyed up and down the Pacific Coast of California, though this was never tested in the Pimería Alta (Officer 1989:50).

The Tucson Presidio was one of many Spanish settlements in the Pimería Alta. To the south were other presidios, as well as Catholic missions, ranches, mines, and Native American communities. These were scattered sparsely across the landscape, usually along permanent water sources that allowed cultivation of agricultural fields (Officer et al. 1996; see also chapters by Jelinek and Brenneman [10], and Barnet Pavao-Zuckerman [11], this volume). The lack of readily available water sources, as well as the presence of hostile Native Americans, limited the number and size of settlements. At times, conflicts, primarily with the Apache, caused many settlements to be abandoned (Officer 1989; Santiago 1994).

The presidio in Tucson was constructed from locally available materials. Initially, a wooden palisade was constructed, probably of cottonwood and willow trees cut along the Santa Cruz River (Dobyns 1976:60). In May 1782, a large Apache attack nearly succeeded in overwhelming the poorly defended fort. The firing of a cannon by Commander Allande surprised the attacking warriors and apparently ended the battle (McCarty 1976:44). Afterward, ongoing efforts to complete surrounding adobe walls were accelerated, and their construction was completed by the middle of 1783. Three-meter-tall walls enclosed a space measuring about 204 meters across, with large towers on two opposing corners. Archaeological remnants of the adobe foundations indicate that they were fashioned from adobe bricks alternating with layers of puddled adobe that was poured in place to hasten construction (Thiel and Mabry 2006). Soil was mined from the exterior of the fort, creating a shallow ditch along the exterior base of the walls, helping to increase their elevation and retard water erosion of their bases. Soil-mining pits were also located on the adjacent floodplain (Thiel 2008a). These soil-mining pits were then used for trash disposal and were the source of much of the archaeological materials recovered during the presidio excavations (Thiel 2008b; Thiel and Mabry 2006). Cattail pollen was recovered from the adobes, indicating that water was drawn from the irrigation canals on the floodplain for construction purposes (Thiel et al. 1995).

The interior of the presidio's walls was lined with dwellings, stables, storehouses, and granaries, with a church centered along the east wall. The commandant's residence was located near the center of the fort, adjacent to a plaza where soldiers drilled. These structures were also built from adobe bricks, most set directly on the ground surface (Thiel et al. 1995). Pine trees for roof *vigas* were cut on the Santa Rita Mountains, about sixty-five kilometers to the south. Two large meteorites were also found in the Santa Ritas in the 1820s and were transported back to Tucson where they were used as blacksmith's anvils (Willey 1987). Cattle hides served as door coverings, and dwellings lacked window glass. Given the small available workforce, it seems likely that at least some of the labor to construct the presidio was conducted by local Native Americans.

THE PEOPLE OF THE PRESIDIO

About sixty soldiers and their families were the first residents of the presidio. Spanish officials were very interested in racial classifications, and this was the case early on in the fort's history. Among the initial inhabitants were twelve Spaniards (of Spanish ancestry), ten *coyotes* (of Spanish and Native American ancestry), three *moriscos* (of African and Spanish ancestry), and one *mulatto* (also of African and Spanish ancestry) (Dobyns 1976:153). Enlistment records indicate continued use of such racial categorization into the 1790s, but afterward race classifications largely disappear from documents generated at the presidio.

Population counts were collected in censuses during the years the presidio was occupied, though these often failed to include local Native Americans. In 1797, there were 295 people present: 101 soldiers, 110 family members, and 84 other civilians (Collins 1970; Dobyns 1972). In 1831 there were 465 residents of the presidio, 193 in civilian households and 272 in military households (McCarty 1981a, 1981b). In 1848, 760 people were counted (Officer 1989:214). An 1851 cholera epidemic killed 122 residents of the community (Officer 1989:387).

After about 1800, few of the newly recruited soldiers came from outside Tucson. Instead, the sons of presidio soldiers were enlisting. No women were arriving from outside the community. As a result, only a handful of potential spouses were available for each man or woman in Tucson. Most residents were of mixed-race ancestry, and people were compelled to not take into account a person's racial background when looking for a husband or wife within the small community (Thiel 2008c). An identical, concurrent pattern of upward movement and abandonment of the caste system also took place in California (Haley and Wilcoxon 2005; Voss 2005). Despite the lack of eligible partners, one custom did remain—residents did not marry local Native Americans.

NATIVE AMERICAN INTERACTIONS

Tucson has been the home of Native Americans for over 4,000 years. The Santa Cruz River floodplain was the location of irrigation agriculture for the last 3,200 years (Thiel and Mabry 2006). When Father Kino visited the Native American village of S-cuk Son, he was impressed by the potential of its agricultural fields. Hugo O'Conor probably viewed this Native American community as a source of potential labor and its agricultural lands as a source of food.

The San Agustín Mission village was primarily occupied by local O'odham. In 1762, the Sobaipuri Pima moved from their villages along the San Pedro River to the mission to escape Apache attacks (Officer 1989:40). The mission population fluctuated due to losses from disease and emigration to other communities. An 1801 census lists 190 Papago, 25 Pima, and 6 Gileño residents living at the mission (University of Arizona Main Library, Parish Archives of Sonora and Sinaloa, Mexico, Microfilm 811, reel 3). Crops and livestock raised by the mission community were sold to the presidio at a reduced cost (McCarty 1997). Smashed cattle bones found at San Agustín indicate tallow production was taking place, the product likely sold to the military or to miners working to the south, useful for greasing wooden wagon axles and the pulleys used to haul ore from mine shafts (Pavao-Zuckerman 2011, and chapter 11 in this volume).

The San Agustín Mission residents and their relatives at Bac often teamed up with the Spaniards in raids against their traditional enemy, the Apache. The Apache frequently attacked O'odham villages in search of food, livestock, goods, and captives. After the arrival of the Spaniards, they frequently attacked the presidio and its nearby fields, killing residents and running off livestock. This antagonistic relationship intensified after the construction of the new presidios at Terrenate and Tucson, and the Spaniards often sent out parties to hunt down and kill Apache in their homes in the mountains north and east of Tucson (Officer 1989).

In 1792, the Spanish government agreed to provide a group of Apache with food, clothing, and tools in exchange for a guarantee that they would live peaceably at the presidio. The *manso* Apache settled northwest of the fort and maintained a fragile truce with the local O'odham (Dobyns 1976:98; McCarty 1976:61–63). The Manso Apache served as a conduit of information, warning the fort when they heard that their mountain relatives were planning raids (Officer 1989; McCarty 1997).

Presidio residents traded extensively with the local O'odham and the Manso Apaches. Besides labor, the Native Americans offered firewood, hay, wild game, and gathered foodstuffs including cactus fruit, saguaro syrup, and mesquite flour. Residents of the fort could also obtain these items through their own efforts, though it made more sense to rely on the Native Americans. When recovered from archaeological deposits, the exact origins of these items are impossible to determine; a plausible explanation, however, is that they were derived through exchange with Native Americans.

In contrast, it is easy to recognize local pottery traded by Native Americans to the fort residents. The Sobaipuri Pima manufactured vessels with a distinctive folded rim. Local O'odham began to add manure to pottery by the 1820s, resulting in a black core that allowed water to slowly seep through the vessel, evaporating on the exterior and cooling the vessel contents (Fontana et al. 1962). These characteristics make remains of these products relatively easy to identify in the archaeological record. One of the problems faced by the people of Tucson was the difficulty and cost of importing metal cookware. Iron or brass cooking pots were heavy; expensive; and, when broken, hard to replace. There is no evidence for the production of ceramic vessels by the Spaniards living in the presidio. As a result, O'odham potters at San Xavier del Bac produced and traded to the Spaniards bean pots, which were used for cooking stews and soups, and large bowls, which were used for serving (Figure 12.2). Native Americans also began creating two new vessel forms based upon Spanish prototypes. Flat ceramic *comales* were used as replacements for iron tortilla griddles, and ceramic mugs replaced copper *chocolatero* pots (Heidke 2006). Both were important to Tucson residents, with wheat tortillas and hot, frothy chocolate beverages representing high-status, culturally significant foodstuffs for the soldiers and civilians living within the fortress walls. Chocolate was sent up to the Tucson Presidio in hard blocks. It was a luxurious necessity, a comfort food in difficult times often fed to the sick and one that melted in Tucson's fierce summer heat (Cabezon et al. 2009).

In exchange for these items, the presidio residents offered fabric, brass buttons and buckles, beads, religious medallions, manufactured clothing, blankets, weapons, ammunition, and tools to their Native American allies. Examples of some of these trade goods have been found at the contemporaneous O'odham sites of Guevavi Mission, the San Xavier Mission, and the San Agustín Mission (Robinson 1963; Seymour 2012; Wasley 1956).

In 1795, the Tucson Presidio commander, José de Zúñiga, led an expedition to New Mexico, stopping at the Zuni villages about 300 miles to the north (Officer 1989:68). It seems likely that the soldiers traded items to the Zuni in exchange for a few black-on-white or polychrome ceramic vessels, fragments of which have been found in the presidio (Figure 12.3). The vessels would have contrasted sharply with the red ware and plain ware vessels produced in the Tucson area. A

FIGURE 12.2. *A Piman bean pot found in a trash-filled pit inside the Tucson Presidio (photograph by Homer Thiel).*

small number of Puebloan ceramics from Arizona and New Mexico have been found at most of the Spanish sites in southern Arizona, and are also found at some late prehistoric- and historical-period Native American sites (Ferg 2004). In addition, a limited amount of trade appears to have taken place between the Native American communities; however, the scale and scope of this exchange are not currently well understood (see chapter by Jelinek and Brenneman [chapter 10 in this volume).

PRESIDIO MATERIAL CULTURE

Where did residents get the other items they needed for day-to-day living? The residents of the presidio manufactured only a few items in Tucson. For example, an 1804 report lists only serge fabric and wool blankets produced locally (McCarty 1976:85). The nearest stores where goods could be obtained were in Arizpe. Materials and goods purchased in Arizpe would have been carried north about 230 kilometers by freight wagons and pack trains to the presidio company store and the privately run store at the presidio. An 1804 report explicitly states that no goods were received from San Blas, which supplied the majority of goods obtained by presidios and missions in California (McCarty 1976:85; Perissinotto 1998:18). Supplies were also ordered annually from Mexico City and

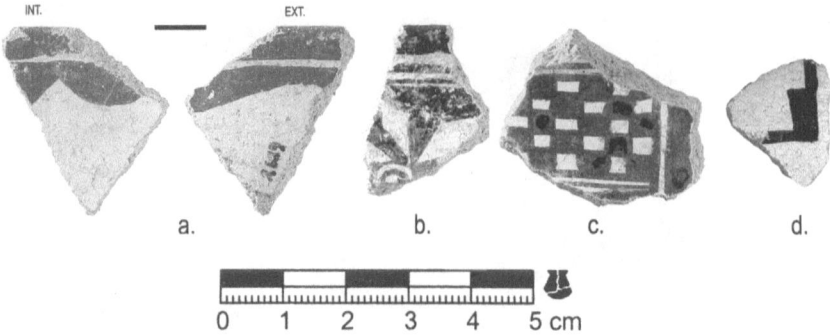

FIGURE 12.3. *Northern Puebloan ceramic sherds found in the Tucson Presidio (photograph by Robert Ciaccio).*

were brought north by agents to Arizpe. Soldiers were expected to purchase their own uniform, weapons, and horses, as well as whatever household goods they could afford (Sugnet 1994:21).

Soldiers traveled to Arizpe monthly to collect the fort's payroll and bring back supplies (Thiel 2005). Few records survive to tell what items were brought back to Tucson. Wax (probably for candles), soap, and chocolate were available at the company store (McCarty 1976:89–90). The Gach store records list a few items sent to Tucson, chief among these was chocolate (Sugnet 1994).

The most common manufactured Spanish goods recovered at the presidio are fragments of colorful majolica dishes made in Mexico (Figure 12.4). Bowls and plates were apparently preferred, with only a few pieces of cups identified. The dishes found in early archaeological contexts are mostly in blue-on-white patterns, some with images of birds in the center of the vessel. These were probably designed to resemble Chinese porcelain or Dutch Delftware vessels. After about 1800, polychrome vessels, with elaborate green and yellow floral sprays or multicolored dots on a light blue background, became popular (Lister and Lister 1982).

Why carry these fragile dishes hundreds of miles to the north from pottery factories to the isolated frontier fortress? Analyses of records for majolica imported into Alta California suggests these were relatively inexpensive and were likely not high-status goods (Voss 2012). For the women of the Tucson Presidio, the symbolism of these vessels was likely a factor. It is easy to imagine that the 100 or so adult women living in Tucson would have wanted to serve meals from the same types of dishes that their mothers and grandmothers had used back in communities to the south in Sonora and further into Mexico. Dining from majolica dishes was something that respectable families did. Majolica is not common at eighteenth- and nineteenth-century Native American sites, with only a

FIGURE 12.4. *Brightly colored Mexican majolica vessels were used by women at the Tucson Presidio to serve meals (photograph by Homer Thiel).*

handful of fragments recovered from the nearby contemporaneous San Agustín Mission (Thiel 2006). At the San Francisco Presidio, uniformity in food preparation and service also took place, both to minimize cultural differences among the residents and to set themselves apart from local Native Americans (Voss 2005), and a similar situation may have existed at the Tucson Presidio.

Other items originating from Mexico that are known to have been brought to Tucson included sturdy glazed cooking bowls, horse gear, and some goods that have left no physical traces, including cloth and blocks of chocolate. Collections at the Arizona Historical Society and the Arizona State Museum in Tucson have numerous examples of bridles, stirrups, and spurs found by ranchers out in the deserts throughout southern Arizona (Thiel 2006). Each presidio soldier was expected to have several horses and a pack mule, and horse gear was likely occasionally lost during expeditions or while managing the presidio's large herds of cattle, horses, and sheep.

Some goods were manufactured in Europe and brought on ships to Mexico then carried north. These included weapons (muskets, pistols, lances, cannons, and ammunition), exotic food stuffs (olive oil, wine, and spices), cloth, buttons, buckles, books, religious paraphernalia, beads, and fine-toothed bone combs (Di Peso 1953).

Clothing-related artifacts found at the presidio include a few brass buttons, some clothing buckles, and beads. One account described how the poorest Sonoran residents wanted to dress above their class (Pfefferkorn 1949:287–88).

Presidio-era documents indicate that each soldier was required to purchase a complete uniform each year and that most owned only a single set of clothes. Members of the Mormon Battalion, who marched to the community in 1846, reported that they traded thread, cloth, and buttons to eager Tucson residents for food (Officer 1989). One might expect to find some of these clothing items in burials in the presidio cemetery. This cemetery is located on the east side of the fort around and beneath the presidio chapel and was in use from roughly 1776 to the 1850s. Burials from the cemetery were excavated in 1969 and 1970 by the Arizona State Museum and in 1991 by Desert Archaeology, Inc. (Thiel et al. 1995). Most interments were wrapped in shrouds, as seen by pins or brass staining, and only a handful of buttons were recovered. It is likely that clothing was so valuable that it was passed down to family members rather than buried with the deceased. Pieces of copper wire were found near the heads of two children in the cemetery, and excavations at the nearby National Cemetery, used from the late 1850s to 1875, revealed that many children were buried with wreaths made from artificial flowers attached to a copper frame. This represents the Catholic tradition of Los Angelitos ("the little angels"), emphasizing the purity and innocence of children, who went directly to heaven at death, bypassing purgatory (Heilen et al. 2010; Thiel et al. 1995:111, 115).

Religious artifacts are occasionally found at Spanish-era sites in southern Arizona. A religious medallion and forty-four small glass beads were found in a soil-mining pit next to the Tucson Presidio. The medallion bore the embossed inscription "Corazon de Jesus y de Maria" (the "Heart of Jesus and Mary") and was worn by followers of Saint Juan Eudes (Thiel 2008b:65–66) Most of these religious artifacts were likely made in Europe. In contrast, the carved statues of saints often found in the missions in southern Arizona were likely constructed in artisan's studios in Mexico.

Although presidio soldiers carried weapons as part of their daily routines, and weapons are frequently mentioned in contemporary documents, only a trigger guard and a ramrod holder have been found in the Spanish-period deposits excavated within the Tucson Presidio (Brinckerhoff and Chamberlain 1972; Thiel 2006). In contrast, during the 1950s excavations at the contemporary Terrenate Presidio, located to the east on the San Pedro River, numerous gun parts were found that were left behind in 1781 when the fort was abandoned due to incessant Apache raids (Di Peso 1956). Gunstock brass decorations that would have adorned the wooden stocks of muskets were found in several rooms. In the early 2000s, Archaeology Southwest developed a public outreach and education program called the Coronado Project. As part of this project, they held a series of events, called "Coronado Roadshows" (Thiel 2006). At these events, Archaeology Southwest staff invited residents of Arizona and New Mexico to bring in Spanish-era artifacts in for identification and discussion (Thiel 2006).

FIGURE 12.5. *Religious medal and forty-four European glass beads found in a soil-mining pit adjacent to the Tucson Presidio. Photograph by Robert Ciaccio.*

At one of these events, a man from New Mexico brought in a Spanish *escopeta* that had been found in a crack in a cliff face in the 1940s (Figure 12.6). The musket was perfectly preserved, with the leather wrapping of the gunflint still in place, and elaborate brass appliqués attached to the stock. It is likely that the soldiers at Tucson had similar weapons and that the brass decorations found at the Terrenate Presidio would have adorned firearms used at that fort in a manner very similar to the weapon shown in Figure 12.5.

Spain cut off trade relations with Mexico after that nation achieved independence in 1821. England then became an ally of Mexico and a new source for trade goods. It had been suspected that soldiers at Tucson used British-made

FIGURE 12.6. *Brass gunstock appliqués on an escopeta found in New Mexico. Photograph by Homer Thiel.*

Brown Bess muskets, but evidence was lacking until the excavation in 1999 of the Francisco Solano León farmstead, located a few hundred meters to the northwest of the presidio. León served in the Mexican military in the 1840s and 1850s, and an English-made Brown Bess trigger guard was found in a soil-mining pit next to his home (Thiel 2005).

Gun flints used in flintlock muskets and pistols had traditionally been manufactured in France. At times, these were difficult to obtain or perhaps too expensive to purchase. Enterprising soldiers or civilians in Tucson made their own from locally available chert. Those flints that were worn out were then reused as strike-a-lights (Sliva et al. 2008).

The overall lack of metal artifacts in Presidio-era features and deposits suggests that recycling of iron and brass items was important. Other recycling was discovered when excavations inside the Presidio blacksmith shop, located on the west side of the fort just south of the Main Gate, led to the discovery of four pieces of prehistoric groundstone on the shop floor. The presidio is built atop a prehistoric site dating to the Early Agricultural and Hohokam Pre-Classic Periods (ca. 400 BC to AD 1150). When examined under a microscope, traces of copper were found pounded into the surface of the groundstones. The blacksmith was using the prehistoric tools, working on the surface of his meteorite anvil, to turn scrap metal into useful items for the presidio residents (Heidke et al. 2004).

After 1821, a small number of transfer-printed ceramics began to arrive in the community from England (Thiel 2005). Decorated with romanticized scenes of faraway places—including cathedrals, bridges, forests, and people—they were basically the only source of information about what the outside world looked like. There were few books in the community, and probably the only illustrated ones were religious texts and songbooks housed at the Catholic churches in the presidio, at the Mission of San Agustín, or at the San Xavier Mission. These were likely largely unseen by the general public. Paintings and statues held in churches were at least visible, but provided little information about contemporary fashions or the outside world. Clues about the use of such ceramics can be gleaned from the excavations of the León family farmstead (Thiel 2005). Excavation of the home yielded brightly colored transfer-print dishes. One can imagine Ramona Elias de León, whose husband, Francisco Solano León, served at the presidio in the 1840s and 1850s, serving her guests hot chocolate in her decorated cups from England, and family friends and presidio personnel eagerly examining the clothing styles and architecture depicted on the vessels.

The farthest trade items brought into the Tucson Presidio were fragile Chinese porcelain cups, carried by vessels from China to Manila and from Manila to Acapulco on the western coast of Mexico, and then carried north on pack trains to the presidio (Robinson and Barnes 1976:161). Only a few pieces of the delicate porcelain have been found in Tucson, suggesting it was a rare luxury item, perhaps used by the better-paid military officers (Barnes 1983).

CONCLUSIONS

Life in the Tucson Presidio was harsh and unpredictable. The military and civilian residents of the presidio had to learn to adapt to the challenges of the Sonoran Desert, the isolation due to their position on the northern frontier, and frequent conflicts with the Apache that created problems with the movement of goods (see Pavao-Zuckerman, chapter 11 in this volume). In response, residents appear to have followed a conservative and frugal approach to life. The material culture and food remains that are found at the presidio indicate practicality, the retention of customs in a new community, and the opportunities presented by a close relationship between the presidio soldiers and civilians and local Native American groups.

When possible, local resources were exploited, especially for building materials and foods, bulky items that would have been impractical to move long distances. The presidio residents offered manufactured goods to O'odham and Apache in exchange for firewood, fodder, foods, ceramic vessels, and information. Money paid by the Spanish or Mexican government to the fort or earned by presidio soldiers was used to purchase necessities from distant shops, things such as arms, ammunition, and clothing, along with a few luxury items such as chocolate and spices. Majolica dishes, which today might seem to be a luxury, were likely viewed as a necessity by presidio housewives, needed to express family roots deeper into New Spain and Mexico. The distance to stores, the dangers and difficulties inherent in transporting goods, and their high cost led to a frugal existence, one where recycling and reuse was an everyday activity. For eighty-one years, residents of the Presidio San Agustín del Tucson endured the harsh conditions of the Sonoran Desert, and while many left for Mexico after the arrival of Americans in 1856, many also stayed and continued on within the community.

REFERENCES CITED

Barnes, Mark R. 1983. "Tucson: Development of a Community." PhD dissertation, Department of Anthropology, Catholic University of America, Washington, DC. Ann Arbor, MI: University Microfilms International.

Brinckerhoff, Sidney B., and Pierce A. Chamberlain. 1972. *Spanish Military Weapons in Colonial America 1700–1821*. Harrisburg: Stackpole Books.

Cabezon, Beatriz, Patricia Barriga, and Louis Evan Grivetti. 2009. "Blood, Conflict, and Faith: Chocolate in the Southeast and Southwest Borderlands, 1641–1833." In *Chocolate! History, Culture, and Heritage*, edited by Louis Evan Grivetti and Howard-Yana Shapiro, 425–37. Hoboken, NJ: John Wiley and Sons. http://dx.doi.org/10.1002/9780470411315.ch33.

Collins, Karen Sikes. 1970. "Fray Pedro de Arriquibar's Census of Tucson, 1820." *Journal of Arizona History* 11 (1): 14–22.

Di Peso, Charles C. 1953. *The Sobaipuri Indians of the Upper San Pedro River Valley, Southeastern Arizona*. Amerind Foundation Publications 6. Dragoon, AZ: Amerind Foundation.

Di Peso, Charles C. 1956. *The Upper Pima of San Cayetano del Tumacacori: An Archaeohistorical Reconstruction of the Ootam of the Pimeria Alta*. Amerind Foundation Archaeology Series 7. Dragoon, Arizona: Amerind Foundation.

Dobyns, Henry F. 1972. "The 1797 Population of the Presidio of Tucson." *Journal of Arizona History* 13 (3): 205–9.

Dobyns, Henry F. 1976. *Spanish Colonial Tucson: A Demographic History*. Tucson: University of Arizona Press.

Ferg, Alan. 2004. "Pueblo Trade with Santa Cruz Villages, circa 1350–1900." *Archaeology Southwest* 18 (4): 10.

Fontana, Bernard L., William J. Robinson, Charles W. Cormack, and Ernest E. Leavitt Jr. 1962. *Papago Indian Pottery*. Seattle: University of Washington Press.

Haley, Brian D., and Larry R. Wilcoxon. 2005. "How Spaniards Became Chumash and Other Tales of Ethnogenesis." *American Anthropologist* 107 (3): 432–45. http://dx.doi.org/10.1525/aa.2005.107.3.432.

Heidke, James M. 2006. "Native American Pottery." In *Rio Nuevo Archaeology, 2000–2003: Investigations at the San Agustín Mission and Mission Gardens, Tucson Presidio, Tucson Pressed Brick Company, and Clearwater Site*, edited by J. Homer Thiel and Jonathan B. Mabry, 7.1–7.94. Technical Report No. 2004-11. Tucson: Desert Archaeology.

Heidke, James M., J. Homer Thiel, and Jenny L. Adams. 2004. "Artifacts." In *Uncovering Tucson's Past: Test Excavations in Search of the Presidio Wall*, by J. Homer Thiel, 67–83. Technical Report No. 2002–05. Tucson: Desert Archaeology.

Heilen, Michael, Joseph T. Hefner, and Mitchell A. Keur. 2010. *Deathways and Lifeways in the American Southwest, Tucson's Historic Alameda-Stone Cemetery and the Transformation of a Remote Outpost into an Urban City. The History, Archaeology, and Skeletal Biology of the Alameda-Stone Cemetery*, vol. 2. Technical Report 96-10. Tucson, Arizona: Statistical Research.

Jackson, Robert H. 1998. "Northwestern New Spain: The Pimería Alta and the Californians." In *New Views of Borderlands History*, edited by Robert H. Jackson, 41–72. Albuquerque: University of New Mexico Press.

Lister, Florence C., and Robert H. Lister. 1982. *Sixteenth Century Majolica Pottery in the Valley of Mexico. Anthropological Papers 39*. Tucson: University of Arizona Press.

Mabry, Jonathan B., and J. Homer Thiel. 1995. "A Thousand Years of Irrigation in Tucson." *Archaeology in Tucson*. 9 (4): 1–6.

McCarty, Kieran. 1976. *Desert Documentary. Historical Monograph 4*. Tucson: Arizona Historical Society.

McCarty, Kieran. 1981a. "Tucson Census of 1831." *Copper State Bulletin* 16 (1): 5–9.

McCarty, Kieran. 1981b. "Tucson Census of 1831." *Copper State Bulletin* 16 (2): 41–47.

McCarty, Kieran. 1997. *A Frontier Documentary: Sonora and Tucson, 1821–1848*. Tucson: University of Arizona Press.

Officer, James E. 1989. *Hispanic Tucson, 1536–1856*. Tucson: University of Arizona Press.

Officer, James E., Mardith Schuetz-Miller, and Bernard L. Fontana, eds. 1996. *The Pimería Alta*. Tucson: Southwestern Mission Research Center.

Pavao-Zuckerman, Barnet. 2011. "Rendering Economies: Native American Labor and Secondary Animal Products in the Eighteenth Century Pimería Alta." *American Antiquity* 76 (1): 3–23. http://dx.doi.org/10.7183/0002-7316.76.1.3.

Perissinotto, Giorgio, ed. 1998. *Documenting Everyday Life in Early Spanish California: The Santa Barbara Presidio Memorias y Facturas, 1779–1810*. Santa Barbara: Santa Barbara Trust for Historic Preservation.

Pfefferkorn, Ignaz. 1949. *Sonora: A Description of the Province*, translated and annotated by Theodore. E. Treutlein. Albuquerque: University of New Mexico Press.

Polzer, Charles W. 1998. *Kino, a Legacy: His Life, His Works, His Missions, His Monuments*. Tucson: Jesuit Fathers of Southern Arizona.

Robinson, William J. 1963. "Excavations at San Xavier del Bac, 1958." *Kiva* 29 (2): 35–57. http://dx.doi.org/10.1080/00231940.1963.11757651.

Robinson, William J., and Mark R. Barnes. 1976. "Mission Guevavi: Excavations in the Convento." *Kiva* 42 (2): 135–75. http://dx.doi.org/10.1080/00231940.1976.11757872.

Santiago, Mark. 1994. *The Red Captain: The Life of Hugo O'Conor, Commandant Inspector of the Interior Provinces of New Spain*. Tucson: Arizona Historical Society.

Seymour, Deni J. 2012. *Where the Earth and Sky Are Sewn Together: Sobaipuri-O'odham Contexts of Contact and Colonialism*. Salt Lake City: University of Utah Press.

Sliva, R. Jane, Jenny L. Adams, and J. Homer Thiel. 2008. "Flaked Stone, Ground Stone, and Manufactured Artifacts from Historic Block 185." In *Archaeological Investigations at AZ BB:13:756 (ASM) and AZ BB:13:757 (ASM), Historic Block 185, Tucson, Pima County, Arizona*, edited by J. Homer Thiel, 55–70. Technical Report No. 2006-09. Tucson, Arizona: Desert Archaeology.

Sugnet, Christopher L. 1994. "Hispanic Ceramics from Santa Cruz de Terrenate." Master's thesis, Department of Anthropology, University of Arizona, Tucson.

Thiel, J. Homer. 1996. *A Summary of Archaeological Investigations in Sunset Park, Tucson, Arizona*. Technical Report No. 96-10. Tucson, Arizona: Center for Desert Archaeology.

Thiel, J. Homer. 2004. *Uncovering Tucson's Past: Test Excavations in Search of the Presidio Wall*. Technical Report No. 2002–05. Tucson: Desert Archaeology.

Thiel, J. Homer. 2005. *Down by the River: Archaeological and Historical Studies of the León Family Farmstead. Anthropological Papers No. 38*. Tucson: Center for Desert Archaeology.

Thiel, J. Homer. 2006. "The Coronado Roadshow." *Archaeology Southwest* 19 (1): 7–8.

Thiel, J. Homer. 2008a. *Additional Archaeological and Historical Research in the Tucson Presidio, Historic Block 181, Tucson, Pima County, Arizona*. Technical Report No. 2006–10. Tucson: Desert Archaeology.

Thiel, J. Homer. 2008b. Archaeological Investigations at AZ BB:13:756 (ASM) and AZ BB:13:757 (ASM), Historic Block 185, Tucson, Pima County, Arizona. Technical Report No. 2006-09. Tucson: Desert Archaeology.

Thiel, J. Homer. 2008c. "Pioneer Families of the Presidio San Agustin del Tucson." Accessed December 16, 2013. http://www.archaeologysouthwest.org/pdf/presidio_families.pdf.

Thiel, J. Homer, Michael K. Faught, and James M. Bayman. 1995. *Beneath the Streets: Prehistoric, Spanish, and American Period Archaeology in Downtown Tucson*. Technical Report No. 94-11. Tucson: Center for Desert Archaeology.

Thiel, J. Homer, and Jonathan B. Mabry, eds. 2006. *Rio Nuevo Archaeology, 2000–2003: Investigations at the San Agustín Mission and Mission Gardens, Tucson Presidio, Tucson Pressed Brick Company, and Clearwater Site*. Technical Report No. 2004-11. Tucson: Desert Archaeology.

Voss, Barbara. 2005. "From Casta to Californio: Social Identity and the Archaeology of Culture Contact." *American Anthropologist* 107 (3): 461–74. http://dx.doi.org/10.1525/aa.2005.107.3.461.

Voss, Barbara. 2012. "Status and Ceramics in Spanish Colonial Archaeology." *Historical Archaeology* 46 (2): 39–54.

Wasley, William W. 1956. "History and Archaeology in Tucson." Manuscript A-767. Manuscript on file, Arizona State Museum, Tucson.

Willey, Richard R. 1987. *The Tucson Meteorites: Their History from Frontier Arizona to the Smithsonian*. Tucson: University of Arizona Press.

THIRTEEN

O'odham Irrigated Agriculture Response to Colonization on the Middle Gila River, Southern Arizona

COLLEEN STRAWHACKER

INTRODUCTION

Colonization has been shown to have sweeping effects on indigenous households in different parts of the world, including Sub-Saharan Africa, Mexico, the southeastern United States, and the southwestern United States, where many of these indigenous groups are subsistence farmers (e.g., Netting et al. 1989; Pavao-Zuckerman 2007; Pavao-Zuckerman and LaMotta 2007; Spielmann 1989; Spielmann et al. 2009; Stone 1994; VanDerwarker et al. 2013). Previously, much of the research regarding colonization focused on the destructive effects that colonization had on indigenous subsistence farmers, including the decimation of population due to introduced diseases, the acculturation of indigenous groups into the colonial regime, and the loss of agricultural biodiversity as indigenous farmers increased their focus on introduced cash crops (e.g., Bolton 1919; Corkran 1967; Hackenberg 1962; Russell 1908; Swanton 1998). In recent decades, however, archaeologists and ethnographers have shown how indigenous communities frequently act as dynamic responders, not passive recipients, to these colonizing groups, sometimes resulting in significant economic success for them.

DOI: 10.5876/9781607325741.c013

"Economic success" here is defined as an indigenous group being able to maintain economic independence from colonizing groups (DeJong 2009; Kowalewski 2006; Netting et al. 1989; Pavao-Zuckerman and LaMotta 2007; VanDerwarker et al. 2013).

While valuable research has been done on the impacts of Spanish colonization on indigenous southwestern populations (e.g., Pavao-Zuckerman and LaMotta 2007; Pavao-Zuckerman 2011; Sheridan 2006; Spielmann et al. 2006, 2009; Tarcan 2005), their groups of focus, including the Salinas pueblos along the Rio Grande and O'odham groups in extreme southern Arizona, were under the direct control of the Spanish missions, resulting in forced tribute payments and new subsistence strategies. The O'odham along the middle Gila River, however, provide an interesting counterpoint to this research. During the 1700s and early 1800s, the majority of Spanish population and influence was restricted to extreme southern Arizona, mostly focused in areas south of Tucson (Figure 13.1), where missions, such as San Xavier del Bac and Tumacácori, exerted control over indigenous populations in the region (Bolton 1919; see also Lauren E. Jelinek and Dale S. Brenneman, chapter 10 in this volume).

Due to fear of Apache raiding along the middle Gila River Valley, the Spanish never missionized the middle Gila River, and the Gila O'odham remained peripheral to colonial developments in the Pimería Alta (Wells et al. 2004; Wilson 1999), leading to differences in the economic development between the O'odham along the middle Gila River and indigenous groups in other parts of the Southwest. The Gila O'odham, then, represented a frontier for the Spanish moving into the Pimería Alta. Despite being a frontier region, however, historic documents indicate that the Gila O'odham were actively trading with the Spanish to the south, mostly through other indigenous groups in the Pimería Alta (Dunne 1955; Ezell 1961), but because they were never missionized, they were not subject to tribute payments to the Spanish (Wilson 1999). Thus, research on the Gila O'odham reactions to colonization can help clarify how groups changed in contexts in which indigenous groups were not under direct control of their colonizing groups.

The O'odham along the middle Gila River also had access to plenty of irrigable land and perennial water, unlike their indigenous neighbors to the south, allowing for productive agricultural land and the potential to irrigate, like their Hohokam ancestors (see Woodson 2010 for extensive background on prehistoric irrigation agriculture along the middle Gila). The Hohokam built the largest irrigation system in the New World north of Peru prior to Spanish contact, which resulted in the production of prodigious amounts of surplus for these desert dwellers. Uncertainty exists concerning the relationship between the prehistoric Hohokam and the historic O'odham in the Phoenix Basin, and archaeological evidence from the period after the Hohokam collapse (ca. 1450) and before first contact with the Spanish by Eusebio Kino in 1694 is scant (Loendorf 2010).

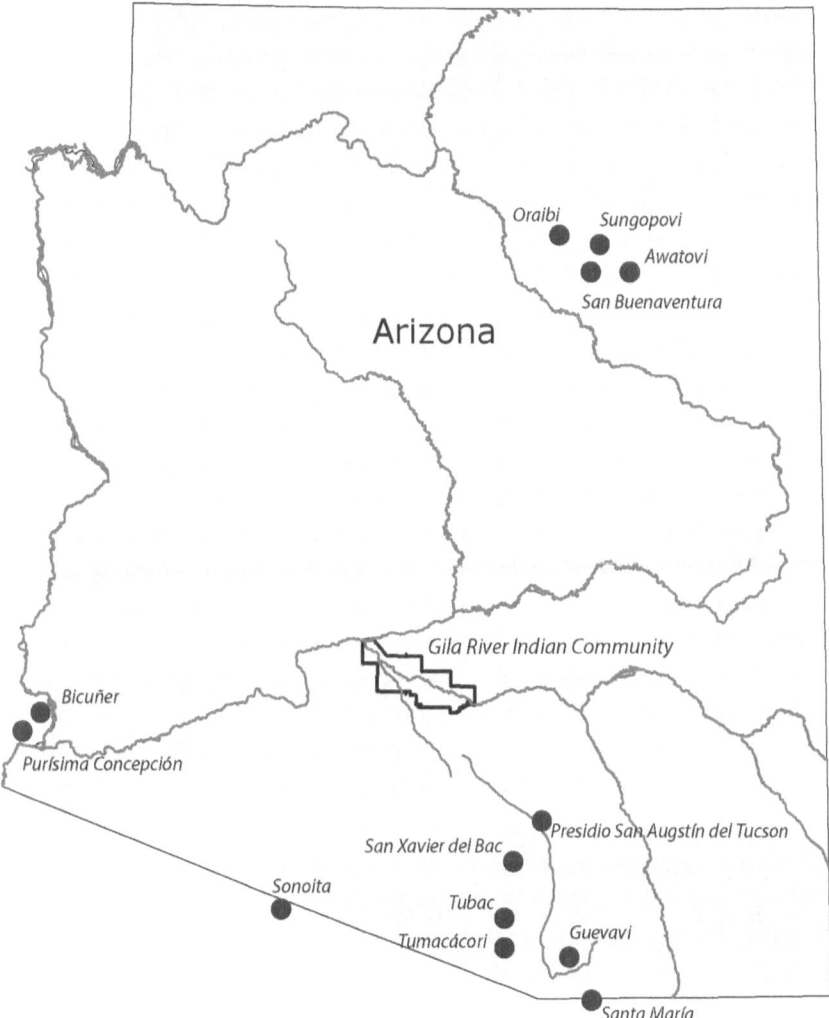

FIGURE 13.1. Map of major Spanish missions and presidios in Arizona and the study area of focus in this chapter. Note the isolation of the Gila River Indian Community from Spanish settlements.

Despite the uncertainly in connection between the Hohokam and O'odham, historic documents can provide insight into how the O'odham altered their agricultural system in response to colonization. These documents indicate that throughout the 1700 and 1800s, the Gila O'odham adapted to incoming Spanish and American groups in ways that resulted in great economic success (DeJong 2009). Historic documents are replete with numerous accounts of how the Spanish and, later, Americans relied on the agricultural production of the O'odham for food and materials (e.g., Dobyns 1961). *How, then, did the O'odham adapt their agricultural system to the influx of new people, crops, and markets into the middle Gila River?* Using demographic, archaeological, and historical data from Spanish and American sources, I argue in this chapter that the O'odham successfully intensified agricultural production throughout the 1700 and 1800s to meet the market demands of incoming Spanish missionaries and American explorers, resulting in great economic success for the O'odham.

The middle Gila River is now managed by the Gila River Indian Community (GRIC; Figure 13.1) providing an excellent opportunity to study the social and ecological effects of the transition from subsistence agriculture to a market economy during the historic period, because the Gila O'odham provide (1) a case study of direct versus indirect colonial impacts on economic strategies, (2) an example study of agricultural intensification in a colonial context, and (3) a reimplementation of strategies of intensification from their prehistoric Hohokam ancestors. With the city of Phoenix rapidly growing outward into the desert formerly managed by the Hohokam and now the O'odham, the GRIC has prevented urbanization along the middle Gila River, preserving archaeological resources that can be linked to historic sources to understand the economic, social, and environmental dynamics during colonization. The chronology used in this chapter is based on major external events that affected O'odham economic strategies. The early historic, or Spanish/Mexican period, ranged from 1684 to 1848. The late historic, or American, period began in 1848 (Wilson 1999).

COLONIZATION AND THE INTENSIFICATION OF RESOURCE PROCUREMENT

Archaeologists working in the US Southwest have documented how indigenous communities adapted to Spanish colonization, including patterns of agricultural intensification, increased animal procurement and processing through the adoption of livestock, and changing crop and, thus, diet diversity (see chapter by Barnet Pavao-Zuckerman, chapter 11 in this volume; Pavao-Zuckerman and LaMotta 2007; Sheridan 1988, 2006; Spielmann 1989; Spielmann et al. 2009; Tarcan 2005; Trigg 2003, 2005). In the northern Southwest, for example, Carmen Tarcan (2005) studied how hunting and diet changed among the Zuni throughout the historic period. The Spanish introduced grazing animals, such as sheep and goats, that the Zuni rapidly adopted, according to zooarchaeological evidence. Tarcan (2005) also found, however, that high amounts of native animals—deer and antelope—were also found in the zooarchaeological assemblage. Tarcan (2005) argues that while the Zuni readily adopted Spanish animals, diet, and technologies, the Zuni also strove to maintain traditional indigenous hunting practices by continuing to hunt deer and antelope.

In southern Arizona, near Tucson, Barnet Pavao-Zuckerman and Vincent LaMotta (Pavao-Zuckerman and LaMotta 2007) argue that the O'odham actively resisted adopting Spanish-introduced livestock during the first part of Spanish missionization. The O'odham around these missions actively slaughtered livestock and refused to participate in their care. They explain, "the O'odham may have viewed the introduction of livestock as a threat to traditional lifeways and intentionally destroyed the animals to repulse that threat. The O'odham had no prior experience with domesticated livestock, and animal husbandry makes demands on labor, scheduling, infrastructure, and land use that were entirely novel to O'odham households" (Pavao-Zuckerman and LaMotta 2007:259). While the O'odham in this part of the Pimería Alta eventually adopted livestock husbandry, especially cattle, it is clear that they actively attempted to maintain indigenous subsistence strategies during Spanish colonization.

This O'odham group was under the direct control of the Spanish and were compelled to pay tribute and to change subsistence strategies in response to direct Spanish demands. The O'odham along the middle Gila River, however, were never under the direct control of the Spanish and were not subject to tribute payment, leaving them free to economically respond to colonization. How, then, did O'odham alter their agricultural system with Spanish colonization? Here, I focus on one specific strategy incorporated by the O'odham in response to colonization: the intensification of agriculture in response to introduced market economies. The intensification of agriculture is defined as any attempt to add more labor to a field in order to increase agricultural production for a given field area. Strategies to intensify agriculture include terracing, multicropping, addition of fertilizer, and, most importantly for the middle Gila River, the construction of infrastructure, such as irrigation canals (Boserup 1965; Erickson 2006; Netting et al. 1989).

AGRICULTURE, ECONOMIC DEVELOPMENT, AND LAND-USE INTENSIFICATION ON THE MIDDLE GILA RIVER

To address how O'odham agriculture changed during Spanish and American colonization, agricultural intensification is analyzed through archaeological, historic, and ethnographic evidence on the middle Gila River during the historic period (1694–1950). These data indicate that with challenges such as variable streamflow, low annual precipitation, and colonization, the O'odham nonetheless created a highly productive agricultural system that created surplus for barter and the market likely using strategies employed by their ancestors—the Hohokam—prehistorically.

I argue in the following sections that the O'odham intensified agriculture as they adopted Old World crops, such as wheat, with the introduction of a market economy with the entrance of the Spanish in the region in the late 1600s. In order to measure the intensification of agriculture during the historic period,

I analyze historic sources from Spanish missionaries (the early historic period, 1697–1848) and the US explorers and military (the late historic period, 1848–1950) to document an increase in population density (with the combination of settlement extent and demographic estimates), the adoption of intensive irrigation, and an increase in maize and wheat yields. These measures indicate that with increasing population density and access to market demand, the O'odham intensified agriculture by adopting intensive irrigation to produce crops to sell to Spanish and American incomers. Other researchers (DeJong 2009; Doelle 1981; Rice et al. 1983; Wilson 1999) have assembled many of these numbers, but their calculations are checked, when possible, and restructured for the purposes of this chapter. These documents provide data on where settlements are located, population size, irrigated acreage, and the amount of crops produced in certain years, and can provide insight into the level of aggregation and crop production over time, both of which are important indicators of agricultural intensification.

Agricultural and Economic Growth during the Protohistoric (1450–1694) and the Early Historic Periods (1694–mid 1800s)

The collapse of the prehistoric Hohokam cultural system ushered in the Protohistoric Period (ca. 1450 to 1694) on the middle Gila River. The Protohistoric Period has been little studied by archaeologists due to the scarcity of archaeological materials, probably due to small and scattered populations at this time (see Jelinek and Brenneman, chapter 10 in this volume; Loendorf 2010; Wells, Loendorf, and Woodson 2004). Early historic observers in the region doubted the relationship between the substantial archaeological remains left by the Hohokam and the small populations remaining on the landscape during the early historic period (Fewkes 1912; Russell 1908). Due to the differences in the archaeological record between the Classic Period Hohokam and the Protohistoric O'odham, some researchers speculated that the Hohokam and the O'odham were distinct cultural groups (e.g., Russell 1908). However, most O'odham have long claimed continuity with the Hohokam, despite the uncertainty in the archaeological record (Loendorf 2010). Recent archaeological and historic research has taken a more nuanced view of the processes affecting historic populations and has strongly demonstrated continuity in artifacts, most specifically lithics and ceramics, between the prehistoric Hohokam and the historic O'odham (Doelle 2002; Loendorf 2010; Wells et al. 2004).

The small, dispersed O'odham populations occupying the middle Gila River Valley were first recorded by Father Eusebio Kino, who arrived in the region in 1694 (Bolton 1919). For information dating back to the arrival of Kino little remains in the archaeological record , so limited archaeological investigation has been done and we are largely reliant on historic Spanish documents for information about the O'odham interactions with the Spanish. (Wilson 1999). While Kino recorded little about the agricultural systems of these Protohistoric populations, he documented five to seven *ranchería* villages spread out along the middle Gila River with no supravillage organization (Winter 1973). With the entrance of Kino also came many Spanish-introduced crops and goods—such as the horse, wheat, and metal tools—which the Gila O'odham acquired shortly after Kino's arrival, though it remains unknown when exactly the O'odham were first introduced to these technologies and resources (Dunne 1955 documents extensive use of these goods in the mid-1700s).

Shortly after the arrival of Kino and throughout the 1700s, Apache raiding of O'odham villages increased throughout the 1700s. The introduction of the horse allowed the Apache to more efficiently steal from the O'odham (Rice et al. 1983; see also chapters by Pavao-Zuckerman [11], and J. Homer Thiel [12], this volume). Kino noted many instances of early Apache raiding throughout the Pimería Alta (the middle Gila River represented the extreme northern section of this region), but raiding did not become an issue on the middle Gila until after his arrival. With the increase in Apache raiding, the O'odham were forced to move their rancherías toward the center of the valley, aggregating in defense against the mobile Apache (Hackenberg 1962; Rice et al. 1983). The danger of raiding also prevented the Spanish from missionizing the middle Gila River, but did not prevent the Spanish from trading with the O'odham through other indigenous groups who entered the middle Gila River to assist with seasonal harvests (Dunne 1955).

In 1821, Mexico gained independence from Spain, ending Spanish control of the Pimería Alta, but little changed for the O'odham on the middle Gila River and their interactions with the Spanish and Mexican colonizers (DeJong 2009; Wilson 1999). The mid-1800s, however, brought many changes at different scales to the middle Gila River. During the Mexican American War, the US federal government took control of the middle Gila River in 1846 and increased the military presence in the region. This amplified military presence led to a decrease in Apache raiding in the mid- to late 1800s, allowing for more people to enter the region. In 1848, gold was discovered in California and the Southern Trail was established through the middle Gila leading to an estimated 60,000 people moving through the region from 1849 to 1851 (Dobyns 1961). These new American explorers relied heavily on the O'odham along the middle Gila, and the O'odham responded by further expanding their irrigated acreage and increasing emphasis on wheat production. In 1854, the Gadsden Purchase officially made the territory south of the Gila River to today's border with Mexico part of the United States. In 1859, the federal government established the first reservation in Arizona—the Gila River Indian Community—officially recognizing the Gila O'odham as a native group in the region (Wilson 1999).

Over the course of these external changes in the 1700 and 1800s, the O'odham adapted to Spanish and American introductions of new crops and goods, Apache on horseback raiding their villages, and colonizers needing access to food sources. Regardless of these rapid social changes, this time was a period of great economic success for the O'odham living along the middle Gila River, as they sold a surplus of crops to the influx of newcomers, who created a new demand for wheat. These incoming groups relied on O'odham agricultural success, and the intensification of agriculture proved to be an economic boon for the O'odham during this time. In the following sections, I argue that during the historic period (1) settlement patterns and demographic estimates indicate increasing population density, (2) increasing population densities led to the creation of a tribal government, allowing for a cooperative structure necessary for a complex irrigation system, and (3) intensive irrigation agriculture and wheat were adopted to meet the demands of a market economy. These factors denote that O'odham agriculture shifted from subsistence-based agriculture, of a kind largely practiced by their ancestors prehistorically, to a more intensive, cash-based agricultural system in response to the introduction of market economies.

Increase in Population Density

One of the main drivers of the intensification of agriculture and land use is increasing population density (Boserup 1965; Netting 1993). To argue this process occurred on the middle Gila, I use data on the settlement extent of historic rancherías and demographic estimates during the historic period. Consequently, O'odham agriculturalists most likely intensified agricultural production to maintain previously high yields of agricultural crops on a smaller extent of land. The increase in population density also had important implications for the ability to create a tribal government and to construct and manage a large-scale irrigation system.

Figure 13.2 shows the extent of Pima settlement along the middle Gila River from 1702 to 1877. Glen Rice and colleagues (1983) previously compiled these data (from Ezell 1961 and Hackenberg 1962) to show the level of aggregation across the middle Gila River during the historic period. The extent of settlement (in miles) shows how much of the landscape along the middle Gila River was occupied during a given year, and thus provides insight into the level of aggregation. For example, a larger extent of settlement indicates that the settlements were more dispersed across the landscape.

As Figure 13.2 shows, the extent of settlement decreased throughout the historic period, as O'odham villagers aggregated together in response to increased Apache raiding. This process continued until the late 1800s, when extent expanded again in response to the loss of water upstream and the reduction of Apache raiding due to the presence of the American military. Although settlement extent

FIGURE 13.2. *Settlement extent of O'odham villages along the middle Gila River during the historic period.*

shrank throughout the historic period, population data are needed to confirm that population numbers remained the same on a smaller extent of land, indicating an increase in local population density. For example, settlement extent could be shrinking due to a loss of population from Spanish-introduced diseases, resulting in extensive mortality for indigenous groups across the Americas.

Figure 13.3 shows the best estimates of population during the historic period and tells a complicated story of demographic highs and lows (Bell 1869; Dunne 1955). These numbers were drawn from estimates in Spanish diaries and, later, US censuses, so they reflect rough estimates of population numbers and not exact counts. Population appears to undergo demographic shifts over the historic period, though it is unclear whether these shifts are real or a product of imprecise estimates made by incoming explorers. Overall, however, the data on both settlement extent and population indicate that population density increased during the historic period, especially from the initial population observed when the Spanish first arrived in the late 1600s, until population loss in the late 1800s due to the

FIGURE 13.3. Population numbers of the middle Gila River Valley from historic documents (compiled by Doelle [1981] from Spanish diaries and American censuses).

reduction of water on the middle Gila River. With population increasing to 4,000–6,000 people after initial Spanish observations, the O'odham still fell victim to diseases introduced by the Spanish (see Garcés 1965 for documentation of vomiting and fevers), but the population lost from disease was replaced by in-migration from other indigenous groups, such as the Cocomaricopas, who sought refuge with the Gila O'odham from the Apache (Bolton 1919; Doelle 1981, 2002).

Regardless of these shifts, population appears to have generally increased throughout the historic period, resulting in increased population density. Many authors cite different reasons for this increasing aggregation. Rice and colleagues (1983) argue that this aggregation is intrinsically linked to Apache raiding, and statements made in early Spanish documents strengthen this argument. Jacobo Sedelmayr, a Spanish missionary, for example, describes unpopulated stretches, or buffer zones, upstream and downstream from the core of O'odham settlements along the Gila River to protect themselves against the Apache in the mid 1700s (cited in Dunne 1955). The aggregation across the landscape is also correlated with increased production of wheat, but that increase in wheat production is likely a product of the aggregation, not the cause, with a greater population density allowing for available labor to construct irrigation canals. Regardless, the aggregation of population to the center of the GRIC could have occurred for defensive or economic reasons and resulted in a population density increase, allowing for the creation of political structures necessary for an intensive irrigation system.

Development of a Tribal Government Necessary for Intensive Irrigation

Population growth and aggregation had important implications for tribal life and leadership during the 1700s. Numerous studies of prehistoric Hohokam irrigation systems indicate that a multivillage organizational system was needed to adequately distribute water and to maintain and construct canals (e.g., Howard 2006; Hunt et al. 2005; Woodson 2010). Without a cooperative or organizational structure, large-scale canal systems would not have been economically viable. Indeed, Kyle Woodson (2003) argues that the lack of an irrigation canal system when the Spanish first arrived was not due to a lack of knowledge of irrigation. Instead, he maintains, low population density and the lack of a centralized tribal government restricted the ability of the O'odham to cooperatively organize a large-scale irrigation system.

In 1694, prior to the aggregation in the mid-1700s, Father Kino observed no centralized authority above the village level (Bolton 1919). By the mid-1700s, new aggregated settlements along the middle Gila River had created a centralized tribal authority, which had not been previously documented during the historic period (Bolton 1919; Ezell 1961; Winter 1973). It appears that a new leader of this centralized tribal authority grew out of the previous position of "war chief," but the beginnings of this tribal leadership remain unknown (Winter 1973). The creation of this position and a tribal council, however, indicates changing social relationships among the previously scattered rancherías. This centralized tribal authority, led by one man known as "Crow Head," organized the middle Gila villages, and Joseph Winter argues, "the growing need for cooperation necessitated by raiding, and possibly by irrigation, fostered the rise of the tribal leader and the tribal council" (Winter 1973:74).

As Winter (1973) suggests, the centralization of leadership, by providing a framework of cooperation for developing more complex agricultural systems, may have been instrumental in the (re)adoption of irrigation among the middle Gila villages, which is documented in historic observations at that time, and the increased production of agricultural crops (Hunt et al. 2005). Thus, the creation of a tribal authority, likely growing out of increasing population density from the aggregation of settlements, allowed for the creation of cooperative agreements for the successful management of a large-scale irrigation system during the historic period, leading to the intensification of agriculture in response to new market-economy demands.

Expansion of Intensive Irrigation and the Adoption of Wheat for a Market Economy

The use of new strategies, including the adoption of large-scale irrigation, to increase agricultural production is another key indicator of the intensification of land use. Early Spanish documents provide important insights into agricultural production along the middle Gila River during the early historic period (e.g., Bolton 1920; Dunne 1955). While they do not provide specific quantities of harvested crops on a defined plot of land, their descriptions are essential to understanding how the intensity of agriculture across the landscape changed during the historic period. These documents provide background concerning how agricultural strategies changed and intensified during the historic period with the construction of large-scale irrigation systems, evidence of the entrance of the O'odham into the market economy, and data that the irrigated acreage expanded and agricultural yields increased throughout this time. These documents indicate that, during the historic period, the O'odham went from cultivating maize, beans, and squash for subsistence purposes without irrigation to cultivating sizeable tracts of mostly wheat (and some maize) with large-scale irrigation systems for sale to the Spanish and the Americans. All of these lines of evidence indicate that agriculture intensified throughout the historic period.

After the prehistoric Hohokam canal system fell into disuse in the mid-1400s, no canals are known to have been constructed anywhere in southern Arizona from about 1450 until 1744 (Bolton 1919; Wells et al. 2004; Wilcox 1981; Woodson 2003). Historians argue whether O'odham groups were even practicing irrigation when the Spanish first arrived (Castetter and Bell 1942; Ezell 1961; Hackenberg 1962; Winter 1973). Spanish missionaries briefly mentioned an irrigation agricultural system on the middle Gila River during the mid-1700s (Dunne 1955; Ezell 1961), but these documents are notoriously unreliable as they rarely focus on the agricultural system of the O'odham. Kino briefly mentioned fields of maize along the middle Gila River in 1697, but did not record the use of irrigation canals (Bolton 1919). In fact, most of the statements made by Kino and one of his traveling companions, Manje, in documents from the late 1600s indicate that no canals were observed at all. While they did not specifically mention irrigation on the middle Gila River, Manje wrote this observation when their expedition had subsequently made it farther west to the Cocomaricopas areas along the Colorado River: "I do not doubt that by constructing irrigation canals they could cultivate much more land, but these natives do not use canals to

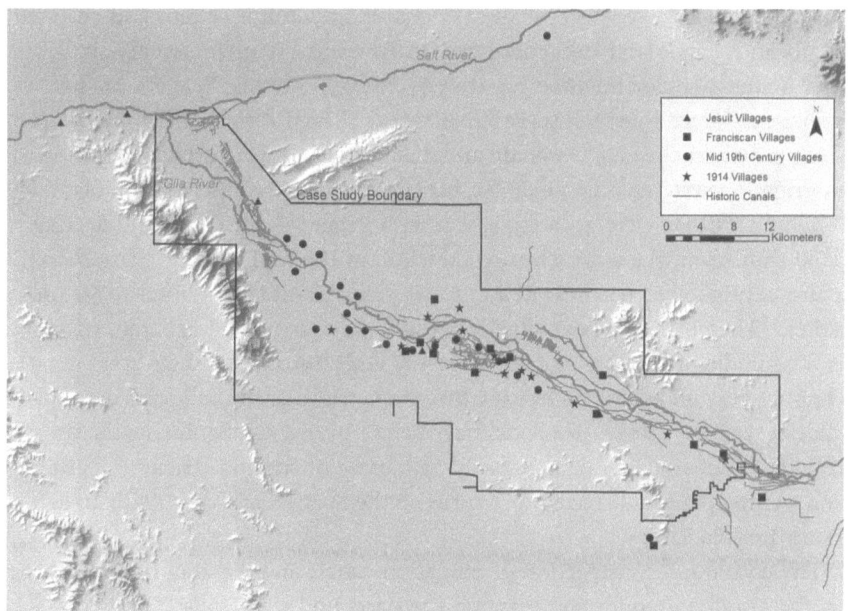

FIGURE 13.4. *Map of middle Gila River historic canals and villages (aggregated through time).*

irrigate their lands; they simply wait for the water and with the great flood the river banks are inundated, and when the flood goes down they plant some of the bends and low spots" (Burrus 1971:438). This statement has led many authors to believe that Manje never observed canal use during his travels throughout southern Arizona (Doelle 1981; Wilson 1999; Winter 1973). Regardless of the uncertainty in the use of irrigation canals at Spanish contact, it appears that the O'odham were practicing extensive agriculture of maize, beans, and squash without the use of intensive, *large-scale* irrigation systems evident later in the historic period (Figure 13.4).

By the time Sedelmayr, arrived on the middle Gila in 1744, one O'odham village out of the seven known to exist at that time was growing Spanish-introduced wheat with river-fed irrigation (Dunne 1955; Ezell 1961). Interestingly, the other villages still cultivated the traditional crops of maize, beans, and squash without irrigation at this time. Sedelmayr documented that the Gila O'odham also produced a considerable surplus, necessitating the use of labor from Tohono O'odham to the south to assist with seasonal harvests. The Tohono O'odham, who were in much greater contact with Spanish missions to the south, ultimately acted as trade brokers between the Gila O'odham and the Spanish, facilitating the trade of agricultural surplus and the increasing initiation of the Gila River O'odham into the emerging colonial barter and cash economy.

By the 1770s, this picture of the O'odham agricultural system had changed significantly, and land use continued to intensify. A mere twenty-six years after Sedelmayr documented his travels, in 1770, another Spanish missionary, Francisco Garcés (1965), observed that wheat rivaled maize as the major crop being grown by the Gila O'odham and that all villages were growing crops with an irrigation system. When Juan Bautista de Anza entered the region in 1776, all O'odham villages were growing wheat with irrigation agriculture, indicating a rapid shift from maize to wheat production in the mid- to late 1700s, though maize continued to be cultivated in some fields (Ezell 1961; Winter 1973). Anza writes, "The fields of wheat which they now possess are so large that, standing in the middle of them, one cannot see the ends, because of their great length. They are very wide, too, embracing the whole width of the valley on both sides" (Bolton 1920:179). Anza, like Sedelmayr before him, also documents the use of Tohono O'odham labor to assist with the harvest of surplus agricultural production and to act as trade facilitators between the Spanish and the O'odham living along the Gila River.

The continued construction of irrigation canals and the adoption of wheat by the O'odham continued through the early and mid-1800s. The mid-1800s was a time of great economic and agricultural growth for the O'odham, as the risk of Apache raiding decreased and the numbers of outsiders entering the region increased. Because of this increasing demand for food from Spanish explorers and the United States military, the O'odham appear to have been fully committed to cash and barter economies by 1850 (Doelle 2002; DeJong 2009; Wilson 1999). Although details of this transition from the barter only to the cash and barter economy remain unclear, the O'odham appear to have shifted from focusing on producing agricultural crops for their own consumption to obtaining goods and other foods in exchange for their crops. Spanish and American colonizers, entering an unfamiliar environment, depended on the O'odham to provide them with food, leading the O'odham to produce crops for the market for which the O'odham received horses, metal agricultural tools, and other goods.

David DeJong (2009) undertook an analysis of agricultural data collected by the US. Bureau of Indian Affairs from the mid-1800s to the early 1900s, documenting the expansion of agriculture and the continued widespread adoption of wheat. Along with showing the increase in farmed acreage in the mid-1800s, DeJong (2009) also documented major changes in crop production. First, the selling of maize to the US military decreased over time and remained secondary to wheat production. The O'odham likely grew more wheat in response to increased demand from the US military. Second, the total cultivation of crops, especially wheat, increased during the mid-1800s, similar to the increase seen in cultivated acreage (DeJong 2009:7).

Figure 13.5 shows the amount of acreage farmed in select years from 1850 to 1921, and Figure 13.6 illustrates changes in wheat and maize production along the middle Gila River by O'odham groups between 1887 and 1899. For the first part of the period, the acreage of agricultural land increased, and the cultivation of maize decreased over time and was secondary to wheat production by the mid-1800s. These increases in irrigated acreage and wheat production during the early and mid-1850s is linked to higher demand and opportunities resulting from the influx of Anglo-American explorers and the military, who needed foodstuffs in this new environment (DeJong 2009; Wilson 1999). This increase in irrigated acreage and wheat production changed, though, with the decrease in water availability in the Gila River. In the late 1860s, non-Native Americans moved into regions upstream, drawing water off the river for their own irrigated fields. By the 1880s, the agricultural productivity of the middle Gila became severely limited due to lack of water, as reflected in the decreased amount of agricultural productivity and irrigable land used during these years (see Figures 13.5 and 13.6). Regardless, the data from the Bureau of Indian Affairs indicates that wheat was rapidly adopted, and maize was essentially abandoned at this time due to the low amount of corn being sold on the market (though it was still likely being grown by the O'odham, for subsistence purposes, which is not reflected in documents of crop sale to non-Native Americans).

It is likely, however, that the O'odham continued to cultivate maize and wheat during different times of the year. Some researchers have argued that wheat was rapidly adopted into the O'odham agricultural calendar for two reasons: (1) newcomers in the region provided a strong demand for the crop, and (2) wheat grew well in the winter months of southern Arizona, while maize grew well in the summer months, the two grains perfectly complementing each other in the O'odham agricultural calendar (Castetter and Bell 1942; Doelle 1981, 2002). Based on these sources, the O'odham planted the first crop of wheat in December in dedicated fields for wheat; a second crop of maize, beans, and squashes in early March; and a third crop of maize in July (Castetter and Bell 1942; DeJong 2011; Southworth 1919). Indeed, many ethnographic and historic sources in the early to mid-1900s also document the O'odham using traditional digging sticks to monocrop maize and wheat in separate fields and during different seasons of the year, though these observations occurred after the loss of water on the Gila, which drastically changed the O'odham's ability to participate in market exchange (see Castetter and Bell 1942; Ezell 1961; Russell 1908).

CONCLUSIONS

Historic and ethnographic sources document a wide variety of changes to the O'odham agricultural system throughout colonization during the historic

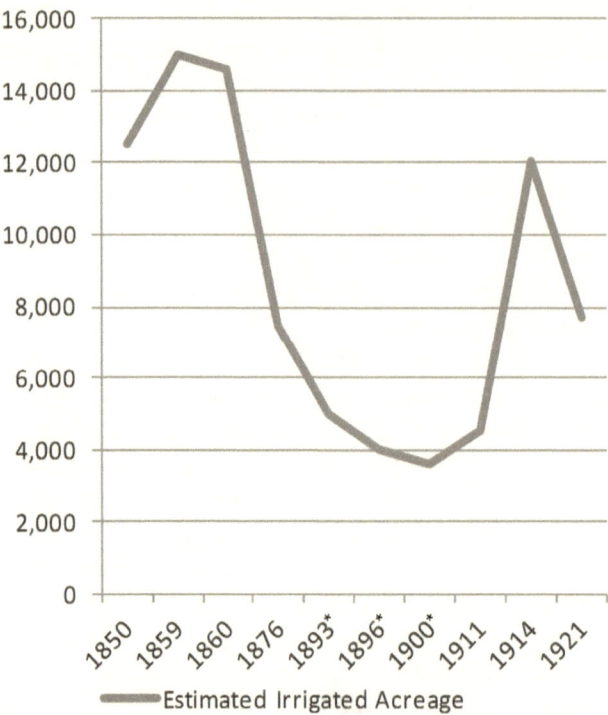

FIGURE 13.5. *Estimated irrigated acreage in the late historic period, select years, 1850–1921 (adapted from DeJong [2009:7]) (* indicates that numbers were listed as "less than" plotted number).*

period. In this chapter, I argued that increases in population density, the creation of a political structure to allow for cooperative irrigation, and the adoption of a large-scale canal system and production of wheat indicate that the O'odham intensified agriculture throughout the historic period in order to meet the market demands introduced by the Spanish and American colonizers. The initial aggregation of O'odham settlements and the introduction of new crops and technologies in the mid-1700s set into motion a complex series of decisions, including the creation of a tribal council, the expansion of agricultural production, the construction of new canals to open more acreage for farming, and the addition of wheat into the O'odham agricultural regime.

The 1700s and early 1800s were a time of great economic success for the O'odham, as they actively participated in a market economy, trading their agricultural crops for colonial wares, including metals, from non-Native Americans entering the region. This economic success exploded over the following decades, as records show the O'odham were selling record quantities of crops to travelers

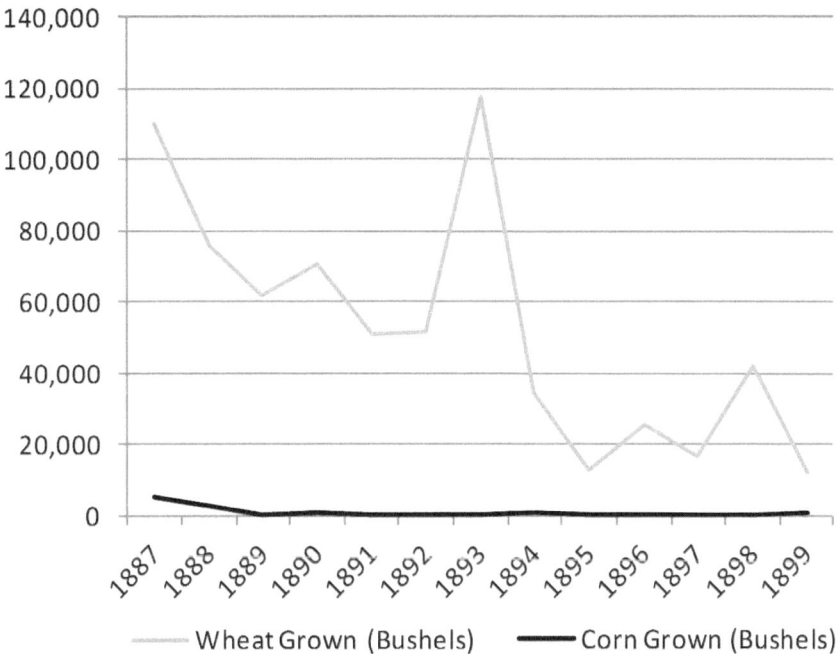

FIGURE 13.6. *Grain production on Gila River Indian Community (adapted from DeJong [2009]; source: US Bureau of Indian Affairs, Annual Report of the Commissioner of Indian Affairs [Pima Agency], 1887–1925).*

and military from the United States (DeJong 2009). Interestingly enough, the O'odham had freedom to adapt to colonization due to the lack of direct Spanish influence and control over the region. The O'odham along the middle Gila River responded to the Spanish colonial regime by maintaining agricultural strategies that had been used by their prehistoric ancestors, the Hohokam, for centuries. Later, to participate in, and meet the demands of, new markets, they turned to traditional practices, including the reintroduction and expansion of irrigated agriculture.

This economic success changed, however, with the loss of water along the middle Gila River in the late 1800s due to non-Native American farmers moving upstream and diverting water for irrigation in areas such as Coolidge and Florence in eastern Arizona. With the loss of water, the O'odham faced mass poverty and starvation. Because agricultural production was greatly reduced at this time, the O'odham resorted to a number of strategies to avoid these fates, including relying on federal food donations (DeJong 2009), moving upstream of designated reservation areas to try to capture irrigation water before the river dried up (DeJong 2011), harvesting mesquite along the river to sell as firewood to the city of Phoenix (Bigler 2007; DeJong 2011), and migrating to Phoenix to obtain available service jobs (DeJong 2011). Despite these efforts, the loss of water resulted in extreme poverty. While the O'odham along the middle Gila River experienced great economic success for the first periods of the colonial era, the increase in population upstream resulted in devastation to O'odham economic and agricultural success—a legacy that persists today.

ACKNOWLEDGMENTS

This research would not have been possible without the support of many people and organizations. This chapter represented one part of my dissertation, which was guided by an incredible supportive committee, including Kate Spielmann, Peggy Nelson, Jon Sandor, and Sharon Hall. This research was undertaken in conjunction with the Pima-Maricopa Irrigation Project (P-MIP) under funding from the Department of the Interior, US Bureau of Reclamation, under the Tribal Self-Governance Act of 1994 (P.L. 103-413), for the design and development of a water delivery system using Central Arizona Project water. Support from many people at the GRIC Cultural Resources Management Program—including Kyle Woodson, David Wright, Chris Loendorf, and Craig Fertelmes—made my fieldwork possible.

Financial support for this research and related laboratory analyses was provided by multiple sources, including the including the Central-Arizona Phoenix Long-Term Ecological Research Project (NSF Grant Number BCS-1026865), the Graduate and Professional Students Association at Arizona State University, the School of Human Evolution and Social Change, the National Science Foundation Graduate Research Fellowship Program, the Coupled-Natural Human Systems Long-Term Vulnerability and Transformation Project (NSF Grant Number ARC-1104372), and the IGERT in Urban Ecology Program (NSF Grant Number 0504248).

REFERENCES CITED

Bell, William A. 1869. *New Tracks in North America: A Journal of Travel and Adventure whilst Engaged in the Survey for a Southern Railroad to the Pacific Ocean during 1867–8.* London: Chapman and Hall.

Bigler, Wendy. 2007. "Akimel O'Odham Agriculture and the Gila River." PhD dissertation, Department of Geography, Arizona State University, Tempe.

Bolton, Herbert E. 1919. *Kino's Historical Memoir of Pimería Alta.* Cleveland: The Arthur H. Clark Company.

Bolton, Herbert E. 1920. *Anza's California Expeditions.* Cleveland: The Arthur H. Clark Company.

Boserup, E. 1965. *The Conditions of Agricultural Growth.* Chicago: Aldine.

Burrus, Ernest T. 1971. *Kino and Manje, Explorers of Sonora and Arizona: Their Vision of the Future. Sources and Studies for the History of the Americas 10*. Rome: Jesuit Historical Institute.

Castetter, Edward F., and Willis H. Bell. 1942. *Pima and Papago Indian Agriculture*. Albuquerque: University of New Mexico Press.

Corkran, David H. 1967. *The Creek Frontier, 1540–1783*. Norman: University of Oklahoma Press.

DeJong, David H. 2009. *Stealing the Gila: The Pima Agricultural Economy and Water Deprivation, 1848–1921*. Tucson: University of Arizona Press.

DeJong, David H. 2011. *Forced to Abandon Our Fields: The 1914 Clay Southworth Gila River Pima Interviews*. Tucson: University of Arizona Press.

Dobyns, Henry F., ed. 1961. *Hepah, California! The Journal of Cave Johnson Couts from Monterey, Nuevo Leon, Mexico to Los Angeles, California during the Years 1848–1849*. Tucson: Arizona Pioneers' Historical Society.

Doelle, William H. 1981. "The Gila Pima in the Late Seventeenth Century." In *The Protohistoric Period in the North American Southwest, A.D. 1450–1700*, edited by David R. Wilcox and W. Bruce Maase, 57–70. Anthropological Research Papers 24. Tempe: Arizona State University.

Doelle, William H. 2002. "Demographic Change and the Adoption of Wheat by the Gila River Pima." In *The Archaeology of Contact*, edited by Kurtis Lesick, Barbara Kulle, Christine Cluny, and Meaghan Pueramaki-Brown, 258–69. Calgary: University of Calgary.

Dunne, Peter Masten. 1955. *Jacobo Sedelmayr: Missionary, Frontiersman, Explorer in Arizona and Sonora, Four Original Manuscript Narratives, 1744–1751*. Tucson: Arizona Pioneers' Historical Society.

Erickson, Clark L. 2006. "Intensification, Political Economy, and the Farming Community." In *Defense of a Bottom-Up Perspective of the Past*, edited by Joyce Marcus and Charles Stanish, 334–64. Agricultural Strategies. Los Angeles: Cotsen Institute, University of California.

Ezell, Peter H. 1961. *No. 5, Pt. 2. The Hispanic Acculturation of the Gila River Pimas*. Memoirs of the American Anthropological Association, vol. 63. Washington, DC: American Anthropological Association.

Fewkes, Jessie Walter. 1912. "Casa Grande, Arizona." In *The 28th Annual Report of the Bureau of American Ethnology*, 25–180. Washington, DC: Bureau of American Ethnology.

Garcés, Francisco. 1965. *A Record of Travels in Arizona and California, 1775–1776*. San Francisco: J. Howell-Books.

Hackenberg, Robert A. 1962. "Economic Alternatives in Arid Lands: A Case Study of the Pima and Papago Indians." *Ethnology* 1 (2): 186–96. http://dx.doi.org/10.2307/3772874.

Howard, Jerry B. 2006. "Hohokam Irrigation Communities: A Study of Internal Structure, External Relationships and Sociopolitical Complexity." PhD dissertation, School of Human Evolution and Social Change, Arizona State University, Tempe.

Hunt, Robert C., David Guillet, David R. Abbott, James M. Bayman, Paul R. Fish, Suzanne K. Fish, Keith W. Kintigh, and James A. Neely. 2005. "Ethnographic Analogies for the Social Organization of Hohokam Canal Irrigation." *American Antiquity* 70 (3): 433–56. http://dx.doi.org/10.2307/40035308.

Kowalewski, Stephen A. 2006. "Coalescent Societies." In *Light on the Path: The Anthropology and History of the Southeastern Indians*, edited by Thomas J. Pluckhahn and Robbie Ethridge, 94–122. Tuscaloosa: University of Alabama Press.

Loendorf, Christopher. 2010. "Hohokam Core Area Sociocultural Dynamics: Cooperation and Conflict along the Middle Gila River in Southern Arizona during the Classic and Historic Periods." PhD dissertation, School of Human Evolution and Social Change, Arizona State University, Tempe.

Netting, Robert McC. 1993. *Smallholders, Householders: Farm Families and the Ecology of Intensive, Sustainable Agriculture*. Stanford: Stanford University Press.

Netting, Robert McC, M. Priscilla Stone, and Glenn Davis Stone. 1989. "Kofyar Cash-Cropping: Choice and Change in Indigenous Agricultural Development." *Human Ecology* 17 (3): 299–319. http://dx.doi.org/10.1007/BF00889021.

Pavao-Zuckerman, Barnet. 2007. "Deerskins and Domesticates: Creek Subsistence and Economic Strategies in the Historic Period." *American Antiquity* 72 (1): 5–33. http://dx.doi.org/10.2307/40035296.

Pavao-Zuckerman, Barnet. 2011. "Rendering Economies: Native American Labor and Secondary Animal Products in the Eighteenth-Century Pimería Alta." *American Antiquity* 76 (1): 3–23. http://dx.doi.org/10.7183/0002-7316.76.1.3.

Pavao-Zuckerman, Barnet, and Vincent M. LaMotta. 2007. "Missionization and Economic Change in the Pimería Alta: The Zooarchaeology of San Agustín de Tucson." *International Journal of Historical Archaeology* 11 (3): 241–68. http://dx.doi.org/10.1007/s10761-007-0030-x.

Rice, Glen E., Steadman Upham, Linda M. Nicholas, and Veronica DaCosta. 1983. *Alicia, the History of a Piman Homestead. Manuscript on file*. Tempe: Office of Cultural Resource Management, Department of Anthropology, Arizona State University.

Russell, Frank. 1908. *The Pima Indians*. Tucson: University of Arizona Press.

Sheridan, Thomas E. 1988. *Where the Dove Calls: The Political Ecology of a Corporate Peasant Community in Northwestern Mexico*. Tucson: University of Arizona Press.

Sheridan, Thomas E. 2006. *Landscapes of Fraud: Mission Tumacácori, the Baca Float, and the Betrayal of the O'odham*. Tucson: University of Arizona Press.

Southworth, Clay. 1919. "The History of Irrigation along the Gila River." In *Hearings before the Committee on Indian Affairs, House of Representatives, Sixty-Sixth Congress, First*

Session, on the Condition of Various Tribes of Indians. Vol. 2., 103–225. Washington, DC: Government Printing Office.

Spielmann, Katherine A. 1989. "Colonists, Hunters, and Farmers: Plains-Pueblo Interaction in the 17th Century." In *Archaeological and Historical Perspectives on the Spanish Borderlands West*, edited by David H. Thomas, 101–13. Columbian Consequences, vol. 1. Washington, DC: Smithsonian Institution Press.

Spielmann, Katherine A., Tiffany C. Clark, Diane Hawkey, Katharine Rainey, and Suzanne K. Fish. 2009. "'. . . being weary, they had rebelled': Pueblo Subsistence and Labor under Spanish Colonialism." *Journal of Anthropological Archaeology* 28 (1): 102–25. http://dx.doi.org/10.1016/j.jaa.2008.10.002.

Spielmann, Katherine A., Jeannette L. Mobley-Tanaka, and James M. Potter. 2006. "Style and Resistance in the Seventeenth Century Salinas Province." *American Antiquity* 71 (4): 621–47. http://dx.doi.org/10.2307/40035882.

Stone, Glenn Davis. 1994. "Agricultural Intensification and Perimetrics: Ethnoarchaeological Evidence from Nigeria." *Current Anthropology* 35 (3): 317–24. http://dx.doi.org/10.1086/204283.

Swanton, John R. 1998. *Early History of the Creek Indians and Their Neighbors*. Gainesville: University Press of Florida.

Tarcan, Carmen G. 2005. "Counting Sheep: Fauna, Contact, and Colonialism at Zuni Pueblo, New Mexico, A.D. 1300–1900." PhD dissertation, Department of Anthropology, Simon Fraser University, Vancouver, British Columbia, Canada.

Trigg, Heather B. 2003. "The Ties That Bind: Economic and Social Interactions in Early-Colonial New Mexico, A.D. 1598–1680." *Historical Archaeology* 37 (2): 65–84.

Trigg, Heather B. 2005. *From Household to Empire: Society and Economy in Early Colonial New Mexico*. Tucson: University of Arizona Press.

United States Bureau of Indian Affairs. 1887–1925. Annual Report of the Commissioner of Indian Affairs. 1857–1859, 1864, 1866–1867, 1869–1878, 1880, 1883, 1887–1889, 1890, 1894–1900, 1904–1905, 1911, 1913–1914, 1919–1921, 1925. Washington, DC: William A. Harris.

VanDerwarker, Amber M., Jon B. Marcoux, and Kandace D. Hollenbach. 2013. "Farming and Foraging at the Crossroads: The Consequences of Cherokee and European Interaction through the Late Eighteenth Century." *American Antiquity* 78 (1): 68–88. http://dx.doi.org/10.7183/0002-7316.78.1.68.

Wells, E. Christian, Christopher Loendorf, and M. Kyle Woodson. 2004. "From Hohokam to O'Odham: Quantitative Measures for Identifying Protohistoric Ceramic Assemblages in the Middle Gila Valley, Central Arizona." Paper presented at the 2004 Arizona Archaeological Council Fall Conference, Tucson.

Wilcox, David R. 1981. "Changing Perspectives on the Protohistoric Pueblos." In *The Protohistoric Period in the North American Southwest, A.D. 1450–1700*, edited by David R.

Wilcox and W. Bruce Masse, 378–409. Anthropological Research Paper 24. Tempe: Arizona State University.

Wilson, John P. 1999. *"Peoples of the Middle Gila: A Documentary History of the Pimas and Maricopas, 1500s–1945." Manuscript on file*. Sacaton, AZ: Cultural Resource Management Program, Gila River Indian Community.

Winter, Joseph C. 1973. "Cultural Modifications of the Gila Pima: A.D. 1697–A.D. 1846." *Ethnohistory (Columbus, Ohio)* 20 (1): 67–77. http://dx.doi.org/10.2307/481427.

Woodson, M. Kyle. 2003. *A Research Design for the Study of Prehistoric and Historic Irrigation Systems in the Middle Gila Valley, Arizona*. P-MIP Technical Report No. 2003-10. Sacaton, Arizona: Cultural Resource Management Program, Gila River Indian Community.

Woodson, M. Kyle. 2010. "The Social Organization of Hohokam Irrigation in the Middle Gila River Valley, Arizona." PhD dissertation, School of Human Evolution and Social Change, Arizona State University, Tempe.

PART 3

Discussion and Comparative Viewpoints

FOURTEEN

The Archaeology of Colonialism in the American Southwest and Alta California

Some Observations and Comments

KENT G. LIGHTFOOT

INTRODUCTION

The chapters in this book present a fresh, state-of-the-art perspective on the complex histories of native and colonial entanglements in the American Southwest using diverse data sets, including archaeological materials, historical sources, and native narratives. In exploring various theoretical questions and methodological approaches to the study of colonialism, the authors examine the complicated social, political, and economic relationships that transformed the Southwest beginning with the Coronado expedition in 1540–42 and continuing through Spanish and later Mexican colonization from the late 1500s to the mid-1800s. The case studies focus on two primary areas: the New Mexico Colony, which encompassed present-day northeastern Arizona to north and central New Mexico, and the Pimería Alta, in the northern Sonora Desert of southern Arizona and Sonora Mexico.

In commenting on these chapters, my purpose is not to impart additional information or historical content on the events and processes of colonialism that unfolded in these two areas, which is superbly done in the introduction (chapter 1) and other chapters in the book. Rather, my purpose is to comment on the chapters from the vantage point of someone who not only has some familiarity with Southwestern archaeology dating back to my graduate student days at Arizona State University in the 1970s, but who has now been working in the adjacent California region for the last twenty-five years. Thus, my goal is to compare the chapters in this book with developments taking place in the archaeology of colonialism in Alta California, and, where appropriate, across the broader Spanish borderlands of North America.

My task is greatly facilitated by John Douglass and William Graves, who present an exceptional introduction to the broad sweep of humanity that engulfed the Southwest during three centuries of Spanish and Mexican colonialism. They not only present a succinct and readable account of the events and processes of colonialism in the New Mexico Colony and Pimería Alta, but they interpret these developments building on the latest theoretical advances in the archaeology of colonialism. As John G. Douglass and William M. Graves emphasize in chapter 1, the multiethnic, polycultural, and multifaceted political relationships that unfolded in the American Southwest resulted in trajectories of both cultural change and cultural persistence that are still evident today. This introductory chapter (along with others in the book) accentuates why the American Southwest is such a superb place to undertake research on colonialism. The region stands out because of its cutting-edge archaeological investigations, its long tradition of notable research in colonial history, and the potential to undertake collaborative research with multiple tribes who have powerful and relevant oral traditions concerning past colonial engagements. Consequently, the American Southwest offers a fantastic opportunity to compare and contrast the practices and processes of colonialism in the broader Spanish borderlands of North America, including Florida, Texas, northern Mexico, Baja California, and Alta California.

In reading and commenting on the chapters, I am struck by both the similarities and differences in how colonial entanglements unfolded in the American Southwest when compared to Alta California. Both areas were explored by the Spanish Crown beginning in the early decades of the 1500s, but while the New Mexico Colony and the Pimería Alta were populated by foreign intruders beginning in the 1590s and late 1600s, respectively, Alta California was not settled by Spanish colonists until 1769. The Franciscan order administered and staffed the Catholic missions established in both the New Mexico Colony and Alta California, as well as in the Pimería Alta when the Jesuits were expelled in 1767. However, the missionaries and other colonists interacted with a diverse range of native societies characterized by distinctive political economies, including complex hunter-gatherers in coastal California and nomadic hunter-gatherers and settled agrarian communities in the American Southwest. It is from this comparative perspective encompassing similarities and differences in the colonial entanglements in the American Southwest and Alta California that I comment on the chapters.

My commentary on the chapters addresses four major themes. The first theme examines early encounters that unfolded between native peoples and Spanish explorers in the American Southwest and Alta California. The second theme is the continuation of exemplary archaeological studies of colonial settlements—particularly presidios and missions—that are providing new insights about the colonists and their interactions with indigenous populations. The third theme concerns the recent trend of emphasizing native political economies and indigenous landscapes in understanding the processes and outcomes of colonialism in the Spanish borderlands. The final theme addresses the importance of studying the archaeology of the recent past to better understand the legacies of colonialism and how they have shaped our contemporary human-environmental interactions and the identity, composition, and political influence of modern communities.

THEME ONE: EARLY COLONIAL ENCOUNTERS

Early Spanish explorations of both the American Southwest and Alta California have received considerable attention by colonial historians over the years (Bolton 1916; Hammond and Rey 1940; Quinn [1542–43] 1979e; Wagner 1924). These studies make it very clear that while both regions were first explored by Europeans in the 1500s, how these expeditions were mounted, supplied, and ultimately interacted with indigenous populations differed dramatically. In reading the chapters in this volume, I am struck by how the distinctive outcomes of these initial colonial encounters may have fostered long-term consequences in the kinds of social relationships and antagonisms that unfolded in later colonial times.

Mathew E. Schmader (chapter 2) presents a provocative analysis of the Coronado Expedition of 1540–42 based on his recent archaeological investigations and a critical reading of relevant ethnohistorical sources. His study describes how the expedition was funded, who participated in it, and the various interactions and negotiations that took place with Southwestern indigenous peoples. He emphasizes that the majority of the expedition comprised *indios amigos* warriors from central and western Mexico (peoples of Tarascan, Tenochca, Tlatelolca, and Mexica descent) who were equipped with their traditional armor and weapons. Schmader's insightful analysis of the expedition's documents reveals common patterns in how southwestern peoples negotiated with the Spanish and Native Mexican intruders, including their use of long-distance information networks to keep abreast of the expedition's movements; ritualized practices in dealing with foreigners (such as orations, food giving, etc.); and various defensive, deceptive, and offensive tactics to thwart the advancement of the foreign intruders.

The Coronado expedition, consisting of 375 European men-at-arms, at least 1,300 Native Mexican warriors, an unknown number of women and various camp followers, and thousands of head of livestock, lived off the land by trading, stealing, or taking by force food and goods from native southwestern communities. It is clear from Schmader's chapter (2) that this practice, combined with the abuse of indigenous women and other hostilities, fostered a recurrent pattern of brutal and violent colonial encounters that sometimes escalated into armed confrontations and pitched battles. The latter is exemplified by the archaeological investigation of Piedras Marcadas Pueblo in New Mexico, where a suite of low-impact geophysical and surface collection methods are delineating the spatial distribution of features and artifacts across the pueblo site. The spatial analysis of artifacts, including sixteenth-century Spanish military objects (musket balls, chainmail, boltheads, etc.), Mexican arms, and Puebloan projectile points, is providing new insights into the strategies of armed conflict that took place between Coronado's men and the Pueblo warriors.

Thomas E. Sheridan and Stewart B. Koyiyumptewa (chapter 9) present another important study of early native encounters with Spanish colonists from a different vantage point—tribal oral traditions. The Hopi History Project, a collaborative venture of the University of Arizona and the Hopi Tribe, is collecting Hopi accounts of their interactions with early Spanish explorers and colonists, many of which have been orally transmitted from one generation to the next over more than four centuries. The Hopi Tribe has a long and lucid memory of these early encounters, including Coronado's army destroying a Hopi village in 1540, which was evidently not described in any known Spanish accounts of the *entrada*. However, many of the recollections pertain to the early mission period (pre–Pueblo Revolt), when, beginning in 1619, the Franciscans established missions in several Hopi villages. The oral narratives highlight the maltreatment of the Hopi people by Coronado and the later missionaries, including the physical abuse of some men and women, and how these colonial entanglements created significant disruptions in their tribal lifeways, cultural practices, and religious activities. While I will return to this notable chapter below, it is clear that more than 400 years after their first encounters with the Spanish, the intergenerational traumatic memory of these events have left deep scars among the Hopi people.

The broader implications of Schmader's (chapter 2) and Sheridan and Koyiyumptewa's chapters (chapter 4) is that the early show of force and brutality by Coronado and his army in 1540–42, which appears to have been reintroduced by some early missionaries in their interactions with local Indian communities in 1600s, set the tone for antagonistic and distrustful relations between tribal groups and Spanish colonists for decades to come.

In comparing these early encounters with those in Alta California, a very different picture emerges. The initial exploration of Alta California, which took place during the period of 1542 to 1603, was undertaken by four Spanish (Cabrillo, Unamuno, Cermeño, Vizcaíno) and one English (Drake) maritime expeditions whose ships made periodic landfalls for short durations in coastal places inhabited by native communities (Bolton 1916; Quinn 1979a, [1584–85] 1979b, 1979c, 1979d, [1542–43] 1979e, [1584–85] 1979f; Wagner 1929). With the exception of these landfalls, the sailors remained on their ships and lived primarily off provisions stored on board. Consequently, a different rhythm of encounters transpired in which California Indian delegations would typically meet the maritime explorers as they landed, greeting them with long orations and gift giving of food and goods that were performed according to ceremonial and honorific protocols (Lightfoot and Simmons 1998). In turn, the explorers exchanged ship's biscuits, clothing (hats, shirts), cloth, and glass beads to the Indian leaders, and performed public masses on the beaches.

Although some abuses took place in the early encounters in Alta California, particularly when sailors stayed in port for any length of time, these coastal interactions rarely led to armed confrontations, raids, and battles, which appear to have been a common occurrence in the American Southwest. How these different kinds of early encounters may have influenced and structured later colonial relationships in both regions is a topic deserving future investigation. But while Native Californian tribes have intense memories of the later Franciscan missionaries and Spanish colonists, I am not aware of any extant oral traditions concerning the 1542–43 Cabrillo voyage. This contrasts sharply with the Hopi's recollections of the dreadful consequences of the 1540 Coronado expedition that transpired more than 400 years ago. It seems clear that the colonial enterprises in the American Southwest and Alta California got off to very different starts.

THEME TWO: RESEARCH ON COLONIAL SETTLEMENTS—PRESIDIOS AND MISSIONS

Several chapters in the volume detail recent archaeological investigations of the Tucson Presidio (J. Homer Thiel [chapter 12]) and Pimería Alta missions (Barnet Pavao-Zuckerman [chapter 11]), and ongoing studies of Hopi Indians in Franciscan missions (Sheridan and Koyiyumptewa; Laurie D. Webster [chapter 4]). They are part of a venerable legacy in the American Southwest of undertaking scholarly archaeological investigations of colonial settlements that examine interactions with indigenous populations. In discussing this work in relation to Alta California, it is important from the outset to understand how this tradition of scholarly research differed from the trajectory of less rigorous, restoration projects that took place during the formative years of California archaeology.

As vividly described by David Thomas (1991a), the influence of Helen Hunt Jackson's 1884 novel, *Ramona*, and the initiation of Mission Revival architecture shortly thereafter excited a flurry of major restoration projects at colonial-age buildings throughout California. Many of the Franciscan missions had been neglected and pilfered in the postmission years, but the majority had been reclaimed and maintained by the Catholic Church since their return by the US government in 1862. By the early 1900s a series of restoration projects were initiated with archaeology serving primarily as a handmaiden for local church groups, historical societies, and restoration architects who were attempting to reconstruct the original appearance of crumbling mission quadrangles and other historic adobe buildings. Unfortunately, as Thomas details, most of these early restoration ventures were based more on a romanticized view of a mythical Californio past than detailed, rigorous academic investigations, which led to many inaccuracies and architectural whimsies.

Early historical archaeology in the American Southwest followed a more scholarly trajectory under the auspices of the School of American Archaeology, later renamed the School of American Research (now known as the School for Advanced Research), and other institutions whose research programs were geared toward the study and preservation of Spanish-era buildings and sites rather than in their reconstruction per se (Cordell 1989:32–33; Thomas 1991a:138–39). While relatively few well-documented archaeological studies of Spanish missions and ranchos took place in Alta California prior to the 1960s (for exceptions, see Bennyhoff and Elsasser 1954; Neuerburg 1987; Treganza 1956; Whitehead 1991), many of the leading archaeologists working in the Southwest participated in the excavation of Spanish-era sites in the early twentieth century (Brew 1937; Kidder 1916, 1924; Montgomery et al. 1949; Nelson 1916; Smith et al. 1966; Toulouse and Stephenson 1960; Vivian 1964). Much of this early interest stemmed from the development of early chronologies, since the Spanish occupations provided discrete time markers for dating ceramic seriations (Cordell 1989:32; Wilcox 2009:162).

The academic nature of early archaeological work in the American Southwest was probably also influenced by land ownership. While many of the Spanish sites in California are now situated in or near heavily urbanized coastal cities, southwestern colonial places (outside of Tucson and Albuquerque) tend to be found in rural areas on federal lands or on (or near) extant Indian reservations. The research protocols and oversight that were employed to work on colonial sites on federal lands and Indian reservations in the American Southwest appears to have differed markedly from those that transpired on private lands in coastal California prior to the 1960s, when many imaginative restorations of Spanish-era buildings took place.

Archaeological research of colonial settlements accelerated throughout the Spanish borderlands beginning in the 1970s, 1980s, and 1990s with the growing sophistication in the theory and method of historical archaeology, as well as the increased funding for colonial archaeological research provided by cultural resource management legislation and the Columbian Quincentenary (Deagan

1983; Farnsworth 1987; Greenwood 1975; Hester 1977; Hoover 1979; Larsen 1990; Lycett 1995; McEwan 1993; Thomas 1987, 1989, 1990, 1991b; Thomas et al. 1978).

Thus, I believe the exemplary chapters in this volume have benefited greatly from the solid foundation of colonial archaeology in the American Southwest that has developed over the last century, as well as by recent advances in the field of historical archaeology.

Homer Thiel (chapter 12) presents a succinct overview of twenty years of research at the Presidio San Agustín del Tucson undertaken by Archaeology Southwest and Desert Archaeology. His chapter contextualizes the historical importance of the Tucson Presidio in the Spanish colonization of the Pimería Alta. The extensive ethnohistorical and archaeological investigations have resulted in a wealth of information about the presidio—how it was built over time, the spatial layout of the community, and the kinds of relationships the colonists had with nearby indigenous populations. A significant contribution of this work is elucidating the social interactions and exchange networks that the presidio community maintained with local O'odham peoples, Mexican towns, and the broader world through the study of a diverse range of material goods recovered from archaeological contexts, including indigenous pottery vessels, majolica dishes, transfer-printed ceramics, buttons, buckles, beads, and so on.

The long-term, intensive investigation of the Tucson Presidio provides an excellent opportunity to examine the similarities and differences of presidio communities elsewhere in the Spanish borderlands. Thiel (chapter 12, this volume) notes that some of the cultural practices revolving around food set the Tucson colonists apart from local native people. A similar observation has been made in archaeological investigations of the contemporaneous San Francisco Presidio in Alta California (Voss 2005, 2008). This observation raises the question about whether similar processes of ethnogenesis that bonded the members of the presidio community together in San Francisco, but distinguished them from local Ohlone Indians, may have been unfolding in Tucson.

Pavao-Zuckerman in chapter 11 examines the zooarchaeological remains from recent excavations at two missions—Mission San Agustín de Tucson, located across the river from the Tucson Presidio, and Mission Nuestra Señora del Pilar y Santiago de Cocóspera in northern Sonora. She focuses on the importance of animal husbandry, specifically the production of cattle and sheep, as a lynchpin in the colonial regional economy. Not only did the cattle offer sustenance for the mission community, but dried meat, hides, and tallow (as evidenced by the heavy fragmentation of the cattle bone) provided much needed food and goods to the nearby presidio, rancho, and mining communities. She also emphasizes how livestock played a critical role in the raiding economy of the Apache groups that terrorized both O'odham and colonial settlements alike in the Pimería Alta region. Interestingly, the proportion of sheep and cattle found at colonial settlements in the Southwest probably varied given local environmental factors, economic incentives, and raiding intensity, with cattle increasing in numbers during peaceful times.

Douglass and Graves, Pavao-Zuckerman, and others in this volume highlight several salient differences in the history of missionization between the American Southwest and Alta California. First, most missions in the Southwest were generally established in extant Indian communities. In California, local hunter-gatherer polities were relocated to central locations where mission complexes were established. Second, as discussed by Pavao-Zuckerman (chapter 11), while the Indian neophytes in Pimería Alta labored in mission agrarian and craft enterprises three days a week, they were allowed to work their own fields for another three days each week. In contrast, California Indian neophytes worked exclusively on mission economic enterprises throughout the workweek, and they did not control their own fields or agrarian products. A third significant difference is the scale and intensity of raiding in the American Southwest by various nomadic groups (e.g., Apache, Navajo, Comanche), which provided a powerful reason for some agrarian communities (O'odham, Pueblo peoples) to decide to enter into alliances with the Spanish. This was never a major factor in the Alta California missions. Finally, the *encomienda* and *repartimiento* systems used to exact tribute and labor from settled communities in the American Southwest by Spanish colonists in the seventeenth century were never formally instituted in Alta California.

While future comparative work still needs to be undertaken to understand how these differences influenced the processes and outcomes of colonial entanglements in the American Southwest and Alta California (Lightfoot, Panich, Schneider, Gonzalez, et al. 2013), it is clear from this volume that the potential of some Southwestern tribes to remain in their ancestral lands in extant villages did not lessen the trauma and stress of colonization, particularly in the 1600s and 1700s. The Hopi History Project makes this point crystal clear (Sheridan and Koyiyumptewa [chapter 9]). Missionary abuses involving corporal punishment, such as those recorded by the colonial government concerning Padre Fray Salvador de Guerra, are still very much remembered by the Hopi.

Webster's stellar study of Hopi weaving (chapter 4) dovetails nicely with the points made by Sheridan and Koyiyumptewa. She shows how the abusive demands for textiles by colonial agents through the encomienda system, as well as by some missionaries, resulted in forced labor practices that involved major transformations in the organization and composition of textile work groups. For example, an increasing number of women worked on cloth production outside of kivas, where men had traditionally woven cotton textiles. Colonialism also resulted in the increasing use of wool, new knitting techniques, and the adoption of imported dyes. Significantly, Webster's painstaking analysis demonstrates that despite the excessive textile demands of colonial men, such as Padre Guerra, in the 1600s; the Pueblo Revolt; and the painful destruction of Awatovi, many continuities were maintained in the production of Hopi textiles, particularly in the weaving of cotton goods for ceremonial use within the Pueblo communities.

THEME THREE: COLONIALISM IN INDIGENOUS LANDSCAPES

A recent development in the archaeology of colonialism is the study of native political economies and understanding how they shaped the direction, intensity, and kinds of colonial interactions that unfolded (Lightfoot, Panich, Schneider, Gonzalez, et al. 2013; Oland et al. 2012; Panich and Schneider 2014; Rubertone 2000; Scheiber and Mitchell 2010; Silliman 2009). Spanish exploration and settlement across the North American borderlands took place in indigenous landscapes populated by diverse polities who had participated for centuries in complex systems of exchange, political alliances, social relationships, ceremonial associations, and raiding/warfare. How native peoples chose to negotiate and interact with colonial intruders was influenced greatly by these extant social, economic, and political relationships. Individuals, families, or entire polities might decide to ally with the Spanish based on the perceived advantages that it might provide them in regards to their access to new kinds of goods, protection from enemies, and providing competitive advantages over political factions. The creation of these new alliances, in turn, would have rippling effects across the landscape that might lead to antagonism and conflict among other rival social entities. Lee Panich and Tsim Schneider's (Panich and Schneider 2014) edited book on the archaeology of Spanish borderland missions makes many of these points in a series of case studies that demonstrate the crucial insights that can be derived by analyzing colonial settlements as embedded places within broader indigenous landscapes.

In reading the chapters in this volume, I believe that archaeologists in the American Southwest may be at the forefront in examining how native political economies and indigenous landscapes influenced the practices and processes of colonialism. In contrast to the archaeology of Alta California, where these kinds of studies are relatively recent (e.g., Bernard 2008; Gonzalez 2011; Hull 2009; Panich 2010; Peelo 2009; Russell 2011; Schneider 2010), there is a longer tradition in the American Southwest of emphasizing native influences in colonial entanglements and how they impacted local histories. I suspect this may date back to those formative studies in Arizona and New Mexico involving the construction of ceramic chronologies using colonial-era sites and materials. Interestingly, this work was not conducted by scholars who specialized in Spanish historical archaeology per se, but rather by anthropological archaeologists interested in the culture history of indigenous societies that transcended both prehistory and history (e.g., Kidder 1924; Nelson 1916). Furthermore, the study of Spanish missions that are situated within contemporary Pueblo communities or on lands controlled or overseen by tribal entities or federal agencies has probably influenced a more native-oriented inclusion in the research designs and protocols of Southwestern archaeologists in a manner that differs substantially from the history of research in the urbanized areas of coastal California.

Archaeologists now working in the American Southwest forefront native agency, cultural practices, and political relationships in the investigation of colonial-era revolts, food ways, regional exchange systems, regional settlement distributions, and the spatial organization of village sites (Liebmann 2012; Liebmann and Preucel 2007; Lycett 2014; Mills 2008; Preucel 2002; Spielmann et al. 2009; Spielmann et al, 2006; Wilcox 2009). Phillip O. Leckman's contribution on the seventeenth-century Puebloan landscape (chapter 3) is an important contribution to this corpus of work. He discusses how Spanish settlements (missions, *visitas*, and *estancias*) were embedded within a Puebloan landscape of nested spatial tetrads composed of fields, shrines, and community lands of villages, which in turn were organized by plazas, roomblocks, and kivas. Significantly, the Spanish founded their *convento* complexes and Catholic churches and chapels, not in the central core of the villages, but in their margins—which is suggestive of the power Pueblo people maintained in controlling space in colonial contexts. Leckman's chapter details the fundamental misrecognitions that the Spanish made in their interpretation of the built landscapes of Pueblo communities, and how this influenced the nature of colonial entanglements that unfolded over time. His analysis of the seventeenth-century archaeological remains at Paako illustrates how the foreign intruders attempted to co-opt the Pueblo landscape through the construction of a chapel (which was not finished), the destruction of at least one kiva, and the alteration of the Pueblo plaza into corrals and a metal-smelting facility. However, despite the various changes initiated by the missionaries, Leckman shows how a Puebloan sense of space and landscape was sustained within indigenous communities and in their broader hinterlands.

Other chapters in this volume illustrate the importance of analyzing colonial entanglements based on an understanding of indigenous political alliances, trade connections, factionalism, and antagonisms in the broader region. Lauren Jelinek and Dale Brenneman (chapter 10) highlight how the American Southwest is ideally suited for this kind of analysis given its long, rich history of archaeological, ethnohistoric, and ethnographic research. They demonstrate how previous studies of ceramics and exchange, in combination with relevant ethnohistoric sources, can be employed to build a better understanding of regional-scale social and economic interactions in the Pimería Alta prior to and during colonial encounters in 1600s and 1700s. Their overview provides insightful information on the political alliances and antagonisms of various O'odham- and Yuman-speaking groups through time and space.

Studies of the Pueblo Revolt (1680) and its aftermath exemplify some of the most sophisticated research in North American archaeology today that is examining how native political relationships influenced the historical trajectory of colonial interactions across broader indigenous landscapes (e.g., Liebmann 2012; Liebmann and Preucel 2007; Preucel 2002; Wilcox 2009). Matthew Liebmann, Robert Preucel, and Joseph Aguilar's chapter (5) is a continuation of this fine work. Here they explicitly examine the alliances and factional rifts that existed between northern Rio Grande Pueblos before, during, and after the Pueblo Revolt. They ask an intriguing question—what happened to the Pan-Pueblo alliance that forced the Spanish out of the northern Southwest? In employing a sophisticated research program to address this question that scrutinizes the archaeological assemblages from Rio Grande mesa villages, they show how detailed petrographic and geochemical analyses of lithics and ceramics can reveal population movements, exchange relationships, political alliances, and factionalism. Their findings raise red flags about traditional interpretations concerning rifts that supposedly took place among some groups based on traditional historical sources. For example, they found evidence that an enduring coalition was maintained between the Tewa, Jemez, and Keres of Kotyiti. But their research also suggests that other Pueblo groups were continually negotiating their participation in this coalition as the political relationships of the indigenous landscape continued to change during the period of 1680–1700.

The provocative chapter by Severin Fowles, Jimmy Arterberry, Lindsay Montgomery, and Heather Atherton on the Comanche expansion into the New Mexico Colony (chapter 6) highlights the importance of undertaking archaeological research in the broader hinterland of indigenous landscapes well beyond the placement of colonial settlements. In presenting a succinct update on Comanche research in western North America, they highlight the impact that Pekka Hämäläinen's (2008) book, *The Comanche Empire*, has had on colonial scholarship given its far-reaching implications for understanding the nature and power dynamics of indigenous and colonial relationships in eighteenth-century and early nineteenth-century interactions in the Southern Plains. They note that despite the importance of the Comanche in structuring Spanish movements, settlement distributions, and alliances with other native groups in northern New Mexico, very little is known about Comanche archaeology. In part this is because the Comanche traveled light and left few identifiable materials behind. But as Fowles and colleagues emphasize, it is also because archaeologists have not been very proactive in their study of Comanche archaeology. They describe recent fieldwork in the Rio Grande Gorge region west of Taos where archaeological remains of Jicarilla Apache, Ute, and Comanche peoples are being detected. At the Vista Verde Site, where a possible buried dance floor and tipi rings are being mapped, a series of spectacular panels of etched rock art have now been recorded. The art style resembles the Plains Biographic Tradition that is found in ancestral Comanche territory in northern Colorado and Wyoming.

Fowles and colleagues' chapter emphasizes that archaeological research of indigenous landscapes is crucial for understanding how native peoples maintained their cultural lifeways and values in the face of colonialism. In the case of Comanche ethnogenesis that unfolded in the Spanish borderlands, this involved cultural innovations and reorganizations that transformed local groups into formidable equestrian military forces. While traditional cultural values were maintained and built upon as evident in the rock art and spatial patterning of archaeological materials, the Comanche adopted horses, guns, knives, and flour into their dynamic way of life.

Similar kinds of research projects are now underway in Alta California. Well beyond the Spanish presidios, ranchos, and missions, archaeological investigations are revealing how native peoples maintained their cultural values and practices while transforming themselves in the face of colonial entanglements. The most innovative work is now focusing on refugee sites where people attempted to keep a low profile from Russian and Spanish colonists (Bernard 2008; Schneider 2010; Schneider et al. 2012). Similar to Comanche sites, these archaeological places tend to be difficult to detect as they are located in concealed places and typically contain relatively few material remains. Furthermore, it is now apparent that California Indians often reused ancestral places that had spiritual meaning and offered excellent vantages for harvesting traditional resources. Consequently, distinguishing these historical contexts from earlier precontact deposits can be challenging, particularly if relatively few introduced foods or goods were intentionally used at these sites (see Graesch et al. 2010; Schneider 2010).

THEME FOUR: THE LEGACIES OF COLONIALISM

The archaeology of the recent past has much to contribute to our understanding of the legacies of colonialism and their impacts on our modern world. As outlined elsewhere, the archaeology of the last two or three centuries can be of great importance to many descendant communities immersed in the contemporary politics of indigenous landscape management practices, cultural heritage issues, identity inquiries, tribal territorial boundaries, federal recognition, and repatriation (Flexner 2010; Hart 2012; Lightfoot, Panich, Schneider, Gonzalez, et al. 2013; Mrozowski et al. 2009; Panich 2013). The archaeology of the recent past can be extremely challenging, however, given the increasingly polycultural and multiethnic construction of local communities and households who differentially participated in the global market economy and increasingly incorporated mass-produced goods and foreign foods into their lives. This is particularly true during the height of American repression in the western United States in the mid- to late 1800s, when many people of color had to disperse, hide, or even change their outward identities to endure (Heizer and Almquist 1971; Lightfoot 2006:281–84). In coastal Alta California, these later historical indigenous archaeological sites are often difficult to detect given the propensity of Native Californians to keep a low profile, such as in refugee sites discussed above, or when they were integrated (hidden) within more complex urbanized environments.

The recent past that transcends earlier colonial times and the present is crucial for understanding how descendant communities negotiated with the emerging modern world and devised strategies for survival and persistence (Panich 2013; Silliman 2009). It is also a critical time for understanding how long-term human-environmental interactions, as instituted by indigenous populations in precolonial and colonial times, underwent significant modifications and transformations with the growth of industrialized farming and ranching that continue to shape our modern landscapes in many rural areas (Lightfoot, Panich, Schneider, Gonzalez 2013; Mrozowski 2006). Several chapters in this volume make significant contributions to the growing corpus of archaeological research on the legacies of colonialism in the American West.

Colleen Strawhacker (chapter 13) presents a case study of how the O'odham people along the middle Gila River in southern Arizona participated in the emerging market economy of the 1700s and 1800s through agricultural intensification. Her broader project is examining how irrigation economies influenced the people and lands of the Middle Gila region in the *longue durée*—beginning with the prehistoric Hohokam communities and continuing with the later O'odham farmers. Strawhacker's chapter focuses on how the O'odham chose to intensify wheat production by initially selling their produce to Spanish colonists, and later to American settlers and the US Army until water was cut off to their irrigation system by upstream farmers in the 1870s. Strawhacker's analysis suggests that an understanding of the agrarian practices of the ancestral Hohokam was retained by the O'odham, and that this knowledge was probably tapped into when they chose to intensify their output from irrigation agriculture. Her project has tremendous potential for examining the social and ecological impacts that agricultural intensification has had on a local region spanning prehistoric, colonial, and later historic times.

I am currently participating in a similar kind of project that is examining the long-term implications of changing human-environmental relationships in precolonial, colonial, and modern times on the central coast of Alta California. But rather than the irrigation economies of the Hohokam and O'odham peoples, this study is examining the advent and modifications of hunter-gatherer landscape management practices, particularly that of prescribed burning to enhance the productivity, diversity, and sustainability of economic plants and animals exploited by local groups. Our interdisciplinary research team is examining how these indigenous management practices underwent transformations in colonial times, and how colonial and later American government prohibitions outlawing fires ignited by California Indians have had a detrimental impact on the health and vitality of coastal grassland and woodland habitats in recent years (Cuthrell 2013; Cuthrell et al. 2012; Lightfoot, Cuthrell, Boone, et al. 2013; Lightfoot, Cuthrell, Striplen, et al. 2013). As Strawhacker (chapter 13) and our ongoing project demonstrate, there is much promise for archaeologists to evaluate contemporary environmental issues in the American West through detailed historical-ecological studies that incorporate landscape management practices of the recent past with those from earlier colonial and precolonial times.

Two complementary chapters by J. Andrew Darling and B. Sunday Eiselt (chapter 7) and Kelly L. Jenks (chapter 8) explore identity construction and the creation of multiethnic communities in the New Mexico Colony during the 1700s and early 1800s. Both chapters illustrate nicely that the creation of the Vecino identity was not based on ethnicity per se, but rather on how people lived—their place of residence and accepted membership in a Hispanic corporate community as tax-paying, property-owning Catholic families. Darling and Eiselt present a succinct historical overview on the demographic rise of Vecino communities as part of the Bourbon reforms initiated to protect the northern Spanish frontier from nomadic Indian raiders and other European colonial ventures in the late 1700s. By receiving land grants and support for military service, Vecino families populated the Rio Grande Valley in increasing numbers after 1790. In undertaking a synthesis of archaeological research in the Rio del Oso land grant, the authors show how significant transformations took place over time from the defensive, segregated nature of early colonial sites to the more open, integrated Vecino settlements where membership was based on property ownership and marriage associations rather than ethnic relationships.

In her detailed examination of twenty-five sites along the Rio Grande Valley, Jenks (chapter 8) discusses the similarities and differences across both space and time in Vecino villages with regard to their spatial layouts, food way, trade practices, and corporate organizations. She emphasizes the difficulties of defining clear-cut "ethnicities" in these late colonial settlements using archaeological materials. She makes an excellent case for why a practice-oriented approach provides a more effective way to analyze late colonial communities. It is through the study of shared practices of space, food, material goods, and economic practices that archaeologists can understand the composition and identify of Vecino villages.

The chapters by Darling and Eiselt and Jenks on the construction of Vecino villages in the Rio Grande provide a nice model for examining the creation of Californio communities in Alta California that also emerged in the late 1700s and 1800s. The latter involved a process of ethnogenesis that emphasized

Spanish ancestry and common cultural practices among a diverse group of people from Sonora, Sinaloa, Baja California, and Alta California. While Barb Voss (2005, 2008) completed a cutting-edge study on the emergence of Californio identities in the Presidio of San Francisco from 1776 to 1821, detailed archaeological investigations of the Californio experience has not been well developed outside the presidio context. While considerable work has been done over the years on rancho archaeology—in the early years through the restoration of adobe structures and then later by Cultural Resource Management (CRM) projects—there have been few syntheses that pull this material together to examine the rise of Californio communities and their relationship to indigenous populations (but see Farris 1997, 1999; Silliman 2004). The Darling and Eiselt chapter, provides an excellent example of how to synthesize the indigenous and colonial archaeological remains from one land grant into a research program. Jenks offers a nice model for undertaking a regional-scale comparative analysis of the spatial layout, architecture, food ways, and artifacts from a range of colonial sites dispersed across a broad area. The archaeology of colonialism in Alta California will benefit greatly by similar synthetic overviews that integrate together various kinds of indigenous and colonial sites recorded by CRM projects and other archaeological investigations within the territories of specific Californio ranchos.

CONCLUSIONS

The chapters in this book highlight why the American Southwest holds such promise for undertaking innovative and leading-edge research in the archaeology of colonialism. For more than a century, a cadre of exceptional archaeologists have made significant contributions to our understanding of the precolonial and colonial histories of the region, providing an extraordinary database for examining cultural change and persistence that transcends the last 500 years. The American Southwest is also well known for its strong tradition of scholarship in colonial history and ethnography. Most important, Southwestern tribal nations retain long and vivid memories of colonial entanglements going back to the Coronado entrada that offer a much-needed native perspective to the study of colonialism. As demonstrated in this book, scholars can employ these different evidentiary sources to evaluate diverse questions concerning the practices, processes, and outcomes of colonialism from the initial stage of exploration, through the early phases of Spanish and later Mexican occupation, and into the American period and contemporary times.

In reading the chapters in this book, I am convinced that the American Southwest has an important role to play in broader, comparative studies of colonialism, particularly in examining distinctive historical trajectories that unfolded in the Spanish borderlands of North America. In comparing the contributions in this book to my understanding of the colonial history of Alta California, I conclude with four observations.

First, while much scholarship has focused on documenting the initial encounters between Spanish explorers and indigenous populations throughout the American borderlands, much less work has been expended on considering the long-term implications of these early engagements. The exploration programs initiated by the Spanish Crown in the American Southwest and Alta California in the 1540s differed dramatically. As detailed by Schmader (chapter 2), the overland Coronado entrada into Arizona and New Mexico lived off the land, appropriated native provisions and goods, brutalized local communities, and engaged in armed conflict with several tribes. The Cabrillo voyage to Alta California maintained stores on the ships, interacted with indigenous populations for relatively short durations during landfalls, and, for the most part, maintained relatively peaceful relations with local groups. The question I raise, particularly after reading Sheridan and Koyiyumptewa's chapter (9), is how did the distinctive outcomes that took place during these initial colonial encounters affect native memories and influence the social relationships and negotiations that took place later when the Spanish returned to settle both areas.

Second, the archaeological investigations of presidios and missions in the American Southwest, as exemplified in Thiel (chapter 12) and Pavao-Zuckerman (chapter 11), present the opportunity for comparing how the colonist's cultural practices and lifeways, as well as their relationships with indigenous populations, developed in different areas of the Spanish borderlands. I have long been intrigued by the distinctive Franciscan mission policies for working with different kinds of indigenous populations, in particular how the process of native resettlement (*reducción*) was implemented among settled agrarian populations and hunter-gatherer societies. However, as Sheridan and Koyiyumptewa (chapter 9), Pavao-Zuckerman (chapter 11), and Webster (chapter 4) illustrate, the ability of some Southwestern tribes to remain in their homeland villages did not reduce the trauma and stress of colonial occupations.

Third, the recent trend of examining the practices, processes, and outcomes of colonialism from the perspective of native political economies and indigenous landscapes may have stronger roots in the American Southwest than elsewhere in the Spanish borderlands. I believe this may stem from the seminal early work of anthropological archaeologists examining colonial-era sites from the perspective of indigenous culture history and chronology rather than as historical archaeologists who specialized in Spanish colonial history. The chapters in the book exemplify this fine tradition of placing at the forefront native agency and history in the archaeology of colonialism. Leckman (chapter 3) demonstrates how a Puebloan sense of landscape and space was maintained in the Rio Grande Valley in the face of Spanish colonialism, while Jelinek and

Brenneman (chapter 10), Liebmann, Preucel, and Aguilar (chapter 5) show why the Southwest is such an exceptional place to study the importance of native political alliances, social relationships, ceremonial associations, factional groups, and antagonisms for understanding the kinds of colonial entanglements that unfolded. Fowles, Arterberry, Montgomery, and Atherton in their presentation of Comanche archaeology (chapter 6) highlight the critical importance of undertaking archaeological research in indigenous landscapes many kilometers from missions, presidios, and *rancho* homesteads.

Fourth, we need to invest more time and energy in the study of colonial entanglements in the more recent past. The period spanning the last two or three centuries is crucial for understanding the creation of our contemporary world and how the legacies of colonialism have influenced our interactions with the environment and the identity, composition, and political relationships of modern communities in the American borderlands. Most of our research on Native American societies still focuses on precolonial and early colonial sites when specific groups can be identified and studied in the archaeological record. It is a much more difficult task to entangle and investigate indigenous archaeological remains from other peoples in late colonial times. Several chapters in this book make considerable progress in our study of the archaeology of the recent past. Strawhacker (chapter 13) presents a research program for examining long-term environmental changes associated with irrigation agriculture that transcends precolonial, colonial, and recent times. Darling and Eiselt's (chapter 7) and Jenks's (chapter 8) investigation of the creation of Vecino villages in the Rio Grande in the late 1700s and 1800s provide an excellent roadmap for examining the construction of similar communities elsewhere in the Spanish borderlands.

Finally in closing, it is clear given the major advances taking place in the archaeology of colonialism as amply demonstrated in this book that another major synthesis of Spanish borderlands scholarship is now needed. The last great overview—the seminal Columbian Consequences volumes—has been on the library shelf for more than twenty years. But I will leave this to my able colleague David Hurst Thomas to ponder...

REFERENCES CITED

Bennyhoff, James, and Albert B. Elsasser. 1954. *Sonoma Mission: An Historical and Archaeological Study of Primary Constructions, 1823–1913*. University of California Archaeological Survey Reports 27. Berkeley: University of California Archaeological Survey.

Bernard, Julienne. 2008. "An Archaeological Study of Resistance, Persistence, and Culture Change in the San Emigdio Canyon, Kern County, California." PhD dissertation, Anthropology Department, University of California, Los Angeles.

Bolton, Herbert Eugene. 1916. *Spanish Exploration in the Southwest 1542–1706*. New York: Charles Scriber's Sons. http://dx.doi.org/10.5479/sil.261021.39088005888821.

Brew, John O. 1937. *The First Two Seasons at Awatovi*. Wisconsin: Menasha.

Cordell, Linda. 1989. "Durango to Durango: An Overview of the Southwest Heartland." In *Archaeological and Historical Perspectives on the Spanish Borderlands West*. Columbian Consequences, vol. 1, edited by D. H. Thomas, 17–40. Washington, DC: Smithsonian Institution Press.

Cuthrell, Rob Q. 2013. "Archaeobotanical Evidence for Indigenous Burning Practices and Foodways at CA-SMA-113." *California Archaeology* 5 (2): 265–90. http://dx.doi.org/10.1179/1947461X13Z.00000000015.

Cuthrell, Rob Q., Chuck J. Striplen, Mark G. Hylkema, and Kent G. Lightfoot. 2012. "A Land of Fire: Anthropogenic Burning on the Central Coast of California." In *Contemporary Issues in California Archaeology*, edited by T. L. Jones and J. E. Perry, 153–72. Walnut Creek, CA: Left Coast Press.

Deagan, Kathleen. 1983. *Spanish St. Agustine: The Archaeology of a Colonial Creole Community*. Gainesville: University Press of Florida.

Farnsworth, Paul. 1987. *The Economics of Acculturation in the California Missions: A Historical and Archaeological Study of Mission Nuestra Señora de la Soledad*. PhD dissertation, Anthropology Department, Department of Anthropology, University of California, Los Angeles.

Farris, Glenn J. 1997. "Captain José Panto and the San Pascual Indian Pueblo in San Diego County, 1835–1878." *Journal of San Diego History* 43 (2): 116–31.

Farris, Glenn J. 1999. "The Reyes Rancho in Santa Barbara County, 1802–1808." *Southern California Quarterly* 81 (2): 171–80. http://dx.doi.org/10.2307/41171943.

Flexner, James Lindsey. 2010. "Archaeology of the Recent Past at Kalawao: Landscape, Place, and Power in a Hawaiian Hansen's Disease Settlement." PhD dissertation, Anthropology University of California, Berkeley.

Gonzalez, Sara L. 2011. "Creating Trails from Tradition: The Kashaya Pomo Interpretive Trail at Fort Ross State Historic Park." PhD dissertation, Department of Anthropology, University of California, Berkeley.

Graesch, Anthony P., Julienne Bernard, and Anna D. Noah. 2010. "A Cross-Cultural Study of Colonialism and Indigenous Foodways in Western North America." In *Across a Great Divide: Continuity and Change in Native North American Societies, 1400–1900*, edited by L. L. Scheiber and M. D. Mitchell, 212–38. Tucson: University of Arizona Press.

Greenwood, Roberta S. 1975. *3500 Years on One City Block: San Buenaventura Mission Plaza Project Archaeological Report, 1974*. Ventura, CA: Redevelopment Agency of the City of San Buenaventura.

Hämäläinen, Pekka. 2008. *The Comanche Empire*. New Haven, CT: Yale University Press.

Hammond, George P., and Agapito Rey. 1940. *Narratives of the Coronado Expedition, 1540–42*. Albuquerque: University of New Mexico Press.

Hart, Siobhan M. 2012. "Decolonizing through Heritage Work in the Pocumtuck Homeland of Northeastern North America." In *Decolonizing Indigenous Histories: Exploring Prehistoric/Colonial Transitions in Archaeology*, edited by M. Oland, S. M. Hart, and L. Frink, 86–109. Tucson: University of Arizona Press.

Heizer, Robert F., and Alan F. Almquist. 1971. *The Other Californians: Prejudice and Discrimination under Spain, Mexico, and the United States to 1920*. Berkeley: University of California Press.

Hester, Thomas R. 1977. "The Lithic Technology of Mission Indians in Texas and Northeastern Mexico." *Lithic Technology* 6 (1–2): 9–12.

Hoover, Robert L. 1979. "The Mission San Antonio de Padua in California." *Archaeology* 32 (6): 56–58.

Hull, Kathleen L. 2009. *Pestilence and Persistence: Yosemite Indian Demography and Culture in Colonial California*. Berkeley: University of California Press.

Kidder, Alfred V. 1916. *The Pueblo of Pecos. Papers of the School of American Archaeology No. 33*. Washington, DC: School of American Archaeology.

Kidder, Alfred V. 1924. *An Introduction to the Study of Southwestern Archaeology with a Preliminary Account of the Excavations of Pecos. Papers of the Philips Academy Southwestern Expedition, No. 1*. New Haven, CT: Yale University Press.

Larsen, Clark Spencer. 1990. "The Archaeology of Mission Santa Catalina De Guale: 2. Biocultural Interpretations of a Population in Transition." *Anthropological Papers of the American Museum of Natural History* 68:1–150.

Liebmann, Matthew Joseph. 2012. *Revolt: An Archaeological History of Pueblo Resistance and Revitalization in 17th Century New Mexico*. Tucson: University of Arizona Press.

Liebmann, Matthew, and Robert W. Preucel. 2007. "The Archaeology of the Pueblo Revolt and the Formation of the Modern World." *Kiva* 73 (2): 195–217. http://dx.doi.org/10.1179/kiv.2007.73.2.006.

Lightfoot, Kent G. 2006. "Missions, Furs, Gold and Manifest Destiny: Rethinking an Archaeology of Colonialism for Western North America." In *Historical Archaeology*, edited by M. Hall and S. W. Silliman, 272–292. Malden, MA: Blackwell Publishing.

Lightfoot, Kent G., Rob Q. Cuthrell, Cristie M. Boone, Roger Byrne, Andreas B. Chavez, Laurel Collins, Alicia Cowart, Rand R. Evett, Paul V. A. Fine, Diane Gifford-Gonzalez, et al. 2013. "Anthropogenic Burning on the Central California Coast in Late Holocene and Early Historical Times: Findings, Implications, and Future Directions." *California Archaeology* 5 (2): 371–90. http://dx.doi.org/10.1179/1947461X13Z.00000000020.

Lightfoot, Kent G., Rob Q. Cuthrell, Chuck J. Striplen, and Mark G. Hylkema. 2013. "Rethinking the Study of Landscape Management Practices among Hunter-Gatherers in North America." *American Antiquity* 78 (2): 285–301. http://dx.doi.org/10.7183/0002-7316.78.2.285.

Lightfoot, Kent G., Lee M. Panich, Tsim D. Schneider, and Sara L. Gonzalez. 2013. "European Colonialism and the Anthropocene: A View from the Pacific Coast of North America." *Anthropocene* 4:101–15. http://dx.doi.org/10.1016/j.ancene.2013.09.002.

Lightfoot, Kent G., Lee M. Panich, Tsim D. Schneider, Sara L. Gonzalez, Matthew A. Russell, Darren Modzelewski, Theresa Molino, and Elliot H. Blair. 2013. "The Study of Indigenous Political Economies and Colonialism in Native California: Implications for Contemporary Tribal Groups and Federal Recognition." *American Antiquity* 78 (1): 89–103. http://dx.doi.org/10.7183/0002-7316.78.1.89.

Lightfoot, Kent G., and William S. Simmons. 1998. "Culture Contact in Protohistoric California: Social Contexts of Native and European Encounters." *Journal of California and Great Basin Anthropology* 20 (2): 138–70.

Lycett, Mark T. 1995. *Archaeological Implications of European Contact: Demography, Settlement, and Land Use in the Middle Rio Grande Valley*. Albuquerque: University of New Mexico Press.

Lycett, Mark T. 2014. "Toward a Historical Ecology of the Mission in Seventeenth-Century New Mexico." In *Indigenous Landscapes and Spanish Missions: New Perspectives from Archaeology and Ethnohistory*, edited by L. M. Panich and T. D. Schneider, 172–87. Tucson: The University of Arizona Press.

McEwan, Bonnie G., ed. 1993. *Spanish Missions of La Florida*. Gainesville: University Press of Florida.

Mills, Barbara J. 2008. "Colonialism and Cuisine: Cultural Transmission, Domestic Practice, and Agency at Zuni Pueblo." In *Cultural Transmission and Material Culture: Breaking Down Boundaries*, edited by L. Horne, B. Bowser, and M. Stark, 245–62. Tucson: University of Arizona Press.

Montgomery, Ross Gordon, Watson Smith, and John O. Brew. 1949. *Franciscan Awatovi, The Excavation and Conjectural Reconstruction of a 17th-Century Spanish Mission Establishment at a Hopi Town in Northeastern Arizona*. Papers of the Peabody Museum of American Archaeology and Ethnology, Harvard University No. 36. Cambridge, MA: Peabody Museum, Harvard University.

Mrozowski, Stephen A. 2006. "Environments of History: Biological Dimensions of Historical Archaeology." In *Historical Archaeology*, edited by M. Hall and S. W. Silliman, 23–41. Malden, MA: Blackwell Publishing.

Mrozowski, Stephen A., Holly Herbster, David Brown, and Katherine L. Priddy. 2009. "Magunkaquog Materiality, Federal Recognition, and the Search for Deeper History." *International Journal of Historical Archaeology* 13 (4): 430–63. http://dx.doi.org/10.1007/s10761-009-0088-8.

Nelson, Nels C. 1916. "Chronology of the Tano Ruins, New Mexico." *American Anthropologist* 18 (2): 159–80. http://dx.doi.org/10.1525/aa.1916.18.2.02a00010.

Neuerburg, Norman. 1987. *The Architecture of Mission La Purísima*. Santa Barbara, CA: Bellerophon Books.

Oland, Maxine, Siobhan M. Hart, and Liam Frink, eds. 2012. *Decolonizing Indigenous Histories: Exploring Prehistoric/Colonial Transitions in Archaeology*. Tucson: University of Arizona Press.

Panich, Lee M. 2010. "Missionization and the Persistence of Native Identity on the Colonial Frontier of Baja California." *Ethnohistory (Columbus, Ohio)* 57 (2): 225–62. http://dx.doi.org/10.1215/00141801-2009-062.

Panich, Lee M. 2013. "Archaeologies of Persistence: Reconsidering the Legacies of Colonialism in Native North America." *American Antiquity* 78 (1): 105–22. http://dx.doi.org/10.7183/0002-7316.78.1.105.

Panich, Lee M., and Tsim D. Schneider, eds. 2014. *Indigenous Landscapes and Spanish Missions: New Perspectives from Archaeology and Ethnohistory*. Tucson: University of Arizona Press.

Peelo [Ginn], Sarah M. 2009. "Creating Community in Spanish California: An Investigation of California Plainwares." PhD dissertation, Department of Anthropology, University of California at Santa Cruz, Department of Anthropology.

Preucel, Robert W. 2002. *Archaeologies of the Pueblo Revolt: Identity, Meaning, and Renewal in the Pueblo World*. Albuquerque: University of New Mexico Press.

Quinn, David B. 1979a. "December 1, 1587: Pedro de Unamuno to the Marques de Villamanrique, Viceroy of Mexico." In *The Extension of Settlement in Florida, Virginia, and the Spanish Southwest*. New American World: A Documentary History of North America to 1612, vol. 5, edited by D. B. Quinn, 401–8. New York: Arno Press and Hector Bye.

Quinn, David B. [1584–85] 1979b. "Fray Andrés de Aguirre to the Archbishop of Mexico: Proposing the Continuation of the California Voyages." In *The Extension of Settlement in Florida, Virginia, and the Spanish Southwest*. New American World: A Documentary History of North America to 1612, vol. 5, edited by D. B. Quinn, 399–401. New York: Arno Press and Hector Bye, Inc.

Quinn, David B. 1979c. "May 5, 1602 to March 21, 1603: Fray Antonio de la Ascension's 'Brief report' of the Voyage of Sebastian Vizcaíno up the California Coast." In *The Extension of Settlement in Florida, Virginia, and the Spanish Southwest*. New American World: A Documentary History of North America to 1612, vol. 5, edited by D. B. Quinn, 413–26. New York: Arno Press and Hector Bye.

Quinn, David B. 1979d. "November 30, 1595: Abstract of the Journal of Sebastian Cermeño on his Voyage up the California Coast." In *The Extension of Settlement in Florida, Virginia, and the Spanish Southwest*. New American World: A Documentary History of North America to 1612, vol. 5, edited by D. B. Quinn, 408–13. New York: Arno Press and Hector Bye.

Quinn, David B. [1542–43] 1979e. "The Voyage of Juan Rodríguez Cabrillo (João Rodrigues Cabrilho) up the Pacific Coast." In *America from Conception to Discovery: Early Exploration of North America*. New American World: A Documentary History of North America to 1612, vol. 1 , edited by D. B. Quinn, 450–61. New York: Arno Press and Hector Bye.

Quinn, David B. 1979f. "'The World Encompassed' Account of Drake's California Visit." In *America from Concept to Discovery. Early Exploration of North America*. New American World: A Documentary History of North America to 1612, vol. 1, , edited by D. B. Quinn, 467–76. New York: Arno Press and Hector Bye.

Rubertone, Patricia E. 2000. "The Historical Archaeology of Native Americans." *Annual Review of Anthropology* 29 (1): 425–46. http://dx.doi.org/10.1146/annurev.anthro.29.1.425.

Russell, Matthew A. 2011. "Encounters at Tamál-Húye: An Archaeology of Intercultural Engagement in Sixteenth-Century Northern California." PhD dissertation, Department of Anthropology, University of California, Berkeley.

Scheiber, Laura L., and Mark D. Mitchell, eds. 2010. *Across a Great Divide: Continuity and Change in Native North American Societies, 1400–1900*. Tucson: University of Arizona Press.

Schneider, Tsim D. 2010. "Placing Refuge: Shell Mounds and the Archaeology of Colonial Encounters in the San Francisco Bay Area, California." PhD dissertation, Department of Anthropology, University of California, Berkeley.

Schneider, Tsim D., Sara L. Gonzalez, Kent G. Lightfoot, Lee M. Panich, and Matthew A. Russell. 2012. "A Land of Cultural Pluralism: Case Studies from California's Colonial Frontiers." In *Contemporary Issues in California Archaeology*, edited by T. L. Jones and J. E. Perry, 319–37. Walnut Creek, California: Left Coast Press.

Silliman, Stephen W. 2004. *Lost Laborers in Colonial California: Native Americans and the Archaeology of Rancho Petaluma*. Tucson: University of Arizona Press.

Silliman, Stephen W. 2009. "Change and Continuity, Practice and Memory: Native American Persistence in Colonial New England." *American Antiquity* 74 (2): 211–30.

Smith, W., R. B. Woodbury, and N. S. F. Woodbury. 1966. *The Excavation of Hawikuh by Fredrick Webb Hodge: Contributions of the Museum of the American Indian Heye Foundation XX*. New York: Heye Foundation.

Spielmann, Katherine A., T. Clark, D. Hawkey, K. Rainey, and Suzanne K Fish. 2009. "'. . . being weary, they rebelled': Pueblo Subsistence and Labor Under Spanish Colonialism." *Journal of Anthropological Archaeology* 28 (1): 102–25. http://dx.doi.org/10.1016/j.jaa.2008.10.002.

Spielmann, Katherine A., Jeannette L. Mobley-Tanaka, and James M. Potter. 2006. "Style and Resistance in the Seventeenth-Century Salinas Province." *American Antiquity* 71 (4): 621–48. http://dx.doi.org/10.2307/40035882.

Thomas, David Hurst. 1987. *The Archaeology of Mission Santa Catalina de Guale, 1. Search and Discovery. Anthropological Papers of the American Museum of Natural History 63, pt. 2.* New York: American Museum of Natural History.

Thomas, David Hurst. 1989. *Archaeological and Historical Perspectives on the Spanish Borderlands West.* Columbian Consequences, vol. 1. Washington, DC: Smithsonian Institution Press.

Thomas, David Hurst. 1990. *Archaeological and Historical Perspectives on the Spanish Borderlands East.* Columbian Consequences, vol. 2. Washington, DC: Smithsonian Institution Press.

Thomas, David Hurst. 1991a. "Harvesting Ramona's Garden: Life in California's Mythical Mission Past." In *The Spanish Borderlands in Pan-American Perspective. Columbian Consequences,* vol. 3, edited by D. H. Thomas, 119–57. Washington, DC: Smithsonian Institution.

Thomas, David Hurst. 1991b. *The Spanish Borderlands in Pan-American Perspective.* Columbian Consequences, vol. 3. Washington, DC: Smithsonian Institution.

Thomas, David Hurst, Grant D. Jones, Roger S. Durham, and Clark Spencer Larsen. 1978. "The Anthropology of St. Catherines Island, 1. Natural and Cultural History." *Anthropological Papers of the American Museum of Natural History* 55 (2): 155–248.

Toulouse, Joseph H., and Robert L. Stephenson. 1960. *Excavations at Pueblo Pardo.* Papers in Anthropology No. 2. Santa Fe: Museum of New Mexico.

Treganza, Adan E. 1956. *Sonoma Mission: An Archaeological Reconstruction of the Mission San Francisco de Solano Quadrangle.* Kroeber Anthropological Society Papers.

Vivian, R. G. 1964. *Gran Quivira: Excavations in a Seventeenth-Century Jumano Pueblo.* Washington, DC: National Park Service, Department of Interior.

Voss, Barbara L. 2005. "From Casta to Californio: Social Identity and the Archaeology of Culture Contact." *American Anthropologist* 107 (3): 461–74. http://dx.doi.org/10.1525/aa.2005.107.3.461.

Voss, Barbara. 2008. *The Archaeology of Ethnogenesis: Race and Sexuality in Colonial San Francisco.* Berkeley: University of California Press.

Wagner, Henry R. 1924. "The Voyage to California of Sebastian Rodríguez Cermeño in 1595." *California Historical Society Quarterly* 3 (1): 3–24.

Wagner, Henry R. 1929. *Spanish Voyages to the Northwest Coast of America in the Sixteenth Century.* San Francisco: California Historical Society.

Whitehead, Richard S., ed. 1991. *An Archaeological and Restoration Study of Mission La Purísima Concepción. Reports Written for the National Park Service by Fred C. Hageman and Russell C. Ewing.* Santa Barbara: Santa Barbara Trust for Historic Preservation.

Wilcox, Michael V. 2009. *The Pueblo Revolt and the Mythology of Conquest: An Indigenous Archaeology of Contact.* Berkeley: University of California Press.

FIFTEEN

Materiality Matters

Colonial Transformations Spanning the Southwestern
and Southeastern Borderlands

DAVID HURST THOMAS

INTRODUCTION

While preparing these comments, editors John G. Douglass and William M. Graves shared with me Kent Lightfoot's (chapter 14) enlightened comparison of the Southwestern papers in this volume with the Alta California experience. These fortunate circumstances afforded me the chance to tailor-make my own contribution in complimentary directions.

I was assigned to draw some parallels and contrasts between the chapters in this book addressing the colonial Southwest and comparable histories now emerging from the Mississippian Southeast. It is my pleasure to do this and because Lightfoot has already commented in detail on the individual chapters, I will frame my own discussion as a more generalized theoretical conversation—drawing upon the themes and specifics of the southwestern chapters, to be sure, but also developing related themes about the importance of materiality and agency as it played out in the "practical politics" of both colonial encounters (after Silliman 2001).

DOI: 10.5876/9781607325741.c015

This discussion is informed by Igor Kopytoff's (1986:66–67) advocacy for constructing the cultural biography of things, interrogating objects in ways akin to asking questions of people—inquiring about the relevant possibilities for understanding status, temporality, and cultural context. Where did something come from and who made it? How far did its use life go? What are its expectations for the future? What are the ideal expectations for this thing? Are there various life stages of this object, and what are the cultural identifiers associated with these? Does a thing's usage change with age? Is there an expected time when the thing is no longer useful? What is its afterlife? William Walker and Lisa Lucero (Walker and Lucero 2000:12) expand these concepts by distinguishing between a biographical approach to artifact genealogies from the more inclusive concept of genealogies of practice (see also Joyce and Lopiparo 2005). Viewing "things as historicized traces of practices" (Joyce 2012a), objects can be animated from static to active through "object itineraries" that emphasize motion and interaction, fragmentation and accumulation—tracking objects moving through time and space, as they entwined with people and places (see also Joyce and Gillespie 2015). Object agency can indeed be archaeologically accessible, and Walker and Lucero (2000) have incorporated agency theory to examine how artifact life histories, ritual, and politics intersect. With this in mind, I will present a comparative inquiry into the biographies of public architecture and singularized objects from the Southwest and Southeast.

PUEBLO COLONIAL WORLDS

Neither the Spanish colony in New Mexico nor that in La Florida was self-sustaining, because both outposts were significantly underwritten by the Spanish Crown, at least partly for strategic purposes. Following standard sixteenth- and seventeenth-century colonial practice, missionaries were stationed near the principal indigenous settlements closely associated with a frontier garrison; inevitably, the proximity of soldiers to the native populations created problems with political meddling, distribution of supplies, and harassment of local women. But Franciscans from both corners of the Spanish Borderlands articulated the critical importance of saving Indian souls if the colonies were to remain in business (see Liebmann 2012:34–35; Riley 1999:86–87; Thomas 2014, 2015).

Franciscan Missions in the American Southwest

Initial prospects for missionization in the Southwest must have seemed bright. "For Franciscans, who insisted that Indians live like Spaniards and tried to congregate them into towns if they did not, the apartment-dwelling Pueblos seemed a godsend" (Weber 1999:4). The Spanish called these apparently permanent towns—and the people who lived there—*los pueblos*, to distinguish them from the more mobile Apache and Navajos (Thomas 2013a, 2013b; see also Phillip O. Leckman, chapter 3 in this volume).

Hispanic optimism was quickly shattered by the realities of fluid Pueblo settlement strategies, often involving annual cycles of seasonal dispersal and aggregation, with households frequently relocating among villages. This was a problem for Franciscans seeking full-time sedentary populations, preferably under the control of a single political leader. Juan de Oñate complained about the lack of solid decision making and governance within Pueblo society: "In government they are free, for although they have petty captains, they obey them badly and in very few things" (quoted in Bolton 1908).

Oñate had put his finger squarely on a dilemma that would bedevil top-down Hispanic colonial thinking for centuries: Who, exactly, are the Pueblo leaders? Who, exactly, makes the decisions? Who, exactly, has the power to negotiate commitments? Where, exactly, does the leadership hierarchy reside? Answering these questions is critical for understanding how and why Spanish and Pueblo trajectories intertwined.

Decision-Making, Factionalism, and Social Agency

Pueblos lived as autonomous villagers, with their decision-making process ramified through differential access to esoteric knowledge and ceremonial objects, social duties, and family/lineage alignments, and inequities in wealth and power (Brandt 1994; McGuire and Saitta 1996). "To the extent that the Pueblos are govern at all," cautions John Ware (2002:94), "they are governed by hierarchies of priests—members of secret sodalities who exercise authority over the ritual, and in many communities, the mundane aspects of everyday life." At least among the Hopi, society (sodality) chiefs had a considerably more important role in political life than conventional ethnographies allow—they were not subservient assistants to village chiefs, but instead independent participants with the groups of decision makers, with village chiefs being merely "first among equals" (Whiteley 1988).

Lee Panich, arguing for "archaeologies of persistence," emphasizes the variability in how native communities negotiated their colonial world (Panich 2013:17). Matthew Liebmann, Robert Preucel, and Joseph Aguilar (chapter 5 in this volume) highlight the pervasive factionalism in Pueblo societies. Citing Edward Dozier (1966), they stress an "endemic ... inherent opposition" to the compulsory dictates of Pueblo authorities leading to the extraordinary level of intracommunity friction before, during, and after the Pueblo Revolt of 1680.

At the core of the Pueblo Revolt were the northern Tiwa, Tewa, and Towa and the eastern Keresan Pueblos. Acoma, Hopi, and Zuni also joined in, though at least one Hopi town (Awat'ovi) had a strong Christian faction (Brooks 2013;

Thomas 2014). The southern Tiwa were divided. The southernmost Pueblos, the Piros and Tompiros, refused to follow along. And even in the heartland of the rebellion, pro-Franciscan factions persisted, leading Po'pay and his colleagues to take sometimes savage actions against those perceived to be wavering or disloyal to the cause (Riley 1999:222–24). As Liebmann, Preucel, and Aguilar (chapter 5 in this volume) argue, the pan-Pueblo alliance "didn't so much break down after 1680 as it was continually renegotiated by Pueblo leaders in response to changing needs within the postrevolt community."

Thomas E. Sheridan and Stewart B. Koyiyumptewa (chapter 9 in this volume) likewise underscore the importance of social agency, local histories, and Pueblo factionalism in their assessment of long-term oral accounts of Franciscan "abusive guests." Emphasizing the constellation of factors that triggered the anti-Spanish rebellion at Hopi, these authors craft narratives from both indigenous and Hispanic sources, stressing that each perspective has "strengths and limitations that need to be understood." Whereas conventional accounts have long privileged the friction caused when the pro-Catholic faction invited Franciscans to return to Hopi after the Pueblo Revolt, Sheridan and Koyiyumptewa argue that Hopi accounts paint a much more complex picture (see also Whiteley 2002). Regardless, the end result was Pueblo factionalism at its worst—"destruction of one of their own communities and the killing of their own people still sear Hopi memories today."

Pro- and anti-Franciscan factions arose in most Pueblo communities, though the precise histories of each are difficult to discern. William Merrill (2009:130) emphasizes that some indigenous Pueblo practices have similarities and parallels to the Catholic rites introduced by Franciscans during colonial times. There is also considerable evidence that power imbalance and gender inequality helped spawn the resulting factions in colonial Pueblo societies. James Brooks (2013:754) argues that Franciscan Catholicism provided a counterbalance to the Katsina religion. Young single males—accorded lower rank and status than the headmen of the medicine societies, sodalities, and Katsina societies—formed the core of neophyte Franciscan enlistees throughout several Pueblo communities.

Katsina ritualism predominantly enhanced masculine ritual power, and in most manifestations, provisions were made to include young males in the ritual organization, to be formalized at puberty. Women were prohibited from acquiring Katsina knowledge among the eastern Pueblos, at Zuni and to some degree at Hopi. The Pueblo Revolt further reflected the chasms separating traditionalists from those drawn to Catholicism, pulling not only on religious sympathies but also "the inequities in power that had crosscut Pueblo society for generations" (Brooks 2013:756). Women likewise did not rank high among Po'pay's priorities for the new Pueblo world. It is small wonder that women in particular were attracted to a Franciscan catechism that honored the lives and suffering of female saints. As Liebmann (2002, 2012:136–42) notes, during the post-Revolt era in the Rio Grande area there are repeated representations of the Virgin Mary in rock art associated with refugee pueblos.

The Pueblo world was structured in ways fostering factionalism and resistance to top-down changes ordered by Spanish colonial authorities (including members of the Franciscan order). The resulting conflicts reflect a pervasive social agency that privileged decisions by factions of actors who were simultaneously operating within contemporary colonial contexts, yet making critical decisions for the future. While such social agency can indeed involve innovation and change, there are also options to reiterate (in whole or in part) what was done in the past (Joyce and Lopiparo 2005:368–70).

MISSISSIPPIAN COLONIAL WORLDS

Comparing the Pueblo and Mississippian worlds, it is difficult to overemphasize the deep-reaching contrasts in decision making and social agency. Hernando de Soto's expedition was structured along medieval lines of Hispanic honor and hierarchy, with social status determined by a complex system of racial gradients and classifications (Hudson 1997:10; Thomas 2013a, 2014). These sixteenth-century Spaniards noticed immediately how closely Southeastern Indian societies were "structurally similar to their own society . . . some Indians possessed more social honor than others" (Hudson 1997:17, 23). The Spanish newcomers knew intrinsically how such hierarchies operated and they insisted that negotiations proceed strictly between paramounts, with everyone else expected to fall in line.

"Inequality was institutionalized in the Southeast" (Hudson 1997:17). The Muskogean-speaking descendants of pre-Columbian powerhouses at Etowah, Moundville, and Ocmulgee lived in what John Swanton (1922:84) termed "a kind of confederacy" built upon relatively short-term and brittle federations of chiefdoms characterized by long-distance trade networks and centralized leadership (G. Jones 1978:179; Worth 2002, 2013a, 2013b). These contact-period Mississippian polities were long committed to maintaining hereditary birthright based on genealogical distance from a single noble ancestor. Dominants belonged to a privileged chiefly class, enjoying great status and wealth. Mississippian subordinates supplied the labor and material resources to underwrite this hereditary inequality (and in the case of the conscripted draft risked their lives in chiefly warfare).

As a result, Pueblo-style factionalism was not manifest in La Florida, and there was no Mississippian equivalent to the "endemic" and "inherent opposition" to Pueblo authorities (Dozier 1966). In the Southeast, disputes within individual lineages were handled internally, and between-lineage misunderstandings were handled by the caciques (locally termed *micos*) and other mechanisms of chiefly governance (which varied considerably in terms of centrality and power). Individual chiefdoms identified closely with their micos and were protective of chiefly authority. At least one of de Soto's prisoners committed suicide rather than betray his mico (Hudson 1976:223, 233). When irreparable disputes arose between towns and lineages, they sometimes split to acquire distinctive social identities, each with its own ceremonial center and ritual practices. Sometimes chiefdoms fused, but in other cases they maintained separate council houses (Blair and Thomas 2014).

In short, the inherently segmented sociopolitical structure of southwestern Pueblos often resisted the sweeping changes brought about by colonial authority. In contrast, Mississippian long-term hierarchical and authoritarian structure was vastly more compatible with the sixteenth-century Spanish colonial system imported to the deep American South.

Franciscan Missions in Spanish Florida

In the wake of the Hernando de Soto, Tristán de Luna, and Juan Pardo *entradas*, the major chiefdoms of the deep interior collapsed into the "Mississippian shatter zone," where the remnants would be spared direct or sustained contact with Europeans for more than 130 years (Ethridge and Shuck-Hall 2009). A wholly different scenario played out in La Florida, where (with rare exceptions) the soldiers and friars stuck close to the Atlantic coastline and Apalachee Province to the southwest. Pedro Menéndez de Avilés established La Florida in 1565 as a strategic Spanish foothold to stave off further French settlements and to safeguard the fleet of the Indies through the Bahama Channel as the treasure-laden ships sailed back to Spain. This strategic significance ultimately ensured a relatively stable source of royal funding, but it also required that Spanish colonists in St. Augustine rely heavily on local Native American populations to buffer against interruptions in external supply lines.

From the outset, Spanish colonists were dependent on the human and natural riches of La Florida. With both slavery and abusive treatment of indigenous people explicitly banned, Menéndez de Avilés and his successors were constrained to ensuring good treatment for indigenous peoples, acting with explicit permission from all Native leaders. This is why the Europeans colonizing Spanish Florida elected to become active participants in indigenous political dynamics, bolstering and reinforcing the political power of traditional Indian leaders. Hereditary chiefs retained considerable internal autonomy over secular matters and ruled using traditional lines of authority.

The seventeenth-century economy of Spanish Florida evolved into an exchange network through which Native populations channeled their surplus food (primarily maize) and labor into colonial St. Augustine. Several indigenous Timucua, Mocamo, and Guale caciques elected to pledge allegiance and obedience to Spanish officials; others did not. Those siding with the newcomers annexed a powerful military ally in the Spanish garrison at St. Augustine. These Native paramounts not only generated new markets for their agricultural surplus, but they also gained access to new tools and technologies to improve their yield.

Clearly, Franciscan friars in both Spanish Florida and the American Southwest served as face-to-face primary agents of directed social change, but the two mission systems were vastly different. Amy Turner Bushnell has long argued that the mission in Spanish Florida "was no theocracy. It was a fully functioning Native town governed by an interlocking set of hereditary and elected native leaders" (Bushnell 1994:28; see also Bushnell 2014). John Worth (2013a) takes things a step further, arguing that Franciscan friars stationed in La Florida functioned in a manner analogous to the modern Peace Corps, granted voluntary admittance into Native American communities to assist in the transition to a new order. While Franciscan missionaries remained at the head of the new church, they did so only within the context of chiefly authority, accepting the continued practice of ancient indigenous Mississippian religion alongside new Christian rites.

The friars occupied unique new roles in the hybrid colonial context of La Florida, operating as cultural facilitators to help bridge the realities of pre-Columbian and colonial Spanish practice. Franciscans assumed economic responsibilities (especially involving intensified agricultural production), negotiated new roles for the military, and interceded at times on behalf of the mission Indians (often shoring up traditional Mississippian hierarchies). By accepting conversion to Christianity and accepting resident Franciscan friars within the local community's jurisdiction, native chiefs could retain authority reckoned through ancient Mississippian hereditary bloodlines, while still drawing on the largesse of the Catholic Church and the Spanish Crown.

Social agency is evident in all quarters. Franciscans assigned to La Florida had to accommodate religious practices other than those they knew previously or necessarily condoned. At times, they objected and resisted. The Mississippian micos and populace tolerated living conditions that differed from their long-term community practices from before. At times, they also objected and resisted as well. But it is clear that Spanish colonial functionaries and hereditary Mississippian nobility alike enjoyed "considerable room for individual interpretation" (Worth 1998:124)—practical politics and social agency in action (see also Blair 2015a, 2015b; Blair and Thomas 2014; Bushnell 2014; Thomas 2014, 2015).

Tribute, Materiality, and the Trappings of Chiefly Power

In the transition from entrada to permanent colonization, as elsewhere in the New World, the Spanish crafted ways (some legal, some not) to extract tribute and exploit the indigenous populations. The *encomienda* (in which trustees held a specific number of Natives in trust) and the *repartimiento de indios* (which distributed Native men to work on a rotating basis for the public good) were the favored "legal" institutions. Some Spaniards also turned to the patently illegal practice of taking Indian slaves—rarely among mission Indians (their labor was exploited in other ways), that is to say, seizing "pagans" beyond the expanding rim of Christendom (Weber 1994:124–29; see also Brooks 2002).

Tribute in the American Southwest was basically a one-way street, with Pueblo households assigned the burden of producing foodstuffs and textiles for the newcomers (see Laurie D. Webster [chapter 4], this volume). By contrast, Atlantic coastal Mississippians had paid and received tribute for centuries, and Guale households knew no other way. Mississippian micos held important offices in local political and religious hierarchies, with tangible social, political, and economic advantages. While inherited status was a necessary condition for leadership, micos found themselves constantly required to shore up their power base through effective manipulation of ritual, access to scarce trade items, and hospitality.

These paramounts had long maintained large-scale, regional systems of tribute, traveling extensively to conduct war, diplomacy, ritual, and participate in complex, rank-enhancing marriage alliances. The trappings of chiefly office included clothing, adornment, and regalia—long staples in the Mississippian world well before European contact (Worth 1998:12–13). The preexisting emphasis on appropriate chiefly attire and the exchange of exotic luxury items such as conch shell, polished greenstone, high-quality chert, and native copper were particularly important between neighboring chiefdoms in transactions that were more symbolic than economic.

The colonial system in Spanish Florida reinforced such long-standing Mississippian power structures by channeling access to indigenous land and labor through hereditary chiefs. By participating in the external colonial Spanish markets, traditional Guale leaders transformed agricultural surpluses, land, and labor—all commodities under their control—into military backing and, perhaps more important, the symbolically charged Spanish goods, including cloth, tools, and beads. In this way, the caciques positioned themselves to receive tribute from both the Spaniards and their own people. "In effect, Spanish Florida became a sort of modified paramount chiefdom through which the chiefly matrilineages of destabilized chiefdoms bolstered their own internal power by subordinating themselves to the Spanish crown" (Worth 2002:46; see also Pearsall 2013).

The pivotal importance of material goods and native labor thus carried over from precontact to colonial times, with selected micos now enjoying exclusive access to new tribute items and prestige items to enhance their chiefly authority (Hall 2009; Francis and Kole 2011:91). To illustrate:

- Early in the colonial era, gifts to caciques included fine woolen friar's cloth, oriental cotton cloth, pressed linen, stockings, silk buttons and braids, Chinese

taffeta, and even firearms such as arquebuses (despite Spanish colonial prohibitions elsewhere; Worth 1998:24).
- Fray Francisco de Ávila was taken captive during the Guale Uprising of 1597; his ransom consisted (almost entirely) of ritually charged items of symbolic tribute: six knives with yellow handles, three bundles of glass beads, six hatchets, one dozen iron axes, four muskets, and a single white blanket (Francis and Kole 2011:table 6).
- In the 1670s, Governor Hita Salazar reported that the Indians preferred to be paid weekly by items of European manufacture, which he judged to have curiously low monetary value—hawks bells in two sizes, knives with black or white hafts, blue or multicolored beads, sheet brass, lengths of blue or red cloth, razors, and scissors (Bushnell 1994:122).

The Spanish often scoffed at these tribute items as simply trifles and trinkets being circulated among naive indigenous leaders. But to the Mississippian micos and those they ruled, these "trinkets" were not merely tokens of Spanish largess. In many ways, such gifts "represented the 'cement' for the colonial system, providing local and regional caciques with visible symbols of chiefly rank and status by way of access to exotic Spanish clothing, food and other items. Chiefs who failed to return from St. Augustine with such gifts might have been far less likely to overlook the more insidious consequences of missionization" (Worth 1998:137).

In effect, these knives with special handles, the lengths of blue and red cloth, and multicolored beads had become sanctified and ritualized out of the Spanish world of *commodities* and into the Mississippian realm of *priceless non-commodities*. Kopytoff (1986:64–68) terms this process "singularization," reflecting the need for societies "to set apart a certain portion of their environment, marking it as 'sacred.'" Through ritual practice, such commodities became "singularized" because they no longer belonged to the usual economic sphere. Such symbolically sacred things include public lands, monuments, state art collections, paraphernalia of political power, royal residences, chiefly insignia, and ritual objects. As noncommodities, they are "priceless" "in the full possible sense of the term, ranging from the uniquely valuable to the uniquely worthless." Symbolic authority typically asserts itself by reserving and exercising the right to "singularize" objects through an extension of sacred power as projected onto "sacralized objects ... [and] biographies of things can make salient what might otherwise remain obscure" (Kopytoff 1986:67, 73–75).

The centrality of tribute items and their role in maintaining the Mississippian chiefly order contrasts vividly with the intra-Puebloan factional egalitarianism that characterized the American Southwest. Paramount chiefs of La Florida competed with one another—sometimes violently—to enter into the Franciscan mission system; by courting the Hispanic newcomers, they defined novel ways to maintain and continue their Mississippian practices—employing ostentatious displays of wealth and status items to reinforce their hereditary status. Oddly enough, the Franciscan mission system provided Mississippian polities a way of projecting past practices into an uncertain future.

The Guale Revolt of 1597

Fray Gerónimo de Oré was not in La Florida in late fall 1597, when Guale Indians burned the churches of coastal Georgia and murdered five Franciscan friars stationed along the coast. But Oré's (1619) remarkable *Martyrs of Georgia* chronicled the details of this bloody indigenous revolt against the Spanish and long remained the authoritative voice of the 1597 unrest.

Until very recently, Borderlands historiographers have been unanimous in accepting Oré's reading of this event as a violent indigenous revolt against Spanish rule—basically an unsuccessful southeastern rehearsal of the Pueblo Revolt that would play out eight decades later. Virtually all modern treatments of the 1597 unpleasantness emphasize Franciscan interference in Guale affairs and missionary opposition to the practice of polygamy (Pearsall 2013). This historiography singles out a Guale Indian named Don Juan as the principal leader against the Spanish, and in most recent accounts of the episode, it is simply referred to as "Juanillo's revolt" (e.g., Gannon 1965; Hoffman 2002; Lanning 1935).

Extensive new documentary and archaeological research has demonstrated that the Guale uprising of 1597 was not an indigenous rebellion against Spanish authority at all (Blair and Thomas 2014; Francis and Kole 2011; Thomas 2013a, 2013b; see also Pearsall 2013; Worth 2002, 2013a, 2013b). Instead, the root cause of unrest actually reflects the underlying tensions and conflicts between indigenous chiefdoms competing for favored status within La Florida. The Spanish colony at St. Augustine had morphed into another powerful Mississippian chiefdom, simultaneously allying with, and competing against, existing Guale, Mocamo, and Timucua chiefdoms. To maintain hegemony during the late sixteenth century, paramount Guale chiefs had become dependent not only on alliances and tribute relationships from lesser Guale polities, but also support from the Spanish government.[1]

Comparing the Guale and Pueblo Revolts

Dozens of Franciscans were martyred in the Pueblo and Guale uprisings, but they perished for very different reasons. The Pueblo Revolt was about overt rejection of forced conversions and tribute demands, crosscutting existing communities of practice and involving many different kinds of people. The friars became the focus of the violence because the conflict was aimed at driving the Spanish away forever. These events "ultimately created a Pueblo people, who had not existed as such prior to the revolt . . . both women and men helped to create this new world out of old forms" (Pearsall 2013:1026).

By contrast, the social agency and materiality that powered the Guale Rebellion of 1597 reflect an internecine struggle about chiefly power (whether mico or Franciscan), a conflict between embattled paramounts locked in bloody traditional warfare. The friars were caught in the middle because the conflict centered on retaining and enhancing favored-nation status within the Franciscan mission system. Coercion and involuntary constraints certainly existed within the missions of Spanish Florida, but such had been the reality for subordinates living in the Mississippian world centuries before the Spanish entradas. In La Florida, both colonists and indigenous people had joined into a social, economic, and political hierarchy that bore considerably more similarity to Mississippian-style chiefdoms than Spanish settlements in the rest of the New World.

Social rank and status remained primary among the Guale people, including those neophytes living in the Franciscan missions of La Florida. The specific conditions that ignited the Pueblo Revolt of 1680 did not exist in Spanish Florida, because of the direct and highly public continuities of precolonial practices. This Spanish colonial–Mississippian hybrid continued to provide the external support necessary to maintain the authority of hereditary chiefs, who kept clinging to time-worn vestiges of traditional rank and privilege "even in the face of near total demographic collapse—along with English-sponsored raids—surviving missions retreated into the shadow of St. Augustine . . . [and] chiefly lineages still survived. Ultimately, the Spanish colonial strategy served to preserve these ancient social systems in a way unparalleled by other forms of European interaction" (Worth 2002:59).

ARCHITECTURE AS SOCIAL AGENCY

The colonial period of New Mexico has long been approached from perspective of informed (if occasionally heavy-handed) readings of textual evidence from the colonial era. So viewed, the Spanish colonial period witnessed a nearly complete disruption of Puebloan society—a landscape in which virtually all Pueblo Indians became Christians, fully subjugated by Franciscans until a handful of rebels and troublemakers touched off the unpleasantness of 1680. This view was fostered by France Scholes (1937, 1942), among many others, and continues to be articulated by those who tended to accept the documentary evidence at face value (Ivey and Thomas 2005). As Sheridan and Koyiyumptewa (chapter 9 in this volume) emphasize, sometimes these documents can be accurate and sometimes they are not.

In fact, several contributors to this volume argued that simple European domination/indigenous resistance models of colonialism must be replaced by agent-centered and practice-based approaches (see also Blair 2015b; Blair and Thomas 2014; Panich 2013:108–9). Matthew Liebmann and Melissa Murphy (Liebmann and Murphy 2010:7, 17–18) highlight problems with the previous "Grand Narratives" constructed centuries after the fact and viewing Spanish colonialism in the Americas as a "clash of cultures." They persuasively argue that modern discourse must transcend these "oversimplified notions of domination and resistance [implying] seemingly self-evident notions of (dominant) cores and (dominated) peripheries, active colonizers and passive colonized and the false dichotomy of indigenous survival versus extinction." These authors likewise criticize the recent generation of so-called resistance studies as flattening out the past, granting social agency to indigenous resistors, but denying equivalent agency to the colonizers. Liebmann and Murphy (2010) call for "bottom up" considerations of colonization, with an explicit recognition of individual and/or collective actions for all players in the colonial communities of practice.

To bring this conversation back to materiality, it is useful to examine object agency as expressed in the architecture of ritual. Although ritual behavior can be everywhere, some ritual practices operate at scales more archaeologically visible than others (Mills and Walker 2008:22). Here, I will isolate several such "ritually charged" spaces in the colonial Southwest and Southeast, paying particular attention to the choices being made about reiterating the past or choosing not to do so (Joyce and Lopiparo 2005:368).

Colonial architecture juxtaposes ritually charged spaces in new contexts. The Spanish colonial use of space was constrained by the utopian Ordinances of the Indies, guidelines for town planning in the New World (though rarely practiced on the Iberian Peninsula). Leckman (chapter 3 in this volume) explores how Spanish colonial spatial perceptions played out at the archaeological site of Paako, where the Ordinances provided a bridge for incorporating the basics of Iberian town planning with long-term indigenous secular (and sometimes ritual) architectures.

Situated within this larger framework, Franciscan custom involved long-established architectural conventions that generally played out, in one form or another, in the missions of the Spanish Borderlands, with the entire mission complex—not just the church and friary, but also the offices, storerooms, workshops, sheds, barns, pens, herds, and fields—becoming virtually a self-contained community. This was certainly the intent of the design, derived from over 800 years of monastic tradition and four centuries of Franciscan development. The Franciscan plan varied considerably in medieval Europe and in renaissance Mexico. Individual friars traveling into the Spanish Borderlands carried with them accumulated monastic experiences. Franciscan friar's practice, then, reflected a degree of social agency in constructing their generation of mission architecture and in the way in which the Catholic rituals would be conducted—based on personal experience in the churches attended as a child, the mission colleges, and the other missions visited, all of which molded idealized plans in the minds of a friars, influencing what was built at the new missions.

The missions of La Florida reflect a hybrid blend of Franciscan and Mississippian spaces. At Mission San Luis de Talimali archaeologists discovered a huge council house (*buhio*) capable of seating 2,000–3,000 people inside (McEwan 2014a, 2014b; Shapiro and Hann 1990). Long the most important feature of Mississippian settlements, the council house functioned variously as the seat of chiefly government, a community meeting place, a place for Black Drink ceremonialism, a locus for interacting with Spanish authorities, and a place to house enemy scalps. The buhio at San Luis fronted the main mission plaza (directly across from the mission church)—the material consequence of a unique blending of indigenous and Franciscan place logic.

Franciscans in Spanish Florida were also confronted by the ball game, a centuries-old custom commonly played between competing villages (with 50 to 100 participants to a side). *Pelota* games typically lasted a half day with omens and rituals attending every aspect of the game; serious injuries were not uncommon (Bushnell 1978). A debate raged within the Franciscan community about whether the ball game was compatible with Christianity—was the ball game a simple athletic contest or a survival of pagan demonic beliefs? The Franciscans initially supported the ball-game complex, arguing that attending the ball games encouraged sedentism among neophytes and increased attendance at mass. The Governor of St. Augustine also reluctantly supported the practice under pressure from caciques anxious to keep tribute relationships and responsibilities intact. But Apalachee paramounts eventually prevailed with arguments claiming that these ancient Mississippian did indeed reflect "pagan" beliefs, especially the symbolism of sun, thunder, and rain deities. When the Apalachee caciques insisted that such non-Christian practices could not be permitted in their mission communities, the Franciscans eventually complied.

The ritualized architecture of La Florida thus reflected a tightly negotiated and sometimes fluid hybrid of Franciscan ideals played out in the context of continuing Mississippian beliefs and materials.

The Kiva as an Object Lesson in Social Agency

Coronado's entrada encountered a ritually charged space they called *estufas*, which today is better known as the kiva. These underground chambers served multiple functions in the Pueblo world, including Katsina dances and rituals and clan or social group meeting rooms. In her dynamite study of colonial materiality, Webster (chapter 4 in this volume) addresses the Southwestern kiva as locus of textile making. The shifting tribute demands imposed by the encomienda required that Pueblo households make twice-yearly payments of cotton blankets, hides, or corn to *encomenderos*, including Franciscans, who sometimes exchanged Pueblo-made textiles southward to Mexico for church furnishings. Among the Rio Grande Pueblos, these tribute requirements ultimately caused significant shifts in the sexual division of labor, and the timing and contexts of textile production, to say nothing of the long-distance patterns of textile exchange. But more isolated Hopi communities, while still impacted by colonial demands, maintained long-term practices of textile production into modern times.

Webster's impressive chapter (4) examines the materiality of textile production by focusing on the nature of kiva practice and architecture at Hopi. Watson Smith (1972:76, 75) argued that kivas were abandoned 1630–80 due to missionary pressure, but Hopi oral tradition suggests that kivas were still used throughout this period (Courlander 1971:160). By tracking diagnostic loom holes in the Pueblo V kiva and nonkiva spaces at Awat'ovi (Smith 1972), Webster concludes that men did indeed manufacture of textiles for tribute on upright looms inside kivas throughout the Franciscan interval, with at least tacit approval by friars. But encomienda pressures likewise appear to have fostered weaving in outdoor, nontraditional settings including public plazas (perhaps reflecting manufacture by women as well). If so, then it would seem the cultural biographies of Hopi textiles maybe have temporarily shifted from their ritualized, noncommodity ("priceless") function to a temporary "commodified" status appropriate for economic tribute (Kopytoff 1986). After the expulsion of the Spanish, the highly gendered system of textile production was "re-sacralized" to long-term Hopi practices (if it ever really changed at all).

Webster (chapter 4) concludes that the geographical remoteness and marginal environment of the Hopi mesas shielded these communities from many of the Spanish labor demands experienced by Rio Grande pueblos, thereby affording them more freedom to maintain precontact ritualized practices. Among the Rio Grande pueblos and elsewhere, more intensive day-to-day interaction with Spanish authorities and the resulting material consequences reflect multiple responses within the ritually charged sacred spaces of the kiva.

The Theory of Superposition

The Southwestern Grand Narrative was most eloquently developed by Ross Montgomery, in an evolved theological metaphor he termed the "theory of superposition" and applied without reservation to Franciscan and indigenous architectural practice throughout colonial New Mexico (Montgomery 1949:143–37; see also Brew 1949:65–67; Ivey 1998:126). The "superposition" argument holds that whenever a prerevolt kiva is associated with a church and convento in colonial New Mexico, the Franciscans must have deliberately built their church over that earlier sacred space to obliterate the pagan past.

Harvard University excavations at Awat'ovi exposed portions of the sacristy and sanctuary of the church at San Bernardo de Aguatubi in Room 788. Montgomery predicted at the time that a desanctified kiva should lie buried immediately below (Smith 1972:59–66). To test this hypothesis, a small pit was dug through the sanctuary near the steps leading up to the *predella* (the altar platform), revealing the top of a masonry wall with a wooden beam emplaced in a socket, buried 1.25 meters below—clearly evidence of the kiva predicted by Montgomery. This was pretty good science as practiced in late 1930s, with an a priori hypothesis expressed and tested on independent data.

Reflecting the Grand Narrative, archaeologists working at Awat'ovi concluded that Franciscans had deliberately and symbolically subjugated Hopi religion by erecting a Christian altar over the sacred ground of the past. Sheridan and Koyiyumptewa (chapter 9 in this volume) agree that by building the church at Awat'ovi directly over a "perfectly preserved kiva," these "abusive guests" were proclaiming that "the Christian God was superior to Hopi gods, that Christian sacred spaces were submerging Hopi sacred spaces." Hopi traditional history and Harvard archaeology thus concur. This specific interpretation—and the larger issue of ritual superposition across colonial New Mexico—has generally been accepted and has not been criticized in print until James Ivey specifically questioned the hypothesis of deliberate superposition at Awat'ovi (1998; see also Ivey and Thomas 2005:211; Thomas 2014).

There is no question that Church 2 at Awat'ovi was built over two intentionally backfilled kivas, one with ceiling beams intact. But does this archaeological fact reflect deliberate superposition? Relative to Church 2 architecture, both buried kivas were offset in an "untidy location," which Ivey attributes entirely to chance alone—suggesting that other similar kivas are probably buried nearby, but the excavators did not look for them. He points out that Church 2 was only a temporary structure, soon to be replaced by a more impressive church building. Did the friars at Awat'ovi had sufficient power and agency to destroy publically one or more kivas then insultingly erect a new temporary Christian church over the top? Ivey argues that the emplacement of Church 2 was the outcome of seventeenth-century Franciscan negotiations with both pro- and anti-Catholic factions at Hopi. Together, they must have agreed to decommission the kiva spaces followed by a careful, orderly, and respectful backfilling process.[2]

Aside from the contested kivas at Awat'ovi, there are no other examples of kivas being deliberately buried beneath Catholic churches in New Mexico, and there is every reason to question the Theory of Superposition as applied to the colonial Southwest (Ivey 1998:132; Ivey and Thomas 2005).

Reverse Superposition

The archaeology of Pecos Pueblo provides another telling example of how the Grand Narrative has continued to color interpretation of Spanish colonial archaeology in the American Southwest.

Shortly after the ruins at Pecos were gifted to the National Park Service in 1965, Jean Pinkley and Alden Hayes excavated (or reexcavated) almost the entire Franciscan convent, finding a well-preserved kiva buried inside one of the rooms. The associated artifact inventory suggested a century-long window for the construction date of the kiva (roughly 1620 through 1720). Rather than address the ambiguity, Hayes instead enlisted the concept of superposition (in reverse). He argued that after demolishing the church and convent in 1680, rebellious Pueblos symbolically reclaimed their land by deliberately emplacing one or more kivas in formerly sacred Franciscan space (Hayes 1974:23–35; see also Ivey and Thomas 2005:211). John Kessell (1979:239) accepted this interpretation of the archaeological evidence, likewise attributing the Pecos convento kiva to postrevolt fervor, when victorious rebels took over the church space and dug a new kiva inside the convento: "The symbolism was clear. The ancient ones had overcome. The saints, mere pieces of rotted wood, were dead."

More recent archaeological evidence suggests a more plausible alternative. Courtney White's (1996) reanalaysis of the bricks and adobe mortar sequence at Pecos makes it clear that the "convento kiva" was constructed during the interval 1630–40—squarely during the height of the Franciscan involvement at Pecos. As at Awat'ovi, it seems highly unlikely that anti-Catholic factions could have built such an outlaw convento kiva with the pro-Franciscan factions still in place (Ivey 1998:125–26, 133). It seems more likely that the so-called postrevolt kiva at Pecos was actually constructed almost a half-century before the Pueblo Revolt—apparently with the participation and approval of Franciscans. Perhaps the convento kiva at Pecos served as training rooms and chapels for mission neophytes—an initial training practice pursued "with great caution" of influential "principal caciques and captains of the pueblo" (Ivey 1998:22; see also Riley 1999:124; Weber 2009).

Ivey (1988, 1998) argues that the prerevolt convento kiva was not unique to Pecos, citing quite parallel structures documented at the Salinas missions of Abó and Quarai (Ivey 1988, 1998:134–38). The kiva at Abó (Figure 15.1) was precisely centered inside the garth (convento patio) during the construction of the first church in 1622–28. Construction of the second church, about 1647–52, disrupted the plan of the convent plaza, and the kiva was unroofed and intentionally filled (see Toulouse 1949 for an alternative interpretation invoking the Grand Narrative). A square convento kiva was also constructed in 1626 at nearby Quarai (Ivey 1988).[3]

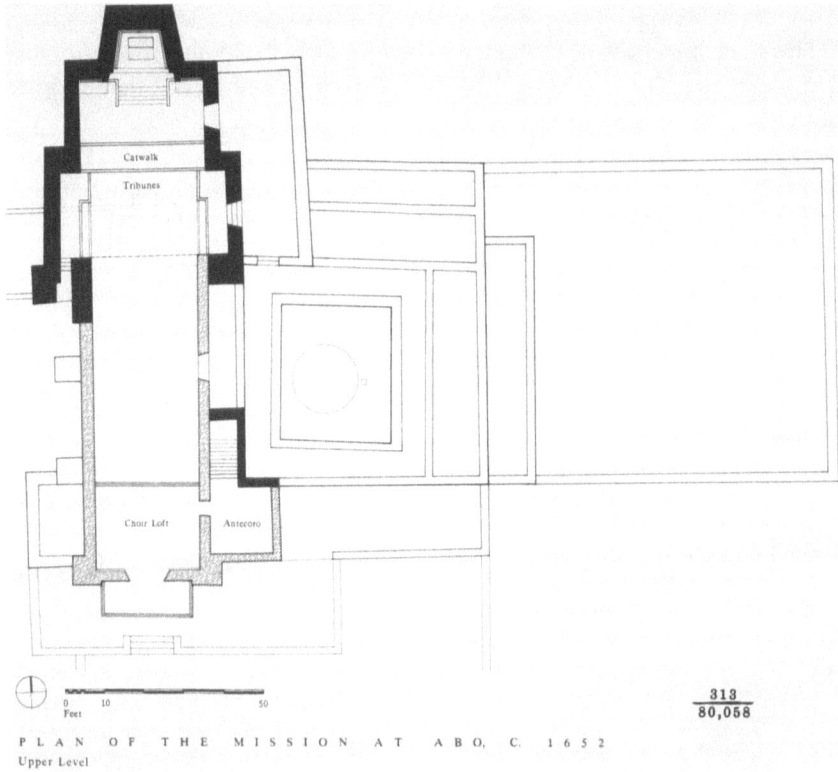

FIGURE 15.1. *Plan view of the Spanish mission at Abó (New Mexico) after its first reconstruction circa 1652. Note the circular "Franciscan kiva" (built between 1623 and 1645), carefully centered inside the convento, adjacent to the church (after Ivey et al. 1991:fig. 4; reproduced courtesy of the National Park Service).*

Convento and Visita Kivas: Historicizing the Mission Experience

The fact of convento kivas underscores the importance of historicizing the colonial experience—not as a monolithic "clash of cultures," but rather as an outcome of specific histories of "accommodation, alliance, ambiguity and ambivalence" on the part of active agents from diverse backgrounds (Liebmann and Murphy 2010:18).

Sometime after New Mexico shifted from a proprietary colony to a royal colony (in 1610), Franciscans followed a plan of more "careful integration" when establishing new mission churches. This was a time of deliberately increased religious tolerance, and there are several recorded cases of replacing friars who were too aggressive in handling neophytes (e.g., Kessell 1979:121; Ivey 1998:129–30, 148nn40, 41). During the interval 1610–45, colonial officials approved and encouraged construction of convento and visita kivas throughout the New Mexico

Province, creating familiar places within the Franciscan mission space where children and others could be taught the basics of Christianity, the catechism, and Spanish culture. David Weber (2009:10–11) concurs, pointing out that (at least during in the early seventeenth century), Franciscans introduced churches into the Southwest only "gingerly" to avoid triggering a backlash among the Pueblos, who vastly outnumbered the newcomers, thus demonstrating "restraint and flexibility that had long European antecedents."

The convento kiva is one of the many "creative architectural provisions" employed by Franciscans throughout the New World, including sixteenth-century "Franciscan mosques" in Mexico (Ivey 1998:123–24). Convento and visita kivas apparently went out of use sometime after 1645, in part because the missions of New Mexico were past the initial phases of proselytization. Spanish colonial policy stiffened further in the early 1660s, when Franciscans hardened their policies to suppress the Katsina activities at Isleta and Pecos, when "indigenous idols" were smashed and kivas deliberately destroyed (Kessell 1979:111; Ivey 1998:144,147n6; Brooks 2013).

Rejection of the Grand Narrative means that understanding the colonial period in the American Southwest no longer requires that either Pueblos or Franciscans have passive roles. The tired dominance/revolution dichotomy grew out an early twentieth-century reading of the documentary research. A more contemporary rereading of the same documents suggests some alternative interpretations, including the kiva as a hybrid colonial form.

THE MISSION BELL AS SOCIAL AGENT

Objects such as Mississippian tribute and Hopi textiles have genealogies and itineraries, some more generalized, but others quite specific and varied (Gosden and Marshall 1999:171). At different points in their life histories, these same objects may also be vested with transient values and meaning (Kopytoff 1986; Joyce 2012a; Joyce and Gillespie 2015; Mills and Walker 2008:10–11). The rest of this chapter considers some of the cultural itineraries experienced by selected mission bells in the American Southeast and Southwest.

Mission bells had a critical importance throughout Spanish American missions, with the churches sporting a *campanario* (or bell tower), which functioned as a "community timepiece" calling the faithful to their evening and morning devotions (Foster 1960:159; Bushnell 1994:82). Franciscan friar and historian Maynard Geiger described how the church bells ruled the Mission Santa Barbara (Alta California) landscape as they "proclaimed the Lord's Day and feasts of saints. Their peels were heard on occasions of national rejoicing. They were rung to greet governors and other distinguished visitors. They lent a merry note to weddings, and in doleful tones lamented the departure from life of both the great and the humble. Thrice daily they called men to prayer 'at morn, at noon, at eventide' . . . in fact, the entire day at the missions was regulated by the bell: prayer, work, and sleep" (Geiger 1956:1). The tolling bells arranged the precisely timed life rhythms of the mission and its community of souls.

Consistent with long-term Spanish tradition, New World mission bells were consecrated and blessed in a ceremony similar to baptism—typically involving exorcisms; application of water, salt, and holy oils; bestowing of a Christian name (after a specific saint, but sometimes for living individuals); and the naming of godparents. One of the original church bells at Mission Santa Barbara (Alta California) was so "baptized" in 1833 during the wedding of Doña María de las Augustias de la Guerra, who became the *madrina* (godmother) to this bell (Walsh 1934:79).

The power of mission bells extends far beyond their role as community timekeeper, with the metonymic oppositions of "life under the bell" and "break up the bells" signaling their metaphorical life and death (after Kopytoff 1986; Gosden and Marshall 1999). Reflecting his personal Franciscan beliefs, Maynard Geiger described the ecclesiastical genealogies of church bells at Mission Santa Barbara (and elsewhere): "Some of the bells played themselves out in the faithful performance of their musical calling. Others sustained injury during the convulsions of nature. Some found an unmarked resting place. Many remain to tell the story of their happy usefulness. Some, while still speaking in silvery tones, are mute with regard to their origin. *Thus bells, like humans, are a varied lot*" (Geiger 1956:1; emphasis added).

Indeed, like humans, most mission bells led more complex existences than implied in a simple life-and-death dichotomy. Many church bells had colorful life histories, genealogies, and itineraries across the Spanish Borderlands. The church bells of Spanish Florida had such social agency that during a 1575 trip to the establish the earliest missions, friars found that merely touching a small bell attracted the caciques and their subordinates in great numbers, offering themselves for conversion and baptism (Bushnell 1994:42).

Life under the Bell (bajo campana)

The mission bell has been taken as a "metonym"—a figure of speech identifying thing or a concept not by its own name, but rather by something closely associated—for the entire Franciscan mission enterprise (Bushnell 1986). "Hollywood" is a common metonym denoting film industry in southern California and "the White House" often signals the executive branch of the United States government (if not the entire government itself).

The metonym *bajo campana* (beneath the bell) reflects the expectation throughout the Franciscan ecclesiastical world that the greater mission communities should live within earshot of the *campanario*. A 1688 account from St. Augustine

(Spanish Florida) cautions that when neophyte Christians run off into the woods, every effort must be made to find and "reduce them under the bell of their *doctrinas*" (Bushnell 1994:96). The metonym "under the bell" has even achieved considerable currency in the archaeological literature of the Spanish Borderlands (e.g., Liebmann 2006, 2012:chap. 2; Lycett 2004; Milanich 2006:chap. 6;).

Putting the Bell into Rebellion

For friars and pro-Franciscan converts living within the "the missioned soundscape" (Mahar 2013), the church bell was a full-fledged member of the community, reflecting a power that blurred the lines between person and thing. But for anti-Christians living in these same communities, mission bells had become a nuisance—literally tolling every facet of their lives, tell them when to eat and sleep, wake and work, pray and attend mass.

Mission bells rang across the Pueblo world for eight decades, meaning that virtually every revolutionary in the Pueblo Revolt of 1680 knew no other existence. These same mission bells were most famously contested by Po'pay, the Tewa firebrand from San Juan who urged the Pueblo rebels in 1680 to "break up and burn the images of the holy Christ, the Virgin Mary and the other saints, the crosses, and everything pertaining to Christianity . . . burn the temples, *break up the bells*, and separate from the wives whom God had given them in marriage and take those whom they desired" (Hackett and Shelby 1942:247; emphasis added). As the violent counterpart to "life under the bell," the metonym of "breaking up the bells" has become a commonplace figure of speech to denote indigenous rebellions against Franciscan authority.

The materiality of both metonyms is confirmed across the Spanish Borderlands. As the Pueblo Revolt spread throughout the Southwest, mission bells were often yanked from the campanario and smashed to fragments; other cases, however, they were protected and revered (e.g., Brew 1949:56; Brooks 2013:756–57; Courlander 1971:163; Hackett and Shelby 1942:1:96, 2: 240; 2:203–6; Kessell, Hendricks, and Dodge 1992:549–550; Liebmann 2012:225n12: Lippard and Ranney 2010:202). Examples of both treatments:

- At Santo Domingo, the church, convent, sacristy, and trappings of the church were initially left unharmed until Po'pay specifically ordered their destruction.
- Rebels at Isleta expressed contempt for Franciscan religion by converting the burned-out church into a cow pen; but the priest's vestments, candlesticks, books, and mission bells were carefully curated, unharmed.
- The church at Hopi was totally destroyed, but the mission bells were removed from the village and sealed up in a crypt below the mesa. A line of stones was laid out atop the mesa and tribal history records that elders sighted along

the stone markers to be certain that drifting stand still covered the unbroken church bells.
- At San Felipe, rebels smashed a hole in one side of their mission bell, then sank it into the Rio Grande.
- The Zias drowned their bells in the Jemez River.
- Bells were shattered at Hawikku, Sandia, and Senecú, and the fragments were disposed in cemeteries.
- At Senecú, Alamillo, and Zuni, the rebellious Pueblos "castrated" their bells by removing their clappers.

Po'pay's edict to "break up the bells" likewise has a distinct materiality.

For more than a century, archaeologists have found fractured mission bells at sites associated with the Pueblo Revolt of 1680. Don Juan Oñate brought two church bells to New Mexico in 1598, and both were recovered in excavations near the site of San Gabriel (Howe 1956). R. G. Montgomery et al. (1949:55, fig. 6) illustrate the two bell fragments they found, superimposing the images on a church bell then hanging at Acoma; they argued that the Awat'ovi and Acoma mission bells had been cast in the same mold. Adolph Bandelier (1881:40–41) reported seeing a single bell fragment from the church at Pecos, and Alfred Kidder (1932:306) excavated eight additional mission bell fragments. Nels Nelson excavated a large mission bell fragment in at San Cristobal (Nelson 1914:59), as illustrated in Figure 15.2. Nelson also found another single mission bell fragment at San Marcos; my own excavations recovered five additional bell fragments (Ivey and Thomas 2005; Thomas 2014, n.d.). More than two dozen mission bell fragments are known from San Lazaro, including four refits and two showing damage from deliberate breakage (Fenn 2004:170–71, fig. 51, plates III and 112).

Each mission bell has a unique life history, and the best known of these come from Pecos and the Galisteo Basin, where the factionalism is well documented (Bandelier 1881; Brooks 2013; Kessell 1979:232; Levine 1999; Riley 1999:223), with pro-Franciscan neophytes living at the southern end of Pecos, literally in the shadows of the church, and more traditional anti-Hispanic factions residing in the older northern section (Liebmann, Preucel, and Aguilar, chapter 5 in this volume). Pecos remained a divided pueblo even after the Spaniards were gone in 1680 (Kessell 1979:7, 26, 223; Kidder 1958:1008).

The genealogies of these particular bell fragments are intriguing. After initial manufacture in a foundry, the bells of Pecos were sanctified by Franciscan ritual, then hung and rung in the campanario at Nuestra Señora de los Angeles de Porciúncula. Kidder (1932:306) is doubtless correct when concluding that the eight church bell fragments he recovered "date from the Pueblo Revolt of 1680 when the mission was sacked." But the perpetrator is unclear (perhaps the anti-Franciscan faction at Pecos, or perhaps Tanoans from the Galisteo Basin).

FIGURE 15.2. *This mission bell was found at San Cristóbal Pueblo in New Mexico's Galisteo Basin (Nelson 1914:59). The bell was almost certainly broken during the Pueblo Revolt of 1680, then subsequently recovered and deliberately placed by pro-Franciscan factions within a "secret kiva" near the destroyed mission church (photograph by Nicholas Triozzi, courtesy of the American Museum of Natural History).*

Another Pecos bell was taken hostage by San Cristóbal rebels as a war trophy, then "killed" in the nearby mountains (Bandelier 1881). Figure 15.2 shows the bell piece found by Nelson in a "secret" mission-period kiva at San Cristóbal, where it was apparently being venerated. Nelson (1914:57–59) mused over whether the Pecos and San Cristóbal bell fragments might match up, and we're currently working on such possibilities (Thomas 2014, n.d.).

These object itineraries echo the words of Po'pay about "breaking up the bells" and tell conflicted tales about the internal civil war waged during and after the Pueblo Revolt. While I am unaware of precisely parallel oratory from the Southeastern Borderlands, that same metonymic refrain to "break up the bells" must have resonated in the Muskogean and Apalachee languages because violently fractured bell fragments marked the advent of indigenous uprisings across La Florida (e.g., Francis and Kole 2011; Jones 1970; Jones and Shapiro 1990; Thomas 1988, 2014, 2015).

THE MISSION BELLS OF SANTA CATALINA DE GUALE

So it is that powerful, singularized objects such as mission bells accumulate histories reflecting the social processes of value creation between people and things:

"As people and objects gather time, movement and change, they are constantly transformed, and these transformations of person and object are tied up with one another" (Gosden and Marshall 1999:169–70). Relating materiality to their life histories, it is possible to track the making and unmaking of objects through recourse to so-called fragmentation theory by exploring breakage patterns evident in the archaeological record (Chapman 2000; Chapman and Gaydarska 2006; Knappett 2012:199).

The importance of a signal object and its fragmentation was manifestly obvious during our excavations at Mission Santa Catalina de Guale (1570–1680), where we recovered 163 bronze church bell fragments from the mission complex on St. Catherines Island (Georgia). Most of the bell fragments came from the *atrio* immediately outside the church doorway, throughout the central mission plaza, and along the eastern wall of the friary; a few came from the surrounding pueblo part of the mission. Each bell fragment from Mission Santa Catalina has a specific "object provenience"—the original "find spot," documented in detail during the excavation process (Bushnell 1994; Thomas 1988, 1993).

Understanding the genealogies and itineraries of these objects requires a close consideration of object provenance as well—clarifying the sequences of ownership and meaning, ideally from creation through the social lives and circulation to establish networks of connections between persons and these things (Blair 2015a, 2015b; Chapman 2000; Joyce 2012a, 2012b: 8). Here is my reconstruction of the multifarious itineraries and genealogies of the mission bells of Santa Catalina de Guale, from the sixteenth century to today.

Bells: From Commodities to Singularized Objects

When Pedro Menéndez de Avilés sailed in 1565 to establish the St. Augustine colony and the attendant mission chains, he loaded eight church bells aboard *San Pelayo*, his flagship. A hurricane struck while the great ship was unloading and heretic mutineers took control, immediately setting set sail for Europe. *San Pelayo* and its remaining cargo sank somewhere off the coast of Denmark—perhaps with the mission bells still on board (Bushnell 1986; Lyon 1976:91, 128). Maybe those bells still lie at the bottom of the North Sea, but it is also possible that one (or more) one of them ended up at missions on the Georgia Coast.

One way or another, the bells of Mission Santa Catalina de Guale began their cultural itinerary in a European foundry. As commodities, these bells circulated through the economic system and were exchanged for other things, usually money (Kopytoff 1986:64–68). One such client was His Majesty, the king of Spain, who provided all new colonial missions with a "start-up kit" containing the means necessary to conduct divine worship—especially the vestments, ornaments, and mission bells, plus remittances for the sacraments (Bushnell 1994:84).

Somewhere between foundry and campanario, the church bells destined for *doctrinal* service at Mission Santa Catalina de Guale were transformed through liturgical protocols from the realm of economic commodities to the world of inalienable power. Like Spanish tribute items being transformed into ritualized chiefly Mississippian prestige items, these large bells became "singularized" through Franciscan ritual practice into priceless noncommodities, reflecting the extension of sacred power projected onto "sacralized objects" (Kopytoff 1986:64–68, 73–75).

Franciscan Fray Maynard Geiger (quoted earlier) lyrically expressed how the mission bells of Santa Barbara were "singularized" through baptism and naming, creating distinct object identities and preparing each bell to fulfill its own unique destiny. But Franciscan missions are, by definition and design, multicultural communities with social agency articulated by both colonizer and colonized. Archaeologists must be mindful when such powerful, singularized objects are employed in a colonial setting, because multiple agencies and contingencies are likely in play.

With respect to native North America, María Nieves Zedeño (2009) could identify only a "handful" of such inherently powerful and singularized objects, which she calls *index objects*, with the potential for revealing "relational ontologies [in which] animate objects can and do establish social relationships that parallel those of human social systems" (Zedeño 2009:413). Index objects can and often do speak a universal language of power; indigenous leaders and Franciscan authorities recognized the importance of such ritualized index objects—whether items of tribute or mission bells—in cementing cross-cultural relations in New Spain. In both cases, these priceless noncommodities played agential roles in modifying human behavior and social relations in Mississippian Spanish Florida (see also Brown and Walker 2008:298).

A 1682 court case ruled that local Guale and Timucuan caciques actually "owned" the mission bells of La Florida. When the doctrina of San Salvador de Mayaca was abandoned, friars gathered up the sacred furnishings (including two church bells) and took them away for safekeeping. But local caciques argued that "His Majesty made the grant ... of the said ornaments and bells to their pueblo and no other." Although temporarily without a friar, the caciques asserted that the neophyte community would still get another, and in the meantime, they still owned the bells—gifts so powerful they could not be withdrawn simply because the Indians and the friar chose to close that particular mission (Bushnell 1986, 1994:155, 159; 2014).

This episode highlights the importance of viewing colonial practice not in terms of the Grand Narratives, superposition or syncretism, but rather through an expanded multicultural context where practical politics play out. These sometimes novel, hybrid formulations crosscut indigenous American and European linguistic and religious ideologies—materialized in a uniquely singular index objects such as the mission bells.

For a century, off and on, the bells of Santa Catalina served their agreed-upon, multicultural role—to hang in the campanario and ritually regulate the lives of those who elected to "live under the bell." But this practice was contested by many others, in several ways.

Recommodifying the Santa Catalina Bells

The mission bell and the artillery cannon are "technological twins," in that either can be melted down and recast to assume the form and function of the other (Bushnell 1994:163–65). As Spain's military prowess grew, artisans working in the foundries became national resources, shifting as necessary from casting church bells to casting guns. When Spain ventured onto the global stage as a military power, many church bells were melted down and cast into cannons, with the naming tradition sometimes carrying over to the new firearms.

Pirates plying the La Florida coastline knew this as well. During a 1683 raid on St. Augustine, Governor Juan Marques Cabrera and his troops took refuge inside the *castillo* fortress. Recognizing the scarcity and market value of bronze, the pirates diverted to nearby missions San Juan and San Phelipe, where they stole six mission bells, presumably to be melted down ("recommodified") into a cannon (after Kopytoff 1986:82). Ironically, the bells stolen from the Guale and Mocamo missions may not have been recast. A Spanish spy saw intact mission bells in Charles Town in 1687, and the governor of Florida used this as evidence that the British were providing safe harbor to pirates. If so, the bells of Guale may have been more valuable as (noncommodity) trophies of war than as (recommodified) cannon.

The singularized, sacred role of mission bells was contested on other fronts as well. Bells were rung at all public occasions in St. Augustine and elsewhere throughout Spanish Florida, and at times they figured prominently in the power struggles between the sacred and secular sectors of the Spanish community. Bushnell (1994:150), for example, describes the 1681 "showdown at Sapelo." Captain Francisco de Fuentes (a veteran of the defense of Mission Santa Catalina de Guale a year before) complained that he and his men rushed to arms on Sapelo Island when they heard a bell signaling the *tocsin* (an alarm and call to arms) only to find the *fiscal* calling the mission women together to grind corn at the convento. In the ensuing dispute between Friar Juan de Useda and Captain Fuentes, voices were raised and tempers flared; Fuentes was ultimately excommunicated from the Roman Catholic Church for this (and other disputes) with the Franciscans.

Killing and Resurrecting the Bells of Santa Catalina

Rebellious Guale Indians murdered the church bells at Mission Santa Catalina de Guale in October 1597. At least three mission bells were broken into hundreds of fragments and apparently broadcast across the smoldering ruins of Mission Santa Catalina. Kopytoff (1986:76) calls this "deactivation," signaling the transition from a singularized "priceless" noncommodity into worthless junk. Intriguingly, these bells were killed not by local Guale neophytes, who literally lived under the same bells; these church bells of Mission Santa Catalina were destroyed instead by enemy Guale from a rival non-Christian chiefdom, who also killed five Franciscans (including Fray Miguel de Auñón and Fray Antonio Badajoz, both stationed at Mission Santa Catalina de Guale). These rebellious Guale ransacked Franciscan missions along the Georgia coastline, not only burning churches and breaking bells, but also torching the rival Guale council houses and cacique residences along the way.[4]

Franciscans returned to Guale territory nearly a decade after the rebellion, in March 1606, to refurbish Mission Santa Catalina de Guale and establish four new missions as well (Blair 2015b; Blair and Thomas 2014;Francis and Kole 2011:7). Over the next seven decades, members of the Santa Catalina de Guale mission community collected four dozen pieces of the bells fragmented in 1597, stacking them against the back wall of the new convento. These bell fragments were almost certainly being stockpiled for recasting into rebaptized replacement bells (and a quantity of bronze slag suggests that perhaps new bells were being recast on St. Catherines Island). In the meantime, replacement mission bells rang over Mission Santa Catalina de Guale until 1680, when the mission site was attacked once again, this time by slave raiders from Charlestown. After the enemy retreated, the friars and neophytes at Mission Santa Catalina fled southward to the adjacent Sapelo Island, apparently taking their replacement church bells with them (Bushnell 1994:163).

The 163 bell fragments were left behind where they had symbolically perished in the attack of 1597. Like the martyred brothers Michael and Antonio who died at Mission Santa Catalina de Guale that same day, the church bells were victims of deadly internecine warfare between rival Guale polities. The bells were broken up and tossed around while the priests were butchered on the spot, then hastily buried.

The Bells of Santa Catalina in the Twenty-First Century

With the Franciscan abandonment in 1680, the whereabouts of Mission Santa Catalina de Guale was unknown until 1979, when archaeologists from the American Museum of Natural History found the site and dug there for two decades (Thomas 1988, 1993, 2014). The bell fragments, now perceived as archaeological artifacts, were transported to laboratories New York City, where they remained until 2005, when the entire archaeological assemblage from Mission Santa Catalina was gifted to the Fernbank Museum of Natural History (in Atlanta, reflecting the premise that "what comes from Georgia stays in Georgia").

In 1984, the archaeological ruins of the church at Mission Santa Catalina de Guale were reconsecrated by the Franciscan Order and the Savannah Diocese of the Roman Catholic Church (Judge 1988; Thomas 2014, 2015). Today, (Franciscan) Bishop Gregory Hartmayer is promoting The Cause of the Georgia Martyrs, which seeks sainthood for the five Franciscans killed in the Guale Uprising of 1597. Their bones, if they could found, could become saintly in the eyes of the Vatican, human *relics* "fully capable of saving thousands of lives" (Fr. Conrad Harkins, personal communication, 1985).

SOME CONCLUSIONS

I have drawn upon several themes addressed in the other contributions to this volume, stressing particularly how materiality and social agency played out in the "practical politics" at the edges of Spanish Borderlands (after Silliman 2001). Exploring the "archaeologies of persistence" (Panich 2013:17) emphasizes the variability in how communities negotiated their colonial world, which are (by definition and design) cross-cultural—with social agency articulated by both colonizer and colonized. Throughout, I have stressed the importance of viewing colonial practice not in terms of Grand Narratives, superposition or syncretism, but rather through the expanded multicultural contexts where decision making, accommodation, resistance, and compromise played out.

This chapter highlights the remarkable contrasts between the respective indigenous landscapes in the Southwest and Southeast. The Pueblo world had long resisted top-down authority and with the insertion of Spanish colonial ways, factions in most communities contesting how best to address the changes all around them. Some, particularly those excluded from higher levels knowledge of ritual knowledge and power, embraced innovation and newer ideas. Others chose to reiterate what had been done previously.

Practical politics and social agency cut both ways in colonial communities, and Franciscans across the Borderlands vacillated over how best to achieve their divine mandate to save indigenous souls. Colonial authorities in La Florida deliberately bolstered and reinforced long-term hierarchical structure of hereditary Mississippian micos, who retained a large measure of secular autonomy. The factionalism of colonial Pueblo society lacks a counterpart in Spanish Florida, where indigenous communities were known for their loyalty and protectiveness of chiefly authority. But the paramounts across Spanish Florida competed viciously with one another to curry favor with the Franciscan authorities.

Spanish colonial–Mississippian hybrids provided an external support system for hereditary chiefs who maintained time-worn practices of traditional rank and privilege, even in the face of the withering demographics.

I have particularly foregrounded the Guale Rebellion of 1597 and the Pueblo Revolt of 1680 as complex and violent affairs, at times pitting rival indigenous factions and sometimes polities against a backdrop of adaptations and negotiations. Franciscans and indigenous leaders died in both uprisings, but for very different reasons.

Attempting to ground these events materially, I have explored cultural biographies of some uniquely singular index objects from repurposed kivas and council houses, *pelota* and Katsina ritualism, to sanctified tribute items and the omnipresent mission bells. These sometimes novel, hybrid formulations crosscut indigenous American and European linguistic and religious ideologies. Archaeologists must be particularly mindful when powerful, singularized objects are employed in colonial settings, because multiple agencies and contingencies might well be in play.

And yet, the selected object itineraries reflect remarkably comparable conflicts and legacies, dramatically underscoring the colonial reality that "messages of violence were directed at other indigenous people, not simply the Spanish" (Pearsall 2013:1017). Church bells were murdered at Nuestra Señora de los Angeles de Pórciuncula (Pecos Pueblo) and at Mission Santa Catalina de Guale (St. Catherines Island)—eighty-three years and 2,500 miles apart—but the perpetrators were not locals fed up with *living under these bell*. Rather, these *bells were broken up* by rival indigenous factions and long-term chiefly enemies driven to punish their pro-Franciscan relatives with an unmistakable show of anti-Spanish force. Ironically, battered bell fragments in both the Southwest and the Southeast were sometimes collected, curated, and venerated, perhaps in the unlikely hope that one of contested bells might one day ring out again.

ACKNOWLEDGMENTS

I appreciate the invitation from Douglass and Graves to participate in this project, and I most gratefully acknowledge the assistance of friends and colleagues who helped me prepare this manuscript: Elliot Blair, Ginessa Mahar, Lorann S.A. Pendleton, Anibal Rodriguez, Diana Rosenthal, and Maria Nieves Zedeño.

NOTES

1. Although the 1597 uprising is the best known, several other rebellions are documented in Spanish Florida: in Guale, 1645 and the early 1680s; in Apalachee and Timucua, 1565; in Apalachee, 1647; in Apalachicola, 1675 and 1681. In the previous historiography, each of these uprisings has been interpreted—per the Pueblo Revolt of 1680 model—as violent indigenous resistance aimed at throwing off unwarranted Spanish authority

(e.g., Bushnell 1994; Matter 1975; Thomas 1993; Weber 1994:133). In light of more recent research, it seems clear that most (if not all) of these rebellions reflect warfare between competing Mississippian-style chiefdoms vying for power, access, alliance, and tribute obligations from Spanish St. Augustine.

2. It is also worth noting the degree of continued factionalism evident at Hopi. More than half of the burials (69 of 118) found within the church nave at Awat'ovi were interred after the church had been destroyed. These individuals were laid out in standard Christian fashion (rather than flexed in traditional Hopi style), and several were associated with Catholic grave goods. "Somehow" writes Brooks (2013:761–62) "after the execution of their Franciscan priests and the expulsion of the Spanish presence from the Hopi mesas, some residents of post-revolt Awat'ovi had continued to bury their loved ones in the ruined mission church, accompanied by cherished symbols of both Hopi and Spanish spiritual life."

3. Another likely convento kiva at Awat'ovi was constructed in the middle of the sacred garden, a placement Ivey (1998:141) believes is more than coincidental. The so-called "sorcerer's kiva" at Awat'ovi had a stepped floor resembling an altar, fragments of local clay candlesticks similar to those used in the nearby Franciscan church. Brooks (2013:762) suggests that in this kiva, people "had been experimenting with combining Hopi and Franciscan imagery, paraphernalia and spiritual practices during a painful period of uncertainty about their own future." Other possible convento kivas include Kiva D at Las Humanas and visita kivas at San Lazaro and Giusewa (Ivey 1998:128, 141–142).

4. We estimate that a minimum of three bells are represented in the Santa Catalina collection through XRF analysis of the fragments (using a TRACeR III-V from Bruker Technologies; Mahar n.d.). Breaking up a bell is no easy matter and beyond doubt, dozens of the bell fragments recovered from the mission site show deliberate punch and axe marks around the margins. Despite repeated attempts, we could not refit any of the 163 bell fragments. To me, this implies that a relatively large number of bell fragments remain in unexplored archaeological contexts, probably still buried at Mission Santa Catalina, or (intriguingly) perhaps elsewhere.

REFERENCES CITED

Bandelier, Adolph. 1881. "A Visit to the Aboriginal Ruins in the Valley of the Rio Pecos." *Papers of the Archaeological Institute of America*, 35–135. American Series, vol. 1. Boston: A. Williams and Co.

Blair, Elliot H. 2015a. "Glass Beads and Global Itineraries." In *Things in Motion: Object Itineraries in Archaeological Practice*, edited by Rosemary A. Joyce and Susan Gillespie, 81–99. Santa Fe: School for Advanced Research Press.

Blair, Elliot H. 2015b. "Making Mission Communities: Population Aggregation, Social Networks, and Communities of Practice at 17th Century Mission Santa Catalina de Guale." PhD dissertation, Department of Anthropology, University of California, Berkeley.

Blair, Elliot H., and David Hurst Thomas. 2014. "The Guale Uprising of 1597: An Archaeological Perspective from Mission Santa Catalina de Guale (Georgia)." In *Indigenous Landscapes and Spanish Missions: New Perspectives from Archaeology and Ethnohistory*, edited by L. M. Panich and T. D. Schneider, 25–40. Tucson: The University of Arizona Press.

Bolton, Herbert E. 1908. *Spanish Explorations in the Southwest, 1542–1706*. New York: Barnes and Noble.

Brandt, Elizabeth. 1994. "Egalitarianism, Hierarchy, and Centralization in the Pueblos." In *The Ancient Southwestern Community*, edited by W. H. Wills and R. D. Leonard, 9–23. Albuquerque: University of New Mexico Press.

Brew, J. O. 1949. "Part II: The Excavation of Franciscan Awatovi." In *Franciscan Awatovi: The Excavation and Conjectural Reconstruction of a 17th-century Spanish Mission Establishment at a Hopi Indian Town in Northeastern Arizona*, edited by R. G. Montgomery, W. Smith, and J. O. Brew, 47–110. Peabody Museum of Archaeology and Ethnology, Papers, vol. 36. Cambridge, MA: Harvard University.

Brooks, James F. 2002. *Cousins and Captives: Slavery, Kinship, and Community in the Southwest Borderlands*. Chapel Hill: University of North Carolina Press.

Brooks, James F. June 2013. "Women, Men and Cycles of Evangelism in the Southwest Borderlands, A.D. 750–1750." *American Historical Review* 118 (3): 738–64. http://dx.doi.org/10.1093/ahr/118.3.738.

Brown, L. A., and W. H. Walker. 2008. "Prologue: Archaeology, Animism, and Non-human Agents." *Journal of Archaeological Method and Theory* 15 (4): 297–99. http://dx.doi.org/10.1007/s10816-008-9056-6.

Bushnell, Amy Turner. 1978. "'That Demonic Game': The Campaign to Stop Indian Pelota Playing in Spanish Florida, 1675–1684." *Americas* 35 (01): 1–19. http://dx.doi.org/10.2307/980923.

Bushnell, Amy Turner. 1986. "The Bells of Spanish Florida." Unpublished manuscript on file, Department of Anthropology, American Museum of Natural History, Johns Hopkins University, New York.

Bushnell, Amy Turner. 1994. "Situado and Sabana: Spain's Support System for the Presidio and Mission Provinces of Florida." Anthropological Papers of the American Museum of Natural History 74. New York: American Museum of Natural History.

Bushnell, Amy Turner. 2014. "'These People Are Not Conquered like Those of New Spain': Florida's Reciprocal Colonial Compact." *Florida Historical Quarterly* 92 (3): 524–53.

Chapman, John. 2000. *Fragmentation in Archaeology: People, Places and Broken Objects in the Prehistory of South Eastern Europe*. London: Routledge.

Chapman, John, and Bisserka Gaydarska. 2006. *Parts and Wholes: Fragmentation in Archaeological Context*. Oxford: Oxford University Press.

Courlander, Harold. 1971. *The Fourth World of the Hopis*. Albuquerque: University of New Mexico Press.

Dozier, Edward P. 1966. *Hano, a Tewa Indian Community in Arizona*. New York: Holt, Rinehart and Winston, Inc.

Ethridge, Robbie, and Shari M. Shuck-Hall, eds. 2009. *Mapping the Mississippian Shatter Zone: The Colonial Indian Slave Trade and Regional Instability in the American South*. Lincoln: University of Nebraska Press.

Fenn, Forrest. 2004. *The Secrets of San Lazaro Pueblo*. Santa Fe: One Horse Land and Cattle Company.

Foster, George. 1960. *Culture and Conquest: America's Hispanic Heritage*. Viking Fund Publications in Anthropology No. 27. New York: Wenner-Gren Foundation for Anthropological Research.

Francis, John Michael, and Kathleen M. Kole. 2011. "Murder and Martyrdom in Spanish Florida: Don Juan and the Guale Uprising of 1597." Anthropological Papers of the American Museum of Natural History No. 95. New York: American Museum of Natural History. http://dx.doi.org/10.5531/sp.anth.0095.

Gannon, Michael V. 1965. *The Cross in the Sand: The Early Catholic Church in Florida, 1513–1870*. Gainesville: University of Florida Press.

Geiger, Maynard. 1956. *Mission Bells of Santa Barbara: Their History and Romance*. Santa Barbara: Mission Santa Barbara.

Gosden, Chris, and Yvonne Marshall. 1999. "The Cultural Biography of Objects." *World Archaeology* 31 (2): 169–78. http://dx.doi.org/10.1080/00438243.1999.9980439.

Hackett, C.W., ed., and C.C. Shelby, trans. 1942. *Revolt of the Pueblo Indians of New Mexico, and Otermin's Attempted Reconquest, 1680–1682*. 2 vols. Coronado Cuarto Centennial Publications, 1540–1949. Albuquerque: University of New Mexico Press.

Hall, Joseph M., Jr. 2009. *Zamumo's Gifts: Indian-European Exchange in the Colonial Southwest*. Pittsburgh: University of Pennsylvania Press.

Hayes, Alden. 1974. *The Four Churches of Pecos*. Albuquerque: University of New Mexico Press.

Hoffman, Paul E. 2002. *Florida's Frontiers*. Bloomington: Indiana University Press.

Howe, James. 1956. "Spanish Bells in New Mexico." *New Mexico Historical Review* 31 (2): 148–53.

Hudson, Charles. 1976. *The Southeastern Indians*. Knoxville: University of Tennessee Press.

Hudson, Charles. 1997. *Knights of Spain, Warriors of the Sun: Hernando de Soto and the South's Ancient Chiefdoms*. Athens: University of Georgia Press.

Ivey, James E. 1988. *In the Midst of a Loneliness: The Architectural History of the Salinas Missions*. Southwest Cultural Resources Center Professional Paper 15. Santa Fe: National Park Service.

Ivey, James E. 1998. "Convento Kivas in the Missions of New Mexico." *New Mexico Historical Review* 73 (2): 121–52.

Ivey, James E., and David Hurst Thomas. 2005. "The Feeling of Working Completely in the Dark: The Uncertain Foundations of Southwestern Mission Archaeology." In *Current Views on the American Southwest*, edited by L. S. Cordell and D. D. Fowler, 204–19. Salt Lake City: University of Utah Press.

Ivey, James E., Marlys Bush Thurber, James T. Escobedo Jr., and Tom Ireland. 1991. *The Missions of San Antonio: A Historic Structures Report and Administrative History, Divisions of Conservation and History, 1987*. Denver: Southwestern/Intermountain Cultural Resources Center, National Park Service Professional Papers.

Jones, B. Calvin. 1970. "Missions Reveal State's Spanish-Indian Heritage: Florida Division of Archives and Records Management." *Archives and History News* 1 (2): 1–3.

Jones, B. Calvin, and Gary N. Shapiro. 1990. "Nine Mission Sites in Apalachee." In *Archaeological and Historical Perspectives on the Spanish Borderlands East*. Columbian Consequences, vol. 2, edited by D. H. Thomas, 491–509. Washington, DC: Smithsonian University Press.

Jones, Grant D. 1978. "The Ethnohistory of the Guale Coast through 1684." In *The Anthropology of St. Catherines Island. 1. Natural and Cultural History*, edited by D. H. Thomas, G. D. Jones, R. S. Durham, and C. S. Larsen. Anthropological Papers of the American Museum of Natural History 55 (2): 178–210. New York: American Museum of Natural History.

Joyce, Rosemary A. 2012a. "Life with Things: Archaeology and Materiality." In *Archaeology and Anthropology: Past, Present and Future*, edited by D. Shankland, 119–32. Oxford: Berg.

Joyce, Rosemary A. 2012b. "From Place to Place: Provenience, Provenance, and Archaeology." In *Provenance: An Alternate History of Art*, edited by G. Feigenbaum and I. Reist, 48–60. Los Angeles: Getty Research Institute.

Joyce, Rosemary A., and Susan Gillespie, eds. 2015. *Things in Motion: Object Itineraries in Archaeological Practice*. Santa Fe: School for Advanced Research Press.

Joyce, Rosemary A., and Jeanne Lopiparo. 2005. "PostScript: Doing Agency in Archaeology." *Journal of Archaeological Method and Theory* 12 (4): 365–74. http://dx.doi.org/10.1007/s10816-005-8461-3.

Judge, Joseph. 1988. "Exploring Our Lost Century." *National Geographic* 173 (3): 330–62.

Kessell, John L. 1979. *Kiva, Cross, and Crown: The Pecos Indians and New Mexico 1540–1840*. Washington, DC: National Park Service.

Kessell, John L., Rick Hendricks, and Meredith D. Dodge. 1992. *By Force of Arms: The Journals of Don Diego de Vargas, New Mexico*. Albuquerque: University of New Mexico Press.

Kidder, Alfred V. 1932. "Artifacts of Pecos." Papers of the Phillips Academy Southwest Expedition No. 6. Andover, MA: Phillips Academy.

Kidder, Alfred V. 1958. "Pecos, New Mexico: Archaeological Notes." Papers of the Peabody Foundation for Archaeology No. 5. Andover, MA: Phillips Academy.

Knappett, Carl. 2012. "Materiality." In *Archaeological Theory Today*, 2nd ed., edited by I. Hodder, 188–207. Cambridge: Polity Press.

Kopytoff, Igor. 1986. "The Cultural Biography of Things: Commodization as Process." In *The Social Life of Things: Commodities in Cultural Perspective*, edited by A. Appadurai, 64–92. Cambridge: Cambridge University Press. http://dx.doi.org/10.1017/CBO9780511819582.004.

Lanning, John Tate. 1935. *The Spanish Missions of Georgia*. Chapel Hill: University of North Carolina Press.

Levine, Frances. 1999. *Our Prayers Are in This Place: Centuries of Pecos Pueblo Identity*. Albuquerque: University of New Mexico Press.

Liebmann, Matthew J. 2002. "Signs of Power and Resistance: The (Re)Creation of Christian Imagery and Identities in the Pueblo Revolt Era." In *Archaeologies of the Pueblo Revolt*, edited by R. W. Preucel, 132–44. Albuquerque: University of New Mexico Press.

Liebmann, Matthew J. 2006. "'Burn the Churches, Break up the Bells': The Archaeology of the Pueblo Revolt Revitalization Movement in New Mexico, AD 1680–1696." PhD dissertation, Department of Anthropology, University of Pennsylvania, Philadelphia.

Liebmann, Matthew J. 2012. *Revolt: An Archaeological History of Pueblo Resistance and Revitalization in 17th Century New Mexico*. Tucson: University of Arizona Press.

Liebmann, Matthew, and Melissa S. Murphy. 2010. "Rethinking the Archaeology of "Rebels, Backsliders, and Idolaters."." In *Enduring Conquests: Rethinking the Archaeology of Resistance to Spanish Colonialism in the Americas*, edited by M. Liebmann and M. S. Murphy, 3–18. Santa Fe: School for Advanced Research Press.

Lippard, Lucy R., and Edward Ranney. 2010. *Down Country: The Tano of the Galisteo Basin, 1250–1782*. Santa Fe: Museum of New Mexico Press.

Lycett, Mark T. 2004. "Archaeology under the Bell: The Mission as Situated History in Seventeenth Century New Mexico." *Missionalia* 32 (3): 357–79.

Lyon, Eugene. 1976. *The Enterprise of Florida: Pedro Menéndez de Avilés and the Spanish Conquest of 1565–1568*. Gainesville: University Presses of Florida.

Mahar, Ginessa J. 2013. "Measuring the Missionized Soundscape." Paper delivered at the Southeastern Archaeology Conference, Tampa, Florida.

Mahar, Ginessa J. n.d. "Church Bells." Unpublished manuscript on file, Department of Anthropology. New York: American Museum of Natural History.

Matter, Robert A. 1975. "Missions in the Defense of Spanish Florida, 1566–1710." *Florida Historical Quarterly* 54 (1): 18–38.

McEwan, B. 2014a. "Colonialism on the Spanish Florida Frontier: Mission San Luis, 1656–1704." *Florida Historical Quarterly* 92 (3): 591–625.

McEwan, B. 2014b. "The Historical Archaeology of Seventeenth-Century La Florida." *Florida Historical Quarterly* 92 (3): 491–523.

McGuire, Randall H., and Dean J. Saitta. 1996. "Although They Have Petty Captains, They Obey Them Badly: The Dialectics of Prehistoric Western Pueblo Social Organization." *American Antiquity* 61 (2): 197–216. http://dx.doi.org/10.2307/282418.

Merrill, William L. 2009. "Indigenous Societies, Missions, and the Colonial System in Northern New Spain." In *The Arts of the Missions of Northern New Spain, 1600–1821*, edited by Clara Bargellini and Michael K. Komanecky, 122–53. Mexico City: Antiguo Colegio de San Ildefonso.

Milanich, Jerald T. 2006. *Laboring in the Fields of the Lord: Spanish Missions and Southeastern Indians*. Gainesville: University Press of Florida.

Mills, Barbara J., and William H. Walker. 2008. *Memory Work: Archaeologies of Material Practices*. Santa Fe: SAR Press.

Montgomery, Ross Gordon. 1949. "Part III: San Bernardo de Aguatubi, An Analytical Restoration." In *Franciscan Awatovi: The Excavation and Conjectural Reconstruction of a 17th-century Spanish Mission Establishment at a Hopi Indian Town in Northeastern Arizona*, edited by R. G. Montgomery, W. Smith, and J. O. Brew, 111–239. Peabody Museum of Archaeology and Ethnology, Papers, vol. 36. Cambridge MA: Harvard University.

Montgomery, R. G., Watson Smith and J. O. Brew. 1949. "Franciscan Awatovi: The Excavation and Conjectural Reconstruction of a 17th-century Spanish Mission Establishment at a Hopi Indian Town in Northeastern Arizona." *Peabody Museum of Archaeology and Ethnology, Papers*. Vol. 36. Cambridge MA: Harvard University.

Nelson, Nels. 1914. "Pueblo Ruins of the Galisteo Basin, New Mexico." Anthropological Papers of the American Museum of Natural History 15 (1). New York: American Museum of Natural History.

Oré, Luis Geronimo. 1619. *Relación de los Mártires que a Avido en las Provincias de la Florida*. Madrid.

Panich, Lee. 2013. "Archaeologies of Persistence: Reconsidering the Legacies of Colonialism in Native North America." *American Antiquity* 78 (1): 105–22. http://dx.doi.org/10.7183/0002-7316.78.1.105.

Pearsall, Sarah M. S. 2013. "'Having Many Wives' in Two American Rebellions: The Politics of Households and the Radically Conservative." *American Historical Review* 118 (4): 1000–28.

Riley, Carroll L. 1999. *The Kachina and the Cross: Indians and Spaniards in the Early Southwest*. Salt Lake City: University of Utah Press.

Scholes, France V. 1937. *Church and State in New Mexico, 1610–1650*. Albuquerque: Historical Society of New Mexico.

Scholes, France V. 1942. *Troublous Times in New Mexico, 1659–1670*. Albuquerque: Historical Society of New Mexico.

Shapiro, Gary N., and John H. Hann. 1990. "The Documentary Image of the Council Houses of Spanish Florida Tested by Excavations at the Mission of San Luis de Talimali." In *Archaeological and Historical Perspectives on the Spanish Borderlands East.* Columbian Consequences, vol. 2, edited by D. H. Thomas, 511–26. Washington, DC: Smithsonian University Press.

Silliman, Stephen. 2001. "Agency, Practical Politics, and the Archaeology of Culture Contact." *Journal of Social Archaeology* 1 (2): 190–209. http://dx.doi.org/10.1177/146960530100100203.

Smith, Watson. 1972. *Prehistoric Kivas of Antelope Mesa, Northeastern Arizona*. Papers of the Peabody Museum of American Archaeology and Ethnology 39 (1).

Swanton, John R. 1922. "Early History of the Creek Indians and Their Neighbors." *Bureau of American Ethnology Bulletin* 73.

Thomas, David Hurst. 1988. "Saints and Soldiers at Santa Catalina: Hispanic Designs for Colonial America." In *The Recovery of Meaning: Historical Archaeology in the Eastern United States*, edited by M. P. Leone and P. B. Potter, 73–140. Washington, DC: Smithsonian Institution Press.

Thomas, David Hurst. 1993. "The Archaeology of Mission Santa Catalina de Guale: Our First Fifteen Years." In *The Missions of La Florida*, edited by B. G. McEwan, 1–34. Gainesville: University of Florida Press.

Thomas, David Hurst. 2013a. "Honor and Hierarchies: Long-term Trajectory in the Pueblo and Mississippian Worlds." In *Native and Spanish New Worlds: Sixteenth-Century Entradas in the American Southwest and Southeast*, edited by C. Mathers, J. M. Mitchem, and C. M. Haecker, 251–73. Tucson: University of Arizona Press.

Thomas, David Hurst. 2013b. "War and Peace on the Franciscan Frontier." In *From La Florida to La California: The Genesis and Realization of Franciscan Evangelization in the Spanish Borderlands*, edited by T. J. Johnson and G. Melville, 105–30. Berkeley: Academy of American Franciscan History.

Thomas, David Hurst. 2014. "The Life and Times of Fr. Junípero Serra: A Pan-Borderlands Perspective [A Tibesar Distinguished Lecture]." *Americas* 71 (2): 185–225. http://dx.doi.org/10.1353/tam.2014.0119.

Thomas, David Hurst. 2015. "Bilocating the American Mission Borderlands with Saint Serra." *Boletin: Journal of the California Mission Studies Association* 31 (1): 5–34.

Thomas, David Hurst. n.d. "The Archaeology of Mission San Marcos." Manuscript in preparation, American Museum of Natural History, New York.

Toulouse, Joseph R., Jr. 1949. *Mission San Gregorio de Abó: A Report on the Excavation and Repair of a Seventeenth-Century New Mexico Mission*. Monographs of the School of American Research, no. 13.

Walker, William H., and Lisa J. Lucero. 2000. "The Depositional History of Ritual and Power." In *Agency in Archaeology*, edited by M. Dobres and J. Robb, 130–47. London: Routledge.

Walsh, Marie T. 1934. *The Mission Bells of California*. San Francisco: Harr Wagner Publishing Company.

Ware, John A. 2002. "Descent Group and Sodality: Alternative Pueblo Social Histories." In *Traditions, Transitions, and Technologies: Themes in Southwest Archaeology*, edited by Sarah Schlanger, 94–112. Boulder: University of Colorado Press.

Weber, David. 1994. *The Spanish Frontier in North America*. New Haven, CT: Yale University Press.

Weber, David. 2009. "Arts and Architecture, Force and Fear: The Struggle for Sacred Space." In *The Arts of the Missions of Northern New Spain, 1600–1821*, edited by C. Bargellini and M. K. Komanecky, 2–23. Mexico City: Antiguo Colegio de San Ildefonso.

Weber, David J., ed. 1999. *What Caused the Pueblo Revolt? Boston*. Boston: Bedford/St. Martin's.

White, Courtney. 1996. "Adobe Typology and Site Chronology." *Kiva* 61 (4): 347–63. http://dx.doi.org/10.1080/00231940.1996.11758314.

Whiteley, Peter. 1988. *Deliberate Acts: Changing Hopi Culture through the Oraibi Split*. Tucson: University of Arizona Press.

Whiteley, Peter. 2002. "Archaeology and Oral Tradition—The Scientific Importance of Dialogue." *American Antiquity* 67 (3): 405–15. http://dx.doi.org/10.2307/1593819.

Worth, John E. 1998. *Assimilation*. The Timucuan Chiefdoms of Spanish Florida. vol. 1. Gainesville: University Press of Florida.

Worth, John E. 2002. "Spanish Missions and the Persistence of Chiefly Power." In *The Transformation of the Southeastern Indians, 1540–1760*, edited by R. Ethridge and C. Hudson, 39–64. Jackson: University Press of Mississippi.

Worth, John E. 2013a. "Catalysts of Assimilation: The Role of Franciscan Missionaries in the Colonial System of Spanish Florida." In *From La Florida to La California: The Genesis and Realization of Franciscan Evangelization in the Spanish Borderlands*, edited by T. J. Johnson and G. Melville, 131–42. Berkeley: Academy of American Franciscan History.

Worth, John E. 2013b. "Inventing Florida: Constructing a Colonial Society in an Indigenous Landscape." In *Native and Spanish New Worlds: Sixteenth-Century Entradas in the American Southwest and Southeast*, edited by C. Mathers, J. M. Mitchem, and C. M. Haecker, 198–204. Tucson: University of Arizona Press.

Zedeño, María Nieves. 2009. "Animating by Association: Index Objects and Relational Taxonomies." *Cambridge Archaeological Journal* 19 (3): 407–17. http://dx.doi.org/10.1017/S0959774309000596.

Contributors

JOSEPH AGUILAR
University of Pennsylvania
aguilarj@sas.upenn.edu

JIMMY ARTERBERRY
Comanche Nation
jimmya@comanchenation.com

HEATHER ATHERTON
Independent Scholar
hnatherton@gmail.com

DALE S. BRENNEMAN
Arizona State Museum
daleb@email.arizona.edu

J. ANDREW DARLING
Southwest Heritage Research
jadarlin@swheritage.com

JOHN G. DOUGLASS
Statistical Research, Inc. and
University of Arizona
jdouglass@sricrm.com

B. SUNDAY EISELT
Southern Methodist University
seiselt@mail.smu.edu

SEVERIN FOWLES
Barnard College, Columbia University
sfowles@barnard.edu

WILLIAM M. GRAVES
Logan Simpson and University of Arizona
wmgraves@email.arizona.edu

LAUREN E. JELINEK
Bureau of Reclamation
laurenejelinek@gmail.com

KELLY L. JENKS
New Mexico State University
kljenks@nmsu.edu

STEWART B. KOYIYUMPTEWA
Hopi Cultural Preservation Office
SKoyiyumptewa@hopi.nsn.us

PHILLIP O. LECKMAN
Statistical Research, Inc. and
University of Arizona
pleckman@sricrm.com

MATTHEW LIEBMANN
Harvard University
liebmann@fas.harvard.edu

KENT G. LIGHTFOOT
University of California, Berkeley
klightfoot@berkeley.edu

LINDSAY MONTGOMERY
University of Arizona
lmmontgomery86@gmail.com

BARNET PAVAO-ZUCKERMAN
University of Maryland
bpavao@umd.edu

ROBERT PREUCEL
Brown University
robert_preucel@brown.edu

MATTHEW F. SCHMADER
University of New Mexico
mschmader@unm.edu

THOMAS E. SHERIDAN
University of Arizona
tes@email.arizona.edu

COLLEEN STRAWHACKER
University of Colorado at Boulder
colleen.strawhacker@colorado.edu

J. HOMER THIEL
Desert Archaeology, Inc.
homer@desert.com

DAVID HURST THOMAS
American Museum of Natural History
thomasd@amnh.org

LAURIE D. WEBSTER
University of Arizona
ldwebster5@gmail.com

Index

Page numbers in italics indicate illustrations.

Abiquiú, 165, 192, 196, 223
Abó, 20, 23, 394, *395*
abuse, by Spanish, 240, 243–49, 255–56, 358
acequia systems, 92, 195. *See also* irrigation
Acoma (Acuco), 12, 60, 106, 119, 127, 227, 241, 245, 381, 399; post-Revolt period, 23, 143, 145
adoptions, and Rio del Oso lineages, 198, 199
agency, social, 380, 385, 390–91
agriculture: Hopi, 129–30; on middle Gila River, 332–34, 338, 342–48, 367; O'odham, 290–92, 335–36; Spanish and Pueblo practices, 92–99, 106; Pimería Alta, 28, 293–94; Vecino, 227, 228
Aguilar, Nicolás de, 120
Ak-Chin Indian Community, 277
Akimel O'odham, 26, 275
Alameda (NM), 63, 69
Alamillo, 399
Alarcón, Hernando de, 266, 276
Albuquerque, 191

Albuquerque Basin, 12, 53
Alcanfor, 53, 54, 57, 63
alliances, 199, 272; in La Florida, 384–85; with native warriors, 16, 17; pan-Pueblo, 143–44, 382; Pimería Alta, 266, 278–79; post-Revolt period, 145–49, 152–53; Rio Grande Pueblos, 22, 31–32, 365
Alta California, 8, 33, 215, 304, 320, 362, 366, 367, 370; Californio identity, 368–69; colonialism in, 356–57; early European encounters in, 358–59; ethnogenesis in, 32, 361; identity transformations in, 18, 32; livestock in, 293, 297, 300, 301–2; mission restoration projects, 359–60
Altar River, 267, 272, 274, 279
Alvarado, Hernando de, 53, 55, 60–61
American period, 225, 229
Analco, Barrio (Santa Fe), 17–18
animal husbandry, in Pimería Alta, 293–95, 296–97

417

animals, domestic, 21. *See also* faunal remains; zooarchaeology; *by type*
Antequera (Oaxaca), 17
Anza, Juan Bautista de, 344
Apaches, 5, 145, 214, 267, 274; ceramics, 227, 228; and Comanches, 159, 162–63; in Pimería Alta, 27, 29, 30, 272, 302, 314, 315, 332, 340–41; post-Revolt interactions, 143, 147; raiding by, 151, 302, 337, 361; in Tucson, 317–18
Apalachee, 391
archaeology, and documents, 50–51; ethnic markers in, 229–30
architecture, colonial period, 390–91
Arenal, 63; Coronado's attack on, 54, 58–60, 66
Areneños, 26, 28–29, 271, 275, 276, 278, 279
Argüello, Fernando de, 250
Arivaca Valley, 267
Arizona, 215, 264, 370. *See also* Pimería Alta
Arizpe, and Tucson Presidio, 319–20
Arkansas River, Comanches on, 162
armas de tierra, 53
armor, bison hide, 173
Astialakwa (LA 1825), 145, 148–49, 152
Athabaskans, 5, 12, 21, 143, 166, 192. *See also* Apaches; Jicarilla Apaches; Navajos
Augustias de la Guerra, María de las, 397
Ávila, Francisco de, 387
Awat'ovi, 116, 119, 122, 132, 407(n2); cotton at, 129–30; destruction of, 120–21, 133, 136(n7), 251–52, 253; Franciscan missionaries at, 20, 241; kiva-church superpositioning at, 393, 407(n3); textile production at, 123, 124–25, 126, 127–29, 136(n6)

Bac, 293, 297, 303, 312, 318, 325
Bacoachi, 269, 271, 279
Bandelier, Adolph, 251
barrios, of indios amigos, 17
battles: Coronado-Zuni, 53; rock art scenes of, 166, *175*, 177–78
Baviácora, 274
Bearhead Peak obsidian source, 148
bells, mission, 396–405, 407(n4)
Benavides, Alonso, 105
Bigotes, 60–61
Boletsakwa (LA 136), 145, 148, 150, 151, 152
bone grease production, in Pimería Alta, 300–302
Bonilla, Leyva de, 15
borders, boundaries, cultural concepts of, 100
botanical remains, at Hispanic sites, 221, 223, 224, 225, 227

Bourbon reforms, 188, 190–91, 205, 368
brazilwood, 123–24
buhio, 391
burials, 122, 125, 132, 322, 407(n2)

Cabeza de Vaca, Álvar Nuñez, 51
Caborca, 30, 270, 271
Cabrera, Juan Marques, 403
Cabrillo, Juan Rodríguez, 359, 370
caciques. *See* micos
Caddoan speakers, 12
Cahuilla, Lake, 275
California, 337; indigenous land use, 367–68; historic restoration projects, 359–60. *See also* Alta California
Californios, 32; identity as, 368–69
Camino Real, 228
campsites, 168; depictions of, *172*, *173*, *175*, 176–77
canal systems: Hohokam, 332, 367; on middle Gila River, 336, 341–42, 343–44; Pueblo, 92, 93, 94. *See also* acequia systems
Cananea, 269
Canito, 269, 271, 272
cannons, and church bells, 403
Cañones region, 197
captives, 17, 164, 182(n6), 198, 223, 387
Carnue Plain, 221
Casitas Red-on-brown, 223
Castañeda de Nájera, Pedro de, Coronado expedition history, 55–62
Castaño de Sosa, Gaspar, 15, 18, 68–69
Castillo, Blas del, 269
Catholic Church, 241, 255, 360, 405; women's empowerment, 382–83. *See also* Franciscans; Jesuits; missionization, missions
Catiti, Alonso, 153
cattle, 92; cattle industry, 361–62; in New Mexico, 92, 225, 228; Pimería Alta, 266, 293, 297–98, 299–300, 304, 361; raiding and, 302, 303
ceramics, 316, 363; at Hispanic New Mexican sites, 221, 222, 223, 225, 227–28; Jicarilla Apache, 164, 166, 202; pan-Puebloan, 22–23; in Pimería Alta sites, 264, 265–66, 276–77, 278, 318–19; post-Revolt era, 145–47, 152; religious knowledge and, 23–24; Sobaipuri, 273–74
ceremonial societies, at Hopi, 251–52
Cerro Colorado (LA 2048), 145, 148, 152
cerros de trincheras, 265
CGDDs. *See* Corn Growing Degree Days
Chaco Canyon, 150

Chalchihuites (Durango), 17
Chama River region, 12, 214, 228; Hispanic sites, 223–24, 227
Chamuscado, Francisco Sánchez, 13, 67
Chiapas, 17
Chichimecas, 17
chiefdoms, Southeastern, 383–84, 386–87
Chili (NM), 197
Chinarras, 30, 272
Christianity, 134, 150; conversions to, 29, 241; introduction of, 20–21
churches: and kivas, 393–96, 407(n3); in New Mexico, 87, 88. *See also by name*
Cibola, 51, 53
Cicuye. *See* Pecos Pueblo
citizenship, and Vecino identity, 216
Ciudad Real (Chiapas), 17
Ciudad Viejo Sonsonate (Guatemala), 17
climate: during colonial period, 242–43; around Paako, 78–81
clothing: at Awat'ovi, 120, 123, 124–25, 126, 127–29, 136(n6); manufacture of, 228–29; Mississippian chiefly, 386; at Tucson Presidio, 321–22
Coahuila, 17
cochineal, 124
Cochiti, 145, 146, 147, 148, 153
Cocomaricopas, 26, 29, 275, 276, 278, 340
Cócopas, 27, 27, 276, 278
Cocpi, Juan, 244
Colón, Cristóbal, 49, 50
colonialism, colonization, 4, 69, 355, 362; adaptation to, 334–35; in Alta California, 356–57; impacts of, 241–42; indigenous landscapes and, 363–66; Pimería Alta, 25–29, 266–67; power relationships, 24–25, 157–58, 390; relations, 6–7; scholarship on, 369–71; Spanish, 9–10, 380–81; *terra nullius*, 10–11
colonial period, 4, 134, 230; architecture, 390–91; at Hopi, 133–34, 243–49; livestock introduction, 289–90; at Paako, 88–92; textile production, 118–19, 135(n1)
colonists: identities of, 7–8; social agency of, 390–91
Colorado, Hispanic sites in, 217, 224
Colorado Delta, 278
Colorado River, 275
Comanche Empire, The (Hämäläinen), 159–61, 365
Comanchería, 163
Comanches, 5, 32, 106, 158, 166, 179, 182(n4), 193, 214, 365–66, 371; documentation of, 161–62; equestrianism, 180–81; imperialism, 159–61, 175–76; raiding, 192, 196; rock art, 170–78; Taos and, 162–63, 164, 182(n7)
communities: grants of, 191–92; mission, 87–88; Puebloan vs. Spanish concepts of, 76–77, 85–87, 92–93, 100
Concepción, Río, Pima uprising at, 272
confederacies, Southeastern, 383
conflict, 159; in Pimería Alta, 270–71, 275–76, 278; post-Pueblo Revolt, 143, 144; among Pueblos, 70, 151–52
convento complexes: in Pueblo communities, 87–88
conversion, 134, 241
corn (maize), 21; middle Gila River production, 336, 343, 345; New Mexico pueblos, 78–80
Corn Growing Degree Days (CGDDs), at Paako, 78–80
Coronado expedition, 50, 241, 266, 358; archaeological evidence for, 63–67; indios amigos/aliados on, 17, 51–52, 357; Native responses to, 55–62; provisioning of, 52–53; route of, 53–54; in Tiguex Province, 54–55
Coronado Project/Coronado Road Show, 322–23
Coronado y Luján, Francisco Vázquez de, 4, 31, 50, 67; expedition, 51–55
corrals, in Paako plaza, 90, 91, 364
Cosari (Dolores), 270
cotton: at Awat'ovi, 122, 125; cultivation of, 129–30; textile production, 118, 362, 363
council houses, Mississippian, 391
counting coup, rock art depictions of, 178, 181
crops, 227; Old World, 293, 335; at Paako, 93–94
Crow Head, 341
crypto-Jews, in New Mexico Colony, 18
Cuiquiburitac, 26
cultural revitalization movement, at Hopi, 252
Cuna, Juan, torture and death of, 244, 245, 246, 250
Cunixu, Luis, 153
Cuquiárachi, 272

dance floor, at Vista Verde site, 168, 365
dances, Hopi ceremonial, 132
decolonization, Vecino, 189, 203–4
defense, 21; Puebloan, 58–59, 70
diseases, in Pimería Alta, 28, 292, 340
Dominguez, Francisco Atanasio, 105–6
drought, 21, 242
Durango, 17
dyes, in textile production, 121, 123–24

Index | 419

Eastern Keresans, 12, 381
economies, 33, 226, 331–32; Gila River O'odham, 344, 367; La Florida, 384–86; Mississippian, 386–87; native political, 363–65; New Mexico Colony, 18–20
El Cerrito, 224
El Cuartelejo, 162
electrical resistivity (ER), 63
Elias de León, Ramona, 325
El Paraje Rio Oso, 196. *See also* Rio del Oso grant
El Paso, 12
El Salvador, 17
embroidery, 135(n4); Hopi use of, 125–27
Embudo (Dixon), 165
empire, Comanche, 159–61
encomienda system, 19, 85, 118, 241–42, 362; at Hopi, 119–20; in La Florida, 385–88
England Ranch Ruin (AZ DD:8:129[ASM]), 274, 278
epidemics, 242, 292, 314
equestrianism: Comanche, 180–81; images of, 166
ER. *See* electrical resistivity
Española Valley, 146
Espejo, Antonio de, 14, 18, 67–68
Espeleta, Francisco, 250–51
Espeleta, José de, 250, 251
estancias, 87
Esteban (Estevan) de Dorantes, 3–4, 53
Estrada, Beatriz, 51
ethnicity, 229–30
ethnogenesis, 32, 188, 361, 366, 368–69
ethnohistory, Pimería Alta, 269–72, 275–76
Eudeves, 26, 27, 271, 280(n2)
exchange network, La Florida, 384–85, 386–87
expeditions, Spanish, 13–15, 67–69
explorations, New World, 49–50, 370

factionalism, 31; post-Revolt Pueblo, 149–52, 365; Pueblo society, 381–83, 407(n2)
families, on Rio del Oso grant, 197–99
faunal remains: at Hispanic sites, 221, 222, 223, 224–26, 227; at Pimería Alta sites, 295–300, 304
feathers, symbolism of, 23
Fernández de la Fuente, Juan, 272
field houses, Paako, 93
Figueras, José de, 250
fire, indigenous use of, 367–68
Franciscans, 26, 356, 360, 403; architectural norms, 390–91; bajo campana and, 397–98; at Hopi, 32, 120, 122, 132, 240, 241, 255, 358; in La Florida, 384–85, 405–6; martyrdom of, 388–89; missionization, 380–81, 395–96; in New Mexico Colony, 20–21, 22, 99, 100; and Pueblo factionalism, 382–83
Frontera (Sonora), 26
frontier, 5, 18
Fuentes, Francisco de, 403

Gadsden Purchase, 337
Galisteo, 76, 106
Galisteo Basin, 12, 53, 101, 102, 146, 399
Gallup Diocese, apology issued by, 255
Garcés, Francisco, 344
Gaybanipitea (AZ EE:8:15[ASM]), 272, 273, 275
gender roles, 21; in textile production, 118, 130–31, 134–35, 136(n6), 392
genealogy, Rio del Oso grant, 197–99
genízaros, 206(n3), 223
gente de razón, 8, 215
Georgia, Spanish missions in, 401, 404. *See also* La Florida
gift giving, California tribes-maritime explorers, 359
Gila River Indian Community (GRIC), 333, 334, 337, 367
Gila River Valley, middle: agriculture in, 335–36, 343–48, 367; irrigation systems in, 342–43; leadership in, 341–42; O'odham in, 275, 332–34, 337–41, 343–44; Protohistoric Period in, 336–37
Gileños, 26, 29, 275
glaze ware, Mexican, 228
goats, 92, 96, 297
Gojia, 202
Gómez, Elena, 120
Gran Quivira, 23
grants: to Spanish colonists, 191–92, 193; Vecino, 193–95
Great Plains, Coronado expedition on, 55, 61
GRIC. *See* Gila River Indian Community
Griego, Juan, 152
Guale, 384, 386, 389, 406–7(n11); and mission bells, 402, 404
Guale Rebellion, 387, 388, 389, 404, 405
Guatemala, *indios amigos* barrios in, 17, 18
Guerra, Salvador de, 120, 133; abuses of, 243–45, 253
Guevavi, 267, 269, 318; livestock at, 297, 299–300
guns, 170, 173
Gutiérrez de Humaña, Antonio, 15

Halyikwamai, 27, 276, 278
Hämäläinen, Pekka, *The Comanche Empire*, 159–61, 365
Hartmayer, Gregory, 405
Hawikku, 53, 59, 399
Herrera, Cristóbal, 197
Herrera, Juana, 196
Herrera, Juan Manuel de, 195–96, 197
Herrera, Juan Pedro, 197
Hia Ced O'odham. *See* Areneños
hides, hide processing, 304–5; intercolony trade in, 301–2, 305
Hímeris, 269, 271
Hisatsinom, 252
Hispanic sites: in Chama Valley, 223–24; in Rio Grande Valley, 217–23
Hispano-Chicano identity, 188
Hispano Homeland, 187–88, 205
Hispanos, 162, 187, 206(n11); identity construction, 368–69. *See also* Vecinos
historical societies, in California, 360
Hohokam, 264, 265–66, 291, 336; agricultural system, 332, 367
Home Dance, and Sitkoyma, 246–48
Homestead Acts, 229
Hopi, Hopi Mesas, 8, 11, 117, 242, 393, 407(n2); adoption of wool, 121–23; colonial period abuse of, 243–49; and Coronado expedition, 56, 358; cotton cultivation at, 129–30; and destruction of Awat'ovi, 251–54; dyes used at, 123–24; embroidery at, 125–27; and Franciscan missionaries, 20, 32, 255, 358; historical trauma, 254–56, 358; knitting at, 124–25; mission bells at, 398–99; mission era, 131–32, 362; oral histories, 239–40; post-Revolt period, 143, 145; and Pueblo Revolt, 250, 381, 382; Spanish conquest and missionization, 240, 241–42; textile production, 31, 115–16, 118, 119–21, 127–31, 133–35, 362–63, 392; way of life, 252–53
Hopification, 8
Hopi History Project, 358, 362
Hopi Independence Day, 256
Hopi language, 12
Hopi Tribe, 255
hornos, on Rio del Oso grant sites, 199–200
horses, 96, 161, 292; Coronado expedition, 57, 58; in rock art, 166, 170, 171–73, 174, 175, 178
household complexes: in Rio del Oso grant, 199–200; at San Lorenzo, 200–202
Huachuca, 269, 280(n1)
Huachuca Mountains, Spanish cattle in, 266

hunter-gatherers, 12, 28; in California, 356, 362, 367–68
hunting, 21, 334; garden, 290–91, 304

Ibargaray, Antonio de, 120, 133, 243, 244–45
iconography: Comanche, 170–78; post-Pueblo Revolt, 23
Ideal Site, 227
identity, 16; civic, 215–17; Comanche, 176, 182(n4); construction of, 368–69; New Mexican cultural, 213–14; pan-Pueblo, 22–23; transforming/reinventing, 8, 18, 25, 31; Vecino, 187–88, 189, 205, 214–15, 229–30
imperialism, Comanche, 159–61, 175–76
Ímuris, 269
index objects, 402
indigenous groups, 7, 214, 366–67. *See also by name*
indigo, 123–24, 132
indios amigos, 16; on Coronado expedition, 4, 51–52, 67, 357, 358; in New Mexico Colony, 17–18
indios bárbaros, 161
information networks, long-distance Pueblo, 55–56
Inquisition, in New Mexico, 245
irrigation: colonial period, 92, 106, 195, 342–43; Hohokam, 332, 367; on middle Gila River, 336, 341–42, 343–44
Isleta, 72(n3), 102, 119, 182(n6), 227, 245, 396, 398
Isleta del Sur, 227
Isleta Red-on-tan, 221

Janos, 30, 267, 271, 272, 274, 279
Jaramillo, Roque Jacinto, 195–96, 197
Jemez, 12, 106, 119, 125, 150, 245, 252; alliances, 152, 153, 365; obsidian at, 148–49; post-Revolt ceramics, 22, 23, 146–47
Jemez Mountains, 62
Jemez River, 12
Jesuits, in Pimería Alta, 25–26, 27, 29, 30, 271, 279, 312, 356
Jicarilla Apaches, 163–64, 193; ceramics, 223, 227, 228; Rio del Oso Valley, 199, 202; in Rio Grande Gorge, 165–66, 365
Jocomes, 27, 30, 267, 271, 272, 274, 279
José María Martínez Site, 224
Joshevama, Elgean, 239–40
Juanillo's revolt, 388
Jumanos pueblos, 12
justice system, Pueblo, 57–58

Index | 421

Kastiilam, 239
Katsina Buttes (Kaktsintuyqa), 246, 247–48
katsinam, 23, 252, 382–83, 396; and mission activity, 246–48
Kechiba:wa, 90
Keresans, 119, 143, 147, 252, 381; alliances, 152–53, 365; conflicts with Tewas, 151–52; and Coronado expedition, 62, 70; post-Revolt ceramics, 22, 23
Kewa (Santo Domingo Pueblo), 62, 147, 152, 245, 398
kilts, embroidered, 127
Kino, Eusebio Francisco, 25, 26, 266, 267, 317, 342; missions established by, 290, 292, 293, 312–14; travels of, 269–70, 275
kivas, 86, 89; and churches, 20, 241, 393–96, 407(n3); functions of, 391–92; textile production in, 116, 127–28, 130–31, 136(n6, n8)
knitting, adoption of, 121, 124–25, 127
knowledge, hidden religious, 23–24
Kotyiti (LA 295), 145, 146, 147, 153; alliances, 152, 365; obsidian at, 148–49

labor, 21, 27; colonial period, 118, 241; exploitation of, 18–19; mission, 26, 119–21, 133, 290, 294, 304; repartimiento, 385–86; textile production, 120, 362
La Florida, 33, 380, 383, 389, 391; church bells in, 397, 400–405; encomienda and repartimiento in, 385–88; Franciscan missions in, 384–85, 405–6
Laguna, 12, 119, 227
La Navidad, 50
land, land tenure, 206(n6), 362; exploitation of, 18–19; marriage patterns and, 197, 198–99, 205; Pimería colonial, 293–94; Vecino, 192–93; Vecino, 193–95, 204, 215, 368
land grants, 214, 224, 311; to Spanish colonists, 191–92, 193; Vecino, 193–95, 204, 207(n10). *See also* Rio del Oso grant
landscapes, 367; cultural concepts of, 31, 76–77, 99–100; indigenous, 363–66
land use, 195, 229; indigenous, 367–68, 370–71; Paako, 31, 77; Pueblo, 76, 99–100; Spanish, 92–93
La Placita, 224–25, 227, 228
La Puente, 223, 224
Las Casitas, 223
Las Huertas land grant, 227
La Soledad, 221
Las Trampas, 192
Las Vegas (NM), 228

Laws (Ordinances) of the Indies, 86, 390
leadership: Gila O'odham, 341–42; post-Revolt, 144, 150, 152, 153; Pueblo, 381–82
León, Francisco Solano, 311, 324, 325
Lightning Arrow Site, 166, 167
lithics: at Hispanic sites, 221, 223; post-Revolt period distribution, 147–49
livestock, 58; butchering and rendering, 300–302; introduction of, 289–90; at Paako, 96–98; in Pimería Alta, 292–95, 296–300, 303–5, 335; raiding of, 30, 302–3; Spanish land use and, 92–93
Lobato, Juan Cristobal, 197
Lobato, Juan José, 196, 197, 206(n8)
Lobato, Polito, 197
looping, 124–25
López de Cárdenas, Diego, 53, 57, 58, 61
López Sambrano, Diego, 250
Los Ojitos, 224, 225, 228
Lowland Patayan, 277, 278

Màasaw, 252
macanas, macahuitls, at Piedras Marcadas Pueblo, 67
Magdalena, Río, 267, 269, 271, 279
majolica: in Alta California and Pimería Alta, 320–21; in New Mexico sites, 222, 224, 228
Malacate, Antonio, 153
Manby Trailhead Site (LA 102341), 167
Manje, Juan Mateo, 267, 276; on floodwater farming, 342–43
Manso Apaches, 317–18
Mansos, 12, 272, 274
mantas, 126–27, 245
Manzano region, 101
Maricopas, 26
maritime expeditions, California, 359
marriage patterns: and land grants, 197, 198–99; O'odham-Cocomaricopa, 275; in Tucson, 316–17; Vecino, 205, 368
Martyrs of Georgia (Oré), 388
matanzas (mass killings), 30
matrilineages, Mississippian, 386
men, 382; Pueblo textile production, 118, 119, 130–31, 134–35, 136(n6, n8), 362
Menchero, Miguel de, 196
Mendizábal, Bernardo López de, 118, 245
Mendoza, Antonio de, 3, 4, 51
Menéndez de Avilés, Pedro, 384, 401
mesa-top communities, post-Revolt, 145, 365
Mesoamerica, influence of, 4–5
Mestas grant, 197, 207(n11)

metal artifacts, from Coronado expedition, 63–66
metallurgy: Paako plaza, 90–91, 364; Tucson Presidio, 324–25
meteorites, 316
Mexican American War, 337
Mexicas, 4; on Coronado expedition, 51, 357
micos, 383–84; exchange system, 386–87
migrants, post-Revolt era, 145–47
militarism, Comanche, 160, 162–63, 177, 178
military, 17, 191, 314, 344
milpa agriculture, 106
mineral resources, Pimería Alta, 27
mines, supplies for, 301, 304–5, 361
Mishongnovi (Musangnuvi), 119, 241, 244, 251
missionaries, 8, 13–14, 68, 100; abuses by, 243–45, 255–56, 362. *See also* Franciscans; Jesuits
missionization, missions, 99, 332, 356–57, 362, 363, 364, 370; bells at, 396–405; Franciscan, 380–81, 382–83; at Hopi, 121–22, 131–32, 133–34, 240, 241, 245, 255, 358; in La Florida, 384–85; livestock butchering and rendering, 300–302; in New Mexico Colony, 19–22, 87–88, 389; in Pimería Alta, 25–29, 266–67, 271, 292–95, 296–97, 302–5, 359; ranching at, 296–97; recruitment by, 21–22; restoration projects at, 359–60; textile production at, 119–21, 127–28
Mississippian Southeast, 379, 391; colonial era, 383–88
Mocamo, 384, 388
Moho Pueblo, 62, 63; Coronado's siege on, 54, 59, 60, 61, 70
Montgomery, Ross, theory of superposition, 392–93
Moreno, Pedro, 244
Morlete, Juan, 15
Mormon Battalion, 322
Mototícachi, 272
mulatos, 8
multiethnicity, of New Mexico Colony, 16–18
Musangnuvi (Mishongnovi), 119, 241, 244, 251
Muskogean-speakers, 383

naborias (*auxiliares*), 17
Nahuatl speakers, 4
Narváez, Pánfilo de, 4
Native Americans. *See* indigenous groups; *various groups by name*
Navajos, 5, 145, 151, 193, 214
Nébomes, 26, 27, 271, 280(n2)
neophytes, control of, 362, 398
New Indian History, 158

New Mexico, New Mexico Colony, 5–6, 9–10, 303, 370; alliances, 31–32; Bourbon reforms in, 190–91; civic identity in, 215–17; Comanche role in, 159–60, 161–62, 365; cultural identity in, 213–14; Dominguez's description of, 105–6; economy of, 18–20; establishment of, 11–12, 15–16; frontier, 103–5; identity construction, 368–69; missionization in, 20–22, 356; multiethnicity of, 16–18; reestablishment of, 24–25; resistance in, 22–24; Spanish vs. Pueblo role in, 157–58
Niza, Marcos de, 3–4, 19, 51, 266
nomadic groups, 106; archaeological evidence of, 274–75; Puebloan relations with, 103, 104–5. *See also by name*
Nombre de Dios (Durango), 17
Northern Tewa, 381; ceramics, 221, 223, 227
Northern Tiwa, 12, 381
Nostrand, Richard, on Hispano Homeland, 187–88, 205
Nuestra Señora de los Angeles de Pecos, 87
Nuestra Señora de los Angeles de Porciúncula (Pecos), 399, 406
Nuestra Señora del Pilar y Santiago de Cocóspera, zooarchaeology, 295–96, 297, 299, 303, 304, 361
Nuevo León, 17

Oacpicagigua, Luis, 28
Oaxaca, 4, 17
objects; agency of, 380; index, 402; ritual and tribute, 387–88
obsidian, 62, 67; distribution of, 147–49
Ocheguene, Joseph, 244
O'Conor, Hugo, and Tucson Presidio, 314, 315
Ohkay Owingeh (Yunque-Yunque), 15, 69, 165, 202
Ojeda, Bartolomé de, 143, 250–51
Oñate, Juan de, 15–16, 17, 399; colonization, 69, 85, 241
Ontiberos Site, 224–25, 228
O'odham, 33, 312, 364; agriculture, 335–36, 343–48; distribution of, 267–68; on middle Gila River, 332–34; missionization of, 293–94, 362; population changes, 338–41; regional interactions, 269–72, 275–76, 278–79, 280(n2); seasonal movements, 290–92; Spanish and, 266–67, 336–37; tribal leadership, 341–42; Tucson area, 317–19
Opas, 26, 275
Ópatas, 26, 27, 30, 267, 294; and O'odham relations, 271–72, 279, 280(n2)

Index | **423**

Oraibi (Orayvi), 119, 241; factionalism, 149, 151; missionary abuses at, 243–45, 248–49
oral traditions, 144, 162; Hopi, 32, 132, 239–40, 241, 243–49, 254–55, 358
Oré, Gerónimo de, *Martyrs of Georgia*, 388
Ortega, José María, 197
Ortega, San Juan, 197
Oseca/Osera/Osara, 275

Paako (San Pedro; LA 162), 20, 364; agriculture at, 93–95; cultural setting of, 82–85; isolated location of, 100–105; land use, 31, 77; livestock at, 96–98; natural setting, 78–82; plazas at, 88–92; sheepherding camp at, 98–99
Padoucas, 161–62. *See also* Comanches
Pajarito Plateau, 146
Palmer Drought Severity Index (PDSI), 242
Papago Plain, 273
Paraje de Fra Cristobal, 219, 221
Parral (Chihuahua), Pueblo textiles in, 118
Patayan complex, 264, 277, 278
Patokwa (LA 96), 145, 147, 148, 150, 151, 152
PDSI. *See* Palmer Drought Severity Index
Pecos Pueblo, 11, 12, 22, 87, 106, 131, 143, 150, 227, 394, 396; Coronado expedition at, 53, 55, 56, 60–61; mission bells at, 399–40, 406
Pecos River, 214, 224, 228
Pee Posh, 26
pelota, 391
Pelotte, Donald, 255
Peñalosa, Diego de, 132, 245
penitentes, 203–4
Peralta, Pedro de, 15
Perea, Esteban de, 241
Pesede'uinge (LA 299), 199, 200, 201
Pétriz de Cruzate, Domingo Jironza, 250–51
petrographic analysis, of post-Revolt ceramics, 146
Pfefferkorn, Ignaz, 300
Phillip III, 16
Picuris, 11, 12, 162, 165
Piedras Marcadas Pueblo, 31, 69, 358; archaeology of, 63–67
Pilar Morada Site (LA 55948), 167
Piman language, 26
Pima Revolt, 267, 293, 296, 312
Pimas (Gileños), 26, 29, 267, 269, 275
Pimas Bajos, 26, 271, 279, 280(n2), 290
Pimería Alta, 5–6, 32–33, 263, 312, 314, 315, 332, 359, 364; archaeological record in, 264–66, 268–69, 272–75; butchering and rendering activities in, 300–302; colonialism, 25–29, 356; documentary record on, 267–68; ethnic group relationships in, 269–72, 275–76, 278–79; native revolts in, 29–31; native settlements, 27–28; ranching in, 292–95, 296–97, 302–5; Spanish exploration and colonialism, 266–67; subsistence pattern in, 290–92; zooarchaeological evidence, 295–300, 361–62
Pinacate, Sierra, 277, 278
pirates, and mission bells, 403
Piro-speakers, 11, 12, 116, 118, 143, 242, 382
Pitaitutgam (AZ EE:8:15[ASM]), 272, 273, 274
Pitic, 26
Plain Black, 221, 222, 223, 225
Plain Red, 222, 223, 225
Plains Apaches, 12; and Comanches, 162–63; and Paako, 104–5
Plains Biographic Tradition, 166, 170, 366
Plains Sign Language, 175
Plaza Colorada, 197
plaza communities, Hispanic, 197, 219–25
plazas: Paako, 88–92, 364; town orientation around, 85–86, 364
Po'pay: on destruction of mission bells, 398, 399, 400; leadership of, 144, 150, 152, 153, 382
population: Hispanic New Mexico, 191, 192–93, 194–95; Pimería Alta, 263–64; Rio Grande Pueblos, 241–42; Tucson presidio, 316–17
Porras, Francisco de, 241
Posada, Alonso de, 245
postrevolt period, 9; alliances, 145–49, 152–53, 382; factionalism, 149–52
power structures, 7; in New Mexico Colony, 24–25
presidios, 26, 28, 30, 33, 370. *See also* Tucson Presidio
Presidio San Agustín del Tucson. *See* Tucson Presidio
projectile points: at Piedras Marcadas, 67; Sierra Pinacate, 277, 278
Protohistoric Period, middle Gila River, 336–37
Puaray, 68, 69
Pueblo Blanco, 102
Pueblo de la Cruz, 59, 63
Pueblofication, 8, 25
Pueblo V period, 158
Pueblo Revolt, 22–24, 116, 250–51, 365, 388–89, 405; factionalism and, 381–82; Hopi and, 122, 133; mission bells and, 398–40; weather prior to, 242–43
Pueblos, 8, 92, 115, 200, 221; capitulation by, 60–61; colonial power relations, 24–25;

Coronado expedition, 4, 56–62, 357–58; decision-making in, 381–82; early Spanish descriptions of, 75–76; encomienda and repartimiento systems, 19, 241–42; factionalism, 149–52, 382–83; landscape concepts, 76–77, 99–100, 364; long-distance information exchange, 55–56; missionization of, 20–21, 362, 389; in New Mexico Colony, 11–12, 157–58; and nomadic groups, 103, 104–5; and Oñate, 15–16; plazas in, 85–86, 88; post-Revolt relationships, 143–49; Spanish governance of, 380–81; textile production, 116, 118–19, 124
Puname-area polychromes, 221, 223, 225
Puname Polychrome, 222
Purgatoire River, Hispanic sites on, 224

Quarai, 20, 23, 245, 394
Quechan, 27, 275, 278
Quera, Francisco, 244
Querechos, 12
Quíburi (AZ EE:4:11 [ASM]), 269, 271, 272
Quíquimas, 27, 276, 278
Quivira, 53

raiding, raids, 21, 151, 163, 166, 182(n6), 196, 362; Comanche, 159, 177; in New Mexico Colony, 106, 192; on O'odham, 337, 340–41; in Pimería Alta, 271, 294–95, 302–3, 305, 361; in Sonora and Pimería Alta, 30–31
Ramírez de Salazar, Francisco, 272, 279
rancherías, 28, 267, 269, 312, 337
ranching, ranches: in New Mexico, 195, 219, 221–23; in Pimería Alta, 28, 266, 292–95, 296–99, 302–5, 361
Ranchitos Polychrome, 221
Rancho de Chama, 196
Ranchos de Taos, 192, 221, 228
rebellions, 405; La Florida, 400, 404, 406–7(n1); in Pimería Alta, 271–72. *See also* Pueblo Revolt
Reconquest, 88, 189, 251
Red Mesa Black-on-white, 222
reduccion, 290
redware, post-Pueblo Revolt, 22–23
refugee pueblos, 383
regalia, chiefly, 386
religion, 21; post-Revolt Puebloan, 23–24
repartimiento system, 19, 118, 362; in La Florida, 385–88
requerimiento, 57
resistance, 8, 390; to Coronado expedition, 54–55, 58–60; Hopi, 243, 251; in Pimería Alta and Sonora, 29–31; Pueblo, 22–24, 133–34. *See also* Pueblo Revolt; rebellions
respect system, Pueblo, 57–58
revolts, in Pimería Alta and Sonora, 29–31. *See also* Pueblo Revolt
Rio Abajo region, 12, 217; Hispanic sites, 219–21
Rio Arriba, 217; Hispanic sites on, 221–23
Rio del Oso grant, 189, 207(n10), 368; archaeology of, 199–202; genealogy of, 197–99; history of, 195–96
Rio del Oso Valley: archaeology of, 199–202; occupation of, 202–3
Rio Grande Classic Period, 82
Rio Grande Coalition Period, 82
Rio Grande Developmental Period, 82
Rio Grande Gorge, archaeology of, 164–75, 365–66
Rio Grande Pueblos, 11, 12, 70, 161; alliances, 31–32, 365; Coronado expedition and, 53–54, 69; plain redware, 22–23; population decline, 241–42; settlement patterns, 100–101, 143; textile production, 131, 132, 392. *See also by community; language group*
Rio Grande Valley: landscape use, 370–71; Hispanic settlements in, 217–23, 368
Rio Medio, 217; Hispanic settlements on, 219–21
Rio Pueblo, sites on, 164–65
rock art, 168, 182(n5), 383; battle depictions in 177–78; Comanche, 170–79, 180, 365–66; Jicarilla, 166, *167*
Rodríguez, Augustín, 13–14, 67
Romero, Diego, 132
Rosas, Luis de, 118
Ruiz, José, 196

St. Augustine, 384–85, 388, 391, 398, 401, 403
St. Catherines Island, bell fragments from, 401
Saitude band (Jicarilla), 202, 203
Salazar, Hita, 387
Salinas pueblos, 10, 23, 242, 332
Salinas Red, 23
Saltillo, 17
Salvatierra, Juan María, 276
San Andrés, 270
San Antonio de Los Poblanos, 219
San Antonio Pueblo (LA 24), 82, 100
San Agustín de Tucson, 317, 318, 325; establishment of, 312–14; livestock at, 297, 303; zooarchaeology of, 295, 299–300, 304
San Bernardo de Aguatubi (Awat'ovi), 393
San Cristóbal, 153; mission bell from, 399, 400
Sandia, 69, 399

Index | **425**

Sandia Mountains, 78
Sand Papagos. *See* Areneños
San Esteban de Nueva Tlaxcala (Saltillo), 17
San Felipe Pueblo, 62, 78, 102, 147, 153, 399
San Francisco (CA), 215, 361; presidio, 321, 369
San Gabriel, 15
Sangre de Cristo Micaceous, 222
Sangre de Cristo Mountains, 224, 225, 227
San José de Baviácora, 274
San José de las Huertas, 192, 219, 227, 228
San José de Los Ranchos, 219
San Juan mission (La Florida), 403
San Juan Pueblo (Ohkay Owingeh), 15, 69, 165, 202
San Juan Red-on-tan, 223
San Lázaro, 102, 153, 399
San Lorenzo, 196; archaeological evidence of, 200–202
San Luis de Talimali, 391
San Luis Valley (Santa Cruz River), 267
San Marcelo de Sonoyta, 270, 276, 278
San Marcos Pueblo, 146, 147
San Miguel (El Salvador), 17
San Miguel de Carnué, 192
San Miguel del Vado, 224, 228, 229
San Miguel River, 271
San Pedro (NM). *See* Paako
San Pedro Arroyo (NM), 78, 93; as Paako water source, 81–82; Plains Apache sites, 104–5
San Pedro Mountains (NM), 78
San Pedro River Valley (AZ), 269, 272, 279
San Pelayo (ship), 401
San Phelipe mission (La Florida), 403
San Salvador, 17
San Salvador de Mayaca, 402
Santa Ana de Cuiquiburitac, 26
Santa Ana Polychrome, 221
Santa Ana pueblo, 62, 106, 152, 153, 227
Santa Barbara mission, bell at, 396–97
Santa Catalina de Guale, bells from, 400–405, 407(n4)
Santa Clara Constitution, 149
Santa Cruz de Gaybanipitea (AZ EE:8:15[ASM]), 272, 273, 275
Santa Cruz de la Cañada, 191, 196
Santa Cruz del Pitaitutgam (AZ EE:8:15[ASM]), 272, 273, 274
Santa Cruz de Terrenate (AZ EE:4:11[ASM]), 26, 272, 274, 322
Santa Cruz River, 266, 267, 269, 274, 279
Santa Fe, 15, 17, 118, 191; structure of, 86–87
Santa Fe Trail, ceramics imported on, 222–23

Santa María, Agustín de, 250
Santa Rita Mountains, timber from, 316
Santa Rosa de Lima de Abiquiú, 223
Santiago (Guatemala), 17
Santiago Pueblo (New Mexico), 63
Santo Domingo, 62, 147, 152, 245, 398
Santo Domingo Basin, 101
San Xavier del Bac, 293, 297, 303, 312, 318, 325
Sapelo Island, 404
scalp dances, at Taos, 164
School of American Research (School for Advanced Research), 360
S-cuk Son, 312–13. *See also* Tucson
seasonal movements, O'odham, 290–91, 294
Sedelmayr, Jacobo, 276, 340, 343
sedentism, rotating, 98, 99
Senecú, 399
Seris, 27, 29, 30
settlement patterns, 28, 145; northern Rio Grande, 100–101; Spanish colonial, 192–93; Vecino, 193–95
sheep, 361; at Hopi, 121–22, 133; in Pimería Alta, 297–300, 302–3, 305
sheep/goat remains, 92, 96, 118, 119; at Hispanic sites, 221, 222, 223, 225–26
sheepherding camp, at Paako, 98–99
Shongopovi (Songòopavi), 119, 120, 241, 244, 251
shrines, 77, 86, 88
siege, on Moho, 54, 59, 60, 61, 70
Sitkoyma, torture and death of, 246–49
slaves, in La Florida colony, 386
slingstones, at Piedras Marcadas Pueblo, 67, 68
smallpox, 242, 292, 314
smelting, in Paako plaza, 90–91, 364
smoke signals, Puebloan, 56
Sobaipuri Plain, 273, 274
Sobaipuris, 26, 269, 271, 272, 278, 279, 317, 318; archaeological evidence, 272–75
Sobas, 26, 267, 270–71, 279
social hierarchies, Mississippian Southeast, 383–84, 386–87, 389
Socorro, 11
soldiers: Tucson Presidio, 314–15, 316–17, 322; weapons, 323–24
Songòopavi (Shongopavi), 119, 120, 241, 244, 251
Sonora, 264, 303; native revolts and resistance in, 29–31; Spanish settlement of, 26, 27–28, 266
Sonora, Río, archaeology, 274, 278
Sonoyta, 270, 276, 278
Soto, Hernando de, 383
soul wounds, 254

Southeast. *See* Mississippian Southeast
Southern Tewa, 12
Southern Tiwa, 12, 119, 227, 382
Southwestern Grand Narrative, 392–94
space, 364, 393; cultural concepts of, 76–77, 370–71
Spaniards, 124, 279, 357; concepts of landscape, 76, 77; dependence on Pueblos of, 157–58; ethnogenesis, 188–89, 361; introduction of livestock, 289–90; land rights concepts, 99–100; and O'odham, 336–37; town structures, 86–87; village establishment, 192–93
Spanish Empire, 10, 380; frontier of, 5, 103–5
Spanish entrada, 3–4, 57, 292; exploring expeditions, 13–15, 67–69, 357–59, 383; trauma of, 240
spinning technology, at Hopi, 128–29
substance abuse, and historical trauma, 253–54
subsistence strategies, 98; hunter-gatherer, 367–68; Pimería Alta, 290–92
Sumas, 30, 271, 272, 274
sun katsina, and Virgin of Guadalupe, 9
superposition, theory of, 392–93

Tabira Black-on-white, 23
Tabira Polychrome, 23
Taino, 50
tallow production, Pimería Alta, 300–302, 304, 305
Tamarón, Bishop, 164
Tanos, Tanoans, 12, 143, 153, 252
Taos, 11, 12, 143,165, 245; Comanches and, 161, 162–63, 164, 170, 182(n7)
Tarascans, 4; on Coronado expedition, 51, 357
Tenochas, on Coronado expedition, 51, 357
Tepehuan, 275
terra nullius, 10–11
Terrenate, 26, 272, 274, 322
Teuricachi Valley, native attacks in, 271, 272
Tewa, 12, 143, 221, 252, 381; alliances, 152–53, 365; conflicts with, 151–52; at Kotyiti, 146, 147; post-Revolt ceramics, 22–23
Tewa Basin, 98
Tewa Polychrome Series, 221, 222, 223, 225
textile production, 132; embroidery, 125–27; Hopi, 115–16, 119–21, 127–29, 130, 134–35, 136(n6), 362–63; knitting, 124–25; Pueblo, 118–19, 392; Vecino, 228–29; wool in, 121–23
Teya/Jumanos, 12
Tiguex Province, 53, 69; contact period archaeology, 63–67; Coronado expedition and, 54–55, 56, 57–58, 60–61, 62; defensive tactics in, 58–59; textile production, 116, 118

Tijeras Creek, 78
Tijeras Pueblo (LA 581), 82
Timucua, 384, 388, 402
tipi rings, Vista Verde site, 168, 169, 176, 365
Tiwa, 31, 63, 69, 143, 252; Pueblo Revolt, 381, 382; textile production, 116, 118, 119
Tlatelolcas, 51, 357
Tlaxcaltecas, 4, 17
Tohono O'odham (Papagos), 26, 267, 275, 343; settlement pattern, 28–29
Tolar Site (WY), 175, 177
Tompiros, 12, 98, 101, 382
Tonque, Arroyo, 78; watershed, 81–82
torreones, 200
Tota'tsi, 248–49
Totonicapán (Guatemala), 17
Towa, 12, 381
town planning, Spanish, 86–87
trade, trade networks, 132, 164, 202, 318, 343, 387; intercolony, 301–2, 305; post-Revolt, 146–47, 152; Tucson Presidio, 319–25; Vecino, 227–28
trauma, historical/intergenerational, 240, 253–56, 358, 362
treaties, Spanish-Indian, 193
Treaty of Guadalupe Hidalgo, 160
tribute, 19, 241; La Florida, 386–87; Mississippian system, 386–88; Pueblo communities, 21, 85, 115, 133, 245; textiles as, 118–19, 120–21, 392
Trincheras, 264, 265
Trincheras Plain, 274
Trujillo, José, 250
Trujillo House site, 223
Tubac, 267, 312; livestock at, 298–99; presidio at, 28, 30, 314
Tubutama, 30, 272, 279
Tucson: archaeological research, 311–312. *See also* San Agustín de Tucson; Tucson Presidio
Tucson Presidio, 359, 361; construction of, 315–16; establishment of, 314–15; livestock at, 295, 298; metallurgy at, 324–25; and Native Americans, 317–19; presidio life, 33, 325–26; residents of, 316–17; trade goods at, 319–24
Tucubavia, 269–70, 271
Tumacácori, 299, 312
Tunque, 78, 100
Tunyo (LA 23), 145, 146, 152, 153
Tupatú, Luis, 144
Turco, El, 61

Ulibarri, Juan de, 162
US military, and Gila River O'odham, 344
Upper Pimans, archaeology, 277
Upper Pima Revolt (1751), 28
uprisings. *See* Pueblo Revolt; rebellions
Useda, Juan de, 403
Utes, 143, 193, 214; and Comanches, 161, 182(n4); raids by, 151, 196; in Rio Grande Gorge, 165, 166, 365; rock art, 167, 182(n5)

Valdez, Antonia Rosa, 197
Valdez, Ignacio, 195, 206(n7)
Valdez, José Antonio, 196, 197, 207(n10)
Valdez, Juan, 195
Valdez, Juan Bautista, 197
Valdez, Rosalía, and Rio del Oso grant, 195, 197
Valencia, 219
Valladolid, 76
Vargas, Diego de, 17, 24, 143, 145, 152, 196, 251
Vecinos, 206(n4); archaeological identity of, 217–25; identity as, 188, 214–17, 229–30, 368–69, 371; identity restructuring as, 25, 32; legal recognition as, 189–90, 205; settlement pattern, 193–95, 203–4; subsistence and economy, 225–26; trade, 227–28
vecinos de razón, 215
Velasco, Luis, 68
Ventana Cave (AZ Z:12:5[ASM]), 276–77
Vicente Valdez Site, 221
Vijil, José Ramón, 196
villages, Spanish colonial, *190*, 191–92
violence, 9, 19, 24, 240; Coronado expedition, 53, 54–55, 58–59
Virgin Mary, images of, 383
Virgin of Guadalupe, 9
visitas: at Hopi, 116, 119, 241; at Paako, 89–90; in Pimería Alta, 295–96, 313–14
Vista Verde Site (LA 75747), 165, 168, 169, 179; rock art, 170–78, 181, 365–66

Wàlpi, 116, 119, 121, 125, 127, 130, 241, 251; textiles, 123, 127–29, 134
warfare: Comanche, 159, 160; among Pueblos, 151–52

warriors, native, 16, 17, 176
warrior societies, in Rio Grande Pueblos, 70
water control/harvesting systems, Pueblo, 92, 95, 98
water sources: for O'odham, 291–92; around Paako, 81–82
weapons, 67, 358; presidio soldiers, 323–25; Spanish, 322–23
weaving: dyes used in, 123–24; as gendered role, 21, 392; at Hopi, 31, 115–16, 127–29, 133, 362–63; in Spanish colonies, 118, 135(n11)
wedding ceremonies, Hopi, 247, 248
wheat, 29, 293; middle Gila River production, 336, 341, 342, 344, 345, 367
Whetstone Plain, 273, 278, 279
Wichita-speakers, 12
women: and Catholicism, 382–83; textile production, 118, 119, 134, 362
wool, 118, 119, 225; embroidery, 125–27; at Hopi, 121–23, 124, 130, 133, 362
Wuwtsim, 252

Xauian, 61
Xiveni, Juan, 243

Yaqui Revolt, 28
Yaquis, 26, 28
Ybargary, Antonio de, 120, 133, 243, 244–45
Yuman speakers, 26, 267, 275–76, 278, 364
Yumas (Quechan), 27, 275, 278
Yunque-Yunque (Ohkay Owingeh), 15, 69, 165, 202

Zacatecas, 13
Zepe, El, 153
Zia, 62, 70, 106, 147, 153, 399; ceramics from, 146, 227; conflicts with, 151–52
zooarchaeology, of Pimería Alta sites, 295–300, 304, 361–62
Zuni, 4, 18, 23, 58, 90, 106, 119, 132, 145, 241, 334; Coronado expedition and, 53, 56, 57, 60; embroidery, 125, 127; Pueblo Revolt, 381, 399
Zúñiga, José de, 318
Zuni language, 12

www.ingramcontent.com/pod-product-compliance
Lightning Source LLC
Chambersburg PA
CBHW060510080526
44586CB00012B/447